D0055241

Also by Peter Greenberg

The Travel Detective Flight Crew Confidential:
People Who Fly for a Living Reveal Insider
Secrets and Hidden Values in Cities
and Airports Around the World

Hotel Secrets from the Travel Detective:
Insider Tips on Getting the Best Value,
Service, and Security in Accommodations
from Bed-and-Breakfasts to Five-Star Resorts

The Travel Detective

The Travel Detective

How to Get the Best Service and the Best Deals from
Airlines, Hotels, Cruise Ships, and Car Rental Agencies

PETER GREENBERG

VILLARD   NEW YORK

Copyright © 2001, 2005 by Peter Greenberg

All rights reserved.

Published in the United States by Villard Books, an imprint of
The Random House Publishing Group, a division of Random
House, Inc., New York.

VILLARD and "V" CIRCLED Design are registered trademarks of
Random House, Inc.

An earlier edition of this work was published by Villard Books,
an imprint of The Random House Publishing Group, a division of
Random House, Inc., in 2001.

Grateful acknowledgment is made to the following for permission
to reprint previously published material:

UNITED AIRLINES: "Automated Baggage Tag" graphic and
"Breakdown in Ticket Pricing Information." Reprinted by
permission of United Airlines.

Library of Congress Cataloging-in-Publication Data

Greenberg, Peter.
  The travel detective: how to get the best service and the best
deals from airlines, hotels, cruise ships, and car rental agencies /
Peter Greenberg.
    p. cm.
  ISBN 0-8129-7380-1
  1. Travel.   I. Title.
  G153.4 .G74 2001
  910'.2'02–dc21   00-069329

www.villard.com

Printed in the United States of America

9   8   7   6   5   4   3   2   1

This book is dedicated to my mother, who always encouraged me to travel; to my sister, who understands why I still travel; and to my late father, who continues to show me the way home.

CONTENTS

8 Final Thoughts on Resources, Tools, Websites: And What to Do When It All Goes Wrong 423

PREFACE

Some years ago, when I was trying to find my way as a writer, I had lunch with a good friend who is also a gifted journalist, Chris Barnett. I had worked for nearly seven years as a correspondent for *Newsweek* and had traveled extensively while on the job. So frequently was I on airplanes, in fact, that I kept two packed suitcases in the trunk of my car.

But at *Newsweek* I was a generalist, assigned to one of the magazine's bureaus on the West Coast. I could—and did—write for different sections of the magazine each week. After six years, I was drifting, looking for a way, as a writer, to pursue my creative passions and to focus.

It didn't take long for Barnett to put the pieces together. "You should be a travel writer," he said. My response? I laughed. In those days, most of the travel writers I knew were failed journalists, escaped librarians, or schoolteachers looking to find someone who would give them a free cruise. In fact, not that long ago, most travel journalism was more or less an oxymoron. And travel sections of newspapers were perceived as nothing more than advertising vehicles.

But Barnett proceeded to convince me. After all, he argued, I loved to travel. More important, I loved the process of travel. Even on stories that had nothing to do with travel, I could be found up in the cockpit talking to the pilots or in the galley with flight attendants, and on cruise ships I'd be on the bridge talking with the officers.

No one was writing about travel as news, or explaining the process of how things really worked.

It began with a weekly column in the *Tribune,* The Savvy Traveler (a name I later gave to my close friend Rudy Maxa, who was at *The Washington Post* when I was at *Newsweek,* and who then started a very successful National Public Radio show as well as a newsletter bearing the same name).

And it soon expanded to nearly sixty newspapers. It was the first investigative travel column—it didn't address subjects like "Lovely London" or "Beautiful Bermuda." Instead, I wrote about which cruise ship was a mechanical disaster, as well as which had a great safety record; which hotel had a pattern of bad fire safety, as well as which trained its staff well; which airline consistently lied to consumers about its pricing, as well as which performed ethically and professionally.

Pete Seeger once said he knew the difference between education and experience. Education, he suggested, was when you read the fine print. Experience is what happened if you didn't.

This book is all about experience. About process. And about how to navigate that fine print.

When I began the task of revising and updating this book, I was confronted with what seemed to be an obvious challenge—that so much of the travel experience had become radically different since 9/11, that the rules of travel had been changed forever.

But what I discovered is that, with the exception of security, safety, and terrorism issues (see Chapter 2), not much had changed at all, and that was even more disturbing. Many airlines were being run by atrocious management before 9/11. And the same airlines (some would argue, *more* airlines) are being run by bad management today. Airports were designed by people who never spent time in airports before 9/11, and with few exceptions, even the new or "new and improved" airports are being designed today for planes, not people. And many hotels were being modeled after airlines and airports—not as experiences we wanted, but as commodities we endured.

First, the airlines.

Any airline that insists its financial problems were started by 9/11 is in serious denial. Their problems were, if anything, *accelerated* by 9/11.

Within days of the terrible tragedy, most major airlines closed city ticket offices, virtually abandoned paper tickets, and did everything possible to eliminate human contact with their customers.

But it didn't stop the hemorrhaging. In 2002, the ten largest airlines in the United States lost $5.5 billion. And the losses keep getting worse. In the past three years, the major carriers have somehow managed to lose more than $20 billion. In the first half of 2004, Delta Airlines achieved the almost unthinkable: The carrier burned through three quarters of a billion dollars, and in the fourth quarter the loss ballooned to 2.1 billion.

The irony is that, at the same time, more Americans are traveling now than before 2000, and the airlines are in their worst shape in recent memory. Air passenger traffic is up 18 percent, and yet, as you are reading this, more than 50 percent of all airline capacity in the United States is under the control of U.S. bankruptcy courts.

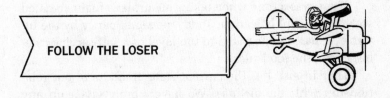

FOLLOW THE LOSER

Today, with exceedingly few exceptions, airlines have become so obsessed with cost that they have totally forgotten value. To make matters more absurd, we are actually measuring the success of airlines by which ones can lose money *longer.*

One by one, these airlines are playing a dangerous game of follow the loser.

Recently, I was a first-class passenger on a United Airlines flight between Los Angeles and Denver. Shortly after takeoff, one of the flight attendants asked what I might like to drink. I asked for a Diet Coke. She returned soon after with my soda and with a small packet of peanuts.

So far, so good. Until, that is, I made the terrible mistake ten minutes later of asking for a second packet of nuts.

"I'm sorry," she apologized. "But in first class, only one per person." She simply shrugged. "That's our policy."

In first class?

"So tell me," I said, laughing, "If that's the case, what's going on in coach? Are they lowering lifeboats and firing flares?"

She didn't laugh.

To me, the nut incident was indicative of the state of thinking of many of the major, so-called legacy airlines. And I was—and am still—convinced that somewhere inside the headquarters of United, there's an accountant in the midst of an orgasmic frenzy, thrilled at the notion that he saved the airline about 6¢ by holding back on my second packet of nuts. At the same time, the airline lost me as a $2,000 passenger.

There was a time when taking an airplane flight signaled wealth and sophistication. Today, powered partly by the Internet, it has disintegrated to the level of a self-service cafeteria. And the food sucks.

Therein also lies the current state of affairs of our relationship with the airlines. We have simply given up any hope of a pleasurable experience. Now we simply aspire to arrive safely.

What the airlines promote as progress and expediency has become nothing less than a demographic disconnect among a majority of passengers. Many are flying JetBlue, Air Tran, easyJet, or Ryanair to get to their luxury ski chalets or yachts.

However, as Lily Tomlin once said, it's going to get a lot worse before it gets . . . worse. A majority of airlines are now part of a vicious circle consisting of an antiquated business plan, weak finances, and low morale, and that can easily become a deadly combination.

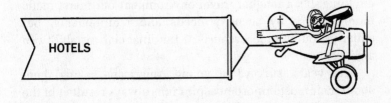

HOTELS

Here comes the Lily Tomlin part: A frighteningly large number of hotels are following the airline model, obsessed with cost at the expense of service and human interaction.

Nickel-and-diming is at an all-time high, and in many hotels, service and human interaction have been replaced with kiosks; amenities have been replaced by "profit centers."

And yet, even in the face of a dismal economic diagnosis for the airlines and a world of diminished service expectations at hotels, we remain addicted travelers. We live and breathe the promise and—if we're lucky—the experience of travel.

Welcome to the world of the New Normal. And the challenge in that world—for both the providers of travel as well as the travelers themselves—is to avoid commoditizing what was once an experience we aspired to and, indeed, coveted.

What remains and, in fact, what keeps us traveling is the staggering potential of travel, its power to mend a fractured world, to bring us together. Not just to commiserate about shared bad experiences but to embrace other cultures, and to build bridges of understanding.

This book has been totally updated and revised. But my basic—and sometimes overriding—principles of travel, for better or worse, remain. I first wrote this book out of my need—and, I'll presume, yours—to avoid being a travel victim, to beat the airlines, hotels, and cruise lines at their own game, playing by *their* rules. That philosophy remains. If anything, it's a tougher travel environment out there, made more intense by security needs and requirements, but equally troublesome because of the financial instability of airlines.

For years, surveys of young Americans asking them about their most important aspirations always resulted in the same three responses about goals. Number one: getting married. Number two: having a family. And number three: traveling. I won't profess to help you achieve those first two goals. Hopefully, this book will help you realize the third.

ACKNOWLEDGMENTS

Harriet Choice at the *Chicago Tribune* took a big chance on me, and for that I will always be grateful. Grateful as well to Jerry Hulse, a tough editor and a great boss, the former travel editor of the *Los Angeles Times.* When Jerry decided to run my column, my work was nationally recognized. Jerry will always be a giant in my eyes because he did it all—Not only did he edit a complete Sunday newspaper section each week, he also wrote for it, and, sometimes it seemed as if he wrote all of it! Thankfully, he knew what he was writing about. And I like to think he felt the same about me. He will always be missed, and he will always be remembered.

Thanks, too, go to Michael Jackson, who will always be the dean of radio talk show hosts in my eyes, and who was enormously generous in allowing me time on his show. He is one of the few radio interviewers who understand the questions they ask as well as why they ask them, because he always does his homework beforehand.

Over the years, I have been blessed with assistants who also became friends—they helped me so much, and they had many things in common, among them that they are strong and incredibly capable women: Jodie Sternberg and Meredith Patterson, Jessica Nathan, and the rock-solid Jessica Milligan. Last but not least, Jill Gable, who held down the fort and organized my life while I crossed every time zone.

I have so many people to thank in the travel industry itself that my biggest fear in writing these acknowledgments is the highly likely possibility of forgetting some. And so I apologize now for any omissions.

Having said that, there are the legendary and unforgettable hoteliers who helped me and pointed me in the right direction, even if what I found out wasn't always flattering to them or their hotels: Stan Bromley and Wolf Hengst at Four Seasons, two men who really know how to run hotels; Wolfgang Hultner of the Mandarin Oriental in San Francisco, and John Toner, who was arguably, and singlehandedly, the Ritz-Carlton in Maui, both of whom have mastered the art of making the impossible look effortless. I was in New York with John Toner and Ed Mady, another great GM of the Ritz-Carlton San Francisco, on 9/11. Timing is everything: They were scheduled to meet with all their general managers on the morning of September 12 at Windows on the World.

Bill Marriott continues to amaze me by being so accessible and helpful; then there's the legendary Kurt Wachveitl at the Oriental in Bangkok, who *is* the Oriental in Bangkok; and Tom Guertner and Bill Black, both veterans of the Regent hotels in Hong Kong and in Bangkok. (The Regent is now an InterContinental in Hong Kong, and it's a Four Seasons in Bangkok.) Black is not just a GM, but a teacher. He can explain Thai culture and nuance—and service—better than anyone else I know. Speaking of legends, there's Sally Bulloch, who personified the Athenaeum in London until she did what all of us felt was the impossible—not only did she fall in love, she left London for South Africa! But Sally remains the role model of limitless energy, and in my mind will always be the consummate hostess. Even from the far reaches of the southern hemisphere, she remains the go-to person—she knows everything and everybody—and shares her information with an impossible combination of great flair and discretion. Thanks to Jon Tisch, who has been a friend and supporter, even when he didn't have to be.

Most guests who have stayed at the Mark Hotel in New York didn't know the name Birgit Zorniger. But she knew their names, and, thankfully, she knew mine. She quietly, efficiently, and with limitless strength turned the hotel into a gracious home. It is almost an understatement to say that this book would not have been possible, or even conceivable, without the incomparable Raymond Bickson, the legendary general manager of the Mark, whom I unabashedly worship as a hotelier but above all as a friend.

Given the inevitable turnover in the travel business, Raymond is now doing what Raymond does best: not just managing one hotel in New York, but running more than sixty of them worldwide for the Taj group from his new home base in Mumbai. And Birgit is there, right alongside him, continuing to make magic for her guests.

Thanks also to Jane Mackie, Deb Bernstein, and Katie Meyer—all formerly of Starwood hotels—for always having answers for every one of my questions. Jane is now at Loews hotels, Deb is an independent PR person, and Katie, after a stint at Meridien hotels in London, has returned to the United States and is now at Hyatt in Chicago.

And some true professional public relations women: Vivian Deuschl, Stephanie Platt, and Colleen Evans at Ritz-Carlton, who have been so generous with their time, their support, their information, and their honesty. I can't just thank them. Instead, I have to say "my pleasure and certainly" for reasons they know all too well. And that now includes Julia Gacjak, who relocated from Asia to Washington, D.C. for Ritz-Carlton. Also thanks to Lou Hammond, Yvonne Middleton, Jeannie Datz, Anita Cotter, Nancy Friedman, and Florence Quinn, who know the difference between promotion and presentation, puffery and the truth.

Anchors of thanks aweigh to Julie Benson of Princess, Mimi Weisband of Crystal, Liz Jakeway of Celebrity, and Morris Silver and Virginia Sheridan, who worked so hard with me in reporting the launch of the *Queen Mary 2*.

A special, special thanks to Sheila Donnelly, my dear friend, and one of the most wired, informed, smart people I know. Outside of being a great PR executive, she understands marketplace reality and was never afraid to tell the truth, even when it hurt. She was always there for me as a constant and selfless source of support, inspiration, and direction.

My love-hate relationship with the airlines includes some people who still helped me immeasurably—Tim Doke at American, Jon Austin at Northwest, Mark Abels at TWA, and Joe Hopkins and the late Chuck Novak at United. None of these men are with their airlines anymore, and Chuck is flying high. Then there's Ned Walker at Continental, Stephanie Ackerman at Aloha, Tom Wright and Scott Mowrer at Cathay Pacific, Gareth Edmonson-Jones at JetBlue, John Lampl at British Airlines, Peter McLaughlin and Ken Groves at Qantas, and John Selvaggio at Delta, who left to start Song. And then left Song. But that's another story . . .

My column is no longer syndicated in newspapers. It now is available to a much wider audience—and is updated every three days—on the Internet, at TravelNewsToday.com.

At NBC, I have been lucky to work with some great producers, ranging from Beatrice Myers and Kim Bondy to the total professional, Linda Finnell, who never asked me for anything other than hard, good work—when she wasn't gently asking me to get out of her office!

At the Travel Channel, Jay Feldman, with whom I once worked at KNXT in Los Angeles, hired me on as chief correspondent and developed a great and ambitious show, *Travel Daily*, along with another KNXT alum, Nancy Jacoby, who served as executive producer.

And most recently, Steve Cheskin, who didn't have to keep me at the channel when he came on board, but, thankfully, did. I'm still there, thanks to Billy Campbell, who embraces the notion—and then acts upon it—that travel news is must-need, must-use information.

My career as a television journalist specializing in travel was actually started by Merv Griffin, who first allowed me a national audience; then came the steady hand of Jack Reilly, who brought me to *Good Morning America*. Seven years later, when Jack left ABC, I moved over to NBC and the *Today* show, and it was—and is—the experience that changed everything. Bryant, Matt, Katie, Al, and Ann welcomed me to their special family. Few people outside of television know how hard their job really is, and even fewer know how easy they make mine.

Most important, it is Jeff Zucker, the former executive producer of the *Today* show (and now president of NBC Entertainment) to whom I will always owe my success. When people ask me if I think I'm lucky, I tell them I became lucky when I met Jeff. He truly recognized travel as news, and treated it as such. First, he invited me on the show as a guest. Then he asked me to stay. A tougher, more fair boss I will never find.

I can think of few things more fulfilling than travel. In the course of writing this book, in fact, in the course of my entire career as a journalist, I have had the wonderful opportunity of meeting and spending time with literally hundreds of the most important people in travel: bellhops, skycaps, ticket agents, train conductors, flight attendants, cabin stewards, taxi drivers, doormen, waiters and busboys, maids, ramp drivers, maintenance jockeys, security officers, airplane cleaners. They were also some of the most interesting people I will ever meet. I learned so much from them, and I will forever be in their debt, as an author as well as a traveler.

My heartfelt thanks to Ginny Carroll, at North Market Street Graphics, for the copyediting of this book, who exhibited saintlike patience and understanding; and to my book agent, Amy Rennert, for her persistence in first believing in this book and its author, and then remaining on my case and helping me to stay the course to finish it. Not quite last, and certainly not least, thanks go to my editor, Bruce Tracy, first for his vision in understanding the need for this kind of book, for his guidance, and for his incredibly polite behavior in waiting for this often delayed flight.

Finally, I am indebted to Kari Haskell of *The New York Times,* for tirelessly organizing the mountains of constantly changing information, following endless but essentially important paper trails, for tracking down previously unreachable or unwilling sources, and for researching this book.

P.G.

The *Travel*
Detective

1

Before Leaving

GETTING WHAT YOU WANT
BEFORE THE FACT

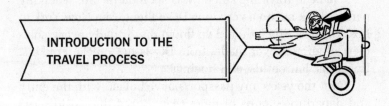

INTRODUCTION TO THE TRAVEL PROCESS

Most of us love to travel. That's the good news.

The bad news: We hate the process of travel.

We've been abused. And after each trip, we tell ourselves we'll never do it again.

And yet we can't wait to do it all over again. So we do.

To many people, travel remains a voyage—or a flight or an interstate trip—of discovery. But to most of us, travel remains a ritual of reassurance. Where there's a whim . . . there's a way. And even though we hate the process, we continue to travel.

Last year, more than two million people traveled by air. The average American traveler is forty-seven years old. Of all American adult travelers, 57 percent are men, 64 percent are married, and 33 percent have children.

We travel to escape, or to explore, or to rest. Travel is, for many of us, an exercise in renewal or a test of our limits. And some of us travel simply because we *can*.

And we *do*. In a recent American Express study of two hundred developing and developed countries, travel and tourism were found to be the biggest industry. In fact, if travel and tourism were a country instead of an industry, its gross national product (GNP) would rank among the top five in the world.

As an industry, it is one of the world's largest employers—one of every sixteen jobs worldwide is held by someone in the travel business.

I've been traveling since I was six months old, when my parents took me on a very long DC-6 flight from New York to Los Angeles. Since then, I've flown on virtually every commercial aircraft ever made, from DC-3s to Comets, Fokkers, Ilyushins, Fairchilds, and Boeings.

Over the years, my passports have bulged with the entry and departure stamps of more than 120 of the world's 193 countries. And many readers of this book have passports that are fatter than mine.

There has been an exponential jump in the number of travelers and in the frequency of their trips. In 1978, at the beginning of airline deregulation in the United States, only about 17 percent of all adults had ever taken an airplane flight. With deregulation came dozens of new airlines. Airfares started matching bus fares, and the numbers of passengers soared. Today, more than 84 percent of adults have flown. An impressive number, but also a scary one because a majority of that 84 percent feel abused by the process.

But the key question remains: Are we tourists or travelers?

My definition of *tourist* is "victim waiting to happen."

I know very few people who define themselves as tourists. Instead, they call themselves *travelers.* But that doesn't mean they're *good* travelers.

I always get a laugh on Mondays. That's when my incoming-call volume soars. Nearly everyone who calls is angry. They've just returned from a trip and there were problems. The calls seem to share the same structure, language, and intonation.

"It was a HORRIBLE flight," one will say. "The service was TERRIBLE." And, they add, they will NEVER do it again.

"Really?" I respond. "A horrible flight?"

"Absolutely," they answer. "Horrible."

"Let me ask you something," I continue. "At any time during your flight did the airplane hit a mountain and disintegrate?"

"No."

"And when you landed, did the wing hit the runway and did you cartwheel and explode?"

Again, "No."

"And," I conclude the questioning, "are you calling me from your . . . destination?"

"Yes."

"Well, hang up the phone. It was a GREAT flight. You arrived!"

However, a funny thing happens between the time my phone rings on Monday and when it rings again—the same person is calling—on Thursday.

The person who insisted that his or her experience was horrible on Monday, that he or she would *never* do it again, is now in a mild panic. Why? Because it's *Thursday* and the person is desperate for the information needed to get to the airport, get out of town, and try it all over again!

We have become a nation of travel junkies. And our addiction seems to be incurable.

Yet for many of us, the decisions concerning the *process* of travel are flawed. We have a serious entitlement problem. Half of us don't think we're entitled to anything when we travel. And the rest of us think we deserve *everything*.

Result: a nation of unhappy, but addicted travelers.

So, what do we *really* want when we travel?

Chances are, if you've traveled lately, you now have a list. You may not have written it down or committed it to memory, but you've got it—your list of all the ways a trip can be ruined.

What tops that list as the one item or experience that guarantees your vacation will be a disaster?

A few years ago, travel researcher Stanley Plog decided to find out, and the results might surprise you. They seem to indicate that, on the whole, we don't do our homework as travelers before we take our trips. We do little research or planning.

To find out our pet travel peeves, Plog tracked travel trends and preferences for virtually every major hotel and airline in the United States. He then picked a random sample of the U.S. population with annual incomes above $20,000. Plog's staff asked the travelers to rate—on a scale of 1 to 10—the thing that they felt ruined their trip the most.

Was it rude people? High prices? Feeling ripped off by locals? How about weather, crime, bad food, or a feeling that the destination visited was too much like other places they've visited?

No. First on the list of factors that ruin a trip was dirt. That's right, *dirt*. Hoteliers and housekeepers, take note: Of 13,526 travelers surveyed, 77 percent said that if a hotel is dirty or rundown, the trip is ruined.

Second on the list? Dirt again. Of those surveyed, 72 percent indicated that if things were "dirty everywhere," their trip would be similarly destroyed.

What about the actual expense of a trip? After all, aren't we all looking for a great deal when we travel? Expense ranked fifth on the list of trip spoilers, behind "poverty."

Poverty? Forty-three percent of the travelers indicated that if there was "poverty evident" at their destination, their trip would be a bummer. Forty percent cited the high cost of a trip as the number one trip destroyer.

There were lots of surprises among these responses, and no one was more surprised than Plog, who has been doing specific travel research for nearly thirty years. To Plog, the survey was a stunner.

A majority of those surveyed want things to be tidy, clean, almost antiseptic, and well planned. They want no surprises when they travel.

These travelers don't take risks. In fact, when Plog listed things like "too many tourist traps" or "too many fast-food outlets or souvenir shops" as candidates for ruining a trip, or suggested that the destination was "too much like other places visited," no one seemed to care.

Why is that significant? Think about what the findings really say. *We* pick cleanliness and organization, but we neglect to note the rampant development that tends to destroy foreign cultures.

That's like going to a McDonald's in a foreign country because you are familiar with its clean operation and prefer not to discover something new about a place, its people, and its customs. In fact, only 9 percent of those surveyed thought their trip would be ruined if the place they picked was "too much like other places visited."

Another interesting finding: The number of sophisticated American travelers is growing, but the bulk of American travelers don't do adequate trip planning, and they are willing to concentrate more on cleanliness than on culture, and more on known creature comforts than on price.

We are also geographically challenged as a people. Only 25 percent of all Americans actually hold a passport, and fewer use one.

I heard this story about a couple who had just returned from their vacation.

"Where did you go?" a friend asks.

"Aruba," they respond happily. "We had a great time."

"That's terrific," their friend says. "And by the way, where *is* Aruba?"

Without hesitation, the husband shrugs, then answers, "I don't know . . . we flew!"

The point is—hopefully—that while we know some of these people, we desperately do not want to *be* these people.

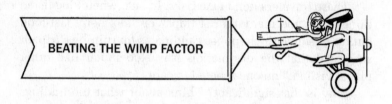

BEATING THE WIMP FACTOR

What's amazing is that our vacation couple actually went to Aruba and weren't scared of the island country.

But how much do we really know about travel? About where we are going, what we are experiencing, and, yes, even where we are?

Two nationwide surveys have attempted to find out. The results are surprising, amusing, even disturbing. And they reveal some widely held misconceptions that Americans harbor about travel.

The National Geographic Society conducted an international study in 1988 to determine how the United States compares with other countries in geographic literacy, and Americans ranked near the bottom in the test of geographic knowledge. Only Italians and Mexicans scored lower.

Adults in nine countries (including France, Japan, Sweden, and the United Kingdom) were asked to locate thirteen selected countries. The Swedes came in first, averaging about twelve places out of a possible sixteen.

Not only did the Americans score poorly, but our eighteen- to twenty-four-year-olds who took the test performed abysmally. They averaged only 6.9 places right—worse than their counterparts in all other countries. Only 15 percent could name the world's largest city—Mexico City. In another survey, none could point to Iraq on the map, and about the same number had trouble finding Illinois!

Fourteen years later, in 2002, the NGS repeated the study, and the results were just as staggering. The worldwide quiz of about 3,000 eighteen- to twenty-four-year-olds showed little or no improvement in young adults' grasp of geography. The United States was second to last among the countries that participated. And sadly, about 11 percent of young U.S. citizens couldn't even locate *the United States* on a map! The 2002 results were even more disturbing considering that despite the threat of war in Iraq and the daily reports of suicide bombers in Israel, less than 15 percent could locate either country. And 83 percent couldn't find Afghanistan.

So much for our geographical knowledge. What about basic travel common sense?

Omni Hotels conducted a survey to try to determine Americans' travel IQ. Some of the results: Seven out of ten Americans don't know the difference between a direct and a nonstop flight. More than six out of ten Americans are not sure whether they must pay travel agents a commission for their services. And nearly half think it is cheaper to drive an automobile than it is to take a plane to a destination.

How many time zones does the United States span? Seven out of ten Americans surveyed by Omni said four. The correct answer is eight: Atlantic (including Puerto Rico and the U.S. Virgin Islands), Eastern, Central, Mountain, Pacific, Alaskan, Hawaiian/Aleutian, and Samoan.

Test yourself on some other questions asked in the Omni survey.

True or false? The economy-class section of a plane is at the rear, behind full-fare, coach-class seats. False again. But more than six out of ten Americans think it's true. Economy class is not a physical section of any plane. It's a fare category.

The Omni survey also revealed what Americans *do* know about travel. For example, 83 percent knew that a federal law prohibits smoking on domestic flights.

About 67 percent knew that airlines have the legal right to give your seat away if you check in at the gate after the designated time. And 64 percent were correct in identifying a major area of airline confusion. You are not entitled to any compensation if an airline bumps you from a flight but is able to get you to your destination within an hour of your original arrival time.

If the delay is more than one hour, you are entitled to *denied boarding compensation* (DBC) equivalent to the one-way fare to the destination but not more than $200. If the delay is more than two hours, compensation must be doubled. Each airline may also offer bumped passengers a voucher for a free flight in lieu of the DBC.

Finally, the Omni survey asked Americans whether they needed a passport to travel to Mexico, Bermuda, the Bahamas, Puerto Rico, Toronto, or Honolulu. The majority of Americans—60 percent—knew a passport was not required to travel to any of these destinations. However, one out of ten Americans surveyed thought a passport was required to visit Honolulu.

Ouch!

The sad fact remains that Americans can be some of the least adventurous people in the world when it comes to travel. In the summer, we go to Europe. In the winter, we go skiing. We're easily scared by world events. One terrorist incident, and we retreat.

And yet a statistical look at the real numbers concerning travel, safety, and terrorism might surprise you.

Between 1992 and 1999, according to the U.S. State Department, ninety-two American *civilians* were killed by acts of political terrorism overseas.

Want a scarier statistic? Can you guess how many of us slip, fall, injure ourselves, or even die, each year, stepping out of our bathtubs? According to the Consumer Product Safety Commission, it's a staggering 214,973. (That works out to around 600 of us each day!)

So every time friends of mine balk at traveling overseas because of safety concerns, I tell them not to worry. They're free to stay home and take a bath instead. But I caution them: They're on their own!

With exceedingly few exceptions, it is still safe for Americans to travel virtually anywhere in the world. In fact, in recent years, the U.S. government prohibited Americans from traveling to only two countries. The first is Lebanon—and that travel ban was removed in 1997. The other is Libya, and travel restrictions to that country were lifted in 2004.

But what about North Korea, Vietnam, Nicaragua, Iran, South Africa, Ethiopia, or Haiti?

Before you wince and run for cover, consider this: You can get there from here. And with a little advance planning, you can have a great time while learning something about the rest of the world. A growing number of specialty tour and travel agencies offer such trips on a regular basis. And you don't have to be a mercenary in military fatigues to sign up.

The U.S. State Department is no longer cautioning Americans about travel in Russia within a 100-mile radius of Chernobyl, and travel to Kiev (about 60 miles from the site of the April 28, 1986, nuclear disaster) is slowly rebounding.

Grenada, the beautiful 13-by-21-mile Caribbean island known largely because of the 1983 invasion by the United States, is still eagerly awaiting American tourists.

How can you find out the score before traveling somewhere?

The U.S. State Department issues "advisories" and

stronger "warnings" about trouble spots around the world. Currently, the State Department has issued these alerts on a few dozen locations within eight geographic regions. The advisories and warnings concern civil unrest, natural disasters, and disease.

Information on the latest travel advisories can be found on the Internet at http://travel.state.gov. In addition to information on the Internet, travelers may obtain up-to-date information on security conditions by calling 888-407-4747 toll-free in the United States, or outside the United States and Canada on a regular toll line at 317-472-2328.

Some advisories are strongly worded and should be heeded. A few years ago, one advisory on Afghanistan warned that "a high level of risk" existed there. Prospective travelers were informed that the U.S. embassy had been evacuated of all American personnel. It stated that anyone who had to go to the region should avoid travel on the national airline, which had an extremely poor maintenance record.

Fair enough.

Another advisory warned against trekking along the Thailand-Burma (Myanmar) border, since there were reports of bandits and drug traffickers.

Other travel advisories should simply be interpreted with a large dose of common sense. Because the situation in the Middle East continues to be tense, the State Department warns us to refrain from traveling there and adds that if we do go there we should stay away from large crowds and avoid taking buses.

What kind of advice is that? I've lived in Los Angeles for nearly thirty years and I stay away from large crowds and buses *here*!

Translation: The words "State Department advisory" carry an unfortunate negative connotation. If I told you there was a State Department advisory on Turkey, would you refrain from going there? Many of you would, merely after hearing the word "advisory."

Now, let's look at what a recent advisory said: U.S. travelers should be aware that Turkish drivers pass on the right as well as the left. Here's a brief news bulletin: Cab drivers do that all the time on the East River Drive in Manhattan!

The important distinction here is that just because the State Department issues an advisory does not necessarily mean that a country is unsafe. It just means the U.S. government is covering its rear, and with good reason.

In early December 1988, the U.S. embassy in Helsinki received what was regarded as a "credible" threat: a U.S. airliner would be blown out of the sky during the Christmas holiday, on a flight from London or Frankfurt to the United States.

The State Department took the threat so seriously that it immediately informed all U.S. embassy personnel worldwide to avoid taking U.S. airlines during the holiday period. One small problem: The State Department neglected to inform U.S. citizens.

On December 21, 1988, Pan Am Flight 103 was blown out of the sky over Lockerbie, Scotland. From that moment on, if someone tears a fingernail in Peru, has a purse snatched on the streets of Montego Bay, or slips and falls in Oman, the State Department rushes to issue an advisory or bulletin.

The net result: Those advisories fuel our fears—often unnecessarily.

For example, Fiji experienced two coups in 1987, and the State Department issued advisories. Few Americans traveled there. But there was hardly any violence, and no foreigners were killed. Another coup in 2000—the same drop-off in tourism and the same U.S. casualty count: zero.

Place the State Department advisories in their proper perspective as they relate to your specific travel needs.

Certain myths do persist. Just ask the Turkish government how many Americans didn't go to Turkey—and still don't go there—after viewing the movie *Midnight Express.* Or ask the Greek government what happened after the *Achille Lauro* incident, which didn't even occur in Greece.

In part due to security concerns, initial reports indicated that foreign tourism in Greece was down 12 percent in July 2004, just prior to the start of the Summer Olympic Games held in Athens. However, once the Games began, followed by glowing media coverage, bookings for the following September and October increased 10 percent over the same period in the previous year.

Until recently, the United States took a hard line against any of its citizens traveling to Cuba or North Korea. Does that mean you can't go to those countries? Absolutely not. What it does mean is that no U.S. travel agent can sell you a ticket or book you a hotel room there.

If you want to go to Cuba, Canadian travel agencies can easily arrange such a trip and will obtain the proper Cuban visas. (The U.S. Treasury Department says American citizens may not spend U.S. currency in Cuba without a "license.") And any U.S. travel agent can book you a flight to Beijing (for separate flights to Pyongyang) or Bangkok.

At the height of our government's problems with the Sandinistas in Nicaragua, 40 percent of the hundred thousand tourists who went there in 1984 were Americans. Did the American tourists shoot it out with the Contras or the Sandinistas? No—many of them went to the beach.

I have always argued that an advisory is just that—an advisory. You are well advised to read it. But I strongly encourage you to put any advisory in perspective.

Recently, a friend told me she would not be getting off

her cruise ship when it docked in Lisbon, because she had heard there was a State Department advisory. Had she read the advisory? No. She made her decision simply because one had been issued. Well, I *did* read the advisory. It warned only of an increase in pickpocketing and purse snatching in the Portuguese capital. Based on that warning, she should *never* get off the ship at *any* port!

Not surprisingly, the Middle East and Asia are targets of a continuous flow of State Department advisories. Some are specific and quite helpful.

For example, in Indonesia, a number of groups identifying themselves as Islamic organizations showed up in some areas of the country. They demanded names of American guests and delivered an ultimatum that U.S. citizens must leave Indonesia within forty-eight hours. The State Department advised Americans to "defer" travel to Jakarta. And for those Americans already in Indonesia, the State Department advised "extreme caution" in their travels.

In this instance, there was a credible, implied threat, and the State Department's advisory was to be taken seriously.

However, Indonesia is a country of more than seventeen thousand islands, and the major tourist areas of Bali, Sumatra, and North Sulawesi have traditionally remained calm during times of major unrest in Jakarta. And yet, would that State Department advisory keep most people from going to Indonesia? Yes.

And I say this even in light of the terrorist bombing in Bali in October of 2002, which killed 202 people and wounded 209 others. I flew to Bali three months after the tragic events. I was the only American on the Cathay Pacific flight from Hong Kong. I was also one of just three Americans at the luxurious Four Seasons Resort on Jimbaran Bay. I never felt unsafe or threatened—just pampered.

So there lies the sad story of State Department advisories. I support the efforts of any government to inform its people of inherent dangers abroad. But I also support an effort to arrive at a definition of terms for when a danger is real.

Based on the current State Department criteria for issuing most advisories, if our government issued advisories for most U.S. cities, using the same State Department criteria for determining danger and other warnings, none of us would ever leave our own towns.

As a result of 9/11, the Department of Homeland Security created a color code to indicate threat conditions. As of this writing, the code has been raised to orange five times.

1. **Low condition (green).** This condition is declared when there is a low risk of terrorist attack.

2. **Guarded condition (blue).** This condition is declared when there is a general risk of terrorist attack.

3. **Elevated condition (yellow).** This condition is declared when there is a significant risk of terrorist attack. Surveillance of critical locations will be increased and emergency plans should be coordinated as appropriate with nearby jurisdictions. Officials should assess whether the precise characteristics of the threat require the further refinement of preplanned protective measures and implement, as appropriate, contingency and emergency response plans.

4. **High condition (orange).** This condition is declared when there is a high risk of terrorist attack. Necessary security efforts should be coordinated with federal, state, and local law enforcement agencies or any National Guard or other appropriate armed forces organizations. Additional precautions should be taken at public events and possibly alternative venues or even cancellation should be considered. Prepare to execute

contingency procedures, such as moving to an alternate site or dispersing the workforce. Threatened facility access should be restricted to essential personnel only.

5. **Severe condition (red).** This condition reflects a severe risk of terrorist attack. Under most circumstances, personnel should be increased or redirected to address critical emergency needs. Assign emergency response personnel and pre-position and mobilize specially trained teams or resources. Transportation systems should be monitored, redirected, or constrained, and public and government facilities should be closed.

Personally, I think the color-coded alerts are absurd. Few of us pay attention to them or even know what we are supposed to do when a color changes. I think I have a better idea. From now on, when the homeland security folks change the color of an alert it should mean that all of us should dress in that color that day. We could all wear red or orange or yellow, depending on the alert level. This would have the same impact as the current alert system, but at least we'd all have something to talk about that day.

One piece of additional advice: You don't have to depend on just the U.S. State Department for advisories. An excellent alternate source is the British Foreign and Commonwealth Office (FCO, at www.fco.gov.uk).

Bottom line: Read the advisories, but use them *only* as advisories and not as outright prohibitions. The State Department currently has no fewer than three dozen such advisories warning of certain dangers abroad.

If an advisory tells you to defer all travel to a particular country or indicates that all Americans there have been urged to leave—as recently occurred with Iraq—you should definitely avoid going to that country. And as long as you are reading State Department advisories, consider reading some of the advisories foreign governments give *their* citizens about traveling to certain locations.

One of the most informative (and often more candid) sources about medical situations abroad is also the FCO (Great Britain's equivalent of our State Department). It's particularly useful for medical information concerning foreign locations—specifically, disease and epidemics.

As with U.S. State Department advisories, the FCO messages are meant only as advisories and should be read in that context. You can access the reports easily at www.fco.gov .uk/travel/.

If an advisory simply states that you should avoid going to a particular region of a country because of political instability or an outbreak of disease there, just avoid that individual region. You don't have to avoid the entire country.

Keep a generous dose of common sense on hand.

What should you do overseas if you believe there's a potential problem?

First, consider some obvious precautions:

- Don't advertise yourself as an American. Don't wear excessive amounts of jewelry. Don't look like a bad golfer or a professional tourist. (Keep those plaid pants in your suitcase; leave the stupid logo T-shirts at home.)

- On an airplane or at an airport, there is no need to show your U.S. passport unless an airline official or customs agent demands to see it.

- Pick a window seat. Though I personally prefer the aisle, my friend Neil Livingston, chairman of Global Options (an international risk management firm), insists that few terrorists or hijackers will climb over two other people to get to you. He maintains that more than likely, they'll pick the person in the aisle seat as a hostage or target for violence.

Think about this: If the commonsense advice is "Stay away from large crowds," then why travel in one? If there ever was an argument against group tours, this is the best one. And if you must take a group tour, when checking in to a hotel or major tourist site, don't stand with the entire group at the counter or the entry gate.

What happens if a real problem erupts?

This is where I will be accused of being unpatriotic. In the past, when I have been in dangerous areas, the absolute last place I head for is the U.S. embassy. Think about it. The U.S. embassy is the first place that either is attacked or, in anticipation of a threat or attack, is immediately closed, even to its own citizens.

Instead, head for the Canadian embassy. Recent history proves that our neighbors to the north are the real heroes when the proverbial you-know-what hits the fan.

If you're ever in a difficult area or you're concerned, worried, or need information, and it just so happens to be a Friday, definitely head for the Canadian, British, or Australian embassy. Why? In the diplomatic world, these embassies traditionally hold TGIF parties. If you're particularly nice, you just might get invited. And if, for example, you're in the middle of dusty Khartoum—a broken-down city that looks like it was evacuated in 1955 but someone forgot to tell a few million people—it can be most comforting to be invited to one of these parties!

It has been argued that travel does more to promote world peace than just about anything else. Slowly but surely, Americans are beginning to realize that they can visit most countries without undue fear. They can vacation in Central and South America, and they can visit Eastern European countries and the Middle East safely.

By the way, if you're *that* concerned about safety—or even potential hijacking—you might think about making your travel plans on charter flights. The hijacking risk is severely reduced when you travel in this manner. Most terrorists won't even consider a charter flight. Charters rarely leave or arrive on time, and some cancel at the last minute. And after all, how many terrorists book at least thirty days in advance?

Well-informed travelers who break down misperceptions are doing all of us a great service. The first thing these travelers pack is common sense.

That's what this book is about—common sense, and beating the airlines, hotels, cruise lines, and rental car agencies at their own game, playing by their rules. If you look around you, you'll see plenty of disclaimers masquerading as advice on or in virtually every product you buy. In case you needed further proof that the human race is doomed on account of stupidity, here are some actual label instructions that have been found on consumer goods:

- *On a bar of Dial soap:* Directions: Use like regular soap.

- *On some Swanson frozen dinners:* Serving suggestion: Defrost.

- *On a Sears hair dryer:* Do not use while sleeping.

- *On a bag of Fritos:* You could be a winner! No purchase necessary. Details inside.

- *Printed on the bottom of one grocery chain's box of tiramisu dessert:* Do not turn upside down.

- *In England, printed on Marks & Spencer bread pudding:* Product will be hot after heating.

- *On a bottle of children's cough medicine:* Do not drive car or operate machinery.

- *On a bottle of Nytol:* Warning: May cause drowsiness.
- *On a Korean kitchen knife:* Warning: Keep out of children.
- *On a string of Chinese-made Christmas lights:* For indoor or outdoor use only.
- *On an American Airlines packet of nuts:* Instructions: Open packet, eat nuts.
- *And my favorite, on a hotel shower cap:* Instructions: Fits one head.

OK, so much for overly cautious lawyers trying to protect their deep-pocketed clients from outrageous litigation. And so much for what most of us would easily classify as the obvious.

Here's something else that's obvious: Travel isn't much fun these days. And we don't need a set of self-evident instructions to figure that out.

I'll try to stay away from the painfully obvious as we explore the ridiculous and often draconian world of the travel experience. The advice I'm offering in this book comes from my own travel experience, as well as the experiences of countless other road warriors who have been kind enough to share some of their secrets with me.

2

The New Normal

HOW I LEARNED TO STOP WORRYING AND LOVE THE NEW SECURITY PROCEDURES

There are moments you remember because they define your life—the birth of a child, a marriage, hitting a home run in the bottom of the ninth to win that softball game. And there are moments you can never forget because they forever define our collective *lives.* We know exactly where we were when we heard the news that JFK had been shot in Dallas, when we watched Neil Armstrong walk on the moon, and when we first heard that an airplane had hit the World Trade Center— especially when we saw the second airplane, the United Airlines 767, smash into the south tower.

And ever since that September morning, our lives have not been the same.

On the morning of September 11, 2001, I arrived early at the NBC studios at Rockefeller Plaza. I was scheduled to make an appearance that morning on the *Today* show. It was a glorious, sunny fall day, with almost unlimited visibility. Outside the studio, a large crowd had assembled for the morning ritual of watching the show. I remember there were some firemen there, handing out small toy fire trucks. Why? It was national 911 day, and they were there to help promote awareness of emergency services across the United States. One of them handed me a small red truck.

Inside the studio, Matt Lauer was interviewing an author, Richard Hack, about his new book. I was in the greenroom on the second floor with some of the other guests. Suddenly, Matt stopped the interview in midsentence as the screen switched to a long shot of the north tower of the World Trade Center, smoke billowing out of the upper floors.

The early report, Lauer said, was that it appeared a small plane had flown into the tower. I looked at the television monitor, at the initial devastation to the upper floors. I tried to put the size of the damaged area into some kind of perspective. It was too wide a hole, too much damage for one small plane to have caused, I thought.

I ran downstairs to the basement control room, where producers were scrambling to get more information. "That was no small plane," I told executive producer Jonathan Wald. "It could not have been a small plane. And in this kind of weather, pilot error can't be a factor. This was no accident. . . ." But I was only going on intuition. It was too early to make that kind of definitive claim on national television.

Then suddenly, as the world watched with us, we noticed a tiny blip on the horizon, a small dot in the air approaching the south tower. On the long shot we were all seeing, we first thought it was a rescue helicopter. But as it got closer, and in the instant it took me to realize it was moving much too fast to be a helicopter, it happened. The plane came quickly into view and before anyone could react, a United Airlines 767 sliced right into the south tower, a ball of flame exiting the building.

I stayed at NBC that day, reporting continuously for the network, for CNBC, and for MSNBC.

As I worked the phones, talking to sources, it soon became obvious that these four planes were picked for a reason. Each was scheduled on a transcontinental flight, meaning they were all loaded with fuel. Each of the planes was the first or second flight out in the morning. I then confirmed that each aircraft had overnighted at its respective airport the previous evening. It didn't take long to figure out what the plan was.

Within an hour of the incident, I walked into Studio 1A and handed Katie Couric a handwritten note, which she read on the air. These fuel-loaded planes had been picked for a reason. They were nothing less than flying bombs, aerial weapons of mass destruction.

Later, walking to my hotel on a deserted Fifth Avenue shortly after 1:30 A.M. on September 12, I continued to be troubled by a number of unanswered questions. How were these hijackers, these terrorists with limited flight training, able to hit three of their four targets with such deadly accuracy?

I watched the repeats of the horrendous videos of the second plane flying into the south tower. One of the videos, shown on CNN, was taken from a different vantage point—from a position south of the south tower—and it showed the plane, from behind, flying directly into the building. It was a fascinating perspective to watch, because in slow motion the building seemed to simply absorb and digest the aircraft. There was a delay before we saw the fireball. (I was later told by an astrophysicist that this meant the plane was actually flying faster than its own explosion.)

I couldn't get that image out of my head. And then it hit me. I had seen that image before . . . when I played on my computer with a flight simulator program.

It was Microsoft Flight Simulator 2000. And in that program, I could fly a jet to O'Hare, to Washington National, to LaGuardia or JFK. And I could program the screen to give me different perspectives, including one from behind the plane as I flew it.

I remembered that once, playing with the simulator, I had decided what it would look like—what the computer would show on the screen—if I flew my plane under the Golden Gate Bridge in San Francisco. Next I tried flying around downtown Chicago, and perilously close to the John Hancock building. Then I flew the simulated aircraft around the World Trade Center and the Empire State Building in Manhattan. Twice, when I miscalculated, I actually hit the bridge. In another case, I tried to fly between the two antennae of the Hancock building and crashed.

And that's when that image hit me. It almost matched

what I was watching on that CNN video of the United 767 hitting the south tower.

Two days later, as the names of some of the hijackers became known, as reports surfaced that investigators were searching some apartments in Florida where the terrorists had stayed, I called one of my law enforcement sources and asked him if they were finding any useful evidence at the last known locations where the terrorists had stayed. "Yes," he said, "we're getting some pretty interesting stuff. And we found some of their computers."

I then took a shot. "Microsoft Flight Simulator 2000 on any of those computers?" I asked. There was silence on the other end of the phone. "Yes," he said quietly. "It looks like these guys just practiced at home."

I ran over to NBC, and they sent a researcher out to buy the Microsoft software. We installed the software, and then looked at the book that came with the simulator. And that's when we saw it. The book contained the exact coordinates of the World Trade Center (then part of the approach to La-Guardia), as well as the Pentagon (part of the approach to Washington National Airport). Within an hour, people with hardly any flight experience were sitting in front of the computer screen and were easily able to "fly" right into the WTC and the Pentagon. That night, we reported the story on *Dateline*. The next day, Microsoft recalled the product from store shelves across America.

As the investigation continued, America quickly became familiar with the uses for box cutters and obsessed with airport security. The hijackers had apparently used the box cutters to slash the throats of the pilots and some passengers on the doomed planes.

In short order, the U.S. government created the Department of Homeland Security, complete with cabinet-level status, which grew quickly to 180,000 employees. And the protocol of taking an airplane flight would change forever.

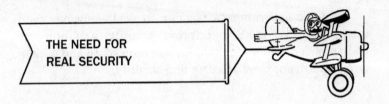

THE NEED FOR REAL SECURITY

Any frequent flier could have told you on September 10 that airline and airport security was bad, even laughable. It wasn't as if no one knew how dire the situation really was.

FAA NEEDS PREBOARD PASSENGER SCREENING PERFORMANCE STANDARDS. . . .

AVIATION SECURITY: URGENT ISSUES NEED TO BE ADDRESSED. . . .

DEVELOPMENT OF NEW SECURITY TECHNOLOGY HAS NOT MET EXPECTATIONS. . . .

These newspaper headlines didn't run in 2004, 2003, 2002, or even in 2001. They are from . . . 1987, 1990, and 2000.

There are those like Max H. Bazerman and Michael D. Watkins, the authors of *Predictable Surprises* (Harvard Business School, 2004), who argue, convincingly, that "September 11 was not only a predictable surprise, it was a predicted event." Indeed, Bazerman, a Harvard Business School professor, reported that fifteen months before September 11, a U.S. General Accounting Office report warned that "the trend in terrorism against U.S. targets is toward large scale incidents designed for maximum destruction, terror and media impact."

The 9/11 scenario became that much easier once you acknowledged that the true value of airport security was only as a psychological deterrent to emotionally disturbed people.

And the government's reaction to 9/11—however well intentioned the push to improve security, and however badly needed—failed to embrace common sense and a long-term, intelligent view of safety and security.

MORONS IN UNIFORM: THE DEATH OF COMMON SENSE

No one can, should, or, in my case, will dispute the need for tougher security at airports, train stations, bus stations, tunnels, bridges, hotels, and cruise-ship ports. And we are certainly throwing a lot of money into security. The total federal government budget for homeland security for 2005 is $23 billion, up 24 percent from 2004 ($18.4 billion).

But it's not just the amount of money we're throwing at the issue. The real problem is how to implement security in a way that actually provides real protection, prevention, or deterrence without sacrificing common sense. And sadly, despite all that money and even with the best of intentions, we have not done this.

Homeland security has become a necessary illusion. It is a physical impossibility to secure all airline flights. A terrorist dedicated to his cause and willing to die for it can easily beat any system. So anyone who claims that our airport security cannot be penetrated is a liar. At the same time, anyone who demands a 100 percent effective solution to the terror threat is a fool. It cannot be accomplished.

The government has attempted to make us feel that it is at least doing something, and considering the shock we suffered on 9/11, the government does deserve some praise for raising the comfort level.

Still, there is more show than substance. Remember how, in the days following 9/11, the airports were flooded with the U.S. National Guard? One report described them as useless "mannequins," simply standing around at screening points. Then there were the untrained personnel stationed at entrances to airports and parking lots, whose only job was to conduct meaningless "glance and go" car searches.

Since the establishment of the Department of Homeland Security and the hiring of thousands of new airport screeners, I have met dozens of intelligent, polite, and dedicated Transportation Security Administration (TSA) workers. However, many of the policies they are required to enforce and apply are nothing short of stupid. And it makes the situation that much tougher for all of us.

Bad planning and bad policies have led to less-than-kind nicknames for the TSA (Thousands Standing Around, Taking Scissors Away . . .). They are still out there strip-searching nuns, looking for tweezers. They are still playing a ridiculous game of Red Light, Green Light in their hunt for terrorists. And in their pursuit of those terrorists, they have created a worse situation for the very travelers the economy so desperately needs to stay in the skies.

About the only way in which the current TSA workers and their rent-a-cop airport security predecessors differ is that now I can actually discuss their moronic behavior with them in a language they can comprehend.

Since 9/11, passenger profiling regimes have gotten worse, not better. Then there are the physical intrusions, ranging from removing shoes and suit jackets to less-than-gentle pat-downs of female fliers.

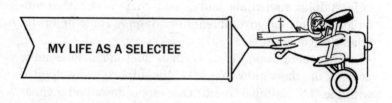

MY LIFE AS A SELECTEE

I have a growing collection of airline boarding passes, each of which has a bold "SSSS" printed on the front. These boarding passes are proof that I am a very special passenger. I get pulled out of line on almost every flight, targeted for secondary screening.

I'm not alone.

My friend Jeff Katz, the former head of Orbitz, has a similar collection of boarding passes, plus an unusual photo collection. He, like me, was always listed as a "selectee." He became so frustrated at being pulled out of line every time he flew that he brought along a small digital camera and actually photographed every TSA agent who searched him. In less than three months, he had a fabulous rogues' gallery of uniformed security folks hanging on his wall.

As a frequent business traveler, I usually fly at the last minute, often on a one-way ticket, and I never check bags. Despite the fact that I am a megamillion miler, a high-yield business traveler, that combination of flight planning, ticket type, and luggageless travel marks me as a distinct target under current profiling practices. As a result, with very few exceptions, my tickets get marked with the dreaded **SSSS**. That's right, I am a selectee.

I might as well change my first name to Ahmed. (Believe me, the thought has crossed my mind.) Just about every time

I go to an airport, I am assured that I will be part of the secondary screening process.

It's absurd. There is no common sense applied. It wastes time and energy. And oh yes, did I mention that it's outright annoying?

At one point, at the Phoenix airport, when I saw my boarding pass coming out of a printer with the **SSSS** printed on its face, I decided to stand my ground. I told the counter agent I wanted to know why I was always a selectee. Could she, perhaps, find out? The agent disappeared behind the counter. When she returned, she handed me a printed form. "Here," she said, "you'll need this." It was a set of instructions from the TSA. "It seems you're on the no-fly list."

The federal government has ordered airlines to turn over personal information about their customers. Under this system, called "Secure Flight," the TSA says it will screen possible terrorists by comparing passenger data with names on two government lists. The "no-fly" list comprises the names of known or suspected terrorists, while a "watch" list names people who should face tighter scrutiny before boarding planes. The no-fly list now has twenty thousand names, and three hundred new ones are added daily. Many are duplicate entries. And this should make you feel safer: There are dead people and even people in prison on the list!

And the reason I was on this list? "Well," she reported, "it seems there's someone on that list named Greenberg, and your name keeps coming up."

I wrote a letter of complaint to the office listed on that TSA instruction sheet (ombudsman@dhs.gov). I have never heard back. And I continue to be taken out of line.

Well, at least I'm in good company: me, Ted Kennedy, and Cat Stevens.

It seems that getting on the no-fly list is infinitely easier than getting off.

A top homeland security official had to apologize to Senator Edward M. Kennedy, who was stopped at airports because a name similar to his appeared on the government's no-fly list of terror suspects. "If they have that kind of difficulty with a member of Congress, how in the world are average Americans, who are getting caught up in this thing, how are they going to be treated fairly and not have their rights abused?" Kennedy asked homeland security undersecretary Asa Hutchinson.

Each time Kennedy was denied boarding and asked airline counter agents why, he was told, "We can't tell you."

And if you think it was bad that Kennedy was put on the list, consider this: Even as a U.S. senator, it took Kennedy three months to get *off* the list! Nevertheless, twice after contacting the TSA Kennedy was stopped again at the airline counter.

The original TSA order, issued late in 2004, forced seventy-two airlines to turn over computerized data for passengers who had traveled on domestic flights during June 2004. The data, known as *passenger name records,* or PNR, can include credit card numbers, travel itineraries, addresses, telephone numbers, and meal requests. And those meal requests have often been used to presume a passenger's religion or ethnicity.

Therein lie the civil liberties issues. As well intentioned as the government order might be, a major problem is that the lists include the names of many people who are not security risks. Furthermore, the lists themselves are often a hodgepodge of inaccurate or outdated information. Perhaps most disturbing is that when the TSA issued the order, the agency allowed for no formal way for anyone mistakenly identified as a terrorist—or those who might have the same name as a terrorist—to get off the list.

The American Civil Liberties Union has filed lawsuits in

San Francisco and Seattle over this issue, demanding that the government explain how wrongly flagged travelers can get off the lists.

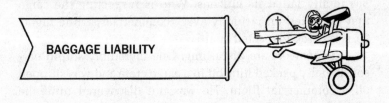

BAGGAGE LIABILITY

Part of the protocol of airline travel after 9/11 dealt with a change in the way checked baggage is handled. Prior to 9/11, U.S. airlines did not match passengers with checked baggage. This meant that anyone, for any reason, could check in for a flight and check their bags, and the bags would travel on that flight whether or not the passenger did. To make matters worse, the bags were never inspected or screened. That was a security breach you could drive a Humvee through.

After 9/11, the government moved with deliberate speed to begin screening checked baggage, and more than a year after 9/11, the TSA began inspecting all checked bags. However, it took much longer for the airlines to actually match passengers with their luggage. And even then, the airlines did the matching only on originating, not on connecting, flights. Another security loophole.

But along with the new baggage screening procedures came additional problems. Passengers could no longer lock their bags. The luggage had to be screened by machine or manually by TSA inspectors. As a result, the TSA ended up paying an average of $110 to each of the fifteen thousand passengers who claimed their possessions had been lost, stolen, or damaged during those inspections.

The TSA had initially settled 1,800 claims in twenty-two

months in 2004. At the same time, two dozen screeners in New York, New Orleans, Detroit, Spokane, and Fort Lauderdale were charged with stealing from checked bags.

But what about air cargo? This is where the government has totally failed its citizens. Who is inspecting the cargo that is carried on virtually every commercial airline flight? Or is it being inspected at all?

The answers are disturbing. One incredibly stupid person actually packed himself in a cargo crate and was shipped on a commercial flight. He was not discovered until the plane landed. Miraculously, he had arrived alive. Alarmingly, only 5 percent of the 2.8 million tons of packages, mail, and luggage are screened.

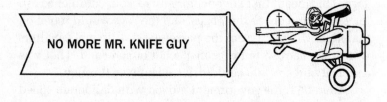

NO MORE MR. KNIFE GUY

There is no doubt—and the statistics certainly prove this—that heightened security since 9/11 has resulted in authorities being able to confiscate a wide variety of weapons, or items that can be used as weapons, on board planes. And they're doing this at passenger security checkpoints.

Of the millions of things seized by the TSA, many were concealed weapons—mostly knives inside belt buckles, canes, and umbrellas. Other things taken from passengers include thousands of cans of mace, cigarette lighters, handcuffs, and the inevitable box cutters.

Some were downright absurd. When I did a *Today* show segment on all the seized items, TSA officials at JFK had them on full display for us at the airport. And sitting right there on the large tables, in between the knives and the scissors and the baseball bats was . . . a small selection of industrial chain saws! Yes, people actually tried to board flights carrying chain saws. These aren't terrorists. These are just truly stupid people!

I now feel so much safer because I am being protected from onboard chainsaws . . .

But the real problem is that most airline passengers in the United States are not screened for explosives before boarding a plane. We merely walk through metal detectors, but we are not screened by explosive detection technology.

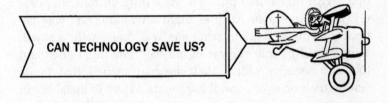

CAN TECHNOLOGY SAVE US?

No. Technology without common sense is counterproductive and wasteful. We are now acutely aware of the case of Richard Reid, the notorious shoe bomber, who tried to detonate his sneaker on an American Airlines flight from London.

And as a result of that incident, I have also changed my choice of footwear. Like thousands of other passengers, I no longer wear shoes that contain any metal. I made this decision with the intention of saving time at security checkpoints.

But it hasn't exactly worked out that way. The TSA has been playing a silly and unnecessary game of Red Light, Green Light. It was a stupid game when I was eight. It's a ludicrous game now. At many checkpoints, passengers have the option of walking through metal detectors without being forced to take off their shoes. In fact, if you ask TSA inspectors whether it's permissible to walk through the magnetometers while still wearing your nonmetallic shoes, they'll say it's your "option." What they won't tell you (but I will) is that if you do walk through, you're immediately taken out of line for secondary screening. Now, that's stupid. Please, treat me like an adult. Just tell me—and everyone else traveling—that if I choose not to remove my shoes, I will automatically be detained. "We don't have to disclose that," one TSA inspector argued. Well, let me disclose that for them . . . and to you. Now you know you don't really have an option at all.

Ready for even more stupidity? Read on. Recently, as I was going through security at Dallas–Fort Worth, I noticed that a TSA officer had pulled aside a fully uniformed, properly IDed American Airlines flight attendant. She was patiently trying to explain what she was doing with a small, 1-inch Phillips screwdriver in her bag. The flight attendant told the security officer that she had carried that petite screwdriver on every one of her flights. Why? To assist her in the galley—to make sure the coffeepot didn't fly out of its holder, to tighten fittings on beverage carts, and so on. He was unimpressed. He told her he had to confiscate the screwdriver. Since I was standing right behind her, I couldn't help but insert myself into their conversation.

"Surely you're not going to take that little screwdriver from this flight attendant," I began.

"Sorry, but it's our policy," he responded (one of my least favorite responses in the universe).

"You realize of course the absurdity of this?" I asked. (He didn't.) "In about seven minutes, this woman is going to board a plane as a working flight attendant, and the very first thing she's going to be given in the galley is an eight-inch corkscrew!"

He was unfazed. Our tax dollars at work: policy taking precedence over common sense.

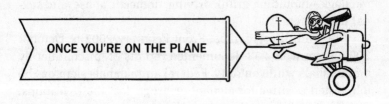

ONCE YOU'RE ON THE PLANE

When it comes to onboard security, there is no middle ground. Either the cockpit door is secure or it isn't.

Which brings up the subject of sky marshals. Are they really needed, and if they are, are they ever effective?

If airport security works, if the cockpit is truly locked and secured, sky marshals would never be needed. In fact, the British Air Line Pilots Association (BALPA) put it best when the United Kingdom was contemplating boarding armed marshals on flights out of Britain. "If we need armed marshals on our planes," the group argued, "then we shouldn't be flying."

I couldn't agree more. The way the air marshal system is currently constructed, the use of sky marshals is more style than substance. The air marshal service has been greatly expanded, from a budget of $4.4 million in 2001 to $545 million in 2003.

But money isn't everything. There are clearly not enough of them. Most of the time, they sit in seat 3B, wear Pendleton shirts, and try to "blend." Are they truly a deterrent? Only in a perceived sense. After all, the concept embodies the Dirty Harry approach. Since sky marshals are not on every flight, it's the *idea* of the marshals, rather than the reality, that security officials are hoping works. Is the hijacker "feeling lucky"?

Do you feel lucky? Consider this recent report from the Office of the Inspector General of the Department of Homeland Security. It examined a review of 504 job applicants, all of whom had been approved as air marshals. One small problem in the report: 161 approved applicants had major red flags—including drunk driving, domestic abuse, and sexual harassment.

But wait, it gets worse. From February 2002 to October 2003, there were 753 documented reports of misconduct by air marshals while on duty. Federal air marshals slept on the job, tested positive for alcohol or drugs, lost their weapons, and falsified information.

Ideally, there should be no middle ground here. There should be a visible, physical deterrent: Install one marshal on every flight, uniformed, and sitting in the jump seat near the front left door, *facing* the passengers, or there shouldn't be air marshals. Period.

That may never happen. Instead, we're left with absurd knee-jerk reactions to 9/11, including the Reagan Rules for flights to and from Reagan National Airport in Washington, D.C. Because flights to that airport use an approach that goes up the Potomac near the Pentagon, the Capitol, and the White House, the government ruled that on flights headed to Reagan no passengers can leave their seats as of thirty minutes before landing. In the case of the New York–to–Washington shuttle, it's quite a circus, since the total elapsed flight time is only thirty-eight minutes. Translation: Once you board the flight, you can't stand up . . . period. Can't go to the bathroom, can't retrieve anything from an overhead compartment, nada.

Before boarding, announcements are made about the rules, and dozens of passengers race for airport restrooms. Then comes the fun part. Fifteen minutes into the trip, a flight attendant comes down the aisle with a drink cart, and just about everyone refuses! (No bathroom trips, remember?)

The stupidity of the Reagan Rules once again presumes that the cockpit is not secure and there are no air marshals on board. We have either secure cockpit doors and uniformed air marshals or the stupid Reagan Rules. Which one do you like the least?

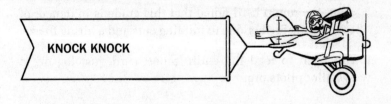

KNOCK KNOCK

And once again speaking of cockpit doors . . . are they secure? The answer: not really. Even pilots have to urinate during a flight, and that means the door is opened at least twice on every flight.

Then there's the actual physical deterrent. In 2004, United Airlines announced plans to add steel cable barriers on five hundred cockpit doors to bar access to the flight deck when the cabin door is open. The barrier can be locked in place when pilots leave the cockpit to use the lavatory or when receiving in-flight meals. Currently, flight attendants block the entrance with a beverage cart when the door is open. That may give some comfort to United's pilots and flight attendants, but when a coalition of airline pilots associations released its own Aviation Security Report Card, it was clear the security problems went way beyond the cockpit door.

The report card assessed various aspects of aviation security such as

- Perimeter security, which earned a grade of "D" due to inconsistencies at the nation's airports.
- Screening of people, bags, and cargo, which earned various marginal and failing grades.

- Credentialing, which scored an "F." Effective airport security requires proper credentialing for anyone with access to the cockpit.
- The federal air marshal program, which received a "C," but the report card noted that this grade is in danger of dropping further due to funding cuts and a hiring freeze.

If you want to read the entire report card, just log on to www.alliedpilots.org.

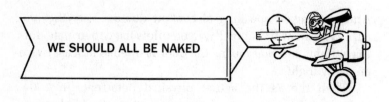

WE SHOULD ALL BE NAKED

When you think about how long the security lines are at most U.S. airports, and how long the delays are, a logical conclusion would be that we should all arrive naked at the airports, holding only our photo IDs and tickets. The scene wouldn't be pretty, but the lines would sure move a whole lot faster.

In all seriousness, the waiting time to go through security at U.S. airports continues to get worse. On average, wait times in 2004 were up 15 percent over 2003. And while there were some noticeable improvements—in Chicago, the wait time to clear security at O'Hare averaged slightly more than five minutes—other airports' performances were downright terrible. The average wait time at LAX: more than twenty-six minutes! (One reason for this is that airports on the East and West Coasts have more originating flights. At least half of O'Hare's passengers, for example, are connecting to other flights and have already cleared security.)

Watch out for airports like Fort Lauderdale on days when cruise ships arrive back in the harbor—the airport is jammed with passengers returning from the megaships, and not one of them has ever learned to pack light.

Certain things are known. There is no uniformity when it comes to the application of passenger security at U.S. airports. And there may never be. Solution: Develop your own consistent rules of travel to minimize the wait time, not to mention the inevitable hassles.

First, we need to change our paradigm for packing—but even more important, *dressing*—for a flight. Our conditioning, of course, is to check our bags and actually dress for travel. It is time to reverse that long-standing ritual. Check no bags on domestic flights—courier or ship them ahead of you. Do *not* dress for the airport; instead, *un*dress.

Before you ever leave for the airport, get a plastic bag and then take everything metal out of your pockets—eyeglasses, pens, keys, spare change, cell phone, Blackberry, camera, and watch—and place the items in the bag. Place the plastic bag in your carry-on bag. (Women need to consider one additional item: If you're wearing an underwire bra, remove it and place that in the carry-on bag as well. Wear a sports bra to get through security.)

In the winter months, wear jackets with lots of pockets, so you can put additional metallic stuff (if you have it) in those pockets. You'll be required to remove all jackets and coats.

Don't hesitate to remove your shoes. (Remember Red Light, Green Light?)

And, of course, don't lock your bags. Baggage locks are, at best, ornamental, and TSA officials will not hesitate to break the locks to inspect your bags.

During holiday periods, do *not* gift wrap any presents. Wrap them after you arrive at your destination, or at least after you've cleared the security checkpoint.

These pointers may help to move the lines faster, but it doesn't mean we're any safer. Even with all the increased security presence and visibility, most airline passengers in the U.S. are not screened for explosives. And neither is most of their carry-on luggage.

In the end, it gets down once again to basic common sense. Don't lock your bags. Don't wrap presents. Have your ID and boarding pass ready. Label your luggage on the outside *and* on the inside. And put your film in your carry-on bag, *not* in your checked baggage.

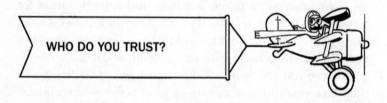

WHO DO YOU TRUST?

Frequent travelers—not surprisingly—are the most vocal complainers when it comes to airport security. They feel they are being singled out, with the irony being that they claim they are the very passengers the airports and airlines should be coveting and pampering.

You can blame that on CAPPS, otherwise known as the Computer-Assisted Passenger Prescreening System—something I have grown to hate. Buy a ticket with cash or travel on a one-way ticket, and you are automatically selected for secondary screening. Ugh . . .

And while some airports actually feature a first-class aisle for faster processing (for first-class or business-class passengers), this doesn't always mean they get expedited treatment.

At the same time, the U.S. is testing a "trusted traveler program"—preemptive security checks that presumably will allow a select few to avoid the dreaded security lines—or at least one of them. Travelers who join the program pay a one-time processing fee of $100 and provide two government IDs as well as biometric data in the form of an iris scan and digital fingerprinting. This information is then run through twenty-two separate government databases to check identity.

This registered traveler program may help only a few people: In order to qualify, you have to fly at least once a week out of your hometown airport, and you have to be a very frequent flier with an airline that is participating in the program.

And then there are some significant privacy issues. Although a majority of frequent fliers say they would be in favor of such a program being implemented across the board—and would actually be willing to pay between $50 and $100 to be processed for such a program—most are unaware that as currently constructed, they won't be saving a whole lot of time. Why? While registered travelers get to stand in their own separate line, the line leads them to a machine that looks like an ATM and reads either their fingerprints or their irises. They still have to go through a metal detector and have their carry-on baggage pass through the x-ray scanners. The only good news: They will no longer be randomly selected for additional screening.

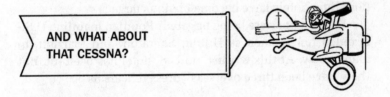

AND WHAT ABOUT THAT CESSNA?

Because of the government's focus on commercial aviation, security at small airports serving private and charter aircraft is inadequate—or nonexistent.

According to a study by the U.S. Government Accountability Office, the Transportation Security Administration still doesn't understand the risks posed by small private planes, fails to issue meaningful threat information to general aviation airports, and can't ensure that charter airlines and flight schools comply with security regulations.

Indeed, it is a challenge for the TSA, considering that there are about nineteen thousand general aviation airports in the United States.

HOSPITALITY IN THE AGE OF TERROR

An overall look at post-9/11 security would easily reveal an obsession with airports and airplanes. But it has always been the contention of many security experts that hotels are prime terrorist targets. After all, terrorists don't go down the path of most resistance, rather, they take the path of least resistance. And while everyone else seems to be focused on air transportation, hotels have become obvious targets.

Which hotels are being targeted? Popular, mainline U.S.-branded hotels such as Hilton, Sheraton, and Marriott, to name a few. At this writing, no U.S. hotel has been hit. But there have been three overseas "dress rehearsals":

- The Sheraton in Islamabad
- The Marriott in Jakarta
- The Hilton in Taba, Egypt

Each hotel was chosen by terrorists because of its brand link with America. But each was also chosen because of the very nature of the security loopholes at hotels: multiple entrances and exits, easy vehicle access, and hundreds of unattended bags in lobbies.

In late 2003, a poll asked more than 2,300 tourists in Southern California what factors they thought were the most important in planning a vacation or a convention. On a scale of 1 to 10 (with 10 being the highest level of importance), these visitors gave security a rating of 8.9. In choosing a hotel, two-thirds said safety was their single most important concern.

Hotels are indeed popular targets. And sadly, most hotel managers—even when confronted with the high potential for terrorist acts at hotels—are not moved to implement proactive, effective security perimeters around their buildings. They have intentionally chosen to ignore the obvious: spacious lobbies, driveways (and in some cases, underground entries), and, of course, the uninspected bags.

Why ignore this? These hotels are worried about market share and fear—that to implement metal detectors and bag scanners in lobbies would frighten their guests. And yet, if the *thinkable* happens—if a U.S.-branded hotel is indeed a terrorism target on American soil—there won't be a hotel or motel that doesn't install the same type of airport technology to screen arriving guests and visitors.

Granted, a Motel 6 in Topeka is probably safer than the huge Hilton in midtown Manhattan, but the principles of proactive security apply across the board. In fact, hotels should model themselves after . . . casinos! I'm serious. If hotels protected their guests the way casinos protected their money, there would be no security issues.

Consider this. When they built the new Borgata hotel and casino in Atlantic City, they installed more than two thousand video cameras to watch the 125,000-square-foot casino floor, 70,000 square feet of event space, 50,000-square-foot spa, 7,100-car parking lot, and access routes to 2,000 guest rooms. The hotel even employs an automatic face-recognition system to screen for known cheats. Officials at Borgata have argued that their security is better than any airport or hotel security, and I believe them.

These are the three security-related questions you need to ask before checking into a hotel:

1. How well does the hotel know its employees? How thorough are background checks? This doesn't apply just to terrorism, but is used to prevent misdemeanors and felonies.

2. Are there security cameras? Every entrance and exit and every hallway should be covered by security cameras, and so should parking lots.

3. Are incoming cars inspected before they pull up in front of the lobby or inside the parking lot?

And be sure to ask the hotel what it is doing to upgrade its security. Remember, security doesn't have to be positioned as a negative. If properly employed, it is a definite positive.

Remember this word: *biometrics.* You're going to be hearing a lot about it.

Biometrics is a system used to identify individuals based on their unique physiological characteristics. Face, iris, and retina scans are among the more advanced forms of biometric identification.

The advantages of the system are significant. Scientists argue that digital finger scans make exit from and entry into the country more efficient for travelers. Perhaps more important are the travelers the system is designed to keep out.

Although the technology works, there are loopholes in the system. For example, fingerprint scanning can't help you if the criminals haven't been entered into the terrorist databases. Nevertheless, the Department of Homeland Security has already started using the system. A pilot program was initiated last summer at O'Hare in Chicago to track travelers' departure data. And the State Department has announced that it plans to issue American passports embedded with facial recognition technology and other detailed biographic data beginning this year.

In the meantime, at least one hotel isn't waiting to try the system.

In 2004, prior to the Democratic National Convention in Boston, Nine Zero Hotel became the first hotel in the world to install an advanced iris authentication system. Starting with the convention, access to Nine Zero Hotel's Cloud Nine penthouse suite, as well as the property's employee and vendor entrance, was secured by this iris identification camera technology. Entrance is granted only to those who are positively identified and who have been previously approved by Nine Zero Hotel.

The system works by combining specially designed camera and software technology to take quick digital pictures of the irises of guests and associates, with no physical contact required. This system works because the iris, the colored part of the eye, is completely unique for each individual, even identical twins. The image is converted into a code in Nine Zero Hotel's private system. In less than two seconds, cameras set up on-site can identify people and grant or deny them entry, even if they are wearing glasses or contact lenses.

Why won't other hotels do this? Remember that as travelers, we vote with our wallets. You should not stay at hotels that don't ask for a photo ID when you check in. You should also avoid hotels that don't ask to see your room key before allowing you elevator access. And you should avoid any hotel that allows unattended, uninspected baggage to pile up on the floor of its lobby.

Once hotel owners and managers realize that we will not patronize hotels that haven't created this kind of proactive security perimeter, change will happen. Or, sadly, we may have to wait until a U.S.-branded hotel is blown up—if history is any indication, it may take a fatal explosion to force hoteliers to think outside the traditional marketing box and do the right thing.

**AND IF YOU THINK HOTELS
ARE BAD SECURITY RISKS . . .**

How about a cruise or a train ride?

Perhaps the saddest thing I have to report is that our bus and train stations, tunnels, bridges—*and* cruise ships—are about as well protected as our airports were on September 10, 2001.

Consider these numbers: In 2003, the North American cruise industry generated $25.4 billion and added more than 295,000 jobs to the economy. Over 9.8 million global passengers took a cruise that year, and spent $12.9 billion in the United States. And yet the CIA has concluded that the most likely way weapons of mass destruction would enter the United States is by sea. According to Stephen Flynn, senior fellow in National Security Studies at the Council on Foreign Relations, "The federal government is spending more every three years to finance the war in Iraq than it has provided over the last three years to improve the security of all 361 U.S. commercial seaports."

Security at seaports means inspecting incoming and outgoing cargo *and* passengers. Since 2001, cruise lines have issued photo ID cards for passengers to use when boarding or disembarking during their cruise. In July 2004, cruise and cargo ships were required to provide manifests of passenger and crew names prior to arrival in the United States. Passengers are now supposedly screened and checked against the U.S. Immigration and Naturalization Service "Prevent Departure" lists, and notice is given to the Coast Guard ninety-six hours in advance of entering a U.S. port. In addition, a 100-yard security zone is maintained around the ship.

All cruise ships now have an onboard security officer as well. The cruise lines also have installed airport-type x-ray machines in most ports to inspect cruise passengers' carry-on luggage. However, many of the people operating these machines, especially in foreign ports, are not thoroughly trained. And what about the heavier luggage that passengers leave at dockside to be brought onto the ship? Many cruise lines will claim those bags are inspected, but in reality they are not.

What's worse? Cargo. According to former homeland security chief Tom Ridge, "Our intermodal seaports are the linchpin of our container-based economy. Rail, truck and ship traffic is highly integrated. A terrorist has plenty of options to move and hide . . ."

Given that information, what are we doing about it? Not much, despite staggering numbers. Very little of the homeland security budget has been properly allocated to examine cargo. At this writing, if the Department of Homeland Security even tried to inspect incoming cargo, it would create mass chaos and force some ports to shut down. The government has not provided the money to support the staff and equipment to do the job. Although the ports have asked for nearly $1 billion in each round of the Department of Homeland Security's Port Security Grant Program, up until now, available federal funding has covered just 13 to 17 percent of that. Compared to what is spent on aviation security, the ports get a nickel to the airline industry's dollar.

The train system fares no better, and perhaps even worse. Compared to airport security, U.S. railroads are a terrorist's amusement park, and all the rides are free.

The March 2004 terrorist train bombings in Madrid that killed nearly 200 people and injured more than 1,800 showed the vulnerability of a major rail system to attack.

Commuter rail systems provide an average 1.2 million passenger trips every weekday in the United States. Amtrak carried more than twenty-four million people in 2004, and let's not forget the freight railroads, which accounted for more than 42 percent of America's intercity ton-miles. That's a lot of freight.

Now consider this: Since 9/11, the United States has spent $11 billion on airline security. How much on rail security? $100 million.

What's worse, the $11 billion has been spent improving security on what already is a closed transportation environment with relatively few access points. The rail system has unlimited access points.

So why not start with baggage screening? The TSA has done a few sixty-day tests at subway stops outside of Washington, D.C. But nothing has moved forward. As with hotel and port security, the money may not be forthcoming unless or until there is a serious attack.

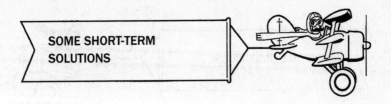

SOME SHORT-TERM SOLUTIONS

"Fly on the damn plane! Calculate the odds of being harmed by a terrorist. It's still about as likely as being swept out to sea by a tidal wave." So says Arizona senator John McCain.

For starters, do not allow yourself to be motivated by fear. It's the worst thing you can do to yourself. Then while you're at it, calculate the real odds of being killed in an airplane accident, a terrorist incident, or the like. At this point, it becomes a no-brainer.

Having said all of this, I continue to fly—partly because I have to, but mostly because I *want* to. When it comes to safety and security, the odds are still overwhelmingly in your favor. At one point between 2002 and 2003, the airlines had more than thirteen *million* takeoffs and landings without a single fatality. Amazing. And convincing.

Part of the solution *is* common sense. Most of us have been conditioned over the years to dress and pack before we go to the airport. It's logical. But logic has nothing to do with the flying experience anymore. My advice—as I've said before and which I follow myself—is to *undress* and *unpack* before I go to the airport. I take everything metal and put it in ziplock plastic bags. I wear slip-on shoes or sneakers. Then when I walk to security, I get to walk *through* security. All I have to do is remove my jacket, take off my shoes, and remove my laptop. If everyone did this, we'd save, on average, ten minutes every time we flew.

AND IF ALL ELSE FAILS . . .

Be the first line of defense in your own travel security and safety:

- At hotels and train stations, unattended luggage spells trouble. Report it.
- At hotels, cars should not be parked in front of the lobby. Complain.
- If you see a "do not disturb" sign on a hotel guest room door for more than twenty-four hours—and unless you know there's a honeymoon couple inside—that's a clear indication that someone wants to deny access to the room. Report it.

And a note about personal possessions . . .

The last thing I want is to contribute to the TSA collection. Before surrendering anything to the TSA, ask whether it's possible to go back out through security. Why? Necessity is the mother of invention, at least at some airports. Now "mailback" kits are being sold at Hudson newsstands in at least thirty U.S. airports including LaGuardia, Portland, JFK, and Fresno. These kits, suitable for mailing sharp objects, contain a padded envelope, a self-sticking cardboard guard, and enough postage to send a 4-ounce package back home. The cost: $6.95—a bargain when you consider how much you spent for that pair of imported tweezers. One caution:

Many airports do not have post offices, and most—for security reasons—have removed mailboxes. So be sure to ask the folks at the newsstand *before* you buy the kit.

Finally, we need to remind transportation and government officials as well as our elected representatives—and last, but not least, ourselves—that perhaps the best deterrent to terrorism, not to mention stress reduction for all concerned, is for all of us to practice random displays of intelligence and common sense, coupled with unexpected acts of self-control.

3

Travel Right

SOME TIPS FROM THE ORIGINAL FREQUENT TRAVELER

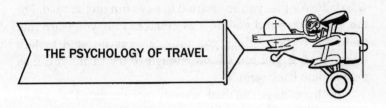

THE PSYCHOLOGY OF TRAVEL

Someone once told me that you know you've been traveling too long when you wake up, panicked, in the middle of the night in a strange hotel room, and you have absolutely no idea where you are.

But, as I learned firsthand—and, I'm ashamed to say, only recently—you've *really* been traveling too long when you get a case of "minthead."

I first heard about minthead when I sat down with another frequent traveler, Jay Leno. At the time, he was doing more than 150 one-night comedy stands a year—and guest hosting on *The Tonight Show*. And he was the most frequent flier I knew.

As we sat in his dressing room at NBC in Burbank, he decided to tell me the frequent-flier meaning of life.

"It's all about minthead," he told me.

Minthead?

"That's right. Minthead," he confided, "is what happens when you get back to your hotel room and go to sleep. But the maid has put a chocolate mint on your pillow, and you end up sleeping on it. You wake up with all this white cream in your hair. If you travel as much as I do, it happens all the time."

In those days, Leno would finish his stint on *The Tonight Show,* pack a carry-on bag with three shirts, two jackets, and an extra pair of pants, and head for the airport and one-night comedy stands across the country.

"Travel isn't fun," he sighed, "and I'm not one of those who believes that you're entitled to have fun on the road. For me, it's work, but if you do it as much as I do, you learn that there are certain things you must always do, and certain things that, if you are stupid enough to try them, you may never come back sane."

In those days, he had already accumulated so many frequent-flier miles that he was one of the top members of the American Airlines and Delta programs. What did Leno do with all his frequent-flier miles?

"Upgrade to first class," he said. "Or I give my friends tickets. But I never buy a first-class ticket. Instead, I buy a full coach ticket and upgrade. Even though the difference between coach and first class isn't that great," he says. "There's not much reason to fly first class. The legroom isn't that much better. The seats are not particularly comfortable. But I like being up front."

The reason, he explained, is simple: He can keep his options open. "I'm like everyone else. I despise delays. I've developed my own approach to coping with it. The trick is to be the first one on the plane under any circumstance. Because once you put your bags in the overhead bin, that's it. There's room for maybe three other people. So I have to be first on. How do I do it? I limp."

Limp?

"When they ask at the gate if anyone needs a little extra time in boarding, I limp up. 'Oh jeez, my leg; oh please, sir.' It always seems to work. But then, as I boarded one flight, I limped to the front, and there was a woman in a wheelchair, and she said, 'Oh, go ahead, dearie, I see you've hurt your leg.' I felt like that guy on the *Titanic* who put on that dress so he could get into a lifeboat."

Of course, Leno was joking. He never limped. He doesn't limp. Oh yes, he doesn't schlepp, either.

Luggage for Leno? Carry-on. Always and only. "Never, never check anything . . . ever . . . under any circumstances. It would be better to throw them away than check them in."

Delays? "I protect myself by checking the schedules beforehand. I always book the first flight out in the morning, and I'm also holding reservations on the next one, and the next one. Sometimes I go so far as to buy two or three tickets, which I cash in later if I don't use them. And since you can always be sure your flight is not going to leave on time, I never book a reservation on the last plane out."

What about delays once the plane leaves the gate and you're trapped, a virtual hostage?

"That's when I use the insulin routine. I begin screaming, 'My insulin! My insulin! I have to have it, and I have to get back to the gate!' That always works." (Leno is not a diabetic.) "Actually," he advised me, "you should employ just about any excuse to get off that plane and back to the gate. Because once you're stuck on that plane, you have no options. You have to assume that airlines push their planes back from the gates on time so that they can say they had an on-time departure. But you have to be prepared to smell a rat."

Weather? In the winter, Leno avoids flying through both Denver and Chicago. "Especially Denver. In Denver, you don't get stuck for hours, you get stuck for days. In the summer, I try to fly through Dallas/Fort Worth on American. Or through Atlanta on Delta."

Seat selection? Leno always sits in an aisle seat. "I don't understand the attraction for a window seat," he said. "You sit there and you're trapped. I also want to be near the door, so I'm first out. So I always get an aisle at the bulkhead because it has extra legroom."

Once seated, Leno prides himself on his mechanical skills and performs some structural work on the airline seat.

Whether he's in coach or in first class, Leno pulls out the middle armrest between the seats.

"On some planes, they make it tough to do," he warned, "and it may require the use of a small adjustable wrench, which I do bring with me. Then I take the bolt out. And the flight attendant will say, 'Those don't come out, sir,' and throughout the course of the flight, I become a little bit like a prisoner tunneling out with a spoon. About halfway through, I'll look at her and say, 'Oh no . . . look! It came out!' Then I'll stretch across the two seats."

Like many frequent fliers, Leno insisted he wouldn't go near airline food. "It's abysmal. You can't even tell jokes about it, because it's no longer funny," he said. "It's beyond bad. I think you have to sample the food on foreign airlines to realize how bad the U.S. food is. To me, first class on a U.S. carrier is now what coach used to be. Everything has been moved back one notch."

Airports? Leno cannot figure out why so many airports are so poorly designed. "For years, you needed a pedometer just to see how far you had to walk at O'Hare," he said. "But the new United Airlines terminal in Chicago is a little better, because at least it gives you the appearance that you're much closer to your plane. Of course, you're not."

All right, what about once he's back on the ground? What about the hotels? Jay Leno has seen the inside of thousands of hotel rooms, and he's offered some choice stories from his experience.

"They've ranged from places where the towels are chained to the wall and you had to dry yourself by rubbing up against it, to suites with every possible amenity. But great goodies in the room don't necessarily make a great hotel," he argued. "It's the attitude of the staff.

"But," he added, "a good hotel tends to be one where I don't really notice it's a hotel. Where the bed is comfortable, the remote control works, and you have a real key, not one of those plastic cards. I think those little key cards are terrible. First, I'm always losing them, and even when I don't lose them, they don't work. And when they do work, I forget my room number."

Another peeve, he charged, is "why some hotels feel they need to glue the remote control unit to the furniture. And they always do it so that it doesn't face the TV. And the unit has this huge lock on it, like I'm going to steal it. You have to be a contortionist to be able to turn on the TV or change the channel."

Leno most despises hotels that try to be something they're not. "If you want to be a classy hotel and have a concierge," he suggested, "why not have a concierge who can speak English? I find this all over. Now, I have nothing against people who speak a foreign language. I come from a family of immigrants. But there's no excuse at a hotel. I was at a hotel recently, and I had just checked into the room. I wanted to watch a comedy program on cable but didn't know if the hotel got HBO. So I called downstairs to the concierge and asked.

" 'Crebblega,' the guy says. I say, 'Excuse me?' And he says, 'Crebblega.'

" 'Crebblega'? What the hell is that? It took me five minutes before I realized what he was saying was 'cable guide.' OK, now we've established the hotel had a cable guide. When I asked the concierge where it was, he said, 'Biroda.' Again, I didn't know what he was saying. This went on for another five minutes until the concierge, who was getting as crazed as I was, said:

" 'It's in the bi-ro-da.' Finally! It was in the bureau drawer."

Leno admitted that he is different from most travelers. After all, he's a celebrity with a forum (*The Tonight Show*), and that gives him a rare natural advantage: He can always invoke the Fear Factor.

"The great thing about being in show business is: People are in dread fear that somehow they will wind up in a *Tonight Show* monologue. Not long ago, I had trouble with my washer. Let's just say it's a brand famous for having a repairman that doesn't work very often. So I called the repair service. They told me they'd send someone out in four days. 'Oh, four days, really,' I say. 'Let me write this down. When I mention this on *The Tonight Show* . . . it's going to be four days. . . .' An hour later, the guy is at the door. So that's the great advantage to being on TV.

"Being in show business is like being retarded," he says. "There are always people along the way to lead you. 'Mr. Leno, come with us.' 'Mr. Leno, walk this way.' You ever hear people talk about celebrities? Sometimes you can hear them whisper, 'He even drives himself to the airport!' "

Is there anything to be said in favor of a life on the road?

"The shampoo bottles. The little shampoo bottles. I haven't bought shampoo in fifteen years. I have hundreds of them. That's how I know when it's time to go on the road again. When I'm down to maybe 1,500 bottles, I call the airline and make a reservation."

Two weeks after I spoke with Leno, I was in a hotel in Denver. I returned from a late dinner and sat down on the bed to watch—as luck would have it—*The Tonight Show*. Five hours later, I awoke in a panic. The television was still on. All the lights in the room were aglow. I had forgotten where I was—couldn't remember the city or the name of the hotel. And my face and forehead felt funny . . . and sticky. Slowly, I put my hand to my face. It was all gooey. Was I bleeding? What happened?

And then I smelled it. Chocolate, with more than a slight hint of mint. It had happened. I had fallen asleep on the mint on the pillow. At that moment, I felt I had been inducted into the official frequent-traveler hall of shame.

But minthead is really the *least* of our concerns when traveling.

When it comes to the travel experience, it seems that we've evolved into a society of people who want to find a line just so we can stand in it. And yet we claim to be desperate for the very information that will help us stay out of any lines.

With luck, this book will help you to avoid the lines and still get what you want from your travel experience.

Indeed, there has been a quantum shift in our travel priorities, not to mention our life philosophy. In a recent travel survey, when people were asked, "Would you prefer more free time or more money?," a majority opted for the extra free time.

Among other trends, business travelers like control over their travel arrangements. A majority like to choose the airline they fly and the hotels they stay in. And if given a choice, a majority of business travelers would never use their companies' in-house travel agency. Why not? Because these people are convinced they can do a better job—and can get a better deal—themselves.

To manage costs, businesses are firing their travel agents and logging themselves on to the Web: Last year, 23 percent of corporations booked their travel online, a figure that U.S.-based market researcher PhoCus Wright expects to rise to 34 percent by 2005. Fueling this trend, many travel sites have launched services aimed at business travelers. Expedia.com's Expedia Corporate and Orbitz.com's Orbitz for Business offer savings of 60 to 75 percent on transaction fees by eliminating the human intermediary. Mark Jones, the CEO of Lastminute.com's new corporate arm, Travelstore.com, says that having employees book their own flights "saves money across the board." In addition to slashed transaction fees, the business-class tickets are generally 10 to 15 percent less; when people make their own arrangements, what the industry calls "visual guilt" often prevails, and they'll book themselves onto the cheapest flight.

The pivotal factor in choosing an airline? A convenient schedule.

And how do we like to spend our time on planes? British, Hong Kong, and Singaporean business travelers like to watch the in-flight movies. American, French, and German travelers seem addicted to in-flight phones, and Asian fliers want to play computer video games.

Here's a no-brainer. Most business travelers say they don't want to sit next to anyone during a flight. (Believe it or not, 40 percent of those surveyed admitted moving their seats so they wouldn't have to sit next to anyone.)

How often do business travelers fly? An average of 5.9 trips per year. Travel for business purposes accounts for 20 percent of all U.S. domestic trips.

Interesting behavioral differences were revealed when the sexes were studied separately. In 1970, only 1 percent of business travelers were women. Today, around 50 percent are women. Women constitute approximately 46 percent of the U.S. workforce and are the fastest-growing segment of business travelers. These women generally think that the positive benefits of business travel outweigh the negative and cite the opportunity to network with new people as the primary advantage. Women are more likely than men to incorporate leisure activities into a business trip. Baby Boomers account for 68 percent of women business travelers, with the rest evenly divided between Gen Xers and Post–Baby Boomers. Among female business travelers, 40 percent are either the sole or the primary wage earner in their households and almost a third have household incomes of $100,000 or more. About three-quarters of them have at least a bachelor's degree.

Women are as likely as men to prefer sitting next to an empty seat on a plane. Also, one woman in ten reports being sexually harassed during a flight.

Households in which one member takes business trips are 72 percent more likely to consist of married people between the ages of thirty-five and fifty-four, and 68 percent of them have a college degree. About 40 percent of these households have children at home, which is higher than the overall average.

There's also a booming interest in family travel. Three of ten adults took at least one vacation with children last year. This finding seems to match other indications that the number of U.S. families consisting of two married parents and their children increased by seven hundred thousand in a recent five-year period.

Business travel volume fell to 197.5 million person-trips in 2002, a 5.8 percent decline from 2001. Overall, business travel comprises 20 percent of total U.S. domestic person-trips. Half (50 percent) of all business person-trips are taken for general business purposes (likely for meetings, presentations, consulting, sales, etc.), 12 percent are taken for the primary purpose of attending a convention or seminar, and 38 percent are made by those traveling for combined business and pleasure purposes. Thirty-eight percent of business/convention/seminar person-trips include air transportation. About one in eight (12 percent) business/convention/seminar trips include multiple adults from the same household; 4 percent include children.

The airlines' once-dreaded Saturday night stay-over restriction has suddenly turned into an ally. If you agree to stay over a Saturday night, your airfare can drop almost 70 percent. Because of this, a number of corporations are encouraging their hardest workers to take the weekend off. Some companies even pick up the airfare for a spouse or significant other. An extra Saturday night is more economical, even with two discount tickets, than paying for one full-fare seat.

The result: happy employee, happy spouse, happy company ledger sheet. And happy hotel.

At least some airlines have started to figure out that their Saturday night restrictions were beginning to hurt their bottom line as well. These airlines have begun to abandon the weekend-night stay rule. In mid-February 2004, Alaska Airlines dropped the requirement for its least expensive advance-purchase tickets on all its flights. America West eliminated the regulation in 2002. And discount carriers like Air Tran, JetBlue, and Southwest had never applied the rule in the first place.

Major airlines are matching other carriers' prices, but they are doing it on a flight-by-flight basis, not systemwide.

Word of mouth continues to play a significant role in travel decisions. Seventy-nine percent of those surveyed said they had confidence in the recommendations of a friend. Only 28 percent reported confidence in the information found in travel advertisements.

Once viewed as a luxury, leisure travel is now considered, by seven out of ten Americans, to be a psychological necessity.

There also seems to be a change in the class of service for airline flights. In 1994, 14 percent of domestic trips were in first or business class. That figure—at least in first class—is dropping.

Then there's the extended business-class trip. In 1994, 10 percent of business travelers were accompanied by a spouse and 3.6 percent brought a child. In 1995, 25 percent took their spouses and 5 percent took a child. Today, nearly 35 percent bring a spouse and 10 percent bring a child.

I found one statistic most amusing. When American Express did a survey of its Platinum cardholders, the company discovered that male Platinum cardholders said the one thing they wanted to take with them on business trips was their spouse. Female Platinum cardholders preferred to take personal items.

Some travel research dollars are spent trying to understand the psychology of travel. For example, psychologists were consulted before the interiors for the Concorde were designed. Because some believed high-speed travel would produce higher levels of tension and stress for passengers, the Concorde interiors were subdued instead of flashy. In the end, the real stress of the Concorde was cost, and it was retired at the end of 2003.

Psychologists continue to be consulted on what makes us happy when we hit the road and makes us angry when the road seems to hit us. A Harvard University study of seven hundred business travelers concluded what we already know: We have a love-hate relationship with travel.

The study found that business travelers fall into four distinct groups:

1. *Tightrope walkers:* Inexperienced travelers "who report high levels of stress and feel they lose a part of their private lives while on the road."
2. *Eagles:* Folks who enjoy business travel "but at the same time admit high levels of stress."
3. *Family-ties:* Married travelers who say that business "puts a lot of stress on their spouses, causing a conflict between career and family."

4. *Road warriors:* People who travel a lot "but report lower levels of stress than other business travelers and are more likely to feel like a hero or warrior on the road."

What do these different groups want? Less stress and an ability to see the humor in situations and a plan for when things go wrong, considering they're dealing with variables over which they have little or no control.

Changing demographic trends can often impact travel psychology. The U.S. population is aging, and because older Americans have been traveling more and rewriting the vacation calendar, off-peak travel is booming.

Average Americans take a day and a half to unwind at the start of their vacation. But one in ten Americans says he or she never unwinds.

And what about vacation "afterglow," that period of feeling good right after a trip? According to an American Express survey, the average vacation afterglow lasts six days. But again, nearly one in every ten of us says it lasts only a day.

This book is about improving the *process* of traveling. It's about realizing that the destination has become incidental to the experience. It's about finesse—understanding the process so we can better handle the product. And in the end, it's about taking some risks, asking some important questions, and thinking outside the box when it comes to both our leisure and our business travel.

Most of all, it's about finding common ground—in the air, at a hotel, inside a rental car, or on the high seas. Travel converts our dreams into the power of discovery.

The bottom line here is that we're all frustrated. We seek information that will help us finesse the process of travel so that we can have a great experience.

Remember, a tourist sees a destination. A traveler *experiences* it.

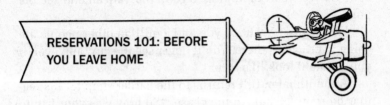

RESERVATIONS 101: BEFORE YOU LEAVE HOME

OK. So much for international acts of terrorism and fear of travel.

Now it's time to discuss some *real* fears about travel, such as making reservations with hotels and airlines, getting a good deal, and asking the right questions.

When it comes to travel, everyone seems to have an opinion. And every time someone asks me for advice, I'm reminded of the story of Bill and Joe.

Bill is sitting in the chair at Joe's barber shop, getting his regular haircut. As Joe is snipping away, he asks Bill, "What's up?"

Bill tells Joe the good news. He's finally taking a vacation.

"Where are you going?" Joe asks.

"Rome," says Bill, excitedly.

"Rome?" Joe says. "Why would you want to go there? It's a crowded, dirty city full of crazy Italians. You're nuts if you go there. So . . . how are you getting there?"

"We got a deal on TWA," Bill replies.

"*TWA?*" Joe yells. "TWA is a terrible airline. They have old planes, their flight attendants are mean, and the airline is always late. So . . . where are you staying in Rome?"

"Well," Bill answers, somewhat hesitantly, "we got a pretty good package at the Hilton."

"That's a dump!" Joe screams. "Without a doubt, it's the worst hotel in the city. The rooms are small and dingy, the service is terrible and slow, and they're way overpriced. And what are you gonna do when you get there?"

"We were sort of hoping to go to the Vatican and see the pope."

Joe laughs. "Yeah . . . you and a million other people are going to crowd in there. You'll never see the guy, and even if you do, he'll look like an ant."

A month later, Bill returns to the barber shop for his regular haircut. Joe cuts to the chase. "So how was your trip to Rome? Let me guess, TWA was the flight from hell."

Bill shakes his head. "Actually, it was great. Brand-new plane, terrific food, and we landed in Rome ten minutes early. But the best part is that because they were booked full, they bumped us up to first class, and the flight attendants couldn't have been nicer."

Joe can't believe it. "Well, I'm sure that hotel was the worst."

Again, Bill shakes his head. "Quite the opposite. They had just finished a major multi-million-dollar remodeling and it's now the hottest hotel in Rome. Even better, because they were fully booked, they upgraded us to the presidential suite at no extra charge!"

"Wait a minute," Joe says, in disbelief. "Don't tell me you actually got to see the pope?"

Bill sighs. "Talk about luck. As we toured the Vatican, a Swiss guard tapped me on the shoulder and explained that the pope likes to personally meet some of the visitors, and asked if I wouldn't mind stepping into this private room. So I did, and five minutes later, the pope walked through the door, and he walked right up to me. And then he actually spoke to me."

"He spoke to you?" Joe asks. "He actually spoke to you? What did he say?"

"Well, not much, but he did want to know where I got that awful haircut!"

So be prepared. If people perceive themselves as travelers, you will inevitably be second-guessed on every travel decision you make.

The key is to make the right decision from the start. Toward that end, it's actually more important to realize which resources you should avoid than to seek out the ones to use. When defining your resources, keep each one in proper perspective.

Let's start with brochures and the brochure mentality. I have a built-in aversion to any word that ends with "st." Can any one hotel, resort, airline, destination, or travel experience be the "best"? The "most"? The "greatest"? The "cleanest"?

How many things are truly "unique"? Is there really only one of them in the universe? And what about the descriptive words "beautiful," "gem," and "jewel"? Are we sick of them already? To navigate the travel maze and negotiate some very good travel deals, you must start by burying the brochures.

Why? How many brochures promise an "ocean-view" hotel room, but when you arrive, you find that you need high-powered binoculars to make out the sea a mile away?

A brochure for a package tour to Russia promises "tickets to the theater where the Bolshoi Ballet performs." Tourists who sign up for the tour are excited at the prospect of seeing first-rate ballet. But it is not to be.

The tourists do indeed arrive at the theater where the Bolshoi performs, but the brochure gave no promise that the Bolshoi itself would actually perform for them. The brochure promised tickets to that theater, and instead of ballet, these unwitting visitors get a disappointing performance of Russian folk songs.

A resort is described as being "five minutes from restaurants, shopping, and entertainment." But the ad doesn't reveal whether those five minutes are spent walking or being beamed to the destination by the cast of *Star Trek*.

One Honolulu hotel claimed in its brochure that it was "steps from the beach." I actually counted, and the result wasn't pretty. If I could have walked there in a straight line, it would have been half a mile away, but there was no direct route to the beach. I had to walk across heavily traveled city streets; through a construction site, a park, and another construction site; and then to the beach. Distance: nearly a mile. That's a lot of steps.

Then there are the visual deceits. A hotel in Santa Barbara airbrushed its brochure photo to show the hotel not just on the beach, but on the ocean itself. Reality: The hotel was across a four-lane state highway. (Translation: If you believed the brochure, went to the hotel with your kids, and told them to go play at the beach, you would have heard the alarming screech of automobile brakes!)

Travel industry brochures must be designed by, written by, and photographed by truly uninspired people. In addition to the overuse of superlatives ("finest," "greatest," "most"), all the women who appear in these brochures are size-two Barbies, standing next to their wooden Kens. There are the inevitable breast-enlarged models holding wineglasses poolside, and, of course, my favorite shot, the hardest-working people in the world of travel promotion: the senior couple dressed in their bathrobes, standing on their balcony gazing blissfully at God-knows-what.

Welcome to the wonderful world of travel promotion and hyperbole, a semantic battlefield where seductive but often misleading descriptions persuade you to journey to a particular country, stay at a certain hotel, fly one airline instead of another, or rent a specific car.

In this highly competitive business, unfair advantage with the language is often taken at travelers' expense.

Most of the time, these descriptive words aren't blatant lies. But in many cases, they are intentionally misleading— or, at the very least, not exactly structured to help would-be visitors find the truth.

If you don't read a travel ad or brochure carefully, you might find yourself the victim of greater expectations about your vacation than logical thinking would otherwise allow.

Here are some of my favorite misleading brochure promises:

- A cruise-line brochure boasts that "you will sail on a classic vessel." Real meaning: The ship is thirty-eight years old and only months away from the salvage yard, if it ever makes it that far.

- "A travelers' oasis." You'd better like solitude. You could be miles from nowhere.

- "Fully equipped spa." Does a solitary exercise bike qualify? You'd be surprised how many hotels think it does.

- "Beautiful swimming pool." Yes, but how large? And where is it located? It may be beautiful but only 10 feet long.

- "You'll love our secluded beaches." Does this mean so isolated that no other services are provided? Or does it mean the beaches are secluded because of the interesting marine life—sharks, perhaps?

- From a package-tour brochure to Egypt: "You will see the Great Pyramids." You will see them, but you won't be getting off the bus as it speeds by.

Then there are the outright lies: "The weather is beautiful all year 'round." That's a statistical improbability and an insult to our intelligence.

Traditionally, the biggest abuses of descriptive language have appeared on package-tour brochures.

Who can forget the ubiquitous airline statement: "Some restrictions apply"? This all-purpose disclaimer has resulted in unending confusion, frustration, and anger.

Then there's the cruise-line brochure that says: "We are proud of our crew, representing 47 nationalities." The idea of a floating United Nations sounds great—until you need to talk with some crew members, only to discover they don't speak English and, in the event of an emergency at sea, won't even be able to communicate with each other!

When tackling any brochure, try to decipher the true meaning of the words used to describe the destination and services.

Before sending in a deposit or paying for your ticket, question your travel agent about what is being promised. If he or she doesn't know the answers, demand that the agent find out.

When booking an airline ticket, remember that a "direct" flight doesn't mean nonstop. It may mean you will make one or two stops en route. If it's a "connecting" flight, you must change planes.

So now you know what it means when Alitalia boasts that it offers the only "direct" service from Los Angeles to Italy. If you want to take a plane from Los Angeles to Rome, be prepared to make a stop in Milan.

Inevitable language problems are associated with tour packages. "Includes superior room"—if anyone can give me the absolute definition of *superior,* I'll send, in return, a matching set of luggage.

The same vagueness often applies to "ocean front" and "ocean view." Does "ocean front" mean that the hotel room actually is fronting the ocean or is facing a distant sea? The words "ocean view" get the worst abuse. At some hotels, the rooms do indeed have an ocean view—provided you bring your own binoculars.

How many times have you seen a very attractive hotel room rate quoted, followed by the disclaimer "double occupancy"? Double occupancy rates mean the price *per person,* based on two people sharing one room.

Ever hear of something called "run of house" rooms? You will often see this term in Hawaii tour packages. It means, quite simply, that you will be given whatever room the hotel feels like giving you. If you agree to a "run of house" room, you are throwing yourself at the mercy of the hotel gods, and your odds of getting a large room, a room with a view, or one with a king-size bed are greatly reduced.

Hungry? Check out various meal packages carefully. In Caribbean destinations, some hotels offer something called "exchange dining." This means that you can eat at specially selected hotels and restaurants as part of a preset meal plan. Caution: Many of these restaurants and hotels define that meal plan on their own exclusive terms—a number of menu items feature surcharges.

Many hotel meal plans are confusing. European Plan (EP) means that no meals are included in the room rate. The American Plan (AP) includes all meals, and the Modified American Plan (MAP) includes two meals (usually breakfast and dinner) as part of your hotel room rate.

Some hotels and resorts allow you to choose either lunch or dinner as your second meal, and, to further confuse things, some hotels market the Continental Plan, which usually means bed and breakfast.

But does this mean a continental breakfast? Not necessarily. In most of Europe chances are that it does mean a continental breakfast: coffee, tea, and rolls. However, in Scandinavia a Continental Plan usually means a full buffet breakfast, although a continental breakfast there doesn't mean a full buffet. A continental breakfast in Scandinavia consists of coffee or tea and a bit of fruit or cheese added to the bread menu, with perhaps a boiled egg or a little salami occasionally. Hotels that offer something called the Bermuda Plan include a full breakfast.

Meal rates can be confusing. At many hotels and resorts, American Plan and Modified American Plan rates are quoted "per person." If your budget is tight, determine before you go what these terms mean at your destinations.

Here are a few more of my favorite seductive (but misleading) terms used to lure travelers to the wrong countries, cruise lines, and hotels:

"Secluded hideaway": Impossible to find.

"Carefree natives": Terrible service.

"Warmed by the Gulf Stream": Cold.

"Cooled by the Humboldt Current": Hot.

"Old-world charm": No bath.

"Family style": You'll be sharing a bath!

"Tropical": Rainy.

"Undiscovered": Not worth discovering.

"Off the beaten path": People have stopped coming here.

"Ocean view": Bring binoculars.

"Beachfront": Hold on to those binoculars.

"Some restrictions apply": Don't even bother trying to qualify for this fare.

And, as mentioned earlier, any descriptive term ending in the letters "st" is usually suspect.

What about guidebooks? Definitionally, they are guides, *not* bibles. But there's another inherent problem. By the time most guidebooks are published, they're already out of date.

So I'm not telling you not to buy them and read them (after all, *this* is a guidebook of sorts), but I am strongly encouraging you to use them only as a point of departure for your travel research.

NOTHING BUT NET

Which brings me to the subject of the Internet. Like the guidebooks, the Net can be extremely useful, but, once again, you cannot always depend on websites to get you what you need.

Currently, everyone and his mother—with the possible exception of *my* mother—has a website. In 2002, according to a Travel Industry Association (TIA) of America study, there were already two billion websites, and a large percentage of them contained travel information.

Some ninety-six million travelers used the Internet in 2002. The number of Americans using the Internet for actual travel planning has increased dramatically since 1997, when only about twelve million Americans were planning and researching travel options online. This rose to about sixty-four million online travel planners in 2002. In 2002, over thirty-nine million people said they had booked travel using the Internet in the past year, up 25 percent over the previous year.

Airline tickets continued to be the most frequently purchased travel products online, reported by 77 percent of all online travel bookers, followed by accommodations at 57 percent and rental cars at 37 percent. The top websites are Expedia, Travelocity, Hotwire, and Priceline.

The rapid growth of travel websites is certainly entertaining, and people driven by low-fare obsessions will find no shortage of supposedly great deals.

For some activities—for example, booking on Southwest

Airlines—the Web is perfect. People who fly on Southwest are price-driven. They want the cheapest deal. They're not on the plane for a movie or a meal (neither is offered) or for luxurious, comfortable seats. Chances are good they'll get stuck in a center seat facing a photo of the bag of peanuts they would have been given two years ago! But that's part of the charm of the Southwest flight experience. Passengers are there only because of price.

Southwest's website has been hugely successful. People can log on, buy their cheap tickets, and log off. Period. In 2000, Southwest became the first airline website to book more than $1 billion in travel!

As a label for other travel websites, I suggest "Supposedly Good Deals" because their offerings all come down to a definition of terms. Want a cheap ticket to Los Angeles? You can find several options available through various sites—Expedia, Travelocity, Hotwire—but what you may not learn there is that your itinerary might require track shoes for sprinting to connecting flights in both directions.

Many informational websites are thinly veiled transactional websites that often don't allow any browsing. Instead, you may quickly find yourself locked into a fare or itinerary, and before you know it, your credit card has been charged.

Please don't get me wrong. I love surfing the Net. But I like *riding* the wave, not getting creamed by it. It is but one informational tool I use. And if you approach the Net this way, you'll be a happier traveler.

Now, having said that, let's get down to the questions you need to ask when you are booking an airline ticket, a hotel room, or a cruise.*

If you don't ask these questions right away, you put yourself at an immediate disadvantage.

---

*You will find more information on the Web in Chapter 8.

AIRLINE RESERVATIONS

Let me give you a typical airline reservation dialogue:

AIRLINE AGENT: Good morning. Draconian Airways. May I help you?

ME: Yes, I'd like to fly from Los Angeles to New York.

AGENT: And when would you like to fly?

ME: I'd like to leave next Thursday and come back a week later.

Anyone find anything worrisome in that conversation?

The minute I told the agent *when* I wanted to fly, I was a dead man. I had given the agent too much information and placed myself at an immediate disadvantage.

Now, consider this approach. This time, the agent isn't doing the questioning. *I* am.

AGENT: Good morning. Draconian Airways. May I help you?

ME: Yes. I'd like to fly from Los Angeles to New York, but before you ask me when I want to fly, can you please punch up on your computer every published fare you have on that route? Thanks. I'll wait.

The wait isn't long. When the agent has punched up the information on the airline's screen, I ask a second question.

ME: OK, could you scroll to the bottom of the list? . . . Great. Now, could you tell me what that fare is?

AGENT: Oh, that's the fare that's only good on Wednesdays at midnight if your middle name is Murray, you own a snowmobile, and you can hop.

ME: And how much is that fare?

AGENT: $249.

ME: [Well, I can fly on Wednesday, change my middle name, and borrow a snowmobile.] I'll take that fare.

The moral of the story: If you volunteer information about when you want to fly, you will invariably be stepped up to a higher fare by the airline. Do it my way and you get to back into the fare, starting at the lowest rate that you can handle, if you're flexible.

One important caution is also a reassurance. Let's say you get an airline agent on the phone who *won't* scroll down on the computer screen. No problem. You dialed a toll-free 800 number. Politely end the conversation, hang up, and *call back!* You *will* get someone to help if you keep trying. A second caution: At least one airline computer system—United—displays the lowest fares at the top of the screen, so you should ask the United agent to scroll *up* instead of down.

Here's an example, a New York–to–San Francisco trip has eleven fares currently listed in United Airlines' computers. They range from full-premium first class, all the way down to a VE21NTV fare, which just about requires that snowmobile. It's a twenty-one-day advance purchase, requires a Saturday night stay, is nonrefundable, and is time-specific. From JFK to SFO, it's valid only on United flights departing between 6:30 A.M. and 12 noon. On return flights to JFK, you can fly only between 6:30 and 8:30 in the morning, or 3:00 to 11:00 P.M.

These are just the basic fares. About 20 others pop up from time to time, depending on the season, the demand, and other factors.

Whenever you buy a ticket, it's imperative to understand the fare basis that is printed (in code) on that ticket. The fare basis codes vary from airline to airline. New fares are always coming on the market, and fares are always dropping out. The ones listed are for United Airlines; though some have expired, they still serve as good examples.

Fare Codes and Definitions (All United Flights)

New York to San Francisco	
Fare Basis Code	*Definition*
PS	Premium first-class product (only on NYC transcontinental flights), one way, no restrictions, refundable (three-class configured flight)
FUA	First-class product, one way, no restrictions, refundable (first United)
CUA	Business class in a three-cabin aircraft, first class in a two-cabin aircraft, one way, no restrictions, refundable (business United aircraft)
YUA	Full-fare walk-up, one way, no restrictions, refundable
BUA	Full-fare walk-up, one way, no restrictions, refundable
BA3	Three-day advance purchase, one way, no restrictions, refundable
ME14NQ	Fourteen-day advance purchase, round-trip, valid all days of the week, Saturday night stay, nonrefundable
MOE14NQ	Fourteen-day advance purchase, round-trip, valid only Tuesday and Wednesday, Saturday night stay, nonrefundable
HE21NQ	Twenty-one-day advance purchase, round-trip, valid all days of the week, Saturday night stay, nonrefundable
HOE21NQ	Twenty-one-day advance purchase, round-trip, valid only Tuesday and Wednesday, Saturday night stay, nonrefundable

New York to San Francisco

Fare Basis Code	Definition
VE21NTV	Twenty-one-day advance purchase, round-trip, Saturday night stay, nonrefundable, valid on certain flights
	Valid only to JFK: 6:30 A.M.–8:30 A.M. or 3:00 P.M.–11:00 P.M. daily
	Valid only from JFK: 6:30 A.M.–12:00 P.M. daily

Chicago to Denver Pricing

Fare Basis Code	Definition
FUA	First-class product, one way, no restrictions, refundable (two-class configured plane)
FUA3FS	First-class product in three-cabin aircraft, one way, no restrictions, refundable
FUA2FS	First-class product in two-cabin aircraft, one way, no restrictions, refundable
YUA	Full-fare walk-up, one way, no restrictions, refundable (full coach, very flexible)
BUA	Full-fare walk-up, one way, no restrictions, refundable (may have to pay fee to change flight)
MFSNR	Walk-up fare, one way, daily, nonrefundable, valid on certain flights (for United)
	Valid only to Denver: 5:50 A.M.–7:15 A.M. or 6:55 P.M.–7:25 P.M.
	Valid only from Denver: 6:00 A.M.–6:30 A.M. or 7:45 P.M.–8:45 P.M.
MA3NX	Three-day advance purchase, one way, valid all days, nonrefundable, fuel surcharge exempt
ME31NX	Three-day advance purchase, round-trip, valid all days, one-night minimum stay, nonrefundable, fuel surcharge exempt
MA7NX	Seven-day advance purchase, one way, valid all days, nonrefundable, fuel surcharge exempt
HA7NX	Seven-day advance purchase, round-trip, valid all days, nonrefundable, fuel surcharge exempt

Chicago to Denver Pricing

Fare Basis Code	Definition
QE7NX	Seven-day advance purchase, round-trip, valid all days, Saturday night stay, nonrefundable, fuel surcharge exempt
HE14NQ	Fourteen-day advance purchase, round-trip, valid all days, Saturday night stay, nonrefundable
HOE14NQ	Fourteen-day advance purchase, round-trip, valid only Tuesday and Wednesday, Saturday night stay, nonrefundable
HA14NX	Fourteen-day advance purchase, one way, valid all days, nonrefundable, fuel surcharge exempt
QE14NRX	Fourteen-day advance purchase, round trip, valid all days, Saturday night stay, nonrefundable, fuel surcharge exempt
VE1423NX	Fourteen-day advance purchase, round trip, valid only Tuesday and Wednesday, Saturday night stay, nonrefundable, fuel surcharge exempt
QE21NQ	Twenty-one-day advance purchase, round trip, valid all days, Saturday night stay, nonrefundable
QA21NX	Twenty-one-day advance purchase, one way, valid all days, nonrefundable, fuel surcharge exempt
QOE21NQ	Twenty-one-day advance purchase, round trip, valid only Tuesday and Wednesday, Saturday night stay, nonrefundable
VA21NX	Twenty-one-day advance purchase, one way, valid all days, nonrefundable, fuel surcharge exempt
VA2123NX	Twenty-one-day advance purchase, one way, valid only Tuesday and Wednesday, nonrefundable, fuel surcharge exempt
WE21NRX	Twenty-one-day advance purchase, round trip, valid all days, Saturday night stay, nonrefundable, fuel surcharge exempt
WE2123NX	Twenty-one-day advance purchase, round trip, valid only Tuesday and Wednesday, Saturday night stay, nonrefundable, fuel surcharge exempt

The fare basis code provides information about the specific fare in addition to the class of service required for booking. Every published fare has a fare basis code. On your ticket, the code appears in the fare basis box. The codes can get confusing. Some tickets represent a combination of fares; thus, more than one fare basis code may exist for each class of service for booking. For example, two fares for H class may exist—one for midweek travel and one for weekend travel.

Airlines distinguish between classes of service and types of fares. Classes of service include first, business, standard, coach, and thrift. Fares usually drop with a lower class of service. For each class except standard there are six main types of reduced-fare tickets: discounted, night, off-peak, weekend, advance purchase, and excursion fare.

	Regular	Premium	Discounted	Night/Offpeak
First	F	P	A	Fn (coach in FC seat)
Business	C	J	D	Cn
Standard	S	W		Bn
Coach economy	Y		B, H, M, Q, T	Qn, Yn
Thrift	K		L, V	Vn, Kn

F and P are relatively the same, as are classes C and J.

Looking at a fare basis number, like the ones listed, the letters following the first letter are usually used to designate different types of fares that distinguish the bucket (see page 90). These letters change often and vary by airline. The first number—for example, 7 or 14 or 21—usually means how many days in advance the ticket must be bought. A number after that—say 2 or 3—is usually the day of the week for which the ticket is valid (this example would be Tuesday or

Wednesday). Following the numbers are restrictions, such as nonrefundable, Saturday stay, and fuel surcharges.

Consider this example: A return fare across the country has the fare basis code HL7LNR (an American Airlines fare). The first letter, H, refers to the class of service for booking (in this case, H class). The L refers to low season, the 7 refers to the requirement for seven-day advance booking, the next L refers to long haul, and the NR means nonrefundable. Presumably, if the ticket were purchased fourteen days in advance or during a high season, both the fare and the fare basis code would be different. Often, you will see the letter X or W, referring to midweek or weekend travel, respectively.

As another example, your fare basis code might be ME7NR. M is the booking class code. E stands for excursion. The 7 and NR indicate that the ticket was purchased seven days in advance and is nonrefundable. The difference between MA7NX and HA7NX (see table) is that the latter is a round-trip.

And now, an important note about the dreaded word *nonrefundable*. Surprisingly, a number of people actually believe that if they buy a nonrefundable ticket and they don't use it, they've lost the entire value of their ticket. They either throw the ticket into a desk drawer or, worse, throw it away, when in fact the ticket has substantial value and can often be applied to the purchase of another ticket. Remember, nonrefundable does *not* mean worthless. In almost all cases—and especially if you change your reservations (or cancel them) *before* the date of your originating flight, you can apply the majority of your original fare against another ticket. Note that refunding a nonrefundable ticket usually incurs a fee.

Why are there so many fares for the same type of coach seat? It all gets down to something called *revenue management,* the dark science of the travel industry, which determines the number of price categories in the plane inventory.

For each flight, an airline allocates only a certain number of seats at each fare level, or *bucket*. That number is a closely guarded secret. In fact, that information is considered highly proprietary. Access to the specific count (how many seats are being sold in which bucket) is limited to only one or two people at any one airline. And if they tell you, they have to kill you.

If the duration given for a bucket expires (21-day advance requirement), then the fare increases to the next bucket rate, but if one bucket sells out, even if the time has not elapsed, you must buy at the next bucket rate (often higher). This is how airlines get you to buy in advance. But the number of seats available at each fare varies from day to day, depending on the airline's revenue management algorithm.

Then there are the different *types* of tickets: student fares, senior fares, group fares, convention fares, Visit USA (VUSA) fares as well as fares to other continents, consolidator tickets, military fares, Internet fares, and RTW (round-the-world) fares.

Student fares are available through Air Tran. Called X Fares, they're available to anyone between the ages of 18 and 22. They are standby fares, priced at $55 per flight segment, with no reserve seating. You must go no more than two hours before a flight. Student Universe offers student fares on Delta and American through a free-membership website, and you can also get student fares through the STA Travel Agent Network.

Senior discounts, which amounted to a 10 percent saving for elderly travelers, have been eliminated by American, Delta, Northwest, United, and US Airways. Continental standardized its senior fares to eliminate confusion; the fares are usually 10 percent lower than fourteen-day advance-purchase tickets, which are often the lowest published fares available. Instead of the flat-rate discount, American, Northwest, and

US Airways implemented new senior fares, and these are not always 10 percent off the lowest published fare. American, Continental, Northwest, United, and US Airways also stopped selling discount coupon books, which were popular with seniors. Alaska, America West, and Southwest retained their senior discount programs.

The Oneworld Alliance (www.oneworld.com) offers its Visit Europe deal, which allows you to fly between cities in distant countries—for example, from Ireland to Russia and the Ukraine or from Finland to Israel, Cyprus, and North Africa. Prices range from $65 U.S. for trips up to 250 miles to $265 U.S. for flights of more than 2,000 miles. There is a two-flight minimum, but no maximum. Oneworld also markets flight deals to Asia, Africa, North America, South America, and Australia and New Zealand.

Star Alliance's European Airpass (www.staralliance.com) features prices and network coverage similar to those of Oneworld but uses Star carriers, while Skyteam's European Airpass (www.skyteam.com) serves non-Europeans arriving via a member airline's intercontinental flights, with fares ranging from $60 U.S. to $205 U.S. per European sector. Emirates (www.emirates.com) and Gulf Air (www.gulfairco.com) offer air passes for first-, business-, and economy-class travel to selected destinations in the Persian Gulf plus Cairo, Beirut, Damascus, and Tehran. First-class fares on Emirates are around $330 U.S., and $290 U.S. for business class and $120 U.S. for economy class; Gulf Air's fares are comparable.

There's more information about specific types of tickets (RTW, air passes, etc.) later in this chapter.

Knowing about airlines' stopover policies can make a substantial difference in the cost and quality of your trip. Terry Trippler, an expert in pricing strategies, routings, and allowable stopovers (at www.terrytrippler.com), knows how to play the game. Learning how to read the airlines' published routing information can give you trip options that you never imagined.

Airline routings list the cities you may fly *through* to get from one destination to another, and there are some points to keep in mind when interpreting them. They use three-letter city codes rather than airport codes (e.g., Detroit is listed as DTT, not DTW, which is the Detroit airport code). A dash (-) means "and," a slash (/) means "or," and an asterisk (*) means "stop." Routing terminates in a city whose code is followed by an asterisk. You must travel through cities in the order in which they are listed, but you can skip any city. You cannot travel through the same city more than once.

Here's an example. Routing #453 for a flight from Minneapolis/St. Paul to Detroit on US Airways reads: MSP-US-CHI-US-PIT-US-DTT*. This means that from Minneapolis/St. Paul you may fly US Airways nonstop, *or* US Airways to Chicago then US Airways to Pittsburgh then US Airways to Detroit, *or* US Airways to Chicago then US Airways to Detroit, or US Airways to Pittsburgh then US Airways to Detroit.

How are all of these rates determined? This is where things get sticky.

Let's say you don't understand the fare bases, you buy a cheap ticket, and, later, you want to change your flight. For example, you bought a $250 ticket and now you want to change the outbound flight (the first leg of your trip). You're in for a painful surprise. When you buy a cheap ticket, you can't disregard the restrictions that apply. If you try to change the ticket, you will end up paying more money than you wanted to. For example, your $250 ticket entitles you to a restricted fare. If you want to change your outgoing flight, you may be told that it will cost $1,000 to make that change. To change any outbound flight after you've bought a restricted ticket can be excessively expensive. Most people don't understand that the price of the ticket is based on the *outbound* flight. It sets the fare for the entire ticket.

Is there any way to get out of paying the extra fees? Here's something that should make you angry. The airlines make more pure profit from their $100 rewriting/change fees on tickets than they make from actually flying you with your original tickets. On principle alone, you should try to do anything within your power—or someone else's—to avoid paying those charges.

And more often than not, your payment of those charges depends on the discretion of the counter agent at the airport. If he or she is in a good mood, the agent can easily waive the charges. On the other hand, if the agent is trying to get high marks for living in the uncompromising world of literal interpretation, then you're stuck with the charge.

Sometimes you just get lucky. At other times, you need to *make* your luck. Too many people look at their flying experience in one-dimensional terms. Every flight is a new flight. It's as if they've never flown before, and, to them, the people who work at the airport are faceless and nameless. Yet these same travelers wonder why they aren't treated better.

To me, it's obvious. They've spent absolutely no time developing a relationship with that counter or gate agent. Got a problem? Quite simply, the airlines can—if they want to—make it all better. It all comes down to the relationship, or relationships, you've built along the way.

Also, it becomes a matter of understanding, and then embracing, a much bigger view of the travel experience. At the same time, it becomes a matter of reducing the travel experience to the very basics.

Why are you really flying? To go from point A to point B. You're really *not* there to be pampered, fed well, comforted, coddled, and cared for. If you believe you're entitled to that kind of attention, you've been brainwashed by too many misleading airline ads.

You're on the plane because it will transport you to where you want to go. But here's the problem. Most people—and, I'm sad to say, a number of my friends—don't get this simple message.

Imagine that Los Angeles was being invaded by outer-space aliens, and there was only one flight at the gate to rescue everyone. Most of my friends would be eaten by the aliens. Why? Because they'd still be at the counter saying, "But I wanted a *window* seat."

No, the concept here is simple: Get on the plane. Period.

The unwritten, unspoken but acted-upon rule is that people who understand the basics—people who at least try to comprehend the actual *process* of travel—are invariably treated better by the airlines.

Short of alien invasion, understanding ticket lingo and codes doesn't have to be an extraterrestrial experience. What follows is a basic primer.

When it comes to tickets and fares, everything is contingent on inventory, as I explained earlier. Every flight has a different inventory. For example, full coach (Y) and full first-class (F) fares are almost always available, and with good reason. They are full-fare, totally unrestricted tickets and give the airline the highest yield per ticket. But you may have only one or two K14NR fares, meaning a discounted, fourteen-days-in-advance, nonrefundable ticket. Or *none* of those fares may be available. It all depends on how many full-fare coach, business, and first-class passengers are already booked on your flight. And perhaps more important, it depends on how many full-fare passengers flew on the same flight last month and last year.

Each airline has a computer-driven model of the projected *load factor* for every flight. It provides a historical pattern that may date back five years. More than anything else, this model determines how an airline will price the inventory for the same flight this year.

It also affects how quickly the airline will break into the inventory and change fares if the projections don't materialize. For example, say Flight 204 from San Antonio to Dallas flew at 82 percent capacity last year, and a majority of the passengers paid full fare. This pattern was consistent with previous years, so an abundance of low-fare seats is extremely unlikely for the same flight on the same day of the same month this year.

But if two weeks before the departure date, the airline realizes that only 61 percent of the plane is filled, the carrier will begin to dump tickets through consolidators, mailings to the airline's frequent-flier program, or the Internet.

How can you find out the exact inventory on a flight—in other words, how many buckets and how many seats are left? The information you get really depends on the questions you ask the agent. Remember, the reservations agent on the other end of the phone is trained to ask you questions that will more or less limit your options.

When you get the lowest fare offered over the phone, make a reservation. You'll have twenty-four hours to pay for the ticket. This gives you enough time to be a comparison shopper. Call competing airlines, and then check the Internet.

Here's another unwritten rule. Let's say an airline will sell you a discount ticket—$400 to fly to Boston from San Francisco—for an 11:00 A.M. departure, but tells you the 8:00 A.M. departure—the flight you *really* wanted—is not available.

When an agent tells you a flight is "not available," the *real* interpretation, in most cases, is that the flight is not available at the fare you want to pay. There could be dozens of available seats. Your retort should be: "But are there *seats* available?" If there are, here's where you can get creative.

Go to the airport at 7:00 A.M. holding your 11:00 A.M. ticket. Go to the counter or the gate and say you came out early and would like to depart early if there's space available. And if there's space, you get to go out on the flight you originally wanted, at the fare you wanted to pay.

Airport airline counter agents are not only encouraged to do this, they are *empowered* to do it by their companies. The logic, from the airlines' point of view, is that the earlier they get people out and fill the departing planes, the better off they'll be if they have a cancellation later and have to spend money for accommodations, meals, and even denied boarding compensation if the later flights operate but are overbooked.

The airline reservations agents will never tell you this. Unless you're traveling during a peak holiday period, this almost always works, and it is totally within the scope of the airline agents' discretion.

THE BEST DAY OF THE WEEK TO BUY CHEAP TICKETS

Believe it or not, there really *is* a best day of the week to make your best deal on an airline ticket, and it's neither Monday nor Friday. It's Wednesday! And there's even a best time on Wednesday to buy that ticket.

Why Wednesday? Thank the small, upstart airlines. In the airline business, fare wars are started by the weakest competitors, and the big guys tend to be the ones to raise fares. And all of that tends to happen on Fridays.

So how did Wednesday become the ideal day to strike a deal?

Let's say Airline A decides to raise fares. It usually does so at a late hour on a Friday night. By Saturday, Airline A's major competitors will probably match that fare increase. Warning: Book your tickets over a weekend, and you might spend a whole lot more than you should.

But what if the major competitors *don't* match the higher fares? Then the instigator of the fare increase drops its fares back down late on Sunday night or on Monday morning. If you already paid a higher fare, you still may be out of luck. Why? Because although you might still qualify for a lower fare and a ticket exchange, that terrible $100 change fee could wipe out your savings!

Here's another example. Let's say upstart Airline B decides to begin a fare war. Again, it happens late on a Friday night. Usually, some (but not all) of the majors will match that fare on routes where they compete with Airline B. Does that mean you should still book tickets over the weekend? Absolutely not. Remember, I said some, but *not all,* of the majors will match that fare. By late Monday, depending on how that new fare is doing in the marketplace, Airline C might jump into the battle and offer an even *lower* fare, so look for all the other airlines to rush to match *that* one—usually by Tuesday—and the war is on. Prices might go even lower on Wednesday. And that's when you strike. Wait any longer than Wednesday, and you may be in trouble. The wars usually end by Thursday morning.

Why? Friday is just around the corner! And the cycle starts all over again.

What's the best time to buy your ticket on Wednesday? One hour after Tuesday midnight (1:00 A.M. Wednesday morning). Why? At about midnight, the airlines usually reload their computers with the latest low-cost fares that were announced the previous day but will be canceled if they are not purchased within twenty-four hours.

THE CLASS SYSTEM

The overall numbers are indeed staggering. By conservative estimates, the airlines update the fares in their computer systems *over 250,000 times a day!* That's how much the allocations of inventory change. Different classes, same economy seats!

In airline reservation computer systems, the allocation of seats into different fare categories is designated by "class-of-service" codes (see page 88). Do not confuse these codes with the actual class of service (e.g., first class, business class, coach—or, for that matter, where you sit on the plane). First class and business class do have their own class-of-service codes, but many different class-of-service codes are used for the coach cabin, even though all of the passengers sit in the same place.

It happens all the time. A full-fare business traveler and the Gen Xer on a budget may sit next to each other in the coach cabin—and often do—but their reservations were made with different class-of-service codes.

So how do you read your airline ticket? Start with the class of service printed on the ticket, and then go to the fare basis. First class is generally coded as F or P, business class is either C or J, and full-fare coach is Y.

Any other letter on your ticket refers to a different—and discounted—fare class. Most of these fare classes have restrictions. They are the dreaded "subclasses," and their letters are: M, B, H, K, Q, T, L, and V. Things get confusing because each airline has a different hierarchical structure for these letters and a different interpretation of the restrictions they represent. These letters, combined with a fare basis, will tell you what your ticket really means.

When you are checking whether a particular flight is available, what you really want to know is which classes are available. If you are looking for a low fare requiring booking in Q class, you must find a flight for which Q class is available.

If you see a fare marked U, you are looking at an Internet fare that can only be purchased online.

See a ticket with an L class? That could be the lowest-class ticket, which has the most restrictions. Generally, L class tickets are not upgradable.

THE AIRLINES' REAL MILEAGE PROGRAM

Most passengers don't know that international fares are based on mileage and North American fares are based on the routing of the trip. International fare tariffs relate to an established amount of mileage—called the *maximum permitted mileage* (MPM)—between every point A and point B. The carriers interested in the traffic between these two points can use their own hubs, provided the maximum permitted mileage is not exceeded.

In the event that the mileage is exceeded by 5 percent (or 10, 15, 20, or 25 percent), a surcharge of 5 percent (or 10, 15, 20, or 25 percent) can be assessed. Beyond 25 percent additional mileage, the through fare must be split and recalculated.

This means that you *can* backtrack on your route overseas, but you can't use your destination as an intermediate point in the same fare breakdown. So when planning an international trip with a number of stops, determine the farthest destination point, go there first, and then return to your original starting point, stopping over en route.

Under MPM rules, you can travel via the same intermediate point more than once, but you can stop there only once. These rules do, however, allow you to play the "open jaw" game.

An open jaw allows you to travel, for example, from Seattle to Miami and then fly to Los Angeles from Miami (with no ticket between Los Angeles and Seattle). Hence, the open jaw. And the fare? Usually, the same low fare as a Seattle-to-Miami round-trip, instead of two full-fare, oneway tickets: (1) Seattle to Miami (point A to point B) and (2) Miami to Los Angeles (point B to point C).

The caveat here is that the distance between points B and C must be less than the distance to and from points A and B. In this example, an open jaw on the Seattle–Miami–Los Angeles ticket is allowed because the distance between Miami and Los Angeles is less than a round-trip between Seattle and Miami.

Another way to look at it: The distance between Los Angeles and Seattle must be shorter than the shortest distance actually flown on the ticket.

OPEN RETURN

If money is no problem, an open return gives you the most options. An open return is a totally unrestricted ticket that allows you to fly between the destination city and your originating city with no set date or flight. You still have to make a reservation when you want to fly, but with an open return ticket, you fly home when you want to fly.

THE CONFUSION OF STANDBY

Standby remains one of the more confusing terms in the airline business. During my college days at the University of Wisconsin, flying standby meant getting a special discounted fare—those were the days of the much-abused student standby fare. At that time, it *was* a fare.

This was the deal: You'd get a student standby card and show up at the airport. If there was a seat, you got to go for half price.

In those days, if a group of us wanted to go to New York for the weekend, I'd phone the airline and make a phony reservation for a family of eight (yes, I actually did this). Then my friends would call and make phony reservations on the same plane for other large families. The airline must have thought it was family reunion time. Within two hours, when I called the airline back, I was told the plane was sold out. Bingo! Run to the airport. Get a cheap ticket. Get on the plane and—surprise!—forty empty seats! There were even standby fares on the New York–to–London route—not just for students, but for everyone—if seats were available.

Thanks to the thousands of college students who, like me, tried this tactic—and given today's more sophisticated computerized airline reservations systems—those fares no longer exist. But they were fun while they lasted.

Today, with exceedingly few exceptions (Air Tran has a limited, restricted standby program for students), standby is simply a status, not a fare.

Lately, the airlines have tried to enforce a rule that you can fly standby only on the same day listed on your ticket (as in, you missed an earlier flight). But that doesn't mean they always stick to that rule. It certainly applies to your originating outbound flight. But what about your return leg? More often than not, as long as you've started your trip and it's your return flight, and as long as there are seats available in the same fare basis as your original ticket, you stand an excellent chance of flying standby on that flight.

If you're flying standby, that means you're also on the waitlist. But a waitlist isn't democratic. It's not first-come, first-served, no matter what the airlines tell you. Getting on the waitlist is easy. But making the jump from the waitlist to an actual seat on the flight you want is something else altogether.

Your status on the waitlist has nothing to do with what time you got placed on that waitlist. It has to do with the class of service, the amount of money you paid for your ticket, and your status as a frequent flier. If all else fails, there's always the hope that the counter or gate agent will like you and look kindly on your plight.

If an airline agent tells you that he or she can put you on the waitlist, ask the agent to interpret that status for you. Don't ask, "How many people are ahead of me?" Instead, ask how many people are ahead of you "with priority status." If they number more than twelve and you're flying on a narrow-body plane, you're not only waiting for Godot, but Godot has a better chance of getting on that flight than you do. Look for alternate connecting flights immediately—or alternate airports.

On a wide-body plane with three classes of service, a waitlist with twelve people is actually promising! Ask immediately: "Is the flight sold out in all classes?" If not, you have an excellent chance of getting off that list and onto the plane.

OK, now you've got the fare you want. Or do you?

These are just the fares in the airlines' reservation computers. They aren't the fares offered on the Internet (by consolidators) or the fares being marketed to specific income and ethnic groups.

OTHER TICKET AND FARE SOURCES

Chances are, you've seen consolidator ads in newspapers. Consolidators offer low-cost round-trip tickets to major destinations around the world: $600 tickets to Hong Kong from San Diego, $478 to Paris from New York, and $500 tickets from Chicago to Madrid. The lowest regular airline fares on these routes often can be twice to three times as much.

Are the consolidators too good to be true? Sometimes.

Consolidators are airline wholesalers who get tickets at fares far below the officially published tariffs, in exchange for committing to sell large numbers of seats for airlines. They sell to travel agents, ticket brokers, and more often than not, directly to the public.

Each airline has a reasonably good estimate of its future bookings. If those bookings are low on certain flights, many airlines will dump tickets on the consolidator market.

The excess inventory is sold to consolidators for a low fixed price. Consolidators then sell these tickets to the public for a small profit. In the past, airlines argued that they didn't dump excess tickets on what was essentially a gray market. But that brings to mind the Claude Rains character in *Casablanca,* who expresses shock and indignation that illegal gambling is going on inside Rick's café, and then collects his winnings from the previous evening.

Through consolidators, the airlines sell seats they otherwise might not be able to sell, and they can say that they have not discounted their tickets. In fact, many consolidator tickets showed that full coach fare was paid (along with endorsements on the ticket that it was totally nonrefundable and nonexchangeable and was good only on that airline on one specific flight).

Is it legal? The Federal Aviation Act of 1958 prohibits the sale of international airline tickets below published fares. But the act—designed to protect airlines—is not being enforced, because the airlines are the ones violating it.

Consolidators thrived for years in this netherworld of dumped tickets. But it's a tougher market these days.

Major international airlines are offering discounts themselves, so the consolidators have little room to maneuver and still offer meaningful discounts. That's where misleading ads have become prevalent. Many consolidators are promoting fares that they cannot deliver.

A few years ago, and after receiving many consumer complaints, New York's metropolitan Better Business Bureau (BBB) decided to investigate. BBB staffers pored through newspaper ads, made calls, and, in some cases, even bought tickets to see which consolidators were telling the truth. They tested one consolidator's ad by trying to buy an advertised high-season cheap ticket between New York and Paris, but they couldn't buy a single ticket.

During the low season, the BBB investigators could buy the advertised low-fare tickets at only one out of five consolidators promoting them. After the BBB complained, it received documentation from a few consolidators that some tickets had been sold at advertised prices.

The situation bordered on bait and switch. It was like an electronics store advertising a new $50 television set and having only one for sale.

The investigation also revealed that, in two-thirds of the cases, BBB investigators would have paid the same amount if they had purchased the ticket directly from an airline, or they couldn't get a confirmed seat or were put on a never-ending waiting list. In each instance, the advertised price was not available, and the investigators were offered a higher-priced ticket.

In fairness, that's not always the case. I surveyed six consolidators' advertising in the *Los Angeles Times*. From three of the six, the advertised price *was* available. And the best deals I found were $179 less than the airline's lowest rate for the same dates.

Here are four rules to live by if you want to play the consolidator game (by the way, I buy tickets from consolidators all the time):

1. Always pay with a credit card. Paying by check offers no protection.

2. Watch out for surcharges. A number of consolidators try to impose an additional charge if you pay by credit card. In New York, where many of these consolidators are based, this violates state law (it doesn't matter where you live; where the transaction takes place is the key).

3. Be aware that many consolidator tickets carry severe cancellation penalties, and most tickets are totally nonrefundable.

4. Make sure you have a confirmed seat. One BBB shopper bought a ticket to Paris, but there was no confirmed seat, and even the waiting list was closed. Then the consolidator tried to charge a $100 cancellation fee!

Most consolidators are not scam artists. They are, in fact, bona fide operations that don't always advertise honestly. That's not to say you can't find savings through consolidators. You just need to be an obsessed comparison shopper.

SURFING THE NEWSSTAND

Sound silly? It's not. Some of the best airline deals overseas can be found right at your local newsstand.

In your neighborhood, look for a newsstand that carries foreign—particularly British—newspapers. Buy any two of them. Take them home, and turn to the travel section. You will see numerous advertisements for great discount fares to virtually anywhere in the world. It's a safe bet that many of the fares will *never* be offered in the United States; some of the destinations aren't even marketed here—especially for discount fares.

As an example, let's say you want to fly from New York to the Canary Islands, or from Chicago to Nairobi. Looking for a discount fare? Good luck. You won't find one.

But you'd have to be dead not to be able to find a great discount fare to London. American, United, Northwest, Continental, and US Airways fly there. So do British Airways, Virgin Atlantic, El Al, Kuwait Airways, and Air India—and I've probably forgotten a few others. With that much capacity over the North Atlantic, London remains an intense discount route.

So getting to London is easy. You can often fly for as little as $298 round-trip—sometimes, for even less.

And that's where the newspapers come in.

Go ahead. Price out the New York–Tenerife (Canary Islands) flight, and you'll be hit—even in coach—with fares that can exceed $1,800.

London is a major international hub. Not only do all the big *and* small airlines fly to there, but virtually every foreign country flies *from* there!

Begin with a cheap fare from New York to London. Now

check the newspapers. I recently found a *round-trip* airfare from London to Tenerife for £89 (that's about $162)!

This theory works on just about any itinerary you could imagine. In fact, it is sometimes cheaper to fly from Los Angeles to London, and then take a cheap flight to Hong Kong or Bangkok, than to take a nonstop flight from Los Angeles to Hong Kong.

ROUND THE WORLD

But what if you want to stop at more than one destination? Point-to-point travel will kill your wallet. Instead, investigate an RTW (round-the-world) ticket. (These tickets are heavily advertised in the U.K. papers.)

Airlines don't promote these fares, and travel agents tend to hate them because they are labor-intensive to process. But if you're stopping in more than one destination overseas, the RTW ticket is more than your friend. It's your lover!

For example, the regular coach fare between Los Angeles and Singapore is $1,300 each way. Other examples: New York City to Rome on British Airways is $800; Chicago to Frankfurt on Lufthansa is almost $900.

If you buy APEX (advance-purchase excursion) tickets, the fares drop, but in most cases you can fly to only one destination, and you are allowed no stopovers or flexibility in departure dates on your outbound or return flights.

Enter RTW fares. They allow you not only tremendous flexibility but also an opportunity—quite literally—to see the world, sometimes for less money than a regular coach fare between the United States and Europe.

Round-the-world tickets have been quietly sold since 1978, when Pan American offered its "Round the World in 80 Days" fare. Initially, the highly promoted fare angered world airlines because the price of the RTW ticket was less than half the cost of a regular economy fare to circle the globe.

When Pan Am flew around the world, the fare made sense to the airline, to customers who wished to combine business with pleasure trips, and to passengers who wished to extend their vacations beyond one or two foreign destinations.

Pan Am ceased operations in 1991, and no one airline currently flies around the world. But the fare lives on.

Almost every international airline offers a special RTW ticket—usually, in conjunction with one or two other airlines. The fares are nothing less than terrific when compared to regular coach and even to other discount routings to foreign destinations.

Remember the Singapore Airlines fare of $1,300 each way between Los Angeles and Singapore? That's $2,600 round-trip. But a round-the-world ticket bought on Singapore Airlines (in conjunction with another airline) can cost as little as $2,806. For just $200 more, you don't get just Singapore, you get the world! I've also found RTW tickets for as little as $1,800 out of London.

Here's what you can do with the RTW ticket. Fly to Tokyo on American Airlines, then on to Singapore, Athens, and Paris, all on Singapore Airlines. In Paris, switch to American, fly to New York, and stop numerous times as you cross the United States on your way back to Los Angeles.

That's just a westbound option. You can also start your flight by heading east on American, United, or Delta and then visit Frankfurt, Brussels, or Bangkok via Singapore Airlines.

Here's the best news: To buy an RTW ticket, you need only make your reservation and buy your ticket fourteen days in advance. There's no minimum stay requirement.

The ticket is good for a year; you can fly when you want. There are two important restrictions:

1. You must continue in the same direction—no backtracking.

2. After you start your trip, if you want to add more cities, the airline will charge you $25 for each change in the original itinerary.

You can buy the same ticket in business class for about $4,411, or in first class for about $6,118. (Some cost comparisons: A round-trip point-to-point business-class ticket between Los Angeles and Paris is more than $7,154, and a first-class ticket checks in at more than $9,615!)

This example is just one of dozens of possible combinations of routes and airlines.

Singapore Airlines has teamed with Star Alliance and Air New Zealand to offer various itineraries. Star Alliance includes Air Canada, Air New Zealand, ANA, Asiana Airlines, Austrian, bmi, Lot Polish Airlines, Lufthansa, Scandinavian Airlines, Singapore Airlines, Spanair, Thai Airways, United Airlines, US Airways, and Varig. Air Canada has also joined with Japan Airlines, and British Airways has paired with American and United to offer similar RTW bargains.

The combinations on RTW tickets are almost endless. Their sheer economy may explain why, with very little promotion or advertising, a growing number of passengers are buying RTW tickets. And they're not just coach passengers.

You will realize even greater savings if you buy your RTW ticket on another continent. One travel agency in England recently offered an RTW ticket for £840 (about U.S. $1,546).

On some RTW tickets, provisions are made for side trips, and some airlines offer discounts on itineraries not flown by them or their RTW partners. (For example, few international airlines have extensive routings in South America, but some offer attractive side packages with local airlines for trips within that continent.)

A typical RTW itinerary might start with a trip from New York to Los Angeles. From Los Angeles you could fly to Honolulu and from there to Tokyo, Seoul, Osaka, Hong Kong, Bangkok, Delhi, Cairo, Athens, and Paris. A European connection could then bring you home to New York.

One of the more exotic RTW itineraries was offered not long ago by American Airlines, Korean Air, and Royal Jordanian Airlines. Passengers flew from New York to Los Angeles, then on to Honolulu on American. From Honolulu to Tokyo, they were on Korean Airlines, which offered a continuing itinerary that included Osaka, Seoul, Taipei, Hong Kong, and Bangkok.

Royal Jordanian flew them from Bangkok to Amman, Jordan, then on to Cairo and Paris. The leg from France to the United States was an American flight.

Itinerary offerings change frequently, but once you're ticketed, you're in.

One of the great things about RTW tickets (other than the fares) is that you don't have to fly to all these destinations. You can fly to as many or as few as you wish, just as long as you circle the globe.

Some travelers book flights to a dozen or so destinations on the route structure of one of the airlines. If they later decide to skip a city or two, they can usually bypass them without incurring additional costs.

Perhaps the best news about RTW tickets is that if you're a member of a frequent-flier program on any of the participating airlines, you can earn mileage. In the airline mileage game, this is tantamount to nuclear fusion. Considering the distances involved, your RTW adventures could conceivably earn enough mileage points to qualify you for a free ticket upon your return.

AIR PASSES

Air passes aren't RTW tickets, but the concept is the same. In conjunction with round-trip tickets between two points, many airlines offer great deals for travel within certain countries or continents. When you buy a round-trip ticket, always check with foreign carriers to see what particular promotions they offer.

In South America, a Latin Pass, for a nominal amount, allows you great flexibility in flying around that continent. British Airways (BA) has seasonal deals featuring booklets of flight coupons. For as little as $50, you can fly from London to many European cities if you've bought a round-trip ticket to London on BA. In the South Pacific, there are similar deals. But remember, you *must* buy these deals when you buy your round-trip tickets in the United States. If you wait until you get overseas, the deals do not apply.

COUPONS

Every once in a while, an airline will issue (or some travel agents will be incentivized to issue) promotional coupons. These coupons offer either a specific dollar discount or a sliding scale, depending on the initial fare you're paying.

An even better coupon is the one that offers a flat percentage off the cost of any published fare. But the next time you see one of these coupons, read the fine print. It may actually benefit you even more. For example, I recently received one of these coupons, and the ticketing instructions, printed on the back of the coupon, specifically delineated the deal: 50 percent off any published fare/itinerary. The key word was "itinerary."

I combined the coupon with another coupon. (I save all those that come my way.) This gave me an upgrade to the next class of service on any itinerary.

I then booked the following itinerary, which included two open jaw tickets, at the cheapest coach fare I could find: Los Angeles to Paris, then Paris to Orlando (open jaw number one), then Orlando to New York, and New York back to Los Angeles (open jaw number two). Total fare on this one itinerary: about $1,526 in coach. I used my 50-percent-off coupon to bring the total fare down to $763, and then assigned my upgrade coupon to the same itinerary. I flew business class or first class on this itinerary for a total fare of $763! And I accumulated lots and lots of future mileage.

ALTERNATE AIRPORTS

Have you considered alternate airports?

On a flight from Los Angeles to New York, you can get even cheaper fares by flying from secondary or tertiary airports—Burbank, Ontario, Long Beach, or San Diego—to Newark, LaGuardia, or Islip instead of Kennedy (JFK).

My favorite plan is to pick airports where JetBlue flies and also competes with some of the major airlines. For example, a one-day-in-advance reservation from LAX to JFK on American results in a $1,400 airfare in coach. But the same one-day advance reservation from Long Beach airport, where American is slugging it out with JetBlue, drops the fare to about $460, a significant saving. The same happens in Oakland between JetBlue and United.

Every once in a while, even JFK becomes the desired alternate airport. Most people don't realize that, of the three major New York area airports, JFK is the *least* congested. With the exception of the 3:00 P.M. to 7:00 P.M. time slots, when most international flights either arrive or depart, JFK is operating at nowhere near its capacity.

This fact wasn't lost on the folks who started JetBlue as a low-fare airline early in 2000. JetBlue flies between JFK and Orlando, Fort Lauderdale, and Tampa (Florida), Buffalo (New York), and other East Coast cities. It has expanded to offer flights to the West Coast, as well as to Puerto Rico and the Dominican Republic.

Consider this: A one-way walk-up fare between New York and Orlando, flying out of congested LaGuardia on American Airlines costs an average of $560—one way! Jet-Blue now offers several prices for a New York–to–Orlando flight; the cheapest is $158 round-trip. And on some flights, the taxi time and delay time out of LaGuardia exceed Jet-Blue's flight time from JFK to Orlando!

One of the best airports for discount pricing is Newark (New Jersey). So many low-fare carriers fly there that the majors often match their fares.

The same deal can often be found at Kennedy. Ask. Then ask again. Airlines may not always volunteer their time-specific discounts.

For example, American Flight 34 is an 8:00 A.M. departure from Los Angeles to JFK. It is not an inexpensive flight. But if you ask about a time-specific discount on the same route, American throws in its 7:00 A.M. departure, and there are significant savings.

Most of the time, that flight actually begins in Honolulu as the red-eye to California from Hawaii. American then needs to get the aircraft to New York so it can assign the plane, later that day, to the profitable 5:00 P.M. or 6:00 P.M. premium flights back to Los Angeles. And those are the flights you want.

Other positioning flights are deeply discounted by the airlines. Check the flight schedules for unusual departures.

For example, Northwest Airlines has a late-night (10:55 P.M.) departure from Detroit to Washington, D.C.

Does anyone ever take that flight? No. Then why is it scheduled? Because Northwest flies the aircraft to Washington, where it undergoes basic overnight maintenance and becomes the popular first flight out of the District to Detroit the next morning. During that night positioning flight back to the nation's capital, you can practically go bowling on the plane. It is *that* empty . . . and is often priced accordingly.

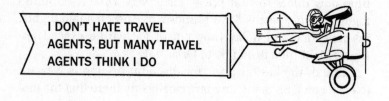

I DON'T HATE TRAVEL
AGENTS, BUT MANY TRAVEL
AGENTS THINK I DO

Once, for a segment I was preparing for ABC's *Good Morning America,* I decided to see how competitive travel agents were and whether I could get better fares on my own.

I polled thirty travel agents around the United States. I asked them all the same question: "I'm traveling tomorrow between city A and city B. What's the lowest fare you can get me?" I then called individual airlines and asked the same question. In every case, I got a lower fare from the airline.

We aired the segment on *Good Morning America* a week after the survey, and we talked about the results. In one case, the fare differential between the travel agent's price and the price I got directly from the airlines was something like $831.

That was a major blow to travel agents. Before I was off the air, ABC and its affiliated stations around the country were inundated with angry telephone calls. Within two hours of airing the segment, an organized letter-writing and faxing campaign began, led by the American Society of Travel Agents (ASTA).

Each letter or fax had essentially the same message. Each claimed that I was irresponsible, unfair, and biased against travel agents, and each demanded that ASTA appear on *Good Morning America* to dispute my report.

By the end of the first day, the angry letters and faxes numbered seven thousand. By the next day, incoming messages were up to fourteen thousand, a one-time record of negative responses.

I had not yet returned to Los Angeles. I was called in to the New York office of Phil Beuth, the executive who ran *Good Morning America.* "What is this all about?" he queried. "This is the most negative response to a segment I've ever seen. Have we been fair here?"

I reminded him that, without exception, every letter was from a travel agent, and each letter's wording was virtually identical. I asked him, "Have there been any angry letters from consumers complaining that I saved them $831?" We agreed that, in the interest of fairness, we should invite ASTA to appear on the show.

ABC then invited ASTA to send a representative to the show the following week, to discuss the segment. ASTA refused, insisting that they would not send someone to any show on which I would also appear. I countered that I would simply sit and say nothing during the first four minutes of a six-minute segment, to give ASTA the opportunity to state its case. Again, ASTA refused.

I then got on an airplane and returned to Los Angeles. A funny thing happened during my transcontinental flight home. ABC producers, confronted with thousands of protesting letters from individual travel agents, each demanding to come on *Good Morning America,* decided to simply pick one at random and extend the same invitation that was delivered to the ASTA executives.

When the ASTA executives heard about this proposal, they did an about-face and sent Richard Knodt, then their chief operating officer, to New York. ABC called and told me to fly back.

The resulting ABC segment made history, of sorts. Tape from that segment is now being used during media training sessions for executives, to teach them what *never* to do or say on a talk show.

I later found out that the segment was a catalyst for one top airline executive who was watching the show that morning.

Knodt argued that my "conclusion that consumers should shop airlines themselves to ensure the lowest fare is like instructing your three-year-old to jump in the water and hopefully swim."

He said that my survey was unfair, and he argued that a travel agent in Boston couldn't be expected to know the lowest fare between Miami and San Francisco.

What? "But isn't that your job? Isn't that what you're supposed to do?" asked cohost Nancy Snyderman.

"Well," Knodt responded, looking at me, "he's smarter than the average consumer and knows all the flights and routes."

"Wait," I interrupted. "Let's look at the facts. All I did was call thirty travel agents at random. These were cold calls. An even playing field. And I asked them what the lowest fare was between two cities. How smart do you have to be to ask that question?"

At that point, the entire segment headed south. I then explained not only my survey but the results from two similar price-challenge surveys by independent, nonprofit consumer research groups in Washington, D.C., and San Francisco.

Of thirty agencies surveyed by the San Francisco "Bay Area Consumers' Checkbook," only two agents were consistently able to find the lowest prices. In a similar survey of one hundred D.C.-area travel agents, most failed the price challenge.

For ASTA to say that consumers who seek out low airfares on their own are like three-year-olds about to drown is an insult to most travelers. I argued that anyone who had a telephone and a little extra time could often achieve substantial savings by being a good comparison shopper.

So, what is ASTA's grievance with me? In correspondence to travel editors at various newspapers, Knodt argued as follows:

- Consumers don't normally call travel agents in Chicago to ask them the lowest airfare between San Francisco and New York. They would normally call a travel agent in either San Francisco or New York. But that's exactly what I did. Thirty out of thirty travel agents failed the price challenge.

- Because I possess more travel and price knowledge than the average consumer, the test was unfairly weighted. I accept the compliment, but I called agents and airlines and posed the same question in the same manner that any consumer would. I merely explained my travel itinerary and asked for the lowest airfare. You don't need any extra knowledge or special travel experience to ask that simple question.

- "Left alone with the virtual morass of everchanging airfares," ASTA's Knodt claimed, "consumers can waste valuable time as they are left sinking in the ocean of fares, schedules, and carriers to choose from." My response: Armed with nothing other than the toll-free numbers of the airlines, it took me only twenty minutes to get the lowest prices for each pair of cities, and, in the San Francisco–to–D.C. example, I saved more than $800. I think that was time very well spent.

In a follow-up piece, I said that, in an ideal world, travelers should be able to find a travel agent who would consistently get them the lowest fare and the best deal. But in the real world, this does not often happen, and here is why:

- Travel agents have traditionally worked on a commission basis for airlines, cruise lines, hotels, and rental car companies. Commissions to U.S. travel agents were reduced to 8 percent in 1995, to 5 percent in 1999, and in many cases were eliminated completely in 2002. Nevertheless, if a travel agent does work on commission and offers a customer a lower fare, that agent must be willing to accept a lower commission. What's the incentive to do that? Your continued business. Conclusion: If you can find an agent who will do that, use that agent. If not, do the agent's work yourself.

RESERVATION COMPUTER BIAS

Around the time of my survey of travel agents, the U.S. Department of Transportation (DOT) was conducting a sweeping investigation into the relationship between agents and the computer reservation systems supplied by individual airlines. Were the proprietary computers placing undue influence on the travel agents to favor particular airlines?

As part of its in-depth review, the DOT was looking closely at these issues:

- *Override commissions.* Most travel agents then operated on an average commission of 10 percent. An airline ticket bought from a travel agent for $400 gave the agent $40 profit. But there were also override commissions, and few agents disclosed them to travelers. Some airlines paid as much as 23 percent commission to agents who steered business to them. One cruise line recently offered 20 percent commission to agents. That's a significant incentive. But how does that benefit consumers? More often than not, it doesn't. The powerful economics of override commissions often mean that some travel agents will feel pressure to book you on the flight or cruise or at the hotel where they make the highest commission.

- *Secret software.* Some large travel agencies created their own "secret software" to indicate the suppliers that paid override commissions. Their computers displayed the names of these airlines, hotels, and cruise lines first on the lists that scrolled through agents' screens.

And then came the whammy. A few months after the *Good Morning America* segment ran, Delta Air Lines fired the first shot—a big one—below the waterline of most travel agencies. Delta announced commission caps. And within days, almost every airline matched Delta's cuts. The travel agency business would never be the same. (Later, I found out that tapes of the original and subsequent *Good Morning America* segments were shown to Ron Allen, then head of Delta Air Lines. He told me in an interview that the *Good Morning America* pieces served as major catalysts in his making that commission decision.)

At that time, one of the holdouts on the commission cuts was TWA. It misjudged travel agents' real power when it kept its commission rate at a flat 10 percent. ASTA also misjudged its members' power when it announced that it would boycott airlines that cut commissions.

Six months later, the numbers were unavoidable and sent a major wake-up call to the entire travel industry. Who had the real power? *You did!*

How much new business came over to TWA when it kept the 10 percent commission? None. (TWA was later purchased by American.) How much business did the other airlines lose when they cut their commissions? None.

Why? The relationship between consumers and travel agents had changed. Air travelers are loyal to the frequent-flier programs of which they are members. They no longer ask travel agents for airline advice. They *tell* the agents which airline they want to fly on. Period.

With no strong commission structure to financially protect them, many travel agents went out of business.

The ones who survived—indeed, the ones who succeeded—became much better travel agents in the process. These agents understand that their financial well-being no longer comes from a ticket transaction. It grows by providing service and up-to-date information on *everything,* not simply what time a plane leaves and arrives.

As a result, many travel agents began to specialize, focusing on particular market niches. We are now seeing travel agents who are experts on specific destinations or experiences. They specialize in cruise ships, East Africa, barge trips, travel for people with disabilities, and so on.

Today, we consult travel agents the way we seek medical help. We don't see a podiatrist if our arm hurts us, and many of us now consult more than one travel agent.

For their part, travel agents are moving quickly into a service fee mode. Many charge between $20 and $100 (or more) for finding us great experiences and, yes, even great deals. And those agents deserve every penny they are charging.

Commission caps made travel agents proactive and service-oriented instead of transaction-oriented. For smart travelers and smart travel agents alike, it was—and continues to be—a win-win situation.

One caution: Secret override commissions still exist between airlines and travel agents. When shopping for a travel agent, you owe it to yourself to ask the agent to reveal whether he or she has any override commission or "preferred supplier" relationship with any airline, cruise ship, or hotel. It lets the agent know—or serves as a reminder—that you expect him or her to work for you first.

A FINAL NOTE ABOUT TRAVEL AGENTS

The change in the role of travel agents, particularly in relation to consumers, has been nothing less than dramatic, not only because of the speed at which this change has happened, but because of its impact.

No one understands that better than Matthew Upchurch, CEO of Virtuoso, a consortium of expert travel agents around the world. Upchurch not only tells other travel agents how to survive, he shows them how to succeed by pointing them back in time.

Upchurch puts it all in proper perspective when he says that to understand the function and the service of a travel agent, "We've gone back to the future.

"A lot of people forget that, prior to deregulation and prior to the advent of sophisticated airline computer reservations systems, the majority of airline tickets were actually processed by the airlines and not by travel agents."

He reminds us, "There used to be a lot fewer agents in this country. The process was fairly simple. There used to be four airfares: day coach, night coach, day first class, and night first class. And it was a regulated environment. And if you flew from New York to London, whether it was on BOAC, or Pan Am, or a lot of those airlines that aren't around anymore, you paid the same fare, regardless of what airline you flew."

So why did people go to an agent? In those days, it was very easy to go directly to an airline and book a flight. Upchurch argues that you went to agents because of their expertise, their service, and their knowledge beyond just booking that particular ticket.

But in the early 1970s the airlines introduced their computer reservations systems, or CRSs, and in 1978 deregulation hit. Suddenly there was an explosion of mergers and a complexity of airfares.

"Imagine the next thing that happens," Upchurch suggests. "Take all the airlines, which are not exactly known for their labor relations and their treatment of their employees— and all of a sudden they talk among themselves, and they come to the same conclusion. 'We've created these computer systems but if we put them in front of our own people and ask that staff to take phone calls both from consumers and from agents, we're going to have to hire hundreds, if not thousands, of these people. And God forbid that they want health insurance. God forbid that they want a pension plan. And God forbid they sue us for carpal tunnel syndrome or God knows what, and unionize, and walk out on us. Gee, maybe we should take these computers and turn around and *give* them to travel agents. And here's the best part: Then we can tell them what we're going to pay them without any problem. And they won't have collective bargaining, and they don't get health benefits or a pension.'

"It was brilliant," concludes Upchurch. "And it easily became one of the . . . largest outsourcings of labor in the history of the country."

Indeed, compared to having the airlines process tickets by themselves, enlisting the travel agent community was a much less expensive way of handling ticket distribution. The airlines had effective outsourced labor, using their new technology.

"It created an artificial monopoly," Upchurch argues, "with information and fares and rates, for almost twenty-seven years."

Then the technology caught up. Enter the Internet.

So then what happened? The airlines started introducing direct booking via the Internet. The technology was available to the public, and the public seized it. The airlines were quick to create a direct booking mechanism, and, when coupled with commission cuts, travel agents found themselves in deep trouble.

Or were they?

Initially, virtually everyone predicted the demise of all travel agents. But it didn't happen. Upchurch knows why. "People thought they could just go out and, with the Internet, do all their own booking themselves. For commodity purchases, like an airplane seat on Southwest, they could indeed do it. But for just about everything else, they soon found out they needed help—not in the physical booking of a trip, but in the details, in the information they needed."

And so, we've come full circle.

More people *are* booking direct, but even more people are traveling, so the numbers have gone higher for travel agents. Ten thousand Baby Boomers are turning age fifty-five *every day* in this country, and they all want to travel—or travel *more.*

"Boomers also are the most traveled, best educated, most

connected group of consumers in the history of mankind," Upchurch reports. "This group is a tough audience and travel is at the top of their list. Times have definitely changed. The World War II generation and the Depression Era generation . . . saw travel as a luxury. The Boomers see travel as a God-given right."

In satisfying that desire, they want added value. The good news for all of us is that travel agents have come to realize that they have to provide that added value in order to stay in business.

Today's travelers don't want to "talk to some airline person . . . they don't trust," Upchurch warns. "They just want to talk to somebody who cares. What's amazing to me is that, in one of the presidential primary debates, one of the questions that was asked was: 'What are you going to do about airline service?' This was in a presidential debate! Now if I were an industry, I'd say, 'By golly, we have a problem.' " Indeed, there has been a problem. "So what are travel agents selling?" Upchurch asks. "We're selling information, relationships, and connections."

But in that environment, Upchurch has learned that the travel industry continues to make a mistake. It tries to sell travel based on the price rather than on the perceived merit or the experience of the trip.

He calls it "the NBA courtside-seat syndrome." "The same person that will sit there and pound down to the last dime on some sale of something—in fact, you would have thought that they didn't have two nickels to rub together— will stop at nothing to pay $1,000 a ticket for NBA courtside seats. Because they want that experience. Because it's not the money. It's the perceived value of the experience. And that's what travel is all about," Upchurch reports.

"Today, consumers are overwhelmed with information,"

says Upchurch. "In fact, one of my favorite quotes is that 'in a world of limitless opportunities and limitless information, the only scarcity will be human attention.' If a travel agent can be an aggregator—somebody who can filter the information that someone trusts—then that is the travel agent I want. . . . The new travel agent engages . . . customers in a dialogue about what their aspirations are. And that information gets shared. So . . . all of a sudden, we know that there are 500 people in the United States . . . customers of our members, who've always wanted to go dog sledding. And then the travel agent can make that happen, as a specialist in dog sledding.

"But the most interesting development," says Upchurch, "is that the airlines have felt, for a long time, that they *own* travel agents. After all, they provided the agents [with] their computer systems. And they made those agents perform— sell their particular airline—to *keep* that computer system."

Do the airlines own the agents?

Upchurch says it just isn't so. "A long time ago, the Boston Consulting Group did a study for the airlines to try to determine that airline–travel agent relationship. What's amazing," Upchurch laughs, "is that the airlines would go out and pay a consulting company—God knows how many millions of dollars—to tell them the most obvious. Who is going to decide the fate of travel agents? The customer, not the airlines. But, the airlines had seen us as something that they created, as an extension of their distribution system."

That was then. This is now. Savvy travel agents are embracing a collaborative model of doing business, of getting to know their customers, of focusing less on the actual ticket transaction—its speed, accuracy, convenience, and price— and more on understanding the experiential needs of their customers.

Yes, there are people who prefer using ATMs to dealing with tellers at banks. But travel is more sophisticated. "Ten years ago, somebody could walk into an agency and say 'I want to go to South Africa.' And they probably would consider the agent an expert on South Africa if [he or she] just even knew the country of Namibia existed and could point to it on the map. Today, that person calls the agent on the phone, and if you haven't been there in the last twelve months, if you don't have personal contacts, if you don't know the elephant migration patterns, you're not an expert."

The travel agency–customer relationship is a combination of collaborative and expertise models. It's similar to the way people now deal with their doctors.

"We're no different," Upchurch argues. "In the old days, you'd go to your doctor and whatever he said you took as gospel. . . . Now, people go and research stuff and walk into their doctors' offices and say, 'Well, what about this drug, or what about this alternative means of treatment?' They want to be connected with somebody who's a professional to help validate the information they've already researched on their own."

But there's something else at work to justify a strong traveler–travel agent relationship. In this world of experiential one-upmanship, everyone is looking not just for a better deal but for a better, more fulfilling, and often more stylish experience. Just ask Anna Scully, an excellent travel agent in McLean, Virginia. "The real reason you need a great relationship with a professional travel agent," she argues convincingly, "is that you can't upgrade *yourself.*"

Still, you need to do your homework—as in any relationship—and the first order of business is to question your agent's loyalties. If your agent has a preferred supplier relationship that can benefit you when hotels or resorts are officially sold out, and that results in you getting a room when others can't, that's a good thing. If, on the other hand, your agent constantly steers you in the direction of that preferred supplier because the agent is getting override commissions from that supplier, that's a very bad thing. Use your own common sense, and don't be afraid to ask your travel agent which, if any, preferred supplier relationships exist *before* making that travel commitment.

In 2002, some fifty-four million adults, or about 26 percent of all Americans, said they used a travel agent to book at least one business, pleasure, or personal trip, flight, hotel room, rental car, or tour within the past three years. An increasing number of Americans are using the Internet to book travel, so it is not surprising that the number using travel agents has decreased from 32 percent in October 1999. Baby Boomer travelers, ages thirty-five to fifty-four, constitute 43 percent of travel agent users, while Generation X and Y travelers, ages eighteen through thirty-four, make up about 33 percent. Travelers booking through travel agents are more likely than overall travelers to be male, have some postgraduate education, and have an annual household income of $50,000 or more.

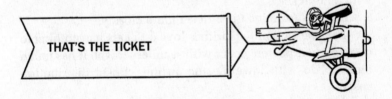

THAT'S THE TICKET

Getting the best deal on an airline ticket is a game, with winners and losers. What does it take to be a winner? A strategy. Following is some strategic advice for playing the airline ticket game.

I DON'T HATE TRAVEL AGENTS,
BUT I DO HATE E-TICKETS

Before I tell you about electronic tickets (e-tickets), let me tell you a little about my mother. She cornered the market on rotary phones, manual typewriters, and carbon paper. She didn't understand fax machines, cell phones, or pagers. The Internet wasn't another planet to her—it was another galaxy!

But my mother and I agreed on one thing: our loathing for e-tickets.

Since 1995, airlines have been offering, promoting, and, in some cases, virtually *forcing us* to use e-tickets.

When they were first introduced by United Airlines, the official spin was that the airlines were giving us electronic tickets as a big present.

A present? An e-ticket, we were told, would give us the opportunity for "seamless" travel. We could make a reservation and then, with no paper ticket or document in our hand, we could simply show up at the airport, go right to the gate, show a photo ID, and board our flight.

Indeed, in principle, you could—and you can—do this with an e-ticket.

But let's examine the e-ticket more closely.

The real reason the airlines love e-tickets has nothing to do with their passengers or with seamless travel. It has much more to do with lowering the airlines' ticket distribution costs.

By some estimates, the cost of processing an e-ticket runs about 22¢. A paper ticket costs an airline closer to $10.

Have the airlines lowered their costs? Indeed they have. In fact, once they started using e-tickets, airlines continued to close more and more city ticket offices. In some cities, when ticket counter agents leave their jobs, they are not replaced.

Within weeks (although it seemed like days) after 9/11, the major airlines rapidly accelerated the closing of ticket offices. In my estimation, it was—and remains—a sad moment in the history of U.S. airlines. The decision was based solely—and obsessively—on cost, not value, and the fallout in terms of the dissolution of long-term customer-airline relationships continues as a result.

Some travelers actually fear that in the not too distant future we will arrive at the airport to confront nothing more than an airline version of an ATM machine. There will be *no* human contact!

Ask the airlines about e-tickets and they will boast that their own surveys show that more than 70 percent of their customers *like* e-tickets. Besides, they claim, you can't lose an e-ticket.

What the airlines *won't* tell you is that they have preprogrammed their computers to automatically issue e-tickets unless the passenger demands a traditional paper ticket. They have also incentivized the ticket transaction by offering passengers mileage bonuses or even fare discounts if they book online and purchase an e-ticket.

So why do I hate e-tickets? Forgetting for the moment that customer service has been decreased in the process, I'm even more worried that e-tickets, by their very definition, immediately limit our options and, in some cases, remove them entirely.

Let me explain.

Unless you have a propensity for losing your tickets—at which point I might actually suggest that you *do* use e-tickets—the e-ticket is *not* your friend.

Here's a recent example. I was flying with two friends from Washington, D.C., to Los Angeles on an early morning American flight. I was holding a paper ticket. My friends had been electronically ticketed.

On the way to the airport, they called me a dinosaur because of my allegiance to the paper ticket. "It's just one more piece of paper to carry," one of them said. "One more thing to lose."

Again, I made my argument that unless you often lose your tickets, there was still nothing to recommend the e-ticket.

When we arrived at the airport, we were confronted with bad news. The American flight was delayed. Our 767 would not be leaving for at least four hours.

I didn't jump into the ever-growing line of disgruntled fliers waiting to rebook. I ran to the nearest phone, called the toll-free number for American, and asked to be put on the next available flight, which was, in this case, a United 747.

I simply walked over to the United gate, where the plane was about to leave, showed my paper ticket, and away I went. My friends were last seen in that American Airlines line. Why? They had to stay there to turn their e-ticket into the paper ticket they should have had in the first place!

There's another downside to the e-ticket. If you change your flights frequently or you have a sudden change of plans, you may be at a distinct disadvantage with an e-ticket—Not in terms of rebooking, but in terms of *remembering*.

Example: You're booked on a round-trip e-ticket from Miami to Boston. You fly your original segment from Miami to Boston. But when you arrive in Boston, your itinerary changes. Instead of returning to Miami, you have to fly to New Orleans and then return to New York. So you buy an additional ticket to New Orleans and then to New York.

With a paper ticket, you have a physical reminder that you never used that first return portion of your ticket back to Miami. And that return portion *can* be used. It has value.

However, with an e-ticket, a majority of fliers tend to forget they never used that return portion. The airline keeps the revenue, and you lose not only the money but the option of using that ticket.

Although I stand by my preference for paper tickets, the airlines have conspired to make it exceedingly difficult to get them. Many airlines announced that they will be entirely ticketless by the end of 2006. But until then, I will continue to do everything in my power as a traveler to cajole, flirt with, and finesse every counter agent I meet into giving me a paper ticket without adding on the outrageous fee that can often be as high as $100.

PRICING A EUROPEAN TICKET

There have always been charter operators and airlines that have dumped unsold tickets on the "bucket shop" market—another name for discount travel agencies in Europe. And a few airlines (Aeroflot, for example) continue to sell under-the-counter tickets.

But for most travelers, there are no published discount airfares in Europe. Passengers flying between European cities pay an astonishing average of 73 percent more for their tickets than passengers flying between American cities that are the same distance apart.

The high prices have continued because European airlines have shared an unwritten agreement to keep fares high. Now, however, a few cracks have appeared in the European airfare wall. Deregulation has finally caught up with Europe, and a number of low-fare start-up airlines have been the catalysts.

Years after the European Court of Justice ruled that the fare fixing practiced by most European airlines was illegal, there are now competitive airfares within the Continent.

The revision started when the British government reluctantly allowed British Midland, an independent airline, to compete on free-market terms with then government-owned British Airways between London's Heathrow Airport and Glasgow, Scotland.

Prices on the route dropped, in-flight service improved, and passengers were offered schedule flexibility at a reasonable price.

Soon after British Midland got into the act, KLM began offering one-way fares as low as $49 (U.S.) between Amsterdam and London. British Airways matched the fares. Again, passengers were happy, traffic increased, and the airlines made money.

Shortly after the European Court's decision, Air France proposed Europe-wide fare cuts of as much as 34 percent. More recently, a fare battle erupted over the Irish Sea. Ryanair discounted its fares between London and Ireland, prompting British Airways and Aer Lingus to cut their prices as well. Now, EasyJet, Virgin Express, and Go are operating as low-cost, low-fare intra-Europe carriers.

Not only have fares dropped, but smaller nations' flag carriers—Icelandair, Royal Jordanian, and Air India—are now undercutting fares of some of the bigger airlines on long-haul intercontinental routes.

A coach seat on a U.S. carrier (or on Air France, for that matter) between New York and Paris runs $842 for a round-trip. Icelandair sells the same seat for $975 and Swissair for $646.

And thanks to the Internet, American travelers can buy a number of deals in the United States before they leave home. Europebyair FlightPass (www.europebyair.com) lets you country-hop all over Europe for just $99 per flight. These "open" passes let you fly one-way, nonstop to cities all over Europe, starting or ending anywhere you want. Europebyair makes it easy—no blackout dates, no fare zones, advance reservations on the go, valid for 120 days, no minimum purchase, and reservation changes are allowed.

Remember that liberalized routes and the authority to cut fares don't automatically lead to lower prices and better service. But demand does. Which brings me to a different way to find cheap tickets: the ethnic route.

A hidden discount world can be found among travel agents operating within ethnic communities in the United States.

Want a cheap flight to Korea from Los Angeles? Head to Koreatown and buy the ticket from just about any Korean travel agent. In New York, Kosfo Travel sells, for $236, a ticket to Seoul that normally prices at $1,350.

Heading for Argentina? Check out Holdy Tours in San Francisco. A normal $1,300 round-trip to Buenos Aires goes for just $816, including tax.

The same is true for tickets purchased for flights from the United States to India, Pakistan, Brazil, Ireland, Israel, China, and South Africa. Even Japan, not known as a discount destination, can suddenly become one if you go through an ethnic agent/discounter. A normal $850 ticket from Los Angeles to Tokyo suddenly costs $650 if you buy it from a local ethnic travel agency.

SPLIT TICKETS

A weak currency may be a friend that makes a split ticket worthwhile. Split ticketing, or currency differential ticketing, is totally legal, and if you're flying first class, business class, or full-fare coach, the savings can be substantial.

Here's how it works. You purchase two separate one-way tickets instead of a round-trip ticket. You buy your outbound ticket in the United States and pay in dollars, and you buy a ticket for a one-way-ticket flight back to the United States from the foreign destination, and pay in local currency.

Always check the fare (in local currency) of your return flight first, to determine whether the saving will, in fact, be significant. Many times, the difference is huge.

The cost of a one-way business-class ticket on Alitalia from New York to Milan is $3,302. But the Milan–to–New York business-class ticket, paid for in euros, totals out at $2,913. The split ticketing saves $389.

From Los Angeles to Bangkok, a round-trip business-class ticket on Thai Airways would run you $3,301.50 if purchased in the United States. Instead, buy a one-way ticket from LAX for $1,646.70 and buy your return ticket in Bangkok for $1,002. You'll save $644.

From New York to Paris, Air France will charge you $5,972 for a round-trip business-class ticket. Instead, buy the one-way flight for $2,986, pay for the return in euros, and save about $600.

If you must fly frequently between two international destinations, you can maximize your savings by purchasing a one-way ticket from the United States to that destination. When you arrive there, buy a round-trip ticket for your trip home and your next return overseas.

"INEXPENSIVE" DOESN'T JUST MEAN THE BACK OF THE BUS

Yes, it's even possible to get discounted first-class and business-class seats. The bucket shops and British newspapers advertise them.

Once again, if you can construct routings that take advantage of currency fluctuations and other marketing inconsistencies, you can get serious discounts in the front of the cabin.

If you're in Hong Kong and want to fly business class to London, Cathay Pacific sells that ticket for $5,683. But if you're flying from Seoul to London (via Hong Kong), Cathay will put you on the *same flight* to London for just $3,584. So how do you take advantage of this lower fare without flying hundreds of extra miles out of your way?

Smart travel agents will book the Seoul–Hong Kong–London flight for you, and will then cancel the Seoul–Hong Kong portion. You simply throw away the first coupon and board the plane in Hong Kong.

Because these are *not* restricted tickets, you don't run the risk of being denied boarding. They are the full-fare business-class tickets on that route.

Officially, Cathay states that "we may not honor your ticket if the first flight coupon for international travel has not been used and you commence your journey at any stopover."

That's theoretically true, but as long as (1) the first coupon is pulled by you, (2) the original reservation is canceled, and (3) the onward reservations are intact (that's where your travel agent comes in), you're in excellent shape. Remember, travel agents can't and don't advertise this service, but in Asia they all do it. It is an unwritten and unspoken daily practice.

The worst that could happen? On rare occasions, you might be challenged and made to pay the difference. Again, it is *not* illegal, but the airlines frown on it.

THE COMMON-RATED PLOY

Go beyond split tickets between the United States and foreign countries; look at some of the split ticketing *between* foreign countries. For example, many airlines charge the same fare from the United Kingdom to their main headquarters airport and to various other destinations reached by changing planes at that main airport. When that happens, these destinations are called *common-rated*. And free stopovers are often allowed.

Let's say you're traveling to the South Pacific. If you're headed to Christchurch, in New Zealand, that city is common-rated with Auckland, the main airport where Air New Zealand is headquartered. How does this work for you? If you book a cheap flight to Auckland and then want to fly to Christchurch, you're getting ripped off. Instead, book your flight to Christchurch and get a free stopover in Auckland.

Another example: If you're flying from London to Malaysia, don't book a nonstop from London to Kuala Lumpur. Book the ticket as London to Penang, or Langkawi, or another Malaysian destination, and get essentially a free stopover in Kuala Lumpur. (Singapore Airlines common-rates Penang and Kuala Lumpur with its own main airport at Changi, in Singapore, so the same booking principle would apply.)

THROW IN A HOTEL EVEN IF YOU DON'T NEED ONE

On the surface, this tactic makes no sense at all, until you begin to understand how large blocks of airline seats are presold to tour operators who also control similar numbers of hotel rooms.

In the United States, getting an inexpensive ticket to Hawaii seems impossible, until you throw in a hotel room.

Large discount operators, like Pleasant Holidays, book huge blocks of seats on flights between West Coast cities and Honolulu and Maui. They offer those seats as part of heavily discounted land packages—for example, six days in Honolulu, *with hotel,* for $498. A similar deal in Maui goes for $565.

If you're trying to get to Hawaii at the last minute and the cheapest round-trip ticket is $1,400, book the Pleasant Holiday deal, with the hotel package, even if you know you won't use the room. It's still a better deal.

The tour operator won't love having an empty room, but you're reimbursing some of the revenue spent for a seat that would otherwise go empty.

The same tactic can save you money on a number of other long-haul flights. For example, Qantas may sell you its cheapest Los Angeles–to–Sydney coach ticket for $1,000, but Qantas Vacations, its own subsidiary, has a deal for airfare *and* hotel for $798.

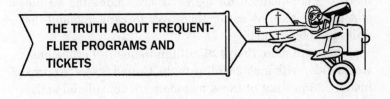

THE TRUTH ABOUT FREQUENT-FLIER PROGRAMS AND TICKETS

In the airline marketing business, it's called a "pledge of allegiance": loyalty to a particular airline because of membership in its frequent-flier program.

We have become a nation of mileage junkies, and we will do just about anything to earn those miles. I have friends who will fly extra flights or extra segments or will completely reroute themselves so they can earn enough miles or segments to qualify for "free" tickets.

But here are the real questions:

- Now that you've earned all those miles, what chances do you have for redeeming them?

- Perhaps more important: How much did it really cost you to earn those miles, presuming you really can redeem them?

The numbers are nothing less than staggering. Since they began, in 1981, airline mileage programs—and, later, hotel frequent-flier/stay programs—have become some of the most popular marketing ideas ever created. How popular? Let's look at some numbers.

More than 61 million Americans are members of at least one airline or hotel frequent-flier/stay program. (United Airlines boasts that more than 38 million people have enrolled in its Mileage Plus program alone.)

And there are more programs than ever. Because of the increased competition for market share among the airlines and hotels, it's now easier than ever to earn frequent-flier miles or hotel points.

There are more than 120 million frequent-flier members worldwide, with most residing in the United States. Approximately 28 percent of those members are considered active. The largest program? American, with more than 45 million members. And in 2001, twenty years after the start of the program, the airline still managed to enroll about 10,000 new members a day. In fact, my friend Randy Peterson, who edits Insideflyer.com, reports that loyalty programs grow at the rate of 11 percent each year.

Add some new marketing partners, and it's now possible to earn mileage for everything short of breathing. You can get miles for buying flowers, refinancing your home, buying stock, and exercising at health clubs. At some Las Vegas casinos, you even get mileage for playing slot machines! In Volusia County, Florida, newsworthy in 2000 because of the post–Election Day voter recounts, you can reportedly get mileage by handling corpses.

Ways to Earn Frequent-Flier Miles

1. **Flying** (43 percent) It might seem that frequent buyers are outnumbering frequent fliers, but flying is still the number one way to earn miles.

2. **Credit card** (19.7 percent) This method is very, very popular—and this doesn't take into account all of the miles that people earn with American Express and Diners Club, since we are only able to count those miles when they are redeemed.

3. **Elite bonuses** (10.6 percent) Though small in numbers, elite members earn significant additional miles as a result of their status.

4. **Telephone, including wireless** (9.3 percent) The interesting thing here is that many of the miles earned are from the sign-up bonuses, which can average five thousand to twenty-five thousand miles.

5. **Flight bonuses** (6 percent) These include the double and triple miles bonuses, as well as the bonus miles that airlines give to their members.

6. **Hotels** (4.9 percent) Hotels have their own programs, and a sizable number of members still collect hotel points rather than airline miles from their hotel stays.

7. **Shopping** (3.1 percent) This may be the fastest-growing category. With programs like ClickRewards, as well as the emergence of several frequent-flier-affiliated online shopping malls, look for this one to skyrocket.

Ways to Earn Frequent-Flier Miles

8. **Car rentals** (1.4 percent) This used to be much higher, almost 8 percent. But when car rental companies reduced the number of miles members earn to the dollars they spend on the rental car, this number tumbled.

9. **Personal financial** (0.9 percent) Also among the fastest-growing categories with home mortgages, insurance, stock trading, and car purchases contributing to the growth.

10. **Flowers** (0.6 percent) Not everyone trades stocks online, but most everyone has bought flowers to earn miles. The average number of miles isn't great, but the number of people doing it is very high.

(From Insideflyer.com.)

OK. So much for the good news. Virtually everyone is out there accumulating miles. In fact, according to most estimates, more than 47 percent of all mileage earned today is earned on the ground. You don't have to fly to get miles.

As a result, there are nearly ten *trillion* unredeemed miles in frequent-flier accounts. As airline traffic has hit an all-time high, frequent-flier mileage has jumped an estimated 30 percent—much of it earned by people who aren't even frequent fliers.

There can be no doubt that the frequent-flier program is one of the cleverest marketing strategies ever devised. But to get us to join and then obsessively earn those miles, the airlines have also had to get us to embrace the notion that we will actually be rewarded for our loyalty to one airline.

And that, sadly, has created a false sense of entitlement among thousands of passengers. Miles have become the global currency of frequent fliers. We look at our mileage statements as often as our bank statements. In our conversations with other passengers, we try to one-up each other with the number of miles we've earned. And when we earn the miles, we actually think we can redeem them.

Q: How do you redeem those miles?

A: Not easily.

Airlines are reluctant to displace revenue passengers and give away free tickets, even though these programs were designed to reward us for our loyalty to a particular airline. Promises were attached to having millions and millions of miles in our accounts. We gave these companies our pledge of allegiance.

What did we get in return? Want to go to Des Moines on a Wednesday? No problem. Want to cash in those hard-earned frequent-flier miles to take that dream trip to Hawaii? Forget it.

The same response applies to upgrades, only the situation is actually worse. Want to use your mileage to upgrade that inexpensive coach ticket to first class on that Des Moines flight? Even that might now be a problem. At Northwest, no matter how many miles you've earned, if you bought your seat at an already discounted rate, you're last in line for an upgrade. At United, last-minute Internet fares or tickets bought through an online discounter are usually not upgradeable.

Want to book a room in Buffalo in February? No problem. Want to cash in your frequent-stay points for that Arizona spa during the same month? *Fuggeddabouddit.*

Recently, I realized that I had accumulated enough miles to qualify for a free ticket to Hawaii on United Airlines. I followed the airline's instructions and called to make a reservation between New York and Honolulu. I thought I would fly over for about five days—five months later, in late March. On the other end of the line, the United Airlines reservation agent started to laugh.

"You're flying on an award ticket?" she asked. "Won't happen," she said. "Every flight is already sold out."

For March? Five months from now?

Sure enough; she checked. From March 1 through March 31, not a single seat was available.

Then she checked April. Nothing. Then May, June, July, and August. Still booked solid.

"Couldn't I fly standby?" I asked.

"No, sir," she said. "You are not allowed to fly standby on a frequent-flier ticket."

After I stayed on hold for twenty-two minutes (I timed it), she found one flight, with one seat available, on September 16 (a Saturday), leaving from New York's LaGuardia Airport and stopping in Chicago and Los Angeles before landing in Honolulu.

And a return flight five days later? No luck again. The earliest date I could get was September 25, nine days later.

I grabbed it.

Did I really want to go to Hawaii on September 16 for nine days? No, but there was a method to my madness. The goal here was to get a paper domestic award ticket in my hands, even if the dates were wrong.

I hung up the phone from the frequent-flier desk and then called the normal reservations number at United. I repeated my New York–to–Honolulu request without mentioning that I was flying on a free ticket. For laughs, I thought I'd mention I wanted to go on March 1.

"How many will be traveling?" the agent asked me, without hesitation.

For more laughs, I said, "Eight."

She didn't laugh. She booked the reservation.

And just to make sure this wasn't some computer snafu, I called United twice again and each time picked another date, one in late March and another in mid-April. I was easily able to reserve four seats on the late-March flight and three seats on the mid-April departure. (I later canceled all three phony reservations.)

In each case, the transactions took less than four minutes. On the first call, no "free" seats were available for nearly seven months. On the second, third, and fourth calls, only revenue seats were available on virtually any flight I wanted.

My reservations experiences made me a member of a growing group of passengers who come face-to-face with the less-than-friendly skies of yield management and capacity control, the methods airlines use to restrict discount or free tickets on every flight in their schedule.

And what happened on March 1? I simply went to the airport with my paper tickets. I showed them to the agent and explained that I would like to fly out to Hawaii earlier than stated on the ticket.

I showed up for the exact flight on the same itinerary printed on the paper ticket. The only things different were the dates. Guess what? There were plenty of seats on my flight. The agent pulled the coupons, issued a boarding pass, and I was on.

The reality: The airline cannot initially issue a standby ticket on a frequent-flier award. But once a paper ticket is issued and as long as you don't change the cities on the ticket, if there's space on the flights, you're on.

The airlines won't tell you this. But I just did.

As long as you're flexible and do a little advance homework (calling the airlines to find out if revenue space is available on your desired flights), you'll be fine. (Suggestion: Always book the first flight out of any city on your original award ticket).

These airline practices—failing to disclose or responding with misleading information—continue to be high on the list of passengers' complaints filed directly with the carriers or with the U.S. Department of Transportation, along with complaints about lost baggage, delays, deceptive airline flight labeling, and, last but not least, deceptive airline advertisements.

In the United-to-Hawaii case, I got lucky. I figured a way around the blockade the airline erects to make it virtually impossible to redeem miles for desired flights on desired routes.

The situation looks like it can only get worse. The annual 10-K reports the airlines file with the Securities and Exchange Commission (SEC) reveal even more disturbing figures. Here's a statistic that might make you sick: Although most major U.S. airline award programs no longer have unused miles that automatically expire, in 1998 62 *billion* miles expired unused.

Want to guess how many unredeemed travel awards there are at Northwest? According to the airline's filing with the SEC, there were more than 7.8 million in 2003. United says more than 10.5 million unredeemed awards are in its system. USAir has more than 7.0 million awards waiting to be redeemed.

Will they ever be redeemed? Some, yes; most, no. Throughout the industry, it is estimated that 75 percent of all frequent-flier miles are never redeemed or go unused, and, yes, some still expire.

In another indication of how some airlines are doing everything possible to make it difficult to redeem miles, United, in what can only be described as a brain-dead decision, announced in the summer of 2004 that if members of their program wanted to actually talk to a *human being* to redeem their miles, it would cost them $15! (I can just imagine the next brilliant idea from United: If you want to talk to a *nice* person to redeem your miles, it's $25.)

In the case of the "pudding man," the airlines would have paid considerably more to talk to him *before* he figured out an ingenious way to earn miles.

Meet David Phillips, whose mileage story is one of the wildest I've ever encountered. In 1999, while he was grocery shopping, Phillips happened on a special mileage promotion offered by a manufacturer and the airlines. The deal: Buy ten Healthy Choice products and get 500 miles—or 1,000 miles for purchases made before June 1999.

It didn't seem like such a great deal until he got to the pudding section of the store. And then he saw them: small Healthy Choice chocolate fudge pudding cups at only 25¢ apiece. He quickly did the math. If he spent just $62.50, he would get 25,000 miles. That's one *very* cheap coach ticket!

He ran home, told his wife of his discovery, and then headed to the bank. Within hours, Phillips was transformed from a mild-mannered civil engineer at the University of California at Davis into . . . PUDDING MAN!

Phillips did some more math and realized that if he moved fast, he could accumulate enough miles to fly halfway to the moon. In short order, he raced around to every supermarket chain in the Sacramento area, wiping them out of Healthy Choice pudding. And in just a few days, he had spent some $3,000 on 12,150 cups of pudding. That translated into an accumulation of 1.22 million miles!

And what did he do with all the pudding? He donated most of it to charity (after taking a healthy tax write-off).

Phillips didn't stop at $3,000 for 1.22 million miles. He was now addicted. So when a group of Latin American airlines offered anyone a million miles if they bought some-

thing called a Latin Pass and flew all ten airlines in a specified time period, he ran to the airport.

OK, so what did Phillips do with all the miles? Like the
rest of us, when he went to redeem them, he ran into problems—capacity controls, blackout dates. When last I
checked, he was sitting in Sacramento with a whole lot of
miles, but no place to go.

The problem is compounded when you realize that not
only do the airlines award miles to travelers, but they sell
them to marketing partners such as Healthy Choice, Hilton,
Starwood, and Citibank, which, in turn, offer promotions
like the pudding deal.

Airlines are reluctant to reveal exact deals, but, on average, the partner companies are paying about 2.5¢ a mile.
From the airlines' point of view, even if the miles *are* redeemed, that outcome can be more profitable than selling
some tickets and operating the actual flights!

Even if you're short on miles, the airlines are there to
help. Are you just shy of enough miles to get that free trip?
United Airlines will sell you miles at $55 per thousand.
American Express will sell you a thousand miles for $28. A
USAir offer will get you a ticket for the first private flight in
space—for 10 million miles.

What's happening? The airlines now see their mileage
programs as profit centers rather than loyalty programs—the
role initially envisioned. And the airlines are striking so
many deals with other marketing partners that the real value
of the frequent-flier programs is becoming steadily diluted.

The airlines know that these free-mileage seats are prepaid out of loyalty, but with players like Priceline.com in the
competition, the airlines are apparently thinking that if they
can get money for seats, they'll take it instead of giving the
seats away. As a result, *free* comes in last.

To make matters worse, in the past few years, many airlines, like American and United, added about twenty more blackout dates within the calendar year (that's twenty more dates on which frequent fliers can't redeem miles) and tightened their capacity controls.

All the news isn't bad. Currently, frequent-flier redemption is running at about twelve million free tickets a year. That sounds like a lot, but, spread out among all the airlines, the number is quite small.

Here's the real problem. Under deregulation, no airline is required, by any law, to disclose how many discount seats it has available on any flight. (By contrast, if a car dealer advertises a car at a specific price, state law requires the dealer to list how many cars are available at that price.) There also are no requirements to let anyone know how many award seats are available on planes. As a result, a lot of unhappy frequent fliers who have earned those miles can't seem to use them.

Is there a way around this?

The answer, believe it or not, is *yes.* If the airlines suddenly change the rules in the middle of the game, you may have some legal recourse. Recently, American Airlines settled a twelve-year legal battle and two class-action lawsuits involving changes it made in its AAdvantage program. In 1988, American had been accused of changing the terms of its mileage program without prior notification, thereby making it more difficult to book flights using mileage awards.

A second lawsuit challenged American's second attempt—in 1995—to increase, from 20,000 to 25,000, the number of miles needed to earn a free domestic coach ticket.

Under the settlement terms, American, without admitting any liability, agreed to give about five million members of its mileage program either 5,000 air miles or certificates good for $75 discounts on future flights.

A lawsuit is in the works and expected to be filed in the spring of 2005 claiming that major airlines are guilty of detrimental reliance violations—that they induce people to become members with the strong inference that the minute they achieve that 25,000-mile threshold, they will get a free domestic coach ticket anywhere they want. But when that time comes, the suit alleges, there is an excellent chance that there will be no ticket, because the airlines aren't running a loyalty program but, instead, an illegal lottery. (Stay tuned.)

Short of legal action against the airlines, here are five suggestions for redeeming your well-deserved free flights:

1. Think alternate airports. Not just JFK, but Newark, Stewart, or Islip in New York; Midway instead of O'Hare; Colorado Springs instead of Denver.

2. Be flexible about your departure times.

3. Make airline code-share partnerships work for you. For example, want to use frequent-flier miles on Virgin Atlantic? Well, if Virgin says it has no award seats available, then call its code-share (and mileage) partner, Continental.

   Recently when this happened the passenger was told that Continental didn't have award seats, but could process the passenger's ticket and get him a seat on Virgin! (Remember, it's the same plane, but different availability and inventory.)

4. Never take a no from someone who is not empowered to give you a yes in the first place. Always ask to speak to a supervisor if the airline won't let you redeem miles. At each airline reservation center there is a supervisor who has the responsibility—and the power— to unblock computer locks and release an award seat to you. All you really need to do is—gently, but firmly— remind the airline that its frequent-flier program was

started to reward your loyalty to that airline. In many cases, that's when the seats get released.

5. Beat the airlines at their own game, playing by their rules. Always ask for a paper ticket (remember to avoid the fees) for your award ticket, and keep in mind my United/Hawaii story: When the airline laughs at you and says there are no seats available until the next millennium, no problem. Take the flight number you want—in that next millennium—and then get it paper-ticketed.

Next, call the airline's reservations number and ask whether there are paid seats available on a flight you want to take in three weeks. If there are, then take your mileage ticket—that paper ticket—to the airport on the day you really wanted to fly. Remember, a frequent-flier mile is a contingent liability the airline would love to unload, but not at the expense of a paying passenger. If there are still seats available on the day you get to the airport, you will be boarded at no additional cost—or put on standby for the next flight.

As long as there was space on that plane, I have never been denied boarding by doing this. You just have to be a little bold, a little flexible, and trust in the thought that saying no to you on the phone is a whole lot easier than saying no to you in person.

However, in recent months, some airlines are making it much tougher to fly standby on a *paid* ticket. Even if you want to fly standby on Southwest Airlines on the same day, if you're holding a discounted Southwest ticket, you'll be forced to step up to the full one-way coach fare, which can be as much as $299. And in the latest standby policy switch by an airline, in March 2004 Delta did away with their traditional, humane standby policy. In its place, there's now a fee of $25 for passengers taking a different flight open the same day on the same route. And changes made earlier than three hours ahead are subject to a $100 fee.

ANOTHER LITTLE-KNOWN MILEAGE TICKET GAME

Let's say (1) you want to fly from Los Angeles to New York and back, using a frequent-flier award, and (2) the airline says you can actually go when you want to go. Be creative. Under current airline rules, you can route yourself on that transcontinental itinerary in a way that maximizes your ticket. You can make stopovers and see friends, business associates, and family along the way.

What the airlines won't tell you is that, on most award tickets, you are allowed one stopover en route, either going or coming.

They also won't tell you about a little-known rule. First, you get the free and uncontested stopover. Next, you can connect as many times as you want along the route, as long as you are not stopping over for more than four hours. But suppose your flight into a connection is the last flight of the day (or night). The last-flight-in/first-flight-out rule applies: You can stay the night in a connecting city if the flight you came in on was the last to arrive, and the flight you have to leave on is the next plane in the morning. Many business travelers use this sequence and avoid paying for an extra flight.

But let's say you don't want to risk anything. You want to travel knowing that everything along the way is confirmed.

The standby game is a difficult game to win. Several companies have tried—like WebMiles.

What was the attraction of WebMiles? Quite simply, they offered miles earned in the form of unrestricted free tickets that were redeemable on any airline and any flight. The claim was that as long as there was a seat on the plane, Web-Miles would get you on it.

How did it work? For starters, WebMiles didn't work with airline frequent-flier programs. The miles earned were used to actually purchase tickets from the airlines. Consumers earned these premium miles, or WebMiles rewards, in much the same way other affinity programs worked—by purchasing through online and offline partners, participating in surveys, referring friends and family, and using the Web-Miles MasterCard. Consumers earned one WebMiles reward per dollar spent on the MasterCard, and multiple miles if the MasterCard was used with a network partner. In addition to free round-trip airline tickets, WebMiles offered discounted travel starting with as few as 8,000 WebMiles rewards.

Specifically, WebMiles manufactured WebMiles rewards and then sold them to WebMiles Partners, who distributed the miles to consumers as rewards. When they redeemed those miles for a ticket, WebMiles used a travel partner, Maritz Travel, to provide the free or discounted tickets. Similar to frequent-flier programs, individuals who accumulated 25,000 miles received a free round-trip ticket of their choice, the only limitation being a fourteen-day advance notice. WebMiles claimed it did not enforce Saturday night stays. Then there was an added bonus: The miles earned translated into a purchased fare ticket, so travelers could actually earn miles for flying the reward ticket!

This business model functioned independently of any airline, but unfortunately the model failed. Although WebMiles was a dismal failure, one bank capitalized on the frustration of millions of frequent fliers—Capital One, with its "no hassle" rewards Visa card. As with other Visa cards linked to an airline's mileage program, you earn one mile for every dollar spent. But unlike the other airline affinity Visa or Master-

Cards, the Capital One card costs only $19 a year (instead of $65 for major airline Visa cards), and while you still get one mile per dollar spent, the computation of those miles is done quite differently: For every 9,000 miles you earn, your account is credited with $100. And when you've accumulated enough mileage money, Capital One simply buys you a paid, positive-space ticket. No blackout dates, no rules or regulations. This is a tangible, understandable program that comes with no secrets or disclaimers.

In practical terms, no matter when or how you use your frequent-flier tickets, it's important for you to know—especially if they are "free" tickets issued by the airlines—what they really cost you or your company to earn.

Airlines intentionally keep annual redemption levels to about 8 percent of the available mileage eligible for redemption.

Here's something that might make you angry. Let's talk about what that "free" award ticket cost you, assuming you *are* able to redeem it.

With 47 percent of all mileage being earned on the ground, and with most miles being awarded at a rate of one mile per dollar spent, you can soon discover why these programs are so wildly profitable for the airlines.

The minimum mileage needed for a free domestic coach ticket is 25,000 miles. That means that most people spent at least $11,750 (in real dollars) on goods and services, and the rest on real airline miles, to get to that first eligible tier.

Conservatively, let's say that the other 13,250 miles were earned in the air, and a minimum of $2,000 in airline ticket costs was spent to earn those miles.

At a bare minimum, someone spent $13,250 to earn one free domestic coach ticket. That's one very expensive coach ticket.

Now, prepare yourself to get . . . angrier.

Each airline has to carry these unredeemed miles on its books as a contingent liability, and that liability has to be given a realistic dollar value. The airline also factors in the incremental costs of processing a frequent-flier award ticket, plus the relative costs of food and beverage, fuel, insurance, security, and all the other items that go into processing your ticket, redeeming your award, and putting you in that "free" seat.

It's all based on incremental cost. Example: Let's say a plane ticket sells for $500, but because the plane is going to fly anyway, the marginal (or incremental) cost of carrying one more passenger—slightly more fuel and perhaps a pathetic bistro meal—is not even close to that figure.

Many airlines, like American, value their unredeemed mileage at 40¢ per 1,000 miles. Now, let's do the math. Considering that 25,000 first-tier eligibility for that one coach ticket, the airline estimates its real costs to redeem your mileage, issue you that ticket, and fly you on your "free" flight at a whopping . . . $10!

OK, so now you know how many miles are out there—and, more or less, how many unredeemed awards.

But how can you redeem those miles in a way that is meaningful to you—a way that lets you go where you want to go, when you want to go there?

Perhaps you want to forget about free tickets and use the mileage for something else. A number of new programs can help you spend your miles, or hotel points, on things *other than* airline seats or hotel rooms. And for once, miles may be getting more valuable.

America Online (AOL) and American Airlines will let you turn your miles into money. AOL AAdvantage, for example, will let you buy nonflying stuff such as free AOL time, books and magazines, and CDs. Want a new PalmPilot? It will cost you 78,500 miles.

Another company, Milepoint.com, will allow online

shoppers to trade airline miles for discounts on name-brand electronics, gifts, luggage, and books, at more than one hundred retailers. (Coincidentally, the chairman of the Milepoint .com board is Robert Crandall, a former head of American Airlines, which introduced the mileage programs nearly twenty years ago.) But don't get too excited; the discounts aren't that great. Each mile is valued at just 2¢. If you want a $500 discount from Milepoint.com, you'll have to part with 25,000 miles. (The discounts are all relative. On what price is the discount based? Full retail value rather than the cost to Milepoint.com?)

But again, some companies lost in playing this game. A company called Milespree.com was aimed at people who were already making purchases on the Web. If you registered you would earn a bonus of 8,000 miles, about one-third of the miles necessary for a free ticket. When you bought something at any of four hundred dot.com retailers, you would earn Milespree miles. For 25,000 miles, you earned a free domestic coach ticket. What was interesting about Milespree was that if you made your reservations for that free ticket thirty days in advance, there were no blackout dates. (Milespree actually purchased the ticket; thus, it was not an award ticket.)

But there are still ways to "dump" your miles creatively.

Most airlines offer complete travel packages (airfare, hotel, rental car) for mileage. American offers about three hundred such programs. Others offer deals that combine mileage and nominal cash payments to get opera tickets, fifty-yard-line seats at football games, or cruise-ship holidays.

To be competitive, many hotel programs offer double-dipping. You get points *and* miles for staying at particular hotels in selected cities. (Another word of caution here: The mileage deals and bonuses specify certain hotels, and the rates may vary. Always check whether your deal covers the hotel's full asking price.)

Lodging chains offer some interesting ways for you to spend your points. For example, Days Inn started INNcentives, which is now called TripRewards. This program offers free stays and other goodies to frequent guests of eight hotel chains: Super 8, Days Inn, Ramada, Travelodge, Howard Johnson, Knights Inn, Villager, Wingate Inn, and AmeriHost Inn. The program currently covers 6,397 hotels, with 518,143 rooms on five continents. No blackout dates apply when TripRewards points are redeemed for stays at these hotels.

Travelers who enroll in TripRewards can earn points by doing business with Avis and Budget rental car chains, with automotive service companies such as AAMCO Transmissions and Pep Boys, and with an assortment of merchants such as FTD.com, Lane Bryant, Linens N Things, OshKosh, and Sunglass Hut. TripRewards points can also be redeemed for airline tickets from Air Canada, Delta, or Continental and for various other types of purchases from participating merchants.

Starwood has an extensive redemption program for merchandise as well as experiences.

In the Big Apple, guests of the Sheraton New York Hotel & Towers can trade in their Starwood Preferred Guest (SPG) points for anything from a dinner cruise around Manhattan to a pair of tickets to a Broadway show. At New York City's Essex House, romantics can take a free hour-long horse-drawn carriage ride through Central Park. In Arizona, one of the favorite Starwood redemptions can be found at the legendary Phoenician Hotel in Scottsdale. Guests can exchange points for last-minute spa treatments or, even better, for a dinner for two at the exclusive Chef's Table in Mary Elaine's kitchen. Outrigger canoe rides at the Sheraton Moana Surfrider in Waikiki can also be booked using points.

SPG members earn two Starpoints (Gold- and Platinum-level members earn three Starpoints) for every dollar spent at any Westin, Sheraton, St. Regis, The Luxury Collection,

Four Points, and W hotels. In this program, virtually all charges are eligible, including room rates, food and beverage charges, laundry and dry cleaning fees, telephone calls, and in-room faxes, movies, and video games.

With a Marriot Rewards Visa Card, you can earn points on all your credit card purchases. You can also earn points, based on dollars spent, when you stay at hotels that participate in the Marriott Rewards program. Marriott's alliance with SkyMall Inc. allows Marriott Rewards members to redeem Marriott Rewards points for merchandise and gift certificates during the holidays. Redemption opportunities start at only eighteen thousand points. And then there is the Priority Plus deal offered by Bass Hotels (Holiday Inns, Intercontinental hotels). If you didn't know any better and were judging only from their program, you might think you weren't staying at a Holiday Inn but at the hotel shopping network!

The chain has an extensive sixty-six-page catalog of goodies available for redemption—everything from redeeming your points and creating an incredible vacation package to turning the points into a whopping shopping spree, using retail certificates at places like Best Buy, Sears, and Target. Want to be a fighter pilot? Redeem points and you're in the cockpit. Had your heart set on that chain saw at Target or Sears? Again, you can redeem points for it. The Priority Plus program even lets you redeem points for things that are *not* in the catalog. How? They research your request, assign a dollar value/point value, and, if you have enough points, it's yours.

Some credit cards offer deals, too. The American Express Membership Rewards program allows you to earn points toward a wide variety of travel, entertainment, and shopping rewards just for using your credit card. You earn one point for virtually every dollar you spend, and you can qualify for bonus points as well. For 120,000 points you get to drive a race car, and 220,000 points gets you three days at the Kahala Mandarin in Hawaii.

Why are these programs so popular? One of the reasons is the basic math. Don't be seduced by the prospect of mileage, or even more mileage, unless you can answer whether your miles or points were worth earning in the first place. (Did you take a flight because you were going to fly it anyway or to earn the mileage? Was that impulse purchase influenced by the promise of mileage?) Once you're ready to redeem your miles or points, what's the most financially efficient way to get the best bang out of your miles?

Cashing in 25,000 miles for an airline ticket you could buy for $250 isn't a good idea. But if the ticket would cost you $2,000 to buy, converting miles into money suddenly becomes attractive, especially when it's so hard to get a free ticket to Hawaii. Whether you redeem your miles (or points) for airline seats, hotel rooms, merchandise, or money, always try to remember that if you're earning these miles and points for purchases you'd be making anyway, that's a big bonus. If you're purchasing because you hope to earn miles, more often than not you're costing yourself money.

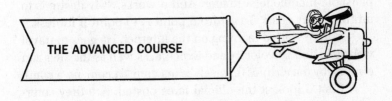

THE ADVANCED COURSE

How do you beat the airlines at their own game, playing by *their* rules? For most of us, understanding airline rules, fares, and disclaimers is the equivalent of translating Sanskrit.

But not for a man I'll call "Dr. Tom." He knows all about

the Talmudic complexities of hidden airline rules, fares, tariffs, and which little known exclusions benefit him.

Dr. Tom flew over 400,000 miles last year, and he did it—
to put it mildly—creatively. The airlines hate Dr. Tom. But
you have to give him credit. He has figured out their game.

When I first met him—on a plane, not surprisingly—he
explained his ethos and his methodology: To find the best
fares, it pays to be vigilant and curious.

"Today, I wanted to go to Washington, D.C., so I checked
routes from San Francisco to BWI—Baltimore. Then I began
to see that all the other carriers were starting to match the
price, not just at BWI, but at Reagan National and Dulles. I
used Baltimore to get me where I wanted to go in D.C." And
he does it all on his home computer.

"It is easy to pay full fare, it is easy to trust a travel agent,
it is easy if you are depending on corporate funding. But
there are people who pay full price, and then there are people who have a great deal of sensitivity. And the airlines recognize this. The airlines have two different distinct markets:
the business market and the dispensable-income leisure
market."

Tom is a business market traveler who acts like a dispensable-income leisure flier. And it works. "My desire is to
minimize my costs. To get from point A to point B for less."

Dr. Tom started learning on the Internet. He goes to travel
websites, like Travelocity and Expedia, as well as the sites run
directly by the airlines themselves (ua.com, aa.com, nwa.com).

"First, I look at the official fares posted. Are they coter-
minus? [Meaning: Does the fare apply to all the airports that
service that area? One example: Is a trip to JFK, LaGuardia,
or Newark common-rated?] Then I look at alternate airports.
And then, once I find a fare I like, I educate myself about the
rules of that fare."

Dr. Tom is a whiz on Expedia. He goes right to the airline

fare list. He fills in his origin and destination cities, and his screen then displays coach-class fares in ascending order.

"Then it gets interesting," he chuckles, "because when you look at that list you will be asked an option, called a fare basis. And that will tell you when the fare is available, as well as blackout dates and routing cities."

The routing cities are key for Dr. Tom. They tell him the different ways he can use that fare not only to maximize the distance he flies (and thus, the mileage he earns) but also to take advantage of any free stopovers in other cities that he can legally manipulate.

"For example, if I want to fly from Los Angeles to Buffalo, I may be able to go through Dallas to New Mexico on the return trip if I fly American. But, on Northwest, I may be able to go through other cities. I find the alternatives to construct the trip to maximize frequent-flier points."

After Dr. Tom has the route he wants, he then goes after "inventory." He checks minimum stay requirements and, of course, advance booking restrictions. When he finds the lowest fare that allows him to route his trip creatively, he's ready to rumble. One weekend, he flew first class on ten Continental flights—five in each direction—and his total airfare was *$198.*

But another game he plays truly maximizes his deals and allows him "phantom" stopovers. As a business traveler, he would normally have to pay ten times as much for the privilege of stopping overnight en route to anywhere. But not Dr. Tom. In the airline business, he's known as Dr. Stopover.

First, here's how it's officially supposed to work. You're flying from Washington, D.C., to San Francisco, but you want to stop and visit your favorite uncle in Minneapolis. Such a visit would constitute a stopover in Minneapolis. Some fares allow free stopovers; others allow stopovers for an additional fee. But most fares do not allow stopovers at all.

So how do you create that free stopover? Many travelers

think that simply by booking a flight that coincidentally stops in Minneapolis, the problem is solved. They can book a connecting flight for the next day.

But it doesn't work that way. You must take into account the *four-hour rule*. If you do not take off from your intermediate point (Minneapolis) within four hours, you have made a stopover. And if your fare doesn't permit one, you're going to be hit with a huge additional full-coach fare to continue your journey.

And let's say that you don't want your uncle to just race out to the airport, have a hot dog with you while you race between planes, and leave. You really want to stay over, but you don't want to pay for it. Enter the phantom stopover.

How does it work? The four-hour rule applies, provided that there actually is a connecting flight departing within four hours.

Dr. Tom books, to Minneapolis, the next-to-last flight of the day that connects with a San Francisco flight. Then he intentionally misses that flight. He is then forced to take the last flight, which has no onward connection that night. (He also understands the standby rules. If he shows up within two hours of the scheduled departure time of a flight on which he holds space, the airline will fly him standby on its next available flight.) And he gets to spend the night in Minneapolis at no extra charge.

Internationally, there is a twenty-four-hour rule. "Sometimes I buy a ticket from L.A. [on a flight] that stops in Miami before going on to Europe," he boasts. "This means that I can legally stay in Miami for twenty-four hours with no extra cost, and take a flight the next day."

The standby rules also work on flights where he doesn't want to make *any* stopovers.

"Let's say I find a fare I like, but there is not a ticket for the time I want to go. But there *is* an available flight that I know I can't make. I will buy that flight anyway, knowing that I will not make that flight, because once I have bought the ticket, the airline cannot change the cost of that ticket." When he gets to the airport, he gets to take the flight he wanted in the first place, but at the lower fare.

He also researches certain routing rules. A number of airlines have maximum transfer rules: no more than four transfers on any one itinerary. Tom books tickets for those flights where he needs to make a total of (surprise!) four transfers.

You would think Dr. Tom never used a travel agent. Wrong. "A good travel agent is worth the payments in commission or service charges, because [the agency's] computers can get you the inventory information you need to construct these routes and fares," he says.

FIGHTING THE BACK-TO-BACK WAR—AND WINNING

Dr. Tom has mastered the art of connections, reroutings, and maximized mileage—not to mention flying standby. I have embraced the concept of the back-to-back ticket.

A few years ago, for a *Today* show segment, I was asked to do a piece on the five questions I am asked most frequently. One of the questions, a no-brainer, was the question I was asked the most: How does someone get a discount seat without having to adhere to the dreaded Saturday night stay requirement?

My suggestion was the back-to-back ticket. Let's say you want to fly to New York from Los Angeles in three weeks, on a Tuesday, but you need to return three days later, on a Friday. Although you're booking your flight and paying for it three weeks in advance, which would normally qualify you for an advance-reservation discount, you don't get that discount because you're not staying over a Saturday night. Result: a full-fare coach ticket that could be as high as $2,000.

Now, using the same scenario, call the airline and make your reservation for the Tuesday flight three weeks from now, but set your return date for sometime a month later. Your fare could drop to as low as $226 round-trip. Then hang up the phone. A few minutes later, call the airline again and make a second reservation, this time for a flight leaving New York for Los Angeles on the Friday three weeks from now, returning sometime a month later. Another $226 fare. For a fraction of what the airline wanted to charge you for one fare, you now have *two* round-trips to New York. If you plan properly, you will get to use both trips, and get double the mileage. Officially—and in reality—you will have satisfied the Saturday night stay requirements for both tickets. Gotta love it!

And everyone watching the show *did* love it—with one major exception. American Airlines went ballistic. In a caustic three-page letter to the head of NBC, the airline charged that I was violating the law, perpetrating a fraud, and misleading NBC's viewers. The letter insinuated that American would take further action if I did not cease and desist talking about back-to-back tickets: "Back-to-back ticketing is a breach of a passenger's contract with American Airlines."

American claimed that "passengers on American who attempt to use back-to-back tickets may be denied boarding, may have the remainder of their ticket confiscated, and may be assessed a charge, which will be no less than the difference between the fare paid and the lowest fare applicable to the passenger's actual itinerary."

I'm not a lawyer, but I have a basic understanding of contracts. If I buy an airline ticket and use only the first portion of the ticket, should I be penalized if I don't use the second half? No. But if I use the second portion and don't change anything, shouldn't the airline honor that ticket? Denying me boarding on a ticket I purchased in my name, for a flight on the date originally specified, and with flight coupons used in proper order could be considered a breach of contract by the airline.

That's what American Airlines was—and still is—threatening to do to passengers who use back-to-back ticketing.

A back-to-back ticket allows me to officially comply with each required Saturday night stay. I am purchasing two separate tickets with different itineraries and using them in order. Simple as that. American claims that the Saturday night stay requirement "is necessary to ensure that these fares are generally used by leisure travelers. Without the ability to enforce this condition, it simply would not be practical for airlines to offer these attractive low fares to consumers."

Perhaps this is true. However, my responsibility is not to ensure financial feasibility for airlines, but to offer consumers practical advice on how to get the best deals within ticketing requirements set by the airlines. I will not stop encouraging consumers to beat airlines, hotels, cruise lines, and rental car companies at their own game, playing by the companies' own rules.

This was the gist of my response to American's letter, and it only served to make the airline angrier.

At that point, it was suggested that I fly to American's headquarters in Texas and meet with the top officials. It was, to say the least, a less than happy meeting.

After some basic pleasantries, the head of American Airlines public relations, holding my letter, pointed it at me. "If you don't cease promoting these kinds of tickets, we will have to take further action."

"Really?" I said. "And what would that be? Would that be to deny me a bag of pretzels on what used to be a meal flight?"

"Not funny," he responded. "If you don't cease to write and report about this, we won't be able to offer these fares to our customers."

"If you don't want to offer these fares, then don't offer them," I countered. "Remember, I don't work for you."

"OK," he said, sounding more serious. "If we discover that you are flying on a back-to-back ticket, we will remove you from the aircraft, deny you boarding, and make you pay a full-fare ticket to reboard the plane."

"If you find out?" I laughed. "Get out your pens and paper." I then told them the flight numbers and dates of the next five back-to-back itineraries on which I was scheduled.

"But let me warn you that I would view your actions as a serious breach of contract and would litigate accordingly and strenuously. I am flying on a ticket I purchased myself, under my own name, on the dates and times specified on that ticket. I am conforming—to the letter—to the contract of carriage. I will also alert other members of the media to the same flight numbers and dates."

Also, I added, I would be using two different airlines. One back-to-back ticket in one direction would be on American; the other, on United.

"But that's a horse of a different color," argued the American official.

"Really?" I responded. "The way I see it, we have two horses in the same race, and they're both winners."

In short order, I received support from a number of consumer reporters, including Joe Brancatelli, who now runs the excellent travel website joesentme.com, and who likened my case to a six-pack of Coca-Cola. In his widely read Internet column, he wrote that if he bought a six-pack of Coca-Cola and drank only three bottles, would the Coca-Cola police come and arrest him?

The upshot of my meeting at American: I continued to

fly back-to-back tickets, I was never denied boarding, and the Coca-Cola police were never sighted.

Indeed, if you want to play the back-to-back game, my advice is this: Protect yourself by buying two tickets on different airlines. In the Los Angeles–to–New York model, buy your Los Angeles–to–New York round-trip on American, and your New York–to–Los Angeles round-trip on United. You'll get the same low discount fares and mileage on *both* carriers! And the best deal is that even if you choose to return later on each ticket, you can still use the return portion of each ticket by paying the $100 rebooking fee per ticket. It remains a great deal.

I am not advocating cheating.

All I have done—and continue to do—is report on a long-standing loophole in airline rules that benefits consumers. If any airline wants to eliminate that loophole, or the Saturday night stay requirement, that's the airline's prerogative. I will certainly encourage consumers to abide by any new ticket restrictions or, where possible, to benefit from them.

THE PROBLEM WITH HIDDEN-CITY TICKETS

As much as I am an advocate of back-to-back tickets, I must caution you about hidden-city tickets.

First, an explanation.

A practice that is a breach of the passenger-airline contract is the hidden-city ticket. Let's say you need to get to Dallas from San Francisco, but there are no discount tickets available. However, an airline is offering a discount fare on its San Francisco–to–Austin flight, which happens to connect in Dallas. You buy the Austin round-trip and get off in Dallas.

Under the airlines' official conditions of carriage, this practice violates a tariff when the passenger attempts to return from Dallas. By not using the Dallas-to-Austin portion of the ticket, the passenger contravenes the condition that states: "Flight coupons of a ticket will be honored only in the order in which they are issued in the ticket booklet."

Most airline computers are programmed to cancel reservations if a passenger does not check in for any portion of the reserved journey. Thus, a passenger using a hidden-city ticket runs the risk of being caught on the return flight.

Is it illegal? No. But when the passenger violates that tariff, the airline reserves the right to deny boarding to that passenger, void the remainder of the ticket, and charge full coach fare for the return flight to San Francisco.

Ironically, there's an exception, and it happens with first-class tickets! Remember, first-class tickets are full fare, and they carry no restrictions as to when you use them or when you fly each segment.

Consider this bizarre fare example. Say you want a first-class ticket between Los Angeles and Green Bay, Wisconsin. No problem. American Airlines will sell you a ticket for about $2,100 and will also let you know that your itinerary will be a nonstop flight between Los Angeles and Chicago, and then a connecting flight to Green Bay. If you call the same airline and ask what a first-class ticket costs for just a simple round-trip between Los Angeles and Chicago, the fare can be more than $3,000! Is this ludicrous or what?

The moral of this story: If you want to fly first class to Chicago, book a first-class ticket to Green Bay and get off in Chicago. You are not flying on a discount ticket, so the airline would either honor your reservation at a later date (should you actually decide you want or need to go to Green Bay) or simply pull the Chicago and Green Bay coupons. You can then make a new reservation and fly home from Chicago for almost $1,000 less than if you had bought a straight Los Angeles–to–Chicago ticket.

What's the reason for this? Airlines like American know the real breakdown when Chicago is the destination. O'Hare is one of America's biggest hub airports, but fewer than 20 percent of the people who fly to Chicago actually want to go there.

Those who *do* want to fly to Chicago, especially in first class, are business travelers who *have* to go. Translation: The airline thinks it can get away with charging a higher fare. And, for the most part, the airline does get away with it.

Still, remember that with the exception of these first-class hidden-city tickets, you run a serious risk of being denied boarding on your return flight. My advice: Don't do it.

In back-to-back ticketing, the situation is different. Passengers are flying, under their own names, on the date, flight, and time listed on the ticket, and they are using the coupons in the order in which they appear in the booklet. They have not sold or bartered their ticket, or changed or altered any reservation. They have followed the terms and conditions printed on each ticket.

In recent years, virtually every session of Congress has seen at least one bill introduced that is specifically geared toward battling airlines' back-to-back and hidden-city ticketing restrictions. And at each session, the bill dies in committee.

The most interesting of those bills was introduced late in 2000 by Nevada Congressman Jim Gibbons. The legislation—called the Consumer Airline Ticket Transfer (CATT) Act—would direct the U.S. Secretary of Transportation to issue regulations prohibiting airlines from penalizing passengers who use hidden-city tickets. It would also stop airlines from penalizing passengers who do back-to-back tickets.

A very interesting part of Gibbons's proposed legislation, which, sadly, never passed, would have allowed consumers to transfer their tickets to another customer without penalty. (After all, if I buy a theater ticket in advance and then can't go to the play, no one stops me from giving that ticket to a friend.)

The Aviation Consumer Right-to-Know Act, introduced in 2000 by Representative Peter DeFazio of Oregon, would directly permit purchase of back-to-back and hidden-city tickets without jeopardy. Not surprisingly, the airline lobby fought that bill as well and it died in committee.

Which brings things full circle. For the moment, I do not advocate the use of hidden-city tickets, but I wholeheartedly endorse back-to-back ticketing.

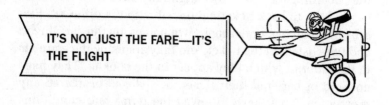

IT'S NOT JUST THE FARE—IT'S THE FLIGHT

Remember that Northwest late-night flight between Detroit and Washington, D.C.? It is one of dozens of flights that I call "secret flights."

These flights are on scheduled airlines. They are published in regular flight itineraries, but few people know they exist. They are either nonstop flights or direct flights that make one stop but do not require a change of planes. And more often than not, these are flights that are not full, offer better service, and are less expensive.

In the United States, where skies have been deregulated, there are few surprises. Still, there are some relatively secret flights. Savvy travelers know—and, in some cases, live by—these secret flights.

And why do the airlines operate these little-known flights? Some of them are simply positioning flights. The airline needs to get a particular aircraft from point A to point B so it can fly a better-known route between point B and point C. The A-B route thus constitutes the secret flight. Or the airline may have been granted something known as "fifth freedom" rights by a host country. Besides having permission to land there, even for refueling purposes, it is allowed to embark and disembark point-to-point passengers.

In the United States, where skies have been deregulated, any airline can fly virtually any route, so there are few surprises. Still, there are some relatively secret flights.

If you're flying between Los Angeles and San Diego, you'd expect United, American, and Delta to handle the route. Indeed, these three airlines operate the majority of the flights between these two southern California cities. And in a majority of cases, the airlines operate small commuter aircraft. United, however, has some positioning flights that use Boeing 737s for the twenty-minute trip.

What I call the secret transcontinental red-eye flights are another variation. No, I'm not talking about the red-eye flights that are nonstop. Indeed, American and United have nonstop late-night flights between Los Angeles and New York. Most leave about 10:00 P.M. and land at JFK just in time for you to get stuck in heavily congested rush-hour traffic into Manhattan. The regular red-eye flights are a bad deal for another reason. Because they leave at 10:00 P.M., they don't give travelers enough time to have a leisurely dinner in Los Angeles. They must rush to the airport in time to get stuck in New York.

Instead, virtually all the U.S. airlines have secret red-eye flights from Los Angeles. They leave shortly before midnight, and they connect in the individual airlines' hub cities. American, for example, has a flight that leaves at 11:50 P.M., connects in Chicago, and lands at LaGuardia at 9:30 the next morning. The cab ride from LaGuardia is shorter, faster, and less expensive because all the rush-hour traffic has already entered the city. United has a similar flight. Delta has a late flight connecting in Atlanta.

Northwest also has secret red-eyes from Los Angeles through Detroit, Memphis, or Minneapolis. Midwest Express departs Los Angeles at midnight, flying through Milwaukee.

The international routes between cities outside the United States make secret flights really shine. Flying from Manchester to Bombay (Mumbai)? One would think the airline choice would be British Airways or Air India. My secret choice: Singapore Airlines' Flight 327, a nonstop 777 flight with superb service. Singapore Airlines' Flight 345 also flies from Manchester to Zurich with a 747.

Between Los Angeles and Tokyo, there are regular Northwest, United, and Japan Airlines flights. But a long-standing international secret flight on this route belongs to Varig's Flight 8836. The Brazilian carrier flies nonstop between Los Angeles and Tokyo.

Singapore Airlines seems to fly everyone else's route. What happens if you're flying between Singapore and London? That's the time to try Emirates Air's Flight 431. It terminates at London but, en route, stops in Dubai for some serious duty-free shopping.

How about Los Angeles to London, or to Frankfurt? Most people don't know that Air New Zealand flies the route—often, for as low as $349 round-trip (or $599 round-trip between Los Angeles and Fiji).

On the Hong Kong–to–Bangkok route, most travelers will choose either Cathay Pacific or Thai Airways. But Gulf Air's Flight 153 is nonstop on its Airbus 340 series. British Airways can fly you between Hong Kong and Manila. So can Swissair.

A number of secret flights into Central and South America start in the United States. And the Santiago–Buenos Aires route is loaded with secret flights. LanChile or Aerolineas Argentinas aren't alone as they crisscross the skies above the two cities. Lufthansa goes from Santiago to Buenos Aires (en route to Frankfurt) once a day, and Air France's Flight 416 flies directly from Paris to Buenos Aires four times a week.

It would be logical to expect that a Rome-to-Madrid route would be flown by either Alitalia or Iberia. But Thai Airways' Flight 942 or Aerolineas Argentinas's Flight 111 also will get you there. If you're headed from Bangkok to Rome, a great secret flight is Flight 15 on Qantas.

The routes, and the "secret" airlines that fly them, indicate that no great air-traffic jam is involved. SAS may have more flights between Copenhagen and Málaga than British Airways, which may have only one per day. Lufthansa has many more flights between Hamburg and Leipzig than SAS. Any of these flights can change seasonally.

Finding hidden airlines on unusual routes is not only fun but can save you money. Remember, some of the secret flights on these routes offer lower promotional or bucket-shop fares, and because so many of them have U.S. partners in their frequent-flier programs, there's an additional incentive to fly them.

With a little planning, you can get better service, a more comfortable plane, and cheaper fares. That's a secret that should be shared.

COURIER FLIGHTS—OVERRATED?

I have a friend who always flew for free. She would check with certain companies, pack only carry-on bags, and go to the airport. Twenty-four hours later, she would be in Istanbul, Hong Kong, London, or Cairo. Once a month I'd get a postcard from Sydney, Rio, or Bangkok.

She flew for a courier service, and as long as she was

somewhat flexible with her time, the price was more than right. It was zero.

The trade-off: She had to fly when the service wanted her to fly, and she returned, often with no notice, when the service wanted her to return. Still, it was a great way to see the world for free, in short bursts of time.

Over the years, thousands of budget travelers have taken advantage of courier flights. But I'm sorry to report that there are few courier bargains left. So many people discovered the deals (you flew for free because it was cheaper for the courier services to buy you a cheap ticket and use your international check-in baggage allowance than it was for them to pay international cargo/air freight bills), that the courier services realized they could make money by selling the tickets. Soon, the total savings were reduced to 75 percent and then to 50 percent.

Some bargains can still be found, but many online offers for discount airline tickets match or beat the courier fares and offer far more options for travelers. Don't jump at courier fares only because you like the concept of discount travel. These days, a courier fare from New York to Paris runs about $550, so you can do better on your own—and you get to take *your own* bags!

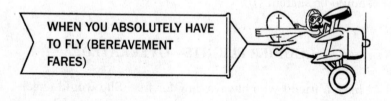

WHEN YOU ABSOLUTELY HAVE TO FLY (BEREAVEMENT FARES)

This is advice about flying the sympathetic and not-so-sympathetic skies. These days, when someone dies, you can get killed financially when you try to get a last-minute compassion or "bereavement" fare so that you can pay your respects to the recently departed.

In theory, bereavement fares are deeply discounted fares supposedly offered by airlines at a time of medical emergency. I say "supposedly" because each airline differs not only in its rules but in how it applies those rules. No airline is *required* to offer these fares; some do it as a courtesy, not because of any government regulation.

Even on the airlines that offer these fares, the definition of terms often changes. What constitutes eligibility for a bereavement fare? On some airlines, a bereavement fare applies only when a member of your "immediate family" dies.

But who constitutes immediate family? No one seems to know. For example, United Airlines says: (1) It will offer a bereavement fare only when a death has occurred, and, (2) "immediate family" means parents and children; grandparents and grandchildren; natural, step-, and adopted children; and half-relations.

And what's the discount on the fare? United will say only that it will handle each case on an individual basis.

In the past, American Airlines has said it will give immediate and extended family members, as a bereavement fare, a 50 percent discount off the minimum fare offered. Continental Airlines waives the fourteen-day advance-purchase requirement and includes just about anyone in the family—nephews, nieces, uncles, aunts, and in-laws.

Northwest expands its discount to include medical emergencies. Its fare takes 70 percent off the full coach fare. Delta, US Airways, and Southwest each have different rules and deals. They range from "Yes" or "No" to "Sometimes" or "Maybe."

Each airline will ask for some documentation or a contact name at a hospital or funeral home to verify the reason for emergency travel.

The discounts offered may occur after the fact and not at the time of booking or payment. On some airlines, what you get is a discount against future flights, and that could kill your wallet.

In effect, traveling at the last minute and asking for a discount because of someone's illness or death may only obligate you to fly the airline again.

So in a time of emergency, what can you do to get a real bereavement fare? The same thing you do when you book your regular flights.

Consider this story. A few years ago, a friend of mine called—in a panic. Her forty-one-year-old cousin, who was apparently in good health, had collapsed and died of a heart attack.

Burial was to be near her cousin's family home in New Jersey, and the man's wife and daughter wished to fly with the body. They had called United Airlines and, after explaining the circumstances, asked for the lowest fare to Newark from Los Angeles.

Could the airline waive its advance-purchase fare? they asked.

The United reservations agent told the widow that because the airline had no published bereavement fare, the lowest possible price she could quote her was $1,176, the full coach round-trip fare.

I called the reservations agent for her, and the agent repeated the same information to me.

"Clearly," I said, "you must have some policy on these situations."

"No," she replied, "we have no published fare and she doesn't qualify for an advance-purchase ticket. Besides," she added, "there are no discount fares available for the flights to Newark."

"But are there *seats* available for that flight?" I asked.

"Yes," she said. "But not at that fare."

"If there are seats available for the flight," I replied, "then surely someone in your office has the authority to override the computer and sell these folks a cheaper seat."

It took another ten minutes before I convinced her that she could, in fact, override her computer, waive the advance-purchase restrictions, and give the two family members a reasonable fare. I told her that not only would the family provide a copy of the death certificate, but the mortuary had informed me that the body would be accompanying them on the same flight (in the cargo hold). "How's that for proof?"

Finally, she relented. The $1,176 per-person fare was dropped to $418.

It is true that United does not have a published bereavement fare. The airline continues to deal with these requests on a case-by-case basis. Translation: There are no guarantees that, in a time of emergency, you'll get a bereavement fare or, even if you do, that it will be compassionately priced.

The airlines are not always to blame. Northwest Airlines saw the death rate suddenly soar in southern California during Easter and Christmas vacation periods. One American Airlines agent told me, "We actually had calls from people saying their grandmother died and the funeral would be on December 25 in St. Thomas." Whoops!

Ultimately, determination of the fare rests with the street-level discretion of individual reservationists or ticket counter agents. And if handled properly, this can do wonders for an airline's public relations.

Recently, an advertising executive from San Francisco—a visitor to Hawaii—approached the American Airlines ticket counter at the Honolulu airport. He had flown from San Francisco to Honolulu and was scheduled to fly back to San Francisco on a discounted and highly restricted ticket.

"I was wondering," he asked the American agent, "if I could change my return flight to Los Angeles instead."

The agent told him that she could, in fact, change his ticket, but the difference in fares would be substantial. "I could waive the additional fare," she then advised him, "if there is a hardship involved."

"I don't think so," the executive said with a shrug. "It's just that my daughter called me last night and asked if I could come to her eighteenth birthday party, and she lives in Los Angeles."

"That's the reason?" the agent asked.

"Afraid so," he said resignedly.

The agent quickly scanned seat availability for the Los Angeles flight. There were plenty of empty seats. She looked up from her computer screen, smiled, and winked. "That's a hardship," she said, as she rewrote his ticket at no additional charge. "Have a nice flight."

A great, true story. But don't count on that kind of response.

Remember: Even if the airline *does* have a bereavement fare and *wants* to offer it, you can often do better by purchasing a last-minute ticket on the Internet. After all, *you're* distressed; why shouldn't you also purchase distressed inventory?

Finally, if you don't want to be a fare casualty, you must do some comparison shopping before accepting an airline's offer of a bereavement fare at a time of loss. If the worst happens, this is the best time to cash in some of your frequent-flier miles. And assuming you can actually redeem them, that's the ultimate sign of an airline's compassion!

4

At the Airport

OK, NOW. YOU'RE PACKED. YOU'VE GOT YOUR PAPER TICKET, YOUR DOCUMENTS. SO, GET READY, GET SET . . .

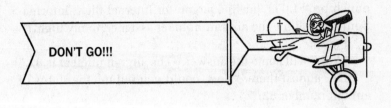

DON'T GO!!!

That's right: Don't leave home yet. You need to make one final call. And most of us regularly *do* make a final call before leaving our home or office to go to an airport.

We call the airline, indicate our flight number, and ask whether the flight is on time. "Yes," we are told, "the flight is leaving on time."

Wrong. When we get to the airport, we discover that the flight has been delayed for four hours. In fact, the plane isn't even on the ground. How did that information snafu happen?

It happened because you didn't word your question in the right way.

When you ask whether the flight is on time, the airline agent can interpret the question as: "Is the flight scheduled to leave on time?" Or if you're calling to confirm an incoming flight, the interpretation might be: "The flight is scheduled to arrive on time."

Are we really interested in the airline's *intentions*? Think about it. The *Titanic* was *scheduled* to arrive on time.

It all boils down to the words you use when you ask the question. Instead of just asking whether the flight is leaving on time, go one step further. Let's say you're booked on Flight 501, from Los Angeles to Boston. It's supposed to depart at 11:00 A.M.

When you call, ask the on-time question this way: "I'm

on Flight 501 from Los Angeles to Boston. Could you please punch up 'FLIFO' [airline jargon for internal flight information] and tell me the aircraft *number* assigned to my flight?"

Pause.

"Yes," will come the answer. "The aircraft number is 82."

OK, almost there. "Now, could you tell me the status of aircraft number 82?"

Pause.

"Sir, aircraft number 82 is in Bangladesh."

Bingo! You now know that although Flight 501 is *scheduled* to leave on time, it has no possible chance of even *arriving* on time at the airport, much less leaving on time for Boston.

Understanding airline schedules means understanding the "cycle" of aircraft. Believe it or not, there are still some folks who believe that their aircraft has been sitting on the ground waiting for them for hours or even for days. Instead, as any airline executive will tell you, schedules are all about utilization of aircraft.

An airplane on the ground earns the airline no money. The key is to schedule aircraft to be in the air as much as possible and, depending on the aircraft type, to carry a maximum number of revenue passengers.

Thus, the cycle. It is not unusual for the flight from Los Angeles to Boston to take off from Los Angeles, land in Boston, turn and fly to San Francisco, and, in less than two hours, become the San Francisco–to–London flight. Two hours after its arrival in London, it is flown to New York, and, ninety minutes later, it turns and heads back to Los Angeles. And that, as an example, is a plane's cycle.

James Gleick, who wrote the excellent book *Faster: The Acceleration of Just About Everything* (Pantheon, 1999), called the cycle the "paradox of efficiency." He tracked American Airlines aircraft number 241, an MD-80 that started its cycle by flying from Phoenix to Dallas, then to Richmond and Norfolk, back to Dallas, and then to Calgary—in one day. The next day, the aircraft flew back to Dallas, then to Los Angeles, and then to Austin, Texas. On day three, it went from Austin to San Jose, Dallas, Nashville, Chicago, and Denver. And so on.

Gleick monitored the MD-80's high-use cycle for an entire week. "Its ramblings are not random," he reported. "They are precisely charted by computers. The goal is a schedule of maximal efficiency."

But if one glitch develops in that cycle, a slight delay can explode exponentially. And suddenly a flight to Boston is, for all practical purposes, nonexistent.

That's why you need information about your aircraft number, not just your flight number.

And now, before ever leaving your home or office, before ever confronting the chaos of the airport, you have enough information to plan your options.

Well, not yet—not until you understand the power of something called Rule 240. You must remember this rule, because the airlines will *never* volunteer it to you.

Rule 240 is actually old jargon for a policy that no longer exists. It referred to a Civil Aeronautics Board (CAB) requirement; in those days when the government supported the perception that it actually controlled and regulated the airlines, the carriers had to tell the board exactly what it would offer passengers if they delayed them or canceled their flights. This covered everything, including free phone calls home, rooms, and meal vouchers. That was then. The airlines are no longer forced to tell the United States what they will provide, but they do have to tell *you* if you ask. In fact—and most people don't know this—it's actually part of the contract of carriage between the carrier and the traveler.

So what does Rule 240 do for you? In its broadest interpretation, Rule 240 deals only with the airlines' minimum responsibilities to you. If you read that contract of carriage, it simply says the airline must deliver you to your destination within two hours of your scheduled flight time. If it can't, it must put you on another carrier at no additional cost, even if it means an upgrade into first class.

So how—or when—does Rule 240 kick in?

The airlines will 240 you only in the event of mechanical delays or delays that are completely the "fault" of the airline, such as misconnections or cancellations. They won't do it for weather delays, acts of God, riots, wars, or labor problems. And it works only in the United States.

Again, the airlines aren't exactly racing to tell you about this rule. This is the one rule that gives you, with one or two exceptions, immediate options in the event of a delay or cancellation of your flight. But you have to ask for it. *No one* at the airline will just offer it.

In the airline business, virtually everyone knows it simply as "240." This is what it says. In the event of the specified "flight irregularity"—if Rule 240 is invoked—the airline must endorse your ticket and put you on the next available flight—not just its own next available flight, but *the* next available flight. (That's one of the main reasons I love paper tickets!)

So in this scenario, you found out real-time information about the status of your flight because you asked for the status of your *aircraft*. And now, armed with this information, you have the weapon you need to take back your options and actually travel from Los Angeles to Boston.

So let's go back to your telephone conversation with the airline agent.

"Now that we've established that there is absolutely no

way my flight is leaving on time," you tell the agent, "I'd like you to 240 me."

And then, before you even leave for the airport, you're truly protected (unless there is a weather problem). And you've saved a lot of time you'd otherwise lose waiting for a flight that isn't leaving or waiting in line for so long that you miss one that *is* leaving.

OK, *now* you can go to the airport.

But wait. *How* you go to the airport also makes a difference.

First, have *someone else* drive you. Have a friend take you or call or hail a cab. Do *anything* necessary so as not to take your own car to the airport.

Then, embrace a contrarian view during heavy "push" times at the airport. At most major airports in the United States, the heavy banks of flight departures are usually between 6:00 and 9:00 in the morning, and 4:00 and 7:00 in the afternoon and early evening.

The key here is to avoid automobile gridlock at the airport. When you are heading to an airport that has divided upper and lower departure and arrival levels, go against the flow. During the high-push times for departures, avoid the departures level altogether. Instead, head for the lower arrivals level. It will be empty. Pull up; no crowd, no waiting. Rent a baggage cart, go inside, and take the elevator upstairs. At some airports, you could easily save up to fifteen minutes of precious time. If people are meeting you at your destination, have them reverse the process as well. When you land, head downstairs, grab your bags from the carousel, and then take the elevator or escalator upstairs where they can meet you at the then uncrowded departures level.

OK, you're at the airport and you've got your bags. Now what do you do?

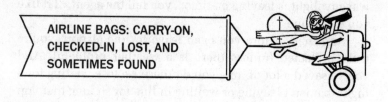

AIRLINE BAGS: CARRY-ON, CHECKED-IN, LOST, AND SOMETIMES FOUND

Airline baggage is one of my favorite topics. If you're like me, you embrace the somewhat cynical philosophy that there are only two kinds of airline luggage: carry-on and *lost.*

I try to carry on as much as possible. Most of the airlines, of course, don't like this. Why? It all gets down to a definition of what actually constitutes a carry-on bag. And sometimes it borders on the ridiculous.

> Which airline has the worst record when it comes to checked bags? In 2003, the most recent reporting year, the honors went to Delta subsidiary Atlantic Southeast, which mishandled 15.41 bags per 1,000 people. American weighed in at 4.45 bags per 1,000 passengers. The best? Alaska, which lost just 2.56 bags per 1,000 fliers.

The U.S. Department of Transportation reports that the airlines lose or mishandle 2.2 million bags annually—two of every one thousand passengers are affected. And even though the airlines claim they are trying to do a better job, many passengers will do everything they can to *not* check their luggage.

They will schlepp it, roll it, push it, even hide it—anything to ensure that it goes onto the plane and remains at their side. And it doesn't matter that it might be an unconventional piece of luggage.

There are some extreme examples. What do the following items have in common: an eight-foot totem pole, a large industrial vacuum cleaner, a refrigerator, and a BMW transmission? These are all items that passengers have attempted—successfully—to take on airplanes as carry-on baggage.

"There are people out there who will try to bring just about anything on the plane," says Debbie Sculley, a Delta airlines ticket counter agent in Los Angeles. "Tires, fenders, drive shafts [car items seem particularly popular], everything short of the kitchen sink." (Kitchen sink? More on the kitchen sink later.)

But as absurd as the carry-on situation has become from the airlines' perspective, it is equally bizarre from the passengers' point of view. Most major airlines seem to be doing everything they can to stop passengers from carrying their belongings onto the plane. At certain airports, carry-on baggage rules are enforced with nothing less than a draconian spirit.

Consider this absurd but true example: I was in Atlanta, on my way to board a Delta flight to Orlando. I carried with me two small, black briefcases. Each contained a computer. As I neared the gate, I stopped at a news kiosk and bought two newspapers and a bag of Gummi Bears. The clerk asked if I wanted a bag for them. I said yes, and she put them in a white plastic bag. I then headed for the gate.

When they called my flight, I dutifully stood in line to board. But when I approached the gate agent who was pulling tickets, he pointed to my bags. "Those yours?" he asked. I nodded. "Sorry, you can't board the flight. You've got too many bags."

Too many bags? Two small briefcases and a third item, a thin plastic bag with a *New York Times,* a *USA Today,* and a package of Gummi Bears?

I'm the first one to understand the difference between

portable and transportable. I know that just because a piece of luggage has two wheels on it doesn't mean it belongs in the passenger cabin. But this was going too far.

"You can't be serious," I laughed.

He didn't laugh. "You either check one of those bags or you don't board."

He was declaring the Gummi Bears an illegal *third* carry-on bag!

He was serious. And he was being ridiculous. I decided to take him at his word.

"All right," I countered. "Since these other bags contain computers, I want to check this bag," I said, pointing to the open plastic bag.

"I can't do that," he said.

"So what do you suggest I do?" I asked.

"You pack that plastic bag inside one of your other bags or you can't board the flight."

"OK," I said, trying to suppress a laugh, "but let me ask you a question of logic. Let's say I do that. And then I board the plane. What do you think is the first thing I'm going to do when I get on the plane? I'm going to unpack the bag. Now, can you tell me what you've accomplished here, other than holding up the boarding process?"

He wouldn't answer. So I packed the two newspapers in the bag, along with the Gummi Bears, and in the process I promised about six people behind me in line that I would share the candy with them once we were on board.

The Gummi Bears didn't last long. But my anger about the incident remains. Why? The underlying problem is that there is no universal agreement on what is and isn't a carry-on. Looking to the government for help? Forget it.

The Federal Aviation Administration doesn't provide a definition. FAA rules require only that cabin baggage be properly stowed, either under the seat in front of you or in the overhead compartment.

Not surprisingly, flight attendants hate the situation. The Association of Flight Attendants (AFA) has been lobbying hard for an industry-standard definition—an FAA rule—for carry-on baggage.

"It's tough," says AFA president Patricia Friend. "We end up in the middle, trying to tell people that there's no room for it in the cabin and it's going to have to be taken off the plane. And that creates a conflict."

The flight attendants are not alone. Another group calling for a federal-standard carry-on bag policy is the Luggage and Leather Goods Manufacturers of America. The LLGMA has also started a nationwide effort to have passengers "think small."

SO WHAT *IS* A CARRY-ON BAG?

What constitutes a carry-on bag depends on the airline, the airport, and the kind of plane you're flying. What is acceptable to one airline is barred by another. And it's gotten downright nasty out there. In 1998, United Airlines tried to limit the size of carry-on bags brought onto its planes by installing restrictive "templates" at security checkpoints. The airline soon enlarged them (even small garment bags were being stuck at the templates), but they proved singularly unpopular.

"We think the templates are a cheap trick," charges Gordon Bethune, the CEO of Continental Airlines. "The reasons why some airlines want to use templates is that it takes the confrontation away from them [and directs it] to a third party—the security guard at the checkpoints. These airlines would like to have a law to take away the rights of the consumers to carry their underwear with them when they fly, and most people don't like to be separated from their underwear."

Continental thought it had gone a long way toward solving the carry-on problem: It spent $15 million on installing bigger overhead bins on its planes. Even the large roll-on bags now fit inside them.

However, at two airports where Continental shared gate space with United, passengers were apparently being separated from their underwear and denied boarding with their carry-on bags that didn't fit United's templates.

Continental got angry and sued United. In the antitrust lawsuit, filed in the U.S. District Court for the Eastern District of Virginia, Continental claimed that United was trying to limit competition by requiring Continental's passengers to conform to United's standards in order to board Continental planes.

"In their quest to prevent customers from carrying their bags on board, airlines like United are thwarting our ability to compete on the basis of offering a superior product," Continental claimed. Shortly before going to trial, United settled out of court with Continental.

In the meantime, it gets worse for passengers who interline—who fly, for example, on a Continental flight from Newark to Atlanta and then change to a Delta flight to Salt Lake City. With the carriers' different rules, passengers could easily have trouble on their connecting Delta flight.

Templates or no templates, the continuing problem is that there is no standard for carry-on bags. Is a purse a bag? Is a laptop computer? On some airlines, each counts as a bag.

Thankfully, at least for the moment, I haven't found an airline that counts overcoats, umbrellas, canes, or small cameras as additional carry-on bags. But they *are* counting, post-

9/11. New rules went into effect severely limiting carry-on bags. You are generally now allowed one small carry-on bag and one "personal" item. But on international flights, some passengers are allowed two carry-on bags and one personal item. It's all very confusing, and while the airlines call them baggage "rules," they are really handled more often as airline policies meant to be bent. It all gets down to who is staffing the first security screening area and who is monitoring passengers as they board their planes.

Although enforcement is spotty at best, here are some of the airlines' current rules (coach class only). American, Southwest, United, Delta, and US Airways each allow one carry-on; Northwest allows one bag plus one purse, briefcase, or laptop computer.

But again, the dimensions vary by airlines. Many carriers put a limit on carry-ons: 9 inches by 22 inches by 14 inches. American shaves that by an inch: 9 inches by 23 inches by 13 inches, which can sometimes be a problem if the bag has wheels and the wheels stick out more than an inch from the bag itself. Southwest allows slightly larger bags: 10 inches by 16 inches by 24 inches.

Carry-on Confusion: Sizing Up the Rules

Airline	Size Limit	Comments
Alaska	10 × 17 × 24″	Size limit is for both bags combined.
America West	Cannot exceed 45″	When space is limited, it may be necessary to limit carry-on bags to one per customer.
American	9 × 13 × 23″	Total of three checked/carry-on bags permitted. Bags limited to 62, 55, and 45 linear inches.

Carry-on Confusion: Sizing Up the Rules

Airline	Size Limit	Comments
Continental	Cannot exceed 51″ or 40 lb	Total of three checked/carry-on bags permitted.
Delta	9 × 14 × 22″	A purse is exempt. Restrictions may apply on certain flights.
Northwest	9 × 14 × 22″	Official carry-on limit is one bag, but exempts purses, briefcases, and laptop computers.
Southwest	10 × 16 × 24″	Purses of reasonable size and food for onboard consumption are also permitted.
United	9 × 14 × 22″	A small purse is exempt. On full flights, you may be asked to check one of your bags.
US Airways	10 × 16 × 21″ 8 × 16 × 24″	Handbags are exempt. Carry-ons may be restricted due to lack of space.

Limits each bag to separate sizes.

Notes: All airlines exempt coats, canes, umbrellas, and reading materials. Some also exempt child seats and baby strollers. Most also restrict a carry-on bag to 45 linear inches (length × height × width).

Source: Based on a chart entitled "Carry-On Confusion: Sizing Up the Rules" from joesentme.com. Copyright © 2000 by biztravel.com. All rights reserved. Adapted by permission of biztravel.com. Source of carry-on size information from the websites of the listed airlines.

Remember the reference to the kitchen sink? Believe it or not, I found an airline that will actually let you board with one of those—that's right, a kitchen sink—as a carry-on.

Just for laughs, I went to a hardware store and bought a double porcelain sink. I took it to LAX, put it on a luggage cart, got it through the security machines, and yes, got it onto a plane as a carry-on!

The airline? The now-defunct but then-new carrier Legend Airlines, based at Love Field in Dallas, was offering fifty-six (all) first-class seats on its DC-9 aircraft flying from Dallas to Washington, Los Angeles, and Las Vegas. "We designed the overheads so that each passenger literally has his or her own bin," says Allan McArtor, Legend's CEO, and a former administrator of the FAA.

"Whether you're a mom with kids, carrying a stroller and a child seat, or you're going on vacation and have a lot of extra gear, or you're a business passenger who needs that extra computer, we'll make room for you," he says. In addition to the bins, the airline offers extra-large closet space on board.

"Our policy," says McArtor, "is that if you can carry them to the gate, you can bring them on the airplane. Do we have a template for bags at Legend Airlines? It's the aircraft door. If you can bring it through the airplane door, you can bring it on."

Sound good? Shortly after I did the interview with McArtor, the airline, hit by high fuel prices and head-to-head competition with American, suspended operations.

So you might want to forget the kitchen sink for a while. Instead, here are my surefire tips for surviving the carry-on chaos:

1. Try to be among the first passengers to board the plane (before all the bins fill up).

2. Use carry-on bags that will satisfy the dimensions of the most restrictive airline on your route.

3. Pack for weight, not just for size. If you can't lift your bag, do not expect the flight attendant to lift it for you once you're on the plane.

4. Never ask at the counter if your bag is approvable as a carry-on. Do that only at the gate. The counter people

will, more often than not, tell you your bag must be checked. The gate people are the best arbiters. If the flight isn't full, they're more likely to let you on with your bag. If the flight is full, they will gate-check it. The good news there is: (a) you know it made your flight and (b) last bag on, first bag off! Be sure to pack at least one of your bags well enough so that, in case you're forced to check it, you can easily do so.

An important note to remember if your connecting flight requires you to switch airlines midtrip. The *second* carrier is responsible for your luggage. Believe it or not, this applies even if the switch wasn't planned and was caused by a flight cancellation. For example, you're flying from Washington to Chicago on United, but St. Louis is your destination, so you must switch to American in Chicago. Even though your original ticket may have been issued by United, American assumes responsibility, in Chicago, for getting your bags to St. Louis.

The subject of checking bags brings up another sore spot: the dreaded excess baggage charges.

Consider this scenario. A friend of mine took a flight on Lufthansa from Los Angeles to Budapest. The plane made one stop—in Frankfurt—and my friend changed planes for his journey to Hungary.

When he had checked in for the outbound flight in Los Angeles, he had two large suitcases and one carry-on bag. The suitcases were full of clothes and gifts for friends in Hungary. The carry-on bag contained documents for a business meeting in Budapest. The two suitcases were checked through to Budapest.

Two weeks later, as he was preparing to leave Hungary, he had less baggage than when he arrived. The gifts had been presented, and most of the business documents had been left for his colleagues. He packed his empty carry-on bag inside one of his two suitcases.

But when he arrived at the Budapest airport for his return flight to Los Angeles on Lufthansa, officials told him he was overweight and would have to pay excess baggage charges—a whopping $254.

Even though it was a Lufthansa flight, the Lufthansa agent actually worked for Malev, the Hungarian national airline, which handles all ground operations for Lufthansa in Hungary. The agent was not in an understanding mood. My friend had only two choices: Either he paid or his bags stayed in Hungary.

Excess baggage charges are among the biggest airline rip-offs—one of the few areas of modern travel where no standardized international rules exist.

Overweight tariffs are applied—or not applied—depending on when you fly, who you are, and the mood of the airline counter agent. It is a capricious, unfriendly, and immensely profitable side business for many airlines, and, more often than not, the unwitting passengers victimized by the charges are left—literally—holding either the bag or an empty wallet.

Airlines can—and do—charge outrageous amounts for excess baggage, especially overseas. The problem stems from the fact that different countries and international tariffs dictate the baggage rules in each place you fly.

In the United States, the Civil Aeronautics Board (it was deregulated out of business in 1978) did something to protect American passengers. It initiated the "piece" system.

On domestic flights, each passenger is usually allowed to check two pieces of luggage and take one carry-on. (Note: Internationally, you can check more.) Generally, each bag can weigh up to 50 pounds. The two bags must not exceed, respectively, 120 inches and 106 inches in total dimensions.

(The carry-on, which can weigh up to 40 pounds on some airlines, theoretically must fit underneath the seat.)

Since 1977, that CAB rule has also applied to international flights arriving in or departing from the United States, regardless of the carrier. But once you leave the United States, you can generally forget the 50-pound allowance per bag. And you had better start jettisoning some of your stuff or preparing to pay for it. In most other parts of the world, bags are weighed. Passengers are permitted to carry 44 pounds (total) in economy class and 66 pounds in first class.

Some airlines will charge you $25, up to $50 per bag over your two-bag limit, but it could be even more than that if your bag weighs more than 50 pounds and exceeds 62 linear inches. There are some exemptions, and this is where your status as a frequent flier kicks in. Some airlines have instructed their counter agents at airports to give up to 10 pounds' leeway for their most frequent fliers and not charge them any extra overweight fees.

For baggage over that amount, you will be charged 1 percent of the regular coach or first-class ticket price per overweight kilo (2.2 pounds). For example, a coach passenger flying between London and Johannesburg and carrying three bags (including one carry-on), each weighing 70 pounds, could be charged about $1,200 for being 166 pounds overweight. Another person, flying between London and Los Angeles and bringing on board the exact same number of pieces and weight of luggage, carries it all for free under the U.S. piece system.

If you have foreign stopovers en route to your final destination, some airlines will charge you excess baggage rates at each stop along the way.

Authorities at Moscow's Sheremetyevo Airport are notorious for not only extracting huge excess baggage charges from departing passengers but also demanding that the fees be paid in hard currency.

To be fair, some airlines do seem to have a legitimate excess baggage problem. Philippine Airlines is regularly plagued with dozens of passengers checking in large, heavy cardboard boxes on their U.S. flights to Manila.

American, which flies an extensive route system in South America, has suffered from excess baggage problems. It is not unusual for the airline to institute a bag cutoff rule, especially during holiday periods. Generally, American does not tell passengers about the cutoff until they arrive at the ticket counter with their bags. Under that rule, excess bags just aren't carried on the flights. If you're flying to the Caribbean during Thanksgiving, no big problem. But at any time within ten days of Christmas, you'd be better off mailing your bags. At that time of the year, a lot of folks come up to Miami to do their shopping, and the return flights are jammed with bags.

So always call first and make sure there is no baggage moratorium on your flight. If you get to the airport and then find out there *is* a cutoff, at the very best, you'll be charged for excess baggage, your bags may not make your flight, and, worse, the airline is then not liable to deliver your bags once they *do* arrive.

A few airlines have tried variations of normal excess baggage formulas. But nothing seems to work. As a result, the excess baggage problem—and airline-by-airline confusion—continues, with no easy solution.

WHAT CAN YOU DO?

With all due respect to airline security (or the lack thereof), I often look for a fellow business traveler who understands my predicament (because he or she has been there before) and appeal to that person to check my bag on the plane as if it were his or her own. I am traveling on the same plane, so the obvious security fears are alleviated.

If you're traveling with your family, remember that each of your kids has the same baggage allowance you do. Use it.

Also consider the aircraft type and whether your bags will actually make it on the flight with you. A fully booked 747 has the capacity to carry all passengers' bags. But a fully booked commuter flight on United Express or American Eagle? Forget it. On the last ten booked commuter flights I've taken, the airlines were batting ten for ten—they delayed at least one of my bags every time, because the planes simply couldn't hold all the passengers' bags. Suggestion: Don't check *any* bags on commuter flights. Instead, walk them to the gate and have them gate-checked. It really works! (Gate-checked bags go into a different compartment in the plane and have a better chance of making the flight.)

You can avoid the problem altogether. Consider FedExing your bags ahead of you. FedEx and other courier services offer discounts for two- and three-day delivery (just send the bags out that far ahead). Virtual Bellhop will do the same thing. Think that's too expensive? How valuable is your time to you or to your business? On average, you will be spending between sixty and ninety minutes checking in luggage for a flight and then, upon your arrival, waiting for your bags to show up on the pickup carousel (assuming they were actually on the same flight with you!).

Depending on the time of day you arrive, that extra waiting time may be the difference between getting from the airport to your destination in a reasonable time and getting stuck in rush-hour traffic. There's also a schlepp factor—lifting your bags, renting a cart, schlepping the bags to and from ground transportation, and so on. Suddenly, sending your bags by courier seems like the *least* costly way to go!

WHEN YOU ABSOLUTELY HAVE TO CHECK YOUR BAGS

Remember, with more airlines forcing us to check our bags, that means more airlines are now losing more bags. Ironically, Delta and United, the two airlines that started putting baggage sizers at security checkpoints to limit carry-on bags, saw their complaint percentages zoom. But since 9/11, with the new carry-on bag rules, Delta's numbers have improved, and complaints against the airline have dropped by half. United reported a similar decrease in complaints.

When an airline loses your bag, you're known as one of the PAWOBs—"passengers without bags." You've seen them wandering aimlessly near baggage carousels at airports, waiting without hope for the luggage that never seems to arrive.

So how do you avoid being a PAWOB, or at least lessen your chances?

Let's start with the bags themselves. First, there's a great deal of difference between portable and transportable. As I said before, just because your bag has wheels on it doesn't mean it belongs inside the airline cabin.

Second, realize that baggage conveyor belts are not your friends. They will eat, mangle, or otherwise destroy anything left dangling on the outside of a bag. Translation: Straps, hooks, and even identification tags stand an excellent chance of being yanked from your bag.

Advice: Clean up your bag before you get to the airport. Take anything—and everything—off the bag that can be pulled, caught, or hooked.

Automated

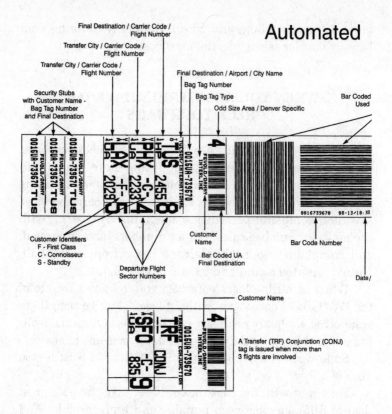

Final Destination / Carrier Code / Flight Number

Transfer City / Carrier Code / Flight Number

Transfer City / Carrier Code / Flight Number

Security Stubs with Customer Name - Bag Tag Number and Final Destination

Final Destination / Airport / City Name

Bag Tag Number

Bag Tag Type

Odd Size Area / Denver Specific

Bar Coded Used

Customer Identifiers
F - First Class
C - Connoisseur
S - Standby

Departure Flight Sector Numbers

Customer Name

Bar Coded UA Final Destination

Bar Code Number

Date/

Customer Name

A Transfer (TRF) Conjunction (CONJ) tag is issued when more than 3 flights are involved

The luggage ID tags the airlines give you are purely ornamental and are almost begging to be stripped from your luggage. Instead, buy some heavy-duty ID tags and put two on each bag. Attach them to different parts of the bag, and not necessarily on the handle. (If the handle breaks, the tag slips off.)

What about the destination tags the airlines put on the bags? How these tags are labeled and how you—and others—read them make a big difference in whether they reach your destination—or, for that matter, *any* destination.

Baggage Tag (United Airlines)

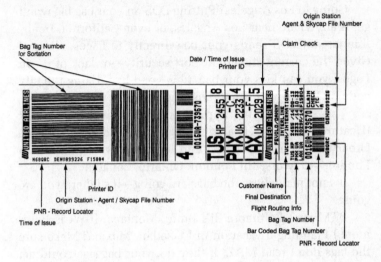

October 1997

Most destination tags today are bar-coded and clearly labeled. If they are generated by machine, they most likely will include your last name, the originating as well as the connecting flights, and the three-letter code of the city that is your ultimate destination.

But not always. It is your responsibility to understand the three-letter code for your destination city *before* you get to the airport. When you make your reservation, ask for that code, write it down, and keep that slip in your wallet. Why? If the proper code isn't on your bag, it could be lost forever.

Here's an example of what happens a lot more than the airlines want to admit.

Going to Los Angeles? Putting LOS on your bag tag won't get it anywhere near Los Angeles, or even California. In airline jargon, LOS sends your bag directly to Lagos, Nigeria! Given the current state of airport security—or lack of it—in Lagos, you can kiss your bag a big good-bye. Using the city code LAX gets your bag to Los Angeles.

The same warning applies with LON instead of LHR (Heathrow) or LGW (Gatwick) if you're headed to London. Otherwise, your bags could end up at the wrong airport in London—or, worse, in London, Ontario, Canada!

It's not just where the bags are going—it's where *you* are going.

BTM isn't Baltimore. It's Butte, Montana. (BWI is Baltimore.) Planning a vacation in Mazatlán, Mexico? Make sure the tags don't read MAZ. If they do, your baggage could get a long rest in Mayagüez, Puerto Rico. MZT is the correct Mazatlán tag. Going to Kansas City? If your bags say KAN, you're in trouble. They'll land in Kano, Nigeria. The correct code for Kansas City is MCI. ALB is Albany, not Albuquerque.

Sometimes, even if the codes are correct, you can be in trouble if they're not written clearly. For example, IND is the correct code for Indianapolis, Indiana, but if it's misread as IMD, it may be a while before you see your bags. Their destination would be Imonda in Papua New Guinea. There's an equally big difference between JSI and JSL. JSL lands you in Atlantic City, JSI in Skiathos, Greece.

Some mistagged-luggage stories are legendary. Some years ago, a gate agent mistakenly tagged all the bags of a charter group headed for Mazatlán with SIN (Mazatlán is in the Mexican state of Sinaloa). When the group arrived in Mexico, there were no bags. A few days later, Pan Am stations around the world received a frantic telex from a confused employee in Singapore. "Is anyone looking for about sixty bags?" he asked. "We seem to be holding a lot of bags for a Mr. Mazatlán."

There are codes for airlines as well as airports. And each year, thousands of passengers show up at the wrong airline ticket counters and may, as a result, miss their flights.

You'll see the two-letter airline identification codes on your airline ticket as well as your luggage tags, if you have to change planes or airlines en route to your destination. In the competitive travel business, airlines fight for these letters. Once an airline gets a code it wants, it fights to the death—and sometimes even beyond death—to keep it.

More often than not, the major carriers get the codes they want. For example, American is AA, United is UA, and Delta is DL. (Pretty easy to remember.)

Overseas, some airlines also get desirable codes (British Airways is BA, Air France is AF), but not always. Finnair isn't FI or even FN. Those codes represent Icelandair and SFO Helicopters. Finnair is AY. Royal Air Maroc isn't RA, RM, or even AM. RA is Royal Nepal Airlines, RM is Wings West, and AM is the code for AeroMexico.

And since most airlines code-share these days, the confusion only gets worse. Pay attention to your ticket as well as your bag tags.

If at all possible, try to get bag tag stubs with the UPC bar code. Ask to have the stubs pasted or stapled inside your ticket jacket. Without them, you're as lost as your bags if the luggage is MIA at your destination.

Always double-check what the skycap or counter agent puts on your bags. It's even more important when your itinerary demands making a connecting flight on the same airline—or worse, interlining among different airlines. Be aware that not every airline has an interlining agreement with other airlines.

For example, you can fly from San Francisco to Chicago on United, transfer there to a Delta flight to Atlanta, and your bags will connect. But if you fly Southwest to St. Louis and then want to connect with American to Los Angeles, your bags will *not* interline. Southwest will connect bags only within its own system, so you'll need to get your bags in St. Louis and then check them in all over again with American. If you have a short connection time (less than sixty minutes on the schedule), your bags may not make the connecting flight. Always ask whether the airlines you'll be taking have an interline agreement if your itinerary requires a connection in another city between two different carriers.

Next comes the hard part. You need to determine the real as well as the emotional value of the contents of your bags.

The good news: The liability limit for damaging or losing bags has been raised to $2,500, but that figure needs to be put in perspective. Most travelers don't realize that the $2,500 figure is calculated "per incident," not per bag, and is based on depreciated value. And there are numerous exclusions for what the airline will *not* cover, including jewelry, furs, and negotiable financial instruments.

For example, United Airlines claims it "won't be responsible for loss or damage to: fragile items, spoilage of perishables, loss/damage/delay of money, jewelry, cameras, electronic/video/photographic equipment, computer equipment, heirlooms, antiques, artwork, silverware, precious metals, negotiable papers/securities, commercial effects, valuable papers, or other irreplaceable items."

Translation: You'll never see anywhere near $2,500 if the airline loses your bags.

On international flights, the risk is even greater. Liability for loss, delay, or damage to baggage is limited to approximately $9.07 per pound ($20 per kilogram) for checked baggage or up to $640 per bag. Translation (using an internationally recognized word): You get *bubkes*.

An additional problem has to do with how much your bags weigh. Remember that 44-pound allowance in coach?

You may notice that on an international flight the counter agent usually weighs your bags and writes their weight on your ticket, as well as on the airline's copy of the ticket, before handing you your boarding pass. Enter the 50-pound limit domestic and international liability.

If the agent actually writes down the total weight, be prepared for virtually nothing if the airline loses your bags.

It all has something to do with the Warsaw Treaty—definitely not a Polish joke—which established the $9.07-per-pound liability on international flights. In a decision handed down in a recent court case, that liability applies only if the airline confirms what your bag actually weighs at the time you check in. It can't assume your bag weighed only 50 pounds—or anything at all.

This rule emerged from a case in which a Silver Spring, Maryland, family—fourteen persons—flew on American Airlines to Santo Domingo for a wedding. The Cruz family had checked twenty-eight suitcases. The airline lost five of the bags. A sixth arrived late and was damaged *and* empty.

Normally, the family would have been severely limited in its ability to recover damages for this. But when the family checked in, the airline forgot to note the weight of the bags.

When the family filed a claim, the airline simply estimated the weight of each bag at 100 pounds and offered to settle the case for $4,535. The family refused. Then the airline raised its offer to $7,500. At that point, Mrs. Cruz retained the services of a lawyer. Coincidentally, she already worked for the lawyer—as his cleaning lady.

The lawyer sued the airline. A lower court dismissed the case and called the omission of the weight a technicality. But a three-judge circuit court panel reversed the lower court's decision and not only reinstated the suit but allowed Mrs. Cruz's request to certify it as a class action.

What does this mean? Judges are now more inclined to go after airlines when they abuse passengers. A suggested reason: Judges, as passengers, have also been abused by the same airlines.

In a recent—and horrendous—legal case, a woman flying to the West Indies boarded the plane with her medication and breathing apparatus. She was told that she had exceeded the normal carry-on limits and that her extra gear would have to be checked. She told the agents that it was required medical gear, but the agents insisted and the gear was loaded in the baggage hold.

During the course of the flight, she became ill. When the plane landed, it was discovered that the airline had lost her gear. She died two days later. Her relatives then sued the airline, claiming that it was indirectly responsible for the woman's death. And a court agreed. This marked the first time that an airline that lost a passenger's bag was found liable for wrongful death.

You don't have to file a class-action suit if the airline loses your bag. But you do need to pay attention. On an international flight, did the counter agent write down the weight of your bags? If you have to file a claim, that detail can significantly affect the settlement you'll receive. You'll also have to provide receipts and dates of purchase for anything lost.

There's a little-known tactic you can use when checking in your bags, but it works only on domestic flights. The airlines don't like to publicize this (in fact, they *don't* publicize it) and would prefer to have you *not* know about something called *excess valuation.*

Here's how excess valuation works. For a charge that averages between $10 and $50 for up to $5,000 of coverage, over and above the standard $2,500 limit, the airline essentially insures the bag. You must request this extra insurance at the ticket counter. Skycaps can't accommodate you. Not all companies offer excess valuation, and, yes, there are some exclusions here, too. But if you have the option and harbor any doubts about your bag's arrival, *buy the coverage.* It's an excellent incentive for the airline to get your bag to your destination.

So is your bag worth at least $50 to make sure it arrives on time and in good shape? In many cases, it's worth a multiple of that.

One essential piece of advice: Assume that if the airline loses your bag, your luggage tags will also be missing. Think of traveling as sending your bags to a bad summer camp. Identify everything twice, or even three or four times. Put two ID tags on the outside of each bag; put another two, in visible areas, on the inside of each bag. And *never* put anything other than your name and your phone number on the tags.

Why? Clever airport crooks look for bag tags with a person's home address plainly listed. These criminals aren't looking to steal the bags. They're looking to unload your entire house! You're traveling, and you're advertising that fact simply by being at the airport. A bag tag with your home address on it is an open invitation for burglars to pay a visit while you're out of town.

Another helpful tip when you're traveling internationally: A number of airports have services that shrink-wrap your bags in thick plastic, for a nominal charge. This is a great idea, for one obvious reason: If your bag has been opened during the trip, you'll know it immediately when you reach your destination.

What happens if you've done all your homework and the airline still manages to lose your luggage? What are your rights? And what can you expect the airline to do until it finds the bag—or worse, if it doesn't?

The answers to these questions vary wildly among airlines and depend on an unspoken caste system: how much you paid for your ticket, what class of service you're flying, where the loss occurred, and your status in that airline's frequent-flier program.

Swissair once offered an immediate debit card, similar to a Visa card. The airline preloaded it with a specific dollar amount and allowed you to buy essentials—clothing, toiletries, and so forth. It was a fresh idea—so fresh, in fact, that the airline canceled it! Swissair currently offers only reimbursement with receipts required as proof of purchase.

Northwest Airlines' current policy is that customers requiring amenities are provided with a kit containing a comb, deodorant, razor, shaving cream, toothbrush, toothpaste, and shampoo. Additionally, customers may be offered transportation credit toward future travel on Northwest, as a gesture of goodwill and an apology for inconveniencing them. Customers may also request reimbursement for additional items they need to purchase as a result of the delay by presenting receipts at the Luggage Service Office at the airport ($50 for the first 24 hours and $25 per day for each day beyond that, up to $150 per ticketed passenger). If the luggage is not located after five days, Northwest's Central Luggage Service (located in Minneapolis) will initiate a more extensive search that includes a detailed description of the bag and its contents and expands the search to other airlines beyond the original destination.

But compensation in the form of a credit is not really compensation; it obligates passengers to spend even more money. To use the credit, they must fly the airline that delayed their bags. It's nothing more than a nominal discount on a future flight.

Yes, it's better than nothing, but let's put this sequence in perspective. The airline emerges in a good position. It can use the credit as a sort of reverse incentive to encourage its baggage handlers to do a better job—to make sure passengers and their bags arrive at the same time and at the same destination.

In the United States, most airlines insist that lost, damaged, or delayed property must be reported within twenty-four hours, and a claim must be made, in writing, within forty-five days. The full description and value of the missing property must be listed. If you need to make interim purchases, United also insists that it "may consider up to a 50 percent reimbursement of the necessities purchased, taking into account your ability to use the new items in the future."

Over at Continental, if your bag is still missing after twenty-four hours, the airline says it will offer you "$35 per day, for a maximum of 3 days—or a total of $105. This is for passengers not arriving at their permanent residence, and original purchase receipts must be presented to the arrival station where the loss occurred."

What if the airline doesn't lose your baggage, and your luggage actually arrives at the same time, and at the same airport, as you do? Are you home free?

Not necessarily. Here's one final tip. Most people don't realize that a majority of airline baggage thieves do not steal the bags themselves. They take individual contents from those bags. And when you're at that baggage carousel waiting for your luggage, you're so happy to see it appear that you don't check to see if everything is still there.

Shrink-wrapping, still available at the Miami airport, eliminates that worry. Strangely, the service is not available at other airports because under TSA (Transportation Security Administration) rules, bags must be unlocked for inspection. (Translation: If your bags are going to be scanned by machine, shrink-wrapping works—unless they have to open the bags. But at airports where only manual inspection is available, shrink-wrapping is, of course, hopeless.)

Remember, once you get home and discover a loss, it's only your word against the airline's—a disadvantage when you try to reclaim the value of your lost goods.

Common Sense Rule 101: If you pack valuables, you're asking for trouble. "Valuable" may describe your prescription medicines, extra eyeglasses, or important phone numbers.

What kind of bags are you using? Expensive Louis Vuitton bags are a screaming advertisement for disappearance. Buy the sturdiest and, yes, perhaps even the ugliest bags. Make sure their construction is sound. Bolted is better than stitched, especially at corner seams.

If you're buying a bag with wheels, check its center of gravity. Not only are some bags with wheels unsturdy, but they can injure you or others!

Hard-sided suitcases often fare worse than soft-sided ones. How do I know this? I tested five of the top suitcases in an unusual way: I took all five, still in their original shipping containers, to Hawaii. There, I opened each one and did some unusual packing. Inside each bag I placed an orange, a banana, an apple, and a coconut. Then I closed the bag. And then, one by one, with the aid of some friends at the Honolulu Zoo, I placed each bag inside the elephant cage.

Forget the commercials showing a gorilla and some bags. This was the real thing! Hard-sided bags lasted an average of one minute before being shredded—literally—by the hungry pachyderms. The bag that won this bizarre durability test was a soft-sided garment bag constructed of bulletproof nylon. There's a lesson there.

Make an inventory of the items packed in each bag. It helps the airlines if they must try to find your luggage. And it helps you later, if you have to file a claim.

Many people worry about look-alike bags being taken mistakenly. It happens all the time, but there's an easy way to prevent this. Tie a bright-colored ribbon on the handle, or use some Day-Glo tape on the side of the bag. Remember, being stylish doesn't count here; retrieving your bag does.

When you arrive at the airport, if your luggage doesn't come off the plane, contact someone immediately. Baggage is often loaded into different compartments of an aircraft, based on destinations or connecting flights. If it is improperly loaded, it continues on. So you need to move quickly to make sure other compartments are checked before the plane continues its journey.

Let's say that you've done all the right things and the airline still manages to lose your bag. And worse, it *never* comes back. The U.S. airlines are quick to claim that 98 percent of all lost bags are reunited with their owners within twenty-four hours. What about the remaining 2 percent? The airlines also boast that half of those are reunited with their owners within seventy-two hours.

Even if you believe the airlines' robust claims, it's time to forget the percentages and look at the real numbers they represent. The remaining 1 percent—the bags that are lost and never found—translates to a staggering 200,000 bags! And where do *they* go? With the exception of some bags that are victims of outright theft, they head for the foothills of the Appalachian Mountains and the small town of Scottsboro, Alabama—an unlikely destination that has now become the depot for all lost luggage.

And within a few days, the bags—and their contents—are on display, and for sale, at the huge Unclaimed Baggage Center.

This tiny northeastern Alabama town has become the top tourist destination in the state. More than a million visitors come each year, from every U.S. state and from forty foreign countries. And for good reason. Some serious bargains can be found in Scottsboro.

The center was started in 1970, when it bought lost bags from Eastern Airlines, National Airlines, and, for a while, Air Florida.

What began as a small warehouse dealing with three airlines has now grown into a huge operation, and its airline list has greatly expanded. In fact, 115 people now work at two huge locations: the main retail space in Scottsboro (30,000 square feet) and a "clearance center" in Boaz, Alabama, about 50 miles away (17,000 square feet).

Here's how it works. When an airline loses a bag and a passenger files a claim, the airline tries to find that luggage. But after ninety days, if the airline is unable to match a bag with a passenger, it pays the claim. (The current baggage liability limit for the airlines is $2,500, but hardly anyone ever gets paid the full amount. The airlines exclude many items from coverage, and those it includes are covered on the basis of depreciated value.)

After the claim is paid, the airline officially owns the

bag. And then the bag and its contents are sold, sight unseen, to the center.

Because of contractual agreements with the airlines, the center's owners (as well as the airlines) refuse to discuss the nature of their arrangement with the carriers or how much they actually pay for the lost bags. "All I can tell you is that our trucks go all over the country picking up these bags." And they don't just handle baggage anymore; they've also added unclaimed cargo. The center's staff separates and catalogs about one million items a year.

On any given day, about seven thousand new items are put on sale. The list includes just about anything you can imagine. Some are obvious—about 60 percent of the store is given over to clothing—but there's also fine jewelry, cameras, golf clubs, skis, and electronics. It's a veritable Wal-Mart of lost airline bags.

To be sure, there are some big surprises when the bags are opened. In recent years, staffers have discovered a camera from the space shuttle (it was returned to NASA) and rare Egyptian artifacts (they weren't returned; they were auctioned at Christie's in New York). Windsurfing boards, kayaks, and boogie boards line the walls of the store. (Question for the airlines: How do you lose a kayak?) Separate display cases are dedicated to Barbie dolls, designer sunglasses, watches, and portable CD players.

But let's not overlook the full suit of armor ($1,000), the $23,000 5.8-carat diamond solitaire ring, or the original $8,000 Versace runway dress—with the price tag attached—which sold for $500. Jewelry shoppers, take note: At any given time, the center has thirty wedding bands and twenty diamond rings for sale.

And there are even more bizarre items: an airplane wing, a coffin, and a constant parade of dentures (they go to the clearance center or get thrown out). The most popular item these days? PalmPilots, which, like all the other stuff at the center, typically sell for about 30 percent of their original retail price. Jewelry is priced at 50 percent of its appraised value.

Hundreds of brand-new items are for sale, still with their original price tags. Merchandise is brought out ten times a day. People often shop for new clothes, as well as other things, before taking a trip or while they are enjoying their destination.

Indeed, on my most recent visit to Scottsboro, I bought a brand-new Mizuno baseball mitt, which retails at $160, for $40; a new pair of pants for $16; and a slightly used large metal suitcase, which normally retails at $825, for just $30.

Every so often, someone goes to Scottsboro and gets the biggest surprise. Not long ago, a man from Atlanta traveled to the Alabama store, looking for a birthday present for his wife. At the warehouse, he found a pair of ski boots. They seemed to be his wife's size, and he thought she would like the color. He was right. She loved the boots and the color. Then she looked at the inside of one boot and saw the initials of her maiden name. You guessed it—she had lost the exact same boots on her honeymoon!

So much stuff comes into Scottsboro, the center now holds special sales: in March, a scuba sale; on July 4, sporting goods; on Labor Day weekend (and I'm not kidding), an art sale. The big daddy—on the first Saturday in November— is the ski sale. Each year, a few hundred people show up the night before and camp out in the parking lot, waiting for the store to open.

In case you can't make it to Scottsboro in person, don't worry. The center's website is www.unclaimedbaggage.com, and you can shop there.

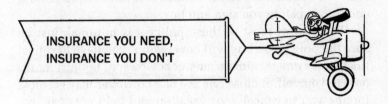

INSURANCE YOU NEED,
INSURANCE YOU DON'T

Let's assume you've got your baggage under control.

Should you insure your *trip*? Or your *life*?

One of the most overrated—and overpriced—things you can do is purchase flight insurance. All insurance is based on actuarial tables, so let's apply one here to prove the point.

The U.S. death rate attributable to airline crashes is just .01 per *billion* passenger miles. A British survey has shown that flying is 176 times *safer than walking*!

Flight accident insurance is truly beneficial only to the company selling the policies. But there is other insurance you absolutely *have* to have. Let's start with the trip itself.

We'll assume that you've negotiated the maze of tour brochure language; you've satisfied yourself that the terms described are in sync with your expectations; you've narrowed down the destination, the tour operator, the length of the trip, the extras, the amenities, and the cost. Now comes the most important part: paying for your trip.

We'll assume that you've budgeted well and can afford the package price. Now comes a crucial moment: What amount/percentage should you pay, and when should you pay it? Are you protected financially in case you must cancel the tour or, in a more dreaded scenario, the tour operator goes out of business before your scheduled departure date?

To protect your money in the event that you can't make the trip, buy cancellation insurance, which is sold by most travel agents. The policies are specific about what they will and won't cover, so read the various clauses, exclusions, and conditions before you sign and buy.

The cost of most of these policies is minimal; just be sure the policy you buy will cover you if you have to cancel the trip for *any* legitimate emergency reason, not just an illness to yourself. A close relative or a coworker may get sick, forcing you to cancel your vacation and help out. Ask, before you buy the policy, whether you will be covered if the tour is canceled because of low subscriber numbers or natural disasters (hurricanes, floods, or earthquakes). These policies are standard and are suggested as basic common-sense protection.

What if the tour operator simply goes out of business? Can you protect your investment against that possibility? Yes, but not in the form of an insurance policy. Instead, do some homework about the tour operator or travel agent *before* you hand over any money. In the past, I've written about the need to pay for your trip with a credit card instead of with cash or a check. But many tour operators will not accept credit cards for payment. (Most travel agents will.)

Many travelers, especially those signing up for package tours or charters, pay with cash. When they are told their money is safe because it's being put into an "escrow account," they think it's *really* safe. Not necessarily.

In the travel business, *escrow* is a secure-sounding buzzword that means nothing. Not only do individual travelers sometimes get burned, but so do their travel agents. Just because your money is placed in escrow, does that mean it is a true escrow account? Is it legitimately being held by the bank under proper regulations and guidelines until after the trip is completed, or does the bank have a very cozy relationship with the tour operator?

Unfortunately, the latter can often be a rhetorical question. A number of states (including Florida, New York,

Ohio, and California) have consumer protection laws requiring tour operators to post bonds or to use escrow accounts to protect passengers' money, but the protection offered is minimal.

Indeed, until recently, these escrow accounts were no different from any other bank account, and now-defunct tour operators were dipping into the accounts to pay the bills for previous trips. When the cycle finally caught up to them, all the money was gone, and thousands of travelers who had already paid for their trips never got the money or what it was supposed to buy.

Don't assume that only poorly capitalized, heavily leveraged newcomers to the tour operator business can be risky. Recently, a twenty-five-year-old tour company—a specialist in trips to the Caribbean, Bermuda, and Mexico—abruptly went out of business and stranded passengers in hotels in the Bahamas and Bermuda.

Specific U.S. Department of Transportation regulations govern tour operators and charter flights. But few travel agents follow the regulations or even know about them, and you may be subjected to a costly lesson.

Here's how to protect yourself when paying for a package tour and/or a charter flight, whether you pay directly or through an agent. First, ask whether the tour operator is a member of USTOA (United States Tour Operators Association). If it is, then it is covered by a $1 million bond that the company cannot access. That money is used solely for reimbursing consumer deposits and payments resulting from bankruptcy or insolvency. Even if the operator is a member of the USTOA, have your travel agent check the operator's relationship with its escrow bank. Does the bank actually exist? If so, what is it doing with the escrow account? Who really controls the account? Is it a true escrow?

To protect yourself when you're paying by check, list the

tour operator *and* the bank escrow account as payees, and, on the memo portion of the check, write the scheduled dates of departure and return. This protects you against the operator's using your funds to pay for someone else's trip.

By the year 2000, approximately sixty million passengers annually were departing by air from the United States, and more than a third of them traveled to developing countries, where the risk of contracting infectious diseases is increased. An estimated 50 percent of international travelers become ill as a result of their travels. In 2000, of all cases of malaria reported to the Centers for Disease Control (CDC), 1,021 were acquired abroad. Of the approximately 400 cases of typhoid fever each year in the United States, 70 percent are acquired while traveling internationally.

The CDC issues different types of notices for international travelers and has defined levels of risk for each type of notice, as well as recommended preventive measures for each risk level. There are four levels of concern, in order of increasing seriousness: In the News, Outbreak Notice, Travel Health Precaution, and Travel Health Warning. Examples range from reports of sporadic cases of dengue in Mexico in 2001 (risk level: In the News) to the SARS outbreak in Asia in 2003 (risk level: Travel Health Warning). These notices are downgraded or removed according to CDC criteria.

You should never leave home without comprehensive travel medical insurance. Every year, more than two hundred thousand Americans get sick overseas. Their illnesses may range from a cold or a stomach virus to a full-blown heart attack. Malaria, hepatitis, and typhoid are often the culprits—or they get hit by a bus!

Whatever health insurance you carry, it probably does not cover you outside the fifty United States. If your insurance does cover you overseas, don't expect it to reimburse you for anything other than emergency treatment expenses.

Most insurance policies do not cover emergency medical evacuation, often the greatest expense when an ill U.S. citizen needs to be brought home.

Travel medical insurance can be purchased through most travel agents or directly from many insurance companies. If you lack this protection, a medical emergency overseas could easily get you into serious financial trouble. Besides ruining your vacation, it could cost you your entire nest egg, your retirement account, and even your house.

Think I'm exaggerating? I remember boarding a Cairo-to-London flight. Occupying two rows of four first-class seats was a fifty-eight-year-old American traveler, lying flat on a stretcher. He had slipped off a curb on a street near the pyramids and had broken his hip. Accompanying him on the plane was a nurse. The man was in pain and had been sedated. The evacuation costs—which involved taking him to a hospital, stabilizing and treating him, and taking him to the airport and placing him on a commercial aircraft back to London and then on to the United States—were more than $120,000.

Some corporate or personal health plans cover you when you're outside the United States, but most don't. Those that do are restricted in what they will and won't pay for. Check the limits and restrictions before you leave town. Don't wait to discover those limits during an emergency.

Often, travelers get confused about their coverage. Travel medical insurance is not trip cancellation insurance. The latter is important and useful, especially if your scheduled trip involves a large, nonrefundable deposit. Cancellation insurance covers you if you are unable to make the trip or if the carrier (tour operator, airline, cruise line) ceases to operate before your planned departure or return date. The policy also kicks in if sudden illness, death, or injury strikes you or a member of your family.

Trip cancellation insurance does *not* cover the medical bills incurred because of that illness or injury. Invest in a comprehensive travel medical insurance policy that not only covers any medical treatment needed on your trip, but, in a serious medical emergency, pays to evacuate you from the area and bring you home.

Buy the policy before you go. Most policies offer coverage for up to fourteen days. (Some can be extended.) Premiums range from $29 to more than $70 per trip; annual policies are also available. The premium might seem high for such a short period, but the coverage is a bargain if you ever need it.

Various policies are offered; read the fine print. For example, one offers medical evacuation, but the evacuation decision is wholly the insurer's. Another policy offers evacuation, but only to the nearest facility where adequate treatment (again, in the insurer's opinion) is available. What you really need is a policy that allows your own doctor direct input into any medical decisions.

The cost of a travel medical policy can vary depending on the type of insurance, the traveler's age, and the cost and length of the trip. According to Jim Grace, president of InsureMyTrip.com, a website that lets consumers compare and buy travel insurance from multiple providers, the price can be less than $100 for minimal coverage for a young traveler to more than $1,000 for an older person who wants more comprehensive coverage.

More than a third of Americans claim not to understand the international insurance coverage provided by their employers or credit cards, and many of them risk traveling without any additional travel insurance, according to a recent survey by RBC Insurance. Since 9/11, most travel insurance has added enhanced terrorism coverage, but not all policies offer the same level of coverage, so it is worth your while to do some comparison shopping on the Internet before you buy.

Some travelers already may have coverage but don't know it. Holders of the American Express Platinum card may now have one very good reason to justify the card's steep annual membership fee. The card offers "travel emergency assistance," including medical evacuation by air ambulance, at no cost to the cardholder.

American Express also offers Global Travel Shield, a portfolio of comprehensive travel insurance products available to all travelers at their website at www.globaltravelshield.com. These packages cover a range of services including emergency medical and dental expenses and medical evacuation.

Visa Business cardholders are eligible for a discount on AIG International Services' International Assistance Membership program, which offers a range of emergency travel and medical assistance worldwide.

America, a travel insurance provider, has joined forces with Continental Airlines to offer protection to travelers who book through continental.com. Access America's Airline Ticket Protector provides coverage for trip cancellation and interruption, as well as twenty-four-hour global emergency assistance for both domestic and international flights.

A key term to look for in the fine print: *guaranteed payments.* If you think getting proper emergency treatment is tough in this country, try getting it abroad without money up front. Shop for a policy that doesn't make you—or the care providers—wait for payment.

A key word to avoid: *reimbursement.* Some policies provide payment only after the fact. You are solely responsible for payment. Blue Cross, for example, will not pay in advance and must preapprove all payments made by the patient and later submitted for reimbursement. When I called to check specifics, a spokesman first said, "If you have a Blue Cross policy and you're covered here, then you're covered abroad." What about medical evacuation? "If you need to be evacuated, we'll take you wherever you need to go." That was their position.

Sounded great. But when I called again, to reconfirm the specific wording of their policies, I got a slightly different answer: "We will pay for all medically necessary treatment." And what does that mean? Who makes that decision? "We need the treating physician to get in touch with us immediately to make that determination," said the spokesman. (Your personal physician needs to be firmly in the communication loop between the doctor on location and the insurance provider, to help make the proper decision—not for the insurer, but for you.)

Under the American Express program, all medical emergency services must be arranged by the emergency assistance officials in advance. AmEx is very clear that "no claims for reimbursement will be accepted."

My advice is that you carry your card with you when you travel and also bring along the phone number of your coverage provider. In the case of a nonemergency, call your provider for hospital approval.

One of the best medical insurance programs is offered by International SOS (ISOS), one of the largest personal and travel assistance companies in the world. For $60, travelers can purchase an ISOS membership for a trip lasting up to ten days. This is money well spent. The package includes a worldwide medical evacuation provision.

In a typical one-month period, ISOS repatriated a man with severe abdominal pain from Portugal back to the United

States; evacuated, from Mexico to Houston, a scuba diver suffering from decompression sickness; and transported a traveler from Siberia to Helsinki for an emergency appendectomy.

My favorite program, MEDJET Assistance, is located in, of all places, Birmingham, Alabama. MEDJET Assistance does a great job of providing emergency medical evacuation and treatment. For $195 per person per year, MEDJET Assistance does the best job for one very important reason: The fine-print disclaimers that you'll find in other policies are virtually eliminated.

For example, on some policies, the determination of when, how, and—most important—*where* you are evacuated *to* is determined by the insurance provider, based on where it thinks the closest available treatment is located.

I don't have to tell you, but I will anyway, that these decisions—in this age of the HMO mentality—are often based on cost versus common sense. If you hemorrhage in Nairobi and your insurance company thinks the closest treatment is in Uganda, that's where you're flown. Considerations of the quality of the blood supply or the capabilities of the doctors in Uganda may not come into play.

MEDJET Assistance officials consult directly with your own primary care physician in the United States, and, based on that consultation, will usually send one of their medically equipped jets, complete with EMT personnel, to bring you back *home.* That's a big difference.

Last but not least, if you get sick overseas, do the same thing you would do at home: Call your doctor. Many times, you can be treated over the phone. If the problem is more serious, don't wait for the hotel doctor. Head straight for the largest local medical center. It's very important to get all records of your treatment—not just for reimbursement, but to allow your own doctor to track what worked or didn't work if the problem continues when you get home.

No matter where you're going, or how, don't assume that you'll have adequate medical treatment available or that you'll be properly covered by your insurance plan. Many travelers on cruise ships assume that because the ship's doctor is featured in the line's brochure, the cruise cost includes free medical care on board. With virtually no exceptions, a ship's doctor is another onboard service that is available to passengers for a fee, as is the photographer or the beautician. Buy comprehensive travel medical insurance that has emergency evacuation provisions.

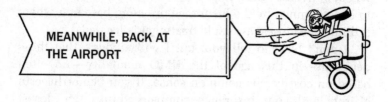

MEANWHILE, BACK AT THE AIRPORT

You've made the right calls. You've protected yourself with appropriate insurance. Not only is your flight on time, but you made it to the airport in one piece. You've got your paper ticket. You've handled your bags.

And now comes a pivotal move: Do everything in your power to avoid the ticket counter.

Why? In the process of travel, the key is to minimize the number of points of abuse. You know this every time you get a gate agent who wants to play only by the rules—you ask the agent a question and he or she answers by telling you all the things you're *not* allowed to do. How helpful is that? All it accomplishes is that the gate agent gets to validate his or her job, and you just receive a list of all the options you can no longer use. Therefore, I empower you to go straight to the gate! So go there. But—not yet!

First, check the departure board. It is not your friend. Like the original "on time" phone call you made, the departure board often lists a *scheduled* departure time, not a real one.

More important, check the arrivals board. If you know your departure gate, check the arrivals board for the same gate. Is there actually a plane at that gate? If so, you have at least an initial indication of whether your flight is still on time.

Either way, keep moving; head at least in the direction of your departure gate. The reason: If you keep moving, you lessen the risk of airport crime.

CRIMESTOPPERS

Most people don't associate airports with crime. They associate airports with travel. After all, if you plan correctly, an airport isn't someplace you go *to.* You go *through* it to get somewhere else.

The very real problem of airport crime is often overlooked by the people who most need to know about it: travelers.

If you don't familiarize yourself with some of the various scams criminals use to rip off travelers at airports, you can easily become a victim. I'm not talking about violent crime—homicide, robbery, or rape. Most airport crime is limited to crimes against property: pickpocketing, luggage theft, and automobile break-ins.

But in almost *every* case, travelers are unwitting accomplices to actual crimes.

How? Most airport criminals count on travelers' goodwill or their nervousness at being in unfamiliar surroundings.

It might surprise you to learn that these airport crooks al-

most always work in pairs. With few exceptions, they practice what police call crimes of "distraction."

Their tactic is to get you to focus on something else.
They will almost always approach a victim and ask a question, or make him or her look in another direction. Or they
will delay the victim so that a crime can occur.

Working in pairs, airport criminals usually target folks
traveling alone. Here are some of the typical distractions
aimed at permanently separating you from your luggage:

- *The phone booth question.* You're standing at an airport
  pay phone, making a call. Your bag is on the floor, alongside your right foot. Suddenly, from the left, a person
  walks up to you and asks you a question that requires
  directions. While you are responding, trying to help, the
  second criminal walks by and lifts your bag. By the time
  you are finished helping the accomplice, your bag is
  gone.

- *The money trick.* You're standing in line, waiting to
  check in for a flight. Alongside you is the luggage that
  you intend to check into the baggage hold, and you're
  holding your purse or briefcase. Someone approaches
  you and points to an area of the airport floor, about 8
  feet away, where three or four dollar bills are visible.
  "Excuse me," the person asks, still pointing to that
  spot, "did you drop this money?" Your first instinct
  might be to put down your briefcase or purse, walk the
  two or three steps over to the money, bend down, and
  pick it up. And the minute you do that, the second
  criminal whisks away your briefcase or purse. The
  criminal will walk quickly away, holding it at chest
  level in front of him or her, so that it is not visible from
  behind.

- *The mustard trick.* You're in line at a ticket counter, a gate, or an airport restaurant or snack shop. Again, you're holding your briefcase or purse. Someone behind you quietly squirts mustard or mayonnaise on the upper part of your back—usually near your left or right shoulder, where you can see it if someone points it out to you. And that's exactly the intent. The first criminal approaches you, tells you that something has been spilled on your shoulder, and offers to help clean it up. Coincidentally, the crook just happens to have a supply of napkins. And your first instinct? You drop your briefcase or purse, and the rest is history. While your attention is focused on cleaning up the mess created by the first criminal, the second is long gone with your briefcase or purse.

- *Auto thefts and break-ins.* The crime suppression advice is the same at airports as on city streets. Park in well-lighted lots, and don't wait until you get to the airport to lock any valuable items in your trunk. Someone could be watching.

- *Conveyor belt tactics.* Crimes that require distraction often occur where travelers are least likely to suspect criminals: security checkpoints at airports.

You're in line to go through the X-ray machine. You've just placed your most valuable possessions—your carry-on bags—on the conveyor belt, when someone steps in line ahead of you. This criminal is armed—not with a gun, but with every piece of metal he or she can find. Inevitably, the audio alarm sounds; he or she is stopped and told to empty all pockets. Of course, not all the pockets are emptied. The full-metal-jacket man walks through a second time, and again the alarm sounds. By the time the security guard deems the person free of metal, his partner—who went through the metal detector minutes before—has stolen your bags.

Never place your bags on the conveyor belt unless you are absolutely sure that (1) you have first placed any of your own metal objects in that separate tray, and (2) your carry-on bags do *not* precede you. The object of this race is to get through the detector before your bags come through the X-ray scanners.

What makes these criminals hard to catch? The person who initially distracts you—with inane questions, money on the floor, mustard, or heavy metal—is never the person who steals. Unless someone actually witnesses the theft and/or detains the thief, there is no evidence against the distracter, and that person cannot be arrested.

Some of the scams border on genius. Here's one scenario.

A limousine pulled up to the curb and discharged a man, his wife, and their child in front of the airline terminal. The driver unloaded expensive Louis Vuitton luggage from the trunk. The family entered the terminal and the wife then went to the bathroom. Moments later, a man rushed up to the husband and said, "Excuse me, sir, but did your wife just go to the bathroom?"

"Yes, she did," he replied.

"Well, I think she had an accident and fell down," said the man.

The husband instructed his son to wait there and watch the baggage as he ran toward the bathroom. As soon as the husband was out of sight, a van pulled up outside and another man approached the child.

"Are you flying out today?" he asked.

The child nodded affirmatively.

"OK," the man said. "I'll load your bags up."

He then proceeded to put all the Vuitton bags in the back of the van, closed the door, and drove off.

When the husband and wife returned, they discovered only their son. The bags were never recovered.

The key is to remain in actual physical contact with your bags. When you're standing at a pay phone, place your bag firmly between your legs.

When you're sitting near a departure gate, try to keep your leg or foot resting on your bag. (It's easy to doze momentarily while waiting for a flight, and that's when luggage can disappear.)

Always put an ID tag on both the outside and the inside of your bag. Luggage thieves will quickly rip off any outside tags, but the inside tags may help you recover something if your luggage is stolen.

When you fill in your ID tags, never write down your home address. Yes, you're going out of town, but why advertise it?

Always use your office address, or simply list a phone number. Some airport criminals have no intention of stealing your bags at the airport. They actually want you to leave town, on time, *with* your bags. They're after a much bigger prize: the contents of your house. Police statistics report all break-ins as home burglaries, but many were initiated as airport crimes in which the homeowners or residents were unwitting participants.

HAVE A SEAT

Whether you're headed to a gate or the VIP lounge (assuming you're a member), another important principle applies: It's not just the flight, it's the *seat*.

Not long ago, the airlines eliminated advance boarding passes. Too many no-shows. But although they didn't eliminate advance seat assignments, they did restrict the number of seats they will allocate in advance for any one flight.

On many airlines, the cap on prior seat assignments runs at about 60 percent of the total number of seats available on a flight. This is an arbitrary figure and can often be overridden by phoning savvy reservations agents.

Which seat do *you* want? Most folks will tell you to get the exit row or a bulkhead seat. Each has its positives and negatives.

But on virtually every aircraft in the air, there are other secret coach seats that the airlines will never tell you about. These seats can actually be better than business-class or even first-class seats, in terms of comfort, privacy, or ease of movement. The airlines tend to make these seats part of the 40 percent they do not allocate in advance.

To protect yourself, you can always ask for an exit row or bulkhead seat. But then plan on getting to the airport in time to get one of the secret seats.

Before I tell you more about the secret seats, let me address the totally overrated concept of window seats. Their only benefit comes on a late-night red-eye flight when you want to lean up against the window. What other possible benefit is there to a window seat?

First, what are you going to look at for six hours? A window seat limits your options. You're essentially trapped for the entire duration of the flight, unless you want to inconvenience your fellow passengers by crawling over them to get to a lavatory.

You can forget about being first off the plane. And if you're last on, you face another uncomfortable and awkward moment as you climb over your seatmates. However, if you prefer to follow Neil Livingston's advice (see Chapter 1), then go ahead and opt for a window seat.

Sitting in an aisle seat requires only two cautions:

1. You run the risk of severe bruising by rogue beverage carts in the aisles.

2. When the plane lands and the captain turns off the seat belt sign, you need to immediately jump up and grab the latch of the overhead bin directly above you. Items *do* shift in flight, and if you aren't first to open the bin, you'll be first to be hit with stuff flying out of it.

Now, back to secret seats. Some statistics: Seven hundred thousand airline seats go unsold every day. Besides the aspects of unearned revenue, airlines hold back the secret seats until they absolutely have to sell them—or until you walk up and ask for one!

Here are just a few of them:

If you'll be flying on an American Airlines 767, there are two secret seats on domestic flights: 17H and 17J. On international flights, these two seats, located across from the galley and actually curtained off as a special section, are designated as "crew rest" seats.

However, on domestic flights, they can be sold as revenue seats. They are also special coach seats: they recline farther, they have footrests, and they give you more space in front because they have their own bulkhead.

Many American flight attendants were angry at me after I disclosed the secret of seats 17H and J on both the *Today* show and *The Oprah Winfrey Show.* But the fact remains that they are revenue seats on domestic flights, and passengers should be allowed to request them. One hint: Since the first edition of this book came out, American has generally restricted assigning seats 17H and J until "airport check-in." Translation: Get to the airport early and ask there. You have a better chance of getting those seats at the airport than over the phone.

If you're flying on an American 757, there isn't a special secret section for you, but there are secret coach seats. Ask for either seat 10A or seat 10F. These are window seats on either the left or the right side of the aircraft.

What makes them so special? Nothing, except that on these planes there is no seat 9A or 9F. Result: You're in a window seat, but you're not trapped. And because there's no seat in front of you, there's no tray table to impale your stomach. You have unlimited legroom, and if you need to get up during the flight, you don't have to crawl or climb to the right or left. Instead, you simply get up and move *forward.*

A similar situation applies on Delta's and United's 757s, but the seat numbers can be different. Look for seat 20A on Delta's 757s or seat 8A on United's 757s.

On Northwest's 757s, look for seat 16F or 15E.

If you're about to board a US Airways 737-200, look for seat 11A or 11F. Again, like the 757s, there is no seat 10A or 10F. Result: serious legroom.

Flying on a United 767, Model 200, and lucky enough to be in business class? Ask for either seat 10A or seat 10F. These are single business-class aisle seats, with petite desk areas on their sides. Very cool.

Overseas, there are also secret seats, and they might really surprise you.

On Swissair MD-11s, you want seat 21A, B, or C.

On British Airways 747s, the real surprise seats are at the back of the plane, and they're center seats at that.

Am I nuts? No. Read on.

The seats you want on those 747s are 51J or 52J on the right side of the wide-body, or 51B or 52C on the left side. Why? Because of the curvature of the plane toward the rear, there are only two seats in each of these side rows: an aisle seat and a middle seat. There is *no* window seat. The result: You have extra room for your legs (you can stretch out almost sideways) and more room for your carry-on bags!

Remember, virtually every aircraft type has them. So when you make your reservations, always ask the agent what aircraft type will be serving your flight. A DC-9 is different from an MD-80; a 757 is completely different from a 767 in the configuration of its seats and aisles.

You can also ask for, and get, seat charts from just about every airline. They are either printed in the airlines' schedule books or visible on their websites. The Official Airline Guide Schedules also feature pages and pages of seat charts for each airline and aircraft type.

Now, let's say you can't get a secret seat. Your scenario is even worse; when you get to the gate, you discover that the only seats left are center seats, and passengers are already boarding the plane. Are you out of luck? Not necessarily.

Exhibiting your best behavior, go to the gate agent and ask, "Could you possibly tell me whether there are any two people flying in coach with the same last name?"

Chances are excellent that at least one couple on the plane is sitting, for example, in seats 15A and 15C, desperately hoping that *no one* will take that middle seat. And that is precisely the seat you want. Ask the agent at the gate—as long as they have only center seats left—if you could have 15B.

Then, when you get to that row, chances are also excellent that the couple will offer to switch with you, and you will get either the aisle seat or the window seat. (Caution: There's always the possibility that the two people in row 15 already hate each other or always ask for the seats they're in and do not want to switch. Still, I'll take my chances.)

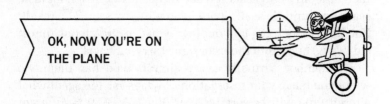

OK, NOW YOU'RE ON
THE PLANE

Let's presume you got the seat you want. Don't get too comfortable. The plane hasn't pushed back yet.

Every time I'm sitting on a plane that hasn't reversed back from the jetway, I'm reminded of a high school science experiment. Start with a glass of water, absolutely full. Carefully, drop by drop, continue to fill the glass. The water is then actually *above* the rim of the glass, held there through surface tension. Continue to add water, drop by drop, until suddenly the last drop breaks the tension. Ripples appear and water flows over the side of the glass.

The airlines have been adding those little drops of symbolic water to our schedules for years.

But there's a whole lot more than surface tension out there. And when it breaks, it explodes.

Airline scheduling—or the lack of it—makes us angry. And we have a right to be.

Most savvy travelers have come to the painful realization that airline schedules are nothing more than attempts at clever marketing on the part of the airlines, and nothing less than wishful thinking on the part of some passengers who actually believe them.

Basic math will tell you that if there are two active takeoff runways at Los Angeles International Airport, and thirty-five departures are listed in airline schedules for 8:00 A.M., thirty-three airlines are, to some extent, bending the truth if not outright lying.

Basic common sense will also tell you that if you publish a schedule that says you will be flying your planes between two slot-controlled airports and claiming a forty-minute turnaround time for each of your planes, you are either lying or in denial.

Here are two examples: the American Eagle operation out of Miami and TED, the "new" airline operated by United, with mostly former United Shuttle routes in Los Angeles and San Francisco.

In Miami, the Eagle operation almost always resembles a chaotic refugee center. Disgruntled passengers are trying helplessly to deal with late, delayed, or canceled flights. It's bad enough that when you finally get to your aircraft, you notice with alarm that the pilot looks about age seventeen and his name is Skippy.

On virtually any given day, the Eagle folks are competing for the title of the world's largest collection of misconnects—harried travelers who never have a chance at making their connecting flights.

In Los Angeles and San Francisco, the crowded TED terminals often resemble Saigon in April 1975. It's a "last flight out" panic scene. Passengers are still bumped and swear they will never go through this ordeal again. And yet, thanks to the power of both the American and the United frequent-flier programs, these same people, expecting the worst, usually return for more abuse. And they often get it. To its credit, United spent more than $30 million to improve Terminal 8 at LAX, and a reconfiguration has created 43 percent more floor space. But it's still not enough.

THE FLIGHT THAT NEVER WAS

One frequent United flier proposed this challenge to me: In a given week, if I flew five round-trips between Los Angeles and San Francisco on the United Shuttle (now TED), I would be lucky if I took off and arrived on time on even one of those five trips. And that's presuming the flights actually weren't canceled.

Guess who won the bet? The other morning I was in San Francisco and had an 8:30 breakfast meeting at an airport hotel in Los Angeles. So I booked the 6:50 A.M. United Shuttle flight from San Francisco to LAX. Of course, when I made my reservation, they asked for my phone number. (I always find this a ludicrous exercise, because no one ever calls me.)

In any case, I arrived at 6:00 A.M. at SFO, handed my ticket to the skycap, showed him my identification and my luggage, and answered all the appropriate security questions. He looked at my ticket and laughed. "Well, you picked the loser."

The loser?

"Yup," he replied. "This flight is always the loser. They seem to cancel it every morning. They already protected you on the 7:30 flight." I love the word *protected*.

How was I protected? When did they cancel the flight?

"Well," the United skycap shrugged, "hours ago . . . maybe even last night." I went inside and was told to go to the gate to get my boarding pass.

The gate scene was another Little Saigon. A few hundred people, tired and angry, had started their day by beating the sun, only to be beaten by the airline.

I gave my ticket to the gate agent. She handed it back to me. My lucky day: a center seat in coach. "Sorry, that's all we have."

"Let me ask you a question," I began. "Why did you cancel this flight? Was it weather? A mechanical?"

"Sir," she deadpanned, "the FAA canceled this flight."

I'm usually the first on my block to blame the FAA for many of the air safety problems that still confront us, but her answer made absolutely no sense.

"The FAA canceled this flight?"

"That's right."

"Excuse me, but unless I'm terribly mistaken, the only time I've ever known the FAA to cancel a flight is when they've grounded an entire airline or after a plane has hit a mountain. *Then* the FAA cancels the flight. Miss, there is no way you can stand there and blame the FAA for canceling this flight. I understand you cancel this flight all the time."

This struck a chord.

"Well, actually, *you people* made us cancel this flight."

She was changing her story, and this was getting good.

"Us?" I laughed. "How did we do this?"

"Frequent business travelers demand that we schedule an early flight and so we do."

How that translated into blaming us escaped me. "Let me see if I'm understanding you. You're saying that we forced you to publish an unrealistic schedule, so you could then cancel the flight and make us angry?"

She saw no humor in this.

"Sir, if you keep this up, I'm going to have to call security."

"You're going to call security because you don't want to answer my question, or because you can't? Or because you know the real answer and it makes you uncomfortable? And what will I be charged with? Somehow violating the airline code of misinformation?"

Soon a supervisor appeared. He couldn't—or wouldn't— answer the question, either. But he didn't call security. He just called the flight. I boarded, sat with my knees touching my chest in my center seat, and missed my meeting in Los Angeles. But I received a few hundred bonus miles.

OK. So much for unrealistic airline schedules.

But wait. There's more. Remember the American Eagle example in Miami—or, for that matter, the United Express operation at O'Hare, or the Delta Connection out of Atlanta?

The commuter operations, in and of themselves, contribute to delays. Let's look at the numbers. Because of the old Federal Railway Labor Act and some scope clauses of the pilot unions, the airlines have been expanding the sizes and frequencies of their regional subsidiaries. The regional fleets have grown in the numbers of aircraft being flown and operated. And, coincidentally, this has been where the most expansion has been occurring in recent years. Due to the act and union scope clauses that limit the size of a regional carrier's aircraft, the regionals are severely limited in the number of people an aircraft can hold.

That's a surefire recipe for delays at major airports. Why? The number of aircraft being flown has increased, but the planes are smaller in size. Yet the same flight rules apply. Each of these smaller planes takes up the same amount of protected taxi space and takeoff separation when it is on the ground, and it takes the same amount of protected airspace while it is airborne.

It will also occupy a terminal gate at each airport. Some airlines argue that they can park more of the smaller planes at the gates, but I haven't seen operational proof of this. At each gate, smaller aircraft are taking up space that could be utilized by larger aircraft.

Why is this happening? The major airlines' reason is money. Pay scales are much lower at the regional, commuter level. The airlines like the smaller planes, and, quite frankly, the pilot unions like them as well. They insist that if the airlines want to fly larger planes, the pilots have to receive a substantial upgrade in pay. The result: continued congestion at the airports.

One airport—San Francisco, otherwise known as the gateway to gridlock—has at least recognized this problem. Think about this statistic *before* flying to or from San Francisco: Current figures show that one out of every four passengers flying out of SFO will not leave the gate at the scheduled departure time. At SFO, aircraft that carry fewer than thirty passengers account for a sizable 18 percent of the airport's takeoffs and landings but only 3 percent of the total number of passengers going to or through SFO. The airport has petitioned the FAA to limit the number of those commuter flights. The airlines, of course, are fighting the petition. Don't hold your breath.

My argument is that it all starts with fudging the schedule.

On one occasion, I was flying to New York from Los Angeles. American Airlines Flight 10 left LAX at 10:00 P.M. and was scheduled to arrive at New York's JFK Airport at 6:07 the next morning. When the red-eye landed at 6:00 A.M., the pilot announced, "Will the flight attendants please prepare for an early arrival?"

Early compared to what?

Ten years ago, the same flight, departing at the same time, was scheduled to arrive in New York at 5:44 A.M. By 1980 standards, we had arrived sixteen minutes late.

Yet officially we had arrived seven minutes early; the flight arrived ahead of the time printed on the official schedule. The real issue is truth in scheduling.

To be sure, the numbers of delays in the air and on the ground are high. In 2003, for example, 17.19 percent of flights arriving at JFK airport in New York were delayed and 14.91 percent of departures were delayed, according to the

U.S. Department of Transportation. And the American air-traffic control system is still suffering the effects of the air-traffic controllers' strike more than two decades ago.

But ever since 1987, the DOT began requiring airlines to report their on-time performance. For years, a flight has been considered "on time" if it departs from or arrives at its gate within fifteen minutes of the scheduled time.

Since the reporting rule went into effect, a number of airlines have been playing with their schedules—adding extra minutes to the official flight times. However, because so many of the airlines have padded their flight times on the schedules, a majority of the on-time performance reports and the final statistics are meaningless for most travelers, and those that get reported do not reflect efficiency in air travel.

I remember an investigative report that the General Accounting Office (GAO) gave to Congress in the mid-1980s. At issue was whether the airlines had adjusted their flight schedules unrealistically, and whether on-time performance statistics reflected improved airline efficiency.

The last year when travelers got even a semblance of a realistic schedule was 1980. A flight from Washington to Chicago took two hours and fifteen minutes. The present schedule shows two hours and forty-five minutes. The airlines claim they're on time, but even the fudged times are exceeded by the airlines more often than not.

Another problem that the GAO discovered was the number of flights delayed or canceled for mechanical reasons. Officially, mechanical problems exempt a flight from being included in on-time performance stats. It's an important exemption, because of safety considerations. On one hand, it could certainly be argued that no one really wants airlines flying broken planes just to support an on-time performance percentage.

However, the GAO investigation found that, although

the DOT "monitors the number of flights excluded . . . from the data for mechanical problems, it does not verify that these flights had mechanical problems."

The most recent DOT statistics show that thousands of flights are excluded from on-time data each month because of apparent mechanical problems. An obvious interpretation: There are a lot of phony "mechanicals." (Remember my canceled SFO-LAX United Shuttle flight?)

To be fair, there *are* real mechanicals, and let's be honest: If they are discovered during maintenance checks, we are thankful.

I am reminded of the time when President Richard Nixon flew to Moscow to meet with President Leonid Brezhnev. After the meetings in the Kremlin, Nixon was scheduled to fly to Kiev. And because of international protocol, he would be flying on Aeroflot within the Soviet Union, not on Air Force One.

U.S. officials were more than a little worried about the safety of the Aeroflot planes. But protocol was protocol. When the Moscow meetings concluded, Nixon headed for the airport, where he boarded the Russian aircraft. The rest of the plane was loaded, the doors were closed, and then the plane sat on the tarmac. And never moved.

Soon, nervous Russian officials approached the plane, and the door was opened. A high-level, embarrassed Soviet military officer walked down the aisle where the president was sitting. With the officer was a trembling Soviet Air Force colonel. Through an interpreter, the military officer addressed Nixon. "Mr. President," he stumbled nervously, "this is the colonel in charge of this flight. We have discovered this plane has broken and cannot fly. What would you want us to do with him?"

Nixon looked up and, without hesitation, responded, "Promote him."

The Soviet officer believed Nixon's answer had been improperly translated. "Mr. President, may I ask you again. This is the colonel in charge of this flight, and the plane is broken. What shall we do with him?"

Again, Nixon answered, "Promote him."

This time, the officer knew he had heard correctly, but he was still in shock.

"Mr. President, why would we want to promote him if the plane doesn't work?"

"Because," Nixon answered, in a rare moment of spontaneous humor, "the colonel discovered the plane was broken *on the ground.*"

Yes, we should be thankful for mechanical delays, even during moments of great embarrassment.

You can believe it was a real mechanical in Moscow that day, just as it was a real mechanical at New York's LaGuardia Airport when now-defunct Eastern Airlines tried to pull a publicity stunt.

Eastern had decided to honor one of its most loyal business travelers, an insurance executive named Michael Cohen. Right before he was about to take his two-thousandth trip on Eastern, the airline announced that it would award Cohen a special commemorative plaque.

The airline alerted the media for the special presentation. However, the plane—which was to fly from Miami to New York—broke down before Cohen could board, and his flight was delayed nearly three hours. To make matters worse, the embarrassed airline towed away the broken plane and replaced it with another that had been scheduled to fly to San Juan, thereby angering the Puerto Rico–bound passengers.

Mechanicals, real or otherwise, contribute to making the published airline schedules laughable.

There's an additional rub to the scheduling scam. Airlines that pad their schedules are somewhat reluctant to do so. If a flight is scheduled at two hours and forty-five minutes instead of two hours and fifteen minutes, pilots have to be paid based on the scheduled time.

Commercial pilots are limited, by FAA rules, to a certain number of flight hours per month. Some airlines are finding that the public relations gains they might be enjoying by announcing improved on-time performance are being outweighed by a shortage of flight crew members toward the end of each month. Ironically, flight cancellations can result.

Finally, there's the problem of language. The next time you are advised to "prepare for an early arrival," you might want to remind the offending airline that our clocks are set ahead only once a year.

In the most recent report on flight operations in the United States, the DOT found that, of 2,322,245 flight operations:

39,180 flights were canceled.

440,538 flights arrived late.

One in five flights either was canceled or arrived late. Not good.

The delay statistics are just getting worse. And the airlines are doing little to fix it. They continue to schedule flights at times when most airports cannot physically handle the traffic. I arbitrarily picked the 12 noon to 1 P.M. time period on a Wednesday, at O'Hare. Not the busiest "push" time of the day, but busy enough. According to airport officials, the greatest number of planes the airport could handle during that period (takeoffs and landings) is 97. Then I checked current airline schedules and found that 110 planes were slated to land or take off in that time period. It's absurd.

If the airlines are truly concerned about air rage among

passengers, they need to address the underlying causes of many of these problems. Phony cancellations are among the main ingredients for air rage.

My unanswered questions to the top management of American, United, and Delta are these:

- Whatever happened to honesty and basic common sense?

- Why do you not instill in your ground staff the ability, as well as the confidence, to tell the truth and to use basic intuition and discretion in dealing with your customers?

- Who told a United gate agent that it was official policy to lie—to say that the FAA canceled the flight?

WHAT DO YOU DO NOW?

You already know why I hate e-tickets. A delay or a cancellation only compounds the problem if you're not holding a paper ticket.

However, if you get to the airport and your flight is delayed *before* you board, do *not* stand in line. Run, don't walk, to the nearest pay phone or use your cell phone. Call the airline's 800 number and ask, on the phone, to have Rule 240 applied (see page 181).

If you've already boarded a plane and a mechanical delay is announced, you've got to think a few things through.

First, are you flying on an airline based at this airport? If you are, your best bet is to stay on the plane. Home-based planes are first in line for mechanical help.

Second, how much duty time has the flight crew logged for that shift? Did the cockpit/cabin crew start the workday on your flight, or did they join it as part of their schedule? Ask. Even an additional thirty-minute delay needed to fix a mechanical can make a crew illegal to fly. If you can get a heads-up on that information as soon as a delay is announced, you'll get a head start toward getting off that plane and being rebooked.

Here's another question to ask. If you're at an airport where your airline is not based, not only will you have to change aircraft types but your crew will also change . . . and additional delays will ensue.

But if your flight is operated by an airline not based at that airport and the clock tells you it's a peak push time for scheduled flights, don't worry about the crew. Worry about *you.* You can do one of two things—or both. First, if the plane is equipped with an airphone, ask a flight attendant for the two-digit toll-free code that immediately connects you to the airline's reservation agents, and get yourself protected right away. (If you're still at the gate, most airlines will allow you to use your cell phone.) Get on the phone, then get off the plane.

This works as long as your flight isn't the last flight of the day. If it *is* the last flight and the delay looks like it will cancel the flight, start the paperwork while you're still at your seat. Protect yourself with a hotel room for the night, possible meal vouchers, some phone calls, and so on.

If no acceptable flights are available, the airline must refund your money if you request it. This policy applies even if you are holding a "nonrefundable" ticket.

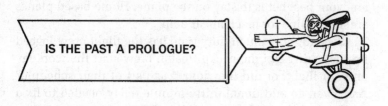

IS THE PAST A PROLOGUE?

The absolute worst delay in history happened on September 11, 2001, in places like Newfoundland and Halifax, Nova Scotia, where dozens of aircraft were grounded for nearly five days. It was the one delay we all tolerated. We had no choice. And perhaps it's no surprise that many of the folks who found themselves grounded in Canada received a blessing in disguise in the tragic events of that day. New friendships were formed. Alumni groups started. On one Delta flight, money was collected for a special scholarship fund for the children of Gander, in Newfoundland. There were even a few marriages directly related to the forced grounding in Canada. It was a terrible but understandable delay.

Most delays, however, are not understandable. Let's not forget what life was like for air travelers during the winter of 1999 and the summer of 2000. They combined to form an apex of frustration and the summit of a mountain of ill will.

Just about everyone in Detroit remembers January 1999. An organizational implosion occurred at the Detroit airport when Northwest Airlines simply became paralyzed. Thousands of passengers were stranded, locked, imprisoned inside their aircraft—many for as long as nine hours.

The cruel and unusual punishment at the airport resulted in a tidal wave of anger manifested by a legislative proposal to finally create an airline passengers' bill of rights.

No less than thirteen bills were introduced in Congress

to force the airlines to be legally responsible for keeping the promises they all too often make and then ignore.

Soon, the airline lobbyists were in full battle mode. They passionately argued to Congress that the airlines were in a much better position to develop, communicate, and implement a series of passenger rights, and no federal mandate was needed.

The lobbyists prevailed, and in time the airlines published their own set of guidelines for customer care. Virtually every statement was surrounded with qualifiers and disclaimers. "Endeavor," "try," and "best efforts" were among the words used to protect the airlines.

And not surprisingly, in June 2000, an interim report from the inspector general of the U.S. Department of Transportation indicated that the airlines, as a whole, were not living up to their promises. Coincidentally, the report was issued in the midst of the most frustrating, anger-inducing period in U.S. air travel history.

WHAT I DID IN THE SUMMER OF 2000

For those who traveled the unfriendly skies during the unfortunate millennium summer of 2000, conditions were almost bad enough to make them stop flying forever.

It was possibly the worst summer for delays and cancellations since air travel began. To discover how really bad it was, I dispatched myself on an ambitious journey.

For two days, I crisscrossed the country on eight separate flights and six different airlines. My mission: to determine whether any airline would be on time. And perhaps more important: to see whether any of them would tell the truth about it.

To give the airlines the benefit of the doubt, I flew first on a Wednesday and Thursday; these are not heavy traffic days. There was no bad weather. With one exception, which wasn't planned, I flew either to or from airlines' headquarters cities or to hub airports they solidly control.

For two days, on a journey that took forty-one hours, from early Wednesday morning until Thursday evening, I virtually lived on airplanes and at airports. Here's what happened.

On Wednesday at 6:00 A.M., I checked in early for the first flight of the trip: Washington, D.C., to Dallas–Fort Worth, on American Airlines. The weather was clear, the sun was shining, and, not surprisingly, every flight on the departure board at Washington's Reagan Airport was posted as being "on time."

Precisely at 7:35 A.M., American Flight 489 pushed back from the gate, and I was off to Dallas. It was an uneventful flight, except for one thing. I arrived in Dallas ten minutes early!

OK, that was good news. And that was the only good news that day.

I then transferred to United Airlines Flight 1604 to Chicago. The flight was scheduled to depart Dallas–Fort Worth for Chicago at 11:15 A.M. The departure board showed an on-time arrival, but when I got to the check-in counter, the agent said the departure would be a few minutes late. How late?

"It will leave at 11:30," she said. OK, so far, so good. A slight delay. And the reason for the delay?

"Weather," she said.

I checked the gate. No plane. I checked the departure board again. It still said 11:15. Then I checked the arrivals board. The plane arriving from Denver for our flight to Chicago wouldn't even be landing until 11:24 A.M.

When I got to the agent at the gate, she said the delay was

because of crew problems. There was no weather problem. And, oh yes, there was no plane.

The only thing we could agree on was that the plane would be late. But how late? It depended on where you got your information. According to the agent, my United flight would now be leaving twenty-three minutes late, at 11:38. (The lesson here: The departure board is not your friend. To put it kindly, it lies all the time. At most, the times listed are best-case, hoped-for times, not real times. In this case, the board wasn't even close.)

A listing for another flight was downright ludicrous. A separate United aircraft coming in from Chicago was listed as landing late (at 12:30 P.M.). But the flight from Dallas to Denver—using the same gate and the same plane—was still listed as an on-time departure at 12:30!

We finally took off for Chicago an hour later, which meant, of course, that we landed late at Chicago's O'Hare Airport. To many passengers on the flight, the delay was not a surprise. They expected it.

When the plane finally landed, the departing passengers were thrust into the chaos of Terminal C. The area was a tableau of frustration and despair. Some passengers were downright angry.

Bill Memefee, a United frequent flier, was steaming. "I am going to Wichita right now. . . . I checked at noon today through the Internet, and United said it was running on time. Then, when I was walking to the gate, the arrivals board showed Grand Rapids inbound flight arriving at 3:47, baggage inbound, Flight 1027, which is the flight in-bound from Grand Rapids going to Wichita. My flight was scheduled to leave at 3:14. But the departure board still says 'on time.' The gate agent tells me it's on time and I say it can't be. I go to check in at the Premier Mileage Plus check-in desk. The lady says it's on time, and I say it can't be; downstairs is showing 'delayed.' She checks the nose numbers and shows a push-back from Grand Rapids at 3:01 Chicago time."

"Now," he began laughing, "if you have a very fast plane that gets here in thirteen minutes, can unload baggage and everything else, then you are on time."

In reality, Memefee's flight was running about an hour late at best. "The real problem isn't the delay," he fumed. "It's that people lie to you. Why can't they just be honest and make it real and fair? That's all I want, I don't expect any special service or anything else. I just like to know what is going on, and I think there is not another soul in this building that wouldn't like the same thing."

The airlines claim that they are giving out accurate information, and they blame an antiquated air-traffic control system. And they blame weather. (To be fair, the weather in the early part of the summer in 2000 was terrible.)

Still, the airlines argue when I suggest that, with about thirty-five planes scheduled to leave from LAX's two runways at 8:00 A.M., thirty-three planes are going to be late. "No," claims Air Transport Association spokesperson David Fuscus. "They're *scheduled* to push back from the gate at 8:00 A.M., then they have to get in line and then they have to take off. That's what airline scheduling means. It doesn't mean wheels up at 8:00 A.M."

U.S. Senator Ron Wyden (D-Oregon) strongly disagrees with that "on time" definition. "I think it's particularly outrageous for airlines to go scheduling above their capacity," he said. "If you take an ideal situation where the weather is clear, there are a maximum number of runways available, they're still scheduling beyond their capacity and that's just not right."

Wyden may have a point. Consider this: At Dallas–Fort Worth, an incredible fifty-seven planes are scheduled to take off within ten minutes, beginning at 6:00 P.M. every day—twenty-two more than the top capacity of the entire airport!

There are some other capacity issues, otherwise known (in football terms) as "intentional grounding." Wyden calls the cancellations of some flights phony. When passenger loads don't materialize, flight cancellations due to "mechanical reasons" coincidentally show up.

"For the life of me," he argued, "I can't figure out why the airlines are unwilling to offer their passengers the same consumer protections that apply everywhere else in the economy. The local movie theater doesn't arbitrarily cancel the three o'clock showing on the weekend because they don't have enough people who bought tickets. But the airlines have been doing that for years."

And finally, there's the flow of information. "There are all sorts of problems about delays," said Wyden. "But the one problem the airlines can do something about is giving the public straight information, and the fact of the matter is: The inspector general of the U.S. Department of Transportation found that some airlines knew about delays four hours before departure and yet they wouldn't tell the flying public. That's just inexcusable."

OK, we're now in Chicago, and there are lots of delayed flights. Passenger service counters are jammed. We're scheduled on United Flight 255 to Denver. A 3:30 departure; the board is showing that it's "on time." We head to the gate. It's a full flight, but somehow the agents are able to board everyone on the huge 777 on time. And within ten minutes of the scheduled departure, we actually push back from the gate.

In airline terms, we're on time. In real terms, we're now right on schedule for waiting on the tarmac. And we do, for forty minutes.

We arrive late in Denver. Things only get worse. While we were flying there, to connect to another United flight to Seattle (a 7:30 P.M. departure), United canceled the 4:30 P.M. departure from Denver to Seattle, making some travelers very unhappy.

When we land—late—lines of travelers are everywhere. A quick look at the departure board is a depressing experience. On one screen, out of eighteen departures, only three are on time. The rest are delayed or canceled.

As expected, our 7:30 P.M. departure is moved back—twice—and we leave late for the third time that day. Some of my fellow passengers have been flying even longer than I have that day. Many of them were rerouted to United by other airlines because their original airlines were even *later*!

We landed in Seattle late. We had just enough time to catch a few hours' sleep before the next day's round of flights began.

Day two started at 5:00 A.M. in Seattle. Again, the weather was surprisingly perfect for our 6:15 A.M. flight on Alaska Airlines to San Francisco (SFO). And the weather had to be perfect on this leg for an on-time departure and arrival.

Miraculously, it was. This is a surprise, considering that SFO has one of the worst on-time performance ratings of major U.S. airports. The airport is plagued with fog conditions and with two runways that are too close together.

Smart travelers claim they will do anything to avoid SFO. But on this day, there were no problems. My America West flight to Phoenix was right on time. Even the gate agents were surprised. So were the passengers. I was now two for two. After landing in Phoenix, I jumped onto a Southwest flight for my short hop to Las Vegas. Would the third flight be the charm?

It was. Another on-time landing in Las Vegas. But that's where my lucky streak ended. I still had to get home to Los

Angeles. The American flight was delayed nearly three hours for a flight that lasted only forty-eight minutes.

Of the eight flights I took, four were late. The United flight to Los Angeles was delayed an hour. Folks at that departure gate weren't happy; the United flight to San Francisco was canceled.

The final score? Remember, I flew on days that weren't full-capacity days. I flew in good weather, and before the escalation of United Airlines' crew-related delays. The departure boards never told the real story, and gate agents gave inaccurate and misleading information.

The moral to this story: Keep your options open. Look at the departure boards to find the lie, and look at the arrival boards to prove it. And do a little homework before you leave for the airport.

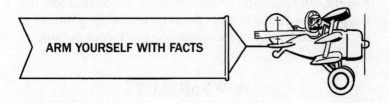

ARM YOURSELF WITH FACTS

Start with your initial reservation. Each month, the DOT publishes a list of the worst-offending delayed flights—their flight numbers, airlines, and routes.

Check the weather at your destination. Based on the most recent DOT report, if you're flying between Washington's Dulles Airport and Seattle, you might want to avoid United Flight 219, which has been late more than 14 percent of the time, although this is certainly not the worst record. (The average delay is forty-five minutes.) You might want to bring a copy of *War and Peace* onto America West Flight 2882 between Phoenix and Fort Lauderdale. It's late 93 percent of the time, and its average delay is fifty-one minutes. Another delay winner is US Airways Flight 1820 between Philadelphia and Boston. That flight is late 81 percent of the time and has a fifty-three-minute average delay. Many more flights are listed. You can easily access this information at the Aviation Consumer Action Project home page (www.acap1971.org) or through the Department of Transportation.

Among other useful on-time websites, check Flight Arrivals and Departures (www.thetrip.com/flightstatus). To check on weather delays, log onto the Air Traffic Control System Command Center (www.fly.faa.gov).

Remember, two hundred thousand flights leave airports each day. Each airport has it own way of calculating departure times. However, for purposes of record keeping, the on-time departure clock starts when the plane's doors close. This clock continues unless the pilot returns for mechanical reasons and *only* if the plane returns for mechanical reasons. If a plane pushes back from the runway and then returns to the terminal for any other reason, the clock does not stop.

HOW BAD IS IT?

A recent survey found that most people spend five years of their life waiting in lines and six months sitting at traffic lights.

And lest you think delays are bad only in the United States, consider this: Lufthansa reports that its aircraft spent more than 5,200 hours in holding patterns over Frankfurt, Munich, and Düsseldorf in 1999.

If the average executive spends an estimated twenty-nine days a year on business travel, he or she spends a great deal of that time waiting at airports or stuck in airplanes. In fact, the average business traveler spends twenty-one days a year simply locked in transit.

Here's an even scarier statistic. In 2000 alone, delays on flights within Europe rose a whopping 30 percent. If you total up the delay time caused by computer failures and air traffic controller and other labor strikes, the total would be fifty-seven *years*!

And if you think that's a long time, fasten your seat belts. A report by the inspector general of the DOT found that the airlines had underestimated the amount of time lost by passengers on U.S. flights by a total of 247 *years*! The DOT report said that 130 million minutes of extra travel time were added to airline schedules between 1988 and 1999—and that was *before* anyone was counting time lost because of delays.

At U.S. airports, delays are no longer seasonal. They are daily. And according to the DOT, the average "dwell time" at airports is now nearly seventy minutes—a new high.

But not only can you check your flight to determine its average on-time performance (obviously, a flight that is an hour late 97 percent of the time will be late for you as well), you can also identify—systemwide—the worst times to try to leave each airport.

Some examples are obvious. Don't count on an on-time departure or arrival from Chicago's O'Hare between 5:00 and 6:00 P.M. on weekdays. National, in Washington, D.C., is about the same. Between 6:00 and 7:00 P.M., it's a real mess. But Dulles is actually worse; 25 percent of all flights leave there late.

At other airports, the worst times to leave might surprise you. At Denver and at Dallas–Fort Worth, the worst time to leave is between 8:00 and 9:00 P.M. New York's Kennedy Airport, which has the fewest flights of the three New York airports, also has the highest concentration of specific time-block flights. Between 6:00 and 10:00 P.M., international flights all compete for taxi and runway space.

LaGuardia Airport, also in New York, was congested beyond capacity several years ago. Yet in 2000, airlines added 200 more flights a day, and they want to add 400 *more*. On an average day, more than 1,390 flights would then land or take off at LaGuardia. And it's only getting worse at LaGuardia. Delta's Song now flies from LaGuardia. So does JetBlue.

Delays are system-related, so LaGuardia can be blamed for a lot of the mess at other airports. It is now the source of one-fourth of all U.S. flight delays. All but two of American's most delayed flights began or ended each day at LaGuardia.

The math is ridiculous. For LaGuardia to process that many flights, it has to cram in eighty-four takeoffs or landings each hour—a physical impossibility.

What can you do about delays? You can protect yourself in a number of ways.

First: Try to book the first flight of the day. If you're flying from an airline's main operation center or hub city, there's a good chance the plane is already on the ground. If you're flying from another city, there's an equally good chance that the aircraft arrived as the last flight the evening before and is ready. Book anything other than the first flight and your chances of a delay increase dramatically.

Second: Get a paper ticket. (However, keep in mind that it can cost $8 to $50 for a paper ticket.)

Third: Know the flight schedules of the route you're on. What airline has the next flight? And the next? If you arm yourself with that information, that's one less phone call or line you have to endure. You can react quickly.

Fourth: Apply Rule 240 (see page 181). It's your best friend.

Fifth: Be a good reporter. Take notes that include the trail as well as the chronology of misinformation.

Sixth: Understand your own status at the airline. If you're a frequent flier, the airline will work that much harder to keep you happy. And whether you fly seldom or often, understand that the price you pay for your ticket often will determine the care you receive if your flight is delayed or canceled.

Who's first when a flight cancels? Full-fare first-class passengers who are members of an airline's frequent-flier program. You bought a discount fare on the Internet? Unless you know your rights, find a seat and sit in it at the terminal. You may be there a while. Many airlines—especially those in financial difficulty, which these days can mean just about all the legacy carriers—will do anything they can *not* to interline their passengers—put them on another carrier's flight—when there is a delay. Reason: They don't want to lose any revenue. So invoke Rule 240. Insist on it. The airline will never openly volunteer that remedy. As an example, right before TWA was bought by American, the airline made an internal policy for airport gate agents that if a passenger bought a ticket from a discount online broker such as Priceline.com and the flight was delayed or canceled, the airline would often make you wait six hours before invoking Rule 240. *Ouch!*

Seventh: You may have status based on where you bought your ticket. In 2000, delays had become so bad that one enterprising online travel e-tailer used to make a guarantee. Biztravel.com started offering refunds for canceled or late flights on American, Continental, US Airways, British Airways, and Air France. Registered users who booked their tickets through the Biztravel.com website would receive $100 if the flight was delayed more than thirty minutes, and $200 for flights arriving more than an hour behind schedule. For flights delayed more than an hour or canceled for reasons other than mechanical problems, Biztravel.com issued a full refund, even if passengers were finally able to use the ticket.

If there was ever an incentive to book online, this one was the best. (Guess what? After supposedly paying out a whopping $1.7 million in penalties under the guarantee, Biztravel.com then revised its deal sharply downward. Instead of receiving $100 for flights 30 minutes late, customers got $25. Flight an hour late? Instead of $200, you got only $50. What does that tell you? Delays are costly, and making guarantees did not incentivize any airline to do better.) The Biztravel.com idea failed miserably as they downsized their offers, and soon Biztravel.com failed miserably—it is now defunct.

Eighth (*but not least*): Understand your legal rights. A number of recent court cases have been resolved firmly on the side of passengers. For years, airlines have tried to have lawsuits dismissed, based solely on the concept of deregulation. The theory is this: Because states can no longer regulate airlines' pricing or scheduling, they cannot have any legal jurisdiction allowing them to enforce any state laws concerning failure to disclose, breach of contract, and so forth.

However, in recent years, the deregulation defense has stumbled. Why? Judges fly, too!

Consider the 168 very angry passengers who were stranded on the tarmac in Milwaukee for six hours on Christmas Eve 1997. United Flight 1536, from Orange County, California, to O'Hare was diverted to Milwaukee's Mitchell Field. Once on the ground, the passengers claimed in their lawsuit, they went without food or functioning restrooms for six hours before their flight was then canceled.

United's attorneys tried for nearly two years to quash the suit. But a Chicago Circuit Court judge let the case proceed. And United, not eager to set any sort of legal precedent by having a class-action lawsuit go against an airline, settled. Each passenger got $500 in cash plus a $500 airline voucher.

In the summer of 2000, when the airline delayed or canceled thousands of flights, the legal cases against United intensified. One particular lawsuit, still pending, sued United for breach of contract and claimed that United, during the summer of 2000, willingly sold tickets on many of its flights, fully knowing that the airline had no intention of operating those flights. And that's *without* weather problems!

Nothing can come close to that one day, in January 1999, at the Detroit airport. It was a horrendous, cold day, but it also was ground zero in the renewed fight for passenger rights.

Improvements have been made at the Detroit airport—specifically, by Northwest—but thousands of angry passengers remain angry.

A friend of mine—a hardworking Northwest counter agent in Detroit who somehow survived the siege of January—called the other day.

"Hey, did you hear our new customer service slogan?" she asked, laughing. "We're not happy until YOU'RE not happy!"

Wait, that's no joke. *We're not happy!*

And while no new federal legislation has been enacted, there are residual rights and tactics that passengers can invoke.

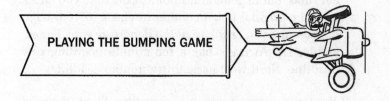

PLAYING THE BUMPING GAME

Your flight is on time, but it's oversold?

Welcome to the wonderful world of bumping, otherwise known as denied boarding compensation (DBC). If you play the game right, it can pay you big dividends.

First, some history. Airline seats are a precious and perishable commodity. Airlines hate to have them empty. And the airlines' sophisticated computer systems have become more accurate in predicting the no-show factor—the 10 to 15 percent of ticketed travelers who simply don't show up for their flights.

The result: Airlines traditionally overbook their flights, sometimes as much as 20 percent, based on the time of year and past years' travel patterns.

When everyone *does* show up, the bump-and-grind games begin.

Almost 800,000 people were bumped from fourteen U.S. airlines in 2003. About 42,000 of these were bumped involuntarily, versus nearly 727,000 who volunteered to take later flights.

Here are the basic rules: If an airline bumps you involuntarily, the DOT requires that airline to cover the cost of your flight, as long as the following conditions apply:

1. You are holding a confirmed reservation *and* a paid ticket.

2. You met the check-in deadline for the flight. This can get a little hairy, so be careful. Each airline has different rules, but in general it's not just the time you check in at the original ticket counter or check in your bags. It's the time you check in *at the departure gate*. For example, US Airways has a ten-minute boarding gate deadline. Northwest has a thirty-minute deadline.

If the airline can get you out on another flight (theirs or someone else's) within an hour of your originally scheduled departure, it owes you nothing. (Translation: Not much to worry about here. I've *never* seen that happen!)

If the airline can get you out between one and two hours of the original departure time, it must reimburse you for the cost of the one-way fare, up to $200. But if it takes them more than two hours, you're entitled to twice the value of your one-way ticket, up to $400.

Once you know the difference between involuntary and voluntary bumping, being bumped can have its finer moments.

Involuntary bumping: You are one of the last to check in, or you never bothered to get an advance seat assignment and the plane is overbooked. Chances are good you're about to get bumped involuntarily. The airlines won't admit this, but if you're flying with only carry-on bags, you stand a better chance of getting bumped, because the airline doesn't have to find and remove your bags before the flight leaves.

Then comes the art, the dance—the finesse, if you will— of the alternative.

Voluntary bumping: Let's say you're holding a ticket for American's Chicago-to-Dallas flight, leaving at 8:00 tomorrow morning. You're going to visit your long-lost Uncle Howie. But the flight is overbooked. When you get to the gate, the airline offers you a free round-trip if you volunteer to give up your seat on the 8:00 A.M. flight and fly later in the day.

Sounds good if it's a Wednesday in early December and you're not in a rush to see Uncle Howie. But before you jump at the free ticket and the later flight, you need to ask some important questions, or Howie will never see you.

Ask: "When is the next flight on which you can guarantee me a *confirmed space* seat?" Don't ever give up a confirmed seat for a standby seat.

Most of the time, your free ticket will be in the form of a voucher that has cash value equal to that of your original ticket. That sounds fair, but once again, some people will be more equal than others. Be careful when accepting that voucher. Be sure to ask, *before* you accept the voucher, whether it is an *unrestricted* voucher. Many vouchers have blackout dates, and some allow only standby travel.

If the wait between flights is long, ask for some other entitlement deals: meals or phone calls (after all, you don't want Uncle Howie to worry).

Now comes the fun part: upping the ante.

In the first scenario, the airline asks for volunteers who will give up their confirmed seats, for which they will be compensated.

But what if there aren't any volunteers? Get ready for an auction.

The DOT mandates the minimum an airline must compensate you when you are involuntarily bumped. But neither a minimum nor a maximum cap is applied to voluntary bumping.

Example: I was on a morning flight to New York. I was already in my seat when the announcement was made that the flight was overbooked and the airline was looking for volunteers. Anyone who volunteered would be given a travel voucher for $500 and a seat on the next flight.

Thirty people jumped up and raced for the exit door. The airline needed only six, and, yes, each got the $500 voucher.

A more rewarding example: A month later, I was on the same flight and the same announcement was made. On this flight, there must have been more experienced travelers, because *no one got up*.

And when no one volunteered, the ante was immediately raised. The voucher offer was increased to $700; still no one moved. Then $900. When the offer was punched again to $1,200, two people got up to claim their prize. But the airline needed four. The voucher deal went to $1,350, and the last two very happy travelers collected their prize.

Some travelers have made the bumping game almost a

way of life. They know, for example, that the first flights from New York to Detroit, New York to Chicago, and New York to Atlanta are always oversold. They carry full-fare tickets on those flights and have no intention of taking those flights. They simply show up at the required times, wait for the overbooking announcement, and collect their vouchers for future flights.

And some, during particularly heavy travel times, have double- or even triple-dipped. If you're bumped from the first oversold flight and the second flight is also oversold, you get bumped again.

During one Thanksgiving holiday, a family of five was able to be bumped four times in one day. They received enough high-value vouchers to be able to take three family vacations that year.

One important note: Whether you play the bumping game by accident or by design, always assume that no matter what other flight the airline puts you on, it may not have removed you from the oversold flight completely. The airline's computers could actually list you as a no-show for your original outbound "bumped" flight and may cancel the rest of your flight itinerary. So if you're bumped, make sure that the gate agent goes back into the computer and protects you on all subsequent flights on which you hold a reservation.

If delays are inevitable, how can you cope? A better question: How can you win?

There are remedies, and every so often some real value is attached to them. But you need to know the game.

As with a standby or waitlist, a caste system is applied by the airlines when something goes wrong. If you're at the bottom of the proverbial food chain, you are about to be "stuck at the airport."

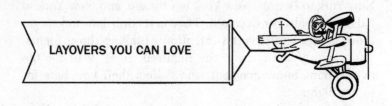

LAYOVERS YOU CAN LOVE

Until recently, being stuck was a fate only slightly worse than death.

The first time I found myself at an airport with a few hours to kill, I was confronted with these depressing choices:

1. Sit in an uncomfortable plastic chair, listen to the tin sounds of Mantovani, and make believe I was in my dentist's waiting room.
2. Sit in *another* uncomfortable plastic chair, insert quarters into a small black-and-white TV set, and watch bad soap operas.
3. Try to guess the ingredients inside the mystery hot dog sold at the combination newsstand/snack bar.

A friend once described waiting at an airport as akin to being "trapped inside a large dirty sock." Indeed, we all have terrible airport stories, and the plots all start with logistics.

Land at Heathrow in London, and despite the long distance between your arrival gate and the immigration and customs queue, you have an excellent chance of finding a free baggage cart within 100 feet of your gate.

Land at LAX, and no carts are to be found anywhere near the gates.

In Zurich, the corridors are a mile long, and carts are prohibited at the gates.

Some airports make it impossible to take rental baggage carts to the gates. And yet at Frankfurt, London, Hong Kong, and other equally busy airports, baggage carts are allowed and encouraged.

My favorite baggage carts are in Frankfurt. Leave it to the Germans to design the sturdiest and most versatile baggage carts I've ever seen. An ingenious design allows them to ride, without ever slipping, on any escalator. The time saved by not waiting for an elevator is substantial.

But saving time at an airport means nothing if you get to your gate and realize you're going nowhere for a very long time.

An entire generation of poorly fed, overtired, and impatient travelers expects nothing more than abuse during airport layovers. Airport food is pedestrian (at best). Airport shopping is limited to overpriced items you never purchase anywhere else. Airport sleeping, while waiting for a flight, requires perfecting the painful art of slumbering in an upright position.

But now, at a growing number of airports, you can shop for things you want or need, eat food that's good (as well as nutritious), be entertained, take a shower, and even sleep in a real bed. You can have a sauna, use exercise equipment, buy a rare book, or use a fully operating temporary office, complete with a secretary, fax machines, and personal computers.

In short, many airports are trying to create a practical extension of travelers' daily life instead of a hindrance to it.

One of my favorites is sitting by the 115-foot indoor mountain stream while planes take off at McGhee Tyson Airport in Knoxville, Tennessee.

Slowly and surely, airports are offering some *fun* to travelers forced to spend time there.

You can eat very well at Legal Seafoods at Logan International Airport in Boston. Fresh crab and salmon are always on the menu at the San Francisco Airport restaurants.

On the concourse level at Mitchell Field in Milwaukee, the Renaissance Book Shop sells new, used, and rare books. This is not only one of my favorite airports (locals like to call it "Chicago's secret airport"), but one of my favorite bookstores—and it stays open until 10 P.M.

At least once a year, I fly into Milwaukee and give myself at least a three-hour layover. I go to the bookstore and usually buy about fifty books. I put them on my credit card and have them shipped, at a nominal fee, to my home in California. No schlepping and no sales tax!

In Rome, the airport offers wine tastings. The international terminal at San Francisco Airport has a five-thousand-volume library and a museum of flight. At Pittsburgh International Airport, there are one hundred separate stores in the Airmall.

O'Hare International Airport, in Chicago, has a "Kids on the Fly" learning and play space in Terminal 2. Developed by the Chicago Children's Museum, the 2,200-square-foot area is equipped with a build-your-own-Chicago Lego™ space, a mock cargo plane to clamber around on, and a fantasy helicopter. Also check out the full-scale model of a brachiosaurus that towers over Concourse B in Terminal 1. A "Back Rub Hub" in Terminal 3 offers chair massage sessions. (When you're facing a long wait at the airport, you might as well be depressed *and* relaxed!)

Airports throughout Europe now offer comprehensive business centers. At Amsterdam's Schiphol Airport, one of Europe's most negotiable airports, you get a private office equipped with a computer and full Internet access. Prices depend on the number of people using the service. Showers are available at the Mercure Hotel for about 12.50 euros. Schiphol also has a museum and a National Geographic store. Or you can visit the airport website (www.schiphol.nl)

for a list of the best places to simply sit and *watch* other planes take off.

Need good travel shoes? Check out Washington, D.C.'s Reagan National Airport. In Denver, ask about a massage. And at McCarran International Airport in Las Vegas, take advantage of a twenty-four-hour fitness center. The fully operational gym has more than 1,500 frequent-flier members. Cost: $10 per day, and monthly memberships are available. Of course, there is also gambling.

Stuck at Dallas–Fort Worth? A golf course at the southwest corner of the airport will rent clubs to anyone stranded at the airport.

If you're delayed in Portland, Seattle, Denver, San Jose, Minneapolis, or San Diego, the latest airport amenity is DVD rentals offered by InMotion Pictures. For about $12, you get the DVD player; the first movie is free and after that the movie titles rent for as little as $4. Savvy travelers rent the player for their round-trip flights and select at least three movie titles. In the event of a delay, they're at least entertained.

Orlando's 15,000-acre international airport is the third-largest in the United States. I actually like this airport. With the addition of a fourth airside terminal, the airport now boasts forty-six name-brand stores, twenty-four restaurants, and a microbrewery. (Beer lovers: Show up on Wednesdays, when the freshly brewed batch is ready.)

I also like having a Hyatt hotel located within the terminal. The 446-room hotel is great for business travelers. If I'm flying in and need to stay at the hotel, I call ahead and have the bellhop meet me in the baggage claim area. I get checked in to my room there while waiting for my luggage—a great time-saver.

Like to shop? The magical Disney Store, Universal Studios store, and Kennedy Space Center store are no surprise.

But there's also a Bijoux Turner store selling fashion jewelry, and none of its eight thousand items costs more than $10.

Miami also has a hotel at the airport, but it is definitely *not* one of my favorites. It closely resembles an original airport hotel—an afterthought that temporarily houses stranded travelers.

But this hotel does have one upside. I'm not keen on staying there, but if you have a few extra hours at the airport, take the elevator to Concourse Level 2 and take advantage of the Miami International Airport Hotel's health club, open from 10:00 A.M. to 6:00 P.M. You can get a dip in the outdoor pool or a run along the rooftop track even if you are not a registered guest at the hotel.

The Hong Kong International Airport has a great Cable & Wireless business center in the check-in hall. If you have enough time, check out the Oriental Massage Center on the Level 6 concourse. I especially recommend the foot massage. You can also visit the Plaza Hair and Beauty Salon for a facial.

England's airports incorporate a concept of "retail therapy." A recent survey showed that because most travelers were so stressed at airports, they spent very little time shopping. Not anymore. Upscale shops at Heathrow (www.baa.co.uk) include branches of Harrods, Pink, Austin Reed, and other well-known stores. Alternatively, just sit on the windy terrace, sip a frozen daiquiri, and watch people come and go. Heathrow also features children's play areas in each of its four terminals.

Singapore's Changi Airport (www.changi.airport.com.sg) offers nature trails, as well as showers and napping facilities at a rate of $30 for three hours. There is also a fitness center. You can go swimming, hit the hot tub, or play virtual reality games.

Are you looking for a bolder airport layover experience?

In Malaysia, at the Kuala Lumpur International Airport at Sepang, you can do a hike along the trails in the jungle nearby.

One of Europe's most complete shopping centers is at the Frankfurt am Main airport. The one-hundred-shop complex opens early and closes late. The stores sell everything from smoked salmon to stuffed toy bears. There are thirty restaurants, two supermarkets, antique and modern art stores, and a Harrods, plus a pharmacy, a dry cleaner, a locksmith, a shoemaker, a porn bookstore, a casino, the biggest airport medical clinic in the world (three doctors and a staff of fifty), and, yes, even a dentist. More than four thousand people— none of whom have any travel plans—flock to the airport each day. If you get tired, there are excellent hotels within the airport perimeter. Using the great baggage carts the airport provides, you can check out of a hotel, walk a very short distance to the airport, and get to your gate in under nine minutes!

Are you traveling with kids? Or do you want to escape from them for a brief while?

At Denver's airport, there are cozy corners at the south end of the Jeppesen Terminal (www.flydenver.com). Concourse A has a great view of the Rocky Mountains.

Philadelphia's airport (www.phl.org) supplies rocking chairs between Terminals B and C.

At LAX, the best place to plane-watch is at the Encounter Restaurant, which rises 70 feet in the air at the center of the airport. Or a free shuttle bus will take you to the nearby Hilton Hotel, where for $10 you get all-day access to the twenty-four-hour fitness center, which has workout facilities, sauna, and steam baths.

Type A people (like me) who dream of 24/7 access to a T-1 line can have that, too, by checking into Laptop Lane (www.wayport.com). Currently, at thirteen airports through-out the United States, in addition to the high-speed T-1 line, you can get your own office with a PC, printer, and fax. There are two laptop ports per cubicle, so you can use your own computer, not just theirs, to access the line.

But before you ever get to an airport, log on to www. quickaid.com—perhaps the most wide-ranging directory of airport websites, with links to almost 160 international airports.

Quickaid.com will also help you locate lounges within airports where it pays to become a member. The Wing, Cathay Pacific's first-class VIP lounge in Hong Kong, is one of the best in the world. It features a complete Elemis Day Spa, two restaurants, a long bar, relaxation rooms, shower rooms, and computer rooms with Internet access. It is not unusual for travelers to arrive at the airport four to six hours *early* for their flights, just to take advantage of the lounge.

The same is true in London's Heathrow, where the British Airways new-arrivals lounge offers aromatherapy sessions, and the Virgin Clubhouse is by now legendary for its vast array of "preflight grooming" opportunities. I may be understating the case, but I have yet to visit this lounge with-out being *annoyed when my flight was called*! This very up-scale, fun oasis in the middle of the chaos of Heathrow makes travelers *want* to go to the airport.

In design and function, the Clubhouse deliberately chal-lenges the traditional airport waiting room in very creative ways. Imagine a facility with a sushi bar, a putting green, a music room (a soundproofed private sitting room equipped with a state-of-the-art Linn hi-fi system and leather sofas), a ski simulator, a hydrotherapy bath, a beauty and haircutting salon, a massage room, a relaxation room, and shower rooms.

The Clubhouse has views of airport runways on two sides

and from the roof. Its library has a few thousand books. My favorite machine here is the Alpine Racer, a ski simulator featuring mounted ski poles for balance and ski steps for rapid turns. Players can choose from three courses that progress in their degrees of difficulty. "Naturalistic" elements such as fog and blizzards are simulated quite realistically.

There is a business center, with all the usual contraptions: computers, a fax, a photocopier, telephones, and access to the Internet and to international financial news services. But most everyone is playing on the ski simulator, or getting a massage, a facial, or a haircut, or eating sushi and hoping their flights will be inexorably delayed.

Travelers who have no such über-lounges use their airport layover time in other, possibly healthier and more constructive, ways. A number of airline passengers landing at JFK and connecting to or from international flights make use of the airport's full-time dental facilities. You can find the airport dentist—Dr. Robert Trager—in Room 2311 in the International Arrivals building. The staff at the dental center is multilingual and often handles the dental emergencies of foreign passengers, though it's not unusual for some regular transiting passengers to visit Dr. Trager to get their teeth cleaned. (At the Frankfurt am Main airport, an excellent full-time dental clinic is also available.)

At Charles de Gaulle Airport in Paris, look for one of the better delicatessens anywhere. (A word of caution: If you're buying any fish or meat or fruit to bring home, ask whether it has been approved for travel to the United States. Many items sold at the delicatessen are not approved by the U.S. Department of Agriculture and might be confiscated upon your arrival in the United States.)

No one is looking for hotels at one of the largest transit airports in the world—Dubai International Airport, in the

United Arab Emirates. Most passengers have just an hour during a refueling stop, but they head immediately for the airport's 22,000-square-foot duty-free shopping complex.

Dubai is a duty-free port, and the duty-free complex offers unbelievable prices for some of the more traditional purchases such as a liter of Johnnie Walker scotch or a carton of Marlboro cigarettes.

I remember when my first late-night flight stopped in Dubai on the way to London from Asia. As I left my plane, aircraft from Ghana, India, Ethiopia, Germany, the Netherlands, Russia, England, and Singapore were lined up, unloading passengers.

For the most part, they weren't really there for the booze and the cigarettes. They had come for the deals on the Rolex Oysterdate watches, the Chanel perfume, kilos of beluga caviar, and gold sold by weight. There's a special room for Cuban cigars and a fur shop where a mink coat sells for $1,800. Want a Mercedes or a Humvee? No problem. The complex sells chocolates, too—about 40 tons of Tobler products per year.

Every once in a while, there's a rush on scotch whiskey. The night I was there, an airplane from Lot, the Polish airline, landed in Dubai on a flight from Delhi. The passengers rushed the store, cash in hand. An hour later, the plane was almost overweight when it roared down the runway toward Warsaw.

In just sixty minutes, the passengers had purchased fifty-eight videocassette players and seventy-eight cases of Johnnie Walker scotch. How the plane ever lifted off the ground remains a mystery. But for those who could forget the cramped and uncomfortable flight, Dubai was a layover to remember.

Today Dubai is still a layover to remember, and duty-free shopping is bigger than ever.

5

On the Plane

JOINING THE UPGRADE BRIGADE, THE AIR YOU BREATHE, AND OTHER (UN)NECESSARY EVILS

 **COMFORT IS ESSENTIAL**

You're almost there. They're about to call your flight to board. Even the departure board is finally telling the truth. It's almost time to go.

But if you're like me, you're an unofficial member of the upgrade brigade. You desperately want to fly in the front of the cabin.

And the scene, all too familiar, is repeated at virtually every airport gate around the world. It's the attack of the "lurkers." Or worse, the "demanders."

Most of us fall into the former category. Come on, admit it: You are a lurker. Or you've been one. You want an upgrade. You go to the counter and ask. The agent tells you that no upgrades are available (you don't believe it) or says that you'll have to wait (you want to believe there's hope).

Doing your best impression of a demented cocker spaniel or a foreign refugee boat person, you hunch your body over, and you slowly shuffle, stalk, and circle the counter at the gate.

But most of the time, you don't get an upgrade.

Trust me when I tell you that, within the United States, the upgrade is overrated. Think about the aircraft type you're booked on. Getting bumped to first class sounds great. But if it's on an MD-80, a 727, or a 737, the first-class section will be crammed. And sitting there is tantamount to being sent to your room as a young child.

I'd much rather take three seats together in coach than fight for an upgrade on a narrow-body plane. When I'm flying, I like to have space to work and read. I'm not there for the movie or the gourmet meal. An open coach seat next to me gets a higher rating than a seat in the full first-class section.

On overseas long-haul, wide-body flights, it's another story. Usually, more seats are available for an upgrade, and more space is available once you're on board. So stop whining about that domestic upgrade and head for the jetway.

On the other hand, some passengers are "demanders."

One of my favorite stories happened at the old Stapleton Airport in Denver. A crowded United flight had been canceled, and a long line was quickly forming at the gate. An airline agent was trying to rebook everyone on the next available flight and on connecting flights.

Suddenly, out of nowhere, an angry passenger pushed his way through the line and slapped his ticket down on the counter. "I have to be on the next flight," he announced, "and it HAS to be first class!"

The agent tried to be nice. "Sir, I've got all these people here, and I'm trying to help everyone. If you'll just bear with me and give me a few minutes, I'm sure I'll be able to help you as well."

He would hear none of this. He raised his voice, as if to make an announcement. "Do you have any idea who I am?" he bellowed.

The agent didn't miss a beat. Without hesitation, she reached down, grabbed the public address microphone from below the counter, and raised it to her mouth. "May I have your attention," she began. "United Airlines has a man at gate 17 who does not know who he is . . ."

The entire line of passengers broke up laughing. The man, of course, was not amused, and stared her down.

"#$*& you," was all he could muster.

Again, the agent was smooth. "I'm sorry," she countered calmly. "But you're going to have to stand in line for that, too."

Guess what? No upgrade.

Again, the bottom line here is to comprehend the reason you're at the airport in the first place: to go from point A to point B. Still, if getting an upgrade is that important to you, remember these basics:

1. Dress for success. Jeans and a backpack just won't cut it.

2. Know the lingo. "Is the plane full?" immediately identifies you as a civilian. The language of the gate— "What's the load today?"—is a better way of asking that question.

3. Is your flight an originating flight and the first flight of the day, or a midday flight waiting for other connecting passengers? If it's waiting for connecting passengers, even if the flight is showing full, you stand a better chance of an upgrade because not all the passengers will connect.

4. *Don't ask* for an upgrade. That's the first sign you're an amateur. Remember, gate agents have been hardened by years of dealing with lurkers and demanders. They *know* why you're there. Often, it's much easier *not* to talk about the upgrade but to employ the "schmooze" tactic. First, you'll always learn something about the airline or the process of travel in that conversation. Second, if the agent likes you and there's a seat available, that's when the upgrade happens. "Can I see your ticket?" the agent will ask, and the unspoken upgrade process has begun.

5. Don't be a lurker or a demander. Just get on the plane. Start by going down the jetway.

What you do next, from the moment you walk down that jetway until you take your seat, will often determine the quality of the flight you're about to take, no matter what section of the plane you're in.

If the airline is preboarding, and you're a member of the carrier's elite program, then by all means preboard. I don't have to tell you that overhead space is at a premium. First come, first stowed.

But unless you're sitting in a window seat in the back of the aircraft, there is no upside to getting in that line. Invariably, you will have to wait for everyone else to show up to fill the center and window seats next to you.

So . . . wait. And when there is no line, start down the jetway. When you get to the aircraft door, don't turn right. Instead, turn *left*. Why? Because you're headed to the cockpit. No, you're not hijacking the plane; you're going to ask an important question: "Are all the air pacs on?" No one in that cockpit will think you're crazy. Instead, they now know that *you* know.

An air pac is part of a plane's air-conditioning and circulation system. Most modern jetliners have at least two. Widebody aircraft have three. Jets were designed to have an almost constant flow of new air through the cabin. Today, about half of the air is recycled; until the 1970s, none of it was. And with more planes flying at full capacity, anecdotal evidence suggests that the low ventilation levels increase the chances that people will get sick.

Here's what is supposed to happen. The air enters through the plane's jet engines. It is compressed and heated by those engines. Then it enters near the cabin ceiling and is circulated through the cabin. Some is recirculated through the plane, but most is purged through the cabin floor.

Many airlines, in an attempt to save money, don't use all their air pacs to do this. Instead, they recirculate old air continuously through the cabin and only purge that old air slowly—or on some flights, not at all. The money saved is significant. On one medium-size aircraft, airlines save $60,000 per year in fuel costs when they simply recirculate the air within the cabin and don't introduce new air.

The people traveling within that cabin generate dust and fibers as well as bacteria and other microorganisms. This dramatically diminishes the quality of the air, and it affects the flow of the air through the cabin. This can easily promote the spread of bacteria and disease.

Think about this: Economy-class passengers on some 737 aircraft are given 8 cubic feet of recirculated air per minute. On some other airlines, first-class passengers on the upper deck of a 747 get 60 cubic feet of recirculated air per minute. Is it therefore a big surprise if a passenger in 5B has the flu and passengers in 17A and 23C then catch the flu?

These days, the recirculated air is generally filtered to trap dust, particulate matter, and microorganisms. Infectious diseases are sometimes transmitted during travel, but evidence suggests that the infection is the result of close contact with other passengers rather than contamination from recirculated air.

The quality of onboard air improved measurably when U.S. airlines banned smoking on their flights. Some airlines, like United, then used new HEPA filters on their flights to remove more particulates from the air. And these high-efficiency filters do reduce the level of airborne particulate contamination. Some airlines deal with this issue better than others. Air France did not eliminate smoking on all of its flights until late in 2000. However, some international carriers still permit smoking, so if you have respiratory problems or a smoke allergy, you should ask about the airline's smoking policy before booking a flight.

Still, unless all those air pacs are operative, the air is, at best, stagnant.

In one study conducted by the Harvard School of Public Health, flight attendants were issued special belt-clipped atmospheric monitoring devices to wear while flying. When those monitors were analyzed, the percentages of carbon dioxide and carbon monoxide were above the lowest acceptable levels listed by OSHA (Occupational Safety and Health Administration) for most office buildings! Add the airborne aspects of altitude and pressure—and dehydration—to the mix and you have a quite unhealthy environment on most flights.

Onboard air is very dry, and thus can cause headaches or itchy skin. The relative humidity in most commercial aircraft cabins is as low as 10 to 20 percent. To counteract this, you should drink plenty of water while flying—bring your own bottled water so you have a ready supply. (See my warning later in this chapter about relying on the airline to supply your drinking water.) If you normally wear contact lenses, switch to eyeglasses for the flight and keep a bottle of natural tears handy. Nasal saline spray can be used to lubricate your nasal passages, and moisturizing lotion can prevent your hands and face from becoming too dry.

On a commercial flight, your blood oxygen level can be 5 to 10 percent lower than normal. If you are in good health, your body can handle this, but if you have a lung condition like chronic obstructive pulmonary disease or cardiovascular disease, you may need supplemental oxygen. Ask your doctor for advice, and if you do need extra oxygen call the airline to find out its policy and charges.

Aircraft type is another factor that can affect air quality. Ironically, some observers think you're getting a better quality of air when you're flying on an older Boeing 727 than when you're on a new Boeing 777. In fact, some reports indicate that on a newer plane you have a higher likelihood of feeling dizzy or nauseated than on other, older airplanes.

After a rash of complaints from flight attendants, the two biggest operators of the 777s—United Airlines and British Airways—are investigating the air quality on those planes.

With the 777, the air pacs may not be the problem. The altitude at which the plane normally flies could be delivering less oxygen. Compounding the problem with the 777 is its size. It is so large that its air-conditioning system has been known to create different kinds of "weather" in various parts of the plane—especially variations in temperature and humidity.

How did this problem surface? Through flight attendants' complaints. In 2000, United's own flight attendants filed twenty-six reports—an unusually high number—of becoming ill on the plane. Next, an ex-pilot and former medical examiner for Britain's Civil Aviation Authority was quoted as saying that a lack of air made him feel "slightly hallucinatory" on a flight from San Diego to London.

United has started to modify the air systems on its forty-three 777s to make the air temperature more consistent throughout the cabin during the entire length of the flight.

Ever notice that you tend to feel colder, the longer you're on a flight? Aeromedical specialists have discovered that your metabolism tends to slow during long flights. So practice the reverse layered look. Pack a sweater in your carry-on bag.

OK, let's recap. You've stopped at the cockpit and asked the pilots to make sure all the air pacs will be turned on. (If you're intercepted by a flight attendant en route to the cockpit, ask the flight attendant to transmit your message. On this one issue, flight attendants are actively on your side. *Everyone* benefits from this.)

Now, on to your seat.

Legend has it that Orville and Wilbur Wright were convinced that people who traveled in flying machines would be most comfortable if they did so lying on their stomachs. That idea made sense when flight distances were measured in hundreds of feet, not in miles.

Thankfully, most aviation pioneers decided against a horizontal, facedown experience and made sitting the preferred flying posture. The first Ford Tri-Motors, which cruised at the leisurely pace of 115 miles per hour, offered stiff wicker cane-backed chairs, but before long passenger comfort became the focus of intense competition among airlines.

One French manufacturer outfitted his planes with overstuffed armchairs and lounging divans. Even the Douglas DC-2 offered its fourteen passengers upholstered contour seats, thick carpeting, and footrests.

In later years, the Boeing Stratocruisers, the Lockheed Constellations, and the DC-7s catered to passenger seat comfort. But the era of passenger comfort seemed to end when the first Boeing 707s and Douglas DC-8s were introduced.

The jet age quickly reduced standard seat distances from 40 to 36 inches, then to 34 and even 32 inches. It was no longer comfortable to fly.

When the jumbos arrived, with ten-across seating in coach, people seemed to stop dressing up to enjoy their flights. Instead, they dressed down, hoping just to survive them.

The airline seat remains a serious problem for many passengers. Few things are less enjoyable than an uncomfortable, narrow, hard seat on a long and crowded flight.

On international runs, most carriers offer—and boast about—sleeper seats in first class. With the 747, airlines returned to promoting seats as part of their advertising campaigns. Pan Am and American had advertised "dining in the air for four" in the upstairs lounges of their 747s. The lounges are gone now, but the seat wars continue. The first sleeper seats were 24 inches wide and reclined fifty degrees. Then the recline was increased to sixty degrees.

So much for first class. In the back of the plane, the airlines increased only the seating density.

In the seat wars, airlines constantly add, and occasionally remove, seats. And because of issues of weight, the airlines are always trying to install lighter seats. At one point, United Airlines added twenty-two seats to its short-haul 737s and still reduced the weight of each plane by more than 1,200 pounds.

Many coach seats still recline only a few inches. On some carriers, passengers hope that the seats don't recline at all. The legroom is so tight that knees get scraped, and when the person in the seat ahead pushes the button and sits back, the meal tray of the passenger behind becomes a bulldozer.

Every airline is different, depending on its market and its competition. Don't expect comfortable coach seats on the TED shuttle between Los Angeles and San Francisco, or on America West flights between Los Angeles and Las Vegas.

About twenty years ago, the ante was upped in the seat wars. Japan Airlines offered "sky beds" on some of its longer 747 flights. For a surcharge of 20 percent above normal first-class fares, the airline provided a curtained six-foot bed and a cotton kimono. But JAL removed them when too many stewardesses complained of being grabbed and fondled on long flights.

Philippine Airlines then offered beds on all of its 747 flights across the Pacific. The airline's "Cloud Nine" service featured fourteen upper-deck berths.

British Airways went much further. Naval architects were hired to completely redesign the first-class cabin. And using the same amount of space, these experts developed incredible fully reclining, spacious beds.

Qantas and Singapore airlines jumped in, and Cathay Pacific, United, and American followed. These single electric/hydraulic seats are engineering marvels; they recline to flat 6-foot, 6-inch beds.

Indeed, the battle for upscale, first-class passengers is heating up. Virgin Atlantic's Richard Branson announced that, by the end of 2000, his airline would be installing *double* beds, complete with enclosures, on long-haul flights. (Don't hold your breath. It *still* hasn't happened yet, and some observers think it's a fantasy that will be shot down by economic realities of weight, space, and cost.)

According to a survey by Skytrax.com, the best flat-bed seats in first class are offered by All Nippon, British Airways, Cathay Pacific, China Airlines, Qantas, Singapore Airlines, South African Airways, and Swiss International Airways.

In the meantime, British Airways extended the upscale seat battle into business class: Flat business-class beds were introduced as well. (In airline economics, 9 percent of travelers—in business class—generate 45 percent of all revenues.)

But what about coach passengers? Remember them? The airlines seem to have forgotten them or are intentionally ignoring them.

In recent years, the space in coach cabins has become even more cramped, if that was possible. High-density seating configurations by most airlines in coach seemed to conspire to restrict and constrict coach passengers into an uncomfortable—and some would claim unhealthy—ride.

A few years ago, American Airlines refitted its planes, adding 3 or 4 more inches between coach seats. When American eliminated seven thousand coach seats from its worldwide fleet, it nevertheless continued its "More Room" campaign, even though there was no indication that it attracted more passengers. Finally, when American recently added seats to 23 percent of its 757 planes, the result was 2 to 3 fewer inches of legroom in coach class.

Despite the introduction of newer-model planes (stretched versions of the MD-80 and the 737), things didn't get better; they got worse. The seats didn't get any wider—and, some airline officials would argue, average passengers *did*.

Anyone who has flown Southwest Airlines knows that it promotes price, not comfort, as a sales perk. But tell that to the Los Angeles woman who sued Southwest in 2000 for discrimination when the airline insisted she was so fat she had to buy tickets for *two* seats.

The airline claimed in its defense that its policy is that "oversized customers" purchase extra seats "for their comfort and safety." And, the airline said, if a flight is full, the portly passengers can request a refund.

One observer noted, "Fat chance!"

Still, anyone who has flown in the "back of the bus" on a 737, 757, or MD-80 aircraft knows that the old joke about your knees pressing against your chest was never really funny.

To make matters worse, American and Continental, among others, are actually flying stretch versions of the 737, with three-plus-three rows in coach, on long-haul transcontinental flights! Some passengers have been known to refuse to board these aircraft, opting instead to wait for later, widebody flights on the same routes. (But even that is a myth. The cabin of a 737 has *exactly* the same dimensions as a 757!)

Are you claustrophobic? The new 737-800 can fly 3,700 miles nonstop and is a very efficient aircraft for the airlines. But its seating configuration crams up to 146 people into a cabin that was designed about thirty years ago for short trips.

Not a pretty picture for passengers, not to mention flight attendants who have to work those flights.

A few years ago, the airlines were confronted with a
problem of excess equipment and excess capacity. In the
1990s, airline profits soared, and companies ordered new
airplanes. But then the Asian economy plummeted. When
OPEC hiked oil prices in 2000 (and airfares started to rise to
adjust for the increased cost of fuel), the airlines found themselves in an awkward predicament. Then came 9/11 and the
ensuing war in Iraq. Oil prices reacted with new highs—to as
much as $40 a barrel.

A case in point is American Airlines, whose turnaround
plan fell short of projections as a result of various factors, including the Iraq war, spiking oil prices, the international
SARS outbreak, sluggish business travel, and fare wars with
low-cost carriers. The airline is attempting to cope through
cost cutting and increased efficiency, but high fuel costs are
difficult to offset. Furthermore, American is losing ground to
low-cost competitors, and its future remains uncertain.

Airlines began to realize that they had more planes than
they needed, and their costs were starting to jump. As a result, they had too many empty planes chasing too few passengers. They simply had too much capacity.

What did the airlines do with the extra planes? United
began using its new Boeing 777s on Chicago-to-Denver
flights, something these planes were clearly not designed to
do and still remain profitable. On certain short-haul routes,
the airline even used some of its Boeing 747-400s. Continental's response was to simply park its excess aircraft.

Besides the general problem of empty seats, in the case
of American Airlines, the seats that were filled didn't net the
airline enough high-yield revenue. Translation: Too many
discount tickets were being sold by too many discount airlines, now including American Trans Air, Independence Air,

JetBlue, TED, Song, and Air Tran. Furthermore, coach passengers were angry about being crunched in the cabin.

Enter American's CEO at the time, Don Carty, one of those angered by the excess capacity in the system. In a surprise move that caught its major competitors off guard, American elected not to park any planes. It decided instead to *park seats.*

In early 2000, American announced that it would begin removing two rows of coach seats from each of its airplanes—systemwide. The absence of those two rows gains space for coach passengers. The 31-inch seat pitch in the coach section went to as much as 36 inches, a significant and noticeable increase in space and comfort.

On the surface, it seemed to be a win-win for both the airline and its passengers. American claimed that no fares would be increased as a result of the reconfiguration. This was a surprise, considering that the move, which affected more than seven hundred aircraft and essentially represented 6.5 percent of American Airlines' total seating capacity, cost the airline roughly $70 million.

Why so much money? Removing seats means readjusting air vents, electrical systems, lighting, computer power ports, and carpeting for each plane.

But wait a minute. Why would American suddenly decide to pull seats from its planes and spend $70 million just to make us more comfortable in coach? Does anyone smell a rat?

Technically, American was correct when it announced that no fares would be increased when the seats were removed. No fares were increased.

Smell the rat yet? You do if you remember our discussion of revenue management. Despite the reduction in capacity, American was convinced it could spend the money, reduce the number of seats, and still make a *bigger* profit in the long run.

The method was quite simple. If there were twenty published discount fares on a particular route, American eliminated about eight of them. In immediate effect, passengers got a de facto fare increase!

"The magic of this," one American Airlines executive quietly boasted, "is that it allowed us to reduce the number of seats and then reduce the number of low fares being offered on any one flight, which will get us a higher percentage of full-fare business travelers in coach."

In airline lingo, American was banking on widening the 14 percent revenue premium gap that it has in the industry. In laypersons' terms, the airline was counting on attracting a higher percentage of full-fare business and coach passengers than its competitors.

American's announcement was a major bombshell within the airline industry, but it is not the first time an airline has announced more space in the coach cabin.

There was TWA, which removed seats from its coach cabins about nine years ago. Indeed, flying coach on TWA soon became a relatively comfortable experience. The marketing folks at TWA loved the idea, but the accountants didn't. Almost as soon as some of us were beginning to settle into the idea of a pleasant coach ride, the airline quietly packed those original seats right back in. But it wasn't enough to save the airline.

Other airlines—Virgin Atlantic, for example—tried to segment the coach market by dedicating a certain number of slightly larger and more comfortable coach seats on each flight. United also tried to do it on some of its longer-haul flights. But those attempts, which only offered certain coach seats to higher-fare coach passengers, didn't apply to the entire fleet. The arrangement was confusing and it angered many coach passengers who felt that they deserved the better seats anyway, given the cost of their flight.

Has the American idea worked? Indeed it has. Based on its de facto airfare increase, American recouped its reconfiguration investment in about a year. (The *average* cost of tickets went up.) And on some of its aircraft (notably the 777s operating across the Atlantic on European runs), the airline quietly *reinstalled* more than thirty seats in coach. So much for promises.

Seat density remains a problem for other airlines. Before 9/11 the United Shuttle, for example, operated Boeing 737-300 aircraft with as many as 134 seats—126 of them in coach. But after 9/11 commercial airlines became even more crowded. Why? Although fewer people were flying, the airlines started using smaller airplanes or reconfiguring aircraft to hold more seats.

In 2002, 640 million people flew (in 2000 it had been 710 million). Airlines rushed to retire 747s and 727s and replace them with high-density 757s, 737s, and 50-passenger regional jets. As a result, the number of passengers actually flying on each plane jumped.

And guess which airline was first on the high-density bandwagon? American. In 2003, the airline quietly announced it was adding back seats to twenty-three of its planes, leaving passengers in coach with 2 to 3 inches less legroom. And they added back even more seats in 2004.

To compound matters, not just at American but also at United, which is operating under Chapter 11 bankruptcy protection, it's not just full planes contributing to more stressful flights, but also thin staffs. Domestic flights that used to be handled by eight flight attendants were now being staffed by only five. International flights that used to be staffed by eleven to fourteen flight attendants were often down to eight.

In 2005, we have come full circle to the age-old price-versus-comfort threshold. For passengers on short-haul flights, how important is price versus comfort? For those who travel on longer-haul routes, what comes first, comfort or price?

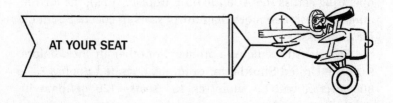

AT YOUR SEAT

You've reached your seat. Expanded legroom or not, you've got to move fast. Put your carry-on into the overhead compartment. Sit down.

Hungry? This moment is key; this is the time to move quickly. Look at your airline ticket. Are you on an even- or an odd-numbered flight? It makes a difference on longer flights that offer meals (and choices of meals). On most airlines, meal orders on even-numbered flights are taken from the front to the back. On odd-numbered flights, meal orders are taken from the back to the front.

Where are you sitting? If you're on an even-numbered flight and you're in the front, no problem. If you're in the middle or at the back, run up to the galley and get your food order in before the plane pushes back.

This advice presumes you're prepared to *eat* airline food, one of the great oxymorons of our time.

Let's be honest. People don't eat airline food because they're hungry. They eat it because they're *bored* or because it comes with the ticket.

You're sitting during the flight. Someone comes to your row and puts a tray of food down. You stare at it. And inevitably, you *eat* it! But, like the quality of aircraft air, it's important to know what is on that tray.

"For breakfast this morning, we will be serving an omelette, which can also be used as a flotation device in the event of an over-water landing."

And still, you eat it!

First, some history. In 1955, Northwest Airlines purchased a series of two-page full-color newspaper ads to promote the launch of its New York–to–Chicago service. However, the ads mostly promoted the "Fujiyama Room," Northwest's downstairs lounge on its Stratocruisers. The illustrations showed a white-jacketed steward offering passengers an elaborate tray piled high with shrimp, egg rolls, and other ostensibly Asian delicacies. The advertising copy was equally fanciful: "Oriental jasmine tea, if you wish. And such meals—juicy steaks, seafood ocean-fresh, salads crisp and cool as salads ought to be." All this bounty was included in the round-trip, first-class fare: $85.70!

Veteran frequent fliers have trouble remembering those days; some insist that those days never happened.

Well, that was then, and this is now. No one complains about the food anymore. Passengers simply expect it to be bad.

A tally of the amount airlines spend on food might confirm a few more suspicions. Domestic airlines spend from 3 to 5 percent of their total operating budget on food service. The percentages include the cost of china, cutlery, and other utensils.

Because so many ancillary costs are included, it's hard to calculate how much an airline really spends, on average, for the meals it serves. The best guesstimates: Most airlines spend less than $5 per passenger per meal. Southwest spends under 60¢ per passenger per meal.

And whenever the airlines can shave a few cents off a meal, they will. "The Olive" at American Airlines, a true story, has gained urban-legend status.

Former American CEO Robert Crandall kept noticing that a single black olive was placed on the top of each salad served with the airline meals. But no one ever ate the olive. He ordered it removed. The cost saved by the airline: about $600,000 a year.

The olive, as we have all discovered, was just the beginning. Some airlines are now employing a caste system in coach. The food you get depends on the price you paid for your ticket.

For example, America West quietly developed a five-tier meal system for coach passengers. The routes with the highest concentration of full-fare business travelers in coach got the best meals. They were served to passengers flying at peak times between Boston and Phoenix or from Las Vegas to Newark. Passengers on a late-night discount flight from Los Angeles to Columbus, Ohio, got potluck.

OK, now that you know how much the airlines spend, can you guess what they are buying?

First, airlines look at detailed time-and-motion studies and compare them with the length of a flight. The goal? To determine which food items can be served on which flights, given the time it takes the flight attendants to prepare and serve a meal, and the time allowed for the passengers to eat it.

During the first twenty years it operated the highly profitable fifty-five-minute New York–to–Boston and New York–to–Washington shuttle flights, Eastern Airlines had no competitors. In the regulated environment of the era, Eastern executives regularly pointed to those dreaded time-and-motion studies that concluded it would be impractical—indeed physically impossible—to offer a meal, a snack, or even a beverage on a shuttle route. So for two decades, the movers and shakers of American business and government rode the Eastern shuttle without being offered even an in-flight soft drink.

But during the heady days of deregulation in the early 1980s, an airline called New York Air was launched to compete with Eastern. And its CEO, the much-despised Frank Lorenzo (he later ran Eastern), did one thing that pleased passengers. He rolled out "the flying nosh," a small, pre-assembled sack of snacks distributed by flight attendants shortly after takeoff.

Delta and US Airways offer snacks on those routes now, and there's hardly a flight that operates more than forty minutes in the air that doesn't at least offer a beverage.

All the market research in the world can't pinpoint passengers' in-flight food preferences. For reasons of cost and simplicity, many airlines have opted to serve cold meals, but they do so at their own peril. For many business travelers, an airline's hot meal may be their *only* meal on a particular trip.

However, hot meals have many problems, beginning with the atmosphere on the plane. Think the onboard air is tough on you? It's harder on the food. British Airways won't talk about its attempt, many years ago, to serve an in-flight soufflé, except to say that soufflés will never be attempted again. Some bread and rolls will never be served again on Singapore Airlines; the flour used didn't work at the planes' altitude. Successes in test kitchens on the ground often fail miserably in the air.

Sometimes a meal is simply positioned improperly. British Airways was shocked when it put something called "Beef Rangdang" on the menu and no one ordered it. Reason: No one knew what it was. The airline renamed the dish "Malaysian-Style Beef Curry," and people ordered it.

But no matter what you call it, food tastes different at 35,000 feet. No one knows exactly why. After his epic thirty-four-hour solo flight across the Atlantic, Charles Lindbergh commented on what his five sandwiches had tasted like.

Today, in-flight catering is a $14-billion-a-year industry worldwide. It employs hundreds of thousands of people. But in an era of major cost cutting, every penny saved counts, even if it means your meal. On average, food service makes up only 1 percent of an airline's costs. (In real dollar terms, that means that most airlines spend only about $3 per passenger on food.) Still, many airlines have already eliminated food altogether, and others are selling food in coach. If you want leather, feather, or flipper, you'd better be prepared to pay for it onboard, or bring it with you.

This can create a serious problem of onboard smells for some passengers, myself included. So many travelers are now buying fast food at the airport and then bringing it on the plane that some passengers are getting sick from the odors. If you're like me, nothing smells worse than the aroma emanating from a McDonald's bag once the meal has been consumed.

Then there are the sheer logistics of onboard food. A jumbo jet preparing to set out on a long-haul flight might be carrying up to forty-two thousand separate catering items.

British Airways, for example, caters more than seventy thousand meals each day out of Heathrow alone. That adds up to 41 tons of chicken, 45 tons of strawberries, 127 tons of tomatoes, and 600,000 pints of milk every year.

So much for the numbers. Next is the moisture problem. Most passengers don't realize it, but hot in-flight meals have been cooked at least twice before they are served. That may explain why some of the dishes are coated with a thick mystery sauce—a pathetic attempt by the airline chef to somehow maintain some moisture in the recooked, reheated food. More often than not, the attempt is a dismal failure.

Sidestepping the quality and the consistency of the food, what are the health concerns? Many airline meals are downright unhealthy. According to one recent study, a meal of a McDonald's Big Mac, french fries, and a strawberry shake is healthier than a typical airline meal.

Consider these facts. A first-class meal on Delta, consisting of Caesar salad, filet mignon, and ice cream sundae, contained 87 grams of fat, 786 fat calories, 1,505 milligrams of sodium (the real killer), and a total of 1,829 calories. (Most doctors recommend that a person consuming about 2,000 calories a day should consume no more than 65 grams of fat and 2,400 milligrams of sodium daily.) Add a soft drink to that mix, and the sodium level soars.

Midwest Express meals are delicious, but they are extremely high in fat: 91 grams. And on Lufthansa, sodium weighs in at 3,477 milligrams for a coach meal.

Yes, you can order ahead and be served a special meal during a flight. Categories of special meals include low sodium, kosher, and lactose-intolerant! And those are just for starters. My advice: If you *must* eat airline food, order the one special meal the airline can't mess up: the fruit plate.

To save money, many airlines have experimented with selling higher-quality food aboard their planes. America West, Northwest, US Airways, Delta, and United test-marketed the idea on selected routes after most domestic airlines either eliminated or cut back food service on domestic flights of four hours or less. When surveyed, three-quarters of airline passengers said they would pay for meals during a flight if no free meals were being served and if the food was good. In response, LSG Sky Chefs sought brand-licensing agreements with partners such as D'Amico & Sons, T.G.I. Friday's, Einstein Bros., Wolfgang Puck Express, and Vie de France and began offering its In-Flight Cafe meals on most domestic flights of 700 miles or more. Lunches and dinners cost $10; breakfasts, $7. So far, the biggest problem with the program is collecting the money from passengers.

Next: the drinking issue. Forget the airborne wine list. It is not your friend. With altitude, pressurization, and dehydration, alcohol is a big no-no. One drink in the air has roughly the same effect as more than two on the ground.

There are also some behavioral considerations. Alcohol is almost always blamed for incidents of air rage on planes. A University of California at Santa Cruz survey demonstrated how seriously the brain is affected by a combination of low levels of in-flight oxygen, low cabin pressures, and alcohol. Add to that the general stress of travel, and you have the unmistakable ingredients of trouble aloft.

"The first thing that goes, with drinkers, is their hearing," one flight attendant told me. "So if you are drinking to excess on the plane, you usually begin to speak very loudly, in which case the entire cabin can hear every word you say. It is not very attractive. But it's also the signal for us to cut you off immediately."

Ironically, airlines began serving alcohol in an attempt to relax passengers and create a feeling that the flight might even be cause for celebration. However, just the opposite has occurred.

Most airlines now carry handcuffs as standard operating equipment on each flight, and the handcuffs are used often. Alcohol is involved in almost every incident that results in verbal or physical abuse. Ration or decline the alcohol.

Doctors tell us how important it is to continually hydrate yourself on flights. OK, we're all in agreement on the need for water. But what *kind* of water? When you see the flight attendant walking down the aisle with a tray full of glasses filled with water, don't just reach for a glass. Instead, ask whether the water is bottled or was drawn from the airline's holding tank. If the answer is the holding tank, don't drink that water. But how do you know where the water is from? On a number of airlines, when the flight attendants run out of bottled water, they refill those bottles with water from the holding tanks. They have a name for it . . . Tappian. Ugh!

And I mean Ugh! in a big way, because airlines have a continuing problem with the bacteria counts in those holding tanks. No one wants to admit this, but those bacteria resemble the characters in the bar scene from *Star Wars*. That's one reason why the airlines dump all those chemicals in the holding tanks and why the water from those tanks tends to have a metallic taste. And if you don't believe me, consider this: Tests performed by the Environmental Protection Agency found traces of coliform bacteria in tap water samples from 20 out of 158 aircraft—including two positive tests for *E. coli!*

If you're at all concerned about where that water is coming from, do what I do. Before flying, go to the store and purchase your own bottled water.

Now for some safety instructions. Interior aircraft configurations differ on almost every flight. Just be aware of one important fact: how far your seat is from the nearest exit. Count the rows to that exit. Why? In an emergency, it is highly likely that there will be no cabin lights. The cabin will be dark and filled with smoke. You will need to feel (and count) seat backs in order to get to that exit door.

What about the safety instructions themselves? Yes, pay attention, but see whether your seatmate is also paying attention—and understands English.

There's real irony in the "safety demo" usually performed by flight attendants or via prerecorded announcements. It concerns the exit-row seats, and here it is:

> Ladies and gentlemen, we ask that each passenger review the safety instruction card in your seat pocket as soon as you are seated. Please contact a flight attendant for reseating if you are assigned an exit seat and do not meet the selection criteria noted on the card. If you are unwilling, unable, or concerned about injury while performing any of the listed functions, you may also request to be reseated. If

you are seated in an exit-row seat, you may be called upon
to assist in an emergency. Follow the directions of the
crew.

Sounds pretty clear, right? But there's one problem. Who
screens the people sitting there to begin with? Under Federal
Aviation Administration regulations, no person may occupy
an exit-row seat if he or she cannot read, speak, and understand instructions in English—or cannot hear well enough to
perform one or more of the applicable instructions. If that
person is hard of hearing or can't speak English, what good
is the announcement?

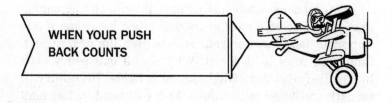

**WHEN YOUR PUSH
BACK COUNTS**

The other day, while waiting to depart from the Orlando airport, I got up from my seat and walked to the first-class lavatory. The door to the cockpit was open and the pilot was
involved in a heated argument with the gate agent. She had
come up to tell him the plane was ready to depart and she
was closing the door.

"Do not close the aircraft door," he shot back. He pointed
to his instruments. "We still have a cargo door open. Why is
it still open?"

"We had about thirty strollers, and we had to put them in
the hold," she responded.

"Well, don't close the airplane door until the cargo door
is shut."

Why was that so important? Because of the ticking clock. This pilot didn't want to be blamed for a delay.

The moment the aircraft door was shut, an internal fax machine on this American Airlines A300 would have automatically transmitted a message to American's headquarters in Dallas. The "clock" would have been started. A second clock would have started the minute the captain released the parking brakes and allowed the aircraft to push back.

A major disparity between the time the aircraft door was shut and the time the aircraft pushed back would have affected the flight's official on-time performance. "If we're going to be late," the pilot later told me, "I don't want to be blamed when, in fact, they were late loading bags."

Luckily, on at least that flight, they were able to quickly close the cargo door, and we were on time. Well, at least we pushed back from the gate on time!

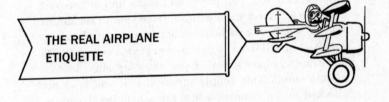

THE REAL AIRPLANE ETIQUETTE

We've all heard about air rage exhibited by passengers. There is also growing air rage among flight attendants. They seem to possess a shorter and shorter fuse in the sometimes not-so-friendly skies.

A flight attendant friend of mine—we'll call her Barbara—has flown for United for more than twenty-five years. She's seen just about everything, and whether you agree with her or not, here's her advice about airplane etiquette, from the flight attendants' point of view.

It starts as you go through security. Please, be ready to go through security when you get to the X-ray belt. It is not necessary to wait for the guard to say, "OK." Walk through one at a time without touching the sides of the machine. Different security machines are set differently at different airports. Just because you did not set off the buzzer at one airport, does not mean that you won't set it off at another. I have known a tea bag (wrapped in an aluminum package) to set off the alarm, and, of course, we all know about the metal underwires in a woman's bra. After you pick up your carry-ons, move to the side and out of the way of others trying to collect their items. Do not reassemble your luggage right next to the conveyor belt.

Whoever said that your plane would be parked directly next to the security check-in? Some airports are large, and the distance from the check-in counter to your gate could be quite far, and lines could be long.

Once you are at the gate, wait in line until the CSR [customer service representative] is ready for you. Do not be talking on your cell phone and make him or her wait until you are done. Be organized. Have your ticket and ID ready. If you have a particular seat or area of the plane you like to sit in, tell them as soon as you begin to check in. Do not expect to have a seat if you show up after the ten-minute cutoff. This simply means that if you have not checked in ten minutes before the scheduled departure, your seat is subject to cancellation and resale. At the very least, it may be given to another passenger who was waiting for a better seat. Do be pleasant and smile—do not blame the agent if the seat assignment you thought you had is not the one the computer gives you. It is not the agent's fault. Do not make up stories about how you were supposed to be in first class or you were supposed to have the whole row to yourself. Trust me, they have heard it all. Do not try to impress them with your status. Keep in mind: You get a lot more flies with honey than you do with vinegar. If you truly were wronged by the airline, not your company's travel department or your travel agent or one of the online travel agents, do not take it out on the ticket agent. Ask to see a supervisor or someone higher up. Deal with the people who can make the decisions.

Board when your row number is called, unless you are waiting for a first-class upgrade. Do not carry on your entire household. Especially, do not try to hide your third, fourth, and fifth carry-ons under your coat, or swung way over the back of your shoulder. We can see them. Do not tell us that you got to carry your household on the last flight. Perhaps it had fewer customers and plenty of room, or perhaps it was the type of aircraft that could accommodate more carry-on bags. Please do not drop off your carry-on items at the first open bin. That is the space for the people in those rows. If you see a pillow or blanket in the bin where you are putting your bags, pull them out first. If they get smashed in behind all the bags, etcetera, they will be of no use during the flight because we won't be able to find them. Plus, it will make more room in the bins for more carry-on items. The bin over your head is not your personal storage space. Several other people must share it. When you reach your row, step in so others can pass by you; *then* store your items. The faster the plane is boarded, the more apt you are to leave on time. If you have a briefcase or other small item, put it under the seat in front of you, to free up more overhead bin space. Many airplanes now have the extended overheads so the smaller rollerboards will fit in lengthwise—wheels down and rolled straight in. This also allows for more storage. Please do not come to the flight attendant with a huge item and say, "Where can I put this? It is too fragile to check and it does not fit in the overhead." Most planes do not have that kind of storage space, and the FAA says, "If it doesn't fit in an approved spot, it cannot be on the aircraft." Same goes for large musical instruments, unless you have purchased a seat for them. Also, if you cannot manage your carry-on items yourself, check them. Something too heavy for you to lift is too heavy for the flight attendant. If your bag must be checked planeside, make sure you give the agent your final destination, to help ensure that your luggage arrives when and where you do.

Once your bags are stowed, sit down and plan to stay there for a while. And during the safety demo, if you don't want to listen, at least be quiet. And besides, it is plain rude to talk while someone else is talking. If you are branded rude and/or arrogant by one flight attendant, the word spreads. When we ask you to turn off your computer or cell phone, do it right away—not in four or five minutes but *right then.* When we tell you that we have to pick up the predeparture beverages in first class, we have to pick up the predeparture beverages. The galley must be completely closed up and secure for takeoff, and that takes a few minutes. Also, if you board three minutes before departure, do not expect to get a cocktail at that time.

Respect the seat belt sign. I have many coworkers who have permanent injuries related to turbulence. They have been floating on the ceiling and have come crashing down to the floor on top of people, carts, armrests, and the like. If the seat belt sign has been on for an inordinate amount of time, and the ride seems smooth, and you really need to use the facilities, you might ask the flight attendants how much longer—or some such thing—in a very polite way. Perhaps the captain has just forgotten. But, please, for your own safety and the safety of those you may come crashing down on, stay in your seats, with your seat belt fastened, any time the seat belt sign is on. Personally, I leave my seat belt on all the time I am in my seat, in case of unexpected bumps.

During the service, try to stay in your seat while the carts are in the aisle. We cannot go back and forward, back and forward, constantly to let you by, or we will never finish the service. We realize that you have to sit with your trays for a while—especially on the larger aircraft—and we try to get back to pick them up as quickly as possible, but it takes even longer if you are milling about during the service. Please try not to be upset with the flight attendant if you do not get your first meal choice. We can only serve what we have, and it is impossible to board 100 percent of everything. If you truly have special dietary needs—if you are allergic to seafood or you are diabetic—bring your own food with you in case we cannot accommodate your needs. Many flights do not serve food, so if you think you will be hungry . . . well, you get the idea. If you call the flight attendant over and ask for coffee, please tell him or her at that time if you want cream and/or sugar or another beverage at the same moment. It is really annoying to the flight attendant to make several trips to the same row within two minutes; plus, there are many other people on board besides you. And a "Please" and a "Thank you" go a long way. You would think that adults would know this, but somehow it is not so. And this applies to first class as well as economy. Remember, you far outnumber us, and we can only be in one place at a time. During the beverage service, please do not hand us a $100 bill and expect to get your drink for free. We are on to this one, and will go to all lengths to get your change; plus, we will do our best to give it to you in singles—just so you won't have to give someone else a large bill. If you do need the flight attendant for something, do not poke her or him—in fact, it is better not to touch the flight attendant at all. If you need her or his attention, raise your hand, say "Excuse me," or ring your flight attendant call button. If you must touch, do so on the arm, very gently.

Do not hand the flight attendants barf bags with dirty diapers in them and do not hand us dirty diapers. We handle food, remember. Dispose of them, in the barf bags, in the garbage. Do not flush them down the toilet. Most flight attendants are happy to hold your child for a few minutes if you need to use the restroom and are traveling alone, but, beyond that, we are not babysitters. We do not change diapers.

Keep in mind the appearance of your area. Can I tell you what the interior of a full aircraft looks like after a flight? We wonder if that is how these people keep their homes. I certainly hope not.

Most flight attendants love their jobs and enjoy being around people. They like to visit with the customers—time permitting. They really do want your flight to be a pleasant experience. Most will bend over backward for you if you are polite, remember to say "Please" and "Thank you," and are generally a nice person. Remember the Golden Rule, and this applies to all persons in the service industry as well: "Do unto others as you would have others do unto you."

OK, kids, got that? Despite the preceding lecture, if you can avoid the beverage carts, and if the seat belt sign is off, you do need to get up during the flight. I'm not talking about a lavatory run. I'm talking about your general health while in the air.

In addition to the air flow, there's your *blood flow*. Sitting in a cramped airline seat can contribute to some serious circulatory problems, according to many medical researchers.

Get up at least twice on flights of five hours or more, dodge those nasty beverage and meal carts, and take a short stroll around the cabin. Recently, numerous reports have surfaced about incidents of what used to be called "economy-class syndrome" and is now given a more specific medical term: deep vein thrombosis (DVT), or blood clots in the legs. Some passengers have reportedly died from it. And it all relates to blood flow and your circulation on board. Dry air in the plane's cabin may increase the risk of DVT. So you really should take that stroll or do some gentle exercises at your seat to stimulate your circulation.

During your stroll, you may want to visit the lavatory. If you thought the holding tanks duplicated the bar scene from

Star Wars, then this room is central casting! This airborne petri dish is nothing less than a bacterial wonderland.

On narrow-body aircraft like a 737, there are only three lavatories for about 150 people. The math is easy. On a full flight, 50 people are looking to use one lavatory. Unless you're traveling with 49 members of your immediate family—well, you get the picture.

Before using that lavatory, realize the epidemiological breeding ground you're about to enter. One of the things you can pack in your carry-on bag is a small spray bottle (not aerosol) of disinfectant. Laugh if you will, but it makes total sense.

Spray the toilet seat; then lift it and spray the rim. After wiping off both, you can sit down. Then, do what a lot of people forget to do: Spray the faucets on the sink. Apply a liberal dose of liquid soap (if it's in the bathroom) to your hands, or, barring that, spray your hands with the disinfectant and then wash with soap.

Although there is no hard scientific evidence, anecdotal history indicates that if you don't get sick from the bad air circulating on a plane, a visit to the lavatory usually exposes you to enough bacteria and viruses to last you a couple of months!

Back at your seat, you might be surprised to see that the traditional airsickness bag may still be in the seat-back pocket in front of you. U.S. airlines use on average twenty million of these bags a year, according to Bagcraft Packaging, the largest supplier of sickness bags. Even though we hardly ever use them for their intended purpose, we've come to expect them anyway. Why? Because they have so many other practical uses.

We use them to dispose of diapers. With the addition of hot water, a clean bag makes a great onboard baby-bottle warmer. On many Caribbean flights, people take the bags for a later use: to hold their wet swimsuits. Strangely, there are even people who like to collect them! (Each year there are conventions for people who love airline "collectibles." Why anyone would treasure a vomit bag from Mohawk or Pan Am is beyond me.)

And some people still do get airsick. But not many.

The biggest problem continues to be adjustment to the pressurization of the aircraft cabin. You know the feeling. You suddenly feel pressure in your ears. They almost feel as if they are locking up as the plane's internal cabin pressure changes. (I'm convinced, as are others, that when small children cry on planes, more often than not they're reacting to the changes in pressure.)

On numerous flights, I wasn't able to clear that pressure. I had to wait until I was on the ground. My ears finally did literally "pop" and clear, but a painful headache became part of the process.

There are ways around pressure problems. Swallowing, chewing gum, yawning, or opening your mouth wide may help. Another option is EarPlanes, special earplugs that equalize the pressure on the eardrums. Or you can try something called the Valsalva maneuver. I learned about it when I was lucky enough to fly F-4s and F-15s in U.S. Air Force war games, at Nellis Air Force Base in Nevada, when I was a correspondent for *Newsweek*. Not only did I learn about the maneuver, I had to perform it before I was allowed to fly in the high-performance fighter jets.

The minute you feel the pressure start to build, sit straight up. Breathe slowly and deliberately—and deeply. Then pull in your stomach and hold your breath. Close your nose with your thumb and index finger and exhale gently against a closed mouth. You should feel your ears start to clear.

What if that doesn't work? One of my flight attendant friends told me her secret, which does work. Ask a flight attendant for a cup *half filled* with very hot water. Then hold the cup level on the right side of your head, and tilt your head so that your right ear rests on top of the lip of the cup. After a few moments, move the cup to the left side of your head and tilt your head so that your left ear rests on the lip of the cup. The steam from the hot water should clear your ear passages and relieve pressure. Be sure to insist on the cup's being only half full, for all the obvious reasons. *Do not pour anything into your ear!*

Obviously, if you're flying with a head cold or existing sinus congestion, you're asking for trouble. Why? Because during descent, air has to reenter your middle ear through the eustachian tube. And here's where the problems occur. If that tube is congested or blocked, that pressure could easily rupture your eardrum. Try using a nasal decongestant one hour prior to takeoff.

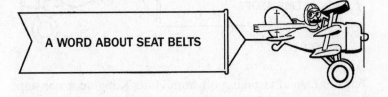

A WORD ABOUT SEAT BELTS

Every airline will tell you to use a seat belt. You are required to wear them for takeoffs and landings. But here's the real irony. The airlines will hate me for this, but we must always remember that seat belts were installed on airplanes when aircraft rolled down runways at 90 to 100 miles per hour. Today, jets take off at around 160 mph and land at about 150 mph. In the event of a high g-force but a survivable "hard landing," studies have shown that passengers do indeed survive the impact, but then die from the resulting trauma. Most often, the seat belt breaks the passenger's pelvis, there is internal hemorrhaging, and the passenger, unable to walk or even to crawl, often dies from the resulting toxic smoke in the aftermath of the "incident."

I'm not going to tell you that you shouldn't wear your seat belts during takeoffs and landings. I'll let you employ your own best judgment. But I *will* insist that you wear a seat belt during the *most* dangerous part of the flight: in the air, when there is a distinct possibility of in-flight turbulence. The most common flying injuries occur at cruising altitude (above 25,000 feet), during moments of unanticipated clear air turbulence (CAT).

How do you feel about becoming an unguided missile in flight? *Don't* wear your seat belt, and you just might find out.

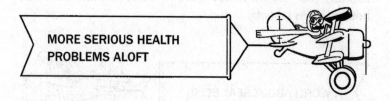

MORE SERIOUS HEALTH PROBLEMS ALOFT

Ten minutes after taking off from Hong Kong on a nonstop flight to Los Angeles, a woman passenger on a fully loaded Cathay Pacific 747-400 suffered cardiac failure.

A woman passenger on a British Airways 747 flight somewhere over India began to bleed internally and was perilously close to losing consciousness.

One hour into a Lufthansa flight from Miami to Frankfurt, a male passenger suffered chest pains and said he was having difficulty breathing.

The Cathay Pacific flight was too heavy to return to the airport. Luckily, there were two doctors on board. One was an English surgeon returning from vacation; the other was a cardiologist from Duke University returning home from a medical conference. The captain set a course for Taiwan and released a locked emergency medical kit to the doctors.

As the pilot dumped nearly 100 tons of fuel, the doctors stabilized the passenger. The plane made an emergency landing in Taiwan, and the woman was taken to a hospital. She survived.

There were also doctors traveling on the British Airways flight. Using the extensive emergency medical kit carried on the plane, and crafting a surgical tool out of a wire coat hanger, the doctors performed an operation to reinflate the woman passenger's collapsed lung. Again, a life was saved.

Although the Lufthansa flight was also carrying an extensive emergency medical kit, it was not immediately opened for the passenger with chest pains. When he tried to lie down in a galley, a flight attendant told him to return to his seat. The captain refused to make an emergency landing and continued on to Frankfurt.

The passenger had indeed suffered a heart attack, and a subsequent examination revealed he had suffered permanent heart damage. He sued the airline, and a federal magistrate awarded the passenger $2.75 million.

These and hundreds of other incidents raise questions about the effectiveness of airline medical equipment, as well as individual airlines' procedures in dealing with in-flight medical emergencies.

Emergencies that are considered life-threatening are rare. In a two-year study, the Federal Aviation Administration (FAA) estimated that about three serious medical problems occur per day on U.S. airlines. There are thousands of flights, and more than 1.5 million passengers boarding planes each day. However, the FAA study was done nearly twenty years ago, and things have changed.

According to 2002 statistics based on forty airlines that use the services of MedAire, a company that provides them with in-flight access to hospital-based emergency room physicians, flight crews called on-the-ground physicians more than 8,400 times for assistance in dealing with in-flight medical incidents and emergencies. Vasovagal (fainting) incidents were the most common, accounting for 21.5 percent of cases, followed by gastrointestinal (15.4 percent), respiratory (10.2 percent), cardiac (9.6 percent), and neurological (8.7 percent). Joan Sullivan Garrett, of MedAire, attributes the overall rise of in-flight medical incidents to the increasing average age of travelers and to stress, and cites the fact that more passengers with health problems are attempting to fly.

Dr. David Streitwieser, medical director at MedAire's MedLink Global Response Center, a 24/7 communications center that manages these remote medical emergencies, says that it's no surprise that vasovagal episodes occur most frequently. "A common scenario occurs when a passenger has been sitting comfortably for several hours then gets up suddenly to use the lavatory," he explains. The passenger becomes very pale and dizzy and then collapses to the floor in an apparent faint."

One thing that has not changed is the different ways in which U.S. and foreign airlines approach medical emergencies, train their personnel, and help passengers in a crisis.

All U.S. airlines train their flight attendants in CPR (cardiopulmonary resuscitation), but it is not a requirement among foreign carriers. That, however, is about the only area in which U.S. airlines have taken the lead in responding to onboard medical emergencies. There is a huge difference in the medical equipment and supplies carried by U.S. carriers and those carried by their foreign counterparts.

It is nice to have a doctor as a fellow passenger, but without proper equipment to help you, the doctor might as well be a circus clown. Had the Cathay Pacific and British Airways incidents occurred on a U.S. airline, the chances of the patients' survival would have been greatly reduced because proper onboard equipment was lacking.

In the United States, the FAA requires aircraft to have one to four basic first-aid kits, depending on the number of passenger seats. With few exceptions, the contents of these kits haven't changed much since the 1930s. They generally include a small assortment of bandages, gauze, tape, scissors, and some new additions—rubber gloves and a biocleanup kit. And in 2004, airlines were supposed to include automated external defibrillators, bronchodilator inhalers, masks for cardiopulmonary resuscitation, and lidocaine.

The emergency medical kit, which is locked in the cockpit, contains no narcotics and can be released by the pilot only to qualified medical personnel. It has a stethoscope, syringes, dextrose injections, and nitroglycerin tablets.

However, until recently most U.S. airlines had only the minimum equipment required by federal regulators. "Whatever the FAA mandates, that's what we carry," said one corporate medical director for a major U.S. airline. "People need to know that we're not set up to be an airborne ambulance or flying emergency room."

Then, slowly, the airlines started getting the message. Qantas realized that it made great economic sense to add more emergency equipment on its flights, most of which are long hauls. A flight diversion for a medical emergency will just about wipe out any profit earned on that particular flight. But if a passenger can be stabilized on the plane, both the airline and the passenger win. Qantas began installing emergency heart defibrillators on each of its airplanes and then trained its flight stewards in how to use them. Almost immediately, the equipment and training paid off. Within days of the installation, passengers who had suffered heart attacks or seizures were revived and stabilized and eventually recovered.

In the mid-1990s, Northwest installed a twenty-four-hour radio patch that let pilots talk with Mayo Clinic specialists. And American Airlines announced it had seven staff physicians on call, to consult with pilots.

But the U.S. carriers still resisted upgrading the emergency medical equipment carried on their planes. The airlines argued that any time a physician uses a kit, it's to stabilize the patient, and that the airline's primary goal at that point is to get the passenger on the ground.

Often, it's as much a legal as a medical consideration. In litigious America, airlines are worried about being sued after the fact. However, every state has a Good Samaritan law whereby individuals who provide well-intentioned first aid in emergencies are exempt from liability.

Foreign carriers don't seem to embrace those legal fears. Emergency medical kits on board Air New Zealand, British Airways, and Qantas planes reveal an entirely different approach to handling medical emergencies.

The Air New Zealand kit is a large orange suitcase filled with instruments, diagnostic and ventilation equipment, suction gear, and a veritable pharmacy of injectable, tablet, and spray drugs to treat everything from cardiac arrest to severe allergic reactions, diabetes, and asthma. And besides providing the kits, the airline offers a detailed protocol for handling medical emergencies ranging from heart attacks and epilepsy to kidney stones.

The British Airways medical kits contain a "delivery pack" in case a pregnant passenger goes into labor on board. Qantas and Virgin Airways carry defibrillators. American Airlines finally agreed to install them on its planes, and, in the height of ironies, the man who was so active in pressuring American to equip its fleet with defibrillators was flying as a passenger on the first day the machines were on the planes, and—you guessed it—he suffered a heart attack. An American flight attendant, newly trained on the unit, used it and saved the man's life.

Now that you know all of this, what can you do to become a better prepared passenger?

If you take any prescription medicine, exercise common sense. Do not pack it in your checked luggage; put it in your carry-on bag. If you have diabetes or epilepsy, carry an identification card such as the diabetes alert card from the American Diabetes Association. Also, bring along your physician's name and phone number and a list of your medications.

If you have a preexisting heart or respiratory problem, remember that aircraft cabins are pressurized to 8,000 feet, and that may contribute to inducing a heart or breathing problem. Always consult your doctor before flying. Or your lawyer. Some of these cases take years to be litigated and resolved, but they may be worth it. In 1998, a fifty-two-year-old California doctor died on an Olympic Airways flight from Athens to New York. His relatives sued, claiming his death was the result of a severe asthma attack caused by exposure to secondhand smoke. The court awarded $1.4 million in the case.

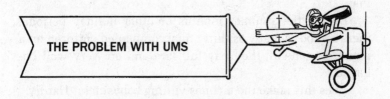

THE PROBLEM WITH UMS

A few years ago, a friend of mine planned to have her six-year-old daughter, Sophie, visit her grandmother in France. But because of schedule conflicts with her own business, my friend couldn't make the trip. She sent her daughter, alone, on a United Airlines nonstop flight to Paris.

When the plane landed in Paris, a United flight attendant escorted Sophie through passport control and customs, and then delivered her to her grandmother, who showed proper identification and signed a release.

Like hundreds of thousands of other children every year, Sophie flew successfully as a UM—airline jargon for "unaccompanied minor." Exact figures are hard to come by, but the accepted estimate, according to the Air Transport Association, is 7 million a year. United estimates that it carries more than 100,000 UMs a year. Continental says its figure is closer to 175,000. Delta's estimate is somewhere around 150,000. Those official numbers appear low. According to the Air Transport Association, the real numbers are increasing almost exponentially.

Given these statistics, it's not surprising that kids are becoming frequent fliers. One big reason for this is the increase in divorced couples and single-parent families, with each parent living in a different city. "We had one kid check in the other day for a flight to Newark," a Continental agent told me. "And his mother gave us his Gold Elite frequent-flier card. We thought it was a joke until we pulled his records. Sure enough, he was commuting twice a month to see his father."

During the summer months or other holiday periods, there can be as many as thirty unaccompanied children on a plane. In general, they pay full fare and are very well behaved.

Does this make the airlines willing babysitters? Hardly.

The airlines take seriously, but often inflexibly, their responsibility for transporting minors. The airlines' contractual concerns are to fly a child and deliver him or her to a responsible adult who will meet the flight at its destination.

No special airline programs or special services are offered for such children, although—as with adult passengers—the efforts of individual crew members and flight attendants can often make the difference between a terrible flight and a great one.

These are the industry's rules:

- No airline will accept an unaccompanied child under the age of five years.
- Children between the ages of five and eight will generally be accepted on nonstop flights.
- Children between the ages of eight and fourteen will generally be accepted on connecting as well as nonstop flights, depending on the airline, and as long as the connecting flight is not the last connection of the day.
- Airlines charge up to $90 each way for a child to fly as a UM.
- Most airlines prohibit UMs on overnight red-eye flights except on long-haul routes where no other schedules are available.

Parents can and should do a number of things to help their unaccompanied children get from point A to point B safely and with a minimum of hassles. The preparation is critical. Try to explain to your child what to expect on a flight—what he or she might see and hear (engine noise, landing gear sounds, and so on).

Pack some important extra things. For starters, your child should be carrying cards that clearly show his or her name, home address, phone number, and destination, and the phone number and name of the person meeting him or her. If possible, include a photo of the person who will meet the child. Some parents make a special zippered pocket in their child's jacket to carry a passport, emergency money, and a plastic-coated ID card full of information.

A child's carry-on bags are critical. Fill at least one bag with small toys, crayons, snacks (including small fruit-juice cartons, and granola bars). Depending on the child's age, include an important travel companion: a favorite toy bear or other animal, or a favorite pillow.

Just as important, instruct your child on some of the things adults take for granted, such as how to make a collect phone call. Tuck in a phone card (after teaching how to use it), a packet of change, and some small-denomination bills.

Nonstop flights are much better (and less expensive) than flights that lead to connections, but that cost keeps going up. In 2003, Northwest and Delta increased their fees for escorting unaccompanied children to connecting flights. They now charge $40 per child for care and attention on nonstop flights, and $75 for kids who are flying alone and must make a connection with another flight. The following chart outlines different airlines' policies for domestic flights. Fees for international travel are generally higher.

Air Tran

Ages: 5–7 nonstop and direct flights only; 8–11 connecting flights

Fees: $25 each way nonstop; $40 connecting

Restrictions: cannot book last connecting flight of the day

America West

Ages: 5–14 nonstop flights only

Fees: $40 each way

American

Ages: 5–7 nonstop and direct flights only; 8–14 connecting flights

Fees: $40 nonstop; $75 connecting

Restrictions: cannot book online; cannot book last connecting flight of the day

Continental

Ages: 5–7 nonstop and direct flights only; 8–14 conecting flights
Fees: $40 one-way nonstop; $75 connecting
Restrictions: no travel 9 P.M.–5 A.M. or last connecting flight of the day

Delta

Ages: 5–14 nonstop and connecting flights
Fees: $40 nonstop; $75 connecting
Restrictions: cannot book last connecting flight of the day

Northwest

Ages: 5–14 nonstop and connecting flights
Fees: $40 nonstop; $75 connecting
Restrictions: no travel 9 P.M.–5 A.M. or last connecting flight of the day

Southwest

Ages: 5–11 nonstop flights only
Fees: none
Restrictions: children under age 5 can travel with children 12 and older

United

Ages: 5–7 nonstop and direct flights only; 8–11 connecting flights
Fees: $60 nonstop and connecting
Restrictions: cannot book last connecting flight of the day

US Airways

Ages: 5–7 nonstop and direct flights only; 8–14 connecting flights
Fees: $40 nonstop; $75 connecting
Restrictions: cannot book last connecting flight of the day

The airlines earn a lot of money for simply assigning one of their flight attendants to do a handoff—walk a child from one gate to another and transfer responsibility to an attendant there. When American changed its fees for UMs from $30 each way to $60 each way, regardless of connections, the airline realized an annual net revenue increase of more than $767,000! Today they charge the same as Delta, and the annual revenue is over $1 million.

There is no federal mandate for airborne staffing or for increasing the number of flight attendants based on the number of UMs on each flight. As a result, on a Saturday flight crammed with kids, harried flight attendants may be unable to serve the adult passengers properly or to supervise the younger ones (or those merely *acting* like children).

Some further advice: After you hand off your child to an airline representative who will escort your UM through security to the gate, don't leave the airport or get a pass. Stay at the terminal and make sure the plane leaves not only the gate but the airport.

People waiting to meet children flying alone should assume that the airline staff (on a domestic flight) will escort the child through the terminal. But if you want to meet the arriving flight *at the gate,* bring proper identification to get a security pass.

If you're a single parent sending an unaccompanied minor to Canada, Central America, or South America, you must produce a notarized letter of permission from the other parent. (Some countries require such a letter from *both* parents.) Always check the rules in advance.

Apply to your child's journey the same basic common sense you would apply to your own. Especially if a connecting flight is involved, *do not* book the last outbound flight of the day to that connecting city. Your child then runs the risk of having to stay overnight in a strange city (hopefully, with airline supervision) if the original flight is delayed or the connecting flight is canceled.

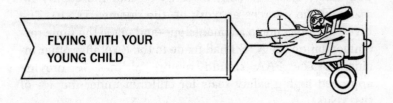

FLYING WITH YOUR
YOUNG CHILD

This situation poses other challenges, not the least of which is safety, especially if you're flying with a child under the age of two years.

Some readers may remember the tragedy of United Airlines Flight 232, which made an emergency landing in Sioux City, Iowa, in July 1989. It was a full DC-10 flight. On board were many parents traveling with their young children. A number of the children were under the age of two years.

Think about this: The FAA requires every airline to properly stow all luggage, and to properly lock and restrain beverage carts and other items before takeoff and landing. But, ridiculously, federal law allows parents to fly with toddlers under age two on their laps and does not require them to purchase seats and restrain their children. In the event of a crash or hard landing, beverage carts stand a better chance than those children.

In the Sioux City incident, the plane hit the runway at an excessive speed—a high-g, extremely hard landing. And that's when the inflexible laws of physics took over. It was physically impossible for any of those parents to maintain their grasp on their children. Many kids became instant missiles. Later, rescue workers found some in overhead compartments. One out of four children aboard died because they were not properly restrained, but many of their parents *did* survive.

In the wake of that crash, the U.S. National Transportation Safety Board (NTSB) investigated and thoroughly researched the g-forces at work on the doomed DC-10. The investigation came to a conclusion—and made the same recommendation the NTSB had made to the FAA after other incidents: The FAA should require airlines to provide approved high-g safety seats for children under the age of two years.

This wasn't the only time the NTSB looked into the child-restraint issue. On January 25, 1990, an Avianca 707 crashed off Long Island, after it ran out of fuel. Of the 159 people on board, 73 survived. The NTSB concluded that, had the one child aboard been in a car seat, it would have survived.

Even when parents want to be responsible, there is confusion and often conflict in the cabin. Since 1982, the FAA has required airlines to let parents bring child seats aboard aircraft, but passengers have complained about conflicts with flight attendants and have reported that some reservation agents dissuaded passengers from bringing car seats on flights.

When I called several airlines to see what they would tell me, I was never dissuaded from bringing a child safety seat aboard because of inconvenience. However, when asked, no representative would say which was safer for a child, lap traveling or traveling in a car seat.

But the NTSB was quite specific. After it evaluated its own tests, it urgently recommended the following to the FAA:

- For children under 20 pounds, a rear-facing restraint seat should be provided.

- For children between 20 and 40 pounds, a forward-facing restraint seat is necessary.
- For children above 40 pounds, a regular belted airline seat is advised.

Under the current procedures, whenever the NTSB makes a safety recommendation, the FAA has ninety days in which to respond. In this case, on the eve of the ninetieth day, the FAA responded with a technically acceptable statement: It would "study" the issue.

The FAA did, in fact, study the use of restraint systems and seats and other contraptions for use on commercial aircraft. Its study, remarkably similar in approach and technique to the NTSB investigation, used baby crash-test dummies in simulated 16-g survivable crashes.

Not surprisingly, the FAA reached the same conclusion as the NTSB: Holding a small child in one's lap is an invitation to tragedy, in the event of an emergency. Belting a small child into a regular airline seat would also be useless.

That's the good news.

Here's the bad news. Since it was mandated into existence by an act of Congress in 1935, the FAA has always been troubled by its schizophrenic and impossible dual mission: (1) to enact and enforce airline safety, and (2) to promote the business of aviation. The two goals don't mix, and when they collide, the FAA has historically opted to act in the best interests of cost benefit or economic impact, which are lobbied hard by the airlines. There are countless stories of absolutely obvious and much-needed safety fixes the FAA has chosen not to order because of their projected cost to the airlines.

The child safety seat issue was no exception.

After doing its own research, the FAA was forced to conclude that the NTSB was right. These seats were needed. So far, so good. But then came one of the lamest reasons ever given for not forcing the airlines to provide these seats for small passengers. The FAA, while announcing that it supported the idea of effective restraint systems, refused to make them mandatory. Why?

(Better fasten your seat belt, so to speak.) The FAA contended that if the federal government required the airlines to provide these seats for young children, the airlines would simply pass those additional costs on to passengers, in the form of higher airfares. The resulting boost in ticket costs would have an undesirable effect: Many people who would otherwise fly would drive instead, and automobile fatalities would be higher.

I'm serious! The FAA actually said this with a straight face. The agency was more concerned with highway safety (clearly not its area of responsibility) than with air safety!

And nothing much has changed, at least on the federal level. In the summer of 2004, the NTSB voted unanimously to recommend—again—to the FAA that they force airlines to provide proper restraint seats for kids under age two. And once again, the FAA used the highway safety argument. This time, the NTSB was prepared, having done its own study of automobile fatalities during times when people chose to drive instead of fly—like after the 1991 Gulf War and in the months following 9/11. And the results? No significant increase in auto fatalities for children under the age of two. Why? Because the parents who drove put their kids in approved car seats. And the Association of Flight Attendants is still pushing for child safety seats for those under age two.

One airline, realizing the importance of the issue, tried to find a middle ground. In 1997, American Airlines announced that although it would not provide these seats, any parent who brought on an FAA-approved seat would be charged a half fare to belt that seat onto the regular airline seat.

How popular is this idea? In a single eight-month period, one airline sold 4,400 discounted child-fare seats.

Later, in federal hearings on the issue, FAA administrator Jane Garvey said the agency was ". . . committed to two things—mandating the use of child restraint systems in aircraft and assuring that children are accorded the same level of safety in aircraft as are adults."

"The FAA goal," she testified, "is getting a child restraint system designed so that it is safe in automobiles and safe in aircraft."

There *are* seats on the market today that fit the dual requirements. Be aware also that *belt positioning booster seats* don't work and have been banned since 1996. They are similar to booster seats in a restaurant, but the seat belt goes through the bottom and the booster's own padded safety belt goes across the child's lap. These seats are not allowed because airplane seats, unlike automobile seats, are designed to collapse forward. If a crash were to occur, a child in one of these seats would be crushed.

The Sioux City crash was only one of many incidents. In 1994, during a DC-9 accident near Charlotte/Douglas International Airport, thirty-seven people were killed, including a nine-month-old in-lap infant who was held by her mother in the last row of the cabin. The child's mother was unable to hold onto the child during the impact sequence, and the baby died of massive head injuries. The mother survived with fractures to her elbow and arm.

Again, the NTSB issued two safety recommendations to the FAA, urging it (1) to require that all infants and small children be restrained in a manner appropriate to their size, and (2) to develop standards for forward-facing, integrated child safety seats for transport category aircraft.

Again the FAA did nothing, despite additional hard evidence gleaned from the NTSB's investigations of accidents in which child restraint system (CRS) seats were in use and provided protection to children—particularly protection against debris. A family that used a CRS was seated in a row directly behind a row in which two passengers sustained fatal injuries. According to the parents, the CRS protected their daughter from being injured.

Until the FAA acts with stronger resolve, the real responsibility for protecting children on flights is (pun intended) in parents' laps.

Here are the current airline rules:

- A child (under twenty-four months) can sit on a parent's lap for no extra charge. Or, if a parent prefers to bring the child's car seat to the aircraft, the seat next to the parent can be purchased for 50 percent of the regular price.
- After the child has passed twenty-four months, a regular-fare seat must be purchased.

Continental allows you to bring a car seat down to the plane, even if you have not purchased a seat for it. If the flight is underbooked and there is an empty seat next to you, they will let you use it for free. If there are no empty seats, they will check your car seat for free. They will also allow you to place the car seat in the overhead bin if there is space and if the dimensions of the seat are less than 45 cubic inches.

United has the same policy as Continental, but the seat is not allowed to be placed in the overhead bins if there is no extra seat.

For a trip that will include a small child, plan in advance. Always ask the airline about its approved seat policy. Find out the real cost of that seat on the plane or the airline's empty-seat policy.

Don't arrive at the airport an hour before takeoff and expect that you can (1) bring aboard a child safety seat and (2) have an empty seat for it. Plan ahead!

When you call and indicate that you will be traveling with a small child, ask about all the requirements the airline has for the seat. Ask about the size, measurement, and weight of the car seat, the direction it must face, the allowable weight of the child, and whether it is necessary to buy a seat.

Some people mistakenly believe that if they show up at the airport and there are empty seats, they can have one for free for their child's safety seat. This is not always true. Call the airlines and ask about empty-seat policies ahead of time. Remember, if you don't purchase a ticket ahead of time and the flight is fully booked, you may have to hold your baby on your lap and have your car seat checked at the gate.

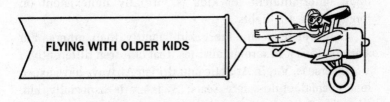

FLYING WITH OLDER KIDS

Ask any parent and you're likely to get the same answer: The airlines couldn't care less about kids. From the counter agents to the gate agents to the flight attendants, it's getting a little ugly up there.

Why? The bottom line: Kids, who don't typically fly first class or business class, aren't big moneymakers. Child passengers account for as little as 5 to 6 percent of an airline's revenue.

Yet if you look at the sheer numbers, children should be given proper recognition.

The number of children flying is growing. Almost 25 percent of households have children who travel. Children under the age of eighteen accompanied adults on more than twenty-six million air trips in 1998, according to the Travel Industry Association of America. That figure was up 30 percent from just two years earlier. And by 2004, the number of flights taken by adults with their kids reached fifty million. A growing number of children of divorced parents are taking to the skies to see parents and family in far-off locales.

Discount airfares and the growing number of unaccompanied minors have combined to make the flying environment less than friendly. Ironically, many of these unaccompanied minors are members of frequent-flier programs and have substantially more mileage than some adult passengers.

With airplanes getting more crowded, the airlines are cutting down on preboarding or more considerate seating for kids. Once in their seats, children face another problem: In-flight entertainment for kids is virtually nonexistent on longer domestic flights.

Some airlines are more kid-friendly than others. For starters, U.S. and foreign airlines treat children differently.

Overseas, Virgin Atlantic and British Airways have excellent special child-safety seats; Swissair is especially kid-friendly. British Airways has a toy chest in its economy sections. Virgin has seatback videos with kid channels. El Al offers both an in-seat TV channel for kids and a special family-seating section.

Singapore Airlines trains its flight attendants for five or six months in often-forgotten arts of assisting with children: changing diapers, preparing formula, milk, and baby meals; sterilizing bottles; and burping a baby. Each aircraft is stocked with diapers, feeding bottles, milk powder, and baby wipes.

Swissair offers preboarding for families with children. Every aircraft is furnished with a changing table, along with children's meals and (on long-haul flights) baby food. Zurich airport has a Lego play area, playrooms, and nursery services.

The domestic airlines most friendly to kids are Southwest, Alaska Airlines, Midwest Airlines, and Air Canada.

For unaccompanied minors, Delta has special supervised play areas called Dusty's Dens at most major airports, featuring soft drinks, computer games, movies, and babysitters. The airline also runs a kids-only frequent-flier program during the summer. Similarly, Northwest has three Kids' Clubs—in Minneapolis, Detroit, and Memphis. Unaccompanied minors can play games, rest, and have a bite to eat—all under supervision.

Continental offers indoor playgrounds at major terminals, while Virgin Atlantic gives kids free backpacks filled with toys when they board. On transatlantic Virgin flights, kids can enjoy Nintendo, in-seat TV with a kids' channel, and ice cream. British Airways has MTV, cartoons, comic books, and loot-filled fanny packs. And many airlines will provide a special kid's meal of chicken fingers, hot dogs, or other favorites, with a day's notice.

In spite of these extras, it's no longer cheaper for children to fly domestically. Carriers have eliminated family-fare discounts in the United States, so be prepared to spend a little more for your vacation.

Some of the bigger U.S. airlines don't score high marks with parents for their treatment of kids. What can parents do? Is there a way to lessen the hassle?

For starters, plan ahead and choose your flights wisely. Adopt my earlier advice about not booking the last flight of the day, especially if you have to make flight connections en route.

Don't book "direct" flights unless there is no alternative. *Direct* does not mean nonstop; it means the plane will make a stop. When you're on a flight that stops, you increase your chances of a weather- or air traffic–related delay. You want to book a *nonstop* flight.

Don't take business flights early in the morning. The best times to travel are on a Tuesday or a Wednesday, around noon. The flights aren't as crowded.

Night flights tend to have fewer delays. Some families like to fly at night so their children can sleep, but I don't recommend it. Just because kids *can* sleep doesn't mean they will, and nothing is worse than a red-eye with wide-awake, screaming children aboard.

Choose a good seat. On some planes, a window seat *behind* the exit row has extra room. (I'm not talking about the exit row; children aren't allowed to sit in that row.) Other passengers will thank you if you choose the bulkhead seat. Why? When (not *if*) your child decides to kick, there's no passenger seated in front of you. Kicking the bulkhead doesn't bother anyone.

On longer international flights, see whether the bulkheads feature fold-down bassinets that can be used in flight. Sit near the front, close to the lavatory.

Many new or refurbished aircraft have incorporated fold-down changing tables in at least one bathroom on board. A few airlines actually provide extra diapers.

Learn how to stay together. One of the biggest problems these days is that, because of increased passenger loads, a lot of airlines separate families on planes and don't seem to care. If this happens, don't expect gate agents to help you. Your best defense here might surprise you. I know of one parent who uses a surefire tactic when all else fails and the airline seats her away from her kids. She buys her kids ice cream cones with not one but two scoops. No napkins. Once her kids sit down, it's only a matter of seconds before the people sitting next to them volunteer to switch places and allow their mother to sit with them.

Get help to the gate. Can you ask the airline to help you get your child or children from the curb to the gate? Not really. At certain airports, such as Chicago's O'Hare and Dallas–Fort Worth, airlines do provide motorized carts for special-assistance cases. That's the good news. The bad news is that these carts are not dependable.

Instead, to get you and your kids and your stuff to the gate in one piece, check in at the curb and tip the skycap more to take you directly to the gate. It's $10 well invested. You cannot depend on any airline personnel to escort you through the airport, but skycaps can and will. (Alexander Hamilton talks.)

Get to the gate early, then seek out a supervisor. Although there may not be a preboarding announcement anymore, this doesn't mean the airline won't preboard you if you ask nicely. My last-resort advice (the airlines will love this): If, for any reason, you can't preboard with your child, then don't board with the masses, either. Instead, wait and board last. Why? You stand a better chance that the airline will realize its mistake and get you a better seat. Standing in a long boarding line with a small child makes things worse for everyone.

Bring food and games. Unless you have prearranged for them, never depend on an airline to provide children's meals, even if they're offered. Instead, bring snacks your child will like—especially snacks that aren't messy. Also bring boxed fruit juices. You can't depend on the flight attendant to make more than two beverage-cart runs during any flight.

Bring games your child likes to play, books, coloring books, activity books, crayons, and that favorite pillow. Extra snacks and activities will be worth their weight in gold in case of unforeseeable delays.

Additional items to bring: diapers, wipes, formula, and snacks for a full day and then some. Be prepared for extra delays or lost luggage. Also bring one or two changes of clothing for your child and yourself.

Finally, take care of your kids' ears. Children's ears are more sensitive than adults' ears to the changes in air pressure on takeoffs and landings. Older kids can chew gum; younger children can drink from a juice box or suck on a bottle. Taking an antihistamine pill the day before the flight will clean out the ears. Parents who have a child with ear problems should ask a pediatrician for medication before the flight.

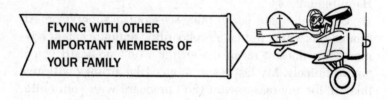

FLYING WITH OTHER IMPORTANT MEMBERS OF YOUR FAMILY

Some readers may have already heard this story.

A woman gets off her flight in Los Angeles and goes to the baggage claim area to get her bags, as well as to claim the kennel holding her dog, which was loaded into the cargo compartment. But when airline baggage handlers remove the kennel from the aircraft, they notice that the dog is dead. They panic and go to an animal shelter in the hope of finding a look-alike dog. They present the woman with a living dog, in the original kennel.

She is shocked when she looks inside. "That's not my dog," she exclaims. "My dog is dead. I was bringing it home for burial."

That story is in the urban legend hall of fame. But among real stories involving airlines' transport of pets, there are many candidates for the hall of shame.

How safe is it to bring your dog or cat on a flight? According to the Air Transport Association, 99 percent of the five hundred thousand dogs and cats the airlines handle each year reach their destination in good health and without problems. That figure sounds impressive, but it means that approximately five thousand animals *don't* arrive safely.

Transportation of live animals is not regulated by the Federal Aviation Administration; however, dogs, cats, and most other warm-blooded animals transported in commerce are protected by the Animal Welfare Act (AWA). The U.S. Department of Agriculture (USDA) is in charge, enforcing the law through its Animal and Plant Health Inspection Service (APHIS). APHIS shipping regulations help ensure that animals covered under the AWA are treated humanely when being transported.

The USDA has levied some heavy fines on airlines that have acted negligently when transporting animals. In 1990, Delta was fined $140,000 when thirty-two puppies, on a flight from St. Louis to Salt Lake City, died from lack of oxygen. A few years later, the USDA fined TWA for improper handling of live animals.

Some transport problems occur because of aircraft design. Newer planes have pressurized and heated baggage compartments, but older aircraft lack ventilation.

Worse is the lack of proper education among passengers and airline workers. If you're shipping your pet in cargo, call the airline first to learn its specific requirements.

Ask about health or immunization requirements for your pet. Airlines and state health officials generally require health certificates for all animals traveling by air. The health certificates should be issued by a licensed veterinarian who has examined your pet within ten days of transport. The vet should also administer any necessary vaccinations or treatments. U.S. territories, Hawaii, and England, among others, require incoming pets to be quarantined. The appropriate government agency or embassy can provide information about such requirements.

How old is your pet? It must be at least eight weeks old and must have been weaned by flight time. Many airlines allow only one adult animal per kennel. Sick, nervous, pregnant, or older pets should not travel by air, nor should certain breeds of dogs and cats because they are susceptible to breathing problems caused by the thin air.

Most likely, you will need to buy an approved carrier/kennel for your dog or cat, but not every airline sells USDA-approved kennels. The design, materials, construction, and ventilation requirements are mandated by law. The kennel you buy should have enough room for your animal to stand up, adjust its position, and turn around. And if the kennel has wheels, they must be removed or made inoperable prior to transport to prevent the kennel from rolling. Be sure to attach a label to your pet carrier with your permanent and travel addresses and telephone numbers.

Your pet will probably have to fly in the cargo hold. Ask if you can watch your pet being loaded; some airlines allow this.

If your pet's kennel is small enough to fit under the seat in front of you, the airline will allow you to take the animal on board, but two conditions apply:

1. Only one pet is allowed per cabin on any flight. On flights that have first, business, and coach class, three pets may travel in the cabin. Southwest flights, which are all coach, allow only one pet.

2. You are not allowed to take your animal for a walk. Even opening the kennel is a big no-no.

But people cheat all the time. The biggest offenders of these two rules? People with small dogs or cats. Some of them literally pack their tiny pets inside their carry-on bags. If the pet goes unnoticed, nothing happens. But more often than not, the owners can't resist taking their animals out once the plane is airborne. Some flight attendants, pet lovers themselves, look the other way. Others tend to enforce the rules.

No one was looking the other way on US Airways Flight 107, a 757 flight from Philadelphia to Seattle. In this funny, somewhat bizarre story, the animal that *did* make it into the passenger section was much bigger than *any* standard kennel.

For those of you who have always wanted to know whether pigs can fly, here's the answer: Apparently they can. Just ask the passengers on that US Airways flight.

How—and why—the airline allowed a 300-pound pig to fly first class on this plane is nothing short of astounding. Evidently, the owners received permission from the airline to bring the porker on board, by producing a doctor's note claiming that the pig was a "service animal"—like a Seeing Eye dog.

According to passengers and flight attendants, the crew first tried to stow the pig in the rear of the aircraft, but it blocked an emergency exit. They then chose to wedge the animal between seats 1A and 1C in the first-class section.

The good news: The animal was well behaved during most of the six-hour flight; it slept most of the way. But when the plane landed, the pig not only woke up, it *got* up, and ran wild through the plane as the 757 taxied to the terminal. It relieved itself as it snorted down the single aisle of the plane. Then it tried to get into the cockpit. Finally, it ran into a galley.

US Airways insisted this was a mistake and would not happen again.

Within days of the incident, the FAA made a startling announcement. It ruled that the pig complied with a Department of Transportation policy that allows individuals with a disability to travel with their "service animals."

Flying is stressful enough for humans, but animals can get really hyper. Some pet owners sedate their dogs and cats, but most airlines and veterinarians discourage this practice because the effects of such medications at high altitudes cannot be accurately predicted. Also, a sedated animal may not be able to properly react to the kennel's movements and could get injured.

Law requires that pets be offered food and water within four hours before check-in, but don't overfeed your pet. Make sure you attach a food dish and a water dish to the inside of the kennel. The dishes should be accessible from the outside without having to open the door. To avoid spilling water, just before the animal is loaded, drop ice cubes into the water dish.

Book your flight well in advance for yourself and your pet and confirm a day or two ahead of the flight that you will be bringing your pet. Try, if possible, to book nonstop, or at least direct, flights, and to travel on the same flight as your pet.

If your pet is lost during transport, speak to airline personnel right away. Many airlines have computer tracking systems that can trace a pet transferred to the wrong flight. If this is not successful, take the following steps to locate your missing pet:

- Contact animal control agencies and humane societies in local and surrounding areas, and check with them daily.

- Contact the APHIS Animal Care regional office closest to where your pet was lost (www.aphis.usda.gov/ac).

- Provide descriptions and photographs to the airline and local agencies. Leave your telephone number and address should you have to return home before your pet is found.

Other problems can occur on connecting flights. Animals might be left exposed on the tarmac in extreme weather conditions. (There are rules regarding the temperature at transfer airports—it must be between 10 and 85 degrees Fahrenheit. USDA guidelines recommend between 45 and 84 degrees.)

What if you discover a problem with your pet after the flight lands? Call a vet immediately and make sure someone from the airline witnesses the problem. Remember, the airlines take a tough position regarding an injury or a death of someone's pet. They will compensate the owner only up to a maximum liability of $1,250. The USDA levies fines, but it doesn't control compensation from an airline to a bereaved passenger.

In one court case, American Airlines argued that it was responsible only for $1,250. A higher court overruled the decision and said that the passenger—whose dog baked to death at 140 degrees in an American cargo hold—could sue for pain, suffering, and inducement to fraud. The judgment against American was $15,000, opening the door a little wider for passengers to seek higher compensation in cases like this.

As a pet owner, watch out for your furry family member to the best of your ability. Your last and best hope: that flight attendants, baggage loaders, and airline captains happen to be pet lovers themselves.

Let's hear it for the captain of United Airlines Flight 231, flying from Washington's Dulles Airport to San Jose, California. Midway in the nearly five-hour trip, an alert United bag loader back in Washington noticed that "Dakota," an African barkless hunting dog, had been improperly loaded into the wrong cargo hold of the Airbus 320. The pilot was alerted by radio and immediately made the decision to divert to Denver.

The dog survived. The captain was hailed as a hero. Oh yes, the movie shown on the flight was *My Dog Skip.*

But the United story is more than overshadowed by some sadder ones. A cat stuck in the cargo hold of an American flight suffered a heart attack and stress. Then there was the story of Boris and Delta Airlines. Boris flew from Fort Lauderdale, Florida, to New York's LaGuardia, but when its owner went to the baggage depot to get the kennel, all Delta employees could show her was a bloody, empty crate. They told her that Boris had escaped and was running around the runways.

Nearly seven weeks later, Boris was found, suffering from serious injuries to his face, frostbite, dehydration, malnutrition, and infection. But despite the owner's efforts to receive some amount of compensation to cover veterinary bills, the airline reimbursed her only the cost of the dog's airfare and of the crate itself.

This one incident resulted in U.S. Senator Frank Lautenberg's introduction of the Safe Air Travel for Animals Act, which was signed into law on April 5, 2000. And that legislation, coupled with a dramatic increase in litigation against airlines for mishandling or killing pets, stirred the airlines to impose even stricter rules (to limit their liability) for accepting pets for travel.

For the moment, the airlines are paying strict attention to the thermometer. Depending on the temperatures in both passengers' originating and destination cities, the airline may refuse to carry a pet because of extremes of either heat or cold.

Every airline has different criteria for their live-animal moratorium, so if you plan a trip with a pet, call and pin them down on exact temperature ranges. If the temperature in either your departure or your destination city, during summer or winter months, is within five degrees of the limits, be prepared to fly without your pet.

Finally, deal with a little reality yourself. Maybe your dog or cat *hates* to fly. Look for a reliable pet sitter or boarding kennel.

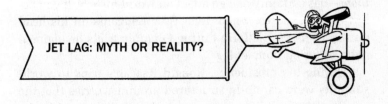

JET LAG: MYTH OR REALITY?

Most of my friends are worried about—some are even obsessed with—the prospect and the effects of jet lag.

How far does that worry extend? Just ask Saudi Arabian Prince Alwaleed Bin Talal Bin Abulaziz Alsaud. When the prince, with his wife, two children, and a seventeen-person entourage, arrived for an eight-day vacation in South Carolina, he decreed that he didn't want to be affected by jet lag. He had a Hilton hotel install $4,000 worth of lights and a volleyball court so that he and his family could maintain their natural body clocks and remain on local Riyadh time. Not only was there a lot of midnight volleyball and swimming, but lunch was served each morning at 2:00 A.M.

Did it work? He never tried it again.

What about special diets, pills, exercise, or eating regimens? I have to admit that the *only* time I ever suffered jet lag was when I actually *tried* one of these "remedies." Millions of travelers complain about it, and very few claim to have conquered it. Jet lag is not a lot of fun.

A flight from Sydney, Australia, to New York, including stopovers, can easily run twenty-four hours, door to door.

But whether you're on a marathon flight to or from Australia, or the shuttle from Boston to Washington, D.C., will jet lag be your constant travel companion? Can you prevent it? Can you treat it? Or is it an unavoidable by-product of jet flight? For some travelers, these may be rhetorical questions.

First, a little history.

Jet lag—some researchers call it *circadian disynchronism*—has certainly had an effect on world history. If you believe such excuses, when diver Greg Louganis hit his head on the 10-meter platform during Olympic trials he claimed to be suffering from jet lag.

During his presidency, Ronald Reagan's trips to world summits were carefully structured around worries that the effects of jet lag might impinge on the crucial decisions he would have to make.

Some diplomats have even cited jet lag as the cause of some of their negotiating mistakes. Before he died, former secretary of state John Foster Dulles actually blamed some of his questionable decisions on jet lag.

Enough about blame or denial. What really constitutes jet lag? Is it, as I sometimes think, merely a state of mind?

Indeed, jet lag is a recognized medical malaise, a disruption of what scientists call the circadian rhythms—the daily individual cycle of sleep and wakefulness. Every time you hop a continent, you upset these rhythms. Jet lag can result in headaches, upset stomach and nausea, and difficulty concentrating and sleeping.

For every time zone that you cross, some researchers say it takes one day for your body to adjust. Many flights from the United States to Europe leave in the evening. If you can take a morning flight that arrives in the afternoon, your body will be more or less on its normal schedule upon arrival. Travelers seem to do better flying west. The body has an easier time setting its clock back.

You need to worry about your internal body alarm clock. When you travel three hours or more, your internal alarm clock goes off three hours earlier (or later) than expected. Synchronization among all of the body's rhythms is lost. Instead of hormone levels dropping while body temperature is rising, both may be increasing. And that's when jet lag kicks in.

There's a whole cottage industry of jet lag diets and computer-generated jet lag schedule programs. A number of airlines, including British Airways and Air New Zealand, offer special aromatherapy kits to passengers or provide treatments once they land.

But a number of researchers and veteran travelers, myself included, believe that what you do before you land makes the real difference.

Doctors have studied the body's internal clock that keeps and controls the body's rhythmic fluctuations, body strength, hormone levels, alertness, sleep, and wakefulness. And they continue to look at how we reset our clock each day with some external cues called *zeitgebers.*

What's a *zeitgeber?* It's a German term for "time giver." Things like light (versus darkness), social activity, alarm clocks, and caffeine help us reset our body's clock every day. But rapid time-zone crossings disrupt the usual fit between physiological rhythms and their *zeitgebers.*

Let's start with what you do before you board your flight. One suggestion that may have merit: Try to hit your body with as many external cues as possible. Stay on the local time of your destination. If it's breakfast time there, have breakfast.

Let's say you're going to England and you're scheduled to arrive the next day at 6:00 A.M. Try to sleep as soon as you get on the plane. If I get on a plane and it's midnight at my destination, I pay attention to that. If they serve dinner right after takeoff and I eat, then my body will think it's 8:00 P.M. again. What you do on a plane should mimic what people are doing at your destination.

Avoid airline food. Most of us eat it not because we're hungry but because we're bored. The moisture problem, the reheating, and other fun things about airline food contribute to creating a digestion problem for many passengers. I can think of few things more conducive to jet lag than eating reheated, dry food at high altitude.

When you're on the plane, walk around. (However, if you feel like sleeping, sleep; if you want to watch the movie, watch the movie.)

And you already know the drill: bottled water, no alcohol. Yes, I know the argument: everyone's metabolism is different, and everyone processes alcohol at varying levels of effect. Alcohol is still not a good idea.

OK, so far, so good. What should you do at your destination?

This key point is the toughest one of all. No matter where you're going, and no matter what time you get there, stay up until at least 11:00 P.M. local time. Needless to say, you will invariably be confronted with an extremely strong urge to take a nap around 3:00 P.M. *Don't do it!* If you do, you will forget your name, where you are, and even why you're there, for at least two days. My advice: Get up, walk around, get some air, shoot some hoops—do anything except succumb to that powerful temptation to take a nap.

The result? If you can stay up until 11:00 P.M. that night, you'll be well on your way to cycling. You won't sleep your full, normal sleep (about five hours), but you will cycle the next night. Follow this timetable when you arrive at your destination and again when you return home. It works in both directions.

Even as I advise all this, I acknowledge that everyone is different and will be affected to varying degrees by the jet flight experience.

Never take any jet lag medication without consulting your doctor. (A traveler might take, for example, melatonin, and then have wine with dinner, at 35,000 feet. That's nuts!)

Some readers may know that the Sydney–to–Los Angeles flight seems interminable, but it's not the longest. New York–to–Johannesburg and Los Angeles–to–Melbourne are longer flights. One of the longest is United Airlines Flight 821, a nonstop service between New York's JFK and Hong Kong. At 7,339 nautical miles, United's Flight 821 was the longest nonstop passenger service in the world. Flight 821 departs JFK daily at 10:30 A.M. and arrives in Hong Kong at 2:10 P.M. (local time) the following day. What time a passenger's body and mind arrive may be a whole different story.

But United Flight 821 is not the longest flight these days. Singapore Airlines, flying an Airbus 340-600, takes that prize with its New York–to–Singapore nonstop flight—eighteen and a half hours.

6

On the Ground

SURVIVING THE CHALLENGE OF TAXIS, HOTELS, MONEY, AND RENTAL CARS

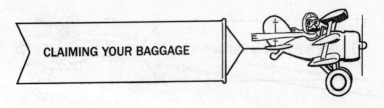

CLAIMING YOUR BAGGAGE

I'm going to make a dangerous assumption here: Your flight landed, and you *and* your luggage were on the *same* plane.

The next hurdle involves the inevitable checked-baggage axiom. You simultaneously checked two bags for your flight. When you land, the first bag off the plane and onto the carousel will be one of yours. The other one will come *last*.

Why waste your time waiting at the carousel—or waste your money renting a baggage cart? Instead, save time *and* money. When you come from the plane, go beyond the baggage claim area to the arrivals area at the curb. There you'll find all the discarded rental baggage carts from the previous flight. You should have enough time to simply walk out, get a cart, and return before your bags show up on the carousel.

Next, push the cart and your bags to the nearest elevator and head upstairs to the departures area, where it will be less crowded and your friends and/or family can meet you.

Suppose there's no one to meet you and you have to take a cab instead. At some airports (New York's LaGuardia, Washington's Reagan, Las Vegas) forget the baggage cart (rented or "found") and hire a skycap. Why? The skycaps get a special courtesy at these airports and get to jump the cab line. Tip accordingly; it's worth it.

THE RIDE FROM THE AIRPORT

If you're like me, you want to get from your plane to a taxi in a minimum amount of time. There are no guarantees that a cab will be waiting, and a huge line of people may be ahead of you.

Here's an idea. Call 1-800-TAXICAB. This clearinghouse will connect you immediately with local cab companies in your destination city. In effect, you're preordering a cab—booking it like a limo, but at a fraction of the cost. If you're short on cash, ask which cab companies accept credit cards. Believe me, you'll save time upon your arrival.

What about the rates? There are only flat-rate cab-ride fares in a few U.S. cities, and in some cities they apply only to certain airports. In New York, the flat-rate fare is $45 plus tolls and tip, but that fare applies only *from* JFK, not in the other direction.

It is important—some would say *imperative*—that the minute you get into a cab, you write down the cab number. Why? You've just come off a long flight and you're not running on all cylinders. You may forget things when you leave the cab—your cell phone, your pocket organizer, or even one of your carry-on bags. Knowing the cab's number may help you retrieve a lost item.

Are you staying in your destination city for more than one day? Tell the driver to make a stop en route. Go to a supermarket or a deli, and have the cab wait for you. Even with the meter running, this is a cost-effective decision. Buy some items that you would like to drink and eat while you're in your hotel room. This will prepare you for your inevitable confrontation with the hotel minibar. (More on that later.)

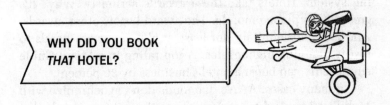

WHY DID YOU BOOK *THAT* HOTEL?

When you're booking a hotel room, clarity means everything. Why did you choose a particular hotel? An advertisement? Price? Word of mouth? A guidebook?

And what do you hope to do at this hotel? Is this a business trip, and you only need a room? Is it a vacation? Does your trip have a combined purpose? What price are you willing to pay, and for what amenities?

Q: What's a four-star hotel? A three-star hotel?

A: No one really knows.

I remember one London hotel's boast that it was the city's only five-star hotel. How did that happen? The hotel awarded the stars to itself!

Sadly, this is not an isolated incident. Many hotels have begun grading themselves. Their brochures are definitely misleading. Biddingfortravel.com, a website devoted to helping us find great deals on Priceline, actually has an entire forum on "hotel misratings."

In many countries, the number of stars is awarded to a hotel by the individual municipal government that has jurisdiction over the hotel's location. The number of stars is based only on the rates the hotel charges, rather than on any quality or service criteria.

Nevertheless, the star search continues. Mobil Guides award stars. AAA gives out diamonds in its guidebooks' rating system. Hotels take these awards seriously. Why? It's great for employee morale. The award begets other awards. And last but definitely not least, it allows certain hotels to justify charging higher rates. A top rating in a Mobil Guide supposedly can boost a hotel's business by 20 percent.

In many cases, AAA's diamonds don't synchronize with Mobil's stars. And what's worse are the criteria. Hotels that are rated three diamonds or three stars are more often than not rated on the basis of their facilities, not their service.

At the upper levels, inspections do rate service. For example, under the Mobil criteria, how long does the registration process take at the front desk? If the hotel can do it in under three minutes and twenty seconds, it rates five stars, under three minutes and forty-eight seconds, it drops to four stars. How about baggage delivery to your room? Under seven minutes and twenty-three seconds, five stars. Under ten minutes and fifteen seconds, four stars. But all of this is subjective. Did the inspector check in at the same time that twenty-three other people decided to check in? Was there a large meeting going on in the hotel, heavily tasking the bellstaff?

So how does this help you? In the long run, it doesn't—although it may be entertaining.

Because of these subjective criteria, I am not a fan of these ratings. If a guidebook gives a hotel five stars because it has a golf course, what possible use is that to me if I don't play golf? I'm more interested in the water pressure in the shower, how the phones work, getting Internet access, how fast the valet parking unit delivers my car, and whether there are enough pillows on the bed. I care less about "fine dining" at hotels. I care more about whether room service can take my order and deliver the food to my room in less than thirty minutes. And there you have my "star" or "diamond" list.

Guidebooks and ratings have another problem. Because they are so subjective, I have a healthy cynicism about the accuracy of any descriptive words that end with "st." My lie detector kicks in when I read that a hotel has been voted "greatest," or "best," or "most," or "finest." You get the picture.

Develop your own criteria for what makes a hotel worthy of your business. For example, what makes a hotel a "resort": A swimming pool? Hardly. And what defines a "health club" or a "spa"? One treatment room and an old VHS Jane Fonda workout tape do not transform a hotel into a spa.

There is one bottom-line criterion for selecting a hotel. When American Express cardholders were surveyed about the most important factor in a comfortable overnight hotel stay, they responded that it was great water pressure in the bathroom. Are you hoteliers listening? Forget the fruit basket welcome. Work on the plumbing!

KID-FRIENDLY OPTIONS

Always ask about amenities in advance of your stay, especially when you're traveling with your kids. Virtually every hotel boasts that it has a great children's program. But knocking out the walls between two guest rooms and installing some large card tables stocked with crayons and Legos does not create a great kids' program.

For many years, with the exception of the legendary Eloise at the Plaza Hotel in New York, kids were either ignored or frowned upon at most hotels. They were considered an annoying encumbrance to hotel staff and other guests. Then, several years ago, a few hotels finally figured out a simple but powerful concept: If you make your property kid-friendly and the kids like it, they're going to bring their parents.

There was another small incentive: the numbers. Children make more than 150 million trips a year, and those trips convert to serious money. So with great fanfare many hotels announced they were suddenly opening their doors to kids and offering special children's programs and activities. However, more often than not, the programs were disappointing. Too many hotels converted one or two guest or meeting rooms, set up a few table-and-chair units, added a few dozen crayons, stacked some cartoon videos on a TV set, and called the offering a "children's program."

But some other hotels quietly created comprehensive, properly supervised, and imaginative children's programs that were innovative, responsible, and safe. Wise hotels followed suit. Today, most hotels at least claim to offer a children's program; in fact, the statistics might surprise you. And the demand for such programs has gone beyond just leisure and vacation travelers.

A survey commissioned by Sheraton Hotels confirmed that, among business travelers, kids have a lot more to say than one might imagine or admit. Of the parents polled, 67 percent said they have refused to go on a particular business trip because it conflicted with their children's activities; 41 percent said they would cut a trip short because of a child's birthday or illness; 31 percent won't travel when a school function is scheduled for their children; and 5 percent would cancel a trip altogether if their children were upset because the parent was leaving.

Translation: As business-traveler parents try to preserve the delicate balance between their work and their family life, the family often hits the road. The kids get to go along.

In many of today's two-income families, executives pack up the kids as well as the briefcase. In the Sheraton study,

60 percent of parents said they have taken a child along on a business trip. (The least significant finding of the Sheraton survey was one of the most amusing. Business travelers who do not take their kids on their trips face a perennial question when they return home: "What did you bring me?" A full 27 percent reported that they bring home a T-shirt.)

In response to the survey's information, the Sheraton chain began offering a family plan. There is no charge for children (seventeen years old and younger) who share a room with a parent or guardian, if the children can be accommodated with the existing furnishings. To make business travelers feel more at home, Sheraton is introducing guest rooms that are more like bedrooms at home than hotel rooms. These rooms feature cozy sleigh beds and oversize desks and work areas. The new look was introduced in more than six thousand hotel rooms as Sheraton renovated its properties in North America. Indeed, Sheraton is just one of a number of major hotel chains oriented toward being kid-friendly—and safe for kids. A number of hotels are going out of their way to "childproof" their rooms—not to protect the hotel from children, but to protect children during their stay at the hotel.

At the Breakers, in Palm Beach, Florida, families with children age three and younger are automatically eligible for a childproof room. If the names and ages of the children were not given previously, they are determined at check-in, and the front desk sends an electronic message to the housekeeping department. Within fifteen minutes, a housekeeping staff member comes to the room and offers to childproof it. Parents may accept or decline this complimentary service. Also, screened and experience-selected babysitters can be booked.

After the childproofing comes the fun part. The guests can choose either a roll-away bed or a Barney, Lion King, or Aladdin sleeping bag. A majority of the hotel's 569 soundproof rooms are now connected, so families can reserve up to five adjoining guest rooms. This feature gives adults more privacy while keeping the kids in close proximity. If children who are age sixteen or younger stay in the same room as their parents, there is no extra charge.

Children of guests can occupy themselves in the craft room, movie room, computer room, or playroom. The Breakers also features the Coconut Crew Interactive Camp, where kids from age three to age twelve can participate in age-appropriate, organized activities seven days a week.

At the Sonesta Beach Resort in Key Biscayne, Florida, when kids between the ages of five and twelve check in with their parents, they can register for the Just Us Kids room. This program includes the Disney Kid Corner featuring kid-friendly furniture, visits from Disney characters, movie ticket drawings, and other prizes.

Families traveling to the Boca Raton Resort and Club no longer need a van to accommodate their little ones' bring-along items, thanks to the resort's new "Boca Tots" program. The tony world-class golf and beach resort caters to a most discriminating group: toddlers. From a menu featuring freshly made baby food, strollers, high chairs, and other paraphernalia available upon request, the Boca Tots program is designed exclusively for children three years old and under. Nearly 10 percent of the resort's guests have babies, so they wanted to make traveling with little ones less stressful and more enjoyable for both the babies and the parents. The program was inspired by the resort's executive chef, James Reaux. He made healthy and delicious baby food for his own children and now does so for the children of resort guests. Meals at the resort come complete with a Boca Tots bib and bottle.

But the hotel goes beyond recipes to more important aspects, such as child safety. As part of the program, guests can request the following items upon arrival: a quality crib with an extra-firm mattress, a high chair, baby bath amenities, child-friendly sunscreen and baby sunglasses, a hooded towel and a washcloth, a baby bathtub, age-appropriate toys, a diaper pail, instructions for reserving babysitters through the resort, a baby monitor (for guests staying in suites), a car seat, a stroller, a humidifier, baby spoons, pacifier/teething toys, diapers (including swim diapers) and wipes, and children's videos.

The Boca Raton Resort also offers Bocabunch, for kids from six to eleven years old, and Boca Sport, for those from twelve to sixteen.

Folks in British Columbia, in Canada, are actively involved in servicing the growing family travel market with an aggressive kid-friendly campaign. The program, run by Kid Friendly, a Vancouver company, goes beyond distribution of cute children's amenities.

"It's more important than just marketing 'Kids stay free' deals," says founder Cheryl MacKinnon. "We are encouraging airlines, hotels, car rental companies, and other attractions to consider elements like safety and accessibility. These range from colorful footstools at counters to kid-friendly play areas in info centers, family parking spots near the front door, interactive/educational games, and giveaways that invite and inspire kids to explore the destination more fully." MacKinnon also has lobbied hotels to start emptying the minibars and using them for storage of formula and other food for babies and young children; ensure that cribs, playpens, skycots, and high chairs meet current safety standards; and provide emergency diapers, blankets, and bottles. "It may sound silly," she says, "but as a parent who traveled with a baby, sometimes—for whatever reason—you need these things to tide you over till the next morning, when the stores open."

At Radisson's Family Approved Hotels, families traveling with children are offered special features, services, and amenities to enhance their stay. There are more than seventy participating hotels in the United States, Canada, the Caribbean, Central America, and Asia. Participating hotels offer, in at least one restaurant and through room service, a children's menu featuring kids' favorite foods. Child-care services are either on-site or are made available via a list of qualified babysitters.

Cots, cribs, and playpens are available upon request. Popular award-winning books and games for children from three through twelve years old can be checked out from a special library. A professional children's librarian from Baker & Taylor, the leading supplier of book and related services to more than one hundred thousand bookstores, schools, and libraries worldwide, recommended a balanced selection of books specifically for Radisson.

A swimming pool is the most popular hotel feature for children, according to family travel research. Childproofing/safety kits are available at the front desk. Families traveling with small children may use them during their stay. Family movies are available on the in-room movie system.

The Hyatt hotels also are trying to be more kid-friendly. At the Grand Hyatt San Francisco, kids can receive a Tonka Toy dump truck filled with candy, fruit, and small toys, and they get to keep the truck. At the Resort at Squaw Creek, at Lake Tahoe, guests can request child seats on the Squaw Valley Shuttle, which transports guests from Reno/Lake Tahoe International Airport to the resort. Childproof safety plugs for a room's electric sockets are available for guests who request them.

The Loews hotel chain does an excellent job of catering to families with children, starting with childproofing. Every Loews property has kits available for guests with small children, which include a night-light, electrical outlet covers, padding for the hard edges of furnishings, a sliding-glass-door lock, and a soft waterspout cover. All kids age ten and under receive a complimentary "Loews Loves Kids" gift bag upon arrival. Kids can also take advantage of a variety of special programs and services such as game libraries, special menus, tours, and supervised recreational programs. Loews provides appropriate DVDs, Game Boys, and social activities for teens as well.

There's a discount on children's rooms that adjoin their parents' room. (Children who are eighteen and under stay free when they share a room with their parents.) Guests have complimentary use of cribs, roll-away beds, and children's sheets. Restaurant menus, room service, and minibars offer children's menus and child-friendly snacks. A "Kids' Kloset" offers games, books, car seats, strollers, night-lights, potty seats, baby bathtubs, baby blankets, and electrical outlet covers for guests to use during their stay.

Can your child say "upgrade"? If so, check in to the Loews Portofino Bay Hotel at Universal Studios Escape, in Orlando, Florida. It features a unique room concept for the hotel's eighteen kids' suites: an adjoining room for children that is accessed only through the main room. Each of the suites is designed with childhood themes and features two single beds, a small table-and-chair set, a beanbag chair, and a separate closet with children's bathrobes and hangers. (Here's a somewhat dangerous thought: Parents also can give their children a separate room card that allows access to the room and lets them make purchases throughout Universal Studios Escape, up to a preloaded spending limit set by the parents.)

Although U.S. hotels have clearly begun to embrace children, most foreign hotels still believe that children should be neither seen nor heard. But there are, of course, exceptions. A few years ago, the Athenaeum Hotel and Apartments in London launched a program in the summer of 2000 for children from four to twelve years old. Each child receives his or her own Arthurnaeum (a lovable brown bear that is the hotel's furry hospitality ambassador), a kiddies' pack containing a coloring book and crayons, a rubber duck for the bath, and a range of children's toiletries (soap, shampoo, bubble bath, talc, mini toothbrush, and toothpaste). A special children's menu has been developed in the Windsor Lounge, and room service and turndown service include milk and cookies. The children also receive a gift voucher to Hamleys, considered London's best-known toy store. Also, children receive free accommodations when staying with their parents in one of the hotel's 34 one- and two-bedroom apartments.

IS THE HOTEL PET-FRIENDLY?

More and more of us travel with our pets. And more and more hotels are developing flexible policies toward allowing pets in guests' rooms.

Even if you are told a hotel is pet-friendly, always ask, ahead of your stay, whether the hotel will require a damage deposit for your animal. Also, are there special pet services? At some hotels, they range from dog walking (by hotel door attendants) to wilder offerings. A hotel in Mexico has installed special exercise treadmills for dogs! One very good website to consult before your trip is BringYourPet.com.

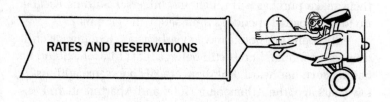

RATES AND RESERVATIONS

The factors that count when you are checking hotel rates are not only supply and demand but also location and season. A special rate at a hotel in Hawaii during the Christmas season? Forget it. However, getting a rate in March may be easy because there are empty rooms.

You need to know how to cut a deal, either before you get there or when you arrive at the hotel. Some desk clerks will throw out a room rate just to see if it will fly; treat it like the first price quoted at the covered bazaar in Istanbul. You know the drill. After hearing the first price, you immediately shake your head and walk out of the stall. If the hotel is 50 percent full at eleven o'clock at night, and the clerk says that rooms are $159, you simply respond: "I'll give you $79 or forget the deal." For most hotels, something is always better than nothing.

What about calling ahead? If it's a convention hotel, it's the beginning of the week, and you're in New Orleans or Chicago and the town is packed, of course you're going to call the hotel before you go there. The question is: Whom do you ask to speak with? The reservations agent? No. Ask for the director of sales. You want to let him or her know you're a corporate person, not some yokel off the street. You might say: "Listen, I was going to talk to the reservations people, but I'd rather talk to you, because I'm going to be coming to Chicago quite a few times over the next several months, and I'd like to work out a rate with you."

Note: Before you contact the director of sales, *do call* the reservations desk and find out the hotel's prices, just to get a basis of comparison. Then see whether you can cut a deal with the director of sales. If so, (1) you've got a deal with someone who's highly placed in the hotel, (2) you've got a contact at the hotel, and (3) you've got a rate that's substantially lower than what you'd pay if you walked in off the street or telephoned for a reservation. A hotel has the same goal as an airline frequent-flier program. It wants your loyalty and your repeat business. If you can give it that loyalty, or at least the perception of it, you will get some deals.

Now that you've been clear with the hotel—and, with luck, have received clarity in return—it's equally important to know the right way to make your reservation.

Like the airlines, hotels also engage in the dark science of revenue management. At some hotels, there may be as many as forty different rates for any one room.

How can you get the best deal? Here are the key factors: what number or extension you call, what day of the week and what time of day you call, how many days you are staying, and to whom you speak.

Let's start with the number that you call. Many of us have been tempted to call a toll-free 800 number for reservations, especially when a booking is desired at any number of large-chain hotels. It's convenient, the call is free, and you can quickly make a reservation at any of the chain's hotels, anywhere in the world. Technically, these facts are correct. Still, you should avoid toll-free 800 numbers for reservations.

A case in point: I had been invited to the wedding of a close friend in Albuquerque, New Mexico. I needed to fly in on a Friday, attend the wedding late on Saturday afternoon and the reception that evening, and fly out early on Sunday morning.

Opting for expediency, I called the toll-free number for Hilton. I asked whether I could make a reservation for a room for two nights, "at the lowest rate," for the Albuquerque Hilton. No problem. The lowest rate they could offer me was $89 per night. Would I like to guarantee that and hold the room via a credit card? Sure. I gave the agent my American Express card number, got my confirmation number, and in less than four minutes, I had made the reservation.

Nine days later, I hopped on the short flight from Los Angeles to New Mexico, grabbed a cab at the Albuquerque airport, and arrived at the hotel. Armed with my confirmation number and prepaid room reservation, I walked into the lobby and headed for the front desk.

There were two people ahead of me in line. The man directly in front of me, also there for the wedding, seemed nervous. While we waited, he told me that he had decided at the very last minute to come to the nuptials and didn't have a reservation. He was taking a chance, hoping there might be a room available. I tried to act concerned, but that wasn't easy since I already had my confirmed reservation.

When it was his turn, he walked up to the front desk clerk, asked whether the hotel had any rooms for that night, and, if so, what was the lowest rate?

"Yes," she replied, "we have rooms."

And the rate?

"Thirty-nine dollars."

What? The lowest rate was $50 *less* than I was paying? There was only one thing to do.

When I approached the desk, I conveniently forgot to mention my earlier reservation and asked the same questions the "walk-in" had asked. Sure enough, rooms were $39.

"Fine," I said, "I'll take one, for two nights."

I whipped out my American Express card and completed the transaction for the much cheaper room.

In the end, both the hotel and American Express still charged me $89 for the room. I disputed the bill, and my claim was simple: The hotel had failed to disclose that there was, indeed, a lower rate available at the time I had made my booking. Therefore, the charge was invalid. In addition, I did not receive the service for which I had contracted—the lowest rate at the hotel. And under the terms of my credit card agreement, I was not liable to pay the charge. Finally, the proof here was easy: I *did pay* the $39 charge—for the same room—with my American Express card. American Express removed the larger charge from my bill.

The lesson here: *Never, ever* call a toll-free 800 number advertised by hotel chains like Hilton, Hyatt, and Sheraton. The 800 numbers are nothing more than clearinghouses for blocks of rooms, which are put on the market at the highest rate the hotels think they can get away with.

It's almost always cheaper to spend a dollar or two on a long-distance call to an individual hotel and negotiate your own rate. There may be thirty-five separate rates that can be used for any room—a corporate rate, weekend rate, senior rate, student rate, auto club rate, and so forth. The *rack rate* is the highest possible tariff published for that room. It's what the hotels charge people who don't know any better. If you pay the rack rate, you should be quietly taken away and put to sleep.

Another word about 800 numbers. The large hotel chains now argue that they have revamped their 800-number reservations systems to provide "rate integrity." The 800 service will offer the exact same rate that would be quoted by the individual hotel if you were to call it directly.

Is this really true? The answer is yes, if you just call the hotel directly and ask to speak to a reservations agent. But, once again, it gets down to *whom* you call and, more often than not, *when* you call. Remember: *Every rate is negotiable.* Usually when a hotel is booked to about 92 percent of capacity, it is much less inclined to lower its rates. But when bookings are under 92 percent, the rate game is definitely on.

There's another unusual formula you can use to negotiate a hotel room: by square footage. At the very least, you'll understand the amount of space you're really paying for— whether your room is indeed the size of a closet or as big as a suite, the square footage formula is enlightening. Size does matter when it comes to determining the true value of a room.

The solution is a simple formula more common in real estate than in travel: Divide the room rate by the number of square feet. So if the room costs $200 per night for 200 square feet, the rate per square foot is $1.

A great example is New York. Most travelers would be surprised to learn there is a huge discrepancy between room rate and square footage costs. Following is a survey of midtown Manhattan hotels including room size (in square feet), room rates, and the calculated rate per square footage.

Prime Midtown Hotel	Rate per Square Foot	Median Room Size	Room Rate
Paramount Hotel	$1.83	130 sq ft.	$239
W Times Square	$1.21	280 sq ft.	$339
Plaza	$1.15	225 sq ft.	$259
Hudson Hotel	$1.12	156 sq ft.	$175
Hilton Waldorf-Astoria	$1.12	240 sq ft.	$269
Le Parker Meridien	$0.91	312 sq ft.	$285
Rihga Royal	$0.65	500 sq ft.	$325
Buckingham Hotel	$0.33	700 sq ft.	$229

THE BEST TIME TO CALL

What's the best time to call to get the lowest rate? If you're simply walking into a hotel without a reservation, it's a no-brainer: 10:00 P.M. on a Wednesday night in February will usually get you an incredibly low room rate. You may even be upgraded to a suite.

For the rest of us, who tend to phone ahead, try 4:00 P.M. on a Sunday. Why? Because the folks who run "revenue management," the people who set the sliding rates for any hotel room, are off on Sundays, and you stand a much better chance of getting a front-desk clerk who just needs to sell a room. The result: a lower rate.

A few years ago hotels tended to be overbuilt, and there were opportunities for bargaining. In fact, more than three-quarters of all business travelers negotiated with hotels and never paid published prices. Keep in mind that, in recent years, though occupancy was down, the *average* daily room rates for hotels in major cities rose by 3 percent per year, with revenue per available room growing by 5.8 percent after increasing only .5 percent last year.

To make matters potentially worse, the meeting and conventions business, which had been devastated after 9/11, is coming back with a vengeance. The result: Available hotel inventory is shrinking. Hotels are doing everything they can to retake control of their inventory, and that includes, in some cases, ending contracts with third-party websites. For example, Intercontinental Hotels totally dropped Expedia in 2004.

Still, an unsold room is the last thing a hotelier wants; it represents revenue the hotel can never recoup. (It's like an airplane flying with an empty seat; the fare is lost forever.) The hotelier will figure that earning something is better than nothing. As an example, in some big-city hotels, the weekend rate may go as low as one-third of the regular nightly rate. Suggest cutting a deal in which that rate is extended throughout the week if you stay in that hotel.

OTHER QUESTIONS TO ASK

When you ask for a price quote on a hotel room, most hotels neglect to mention that the official rate—the rate offered to you, even if it is the lowest available rate—doesn't include occupancy tax or sales tax. Because they're trying to be competitive, the hotels quote only the price for the room. The taxes are add-ons and, in many cities, they are excessive.

In the United States, hotel taxes average 12 percent. The most abusive hidden fee in at least seventeen U.S. cities, including Atlanta, Chicago, and Miami, is a surcharge to finance a local stadium or a convention center.

Not only do these charges add a significant amount to travelers' bills, no one warns that they are coming. Cities get away with burdening travelers with a disproportionate amount of the costs of building arenas because we don't vote there.

How high are these taxes? Here is a tally of occupancy taxes in some cities:

Chicago	14.9 percent
Dallas	13
Los Angeles	14
Houston	15
Anaheim (California)	15
Seattle	15.2
Columbus (Ohio)	15.75

If you call a hotel and the room rate quoted is $150, you know you will be paying more—maybe *much* more. Overseas, the tab can be worse. The dreaded value-added tax (VAT) is slapped onto just about anything, especially hotel rooms.

Be sure you arrive at a mutually agreeable definition of terms. Was the $150 rate quoted to you the cost for double occupancy or for the room? If it was for double occupancy, the real rate is $300 per night. You'd be surprised how many people don't ask about the room rate and don't define the terms ahead of time, only to find out, too late, that their rate is actually double what they expected it to be.

Are there other extras? Is there an additional charge for your kids? Many hotels now have a deal where up to two kids under age sixteen can stay free. But you need to know these details up front, even if the rate quoted is for the room.

Remember, some hotels will do anything to charge you the full rate, even if you're just there for a few hours' sleep. I love this story.

A husband and wife were traveling by car from Key West to Boston. After almost twenty-four hours on the road, they were too tired to continue, so they decided to stop for a rest. They stopped at a nice hotel and took a room, but they planned to sleep for only four hours and then get back on the road. When they checked out four hours later, the desk clerk handed them a bill for $350.

The man exploded, demanding to know why the charge was so high. He told the clerk that although it was a nice hotel, the rooms certainly weren't worth $350. When the clerk told him $350 was the standard rate, the man insisted on speaking to the manager.

The manager appeared, listened to the man, and then explained that the hotel had an Olympic-size pool and a huge conference center that were available for the husband and wife to use. "But we didn't use them," the man complained.

"Well, they are here, and you could have," explained the manager. He went on to explain that they could have taken in one of the shows for which the hotel was famous. "The best entertainers from New York, Hollywood, and Las Vegas perform here," the manager said.

"But we didn't go to any of those shows," complained the man again.

"Well, we have them, and you could have," the manager replied.

No matter what facility the manager mentioned, the man replied, "But we didn't use it!" The manager was unmoved, and eventually the man gave up and agreed to pay.

He wrote a check and gave it to the manager. The manager was surprised when he looked at the check. "But sir," he said, "this check is only made out for $50."

"That's right," said the man. "I charged you $300 for sleeping with my wife."

"But I didn't!" exclaimed the manager.

"Well," the man replied, "she was here, and you could have."

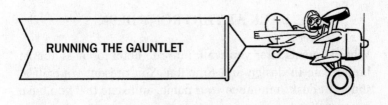

RUNNING THE GAUNTLET

Your cab has brought you to your hotel. In big cities like New York, Chicago, and Miami, where unions rule, be prepared to run the gauntlet of the limited-distance, limited-responsibility army: doormen, bellhops, and others who will help you get from point A to point B—but, you learn, each pair of points measures only about 10 feet.

The doorman opens the door to your cab, helps lift your luggage out of the trunk, and then moves your bags about 5 feet. *Hand extended: tip opportunity 1.*

Then a bellhop appears, places your luggage on a cart, and wheels it roughly 25 feet from the curb, through the doors and into the lobby. *Hand extended: tip opportunity 2.*

Your luggage sits there until you check in. Another bellhop then brings your luggage up and places it in your room. *Hand extended: tip opportunity 3.*

America is a wonderful country. Three separate people to do the job of one person.

Is it any wonder that most savvy business travelers insist on carrying their own bags? The money isn't the issue here. Being forced to support ridiculous excess violates many travelers' principles.

I do not tip the doorman or the first bellhop. I tip the second bellhop according to the amount of luggage I'm carrying. The amount of the tip is sufficient for this bellhop to split the tip with the other two attendants, and I announce that fact when I give him the money.

BACK AT THE FRONT DESK

What happens after you walk into the hotel lobby is almost boilerplate in design and function. You present yourself at the front desk, announce your name, and state that you have a reservation.

The desk clerk checks the hotel's records and, with luck, has you in the system. "Yes, Mr. Jones, we have your room right here."

The clerk will then, most likely, verify your name and address, and the length of your stay.

This is inevitably followed by a routine question: "Could I see a credit card so I can make an imprint?" The request sounds normal, painless, and innocent.

It's anything but.

More often than not, the clerk is *not* making an imprint of your credit card. Instead, without informing you, the clerk swipes the card through the credit card authorization terminal and does something called *blocking.*

This is bad news. The clerk swipes your card, then punches in an arbitrary dollar amount, ranging from your room rate to a wild multiple of that rate. At that moment, anywhere from $100 to $3,000—or more—is "blocked" on your credit card account. The hotel does this to protect itself in case you go beserk at the minibar or steal all the towels.

But here are the problems. First, the hotel doesn't tell you it's doing this. And second, if you use a credit card that has a preset credit line—like MasterCard, Visa, or Discover—you may be in for an embarrassing moment later, when you go to use your card. Unbeknownst to you, your credit line has been maxed out simply by checking in to the hotel!

But whatever you do, *never* use an ATM or debit card to check in to a hotel. Those blocking charges never get reversed. Your checking account is debited, just like cash. And not only does getting that money back take a long time, there's also the issue of all those NSF (insufficient funds) charges on your checks returned as a result of this.

My advice: If you have another credit card with no preset spending limit (for example, American Express or Diners Club), even if you have no intention of paying your hotel bill with it, use it when you check in. That way, when the hotel blocks charges, it won't ruin your day or your stay.

When you check out, ask the hotel cashier to rip up your AmEx or Diners Club invoice. When you see that has been done, pay your *real* charges, and nothing more, with your Visa, MasterCard, or Discover card.

FIVE ESSENTIAL QUESTIONS

After you present a credit card at check-in, but before you go up to your room, five key questions *must* be answered at the front desk. They will affect not only the kind of room you get, but your overall safety and comfort while staying at the hotel.

1. *How close is my room to the construction?* Sound strange? Not in the least. Virtually every hotel is run on cycles of renovation. At any given time, at least one floor, or sometimes an entire wing, is closed down for refurbishment or renovation. The last thing you need is to be booked next to an early-morning jackhammer.

2. *How close is my room to the ballroom?* (Or: *How far above the ballroom is my room?*) There's usually no problem with noise from the ballroom during a party. *After* the party, about 1:00 A.M., there's often a problem. That's when hotel workers are cleaning up, which involves throwing out the used wine and champagne bottles. Ah yes, the blissful sounds of breaking glass.

3. *How close is my room to the elevators?* Some travelers think it's a good idea to be close to the elevators, for both convenience and security reasons. But if you're too close to the elevators, you hear them all night long.

    An aside about what floor your room is on is appropriate here. There is absolutely no advantage to getting a room higher than the eighth floor at any hotel.

    • Reason A: The higher you go, the longer it takes to get there—and to get down from there. At peak morning and afternoon times, a room on a hotel's fortieth floor means an extra ten minutes of waiting *for* the elevator, and more time waiting *in* the elevator as it stops at almost every floor.

    • Reason B: Safety. There's not a fire department in the world that can get above the eighth floor. If you're in one of the high rooms with a great view, in the event of a fire your great view will be of the fire department's futile attempt to reach you!

4. *Is the heating a two-pipe or a four-pipe system?* If it's a two-pipe system, you will either freeze or burn. The newer four-pipe system allows better control of room temperature. Not all hotels have converted to the four-pipe system, which means that you've got to ask about it.

5. *Could you do me a favor: Call engineering and ask what floors have booster pumps?* This is usually my first question, because good water pressure is so important to me. (When you ask, the desk clerk may give you a deer-in-the-headlights look.) Most high-rise hotels have been unable to maintain adequate water pressure in the rooms. So on different (not necessarily alternating) floors, the hotels install booster pumps. Get a room on one of those floors. When you turn on your shower, the pressure will match that of a fire hose!

Back to the front desk. You asked the right questions, you got the right rate, and you got the best room for your money.

What next? You go to the room with the bellhop, even if you have no luggage. Why? For three reasons:

1. Ask the bellhop to remove your hotel bedspread. Hotels do *not* clean bedspreads after each guest. In fact, they may not clean them for weeks. You don't need it, you won't use it, and you don't need me to tell you why you should have it removed. Also, call housekeeping and ask to have three pillows brought to your room. (There's nothing I like less than a hotel bed with just two skimpy pillows.)

2. Don't let the bedbugs bite. That's right, bedbugs are making a comeback in hotels. And what's worse, people who stay in hotel rooms infested by bedbugs often

bring them home. In 2000, the National Pest Management Association reported zero cases. In 2003, there were 390 cases in thirty-three states. And in case you're wondering, bedbugs are small, flat bugs about the size of an apple seed that live in cracks and crevices of beds. Now here's the tough part: They only come out at night to feed on people's blood with a painless bite. So if you wake up in the morning and see white welts on your skin, it's time for immediate checkout!

3. Remember that supermarket or deli stop you made en route to the hotel? The minute you enter the room, ask the bellhop to immediately empty the minibar and inform the front desk.

I *hate* minibars. They are seductive but mean-spirited. (I've had too many dates like that!) Seriously, you must acknowledge the inevitability of a snack attack in your room, but your wallet shouldn't be raped in the process.

Minibars are among the best profit makers in a hotel. Paying $6 for a miniature bottle of soda should be a felony for both parties: the hotel, for charging the outrageous fee, and you, for being stupid enough to pay that amount.

Instead, load up your minibar with the items you bought at the store. During an average two-day stay, you'll save more than $50. Believe me, those overpriced candy bars add up.

The minibar wars have gotten so bad that some hotels have installed Darth Vader minibars. If you even open the door and slightly *move* an item, you are automatically charged for that item, whether you use it or not! You are now forewarned.

The minibars are indicative of the boom in nickel-and-diming at many hotels. These establishments slip insidious, extra, undisclosed charges onto guests' bills, and if you're not careful, you might not even see them or know what they are. Or you might discover the charges only after the fact, when you're checking out.

Here's my hall-of-fame nomination for nickel-and-diming. I was checking in to the Hyatt Regency Hotel in Houston for a one-night stay. I went through the usual ritual, and before handing me my room key, the clerk said, "Oh, you received a Federal Express package. Would you like us to deliver it to you?" (I love stupid questions like this one. I was tempted to respond, "No, please share it with the other guests.") The bellhop walked over, got the FedEx pack, put it with the rest of my luggage, and up we went to my room.

The next morning, when I was checking out, I reviewed my bill. Without explanation, there was an additional $5 charge. When I asked what it was, the reply was a shock. I had been charged to *receive* a FedEx package! I complained. The charge was taken off the bill.

Two days later, at the Hilton in Las Vegas, I was called and told I had received a fax. Would I like it delivered? (Again, I was tempted to respond, "No, please post it in the lobby.") The fax was delivered, and I tipped the bellhop. When I checked out, my bill showed a charge for receiving a fax. Again, I complained, and again, the charge was removed from the bill.

A week later, at the Anatole Hotel in Dallas, I got hit with a double whammy. I had received a fax. The hotel would *not* deliver it. I had to walk about a half-mile to get it, *and* I was charged a fee for receiving the fax!

There's also a nickel-and-diming rip-off involving the in-room safe. Many hotels and resorts now offer these security devices. But many of them don't tell guests that they charge upward of $4 a day for use of the safe. Think about what an in-room safe is saying to you:

1. The hotel doesn't trust its own security system.

2. The hotel doesn't trust its staff.

3. We're going to charge you up to $4 a day to use a safe, when, under every state's innkeeper laws, the hotel is not held liable for the loss of any valuables from that safe. (Hotels are liable—in a limited way—only for theft or loss from their safe deposit boxes, which are available to guests, free of charge, at the front desk.)

Then there's the rip-off of room service, or more precisely, of what comes *with* room service: the double-dipping receipt.

Let's start with a definition of room service. It is a premium service, usually at a premium price, for the luxury and convenience of eating inside your own hotel room. OK; so far, so good.

Understanding that you will likely pay a little more for this service, you pick up your phone and place your order, say for a cheeseburger, a salad, a glass of wine, and perhaps a fruit plate for dessert. Soon (hopefully) there's a knock at your door, and a room service waitperson delivers your meal on a cart. After doing the setup, the waitperson presents you with the bill.

On the surface, most room service receipts look like a standard white-and-yellow copy of a credit card bill. Now, look carefully at that room service bill. It lists the food items ordered and their prices. Next there's a "service charge" (usually under $5) and state sales tax. And then the hotel arbitrarily imposes a 15 to 18 percent gratuity.

Ready for the surprise? Below that space on the slip, is the word *subtotal*.

Subtotal? Yes. Right under the subtotal listing is another word, and the space to its right is left blank: *Tip*.

Another tip? What was the 18 percent gratuity? If you simply look at the subtotal and add a tip, you've just been ripped off. The hotel has double-dipped, courtesy of you.

Now for the biggest rip-off of them all: hotel telephone charges. The good news: Travelers are getting smarter about using their hotel phones. In 2003, the average U.S. hotel made $532 on each room phone—that was 20 percent less than in 2002 and 51 percent less than in 2000. The percentage of total revenue that comes from phones at full-service hotels shrank to 1.7 percent in 2002.

At the same time, hotels have been forced to fully disclose—or I should say, *more* fully disclose—their phone charges to their guests. As a result, many hotels now place "disclosure cards" in their guest rooms. These cards delineate what you will pay to make local and long-distance calls.

I remember one hotel that—quite seriously—put in each room a phone disclosure card that essentially said the following: "Please be advised that the *only* free call you'll ever have at this hotel is if you call another guest room."

The card itself was ludicrous. Many of the guests, myself included, ended up grabbing the card, calling other guest rooms, and asking, "Do you believe this crap?"

Indeed, in any roundup of guests' grievances, nothing else even comes close to the outrageous phone charges—and surcharges—levied by many hotels. If you're like me, you first learned about these charges the hard way: When you got your hotel bill, the phone charges exceeded your room rate!

Hotels often sell their phone services to the highest bidder, frequently known as AOS (alternate operator service), and they don't disclose this arrangement to guests. Alternatively, they may block calls to 800 numbers or toll-free numbers overseas, and often charge as much as $4 per call (not per access) to get these numbers.

In a number of foreign hotels, even when I was able to get through to my MCI or AT&T number to make a call, the call was diverted from the hotel to another operator who asked what number I wanted. When I insisted that the operator identify herself, she revealed that she was a third-party operator for an independent telephone company. Translation: Her company would be placing the call, and when I received my MCI bill, there would be an even higher charge for that call.

Why do hotels do this? By not telling you about the third-party company, they essentially delay your anger by a few weeks. You get your room bill and pay your other charges at the hotel, but the hotel does not add a surcharge for the call. Only when you get home and get your phone bill does the phone arrangement hit you. And the damage has already been done.

Now, let's do the math. Say a hotel charges a minimum of $2 per call, even for toll-free numbers. If you average just ten calls a day from your room (that total is not considered excessively high), you've added $20 a day to your charges.

Is there a solution? Actually, there are two. Hotels and many governments don't like these ideas, but their greed created these solutions, and I heartily endorse them.

1. Use your cell phone at hotels. On the highly competitive cell phone market, prices for air time are at an all-time low. Make your cell phone your only contact phone, and you'll save a bundle.

2. Investigate any number of long-distance phone services that let you program their systems to *call you*. This is an ingenious response to hotel and governmental greed.

Here's how one system, KALLBACK, works. You become a member of the service, and you register your credit card to pay your phone bills. Then KALLBACK (800-516-9993) gives you a special number to call in the Seattle area (where they're based) and your identifying code number. When you're ready to travel to Topeka or Tokyo, you simply call that number and punch in your code. A computerized voice then asks what number you want it to call. Punch in the number of your hotel. Then it will ask whether you want it to call now or later. Punch in "later." Then hang up.

When you get to your location and are settled in your hotel room, go to the phone. Pick it up and proceed to do what others might consider financial suicide: Make a direct-dial call to KALLBACK's number in Seattle. Let it ring once, then hang up. This signals the computer to call you back at the number you originally gave it.

Within thirty seconds, the phone rings at the hotel. When the connection is established and the operator answers, the computer voice asks to speak to you (by name). Your phone rings in your room. You hear the same computer voice asking to speak to you. Simply punch in your code, and the same computer voice then asks which number you want. Punch in the area code and the number, and you're connected. Make as many calls as you want, and pay competitive MCI/Sprint/AT&T rates, without excessive surcharges and taxes. As far as the hotel and the local and/or foreign government are concerned, the call is recorded as a free, incoming call.

Then there is a new system called Vonage, which is on the cutting edge of VOI (voice over the Internet). For as low as $24.99 per month, you take your Vonage box with you on the road. It has a special local number given to you in the city (area code) where you live or work. When you arrive at the hotel, hook it up to the hotel's broadband service, then plug the hotel phone line into it as well. At that point, any call you make from the hotel phone goes over the Internet and is free. A call made to your local number back home rings . . . in your hotel room! Please don't ask me how this works, but it does. I tried it earlier this year in hotels in both Bangkok (a city notorious for excessive phone charges) and London.

One final word about hotel rip-offs. In this case, I'm talking about fire safety and security.

During the past two decades, there have been some disastrous hotel fires: the 1980 blaze at the MGM Grand in Las Vegas (eighty-five dead and almost seven hundred injured); the 1986 New Year's Eve conflagration at the Dupont Plaza Hotel in San Juan, Puerto Rico (at least ninety-seven fatalities); and the 1988 fire at the Heliopolis Sheraton Hotel & Towers in Cairo, Egypt (seventeen dead). In the 1990s, the sad trend continued, with a number of serious and catastrophic hotel fires in Asia.

In the United States today, it may be safer to stay in a hotel than in your own home. In the last two decades the number of hotel fires has declined by nearly two-thirds, even though there are more hotels. Nevertheless, the National Fire Protection Association reported in 1999 that about 4,600 hotel and motel fires occur each year. Fires caused twenty-four civilian deaths and 249 injuries, as well as $115 million in property damage. The fires have focused attention on two serious travel questions: How safe from fire is your hotel room, and how well-protected are you?

Some of the answers may not be comforting. Worse, other answers may not be readily available. This much, however, is known. Cigarette smokers account for 14 percent of hotel and motel fires, and fires of suspicious origin (arson) account for 16.5 percent, according to the Hotel Risk Management Association.

Many hotels are not equipped to report or retard fires effectively, and most hotel guests have no idea how to give themselves a fighting chance before a fire breaks out or how to escape a burning hotel safely.

Think back to the last time you checked in to a hotel. Did the bellhop point out the fire escapes or exits? Was there a smoke detector or sprinkler head in your room? And if the fire escapes weren't pointed out, was there a map or sign in the room to tell you their location?

A lot of the problem can be blamed on outdated municipal and state fire codes. Inadequate codes, combined with a historic unwillingness on the part of many individual hotels (and chains) to upgrade their fire-safety systems, have led to well-documented tragedies. The MGM Grand fire was the catalyst for finally getting officials to strengthen fire-safety codes throughout Nevada. Now sprinkler systems are required in all hotels—old and new—statewide.

In 1987, a bill was introduced in Congress that would have forced most hotels to install sprinklers in rooms. Many hotels, along with the American Hotel and Motel Association, successfully lobbied against the legislation. Even when laws are passed, they are full of loopholes that allow grandfather clauses to exclude hotels already built or to give older hotels many years to make the needed changes.

These days, nearly all hotels have smoke detectors, but many don't have sprinklers.

Some of the larger hotel chains have developed serious guidelines for their properties, such as the following:

1. Fire prevention through controlling the quality of construction and interior-finish materials

2. Design features to retard the spread of fire and smoke

3. Detection alarm systems to alert staff and guests

4. Escape routes and an emergency power supply

5. Fire-extinguishing systems—specifically, sprinklers

If a fire breaks out in a hotel where you are staying, many firefighters suggest that you do everything you can to get out of your room, if possible.

But first, don't just open your room door. Instead, feel the door. If it is very hot, don't open it. Stay in your room. Shut off the air-conditioner, stuff a wet towel under the door, and remove all the curtains or draperies from the window. Next, head for the bathroom. Fill the tub with water—and wait.

If the room door doesn't feel hot, however, drop to your knees before opening it. Then crawl out the door and head for the nearest *stairway,* not the elevator.

The next time you check in to a hotel, ask about its fire-safety system, smoke and heat detectors, and sprinklers. Also inquire about the location of exits. If the staff can't answer these questions satisfactorily, you owe it to yourself to stay somewhere else.

And speaking of leaving your room, here's a side note on security: when you leave your hotel room, put the Do Not Disturb sign on the outside of your door and turn the television on. Why? An intruder or burglar has to think twice before entering a room with both the Do Not Disturb sign *and* the TV on. As an added protection, call hotel security and ask to have someone come to your room to engage the dead-lock bolt to the room from the *outside* when you are leaving the room. (Yes, they can do this easily.) This means that no one can enter the room—including you—without the assistance of a hotel security officer. Few guests know about this tactic, but it really makes your room secure.

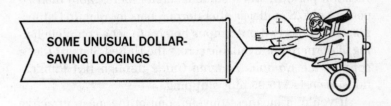

SOME UNUSUAL DOLLAR-
SAVING LODGINGS

You're traveling to Houston or Hong Kong, Peoria or Paris, Los Angeles or London. You have secured an attractive airfare. But where will you stay? You start checking around, only to learn that your four- or five-night stay at a hotel will cost twice as much as the airfare—or more. Even the discount hotels' rates are prohibitive at your destination. What are the alternatives? University dormitories, youth hostels, private apartments, U.S. Forest Service watchtowers, and even coastal yurts are available, at tremendous savings.

Youth hostels have gone considerably upscale, and they're no longer limited to the postadolescent and hippie crowd. Today, many hostels offer private rooms ranging from $25 to $60 a night. For more information and a listing of hostel locations and rates, call American Youth Hostels at 800-444-6111 or visit the website at www.iyhf.org.

Among the world's YMCAs and YWCAs are some surprises, including the Hong Kong YMCA, located next door to the legendary Peninsula Hotel. It offers good rooms, great views, and even a health club, at about $100 a night (a fraction of the Peninsula's price). In New York, a room at the Y can go for as little as $50; in London, where an average hotel room will cost you more than $200 a night, a single room at the Y for eighteen- to thirty-year-olds, is £33, or little more than $100. For more information, call 212-308-2899.

Another great hotel alternative is college dormitories. Dorms eagerly welcome paying guests during summer and vacation periods, when students aren't there. More than 70 percent of U.S. colleges offer dorm rooms for rent. In California, UCLA has two on-campus hotels. To get a complete listing of dorm rooms available across the United States, order a copy of the *Campus Lodging Guide* through B&J Publications. It costs $16.95 plus shipping.

If you're a business traveler, one of the most attractive hotel alternatives (especially for extended business trips) is an apartment rental. More and more folks are reserving flats in London and apartments in Paris instead of booking a hotel. Short-term apartment rentals in Europe and Asia are becoming more popular, for a number of good reasons. The first reason is price. A weekly London apartment rental averages about $875. Amenities include a kitchen, a living room, a dining area—and no minibar. Go to the market, buy what you want at local prices, and stock your own refrigerator.

A number of U.S. firms specialize in finding and renting apartments overseas. Among them are Barclay International Group, 800-845-6636, www.barclayweb.com; B&V Associates, 800-546-4777; Chez Vous (specializes in France), 415-331-2535, www.chezvous.com; and In the English Manner (British manor house agency), 800-422-0799, www.english-manner.com. In Italy, try Italia Reservations, 510-843-0928, www.italiareservations.com, or The Best in Italy, 011-39-55-223-064, www.thebestinitaly.com.

Looking for a really strange hotel alternative? Contact a British company called Distinctly Different (011-441-225-866842). These folks offer former schools, windmills, jails, even a former brothel, all scattered throughout Great Britain, France, Germany, Belgium, and the Caribbean.

Perhaps the strangest hotel alternative can be found at a place called the Ice Hotel in Jukkasjarvi, Sweden, built from thousands of tons of ice and snow and known as the world's largest igloo. The temperature in the rooms ranges from

−3 degrees Celsius to −8 degrees Celsius (27 degrees Fahrenheit to 18 degrees Fahrenheit). That's *cold.* But amazingly,
guests sleep well on beds of (you guessed it) ice covered with
reindeer skins and sleeping bags. There are only eleven
rooms at the Ice Hotel, and, yes, there is a sauna. It is open
only from December through April, and it features new architecture each year. Call 800-528-1234.

Quebec now also has a licensed offshoot of the original
Ice Hotel in Sweden, located only a half hour west of Quebec
City.

There are a number of great lighthouses and light stations around the United States where you can spend the
night. Among them are the Lighthouse Inn in West Dennis,
Massachusetts, 508-398-2244, www.lighthouseinn.com; the
Saugerties Lighthouse in New York state (rooms go for $100
a night), 914-247-0659, www.saugertieslighthouse.com; and
the upscale East Brother Lightstation in Point Richmond,
California, one of the great lighthouses built around San
Francisco Bay. Rates here start at $290 a night; call 510-
233-2385.

My favorite hotel alternative is unique lodgings such as
lookouts and yurts. Scattered throughout U.S. forests are
lookout towers and structures built to house rangers watching for fires. With the advent of specialized radar systems
and other technology, lookout officers have become obsolete,
but the towers still stand. Lookout towers provide the barest
of essentials, but they offer one of the more extraordinary
ways to experience the wilderness. A room with a view is as
low as $25 a night. Check out Oregon and also Montana.

Yurts are circular, domed tents. In Oregon, they are located at nine of the most popular state parks along the Pacific
coast. They have plywood floors, lockable doors, electricity,
indoor lighting, bunk beds, and space heaters. Rents are as
low as $27 a night. For information on the firestation lookout

towers and the yurts in Oregon and Washington, call Oregon State Parks and Recreation at 800-452-5687. For a Montana lookout tower, call Bitterroot National Forest, Sula Ranger District, 406-821-3201.

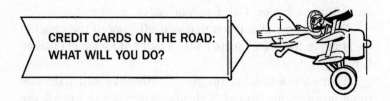

CREDIT CARDS ON THE ROAD:
WHAT WILL YOU DO?

It's a famous American Express commercial: A tourist loses traveler's checks in the Gobi Desert. If you believe the ads, one phone call gets an American Express courier to bush-whack through a forest, climb a peak, or tool through desert sands in a Humvee to bring you your replacement checks, cards, and emergency cash.

Visa and MasterCard make similar claims. Those com-mercials, as well as many printed cardholder agreements offered by MasterCard, Visa, and American Express, prom-ise quick global assistance within twenty-four hours in an emergency.

I decided to test these claims. Did I pick the Gobi Desert? Albania? The Falkland Islands? No. I stayed right here in the good old U.S.A. I chose Rhyolite, Nevada, a ghost town at the gateway to Death Valley. Population: zero. Boasting one working phone booth, Rhyolite is nine miles from Beatty, Nevada, which has hotels and banks.

I used four of my own credit cards:

1. A regular MasterCard from my University of Wisconsin Credit Union

2. A Gold MasterCard from General Motors

3. A First Card Visa Gold card affiliated with United Airlines

4. A Gold American Express card

I started by cutting them in half.

When I called each company's emergency hotline for assistance, I narrated the same scenario: I had lost my credit card, my car had broken down, I was in a ghost town, and the temperature was 120 degrees outside. Could they get me an emergency replacement card and $300 emergency cash?

The University of Wisconsin MasterCard accepted my third collect call. After I was on hold for twenty-five minutes, a supervisor told me to call back in an hour. I did so and got another supervisor, who told me she was "at a loss" and I should call back. I called her an hour later and she suggested I call 911!

Gold MasterCard offers emergency services, including a replacement card within twenty-four hours, and emergency cash—or so the ads proclaim. "Sorry," the representative said, "you're six dollars over your limit, so there's nothing we can do for you."

Perhaps Visa Gold would come to the rescue. After an hour of waiting, I was put through to a supervisor, in Elgin, Illinois, who told me they could—and would—get $300 in emergency cash to me in the desert. Could I call back in an hour? I could. But sixty minutes later, a supervisor said all they could do was wire the $300 to the nearest Western Union office.

"How am I supposed to get there?" I asked the woman on the phone. "Don't you folks at Visa say you're everywhere I want to be? So where are you?"

She said, "I don't know."

"So you're saying I've got to take a hike in the desert?"

"Yes," she answered.

My last hope: American Express. But they too would only wire the money to Western Union.

I suggested that they call Western Union in Beatty and ask whether someone could come to me. After all, there's that indelible advertising image of the AmEx representative navigating the sands.

The American Express representative called the Stage-coach Hotel and Casino, where the Western Union office was situated, and called me back. "Sorry," she said. No one would do it. So realizing that in every case I would have been stranded in the desert (misleading advertising claim number one), I got into the car and drove into Beatty in search of the Western Union office. Assuming—in my scenario—that a Good Samaritan had rescued me from the heat, the sand, and the sagebrush, I wanted to see whether any money was indeed waiting for me.

When I arrived at the hotel in Beatty to collect my $300 emergency money from First Card Visa Gold and Gold American Express, I got a final shock.

The $300 had indeed been wired to Western Union by First Card, but there was no record of money from American Express. Both the hotel receptionist and the manager said they'd never received a phone call from AmEx asking whether they would come out to the desert and get me.

"We get calls from stranded folks all the time," I was told. "We would have been glad to run the money out to you."

So were these credit card companies lying about their emergency services?

Advertising claims notwithstanding, you need to read the fine print on your cardholder agreement, something few of us ever do. There is nothing in the regular MasterCard cardholder agreement that mentions emergency replacement cards or emergency cash. Under the Gold MasterCard agreement, because I had violated the terms by being over my limit—even by six dollars, they were under no obligation to help me.

The Visa Gold agreement reads: "We will work with you to arrange direct delivery or a convenient location for you to pick up your replacement card or emergency cash." Convenient to whom?

The American Express agreement says: "Just request an Emergency Replacement Card, and Customer Service will offer you one of these options:

—Regular or Overnight Mail,

—Pickup at an American Express Travel Service location,

—Hand delivery by courier (in an extreme emergency)."

Being stranded in the desert isn't an "extreme emergency"? What about common sense? Not one credit card customer service representative suggested charging my account and hiring a taxi, tow truck, or rental car to get me out of my predicament. There is an implication in credit card commercials that these companies will help you immediately, no matter where you are. But unless you're actually shooting one of their commercials, I wouldn't count on their help.

OTHER MONEY ISSUES

Do you carry traveler's checks? Do you really need them?

First, let's put them in perspective. With the proliferation of ATM machines worldwide, the need for traveler's checks has diminished. Still, thousands of travelers buy them each year, for their own peace of mind. I understand this. But I don't necessarily accept the concept of traveler's checks in the new global village in which we live and through which we travel.

Indeed, since 1995, annual sales of American Express traveler's checks have declined or remained flat. Visa's traveler's check sales have plummeted to only half of what they were in 1994.

What exactly does a traveler's check mean? When you buy the checks, you are giving the check issuer an interest-free loan. Ever wonder why you get that handy little plastic wallet when you carry them away? The issuer is hoping you *never* use the checks. And even if you use some of them, they're hoping that you will place the rest of the checks in a bureau drawer for later use.

If you're still worried about money security issues while traveling, purchase a minimum number of traveler's checks for emergency purposes only.

Recently, American Express, which has seen purchases of its traveler's checks drop substantially, began offering a different financial product for travelers: a TravelFunds card, which you can preload in advance of your trip (minimum $300, maximum $2,750 during any fourteen-day period). There's a $14.95 charge for the card, but the cool thing is that you can buy it in euros, pounds, or dollars.

FOREIGN CURRENCY EXCHANGE

Use your ATM card worldwide. There are a number of good reasons for this advice. First, you get the current-day exchange rate offered by the local bank to all of its customers; you are not paying an excessively high exchange commission. And the rate you do pay will be 2 to 7 percent better than the rates you'd get if you were exchanging cash or traveler's checks. (However, if you're using credit cards, be careful of the recent trend among some companies to add "transaction fees" for purchases made in foreign countries.)

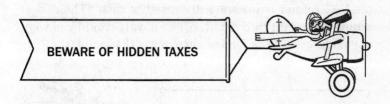

BEWARE OF HIDDEN TAXES

Earlier, I mentioned the dreaded value-added tax, or VAT. When you shop overseas, you are almost always paying extra without knowing it. At last count, about seventy-six countries apply some form of a value-added tax, and this can boost the prices for many goods and services between 3 percent and 25 percent. France's VAT can be as high as 19.6 percent. In Thailand, it's 7 percent. In Argentina, the VAT is 21 percent, and in Finland, 22 percent.

That's the bad news. The better news is that a growing number of countries, many of them in Europe, have several ways for travelers to reclaim the taxes they've paid on items they take with them when they leave and, in some cases, the taxes they've paid on their hotel rooms.

When you're making a purchase, always ask about VAT refunds. The stores, and some hotels, will be only too willing to provide you with the proper forms. Some establishments charge a service fee to process those forms, but this is still found money, and it *does* add up.

In most countries, you need to present these completed, postage-paid forms at the departure airport when you leave. Many countries require that you have the goods with you to show customs officers. This isn't always possible, but bring all of your receipts with you.

Just drop the properly stamped forms in a postbox, and, within about four weeks you will get either a check for the VAT refund or a credit to your credit card. At some airports, the VAT refund is instantly disbursed in cash. (The easiest option: the credit card credit. After all, why would you want to change even *more* foreign currency at that point?)

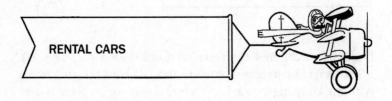

RENTAL CARS

Each year, millions of us rent cars—over fifty million of us, to be exact. Rental fleets now exceed 1.6 million vehicles. Auto travel accounted for 79 percent of all person-trips in the United States compared to just 16 percent for air travel in 2003. And in the past five years, auto travel has increased by 10 percent while air travel has decreased by 2 percent.

There's a very good reason that rental cars are a $15 billion industry. Rates are going up. In 2004, average rental car prices were up $5 per day nationwide, and rates for midsize cars at airports rose an average of 10 percent. More often than not, we overpay for the car and for gas, we buy insurance and other protection services we don't need, and we don't understand other rental requirements and disclaimers.

First, let's look at the rental car and the rate you pay. Getting a great rental car deal is nothing less than weird science. Avis offers six different types of insurance and damage waivers. Hertz has twenty-six—count 'em—different car classes. And because there is no rental car industry pricing standard, companies can do just about anything they want when it comes to what they charge for the same car, on the same day, in any given city.

Think airline fares are confusing? Not long ago, rental car rates at companies like Hertz, Avis, and National filled books the size of municipal telephone directories. Rates have since been consolidated and simplified, but it's still a confusing world out there.

First, how do *you* make a rental car reservation? That dreaded 800 number again? If you use the 800 number, you may get a low rate, but not the lowest rate or the best car. You are calling a national reservations system that displays a rental company's inventory and prices but cannot give you a better deal.

What's the best day to rent a car? Saturday, especially in summer months. Do you think airlines consistently over-book? The rental car companies are just as guilty. If a rental car agency tells you it has no cars available on a Friday, chances are excellent it suddenly will have cars early on Saturday morning, when some of the "committed" weekend reservations don't materialize. Also, weekly renters tend to return cars late on Friday nights.

And just as suddenly, the car also comes with a deal. Again, an empty car sitting unused on a lot is not what the company had in mind.

Deals can be done only at the local level. Why? Rental cars move like a flock of birds; there are seasonal and holiday movements. Also, local agency operations are better judges of their own inventory and pricing. Airport locations have different pricing than in-city rental lots, and, depending on fleet size, they may be more expensive.

So do everything you can to rent locally, but get ready for

some sticker shock. Car rental companies can tack on all kinds of additional fees, from airport taxes to car wash facility surcharges. The best way to avoid surprises on your bill? Ask a lot of questions about hidden charges before you sign on the dotted line.

You need to determine the going rate for the type of car you want to rent. Check out a search engine on the Web that scours the Internet for low rates or check RentalCars.com, a site that tracks deals on rental company websites. If you're traveling within seven days, there may be distressed inventory in the market you're traveling to—check Hotwire.com or Site59.com (and in this scenario the cheapest deal may not, for once, be the smallest car; pricing and deals have more to do with rental car inventory than with car size).

Here are some other questions to ask:

- What if the car I want is not available—will I receive another one, equal to or better than the one reserved, at the same price, or will I have to pay for an unwanted upgrade?

- Do you offer unlimited mileage? Does that include out-of-state mileage?

- What is the average age of the oldest vehicle in the lot? Are there more than 15,000 miles on the average vehicle?

- Do all cars have power windows and power locks? What about ABS brakes?

- Is emergency roadside assistance available twenty-four hours a day? Is the service available out of state, and is there an extra charge?

- I need a child car seat to fit a ten-month-old and a one-year-old. Do you offer seats in different sizes?

HAVE YOU RENTED A CAR LATELY?

At one time, there were fifty different rates for any one rental car. The good news now is that most rental car companies have simplified their basic rates.

Consumers can also save money by seeking out standard corporate discounts or membership discounts available from alumni associations, automobile clubs, and frequent-flier alliances.

Official rates now seem simpler, but ask a lot of questions *before* you rent your next car, or you will be unpleasantly surprised when you get your bill.

What a number of car rental companies don't fully disclose when quoting you *any* rate, discount or not, are the extra fees and surcharges—and they can really add up. Don't believe me? The National Association of Attorneys General has started its own task force in response to consumers' complaints across the country.

This is not the first time the NAAG has looked into possible abuses in the rental car industry. In 1989, the NAAG adopted its first guidelines for industry practices. It addressed the issue of "unbundling" (making the advertised price of a rental car appear artificially low).

Now, more than ten years after the original guidelines were issued, consumers have been hit with additional (and increased) surcharges, fees, taxes, and other surprises sprinkled among the rates. The NAAG now estimates that the actual cost of renting a car may exceed the advertised rate by as much as 75 percent.

Consider this recent scenario. I called Budget Rent A Car and asked about reserving a compact car in Aspen, Colorado, for a midweek rental of two days. Before I could speak to a reservations agent, a recorded voice cautioned me that if I was under twenty-five years of age, restrictions could be imposed, as well as additional surcharges. And, if over twenty-five? "The rate does not include concession fees or surcharges, and your driving record may be checked."

I was then connected to a live agent who quoted me a two-day rate of $109.90 for a Ford Escort, complete with unlimited mileage. That worked out to a daily rate of about $55—a little expensive, but I did get unlimited mileage. "Would you like me to make the reservation?" the agent offered.

"Not yet," I responded. "Are there any other charges?"

"Well, yes," she answered. "There's an eight-and-a-half percent sales tax, as well as a twelve percent surcharge for airport tax."

"That's it?" I asked.

"Yes," came the response.

Well, not necessarily.

Let's do the preliminary math here. The Ford Escort rental fee in Aspen is *not* really $109.90 for two days. Not counting my possible subsidizing of a car wash facility, and counting the 8.5 percent tax plus the 12 percent surcharge (a 20.5 percent hit at the end of the bill), the real basic cost of that rental car is more like $131.88.

Ah, but we're not finished yet. When I showed up to rent the car, I was offered (renters at a number of companies have claimed they were pressured into buying) the collision damage waiver (CDW). Many of us who already own a car and are insured are probably already covered by our own automobile policy. And at Budget in Aspen, the CDW will cost you an extra $16.99 per day.

If I hadn't checked with my insurance company before I flew to Aspen, I might very well have thought that I needed that CDW, and the cost of my two-day rental would have jumped another $33.98. With more than 20 percent tax added, plus $33.98 in CDW, the tab would rise to $165.86.

But we weren't through yet.

Recently, some Budget renters in Aspen were hit with a $3 per day "car washing facility" charge. That's right, they were helping to build a car wash and discovered it only when they received their bill.

As part of my shopping and disclosure test, I called Hertz, Avis, National, Thrifty, and Budget—not just once, but a number of times—to determine whether there was any pattern to disclosures or to rates. The answers: No. I made four calls to Budget, but only twice did they disclose the extra charges; three calls to Thrifty and only one disclosure of the charges. And when I called Thrifty to rent a compact car in Boston, I received no such warnings or disclaimers. The agent simply quoted me the basic rate of $33.90 per day with unlimited mileage. Only when I asked did the agent then acknowledge, after a pause, that, yes, there seemed to be additional charges: a 10 percent airport "access fee," a 4 percent excise tax, and a 5 percent sales tax. Once again, the basic rate, without insurance or other goodies, was pushed to nearly 20 percent above the quoted rate. Then add the CDW, at Thrifty's rate of $16.95 per day.

In the four calls to Budget, the rate quoted changed four times. Each subsequent call netted a lower rate! (Also not quoted: a $10-per-rental charge from the City of Boston to fund its new convention center.)

Some rental car companies will offer to sell you something called PEI—personal effects insurance. In theory, it sounds great. If, while renting a car, something is stolen from that car, you're covered. Not only is it not a great deal, it's insulting. PEI is about the most worthless insurance policy you can buy. Why? Read the fine print. For rental PEI policies to pay off, the car has to be locked, there has to be a forced break-in to the car, and, announced in finer print, most of your valuable items are excluded from coverage anyway. There's a low dollar cap on the amount of coverage, you have to file a police report, and last but never least, many drivers are already covered under homeowner's or renter's insurance policies.

A review of the PEI offered by Hertz reveals that the maximum coverage for all claims is $600 per person, and the total for all individuals in the car is capped at $1,800.

Want a good laugh? Here are the exclusions: animals, contact lenses, currency, tickets, documents, and perishables. Two other items also excluded from coverage are artificial teeth and limbs. With Hertz cars, the message is clear: If you have a dog that has false teeth and legs and is carrying an airline ticket and wearing contact lenses, *don't leave it in the rental car!*

Moral to this story: Before you sign a rental car agreement/contract—or, better, before you make that reservation—demand to know any and all pass-through charges. In Seattle, for example, there's a 5.9 percent car rental tax—in addition to the local sales tax. In Atlanta, the car rental tax is 5 percent.

SOME OTHER AVOIDABLE "SURPRISES"

Always ask whether there is a drop-off charge. Sometimes (and I'm not kidding) the fee can be as high as $1,000! A few companies, like Alamo and Hertz, do not charge for a drop-off in Florida or California if the car was rented within that state.

Then there's the ticking clock. You have to watch out for the twenty-four-hour rate. If you rent your car, for example, on a Wednesday and return it on Thursday, you would expect to be charged for a one-day rental. But what's the grace period? Return it *after* twenty-four hours have elapsed—

even one hour after—and most companies hit you with a second-day rental fee.

Everything I just told you becomes one big foreign-language problem overseas. There, rental car companies, even those bearing familiar U.S. brands, operate as feudal fiefdoms and, more often than not, ignore the rates quoted on U.S.-based reservations.

If you are renting a car overseas, you absolutely *must* keep a paper trail of evidence. Get a confirmation faxed to you. Always reserve and pay with your credit card. This is your only defense against the highway robbery many foreign rental car "local" locations employ to recognize your reservation, and perhaps even to confirm it, but not the terms of the deal.

Remember the dreaded VAT? This is a big whammy on foreign car rentals; it often adds as much as 25 percent of the rental cost. And should you be charged the VAT, ask in advance whether it is at least partially refundable.

There are also highway charges for cars driven in Austria or Switzerland. You'll need to purchase a sticker to avoid paying a fine.

A final word about insurance. Many major credit card companies say that if you rent a car and use their card, your insurance is covered. Not necessarily. Again, it's time to take a walk through the fine-print forest. And on this journey, with few exceptions, you have to be particularly astute. Most credit card companies do, in fact, offer some kind of insurance when you rent a car and use their card. But be careful. Most of this insurance is considered "secondary" insurance; it kicks in only after you've exhausted all your other insurance. If you don't have insurance to begin with, it doesn't kick in at all.

Before you rent, investigate your own automobile insurance policy to determine whether it covers rental cars. If so, you're in. If not, check directly with your credit card company and determine whether it is offering primary or secondary insurance. Hint: If you're renting with a gold or platinum card, there's a better chance that you have primary insurance coverage.

Again, it's a different story overseas. Even if your card offers primary coverage in this country, overseas it might not. At last count, American Express no longer offers collision coverage in Australia, New Zealand, Jamaica, Ireland, Israel, or Italy.

At least one insurance company is offering reasonable rates. According to a 2004 Roper survey, 56 percent of American families will drive to their summer vacation. Access America (Accessamerica.com/drive) offers something called Drive Protection, a policy that covers the entire family and also covers deductible gaps in auto and medical policies, including collision deductibles, auto theft, accident, cancellation/interruption of the trip, belongings stolen from the car or hotel room, and even travel delays caused by severe storms that close roads. It costs about $7 a day and is priced per family.

Watch out for some other rental car whammies. At some resort locations, rental car companies issue cash deposit waivers for some pretty weird things.

Not long ago, I was going to Hawaii. Like many island-bound travelers, I fancied myself wearing a tropical shirt and sunglasses and driving a convertible. The rental car agency offered a "Jeep" at an attractive rate. Excited, I jumped at the deal.

Stupid me. First, it wasn't a real Jeep but a small Geo version of a Jeep, with no storage space or luggage security. Second, everyone renting a car—Jeep or otherwise—should know that there is no approved off-road driving anywhere in the fiftieth state if you're in a rental car. Off-road driving voids your insurance and rental contract.

Third, I was given a surprise waiver to sign and was required to put down an additional $50 deposit. And what was that all about? The convertible top! Under the terms of the waiver, if I didn't return the "Jeep" with the top fastened in the up and closed position, I forfeited the $50.

That seemed absurd. I took the rental agent along an obvious verbal route. "Either the top is really easy to put up, which should mean there would be no waiver, or it's impossible to put up, and that's why there's a waiver."

"No, man," he replied. "It's real easy."

"Then show me," I responded.

He shrugged and then walked out to the parking lot with me. He hit two buttons, two levers, yanked back a handle, and the top was down. "See?" he laughed. "Easy."

But that maneuver put the top *down.* What about putting the top back *up?*

"Here," he said, handing me a two-page instruction book and retreating to the office.

Well, the top *was* down and I *was* in Hawaii, so I drove off.

I went to a hotel that prided itself on individual service. They even provided me a butler, something of an absurdity in Hawaii. Every morning, he would ask if there was anything he could do for me, and I would thank him and decline. Until the last morning, when it was time to drive to the airport and return the infamous "Jeep."

"Yes, there's just one thing I need," I said to him nonchalantly. "Could you just put the top back up on my 'Jeep'?"

"No problem," he said, eager to please, and left my room.

Twenty minutes later, when I looked out from my bedroom window, the butler, two men from engineering, and a room service waiter were surrounding the "Jeep," trying desperately to return the convertible top to the *up* position.

A half hour later, they succeeded. I tipped accordingly, and proudly drove the car back to the airport.

I had beaten the rental car agency. I walked confidently into the office, returned the car keys, and asked for my deposit back. A curious rental car agent looked out the window and seemed surprised: I really had returned the car with the top *up*. He returned my deposit.

Hooray for me. No waiver fees.

But I had not reviewed any of my "refueling options." Most rental car companies now offer the choice of bringing the car back with either a full tank of gas or with the same level of fuel as when the car was first rented. Other companies will allow you to prepurchase a tank of gas at the time of rental for a flat fee, but there's a catch to this. Unless you're bringing the car back on the fumes from an empty tank, it's not an economical choice. And some companies seem to make all of their money on the gas, not on the rental itself— as I was about to find out with my "Jeep." I had escaped the convertible-top waiver, but was about to be shocked by the gas policy.

After giving me back my deposit for the absurd waiver, the rental car agent recorded my mileage and the half-full tank of gas still in the car. He punched a few buttons, out came the receipt, and when I scrutinized the rental car bill, I saw that the company had charged me a $52 refueling charge for 13 gallons of gas! I had brought the car in with a half a tank, and they were charging me for a full tank at $4 a gallon!

Something had to be wrong. I told the agent I wanted to see the supervisor.

He smiled. "I *am* the supervisor."

How could they charge me this much?

"It's our policy to charge for a full tank of gas."

"Even if I bring the car back with half a tank?"

"Yep."

And he wouldn't budge.

Later, I called General Motors and talked to their fleet sales division. First, I asked if they had sold a fleet of rental cars to that company in Hawaii. They had. I asked if the model of the Geo "Jeep" they sold was different from any model I could otherwise buy at a Geo showroom. Yes, there were some differences: the seat covers, the carpeting, and the quality of the radio. That was it.

Everything else was standard? Yes.

Including the gas tank? Yes.

And what is the capacity of that gas tank? 11.1 gallons!

Does the rental company's gas refueling policy constitute a rip-off? Considering that I brought the Geo back with half a tank *and* they were charging me to fill it up *and* they were charging $4 a gallon, the answer would be *yes.* Now, compound this with the crime—yes, the crime. They were charging me to literally *overfill* a tank by nearly two gallons. This was more than a simple rip-off. It was a corporate policy of robbery.

I kept the receipt and wrote about the incident. The company, under penalty of a consent decree hammered out with that state's attorney general, then stopped the practice.

Bottom line: You have rights as long as you keep receipts, get names, and develop an evidentiary paper trail.

Here's another little rental car surprise: Airports are adding up to 50 percent of base rate in taxes and fees. Where rental car companies are charged for being on airport property, a $2.00 to $2.45 charge is passed on to the renter. So use the shuttle to get to your hotel, then pick up your car.

But fees are nothing new. Recently, there was also something called a "turnback" charge for folks who don't buy the loss-damage waiver that rental car companies often force upon consumers, many of whom are covered by their own auto insurance policies.

Let's say you rented a car, didn't buy the company's loss-damage waiver, and had an accident. When you returned the car, the company could hit you with a huge charge for "loss of turnback."

If you don't buy the collision damage or loss damage waiver, a rental car company does have the right to charge you for the cost of repairs, plus a "loss of use" fee to cover the income it would have derived from renting the car during the time it was being fixed. But most car insurance policies held by consumers cover repair and loss-of-use fees.

Loss of turnback, however, is different. It's the money a rental car company expects to lose when it sells a damaged (but repaired) car back to the manufacturer. In some cases, the loss of turnback has run to thousands of dollars.

Budget Rent A Car had been doing this, and the Federal Trade Commission found out because Budget failed to disclose the turnback charge to renters. As a result, no rental car companies are doing this now.

Rental car companies try to impose other insidious charges. Some that they *can* and do impose are within their legal rights. Others are more questionable.

YOUR DRIVING RECORD

Car rental companies can and do ask individual U.S. states to check on your driving record. If you have an abnormal number of accidents, these companies can and will either charge higher deposits or deny you the rental completely.

There's also an extra-drivers fee. If you're renting a car and you have even the slightest notion that another person might drive the car at any time during your rental period, you *must* register that person and provide his or her license at the time you rent the car. It is a legal and insurance nightmare if an accident then occurs and you're not behind the wheel. Some rental car companies simply want you to register the second driver. Others insist upon registration and payment of an additional fee. The companies can legally charge these fees, and as excessive (at least in principle) as they might seem, you must pay them if someone else is going to drive the rental car. You're asking for a heap of trouble if you don't.

Another problem is age discrimination. Many rental car companies make it extremely difficult to rent a car if you're under the age limit. Under twenty-five and asking to rent from Avis or Hertz? Forget it. (Unless you live in New York state. Hertz lost a New York court case on age discrimination there. As a result, renters between eighteen and twenty-four can indeed rent a car. But Hertz slaps them with a *$51-per-day* fee for the underage privilege. The company calls it the "underage insurance differential.")

Other companies' policies vary. If you're between twenty-one and twenty-five years old, you can rent from Alamo, but at a higher rate. The same policy applies with Budget and Dollar.

SPECIAL DEALS

If you look at fleets of rental cars as flocks of migratory birds, you can sometimes get some great seasonal deals.

Magically, rental cars tend to drive away from Florida and Arizona every spring, only to return there in late November. Is this really magic? No, it's oversupply. Companies that own their own fleets are desperate to move those cars in spring and late fall. And who better to do that than *you?*

Hertz, National, Budget, and Avis often offer one-way "drive-away" deals, sometimes for as low as $9 a day, to have renters do them a favor.

If you're interested in a one-way rental, check (or have your travel agent check) with Avis (800-230-4898; www.avis.com), Hertz (800-654-3131; www.hertz.com), or National (800-227-7368; www.nationalcar.com) to see which has the best deal for your preferred itinerary.

WHERE AIRPORT DEALS ARE BETTER

Most of the time, renting a car at an airport boosts the rate because of additional taxes. But there are some strange deals in unlikely places. For example, for reasons that no one understands, a three-day rental from Hertz at the Dallas–Fort Worth airport runs $89, but in downtown Dallas, the same car will cost you $147.

There are never any discounts on car rentals in New York City, especially at an airport, right? Not necessarily. At LaGuardia, a one-day rental of a midsize car from National Car Rental will set you back $76.98, but the same car at Newark costs $42.99. Go figure.

7

At Sea

PLEASE! IGNORE THE BROCHURES

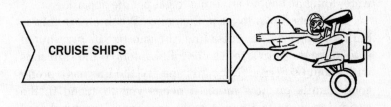

CRUISE SHIPS

On September 10, 2001, the cruise industry was on the threshold of a meltdown. Why? There were too many ships out there. The seas were on sale. Virtually every cruise line was substantially discounting, and in the world of supply and demand, supply was definitely on the consumers' side. Result: A strong buyers' market—worldwide—for any possible cruise vacation.

One of the reasons for this was an unprecedented boom in shipbuilding. Why was this happening? The cruise industry had been insisting that nearly sixty-nine million Americans were interested in taking a cruise in the next five years.

Ten years ago, the same industry officials made the same kind of claim, that forty-four million people intended to take a cruise within the next five years. Guess what happened? They exaggerated. At least half of those forty-four million projected cruise-ship passengers never arrived at the docks.

Despite the no-shows, the cruise-ship industry didn't stop building new ships. In the past, cruise lines built new ships to replace "old tonnage." But in anticipation of (1) a boom in the public's apparent desire to cruise and (2) a lowering of the median age of cruisers, cruise lines had been expanding their fleets almost exponentially.

In the cruise-line business, twenty new ships were contracted to be added by 2008. And as anyone in the cruise business can tell you, an unsold cruise-ship cabin is revenue the cruise line will never recoup once the ship sails. Result:

Cabins were being offered at 1980 prices. The cruise lines were doing just about anything to get people aboard.

It all gets down to basic financing. When a new ship is built, the only way a cruise line can amortize its investment is to make the ship a series of profit centers. If the ship sails with about 80 percent onboard capacity, the line has a pretty good handle on how much it needs you to spend in the casino, on shore excursions, at the spa, and in the gift shop (I should say *shops*) in order to begin to turn a profit.

That's all well and good if demand can support an average occupancy rate of 80 percent. By 2000, with so many new ships coming on line, that figure quickly eroded, despite the fact that about half of the 281 million North Americans are the potential cruise market. Only 30 million are projected to book a cruise in the next three years.

And therein was the problem. Only 12 percent of the American public (according to the cruise industry's figures) has ever taken a cruise. Somehow, more than a few cruise lines converted that figure into an assumption that 50 percent of Americans wanted to take a cruise. Wishful thinking perhaps, but the industry claimed that its own studies show that nine out of ten people who take a cruise plan to do it again.

Then came September 11, and the cruise industry suddenly found itself the unwitting beneficiary of terrorism. How so? It's the one segment of the travel business that could adapt quickly and demonstrably to the staggering drop-off in international travel by Americans following the tragedies at the World Trade center, in Pennsylvania, and at the Pentagon.

Almost overnight, as advance cruise bookings simply evaporated en masse, the cruise lines quickly responded. They could literally move their assets. And they did.

Within a two-month period, most major cruise lines repositioned their ships out of Europe and sailed them to North America, home porting them in U.S. cities, many of which didn't even know they *had* ports. After all, if I mention the words "Love Boat," does Mobile, Alabama, Galveston, or Houston ring a bell? As you're reading this, cruise ships are now sailing out of seventeen North American ports.

Cruises had quickly become a drive-to destination for Americans too afraid to fly over a body of water. Initially, cruise fares dropped as low as $237 for a Caribbean cruise.

In fact, despite a war in Iraq and a weak economy at home, the North American cruise industry was a growing business in 2003, generating a total of $25.4 billion and more than 295,000 jobs. According to the annual study by Business Research and Economic Advisors (BREA) commissioned by the International Council of Cruise Lines (ICCL), the cruise industry increased its total impact on the U.S. economy by 11.4 percent over 2002, while making significant contributions to the economies of those states where their ships now operate.

Since 2000, North American cruise lines have added more than twenty ships and over fifty thousand lower berths to their fleets. Passenger traffic increased during that period by 1.8 million to 9.8 million global passengers, while industry and passenger spending in the United States rose from $10.3 billion in 2000 to $12.9 billion in 2003—a 25 percent gain. And now, the industry reports that a record thirty-seven million cruise "prospects" plan to cruise in the next three years.

Healthy, indeed. In 2003, Carnival Cruise Lines entertained three million passengers, up from two million in 2001, and 450,000 of them were children. About 900,000 of those booked were age fifty-five and older.

Still, the increase in supply is quickly outpacing demand. And that's good news for anyone who seriously wants to take a cruise and save significant money in the process.

In the past decade, dozens of new ships have begun sailing. They have ranged from the 390-passenger *Silver Shadow* to the mammoth 2,976-passenger *Carnival Glory.* That's a lot of berths to fill—in addition to the berths the lines need to fill now.

Get ready to make some deals. The ships are waiting for you. And the deals are so wild that some lines are dumping cabins at rates that now average about $75 a day!

One cruise line lowered prices even further. Forget what it says in the brochures. No one pays those prices, especially when you consider that, at one point, Carnival unloaded some cabins for a weeklong cruise on its ship *Elation* for $367! In July 2004, Carnival was selling five-day Mexico cruises for as little as $279. And Royal Caribbean International was selling five-night Caribbean cruises for $332.

The other good news is that as the new ships come out of the shipyards, cruise lines are repositioning some of their older ships to different, more exotic ports, and discounting those cruises as well.

Here are some great examples of cruise discounts that have been on the market—and constitute reasons to ignore the brochures. For example, the brochure rate for one *Explorer* seven-day sailing was $2,424. But the real selling rate was $1,574. Savings: 35 percent. Take a look at one *Grand Princess* cruise. The brochure rate: $2,583. The real rate: $1,199. Savings: 54 percent. The brochure rate for one Carnival *Triumph* departure was $1,925. But the going rate was $900. Savings: 53 percent.

Here's the point: If you pay the brochure rate, you just paid for all those brochures!

Travel agents and cruise consolidators offer great last-minute deals. For example, Liberty Travel recently offered the following deals:

- A four-night Caribbean cruise for $237 on Carnival
- A seven-day Caribbean cruise on Royal Caribbean for $621

- A four-night Mexico cruise for $211 (unheard-of pricing)
- A twelve-day Caribbean cruise for just $815 on Royal Caribbean

The consolidators, such as World Wide Cruises (800-882-9000), have offered wilder deals:

- A seven-night Barcelona/Athens cruise for $1,199
- A fourteen-night Athens/Dubai cruise for $1,599
- A fourteen-night Sydney/Auckland cruise for $1,799

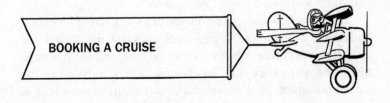

BOOKING A CRUISE

You have to know what you really want in a cruise.

Are you booking the ship to take you to a destination, or is the ship a destination in and of itself?

How physically active do you want to be (or are you allowed to be) on the ship and on shore?

Do you like kids? Will you cruise with your kids?

Or do you want a quiet, romantic cruise?

What kind of cabin do you want? Ignore the wide-angle photography in the cruise line's brochures. If you didn't know any better, you'd think you could entertain the entire state of Rhode Island in your cabin.

Try to remember that you are in your cabin only to shower, sleep, and change clothes. Most people fantasize about spending time in their cabin. The reality is that they are hardly ever there.

After you've determined that you don't need the most expensive cabin on the ship, ask yourself about the view from your cabin. Romantic notions about portholes and gentle sea breezes are nothing but pleasant images of historic ship crossings. Today there are few portholes, and cabin windows do not open. You're in a hermetically sealed, air-conditioned cabin—period. So how important is the view, especially if you're never there?

Think about this: The cabins with the best views tend to be on the higher decks of the ship. A better view, but a rougher ride. Why? Center of gravity. In rough seas, which part of the ship will move the most? Higher decks will roll and pitch endlessly. Lower decks won't.

Embrace a realistic assessment of your needs in a cabin, and book one on the lower deck and inside. It will be cheaper, you'll like it better if you're prone to motion sickness, and with very few exceptions, you're entitled to the same restaurants and onboard activities and experiences as every other passenger. Some other important requirements when you book your cabin: You do not want a room under the disco or the gym, and if you insist on a cabin with a view, make sure it is not blocked by lifeboats or tenders.

There are other questions you need to ask, and all of them concern what the extras will cost. Once again, the brochures can be misleading. Many cruise ships have brochures that feature beautiful photographs of the officers and the crew. There, in dress whites, alongside the other officers, is the ship's doctor. But the doctor is not an officer of the ship. More often than not, he or she is an independent contractor and a separate profit center on the ship.

That was brought into intense focus in 2002. From January to December 2002, the Centers for Disease Control and Prevention confirmed nine Norwalk-like virus outbreaks on cruise ships, three outbreaks of gastrointestinal illness caused by bacteria, and nine episodes whose cause was . . . "not determined."

A few thousand passengers got sick. And the medical care provided by cruise ships varied, as did the cruise lines' handling of what could have been (and in some cases was) a public relations nightmare. Some cruise lines actually operated ships in which there had been a Norovirus outbreak without fully disclosing to newly boarding passengers that there was a continuing problem. Others, like Disney, gave its newly boarding passengers options: They could get a full refund, a week at Disneyworld, or a reservation on a future cruise, or they could go ahead and take the cruise.

With the Norovirus as an exception, just about any medical care you may need on the ship—even the dispensing of an aspirin tablet—will be a separate and often expensive charge. (Not to scare you unnecessarily, but remember that you need to practice some preventive medicine before you board any cruise ship. The potential for the rapid spread of communicable diseases on ships is great, for all the obvious reasons: close quarters, a single air-conditioning system, and so on. Before you sail, get immunized against influenza, typhoid, and hepatitis A.)

This is why, once again, it is imperative that you get your own health insurance and make sure it covers you while you are at sea. As with a land trip, it should also include medical evacuation and repatriation insurance (in an emergency, the insurer will evacuate you from the ship and return you to the best available medical care in the United States).

Ask about the medical facilities on board the ship. Princess Cruises, for example, has a state-of-the-art satellite medical link with the emergency room of Cedars-Sinai Medical Center in Los Angeles. Ship doctors can consult via satellite, review tests and X-rays, and make a more effective diagnosis.

Do you have a physical disability? To their credit, cruise lines were quick to recognize the absolute need to be accessible to physically challenged persons. I have yet to see a cruise ship sailing from a U.S. port that isn't ADA (Americans with Disabilities Act) compliant. Corridors and passageways have ramps. Rooms are accessible to people with disabilities.

This news is refreshing. However, what the cruise lines, for the most part, have neglected to do is use their vast influence to make their port cities accessible to disabled persons. Many passengers confined to wheelchairs must stay confined to the ship at each port. Ask whether the ports you'll visit are as accessible as your cabin.

Shore excursions are major profit centers for cruise lines and are not included in your cruise fare. Do your homework here. Where are you visiting?

Look for "repositioning" cruises; they're the hottest deals around. These are deeply discounted oddball itineraries that are offered when cruise lines need to—literally—reposition their ships from one location to another. More often than not, these cruises are crossings. This is the way cruising was meant to be: long stretches at sea instead of one Caribbean port after another. And the rates for these cruises are well below those of the others because, after all, the line needs to get the ship somewhere, and you just go along for the ride.

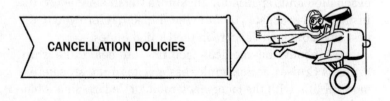

CANCELLATION POLICIES

In addition to medical insurance, you might want to investigate trip cancellation insurance. After 9/11, cruise lines began to relax cancellation policies to ease concerns, but read the fine print! Each cruise line is different. The premium charged for these separately purchased cancellation policies is nominal, and it is worth your investment.

Consider the fine print on one Norwegian Caribbean cruise ticket. In the event the cruise is overbooked or accommodations are oversold, the passenger agrees to the following: "Although space has been booked and confirmed, the accommodations may be withdrawn or boarding denied."

Here's something else. Unless you're an experienced cruise passenger—in fact, unless you're an experienced cruise passenger on a particular ship—beware of booking a cruise online. I'm not saying that you won't get the price you want, but booking a cruise only begins with the fare you pay. Remember, you need to choose a ship, an itinerary, a cabin category, shore excursions, and other options.

Finally, one additional tip that really works: With so many new ships coming on line, book an inaugural cruise. Yes, it will be more expensive, but here's a little-discussed fact. The shipyards building these ships are batting almost a thousand for never delivering them on time. The result: The ships are delayed from going into service. The inaugural cruise is likewise delayed, and the cruise lines give you a full refund and a discount on their next cruise. What a deal!

If you're booking a cruise that includes airfare, be particularly aware of the rights you're giving away to the airline and your route to get you to and from the ship.

Some cruise lines insist that booking your air transportation is totally within their discretion. For example, a family of four living on Long Island in New York booked a cruise out of Puerto Rico ten months in advance on Princess. Then, shortly before departing on their cruise, Princess sent them their itinerary. The cruise line had booked them, in the middle of winter, on an itinerary almost guaranteed to cause trouble. Instead of putting them on a number of available nonstop flights from either Kennedy or Newark airports, Princess put the quartet on a flight from the most delayed airport in the United States—LaGuardia. To make matters worse, the family was booked on a LaGuardia-to-Chicago flight, and then from Chicago to Puerto Rico. (Any look at a map easily shows how ludicrous this route is, even in good weather and flying into and out of airports without delay and cancellation problems.)

Would Princess or their travel agent help this family? No chance. Apparently the family didn't pay something called the *airline deviation fee,* an extra charge that means the cruise line would have guaranteed to put them on a non-stop flight.

Now that you know the questions to ask, here are some questions to avoid.

At about 11:00 P.M. one night, a passenger called the bridge of the cruise ship and asked to speak to the officer on duty. "I'm having trouble sleeping," he said. "Could you please ask the captain to drive between the waves?"

On a Caribbean cruise, a passenger asked whether the outdoor swimming pool was filled with fresh water or seawater. When told it was seawater, she nodded knowingly. "Ah, yes," she said, "that explains why the water is sloshing around."

How about the woman who approached the cruise director on the first night of the cruise and asked, "What time is the midnight buffet?"

Then there was the couple who were into their second week at sea, as part of an eighty-nine-day around-the-world cruise. They walked into the dining room and asked their maître d': "Do the waiters live on board?" When told by the slightly dumbfounded maître d' that, yes, all the waiters did indeed live on the ship, the couple asked, "Does that mean you make all this food here?"

Here's one of my favorites. A cruise passenger walked up to the shore-excursion officer as the ship was sailing from Dubrovnik on its way to Venice, Italy. "Why," he demanded, "didn't they speak English here?"

"Because this is Yugoslavia, sir," the officer calmly replied.

"Well," the passenger shot back, "what about Venice? I suppose we'll have the same problem there?"

Then there was the passenger who pointed to the stairs leading to the upper and lower decks and asked, "Do these stairs go up or down?"

On a cruise into Glacier Bay, Alaska, one passenger asked the ship's officers if they could stop so she could mail a letter.

On another Alaska cruise, after being told the correct temperature, one of the passengers walked up to the captain and inquired, "If it's that cold, what's our altitude?"

Not surprisingly, many silly cruise-ship questions are asked during shore excursions. On a tour of Dalian, a port city in mainland China, one passenger asked her guide, "How much are the condos here?"

Another passenger asked whether it was illegal to wear jewelry in Peking.

Upon docking in Piraeus, Greece, a passenger asked, "How many draculas are there to the dollar?" (He meant *drachmas*.)

On one cruise, a male passenger boarded with five tuxedos, convinced that it was the only outfit he was allowed to wear at sea. On the second day of the cruise, he was gently directed to one of the ship's boutiques, where he could purchase some more casual garments.

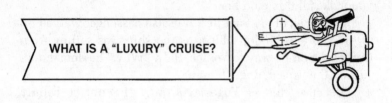

WHAT IS A "LUXURY" CRUISE?

In 1985, when the Italian liner *Achille Lauro* was hijacked by terrorists in the eastern Mediterranean, most of the press described the vessel as a "luxury cruise ship." But the ship was fifty years old when the hijacking occurred, and it had a history of severe problems—a number of fires and at-sea collisions. In 1982, its parent company had declared bankruptcy. The ship itself was seized after Italian government authorities determined that there had been "irregularities" in its casino operations.

So the *Achille Lauro,* seized, abandoned, and bankrupt, sat idle in an Italian port. The Italian government was no longer in the shipping business, and the days of its great liners—flagships like the *Michelangelo*—were long over.

The government didn't want this old ship, so it was leased—for $1—to Chandris Lines, which then marketed the old ship as a down-market, discount cruise ship in the eastern Mediterranean. So much for "luxury."

For a while after the hijacking, the *Achille Lauro* was one popular ship. People booked it not only because of its notoriety, but because they were betting that the odds the same ship would be hijacked twice were extremely slim!

Soon, though, its hijacking history wasn't enough to keep the curious passengers coming. It was chartered to bring Irish and Egyptian soccer fans to Italy for the World Cup games.

A few years later, the ship sank under mysterious circumstances.

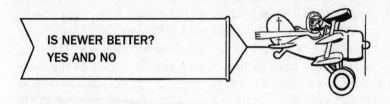

IS NEWER BETTER?
YES AND NO

The only new ship is a *newly built* ship, not a newly named ship.

However, making that distinction doesn't necessarily mean that an older ship is less seaworthy, less comfortable, or less safe. In fact, on a rough sea, I'd much rather be on the old *Rotterdam* than on some of the newer, boxy ships that look like a condominium fell over and somehow learned how to float.

In this era of full disclosure, you have a right to know the genealogy of your cruise ship. It might help you make a better informed decision.

"You'll sail on a classic," reads one cruise ship brochure.

"A ship rich in history," boasts another piece of promotional literature.

It all sounds good, but two questions remain unanswered:

1. How old is your ship?
2. Should its age worry you?

Often, the answers are not easy to find. An "old" cruise ship is not necessarily a floating firetrap or a rust bucket on the verge of submerging. But it's nice to know where your ship has been and how old it is. Such information can help you decide which cruise to take.

As is the case with hotels, some cruise-line brochures

and advertisements have been guilty of using misleading words to sell their cruises. For example, a few years back, one Greek cruise line advertised sailing on the South American Riviera aboard its "new" ship, the *Pegasus.* The ship was hardly new. In fact, it had already sunk—as the *Sundancer,* on June 29, 1984, near Vancouver, Canada. It was then resold to Epirotiki Cruise Lines (based in Athens), refloated, and towed past North America's West Coast and then through the Panama Canal and across the stormy winter swells of the North Atlantic—a slow journey that ended fifty-two days later in Piraeus, Greece. The ship was fixed and then heavily advertised as the "new" *Pegasus.*

It later sank again and was never refloated.

When the *Sundancer* sank the first time, it was declared a total loss, and the insurance company paid up. The parent cruise company then bought a Scandinavian ferry, converted it to a cruise ship, renamed it the *Stardancer,* and brought it to Los Angeles, where it replaced the *Azure Seas.*

The *Azure Seas*?! I first saw the *Azure Seas* about twenty years ago. It was introduced in Los Angeles as a "new" ship sailing from California to Mexico on three-day cruises. But a quick check revealed that it wasn't a new ship. In fact, it was built in Scotland in 1954 and named the *Southern Cross.* It was built to take British holidaymakers to Australia.

The jet age destroyed that market, and it was pulled out of service in 1971. Two years later, a Greek family bought the ship and registered it in Panama, and it became the *Calypso.* In late April 1975, she started cruising in the Mediterranean as a low-class tourist ship. Some cruise-ship aficionados remember that the "captain's dinner" offered passengers a choice between fried chicken and frankfurter sausages in mustard sauce.

The *Calypso* was then chartered by a French company, Paquet Cruises. In 1980, it showed up in Los Angeles as the

Azure Seas, promoted as a new ship doing Mexico cruises. For ten years, she went between Ensenada and Los Angeles. Then *Stardancer* came in and the *Azure Seas* disappeared.

Where is the *Azure Seas* today? Now nearly fifty years old, the ship has been renamed again—this time as the *Ocean Breeze,* running budget cruises in the Caribbean.

And what happened to the *Stardancer*? Its parent company was absorbed by Royal Caribbean Cruises, which renamed the ship *Viking Serenade.* It still sails from Los Angeles but may soon be repositioned to Asia.

To understand a cruise ship's history, look at how often it has changed hands and who has owned it. With few exceptions, most cruise ships older than ten years have probably been owned at least twice. They are, indeed, rich in history—and poor in continuity.

In functional areas, older ships are potentially more troublesome. Plumbing is a major headache on older ships. Electrical problems are a close second. Maintenance costs, not surprisingly, are higher, which might mean that certain maintenance items are deferred because of the expense.

An important question to ask: Was the ship you're booked on built by the line that operates it? If so, chances are that the crew has been thoroughly trained on its equipment, and the engineering staff probably wrote the manuals. If it wasn't, how many years has the ship sailed with this line? If the answer is less than three years, you're dealing with a crew that is still getting to know an older ship.

Interestingly, Carnival Cruise Lines (now the largest in the world) began with an older ship. In 1972, the company bought its first vessel, *Empress of Canada.* On its maiden voyage, the ship ran aground. After an extensive refit (and subsequent renovations in recent years), the ship sailed again. It was called the *Mardi Gras.*

In 1975, Carnival bought the *Empress of Britain* (now

called the *Carnivale*). And in 1977, the company purchased a ship called the *S.A. Vaal,* a liner that had been sailing between England and South Africa, and renamed it the *Festivale.* Since then, Carnival has built all its new ships.

Royal Caribbean Cruises has built all its ships to specifications particular to its markets and cruise areas.

Holland America has built many of its ships, the most famous of which is the *Rotterdam.* The first *Rotterdam* sailed in 1873. Since then, there have been four other *Rotterdam*s, including the current *Rotterdam V,* which was brought into service in 1959 and retired in 1997 (but not scrapped; it became the *Rembrandt*), and now the *Rotterdam VI.* Companies like Holland America maintain the names of their ships, although the ships themselves are different.

The original *Westerdam* (which sailed between 1946 and 1964) was built during World War II as a passenger and cargo carrier, but didn't sail until 1946 because the ship was sunk twice in harbor. The first time, the ship was sunk by the Dutch because they didn't want the Germans to be able to use it. The Germans refloated it and then sank it a second time, near the close of the war, because they didn't want the Dutch to get it. The next *Westerdam* was once the *Homeric,* purchased by Holland America in 1988.

Problems can sometimes occur with successive ownership changes. Perhaps needed renovations—especially safety standard improvements—are not performed because the new owner lacks capital or is not required to upgrade the ship under current laws.

"We've pushed hard to force cruise lines to report incidents, accidents, and ownership changes," says one U.S. National Transportation Safety Board inspector. But the NTSB lacks jurisdiction, in most cases, to demand accurate and current reporting. NTSB records are not accurate because ship companies don't have to report to the NTSB incidents that occur in international waters. The companies can pull a vessel, fix it up, paint it, and sell it. The new owners can give it a new name, and no one will know its former history.

One of the more interesting histories belongs to a ship called the *Regent Sea.* It was built in 1957 for the Swedish American line as the *Gripsholm,* and it sailed for seventeen years as a transatlantic liner. In 1974, it was sold to a Greek firm, Karageorgis Cruises. Renamed the *Navarino,* it cruised Mediterranean, South American, and South African waters until 1981, when a fire broke out. After the ship was repaired, it was put up for sale. The prospective buyer— Commodore Cruise Lines—insisted on a dry docking and thorough inspection before the deal was finalized. As the *Navarino* was being lifted out of the water, the supports gave way and the vessel leaned against one side of the floating dock. The wall collapsed, and the ship flooded through open side ports and foundered with a thirty-five-degree list. Many of the accommodations and all the machinery spaces were underwater. The ship was declared a total loss.

At one point, the ship was going to be towed to Brazil to be used as a stationary floating hotel in São Paolo. But the deal never happened. Instead, it stayed in a shipyard near Athens for a few years.

Then, on November 12, 1985, after undergoing extensive repairs, the ship was sold to Regency Cruises and entered service as the *Regent Sea.* (The ship was later seized when the parent company couldn't pay its bills.)

Anyone remember the SS *Monterey*? The ship, which formerly sailed for Pacific Far East Lines out of San Francisco, was sold to a U.S. company that planned to begin cruising around the islands of Hawaii. But the line went bankrupt. The ship was sold again to a Panamanian company and then chartered to Star Lauro of Italy for twelve- and fourteen-day cruises of the Mediterranean.

Some older ships will never sail again, but they're still floating. Remember the Italian liners *Michelangelo* and *Raffaello*? In 1977, the ships were taken from Genoa to Iran to be used as floating barracks.

The *Victoria,* operated by Chandris, was built in 1936 as the *Dunnotar Castle.* The SS *Britannis* was built in 1932. The fifty-eight-year-old ship was once the *Monterey,* then the *Matsonia,* and finally the *Lurline.*

There are some benefits to sailing on an older ship. For one thing, it actually looks like a ship. Older ships seem to have usable passenger space, plus promenade decks where passengers can truly promenade. On older ships, the passenger cabins can be considerably larger.

In general, older ships usually carry fewer passengers, display a more thoughtful interior design (often using wood), and offer the feeling that you are making a passage rather than simply taking a cruise.

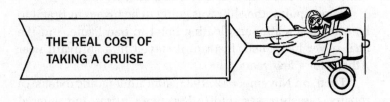

**THE REAL COST OF
TAKING A CRUISE**

My aunt Gail recently sent me the following letter:

There will be no nursing home in my future . . .

When I get old and feeble, I am going to get on a Princess cruise ship. The average cost for a nursing home is $200 per day. I have checked on reservations at Princess and I can get a long-term discount and senior discount price of $135 per day. That leaves $65 a day for:

1. Gratuities, which will only be $10 per day.

2. I will have as many as ten meals a day if I can waddle to the restaurant, or I can have room service (which means I can have breakfast in bed every day of the week).

3. Princess has as many as three swimming pools, a workout room, free washers and dryers, and shows every night.

4. They have free toothpaste and razors, and free soap and shampoo.

5. They will even treat you like a customer, not a patient. An extra $5 worth of tips will have the entire staff scrambling to help you.

6. I will get to meet new people every seven or fourteen days.

7. TV broken? Lightbulb need changing? Need to have the mattress replaced? No problem! They will fix everything and apologize for your inconvenience.

8. Clean sheets and towels every day, and you don't even have to ask for them.

9. If you fall in the nursing home and break a hip you are on Medicare. If you fall and break a hip on the Princess ship they will upgrade you to a suite for the rest of your life.

Now hold on for the best! Do you want to see South America, the Panama Canal, Tahiti, Australia, New Zealand, Asia, or name where you want to go? Princess will have a ship ready to go. So don't look for me in a nursing home, just call shore to ship.

If only that was the case. Despite lower average fares, the cruise industry is consolidating as the result of some failures, more mergers, and the creation of "the big three": Carnival, Royal Caribbean, and NCL. Following Carnival's acquisition of P&O in 2003, the big three now make up roughly 90 percent of North American cruise capacity.

With that kind of inventory control, the basic definition of the "all-inclusive" cruise is disappearing. Remember that $237 cruise price? A lot of folks were shocked to find out that once they boarded the ship, the Diet Coke was $237! (OK, I'm exaggerating, but not by that much . . .)

And as more people fill those berths, cruise lines are giving brokers less latitude on prices. The two biggest operators, Carnival and Royal Caribbean, moved to end widespread rebates—commissions up to 18 percent—to travel agents.

Following the airlines' lead, a number of cruise lines are actually selling more berths than some ships have. Yes, they are overbooking. The difference is that if an airline overbooks a flight, you're entitled to denied boarding compensation. But if you are bumped on an involuntary basis from your cruise, you don't really have any rights. (There is some good news. . . . Since virtually all cruise lines continue selling a cabin category even when space is fully booked, many passengers find themselves upgraded without asking.)

But back to the slow demise of the "all-inclusive" cruise concept. Since more and more cruise lines now charge for just about every extra—nearly everything on a cruise ship is now a profit center—you need to budget accordingly to arrive at a more realistic estimate of what your cruise is really going to cost you. It's a very simple rule of thumb, actually. Multiply your base cruise price by two-and-a-half to arrive at your real costs. If your cruise is $600, count on a final bill of $1,500. That will include what you spend for liquor, extras like ice cream, premium dining aboard the ship, the spa, soft drinks, shore excursions—everything short of the casino. Anything less than $1,500 will be a pleasant surprise.

8

Final Thoughts on Resources, Tools, Websites

AND WHAT TO DO WHEN IT ALL GOES WRONG

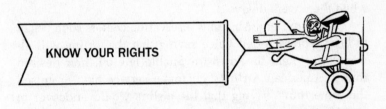

There are those of you who are convinced, perhaps correctly, that the process of travel will only get worse before it gets better.

There are also those who remember, less than fondly, a cold January day in 1999 in Detroit. That was the day when thousands of passengers were kept trapped inside their planes at the airport—some for as long as nine hours.

It was a catalytic moment of passenger rage and justifiable anger. Within weeks of the incident, no fewer than thirteen separate pieces of legislation were introduced in Congress aimed at formalizing the concept of airline passenger rights.

And the airlines moved just as quickly to beg Congress not to do that. Instead, the airlines asked to be given a chance to make some promises of better customer service and improved passenger rights.

And what about all the lawsuits filed in the Northwest Detroit incident? On the eve of a large trial, and more than two years after the snowstorm, Northwest suddenly agreed to pay $7.1 million to thousands of passengers to settle the case (payments ranged from $1,000 to $2,500 per passenger, depending upon how long each was stranded). Meanwhile the airline lobby is still winning in its fight to keep Congress from legislating passenger rights and airline responsibilities.

The airlines then issued nicely packaged "customer care" manifestos, which officially claimed they would tell the truth about offering the lowest fares and improve the flow—as well as the quality—of information to passengers when there were delays.

Callers to Delta Air Lines reservation centers soon began to hear a prerecorded voice saying that the airline will always offer them the lowest available fare on their desired routes. American Airlines' customer service plan promised the same thing, saying that the airline would endeavor to provide the lowest fare.

And then there was the reality. . . . The language used by the airlines was a textbook case in disclaimers: "Try," "all best efforts," "do everything possible."

Really? I decided to test the promise. I called American Airlines to book the ideal discount coach flight: more than three weeks in advance and staying over a Saturday night. The reservations agent asked me what kind of ticket I wanted. I responded "discount coach." The fare quote, for the "lowest" fare, for a flight leaving Los Angeles at 10:00 A.M. and returning six days later from New York at 3:00 P.M., booked three weeks in advance and staying over that dreaded Saturday night: a staggering $785!

That's the lowest fare?

Well, not exactly. What the airline didn't volunteer (so much for "endeavoring") was that if I took their 8:00 A.M. departure on the same day and returned at 8:00 A.M. from New York (again on the exact same dates as the original desired flights) the fare suddenly dropped to $499—almost a $300 saving! Just to make sure they hadn't simply forgotten to mention this deal, I called two times again over the next three days asking for the same flights. Not once were the "flight-specific" deals mentioned. And what are those deals? On transcontinental flights, if you depart LAX before 8:15 in the morning, or between 11:45 A.M. and 1:15 P.M., or if you return from JFK to LAX between 6:45 A.M. and 8:15 A.M. or between 5:45 P.M. and 7:15 P.M., the fares drop dramatically.

But you are not told this. You have to somehow divine it.

Another airline promise made to Congress is better communication when there are flight delays. This case in point involves American Airlines. I was booked on a flight leaving Los Angeles for Las Vegas. Scheduled departure time: 5:05 P.M. But when I arrived at LAX, I was told the flight was delayed until 6:00 P.M. The reason: weather.

Now, here are the real questions:

1. When did the airline know there was a delay? And why didn't they call me? (Yes, they had my number. In fact, every time you make a reservation, the airline asks for your number.)
2. Was it really weather related?
3. Was the new departure time fictitious as well? Where was the plane assigned to my flight at that particular moment?

The answers, as I soon discovered, were less than truthful.

First, the airline knew my plane would be delayed at 3:00 P.M., more than two hours before my flight was scheduled to depart. They just didn't call. And yes, they did have my number.

Second, it wasn't weather related. The aircraft was coming in from Las Vegas, where there were, in fact, no weather problems.

Third, and perhaps most disturbing, was the new departure time information. A further check with American revealed that the plane was then due in to LAX at 5:53 P.M. Assuming the incoming plane was carrying no passengers and needed no fuel, no replacement crew, and no catering, a seven-minute turnaround time was equally absurd.

Then the news got worse. I asked a few more questions and learned that the new arrival time was also a lie. The aircraft hadn't even left Las Vegas when they posted the amended arrival time in Los Angeles.

So . . . what were my options? An American Eagle flight "scheduled" to leave Los Angeles at 5:30 P.M. I raced over to the Eagle terminal, only to discover a plane sitting on the ground with no activity. At 5:20, I asked, "Is the plane leaving at 5:30?"

The counter agent nodded.

"Then when are you boarding?" I asked. "They're just servicing the aircraft," she assured me. I looked out and saw baggage handlers removing luggage from the plane. "Why are they doing that?" I asked. "Oh," she reported, "they are weighing each bag individually."

That was, I'm sorry to report, another lie. In fact, the baggage handlers were taking the bags off the plane because they were taking the plane out of service. And as they towed the plane away from the gate, the departure board was adjusted—unrealistically—to read a new departure time (for a gate that now had no plane) of 5:45 P.M.

At this time, my original—delayed—flight was beginning to look pretty good. The departure board now said it would be leaving at 6:10.

A hopeful sign? Not exactly. I called American and discovered that the flight had only gotten airborne out of Las Vegas at 5:33 and wouldn't be landing until 6:30.

Then American adjusted the departure board to read that the plane would be leaving at 6:30, another impossibility since the plane didn't actually touch down until 6:22.

At this point, I decided to lodge a complaint, and I called the airline. My complaint: I forgive the airlines for weather delays. I certainly forgive the airlines for mechanical delays. I do *not* forgive them for not calling me to communicate their problems, and worse, I do not forgive them for misinformation or false statements.

In every one of these cases, the behavior of the airline limited my options and those of my fellow passengers. So . . . what happened when I complained? The airline representative said someone would get back to me. And a few months later, someone did. I received a form letter of apology from American along with additional credited mileage to my frequent-flier account. Wow.

Here's the question: Could I have done better?

Answer: Yes.

Since 9/11, customer care manifestos are history. And delays at certain cities have become the airport version of "a perfect storm." Clogs at O'Hare delay passengers everywhere. A thunderstorm near Dallas disrupts most of American Airlines' system. And new data show that many airlines actually blame weather for delays when weather had nothing to do with those delays. In fact, among major airlines, the data show that only 3 percent of *all* delays during six months in 2004 were actually caused by extreme weather.

If an airline agent tells you that weather is the cause of a delay, ask the agent to make the case. Why? Remember that under the old Rule 240 (now 120.20), the airline is off the hook if the delay or cancellation is caused by weather. And if weather is not the cause? They're back *on* the hook.

And they were definitely on the hook during the summer of 2004, when more than one in every four flights was late. When travel was back to pre-9/11 levels, airlines were ferrying sixty-five million passengers a month.

So what can you do?

That's what this section is all about: tools, resources, and ammunition. What to do when it all goes wrong.

On the surface, it might seem harder to seek redress. For the moment, the airlines have been able to effectively deflect any federal legislation mandating them to keep their promises. Most cruise ships are officially registered in Liberia, or

Panama, or the Bahamas, making enforcement of safety or service issues that much tougher.

As a result, frustrated passengers are left to write angry letters—to the airlines, to hotels, to cruise ships, to me, and to a growing number of websites devoted entirely to travel complaints.

America's $541 billion travel industry needs to be more responsible. And in many cases, so do you. Toward that end, here are some resources, tools, phone numbers, and websites you should keep handy—and use!

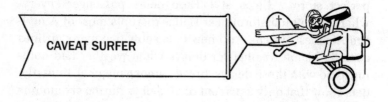

CAVEAT SURFER

Not a day goes by without at least five new websites appearing that are devoted to travel for a specific interest or group, whether it is bicycling tours, art galleries in Cyprus, or one-armed fugitives. There are now more than one million travel websites out there. If you believe current estimates, there are about 143.3 million adults using the Internet for travel purposes worldwide—it seems that if you want to travel, it pays to use the Internet before you leave.

But therein lies the promise—and the problem—of the wild new e-frontier. Sites that at first glance seem to be informational may actually be thinly disguised attempts to get us to buy travel services. Sometimes what they're selling is good. But when we're seduced by apparent access to quick and easy information, we may not be getting what we really want or need.

Which isn't to say travel sites aren't working overtime to

deliver your heart's desire—or at least to figure out what that is. They'll have to in order to survive. The Net has had a seismic effect on the underlying architecture of the travel business, now the largest industry in the world. We're in a brand-new territory, and to determine where the borders are, we're going to need a map.

Let's start with some staggering numbers. In 2003, Americans spent $43 billion on Internet travel purchases, amounting to 20 percent of all travel purchases that year. In 1998, Americans spent only 1.9 billion. It doesn't take a brilliant analyst to calculate how powerful the marriage of the Internet and travel has become. And the honeymoon is just beginning. According to PhoCusWright, an industry research firm, only 20 percent of all travel transactions currently take place online (a figure expected to double by 2008). But there are plenty of window shoppers: the millions of us now researching trips online. The Web has become a sophisticated profiling tool that can point out remote spots we never knew existed and can enhance our entire travel experience. We use the Net as exactly that—a net to gather information and to see the places we're planning to visit. Then we ask it to get us there with the least amount of effort and cash.

Not surprisingly, the Web's most aggressive transformation has occurred in the airline industry: Of all of last year's online travel transactions, 41 percent were for plane tickets. And since the cost of processing an e-ticket is just 30¢, compared with $9.49 for a paper ticket purchased from a traditional travel agent, the airlines want to eliminate the paper option. One key to playing the Internet travel game is to look closely at the new airline marketing partnerships, which will no doubt affect your ability to get the best price online.

Travelocity.com's 2003 third-quarter gross travel sales surpassed the billion mark for the first time in a quarter, easily placing the company in the top five of all e-businesses.

Challenging that behemoth is a beefed-up Expedia.com, which acquired Travelscape.com and other key properties. Then there's the impending consortium of airlines, which, if approved, will combine America's largest carriers and leading foreign airlines into one supersite that offers deeply discounted fares, along with a full menu of other travel services. Meanwhile, Priceline.com is acting as both ticket broker and airline—or airlines, rather—by partnering with United, Delta, and American on its name-your-price site. And let's not forget Orbitz.com, developed by American, Continental, Delta, Northwest, and United.

Sound confusing? It is, even to travel professionals. And until the dust settles, it's all too easy to be dazzled by the technology. It's essential to remember that a visit to the Net doesn't guarantee the best price—or the best of anything. Nor does it take the place of common sense.

The greatest advantage of the Internet is that, with few exceptions, it lets you browse before you buy. So don't assume that just because those five airlines teamed up to form Orbitz.com, you'll get the best prices there. You may find better deals at Expedia.com or Hotwire.com, or even in the newspaper. There are always other places to look, online and off, when you don't find what you want at one of the big Net agents.

Here's an inside tip: When traveling internationally, don't assume that a direct route is necessarily the cheapest one. Let's say you want to fly from New York to Nairobi. No discount fares are available, so your round-trip coach ticket could run upward of $2,000. Airfares from New York to London are dirt cheap, though, with some as low as $298 round-trip. Next stop: Lastminute.com, a British website offering some great travel deals that originate inside the United Kingdom but are available to anyone who logs on. Lastminute.com can't deliver? No problem. Spend five bucks on a London newspaper, such as *The Daily Telegraph* or the *Evening Standard,* and check the travel section. You're likely to find at least a dozen ads offering London-Nairobi round-trip fares for under $400. And yes, you can call them; they take credit cards and will deliver your tickets.

To get the best deals, it's always good to consult the locals. This is true in the United States as well. Want a cheap ticket to Phoenix from New York? Don't look for fares from New York on the usual Net suspects. Instead, log on to 12news.com, the site of the NBC affiliate in Phoenix, and check Internet travel deals. The websites of many local TV stations offer similar services and are worth checking out if the bottom line is your top priority.

Once you get to where you're going, you'll need a place to stay. Hotels came to the Web a bit later than the airlines and are still playing catch-up; in 2000, only 1.5 percent of hotel rooms were booked online. By 2002, 9 percent of hotel rooms were booked online, and in 2004, that number soared to about 22 percent, as hotel websites more aggressively courted travelers. So far, small enterprises that have banded together to make themselves marketable, such as the properties featured at Travelpresskits.com, have had the biggest impact on Net bookings. But it's not only bookings that can benefit hotels. A well-designed hotel site serves a purpose far different from that of an agent's or airline's site: It attracts you, the consumer, by showing you exactly what you'll be getting for your money. And it's much more entertaining than a brochure.

Go to any Four Seasons site and you'll see an example of what I'm suggesting. Many of their locations offer virtual tours that let you look at room interiors or the spa. The best news is that there is little of the pressure to buy that you inevitably feel with most airline sites. And when you do want to book, you're not doing it in the dark.

If price is your main motivator in booking a hotel, the Hotel Reservations Network does a reasonably good job of discounting excess inventory. Want to bid for the room instead? There's Priceline, of course, but now eBay and Yahoo.com have a feature that works the same way. You enter how much you're willing to pay for a room that meets your specs; if the site finds a match, it charges your credit card for a nonrefundable reservation. If you do decide to bid, just remember that there's often a hidden price to pay. With airfare auctions, your flight may not be nonstop and you may not get frequent-flier miles. With hotels, you may not get the miles or frequent-stay points. But if the deal is good enough, the trade-off may be worth it.

What about booking cruises on the Web? The cruise business was one of the last travel sectors to go online, in part because more than 94 percent of all cruise sales are made by travel agents, who can help novices decipher what is often an expensive and complicated purchase. The industry has made a real effort in the past year to come on board the Web, though. Cruises still constitute only a fraction of online transactions, but such a dramatic surge signals something significant.

Perhaps because they were last to launch, many cruise sites are among the best in terms of visual entertainment. One of my favorites is Princess.com. Check out its Live Bridge cams, which give you instant live access to any of its ships around the world.

Talk about aspirational travel! Another great site, Renaissancecruises.com, offers video-enhanced virtual tours. For cruise bargains, try the OnSale marketplace, which recently offered a Celebrity cruise for two to Alaska for $1,199—about $200 less than the same cruise on Celebrity's own site.

Because of unsold ship berth, which means lost revenue

that the cruise line will never recoup, companies have begun to dump inventory directly onto the Net. If you want to actually speak to a travel specialist when booking a cruise (and if you're a first-timer, I absolutely recommend it), Uniglobe.com has agents available to answer your questions via a toll-free number.

More often than not these days, however, traditional agents are being bypassed. The industry has been thoroughly shaken by Darwinian economic forces: The Net will eliminate all vendors that cannot match excess supply to potential buyers with online speed and efficiency.

Does this mean that travel agents will become extinct? No, but they sometimes see themselves as an endangered species. At one point, the American Society of Travel Agents petitioned the U.S. Justice Department to investigate possible antitrust violations by major airlines that partnered in Orbitz, the low-fare site. Agents are particularly concerned about cruise sites, because commissions on ship bookings are the biggest they receive.

Technological advances will also continue to transform how the Internet delivers and promotes travel. According to Pew Research, some sixty-eight million people will have broadband access within the next year. As this trend accelerates, transaction sites will begin to make more and more use of video-streaming technology to better inform visitors and provide greater entertainment value, in the hope that they'll stick around long enough to buy. Smart travel agents will use the same technology to deliver a video e-mail message about where the bargains are.

It hasn't stopped there. When Vodafone (UK), the world's largest wireless manufacturer, forged partnerships with Travelocity and Expedia, the handheld wireless booking engine arrived, allowing travel agents to stream themselves to your

PalmPilot and speak directly to you, wherever you are. The Net has truly changed the travel industry, by putting you in contact with a real human being. Wow, what a concept!

Worried about the security of the last message you had to send from some college kid's laptop in Jakarta? Log on to www.pgp.com, where you can find many different ways to encrypt your files and online correspondence. If you don't want anyone to intercept your naughty e-mail from your sweetheart or the access codes from that novel you're trying to broker to Hollywood, these guys can handle your needs. Go to the freeware section and download their product.

Road warriors John Tedesco and Jeff Grass loved logging on while traveling, but hated coming home to a stack of unpaid bills. So they created a site that lets you pay your bills online from anywhere (Paytrust.com, formerly Paymybills.com). This was not a breakthrough innovation (many banks allow you to do the same thing). But these folks built a better mousetrap. They don't just deduct automatic payments from your account—you're notified by e-mail when a bill is due, and you decide what you want to do and when.

Thanks to the Internet, we can take a sneak peek at what awaits us before we decide to head off for Tahiti. But what about, say, Columbus, Ohio? Certain sites do a good job of covering America's major cities, but information on smaller towns can be more difficult to come by. Poke around a little, though, and the Web yields some surprises.

BEST READ GUIDE INTERNATIONAL

Its globe-trotting moniker notwithstanding, this site (bestreadguides.com) concentrates on small U.S. cities, from Amarillo, Texas ("an outdoorsman's paradise!"), to Traverse

City, Michigan (where "life's a breeze aboard the Tall Ships"). The towns provide lively features and good photos, along with guides to nearby attractions. Angler's alert: Free fishing seminars are held throughout the summer in Brainerd, Minnesota, where walleye and pike are jumpin' in area lakes.

BOULEVARDS AND *WILLAMETTE WEEK*

A good way to suss out information about larger cities is to consult their free alternative weeklies. Boulevards (boulevards.com) acts as an intersection for dozens of such papers around the country. One of the best of these is *Willamette Week* (www.wweek.com), published in Portland, Oregon, which gives you an inside line on artsy gatherings and live club dates. Residents use the print version to make their plans. With a quirky town like Portland, it's a good idea to tap into the underground.

Austin, Texas, is another city with a vibrant alternative scene. A small dose of local knowledge helps unlock its best features, and Austin360 (austin360.com) delivers. In one quick visit, we learned the show times for the Alvin Ailey American Dance Theater, where the best bands were playing, what the garage sales were selling—and, most important, where to find the cheapest gas. Now, that's good juice for the traveler.

Note: Remember that many dot.coms can quickly become *not*.coms. With new sites being added (and disappearing) every day, I can't guarantee that all of these will be there for you. But it's a start.

So with that as my *only* real disclaimer in this book, here are some other choices I particularly like, with the proviso that the Internet is *a* tool, not the *only* tool!

PLANNING A TRIP

Here are two sites to watch. The first is www.hotwire.com, a site backed by a consortium of American, American West, Continental, Northwest, United, and US Airways. The other site is www.sidestep.com. These guys search *all* the airlines' websites for low fares, and then link you to those sites.

LAST-MINUTE TRAVEL

One very creative site is www.site59.com. These folks offer last-minute discounted package deals (it doesn't matter that you get a cheap airfare if the hotel will cost $500 a night). These aren't just great last-minute deals financially, but experientially as well.

FLIGHT DELAYS

The U.S. Department of Transportation can help—a little. It now requires all major domestic airlines to make their on-time record for *every* flight available to the public. Just check online at www.dot.gov/airconsumer.

Want to know where your flight is right now? www.fly.faa.gov has real-time information on flight status and airport operations.

Then there's something called Airport Monitors, brought to you by Passur.com, one of my most favorite sites. Why? It's fun! When you log on to an airport monitor, check out the green and blue planes. The green planes are taking off; the blue ones are landing. This is current airport activity, and these sites are loaded with live, detailed information. Every airport monitor includes maps of the airport and surrounding areas. Here are the current monitors:

Boston Logan (www4.passur.com/bos.html)

Burbank Airport (www4.passur.com/bur.html)

Cleveland Hopkins International (www4.passur.com/cle_test.html)

John Wayne (Orange County) Airport (www4.passur.com/sna.html)

Los Angeles International (www4.passur.com/lax.html)

Traveling on a charter? The Air Transport Users Council website lets you check on which charter carrier has the worst on-time performance: www.auc.org.uk/news/delay99.html.

THE REAL RULES OF AIR TRAVEL

Punch up www.onetravel.com and look for "rules of the air." You'll find simple, easy-to-understand explanations for dozens of airline rules, tariffs, and that document of Talmudic complexity—the airline contract of carriage.

THE REAL TERMS OF AIR TRAVEL

Here's an esoteric site that I like. Call me crazy, but I actually know seating configurations and airplane histories, thanks in part to www.planespotter.com. This site will sell you (for about $8) a great, laminated foldout that gives you a basic explanation and great visual cues to identifying different kinds of planes, configurations, and sizes of aircraft.

WEATHER AND TRAFFIC

Here are some very useful "before you go" sites:

www.weather.com/travelwise

www.nws.noaa.gov/

www.onlineweather.com

And even if the weather is cooperating, there's always the problem of traffic. So log on to www.trafficstation.com for real-time traffic updates from twenty-eight North American cities.

TIME

Just in case you know where you are, but have no idea what time it is where you're headed, www.timeanddate.com will give you the local time in 130 cities around the world.

DIRECTIONS

Try a site called www.mapsonus.com. The site prints driving directions for the way you want to get there—either the fastest route, the geographically shortest, or, if you have the time, the most scenic routes. Another good site, www.mapquest.com, is very user friendly.

Lost at the airport? Then click on www.airlinequality.com/airports, look for "Airports A–Z" and pick your airport.

MONEY

Want to know how many euros it takes to make $20? Do zlotys confuse you? Then log on to www.oanda.com and you'll get fast conversion rates for more than 160 different foreign currencies. You can even print out one of their conversion charts to take with you. Another good universal currency converter: www.xe.net/ucc.

If you're like me, you use your ATM card when you travel. So log on to www.mastercard.com/atmlocator/index.isp or www.visa.com to get ATM locations worldwide.

Want foreign currency *before* you leave town? Visit www.currency-to-go.com. This service promises to get any one of seventy-five foreign currencies to your doorstep overnight for a $10 fee if you order by 3:00 P.M. Eastern time. Order $500 or more and the service even waives the fee!

INSURANCE

Two sites offer important information on virtually every kind of travel insurance: www.travel.state.gov/medical.html will give you information on medical evacuation services, and www.worldwideassistance.com is a good resource for family travel insurance.

Here are some others:

www.berkely.com

www.internationalsos.com

Most of these sites will try to sell you insurance, but when it comes to travel, you probably aren't covered and need it. Perhaps most important, investigate a company called MED-

JET Assistance (medjetassistance.com), which provides medical evacuation and repatriation insurance (I strongly advise you to consider this). Call 800-963-3538.

Also check with www.travelguard.com—these folks even sell trip cancellation insurance and offer storm and hurricane hotline information.

PREVENTIVE MEDICINE

Before leaving home, try out www.who.int or www.cdc.com. Both are great resources for country-specific medical information and where to find medical clinics abroad.

Also, look at www.tripprep.com, which can get you up-to-date information on travel-related diseases and maladies ranging from nausea to yellow fever. Another resource is www.onhealth.com, which takes you to the WebMDHealth home page.

OTHER DETAILS

Looking for more details about your destination, but you don't want the typical brochure promotions? The Zagat guides (www.zagat.com) are great when it comes to restaurants, but now you can get staff views of those same establishments at http://flyinthesoup.com.

PETS

At www.dogfriendly.com you will find a great fifty-state breakdown of which hotels, restaurants, and local cities welcome dogs, not to mention tips about flying with Fido.

PASSPORT INFO

There are about 275 million Americans. But only 25 percent of us have valid passports! Do you have one? If you do, is it valid? If you need a new one or don't have one to begin with, here's what you need to know.

Get one. Period. As hockey legend Wayne Gretzky once said, "You miss 100 percent of the shots you never take."

Need a passport fast? Try www.travisa.com. This site cuts through the red tape, whether you're applying for a new passport or replacing one that you lost. Travisa's stated guarantee is to process your complete application within five hours of receiving it; in some cases, it can have a new passport to you in twenty-four hours. Extensive background resources include visa requirements for U.S. travelers to literally every country, links to government travel advisory sites, and an excellent health section that details which illnesses are prevalent in various parts of the world and how to avoid them.

VISAS AND FEES

It's not just getting the passport, it's knowing which countries require an additional visa before they'll let you in. For that, log on to www.embassy.org/embassies to get a list of every embassy in Washington, D.C. Then link to those websites for the information you need.

LANGUAGE

You've got to start somewhere, so try www.travlang.com—sixteen translating dictionaries that convert basic words and phrases. At least you'll have access to the right words to find the bathroom wherever you are going! Need translations of trickier phrases? Try www.freetranslation.com.

SAFETY

Get all the U.S. State Department consular information sheets, announcements, warnings, and bans at www.travel.state.gov.

Is "danger" your middle name? For practical info ranging from what to pack to what to do if a rhino attacks, there's a site that is a stellar resource for anyone heading off the beaten track. Detailed overviews of global hot spots use a "jump to" box that lets you move from country to country; in Algeria, for example, you'll be warned about bomb attacks in the markets of Algiers. Even those travelers choosing to stick to comfort zones can benefit from handy data such as long-distance access codes from dozens of countries. www.comebackalive. com will land you at a place called "DangerFinder." Before heading to Somalia or other less-than-desirable places, you can find out what you may really be up against.

CRUISE SHIPS

A basic guide to some important information is www. cruiseopinion.com. This site contains more than four thousand cruise ship reviews, and it doesn't pull punches.

Another link is www.cdc.gov/travel/cruiships.htm (*cruise ships* is intentionally misspelled on this site).

CUSTOMS

Worried about what is/isn't duty free? How about what you really can bring into the country? Visit www.customs

.ustreas.gov/travel/trtext.html; click on "Travel," then "Prohibited Goods."

If you need to know what kinds of food you can bring back, try www.aphis.usda.gov.

And remember, those value-added taxes can kill you. But most of us can recoup that VAT amount by getting a customs stamp when we shop. Which countries, stores, and purchases qualify? Go to Global Refund at www.globalrefund.com to find out before you go.

GOING UNDERGROUND

At www.subwaynavigator.com you will find all the routes for all the subway systems around the world.

PROTECTING YOUR LUGGAGE

If you are looking for airports with services that will shrinkwrap your luggage before you check it in, go to www.securewrap.com (currently available only at the Miami airport).

IF YOU'RE DRIVING . . .

Visit www.speedtrap.org. You have to love this site. It actually tells you where "smokey" is—where the cops and/or highway patrols around the United States have set up radar traps to catch speeders.

AIR SAFETY FOR THE TRULY NEUROTIC

If you're truly afraid to fly, or for that matter, travel, here's a terrific site full of instantaneously upgraded statistics bound to impress you, for better or worse: http://worldometers. info/. Want to know, up to the second, how many people have died in airplane, automobile, or train accidents—and that's just for starters? I guarantee you'll fall in love with this site.

SURF CITY

And finally, as long as you're surfing the Net, this discussion wouldn't be complete without a list of the best surfing sites on the Web. You can find it at www.surfline.com (the current surf conditions and even surf cams!).

LET YOUR FINGERS DO THE WALKING

When all else fails, there's always the simple solution of logging on to www.airlinenumbers.com, finding the right listing, and then actually calling someone. Of course, if you're too lazy even to do that, here are some useful numbers:

Access Air 877-462-2237

Aer Lingus 800-223-6537

Aero California 800-232-9820

Aeroflot 888-340-6400

Aerolineas Argentinas 800-333-0276

Aeromexico 800-237-6639

Air Afrique 800-456-9192

Air Aruba 800-882-7822

Air Caledonia 800-677-4277

Air Canada 888-247-2262

Air China 800-982-8802

Air Fiji 800-FLIFIJI

Air France 800-237-2747

Air India 800-442-4455

Air Jamaica 800-523-5585

Air Madagascar 800-821-3388

Air Mauritius 800-537-1182

Air New Zealand 800-262-1234

Air Pacific 800-227-4446

Air Sunshine 800-327-8900

Air Tran Airways 800-AIR-TRAN

Air Vegas 800-255-7474

Air Zimbabwe 800-742-3006

Alaska Airlines 800-252-7522

Alitalia 800-223-5730

All Nippon Airways 800-235-9262

Aloha Air 800-367-5250

America West Airlines 800-235-9292

American Airlines 800-433-7300

American Trans Air 800-435-9282

Ansett Australia Airlines 888-4-ANSETT

Asiana Airlines 800-227-4262

Atlantic Airlines 800-879-0000

Austrian Airlines 800-843-0002

Avianca 800-284-2622

Avioimpex—Interimpex 800-713-2622

Bahamas Air 800-222-4262

Balkan Bulgarian Airlines 800-852-0944

Big Sky Airlines 800-237-7788

British Airways 800-247-9297

British Midland 800-788-0555

BWIA International 800-538-2942

Canada 3000 888-226-3000

Canadian Air International 800-426-7000

CanJet Airlines 800-809-7777

Cape Air 800-352-0714

Cathay Pacific Airways 800-233-2742

Cayman Airways 800-441-3003

Chalk's Ocean Airways 800-4-CHALKS

China Airline 800-227-5118

China Eastern Airlines 800-200-5118

China Southern 888-338-8988

Colgan Air 800-428-4322

Comair 800-354-9822

Condor 800-524-6975

Continental Airlines 800-525-0280

Copa Airlines 800-359-2672

Corporate Airlines 800-555-6565

Corporate EXPRESS—Canada 403-216-4050

Corsair www.corsair.fr

Croatia Airlines www.croatiaairlines.com

Czech Airlines 800-223-2365

Delta Air Lines 800-221-1212

East Coast Flight Services 800-554-0550

Egyptair 800-344-6787

El Al Israel Airlines 800-223-6700

Emirates Air 800-777-3999

EVA Airways 800-695-1188

Finnair 800-950-5000

Frontier Airlines 800-432-1359

Garuda Indonesia www.garuda-indonesia.com

Gulf Air 800-433-7300

Gulfstream International Airlines 800-992-8532

Hawaiian Airlines 800-367-5320

Horizon Air 800-547-9308

Iberia 800-772-4642

Icelandair 800-223-5500

Island Air 800-323-3345

Japan Airlines 800-525-3663

JetBlue Airways 800-538-2583

Jet Express 800-806-8833

Kenya Airways 212-279-5396/818-990-5923

KLM 800-374-7747

Korean Air 800-438-5000

Kuwait Airways 800-458-9248

Lacsa Costa Rica 800-225-2272

LanChile Airlines 866-IFLY LAN

Lauda Airlines www.laudaair.com.au

Leading Air Logistics 800-552-5323

LTU International 888-265-1775

Lufthansa 800-645-3880

Lynx Air International 888-LYNX-AIR

Malaysia 800-552-9264

Malev Hungarian 800-223-6884

Martinair Holland 800-627-8462

Mesa Airlines 800-637-2247

Mesaba Airlines 800-225-2525

Mexicana 800-531-7921

Midway Airlines 800-446-4392

Midwest Express Airlines 800-452-2022

Nantucket Airlines 800-635-8787

Nica Airlines 800-831-6422

North Vancouver Air 800-228-6608

Northwest Airlines 800-225-2525

Olympic Airways 800-223-1226

Pakistan International Airline 800-221-2552

Pan Am 800-359-7262

Philippine Airlines 800-435-9725

Polish Air-Lot 800-223-0593

Polynesian Airlines 800-644-7659

Qantas Airways 800-227-4500

Royal Air Maroc 800-344-6726

Royal Jordanian Airlines 800-223-0470

Royal Nepal 800-266-3725

Ryan International Airways 800-727-0457

Sabena 800-955-2000

SAS Scandinavian Airlines 800-221-2350

Saudia Arabian Airlines 800-472-8342

Singapore Airlines 800-742-3333

Solomon Airlines 800-677-4277

South African 800-722-9675

Southwest Airlines 800-435-9792

Spanair 888-545-5757

Spirit Airlines 800-772-7117

Sri Lankan 877-915-2652

Sun Country Airlines 800-752-1218

Sunflower Airlines, Fiji 800-707-3454

Swissair 800-221-4750

TACA Airlines 800-535-8780

TAM—Transportes Aereos Regionais 888-235-9826

TAP Air Portugal 800-221-7370

Thai Air 800-426-5204

Travelair 800-948-3770

Tropic Air 800-422-3435

Turkish Airlines 800-874-8875

Ukraine International Airlines 800-876-0114

United Airlines 800-241-6522

US Airways 800-428-4322

USAir Shuttle 800-428-4322

Vanguard Airlines 800-826-4827

Varig 800-468-2744

Virgin Atlantic 800-862-8621

WestJet Airlines 800-538-5696

Remember, since these are toll-free numbers, if you don't like what you hear on your first go-around, hang up and try again. Since airlines update their fares more than three hundred thousand times a day, what isn't available at 10:00 A.M. may suddenly become available four minutes later. As long as you are outside the ticketing and payment restrictions window, you lose nothing by calling back.

CAR RENTAL AGENCIES, NATIONAL NUMBERS

Avis	800-230-4898
Budget	800-527-0700
Dollar	800-421-6868
Hertz	800-654-3131
National	800-227-7368

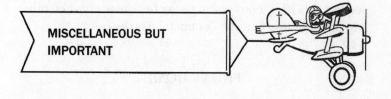

MISCELLANEOUS BUT IMPORTANT

LUGGAGE

I haven't checked a bag domestically in more than eight years. And with good reason. I FedEx my bags, and they don't just go door to door. They go door to room! But there are a number of great services in addition to FedEx, UPS, and DHL that can ship your bags, such as www.virtualbellhop.com,

Luggage Express at www.866shipbags.com or 866-744-7224, and www.gear-to-go.com. Also check www.luggageconcierge. com.

And if you happen to be flying to Hawaii on Hawaiian Air . . . check out BaggageDirect.com. BaggageDirect delivers your boarding passes to your home when they come to pick up your luggage. Without baggage and with boarding passes in hand, all you have to do is walk through security and to the gate.

If you're in Europe and traveling across the continent, check out www.firstluggage.com.

STUDENT AIRFARES AND DISCOUNTS

If you are on a budget and in search of student discounts, try studentadvantage.com, which guarantees a 15 percent discount on Amtrak and Greyhound trips. Also check airtran. com and look for the airline's X Fares, which allow students to travel to any destination the airline flies for as little as $55 per leg. Also log onto www.studentuniverse.com for other unpublished low fares on commercial airlines.

PHONE HOME

Vonage is worth exploring (www.vonage.com). It's an Internet-based service that offers unlimited local and long-distance calling for $24.99 a month. As long as your hotel has Internet access, you're connected. No more hefty hotel phone surcharges!

And if you're in Europe, it's good to know that the continent actually has its own emergency phone number. It's 112. Operators at all call centers speak English.

AIRPORT PARKING

Airport parking gets scarcer each year—especially at holiday time—since no new airport parking lots have been built since 9/11. So check out www.longtermparking.com, which offers free parking coupons and reservations for off-site parking at forty-seven U.S. airports.

What's more, prices can be up to 70 percent lower than those for on-site airport parking.

MORE THAN JUST PARKING

ParkSleepFly.com offers the peace of mind that you won't miss your flight due to airport congestion or unforeseen highway traffic or weather. You receive one night's accommodation, long-term parking up to seven days while away, and shuttle service to and from the airport. In many cases, the hotel rates are competitive with what you would pay for airport parking alone.

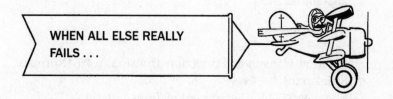

WHEN ALL ELSE REALLY FAILS . . .

THE POWER AND FINESSE OF THE COMPLAINT

When something goes wrong, you want to complain and, more important, you want something done about it.

I'm a great letter writer, but sending a letter to an airline, cruise line, or hotel may just not be enough. You need to develop and maintain a paper trail.

When something goes wrong, be a good reporter. Get names, dates, addresses, phone numbers, witnesses. Then write a letter to the airline, but also send a copy to the appropriate federal agency.

If it's safety related:

Assistant Administrator for System Safety ASY-100
Federal Aviation Administration
800 Independence Avenue, SW
Washington, DC 20591
800-FAA-SURE, 800-322-7873, or the Aviation Safety Hotline at 800-255-1111.

If it's service-related:

Office of Consumer Affairs
U.S. Department of Transportation
400 Seventh Street, NW
Room 10405
Washington, DC 20590
202-366-2220.

And then copy:

Aviation Consumer Protection Division, c-75 (Norman Strickman)
Room 4107 U.S. Department of Transportation
400 Seventh Street, SW
Washington, DC 20590

E-mail the Aviation Consumer Protection Division at air-consumer@ost.dot.gov.

AND IF ALL ELSE FAILS

When that flight is delayed or you discover your hotel room won't be ready for hours, log onto www.sandcastlecentral. com. At least it's something to do while waiting!

INDEX

A

AAA guidebooks, 346
The Acceleration of Just About Everything (Gleick), 180
Access America, 394
Achille Lauro, 16, 414
advance boarding passes, 228
advance-purchase excursion (APEX) tickets, 107
Aer Lingus, 132
Aeroflot, 131, 239
Aerolineas Argentina, 171
AeroMexico, 201
Afghanistan, 11, 14
Air Canada, 109, 325
airfares:
  from alternate airports, 112–113
  basis of, 89–96
  bereavement, 172–176
  class of service and, 84–89, 98–99
  coupons for, 111–112
  deregulation and, 6
  fuel cost and, 284
  increases in, 286, 287
  lowest, 82, 90, 95, 96–98, 158–161, 426, 432–434, 438
  maximum permitted mileage and, 99–100
  Saturday night stay-over, 69–70, 163
  scheduled flights and, 83–84
  senior discounts on, 90–91
  standby, 90, 101–103, 142, 149–150, 160, 259–261
  student discounts on, 90, 450
  through travel agents, 114–118
Air France, 132, 134, 171, 201, 277–278
Air India, 132
airlinequality.com, 440
airline reservations:
  airfare and, 83–96
  to avoid flight delays, 254
  computerized, 118–121, 122, 125
  through cruise lines, 411–412
  flight bumping and, 261
  for pets, 332
  seating and, 228
airlines. *See also specific airlines*
  airfares direct from, 114
  check-in rules of, 12
  child travel policies of, 314–315, 323–326
  class of service on (*see* class of service)
  code-share partners, 148
  complaints about, 6–7, 144, 197
  consortium of, 432, 438
  customer service at, 425–426
  deregulation of, 6, 122, 147, 256, 291
  excess capacity of, 284
  flight bumping by, 12, 96, 257–262
  home bases of, 243, 254
  interlining by, 255
  phone listings for, 446–448
  revenue management by, 89–91, 285

ABOUT THE AUTHOR

PETER GREENBERG is considered the nation's preeminent expert on travel and travel-related issues. Currently the travel editor for NBC's *Today* show, the Emmy Award–winning writer and producer is also the chief correspondent for Discovery Network's Travel Channel.

A former *Newsweek* correspondent, Greenberg is the editor in chief of www.travelnewstoday.com, a weekly online travel newsletter that champions travelers' rights, and each week he hosts a live, nationally syndicated radio show.

Pretty Little Dirty

A NOVEL

AMANDA BOYDEN

VINTAGE BOOKS

A Division of Random House, Inc.

New York

A VINTAGE BOOKS ORIGINAL, MARCH 2006

Copyright © 2006 by Amanda Boyden

All rights reserved. Published in the United States by Vintage Books,
a division of Random House, Inc., New York, and in Canada
by Random House of Canada Limited, Toronto.

Vintage and colophon are registered trademarks
of Random House, Inc.

This is a work of fiction. Names, characters, places, and incidents either
are the product of the author's imagination or are used fictitiously.
Any resemblance to actual persons, living or dead,
events, or locales is entirely coincidental.

Library of Congress Cataloging-in-Publication Data
Boyden, Amanda.
Pretty little dirty : a novel / Amanda Boyden.
p.   cm.
1. Girls—Fiction.   2. Young women—Fiction.   3. Middle West—Fiction.
4. Loss (Psychology)—Fiction.   5. Female friendship—Fiction.
6. Children of the rich—Fiction.   I. Title.
PS3602.O934P74 2006
813'.6—dc22
2005048458

Vintage ISBN-10: 1-4000-9682-0
Vintage ISBN-13: 978-1-4000-9682-4

Book design by Jo Anne Metsch

www.vintagebooks.com

Printed in the United States of America
10 9 8 7 6 5

For all the strong women of my family,
and with great love and thanks to Joseph and my father.

You kept the faith when I did not.

O latest born and loveliest vision far

Of all Olympus' faded hierarchy!

Fairer than Phoebe's sapphire-regioned star

Or Vesper, amorous glow-worm of the sky;

Fairer than these, though temple thou hast none,

Nor altar heaped with flowers;

Nor virgin choir to make delicious moan

Upon the midnight hours;

No voice, no lute, no pipe, no incense sweet,

From chain-swung censer teeming;

No shrine, no grove, no oracle, no heat

Of pale-mouthed prophet dreaming.

—JOHN KEATS

PRETTY LITTLE DIRTY

Look around. Look at the singer and his band. Look at the other hulking things with their bad tattoos leaning against the walls and know that this is not what you believed it would be. Feel your mistake like a steel-toe to the chest.

Decide, anyway, not to cower. Put your mind to it.

You will do this, and you will be good at it. You will give up to the outside everything on your inside. You will reverse your skin like a sweater pulled over your head.

You will show her, them, all of them, every last one of them, how human you are. You will force them to see that you are exactly the same. You will.

Decide, first, that you need another drink.

I MET CELESTE in one of those lucky years of childhood you get before anybody significant dies—before Grandma goes, before your dad's secretary doesn't beat breast cancer, before the pharmacist gets into the car wreck. Celeste fit those years perfectly: me with my illusions of everyone living on into some hazy infinity of old age, Celeste with her surreal beauty, her otherworldly trust, her yellow eyes more gold than green, her skin, her lips, her—god!—her grace. You wouldn't believe how beautiful a sixth-grader could be until you saw her.

Having long known how babies were made—woman and man share love and bodies—I sometimes daydreamed about Celeste's parents procreating in a nonspecific way, making my friend before she existed. I had a lot of trouble imagining mine making me, my mother perpetually medicated by the time I was two, my father entirely asexual as all fathers are in eleven-year-old daughters' minds. But Celeste's parents had done the miraculous; they had made *her*, and I couldn't figure out the genetics of it all.

Celeste's mother, Mrs. Diamond, her face forever defiant (of what I had no idea), stood small and tight and brown as a nut. Mr. Diamond, a booming god of a man, not handsome but there in a sure, ever-present kind of way, danced instead of walked and encouraged you to eat beans and read the newspaper no matter how old you were. You couldn't ignore Celeste's father any more than you could ignore the fact that some wondrous girl actually lived up to the improbable name of Celeste Rose Diamond. No joke.

The Diamonds and my family both moved to Kansas City, Missouri, just days before the start of the new school year, hers from New York, mine from Chicago, both with the intent of placing their incredibly gifted children into the best private school the city had to offer. Celeste and I took our placement exams at the same time. We were coincidentally both young for our class, and there seemed to be some question as to whether or not we could live up to our parents' lauding. Fill in circles with pencil lead. I'd done it my entire young, non-death-filled life. Celeste, apparently, had not.

In a spare schoolroom expressly reserved for such test taking, I lifted my head from my booklet and answer sheet for the first time when the door latch clicked shut and the asthmatic proctor departed with a distinct fart. Celeste laughed out loud. I blushed.

"Hi," she said.

I glanced nervously at the closed door. I wanted to shush her. "Hi," I barely mouthed at the table. I hadn't really seen her yet.

"She doesn't care," Celeste said, throwing a hand up.

I drew the corner of my lower lip into my mouth and started to chew nervously. Studying my booklet in earnest, I shrugged and raised my eyebrows. I held my finger on my question.

"What's number twelve?" she asked.

Judas, I thought. Doughnuts. One short of unlucky. I was in test mode.

"Number twelve," she repeated.

I looked up then, and that's when I saw her, when I first truly saw Celeste, the sixth-grade goddess-to-be just sitting on the other side of the table, staring. I stared back. Years later, when I'd eaten one gram too many of hallucinogenic mushrooms and wasn't sure that what I saw made any sense, I'd blink and stare at a breathing wall in the same way. That way. Blink, blink.

"Hell-*o*," the beauty said.

"Um," I spurted. "Twelve is D. All of the above."

And so it began, with a perfect dozen of sorts. I had never cheated in my life, but from that first moment on I never denied Celeste an academic answer. Nor she me. I don't believe she thought that we were cheating. Somehow over the years I think she decided we were sharing. Just sharing information, maybe in the way she shared her beauty: "Take it; it's yours."

Celeste's own opinion of her physical appearance is exactly what saved her and what doomed her. Her beauty had no more to do with her inherently than a stray dog might. "Yeah," Celeste seemed to say, "Beauty likes me, but really, more, she just follows me around. She hangs out and we play fetch. Beauty drinks out of the park fountain." If her beauty left, certainly Celeste would have noticed, but her mourning would have been minimal. She had no sense of propriety about it. Astonishing, too, when you actually looked at her.

For all the years I knew Celeste her appearance changed as many times, but no matter the dye job, the ugly clothes, the awful choice of eye makeup, she remained undeniably gorgeous. I hated her for it, and I wanted to be her. If I had no other option—and ultimately I didn't—I would simply possess her. She would let me, finally, put a collar on her and call her mine.

I should begin at the beginning.

"D for twelve? Thanks." The girl smiled at me and went back to her circle filling. I glanced at her answer sheet, full of gaps like missing teeth, seemingly marked at random. She was far ahead of me but obviously not doing it the right way. I wanted to tell her that: "You're not doing it the right way." I didn't, though, of course, and thought about skipping ahead suddenly, an idea that had never occurred to me until that very moment. Ever. How had I not figured that out in eleven years of life? Look at how far ahead she was. Hurry up.

Not a minute later, the proctor still absent, this beautiful girl said, "I'm Celeste. What's forty-three?"

I looked at my answer sheet. I'd just colored in a B for thirty-nine.

"What's your name?" she asked.

"I don't know," I whispered, embarrassed.

The girl, Sellest—what kind of a name was that?—laughed again. "You don't know your name or the answer?"

I smiled back this time. She seemed very grown-up. I told her, "I'm only up to forty."

"What's your name?"

"Lisa."

"Lisa What?"

"Lisa Smith."

"That's so nice and normal. What's your middle name?" I watched as she casually closed her test booklet like an adult closing a magazine in a hair salon. "Lisa What Smith?"

"Michelle."

"Wow. Lisa Michelle Smith. How normal."

She seemed to mean it as a real compliment, but my name sounded from that moment onward as bland as cornflakes with no sugar. "Yeah," I said, my voice in my own ears tinny and false. The way her face presented itself, then, right there on the front of her head, was hard to explain. She looked like a live painting. She made you stop what you were doing and pay attention.

"I can't tell you how many times I've had to spell mine or correct teachers and stuff." Her voice dropped off at the end of her sentence, and I could have sworn her cheeks colored. I wanted her to spell her name for me because I was sure that I didn't understand it any better than any of those teachers did.

Instead I asked, "What's your middle name?" and that's when the proctor returned, the door swinging open into our fledgling conversation. I looked down, my finger still on question forty. I didn't look up. I heard Celeste open her test booklet and turn pages like that woman in the salon, flipping leisurely.

The proctor cleared her throat and sternly said, "Girls."

"Hi," Celeste answered.

I continued on with my test taking but could not help glancing at the girl across the table from me more often than I should have.

Certainly the proctor suspected bad behavior. But I couldn't catch Celeste's eye again.

We found out later that we'd both ended up in the ninety-ninth percentile. They were easy tests back at the start of the sixth grade.

I learned how to spell Celeste's name and how to inform other curious students as to its source, how Celeste's parents met of all places at the top of the Eiffel Tower in Paris, the most romantic place imaginable. How *Celeste* was French for "heavenly," for "of the stars." In 1976, few kids our age had unusual first names in Kansas City. In Cowtown. The Dweezils and Moon Units were out there on the West Coast. Still, Celeste's name had a touch of the exotic and more than some glitter about it, and the hometown kids, both the mean ones and the not-so-mean, took a liking to Celeste right from the start. As her sidekick, I fit in well enough under the easy, wide protection of my friend's quick popularity. I wasn't ugly. On the contrary, I was cute and bright, quiet but witty, a fast runner and good dodgeball player. Celeste and I were lean and strong alike. We were both still flat-chested. Without even looking, though, you knew we would always be different.

Celeste had two older sisters in high school already. Being new-comers, too, Diana and Rachel commanded more than their fair share of male attention. Within a month of moving to Kansas City, both of the older Diamond daughters had landed steady boy-friends and would remain regularly attached to some guy or another for the rest of their stays before heading off to equally good col-leges.

As it happened, Diana and Rachel helped prepare Celeste and me for our first truly tactile encounters with the opposite sex, and they are forever linked in my mind to Celeste's and my sixth-grade wilderness camp experience. Besides telling us how not to gross out when kissing for real, these wise older girls provided us with ammunition of the non-garden variety to use with our female class-mates when need be. They prepped us well, gave us lots of good stuff. Gave *me* lots of important information.

My mom had become a ghost of a mother by the time my fam-ily moved to Kansas City. I didn't even really need her permission to go to camp—only Dad's—but she signed her name in her neat script anyway, right beneath his. Experts today might know better what happened to my mother after she gave birth to me and my younger brother just ten months later. But back then, in the wan-ing years of the seventies' sexual and feminist revolution, nobody really knew what her deal was. I truly believe that delivering the two of us destroyed something in my mother. Postpartum depres-sion in the next-to-last degree, just this side of suicide. My mother had no bravery in her, or she would have killed herself at some point in my early life, and then I would have trouble remember-ing her at all. As it is, she simply haunts my past, a filmy figure behind my father, behind Celeste, even behind those two older sisters, who helped my best friend and me through the gauntlet of growing up female. And so armed with crazy, nearly unbelievable information about male and female bodies, about reproductive systems and mating rituals, Celeste and I departed for camp.

John McFarland flirted his ass off, you could say. No, really. For some reason mooning out bus windows would soon be de rigueur in 1976 in Missouri, and John McFarland proved himself a trend-setter. Celeste and I sat next to each other in a seat near the mid-dle of the bus. My twelfth birthday was going to fall during the week at wilderness camp, and I remember we talked about losing our digit repetition—we would have to wait till we turned twenty-two before our digits repeated again. Celeste said she would find a way to have a cake for me. I wanted to believe her, as she truly seemed to believe herself.

Mainly I just looked forward to going for days without washing my hair. And I couldn't wait to rappel. We hunkered down and propped our knees up on the black vinyl back of the seat in front of us. I picked at my chipping nail polish. A round of "99 Bottles of Beer on the Wall" had started earlier.

"What flavor?" Celeste asked loudly over the song, only in its twenties.

"I don't care," I said.

"Yes, you do. What's your favorite?"

I liked almost all cake. I'd had little of it, as my mom never baked, and Dad didn't eat sweets. He said they rotted the brain. "I don't know. Carrot ca—"

Suddenly a loud whoop went up in the bus a few seats behind us, and we craned our necks around. John McFarland stood on his seat dancing, lifting his shirt. Next to John, Peter Alpert clapped and whistled. My first reaction was to look to the front of the bus, where the driver was already frowning, his reflection a pinched face in the large flip-down rearview mirror. The gym teacher, Mr. Rahdart, sat behind the driver and swiveled into the aisle, standing. Celeste started yelling beside me, and I turned just in time to see John McFarland pull down his pants and underwear and stick his bare butt out the open window.

Cruising in the fast lane of a four-lane highway headed straight into the heart of the Ozarks, the bus overtook two sedans, both of which honked at the sight of John's white-cheeked greeting. Probably as a reaction to better hide the little jerk of a kid, the bus driver moved into the slow lane. John McFarland bounced and made kissy-mouth faces, winking directly at Celeste. All of us screamed and laughed. How daring! What a weird thing to do! John was the first in our class to drop trou out the window of a moving vehicle, and none of us could even believe what he was doing as he did it. How could he think—*why* would he think—to do something like that? Continuing to stare in his mirror, the driver drifted right. I watched as a large brown object loomed on the side of the road ahead, a half-crumpled thing that listed into the road like a drunk. I should have called out, but I didn't. And then, just like that, a sign for the Pomme de Terre campgrounds sliced a chunk off John McFarland's ass the size of a twice-baked potato half.

Mr. Rahdart reached John McFarland a split second late, yanking the boy out of the window right after the big warbling clunk of the metal sign. Peter Alpert was the first to react in a way that didn't mean hilarious, in a way that wasn't funny at all. "Jesus Christ, son!" the gym teacher yelled as Peter Alpert scrambled backward off the seat and onto the bus floor. When Mr. Rahdart held up his bloody hands, all the rest of us quit laughing and closed in, sixth-grade hyenas to injured prey.

John McFarland, his face now a slack-jawed mask, slumped as if to sit, but Mr. Rahdart held him up under his armpits. "No! No, no, son, no!"

The bus slowed, gravel pinging on the undercarriage.

"Oh, my god," Peter Alpert said, eyes wide as a doe's. I couldn't stop staring at John McFarland's penis and his testicles, soft-surfaced as fresh apricots, left hanging above his lowered underpants. As I stared, Mr. Rahdart seemed to notice, too, and awkwardly pulled on the waistband of John's underwear. John tugged too, helping the gym teacher, and then cried out like a girl as the backside of his pants scraped his bloodied butt.

"Go, go, go!" Mr. Rahdart yelled up at the bus driver, who had stopped at the side of the highway. "To a hospital!" Mr. Rahdart took off his T-shirt and wadded it. His stomach lolled as the driver lurched back onto the highway. I'd thought a gym teacher would have more muscles. I saw dark hairs dappling Mr. Rahdart's back, a place I'd never realized could grow hair. My own father, pale and thin, had very little hair on his head and none on his chest, much less on his back.

Later, and for years afterward, I wondered three things. First and most often, I wondered what happened to the piece of John McFarland's butt. Did it stick to the sign? Did it fall and get sucked into the bus' wake, only to be run over by other cars? Did it simply drop to the side of the road, where it dried into a concave rind? Was it carried away by animals and eaten in a squirrel nest or shared between baby possums? We didn't yet know then to go searching for the pieces of things, pieces of bodies, to reconnect and reattach. In 1976, in Missouri, we didn't know to try to save fingers or calves or chunks of butt.

I wondered, too, about how the doctors later covered John McFarland's flesh spot. It was a big spot. Where did they pull the skin from? Did it grow in from the edges? We never had a chance to ask John McFarland himself because his father was transferred shortly after the bus trip to camp, and we never really saw John McFarland again after he hobbled down the bus steps and into the Pomme de Terre hospital. Weeks later a neighbor kid two grades lower said he had seen John McFarland on crutches while his family loaded the moving truck, and that his whole butt cheek was gone, that his pants just hung there "like on a board." I sensed an urban myth even then, but nobody could confirm the post-mooning state of John McFarland's butt beyond school administrators and teachers reassuring us that he was recovering, that their former student was just fine.

Third, I wondered what would have happened if Celeste hadn't stepped up that day. Broken rank. "It'll be okay," she said, laying her hand on the gym teacher's fuzzy, bare shoulder as he soaked up John McFarland's blood. "It's not so bad," she told John as he clung to the top edge of the seat back in front of him. "It's not," she said, and somehow she managed to sound normal, and John McFarland looked at Celeste Rose Diamond and smiled.

"It's not?" He almost sounded encouraged.

Celeste shook her head, leaned into him, and whispered something. John McFarland's whole neck and face colored then, and he stood up taller, seemed to buck up under the weight of his injury. She took her seat again, but for the remainder of the ride to the hospital, he glanced at her repeatedly and squared his shoulders or lifted his chin.

I persisted in my questioning. What had she said to him? After a bus ride over three hours longer than it was initially supposed to be, both sections of our sixth-grade class met up at Camp Evergreenshade in the Mark Twain National Forest. Our group, so much later than the other, got stuck with the cruddier cabins, the ones farther away from the bathrooms and in perpetual shade, the result of which was a musty odor that would linger in my sleeping bag until the day, sometime after junior high school graduation, that I stuffed it into a neighbor's garbage can.

Celeste wouldn't give up what she said to John McFarland for years. After a while I stopped asking. She revealed what she'd told him only when all the pressure had disappeared, when I'd not thought about the trip or the boy or the camping week for so long I'd forgotten that I cared at all.

A weirdness permeates any campground, especially a campground designed for "maturing" kids, for soon-to-be teenagers dumbstruck by their own changing bodies. Tromp the kids out in the woods. Crawl them through damp caves. Make them sit in close proximity to one another around a fire. Make them sing. Make them square dance. Make them eat like wolves, they're so hungry after a day of hiking and rope climbing and falling backward blindly into the freckled arms and sweaty necks of class dorks they'd normally spit at. Pull the rug out. Make them learn real things. Make them get it.

The first night we formed alliances.

Two girl cabins and two boy cabins from our busload. Eight cabins total. We were so freaked out by the John McFarland episode that the six of us in our cabin chose beds without any arguing and started clucking away. How could you not want to talk about what happened to the boy?

Celeste and I had already agreed to try to secretly trade with other girls if we didn't get put in the same cabin, but we did. Our luck was good luck at Camp Evergreenshade to begin with. She wanted the bottom bunk, and I wanted the top.

Our no-electricity, no-running-water cabin included Celeste

and me; two other girls who were already each other's best friends and sometimes sat at our lunch table, Lynn L. and Lynne P.; Jennifer, a separated twin crabby without her sister, Jessica; and Wanda, who was black, popular, and cool. The Lynn-Lynnes took a bed together, and Wanda claimed the bottom bunk of the last bed, forcing the lonely twin Jennifer to clamber awkwardly upward, pushing a pea-green suitcase ahead of her.

I aimed my flashlight beam at the rafters overhead. "Whoa." The exposed underside of the roof twinkled with spiderwebs, some spots thick and puffy as cotton batting.

Jennifer squealed.

"Ewww!" the Lynn-Lynnes said.

Celeste stuck her head out from the lower bunk, her mouth open, a pair of blue pajama pants in her hand. "Wow."

"There must be hundreds," Wanda said.

"That is so gross."

"There are poisonous spiders. Brown recluses. Do you think those are brown recluses? I'm not sleeping at all if those—"

"Maybe."

Jennifer crawled down from her bunk, dragging her suitcase. Our six flashlights' dim circles moved around the ceiling.

"Why aren't there any lights in here?"

"Because," Celeste said.

"Because *why*?" Lynn L. whined.

"Why?" Lynne P. echoed.

Jennifer, standing by our bunk, propped her suitcase on her brand-new hiking boots and looked sheepishly at Celeste. "Can I sleep with you?"

I decided on the spot that Jennifer was a wimp and should be forced to go back up to her bed. I bit my tongue.

"How can they make us sleep in here?"

"With spiders!"

"With spiders!"

"Because," Celeste said again.

But, really, why? I wondered. Despite my persistence with the

John McFarland whispering earlier, I'd come to realize that Celeste would tell you what you wanted to hear faster if you didn't ask. If you could help yourself. So I didn't ask.

"Please," Jennifer whimpered. I looked at the lost twin. She might really cry. "Please can I sleep with you?" She raised her eyebrows at Celeste.

"Why?" Lynne P. asked over.

"Please?"

Many years later I decided that women have a rather explainable aversion to crawly things and slithering things because we're naturally protective of our orifices, particularly our most sacred of entrances and exits. Okay. If truth be told I happened to be very drunk at the time, pontificating at the bar to a group of fellow waitresses after the restaurant had closed. But think about it: Women have a really personal, wet "in," meant to nurture, meant to make stuff—if a fetus or a yeast infection or endometriosis can be called *stuff*—*grow*. A bit gross, maybe, but if you were a cold-blooded snake or a chilly spider looking for a warm place to curl up and possibly reproduce, what better spot than a uterus or a ribbed vaginal wall? At Camp Evergreenshade, however, I was still sealed, so to speak. Unlike the others, I had little natural aversion to spiders yet. Celeste, for that matter, didn't seem to be afraid either.

"You can sleep with me, I guess," Celeste answered Jennifer, looking at the small mattress.

"That's pathetic," I blurted. "Don't let her."

"Baby," Wanda teased Jennifer immediately.

Lynn L. crinkled her nose at the ceiling and crept down from her upper bunk. "Well, *I* don't want to be by them either," she said.

"I'm not switching with you," Lynne P. told her best friend. "I'm not going up there."

And the line between the chickens and the dingoes was drawn.

"Do you even see any spiders?" Celeste asked.

I flicked my flashlight around. I couldn't actually see any spiders, just tons of webs. "No," I answered loudly. Proudly. From my upper bunk.

Lynn L. aimed her flashlight beam into a corner and moved timidly toward its sharpening, shrinking circle. She drew in a loud breath and tripped backward. "Ew! There's one, there's one, there's one, there's—"

"Eeewww!" Lynne P. screeched from her lower bunk, picking her feet up off the cabin floor.

Lynn L. screamed too, reactionary best friend that she was, and pounced awkwardly onto Lynne P.'s mattress. Old springs croaked, a metallic clonk sounded in the night air of the cabin, and the Lynn-Lynne bed went down with the graceless aplomb of a tripping, overweight diva. You would think the floor had collapsed for the incredible noise.

Then, of course, we all screamed, scrambling away from the crash, bumping into walls, shrieking in our girliness at the prospect of becoming covered in spiders, perpetuating the contagion of preteen paroxysm.

I don't know why it is that we didn't have a counselor assigned to each cabin. Possibly in the years before exposure of the Catholic Church kind, no one understood the need for direct monitoring (thank god) of either kids or their supposed guardians and actually thought kids learning alone amongst spiders in the Missouri quasi-wilderness was a good idea. But with no counselor or elder in our cabin to calm us down, we tore open the cheap plywood door and piled out into the night. Screaming bloody fucking murder.

Poor Mr. Rahdart, the gym teacher, arrived first, running up barefoot in a sweatshirt and boxers, a Coleman lantern bobbing in his hand. He tore past the full six of us, the Lynn-Lynnes having survived the crash fine, and into Spider Cabin. We watched as he picked up the toppled bunk bed and flung around clothes and sleeping bags, shouting, "What?! What?! What?!"

"Spiders!" Jennifer screamed. She danced a kind of jig in the fallen leaves.

Flashlights bouncing, two college-age women in enormous purple Camp Evergreenshade T-shirts came jogging.

"Spiders!" Lynne P. said breathlessly. "All over. All over!"

"Shh! Girls!" one of the women scolded.

Wanda, Celeste, and I had quit screaming right away at the appearance of Mr. Rahdart and now followed the college women toward the crash site. We pressed ourselves into the doorway, glancing somewhat sheepishly at each other. The women methodically combed the upright bunk mattresses with their flashlights. Mr. Rahdart tried to raise the Lynn-Lynne bed, but it sat crookedly, one metal leg kinked out at a sad angle.

"But all the spiders . . ." Jennifer sort of moaned behind us and then squished through our ranks in the doorway. She drew her flashlight beam in shaky squiggles across the webs.

"Spiders eat mosquitoes," one of the women snapped, "not *girls.*"

"They were crawling all over me," Lynn L. half cried.

Mr. Rahdart stepped to Lynn L. "Let me see." He took hold of her arm. "Come here." His tone of voice let us know exactly how stupid we'd been. He held the Coleman over Lynn L.'s head and squinted sourly. Then he lowered the lantern and made her turn around.

"The spiders don't want anything to do with you, girls," one of the women repeated. "They eat mosquitoes."

Lynne P. suddenly swiped madly at the front of her sweater.

"They're afraid of *you,*" the other woman added. "They only want to eat bugs. They're good spiders." The woman pushed a long breath out of her nose and said to the other, "How many times do we have to give the *Charlotte* lecture?"

I felt embarrassed for our wimpy crew as I watched Celeste nonchalantly back away from us and bend to the ground. Celeste very casually flicked at leaves, just crouching, listening, recovering from our episode, I assumed, or so her posture would have indicated. Then she oh-so-casually inched over behind the more condescending of the two women.

"You girls are *much* bigger than those spiders, and we let them spin in the cabins for *your* benefit. We decide when too many . . ."

Celeste raised her arm.

". . . spiders inhabit a dwelling . . ."

(A *dwelling*?! The woman in her monstrous tent of a T-shirt called our cabin a *dwelling*?)

". . . and harmlessly remove those that need to . . ."

Gently, delicately, incredibly gracefully, Celeste lifted a dry leaf to her beautiful face and twirled it in her slender fingers. As if to study the veining or color in the dim glow of the Coleman. And then she pointed it toward the pontificating counselor and brushed the hairs at the base of her thick neck. Tickle, tickle, tickle.

Choking back a scream, the woman jumped straight into the air. She batted and slapped behind her head. Exactly like any eleven-year-old at wilderness camp.

In my mind, Celeste, the legend, was born.

Leaving, the car breaks down on Highway 99. You are one of seven in a rotting station wagon. Tucked away in the back with your better half, you both sing your lungs out between pulls on a wine bottle when the car wobbles, bucks, and shoots half its drive shaft out behind its rear tires like a massive sparking turd. Watch through the rear window as the following two cars veer and squeal.

Applaud. Think, Good fucking show!

I'VE DECIDED we should all get a "do-over" in life. Just one chance to change one minute of time in the past. If the series of events of our lives continually hinge on one another, each decision or action being a new turn in an infinite maze of possibilities but with no rewind, no way to go back, then I think we should all get a do-over. Celeste and I always allowed each other do-overs when we played badminton in her backyard if we were serving and missed the birdie altogether. You know: a *do-over.* No points lost, it's still your turn, that sort of thing.

I'd take a do-over for telling Celeste about my loss of virginity. And the do-over would be simple: "I *am* still a virgin, Celeste. Trust me." Or something like that. I'd continue to deceive my best friend for the time being, maybe for another few months, or even a few years. It isn't that the event itself ended up being special or particularly horrible for her, but rather that once she'd begun sleeping with guys, she didn't stop. I've always thought that she might have waited far longer on her own. She wouldn't have followed me. And that's the real gist of it: her following me.

Or me following her.

We wouldn't, ultimately, have gone where we did.

In telling her what couldn't be taken back, I think I kindled in her some need to be free of her own virginity as soon as possible. Oh, the slippery slope, the rolling snowball, the . . . the yelling of "Fire!" in the crowded theater of her virgin-minded head. Her maidenhead.

No, we didn't become sluts suddenly. I guess I just think of

Celeste losing her virginity as the fissure in the dike. The crack in the dam.

Celeste's story should be told chronologically, I understand, but that mistake of mine has been on my mind of late. My daughter is nearly eleven, the age at which Celeste and I met. My daughter has years to go, I hope, before she loses her own virginity, but the approach of that repeat-digit age makes me obsess about my old friend.

I know that my being truthful to Celeste some five plus years later, when we were both seventeen, shouldn't have inspired what it did in her. That under the constraints and measures of high school, I shouldn't blame Celeste's behavior on myself, but, fuck, we were each other's best friend. I *knew* that when I told her about how Jim and I had already been having sex for over a month's worth of afternoons, in his attic bedroom while his parents were still at work, that she'd follow suit. How couldn't she? We worked as a unit.

In the months before I told her the complete truth, we'd share boyfriend stories after supper, on the way to school, whenever we could. As far as Celeste knew, Jim and I fooled around only as much as she and Keith did. Which was still plenty far. We knew each other to have given successful hand jobs. We'd both allowed ourselves to be fingered and timidly tasted, although neither of us had experienced orgasms under the control of any guys. Blow jobs were long ordeals we hadn't yet learned to relish. But I repeatedly told her no, that penetration, that the big, *real* S, had yet to occur.

Jim and I had been together longer, six weeks longer, so it was expected that we might eventually get there, to experiencing the ultimate union, before Celeste and Keith. But.

Somehow the first time Jim shoved his erection into me, inside of me, it seemed like a natural extension—as idiotic as that sounds—to what we'd already done. His entering hurt, but not as much as I assumed it would. I would learn down the road that Jim wasn't particularly largely penised. (Martha Stewart echoes in my brain: "A good thing.")

I didn't let Jim move there inside of me long, however, because

Celeste and I were nothing if not well-read on the subject of sex, and I understood how ineffective the withdrawal method could be, how potent preejaculate could be. I told Jim to pull out. "You can ejaculate on my stomach," I said. Amazingly my inexperienced clinical talk didn't deflate Jim immediately. We used condoms and invention after that, and I was lucky. I didn't get pregnant by Jim.

Celeste, by junior year, might be described as having been at her unadulterated best. Her most pristine, least practiced, divinely naive best. For years afterward, she would continue to surpass herself in terms of in-your-face gorgeousness and sheer skill at capture, but in eleventh grade she was simply perfect. Scrubbed and ready.

In 1981 Kansas City, Missouri, at least at our private high school, preppy attire was a given. Celeste lent some creativity to the basic uniform, however. I attempted to follow suit. We didn't actually wear uniforms, but you did want to fit in. Oxfords, khakis, Polos, a few rigorously scrutinized labels of jeans, Izods (*incontesté!*), certain preapproved sweaters, bone-button coats, ski tags on down jackets, loafers, duck boots. You get the idea. Vail or Breckenridge between Christmas and New Year's. Show the exchange students how to make a s'more. Yes, that bad.

But Celeste collected ski tags without ever having been to Colorado and by January wore ten on a cord around her neck. She cut off the too-long bottoms of her father's old oxfords and hemmed them into some retro version of Jackie meets Audrey. She altered her preapproved jeans into cigarette-thin, ass-hugging, drag-your-tongue-if-you're-male-and-you-breathe versions that only she could get away with. If our school's uniform were the nap of a dog, Celeste would rub it at ninety degrees. Not all the way backward, but enough to make the watcher wonder what she was doing.

In 1981, she wore her hair long. We all did. Celeste's hair might not be said to have been her best feature, but it was a mild, light brown, highlighted blond in summer, always thick and wavy in a way none of us yet understood how to achieve, in that way that screamed sensuality when you grew up some: beaches in Italy, hair hanging in clumped saltwater locks. Hot, tangled nights in Asia, anywhere in Asia with mosquito netting and no air-conditioning, hair damp against a temple, twirled around a neck like vines.

You couldn't miss Celeste's eyes, their green-gold color alive with the notes of new leaves and lizards and lucky bamboo, rimmed in fat dark lashes and topped with finely arched brows. Her pupils always looked larger than normal, and it seems ridiculously appropriate now when I read in *Cosmopolitan* or some other magazine in the checkout line that dilated pupils indicate the interest of a viewer, of the owner of the pupils, interest of all kinds. Figure yourself about to get lucky if you're a man staring into the dilated pupils of an objectified woman of desire; she likes you back.

Celeste's eyes were wide-set but not too, and tilted to a degree that would make any woman jealous. Her irises changed color daily, much to the entertainment of the many males at Country Club Plaza High School. Later her eyes would mutate with the wisdom of experience, but then, in 1981, they were spectacular-spectacular, clear, the whites white, the blinking of them a code of intelligence, of an open mind.

She was my best friend.

Her nose revealed nothing of her Hebrew heritage. Instead hers was all Hebe. A most perfect nose. Symmetrical, slim, a whisper of an upturn.

I shouldn't bypass the ears, gentle-lobed shells, their position just slightly high on her head; they provided the added impression of sagacity, a kind of fairy wisdom minus the pointed protuberance of those ears you see sometimes of the furry, fleshy, indelicate kind of smart folks, prone to overgrowth.

Her teeth lined up straight and white and pleasing as possible. One eyetooth slightly crooked to add character. A small mole directly beneath the corner of her right eye, gracing the ideal pitch of her cheek. A chicken pox scar on her long and lithe neck where it met her jawline. Pale freckles in summer, fading into fall.

And then, now, the mouth. Her mouth. Celeste's mouth. I've often wondered if some kind of health concern came into play, some wayward blood disorder or vitamin deficiency. Her lips never needed lipstick they were so berry-stained, so perfectly dark and ripe against the far paler, even skin of her classic chin. (She carried no butter fat beneath her jawbone either, her profile sweet and lifted.) Celeste's mouth would knock out the knees of many a man. Of any man she would choose to have. Her lips were full and rounded and smooth and Cupid-bowed just a little on top. A sculptor could only be so lucky as to find Celeste's mouth there in the marble, alive, her lips curving exactly where a man would want them to curve, would want them to give.

Best still—or worst still, if you happened to be her slighter and shorter best friend—was Celeste's body. Beyond its extraordinary length of limb, its perfect distribution of muscle and bone, of glistening skin, it was the way she used her body that gave it dimension. Elegance and strength and line. But I think that I'll wait to play out that telling; I'll dole it out in the true spirit of the making of the myth. Suffice it to say for now that Celeste was two inches taller than I was.

We had run out in our track cleats to the music-pumping ice-cream truck in the street slowly trolling for kids and were walking back onto school grounds.

"So have you guys done it yet?" she asked again, the same as always.

I still cannot imagine why I couldn't lie that day, why I couldn't say the same, single, solitary two-letter word I had for weeks. "Well . . ." I hedged instead. And it was all over. I'd given Celeste one second and another word, a new word, a stupid, stupid "well," and she knew. She *knew*.

"You're kidding." She looked at me, not wanting to believe yet.

"You're kidding, right?" She held a red-white-and-blue Bomb Pop in her hand; I watched it tilt slowly away from her body like an unaccepted corsage. I didn't budge, didn't smile or wave her off. "When?" she asked almost meekly.

"A while ago." I had no defense. I looked down at my cheap ice-cream cone. It had a flat side to it, like a head deformed by some kind of violent accident. And not nearly enough nuts. The ice-cream head was almost bald. "The first week in April." I took a bite.

Celeste's Bomb Pop dripped onto her shorts, but she didn't notice. We stopped in the grass on the far edge of the shot-put field. "What . . . how did it . . ." Her voice trailed off. Another drop slipped from the phallic tip of her popsicle, glancing off her bare leg. This time she noticed and wiped at her thigh. "What was it like?" she asked, her eyes full of questions and betrayal. She was a smart girl.

"Okay," I answered.

"Did it hurt?"

"Not too bad." She wanted to ask me why I'd withheld, why I'd lied, I could tell, but she didn't. Not there, not then, not at that age yet. Direct confrontation didn't yet factor into our relationship much, and we'd had little need to practice it. I wanted to give her something more, I suppose, so I added, "It's fun."

"It's fun?" She looked so confused.

I swear that I only wanted to defuse the situation, move the spotlight off my lie. "It is. It's fun."

"So it feels *good*?"

"Not at first." I searched around for an immediate simile. "Like, you know, like running or something. At first you're sore and you get blisters—"

"You got *blisters*?"

"No. I mean, it's not great to start, but if you get into it after a while, it can feel good."

"Like 'with yourself' good?" she asked, trying to hide an obvious incredulousness. Masturbation was not the most comfortable of conversations, did not yet rear its common head, so to speak, in every women's magazine in the early eighties. Neither the world wide web nor TV sex talk shows existed yet. The fact that Celeste and I admitted to each other that one could please oneself and not grow black palm hair or go blind was itself an accomplishment. Our masculine track coach, Ms. Harlice (Hard Lice, Hard Face, Lice Face—take your pick) would have assigned extra laps had she heard us talk about such unacceptable things. And drooled all the while.

Like "with yourself" good? "Ah." I sidestepped. "Different, but good." How could I find the guts to tell her then, there, that it'd be up to her, always, the rest of her life, to get off? Or, at the very least, to teach the guy what to do. Maybe I should have.

"How 'different'?" she asked. "What do you mean?" A look fluttered across Celeste's face, and she tacked on, "How long *have* you and Jim been going all the way?" She laid the wet Bomb Pop across her stained tongue.

"Since April," I repeated, muttering. "I said that already."

"What was it . . . How did you . . . What do you use for birth control? Why didn't you tell me?"

I have no idea why I'd never told her. Jim's and my screwing had seemed private at the time, but beyond that I think I must have been embarrassed. And then when Celeste hadn't noticed the next day at school, it got easier by the week to pretend that what Jim and I did in his attic bedroom wasn't all that significant in terms of the overall picture. Fooling around. Sticking a penis in a vagina, big deal. "Rubbers," I managed.

"Yuck," Celeste said, her nose crinkling. I couldn't blame her. Rubbers *were* gross; I wanted to go on the pill. Half the time Jim asked me to use my hand anyway after he'd pushed into me a few times. "What do you do with them afterward?" Celeste asked. "Do they slip off?"

What was she talking about? "What?" Spinning once, I winged my ice-cream cone away like a discus. It landed, cone up, heavy head down, in a corner of the field.

"With the rubbers. Couldn't Jim's mother find them?"

I had never thought about what Jim did with the rubbers, actually. From day one Celeste had done that to me, had made me think of stuff I never, ever would have on my own. "I guess he flushes them down the toilet?" Now I knew that this would probably be the wrong answer, because we all lived in extraordinarily old, showy houses, the kind with columns and stone, slate and ivy, and their plumbing systems were constant sources of irritation for all of our parents, for entire blocks, neighborhood suits erupting from central-plumbing-line disputes. Every girl in our neighborhood knew not to flush tampons, as eventually they would be churned up and spit out onto the sidewalk by the Roto-Rooter man like so many drowned and bloodied white mice.

Duh. Of course you couldn't flush a rubber, a clog waiting to happen. I could just imagine the scene as the nervous words left my mouth: Jim's mother, arms folded and foot tapping, standing next to the Roto-Rooter man, watching the dirty gunk of plumbing water get pumped out onto her front yard when a bloated condom flopped out into the grass, swollen and stinking like a dead fish. No, make that two condoms, once three. We were teenagers, after all. "Oh, Mary, mother of god," she would say, clutching at the gold chain around her throat. "Jimmy!" she would scream. "I never want to see *that girl* in this house again!"

"Maybe he sneaks them into somebody else's trash," I told Celeste quickly. "I don't know."

"I would think you'd wanna make sure . . ." Celeste said, her voice small. We started walking again. Celeste ditched her Bomb Pop in the long-jump sandpit before Lice Face could catch us. Pretending to train long distance, Celeste and I managed to nab the ice-cream man most days of the school week. Now the few bites of my cone weighed in my stomach like lead. I'd made a mistake.

"We need to run," I said, looking around, anywhere but in Celeste's eyes.

"Yeah," she said. And that was that.

Of course Celeste felt the need to catch up. Ketchup. We said that, said, "Ketchup," to each other tagging down the hallways or dragging feet in gym class. The guy she'd been seeing, Keith, played water polo, pole-vaulted, and was a year older. A senior. And being the local winner of the school beauty, he'd been knockin' on Celeste's door for a while.

Celeste picked Keith for the occasion, I believe, because he happened to be in the right place at the right time. Had I not given up to Celeste the fact that Jim and I were screwing regularly, Keith, like all the boys who had come before, would have gone down blue-balled, unsuccessful in his efforts to break a girl like one might a horse.

I'd created a monstrosity of the gravest, most unfixable kind in forcing Celeste to do what—at least in my mind—she shouldn't have done just yet. To learn the ways of the world. To open up her inside. Hook her legs over a pair of water-polo shoulders and let the boy go at it.

Oh, she should have waited years.

Heroin makes you sick the first try. Cigarette smoking too if you're lucky. But if you're not lucky, and you develop a taste, if you're one who senses that cocaine gets better with time, or you're one who jumps out of a plane and becomes an adrenaline junky, or you're one who loves the feel of grease melting over your tongue in the form of pecan pie or thick clam chowder or a fat porterhouse or just plain ol' Doritos by the bagful, and you want to repeat the same comfort and recognizable surprise of that first go, that first indulgence, and yet with each succeeding bite the small hope of true satisfaction slides farther away, then you understand Celeste, at least a little.

After her first fuck, she went looking for a better boy. She always went looking after that.

You've been told it's an underground show. Think mole.
Think basements. Grab her hand and squeeze into the black
place tight as an anus. Wear your gear.

The house music blasts old Stooges and runs a looped
tape of the Three other ones smashing heads with frying
pans, poking eyes, taking rake handles to the face. Stand
around and wait and wait. Wait to hear, "I Wanna Be Your
Dog."

Find ways to occupy the time. You are resourceful now.
Sit and pick the letter I out of the middle of the large scab
on your right knee, hard as beef jerky. Smoke a putrid
Gauloises, the strongest cigarette you can find. Pick out a G
from the scab on your left knee. Do not flinch. It does not
even occur to you to flinch. Invert the G for her to read
when you stand despite the fact that your handiwork is illegible. Tell the others who ask that the scabs are rug burns
from concrete, from sucking on your new boy last week
between cars at the 7-Eleven.

Look around for your new boy and find that he is
nowhere.

There is no sound check.

There is no band.

There is no show.

There is a riot instead.

The battering begins.

You see him finally. Your new boy—the one you have watched pierce his own cheek with a colossal safety pin meant for diapers—dips and bobbles in the center of the creature that sprouts arms and legs. The it, the riot, the monster, consumes other boys, pulls them in from the margins, the marginal boys, like a ravenous cancer. They don't even know they have been taken until they cannot escape. Think *Invasion of the Body Snatchers.* Think you see your new boy eaten. Chewed and swallowed.

Decide you must save him. Know the mistake of your decision before your first step.

$\mathcal{I}$ DON'T REMEMBER getting more than four hours of sleep that first chilly night at Camp Evergreenshade. All six of us had managed to squish into the two remaining bunks, as the Lynn-Lynne bed was a goner. I woke up with Celeste's hair in my face, the two of us curled into each other as neatly as boiled shrimp. Celeste smelled like Breck shampoo and the peanuts she'd eaten on the bus the day before. You could see your breath.

We were giddy and giggly at breakfast in the big common hall, fawning stupidly over the young blond counselor we decided looked exactly like Robert Redford in *The Sting*. Having been united as a force to be reckoned with as a result of backing Celeste's bad behavior with the leaf the night before, every last one of us from our cabin, even black Wanda, bumping elbows and huddling over the table, said that we would marry the blond counselor. We nicknamed him Bobby Bedford. "I'd marry Bobby Bedford tomorrow," Lynne P. said.

"I'd marry Bobby Bedford at lunch," I said.

"No, no," Celeste said, touching our wrists and arms. "Bobby Bedford at *brunch*!"

The conversation took the usual tangential who-could-you-marry? path, this time musical. I decided I could marry Michael Jackson, Roger Daltrey, or possibly one of the Earth, Wind and Fire guys, but not the one with the big teeth. The Lynn-Lynnes both went in for any of the Styx band members. The lonely twin Jennifer opted for Andy Gibb.

"Robert Redford," Celeste said.

"But who *else*," Lynn L. demanded, shoveling scrambled eggs into her mouth.

"Who else?" I asked more nicely. If we pushed we'd get nowhere.

Celeste drank her milk and then said, "James Dean."

"Who?" Jennifer asked.

"Who's that?" the Lynn-Lynnes wanted to know.

I knew only because Mr. Diamond, Celeste's dad, had a framed promotional photo of the cast of *Giant* in his study. Mr. Diamond had a crush on Elizabeth Taylor. "He's a dead movie star," I got to say on Celeste's behalf.

"He was so handsome," Celeste said dreamily.

"He's dead?"

"If he's dead, dead doesn't count."

"Celeste says *John McFaaaarland.* She likes missing-butt men."

"Missing buttmen!"

"Missing buttmen!" We laughed and I actually shot a hunk of eggs out of my nose, which, of course, made us all spit up food and milk into our trays and laugh like girls crazed, in that way that makes you think when you're not one of the group that they must all be laughing uproariously at *you.* Buckling over, faces contorted, stomping feet beneath the table. That way. My nose burned. Somebody burped really loudly. By now we were solidly bonded. (I've looked some of those girls up the last few years. Wanda and I exchange Christmas cards. She's a French teacher in D.C.)

We got scolded by Mr. Rahdart, unfortunately, not by Bobby Bedford. We were becoming The Bad Girls. We couldn't have been happier about it.

The woodlands, if you can call them that, are inimitable in central Missouri. They're stringy-thick and raggedy, sort of—like rednecks, messy-haired and gape-toothed and poisonous. They're full of stragglers and hangers-on, weird undergrowth and low, flat caves, bark-shedding trees and patchy-furred rodents.

Precisely because of this, the central Missouri woods are not a place many well-to-do parents of the well-to-do areas of Kansas City would have their children partake in life-impacting events. If parents had been allowed to come along to Camp Evergreen-shade, very few children would have remained behind the next day.

Ticks. Lots of ticks. Snakes. Questionable building structures, including the dining hall, the cabins, the docks, the equipment huts. Mildew. Crumbling paths, disintegrating rappeling cliffs, collapsing wells. Poisonous spiders. Mosquitoes. Fleas. Mice. Rabid squirrels. Rabid raccoons. Rabid bats. In the caves. Where children spelunked.

That first full day consisted of hiking and hiking and trudging and hiking. We were supposed to be looking for and journaling specific types of flora and fauna, and being the preprogrammed overachievers that we were, we actually tried. Our regular class teachers weren't even at Camp Evergreenshade, so our behavior may or may not have ever been reported back to the powers that be, but we thought that we should try. Well, we tried for a while.

Lynn L. got cut out into another hiking group, and Jennifer was accidentally reunited with her twin Jessica for the day, but the rest of us remained intact, joined by five boys. Oh, the boys.

I can only remember two of their names anymore, largely because—beyond the obvious reason I'm getting to—those two boys continued to grow ever more popular and good-looking over the spread of the junior high and high school years. William Hirsch and Josh Bonn. The two of them would end up hanging out with a third guy who transferred over in the tenth grade, who everybody weirdly called Gunther, even though it wasn't his name.

But at sixth-grade wilderness camp, these two, William and Josh, were the cutest and bravest and funniest and smartest, and Celeste and I fell all over each other whispering and scheming, our brains tingling with the information Celeste's sisters, Diana and Rachel, had imparted to us: Boys' penises got *hard*. They didn't just actually droop there all the time, like when your dad was pee-ing. Diana and Rachel had had to draw Celeste and me pictures of

coitus; we just couldn't understand how a penis, hanging down-
ward, would fit into a vagina tilting upward.

In Rachel's room at the Diamond house, Celeste was the first to
go get a notebook and a pencil. We gathered around on Rachel's
big double bed. Celeste drew a penis in the shape of a J. "Like
this?" she asked plainly, looking up at her sisters.

I desperately wanted to know and chewed on my tongue, glancing from the paper to the pretty faces of Diana and Rachel. I didn't
really understand how a body part could go from soft to hard. I
mean, I could flex my bicep, and it got a bit harder, but it took
some effort. Did boys' penises become hard because they flexed
them hard? It seemed like a lot of work.

"No!" Rachel laughed, looking at Celeste's drawing.

Diana laughed too and dragged the notebook on the bedspread
toward her. "But it's a good guess, I guess. Here." Diana, a bit of
an artist, took her time portraying the erect male genitalia while
explaining the difference between flaccid and excited. Her drawing was very careful. Shaded. She drew pubic hair for us; she drew
veins; she delineated the spongy, blood-filled columns that comprised your garden-variety erection.

"It looks like a mushroom," Celeste said bluntly.

It did. What Diana had drawn looked, more or less, like a long-
stemmed mushroom. I wanted to back up my friend. "It does," I
said.

Diana and Rachel laughed again. Laughed knowingly, which is
irritating as hell when you're out of the know. Celeste and I tried
to be patient.

"That's kinda right," Rachel said, studying Diana's sketch. "A
hungry mushroom," she added, and both of them cracked up.

Eventually Celeste and I got the whole story, the more-or-less
story. The technical, clinical, unfathomable explanation of the
opposite sex's plumbing and how guys used it. At the time you
could have told me that a boy grew a three-fingered prong out of
his penis to impregnate a woman—you could have carefully rendered an exact replica of one on paper—and I wouldn't have been

more surprised. The mind reels. Remember? You think about the weirdness of your grandparents humping to create your mom, your baby brother's baby penis floating in the bathtub and what that little floating nub of flesh would eventually do to grown women. Ew. So Celeste and I had tried to become adjusted over the past week to how the male body announced itself to women's bodies: ta-da!

Out on our wilderness hike, journals and "floor-funna" lists in hand, we scanned the ground for leaves to match up with the pictures on the list, wrote brief descriptions of the leaves and the trees from which they came, and looked for birds in the half-bare branches. And we were supposed to note any and all wildlife we encountered. We were actually told that. "Note any and all wildlife you encounter." In our hiking group's case, these instructions were provided by none other than the second T-shirt-tent-wearing college woman, the one Celeste hadn't scared. Even so, this one was obviously not too receptive to our remaining group of girls, and stuck largely to overseeing the boys. Her name was Janet, and Janet attended college in Lawrence, Kansas, studying something in some department that we didn't care about or listen to.

"Look," Janet said, pointing, her hand on the shoulder of one of the boys, directing his bored gaze up to the treetops. "See the bird? What sort of bird is that?"

We started making fun of Janet almost immediately.

"Look," Celeste said, pointing at the dirt path, snaking her arm around my waist. "What sort of ground is that?"

"Look," I responded, pointing at her hiking boot. "What sort of poo is that?"

We still had Wanda and Lynne P. with us, and while the morning hike puttered out in the woods, the conversation gained momentum. Eventually we all just sat down in a small clearing. Janet decided to try to regain control. "A good idea. Let's all take a rest." She shoved around some logs and brushed off the tops of stumps. "Yes," she added. "Let's all sit for a while."

How could you not make fun? How could you not laugh? By this point, the boys, at least the confident, cute boys, William and

Josh, had started to infiltrate us girls, and we let them. We gave them encouragement. Lynne P. "accidentally" poked Josh in his thigh with a stick. Celeste boldly asked William how many birds he'd written down in his notebook. I watched William crack his notebook halfway and hold it there rather than speaking, forcing Celeste to inch down the log she sat on and lean in closer to him to look.

I asked the boy nearest to me at the moment, one whose name I no longer remember, the same question. "How many birds do you have?"

"Two," he said dully.

I decided to go for Josh, as Celeste had obviously cornered the market on William in a matter of seconds. Lynne P. would recover.

"Now," Janet said, brushing her hands on her jeans. "How many of you have found all the types of trees on your list?" Janet had some kind of seedpod or piece of bark stuck in her frizzed hair.

I picked up a black acorn and threw it at Josh, then pretended I'd done no such thing. Janet hadn't seemed to notice. Nobody raised a hand about identifying all the trees.

"Nobody?" Janet plaintively searched our faces as we lowered our gazes one by one into the almost empty pages of our journals.

Something hit my collarbone. An acorn fell onto my drawing of a nondescript branch. I looked up to see Josh studying his finger-nails. My heart raced.

"They're all here. You should have been able to spot all of the different types of trees at this point." Janet bent from her stump seat to the ground and retrieved a leaf. A plain leaf in a plain leaf shape. "Now, let's take a look at this leaf. William?"

We raised our heads to look at William. How would he be clever? How much of a smart-ass could he be and get away with it?

"Ah," he said. He suddenly took a professorial pose and rubbed an imaginary beard. "It's a leaf," he proclaimed haughtily.

We laughed. Of course we laughed. Who cared what kind of leaf it was? All for one and one for all. What would they do? Fail us in Introduction to the Leaf?

Another acorn hit my shoulder. Butterflies beat inside my chest. Josh was *so* cute. I bent over to pick up a small rock by my boot.

"Well, *silly*, we know it's a leaf." Janet smiled sweetly at William.

Oh, my god! Janet the counselor had a crush on a twelve-year-old boy. I looked quickly at Celeste, who gave me the same look back. *I know! Can you believe it?!*

William blushed then. We all stared at Janet, who, as if realizing the error and transparency of her words, blushed as well. And, oh, if her blush wasn't fuel to the fire, I don't know what could have been. We ran with it.

"Miss Janet calls William '*silly*,'" Wanda started in an exaggerated black voice that meant at the very same time, *I dare you, Janet, to call me on what I just said or how I said it, because I know how to get you fired faster than we're about ready to eat you alive.*

Josh and another boy ooohed.

Lynne P. repeated, "'*Silly!*'" She looked straight at Janet.

The sharks had bumped their prey. Tenderizing. I took the opportunity to throw the little rock at Josh. I'd intended to just sort of fling it his direction, but in my haste I threw it harder than I'd meant. Not even close to a smooth river stone, the rock drilled Josh right above his temple.

"Shit! Ow!" he yelled, his hand darting to his head. He glared at me then, and I knew I'd screwed up. Everyone turned from Janet to Josh.

I'm sorry, I mouthed.

He frowned, pulling his hand away and looking at what were actually already bloody fingers. Oh, shit, had I messed up. Josh's head now blossomed an abstract red rose, a sloppy Jackson Pollock.

Quick as a wink, cute as a button, Janet bolted to Josh's side. "Let me see," she nearly cooed, pulling at the hand Josh was holding over his wound, on his owie. "Let me see."

"God!" Josh balked.

Now Janet cut the crap. She grabbed Josh's wrist and directed, "Don't. Stop it." All of a sudden she looked strong. She pulled his hand away, bunched her brow, then put his hand back. She knelt at the fallen log seat and snapped her fingers behind her back. "Gimme my pack," she demanded of no one specifically.

Celeste stood, picked up Janet's backpack, and carried it over to the disaster of my doing. Celeste bent at the waist and looked at Josh. "Let me see," she said, and Josh took his hand away as if hypnotized. She bent nearer. "It's not so bad," she said.

Déjà vu! Where'd I heard that before? Duh-hay. Less than twenty-four hours ago? Celeste Nightingale Diamond to the rescue. Despite the fact that I felt nearly frozen with the fear of what I'd done to cute Josh, I could not, would not let this happen. She already had William. I stood up and crunched through the leaves to stand next to my best friend. Josh's fingertips, back on his head, were glazed with blood.

Janet rummaged in her backpack, talking into the mouth of it. "I have a first-aid kit in here. We're fine, we're fine." She pulled out a white metal box with a red cross on the lid. "Here," she said, opening the box. An ancient-looking roll of yellowed gauze half crumbled as she extracted a tongue depressor from the box's center.

"My dad has one of those from the war," Lynne P. piped up, moving in.

"We have a box like that in the basement," one of the other guys said, standing. Everybody else followed and surrounded Josh.

"Damn. We need to clean the wound," Janet said.

"Which war?" another guy asked.

"It wouldn'ta been white. The box would be green."

"Same *diff*," Lynne P. said snidely.

"No, it's *not*," the boy retorted.

"Where? Wha—" Janet fumbled with old metal tubes of ointment. "Jesus." She set the first-aid kit on the ground and stood up. Janet took off her down vest and then her flannel shirt and then her purple Camp Evergreenshade T-shirt! Eyebrows raised; mouths opened like airplane hangars. Wide enough for hundreds of flies to come and go at will. What was she doing? Copying Mr. Rahdart? Did adults just get naked at camp? Janet had a beige bra on and really good boobs and a pretty flat stomach. I realized then that she must look a lot better naked than in clothes. I wondered when that would be the case with me, if ever.

Janet covered up fast again with her flannel shirt and then stuck the hem of the big T in her mouth. Josh's head kept bleeding, and his face now looked more gray-white than flesh-colored. My vision went sort of swirly; I felt bizarre, out there in the woods, watching a stranger take off her clothes and a cute boy I liked bleed from getting hit with a rock that I had just thrown at him. Janet started ripping. Oh. She folded up a square of the T-shirt fabric and wiped at Josh's head. "Somebody get the thermos," Janet directed.

Three of us went for the backpack. We understood now. We could make sense of what Janet was doing.

"Open it. Take off the lid."

William unscrewed the thermos lid.

"Here. Pour water on this." She took the cloth away from Josh's smeary head.

William overreacted and sloshed out a big spill, the water darkening Janet's jeans.

Janet wiped at Josh's wound with the wet cloth while he frowned. We could see the damage now. It wasn't bad at all, just a tiny cut, but a real gusher. A bleeder. One of the other boys actually honked out an ugly laugh. "That's it?" he said.

"What?" Josh said, looking around at us from his log seat.

"It's nothing," one of the other boys said, one with braces and glasses, the one with the matching antique first-aid kit in his basement.

Celeste smiled. "I told you so."

Josh and I sighed at the same time, I noticed. I thought he might have noticed, too.

Janet dug through the ointment tubes again. "I doubt you'll need stitches, maybe one at most, but we should go back to the nurse to make sure." She didn't seem to find what she wanted. She tore a long strip from her T-shirt this time and tied it around Josh's head. As the color came back to his cheeks, I thought how ruggedly handsome Josh looked.

"Looks good," William announced.

The braces-and-glasses boy turned away and found his journal. "I'm so sure," he said.

Ultimately the hike couldn't have turned out better—the perfect addition to The Bad Girls' growing reputation. And this time it was me. It was *me*! On the trudge back Josh forgave me, sort of, by making fun of my pitching arm, and then William joined in, as did all the girls.

Janet ended up being kind of okay too. Wanda got her to tear us all T-shirt head strips, except for two of the other boys who didn't want one. We straggled theatrically into the main camp, limping, tripping, crawling, and groaning as loudly as we could, a bunch of rowdy veterans, our purple bandages the signifiers of untold trials and tribulations in the true wilderness, a wilderness of makeshift first aid and quick thinking.

By suppertime in the common hall, everyone knew about what had happened, although the story had mutated as fast as any story could through a grapevine of excitable sixth-graders away from home. Josh had been dealt a gushing blow, a huge dent in his forehead that bled for over an hour. Janet was the cool slutty savior counselor every boy now hoped to catch a glimpse of in the showers. I had a fastball to rival any guy's, and better still, two new nicknames: Lisa Smith-and-Wesson, or just Colt.

I suppose sixth-grade camp is the first place where you really get a taste of adulthood bigger than that swallow of beer at Grandma and Grandpa's on Sunday. Unfortunately the taste involves forced singing en masse, dancing of both the square and disco kind, archery and human chessboards, rope ladders, cold, wind, dirt, fire, bad morning breath, armpits just starting to stink, glimpses of unfamiliar flesh, and maybe failure on a truly personal level, maybe throwing up, maybe refusal and maybe betrayal, maybe stitches, maybe a lip burn from a marshmallow on the end of a roasting stick that ends up looking exactly like a cold sore, maybe chiggers, maybe athlete's foot, maybe success, maybe new popularity, maybe a first kiss.

They took great strides at Camp Evergreenshade to keep the boys separated from the girls when not contained or overseen. Or so we were led to believe. Celeste somehow decided, though, that the counselors and Mr. Rahdart and the assistant directors and the nurse—well, all of the adults, actually—just crashed out because they were so tired after dealing with us kids for the whole day. She said it'd be easy to go hang out with the boys if we wanted to. And we wanted to.

William and Josh put us up to it on night three. Celeste reassured us. Our girls' cabin was supposed to meet their boys' cabin out in the boathouse, a dingy unused structure, for a game of Spin the Bottle and then (*then!*) Truth or Dare. Such elaborate scheming.

The six of us—even Jennifer, stretching her newly independent twin wings—agreed nervously. At eleven o'clock. In the boathouse. My god, it's a bad movie, isn't it? But then again nearly everything from adolescence takes on those sorts of silly proportions: "in Jamie Johnson's basement, at midnight, in the laundry room"; "on the deck of Kiki's boat with her dad below deck!"; "on top of the park jungle gym—I have no idea what time, but it was really dark and I almost fell off!!"; "in the boathouse at eleven o'clock."

And, oh, the best-laid plans.

Eleven o'clock seemed aeons away. What could we wear? It wasn't as though any of us had really packed for the event.

We didn't really disprove many stereotypes either. A lot of squealing all around. Lots of rolling on bunk beds and thrumming heels on mattresses and just dying. The anticipation was enough to bring on a full pileup on the brand-new Lynn-Lynne lower bunk.

"Show me again," Lynne P. said to Celeste when we'd unpiled.

Celeste raised her forearm to her mouth and kissed it.

Lynne P. and Lynn L. scooted in, their noses pressed to some invisible candy store window. They watched Celeste's mouth intently. I'd already practiced, having carefully studied Rachel and Diana kissing their own arms. Jennifer brushed and brushed and brushed her hair, looking nervous. Wanda laughed and played solitaire on her upper bunk; she claimed to have been kissing a boy from her church confirmation class for over three weeks. We didn't even think about the spiders anymore.

Nobody wanted to kiss the boy with glasses and braces.

"What if his braces cut my lips?" Lynn L. asked.

"They won't," Wanda said.

"You wouldn't be kissing his teeth anyway," I assured her. "You'd just have to kiss his lips."

"Maybe he'll take off his glasses," Jennifer offered.

"Ick," Lynne P. said. "I really don't want to get him."

I didn't either. "Maybe he looks better without his glasses," I said, thinking that there was no way I'd get anybody but Josh, Josh, Josh. . . .

"He'll be cute," Celeste proffered.

"Who?"

Celeste said the glasses guy's name. "He will, in high school, when he gets his braces off and maybe some new glasses."

"No way!" I hollered, and flopped onto the Lynn-Lynne bed again.

"Yes way," Celeste said, and sat on me.

"No way," I squeezed out. "No way!"

Big pileup.

I was voted to be first out. The scout. "I think Colt should be the scout," was exactly what Celeste had said.

"Me?" I asked, secretly and immediately proud of the nomination.

"I agree," Wanda said solemnly.

I'm sure I beamed. "Yeah?"

"All those in favor of Colt being the scout," Celeste said, "say 'aye.'"

There were no dissenters.

Out our door, I humped along the walkway like a possum. I crouched to avoid the windows of the two cabins I passed, another girls' and another boys'. I made it to the end of the row and stopped, surveying the clearing, the lush lawn leading toward the communal hall, the showers, and the adult residencies. Just as Celeste had predicted, I didn't hear any adult voices or see any sign of them. I hunkered at the edge of Our Boys' cabin, the one our amours usually slept in, but they had already departed as planned. Oh, the thought of the warm and foreign smells of their sleeping bags! I thought about going inside for a second and trying to find Josh's bunk. I would bury my face in his duffel. I would lie flat on his mattress and drape the musty, dirty leg of a pair of his blue jeans over my eyes and nose and mouth and inhale.

Mad dash across the green. Dart around the showers, somebody's in there, down onto the rocks, ow, stubbed my toe in my best pair of worn-out Tretorns, scamper like a fawn onto the path to the boathouse onto the deck, knock on the door tap tap no louder than a mouse. Come on, louder, you're Colt with the aim, with the arm. You're Colt the scout. Knock, knock.

It was William who answered. "Hi," he said. "Where's the rest?" He looked right past me, and in that brief moment, the starter spore lodged itself under a rib of mine, the future rampant malignancy of "Shouldn't I, alone, be enough?" I hardly recognized it then, at that moment of my scouting debut, but that vapid, empty desire to be the one to which all eyes turned would proliferate through high school and beyond.

"They—we're coming," I said. "I'm the scout."

William let out a laugh I couldn't quite interpret. "Damn." He chuckled, sounding for all the world like a complete grown-up, one who at the moment was making me feel infinitely young and uncertain. I've decided since then that William's laugh revealed him to be the real stuff: adult flesh and blood. A man in boy's clothing. I'm sure on some gut level I felt hormonally underprepared for the late-night adventure to come, underdeveloped in the way where faking tits with toilet paper in a trainer bra just wouldn't cut it—couldn't even touch it. I was still just a kid. But I didn't care. "Go get them then," he said.

"Duh," I snapped. "We had to know if you were gonna fake us out."

"Duh," he snapped back. "As *if*, like we'd really tell you to come here and then not show up. You're the ones who'd be chickening out."

"Well, I'm here, aren't I?" And I was there. The scout.

William made a puffing noise through his lips and rolled his eyes, then retreated away from the door and into the darkness of the boathouse. "Hurry up," somebody hissed from the dank black.

I crabbed my way back to our cabin. "It's clear," I said breathlessly to the rest. "Let's go. Follow me."

"Are they there?" Lynn L. wanted to know.

"Yes. They said to hurry. Hurry up."

As a group we were definitely louder. I arm-gestured and we galumphed ahead, girly elephants tiptoeing through wilderness camp on our way to a few innocent games of Spin the Bottle and Truth or Dare. I knocked again on the door of the boathouse. It creaked open. William stood behind it and ushered us in.

Water slapped the undersides of unseen stuff, wood and foam things, and made a sloppy sucking and sloshing sound in the corner somewhere. We girls couldn't see at all; our eyes hadn't adjusted. A flash of a match and then another one exposed the faces of the boys sitting on the floor arranged in a tight half oval. Josh stood up and held his flame out to William, who lit a cigarette, and the boathouse filled with the distinct smell of Salem menthol tobacco, the same cigarette my father smoked well into his fifties.

We girls teetered some in the dark, trying to find our balance, crowded together in anticipation. In unspoken fervor.

"Hey, dorks," William said quietly. "Sit down." He swung the glowing end of his cigarette in an arc, indicating that we should complete the oval.

"Hey, dorks," Celeste whisper-greeted back, she being the only one of us who could speak at the moment.

Josh sort of laughed, but the rest of the boys sat silently in what was surely their own nervousness. The matches burned out as we settled in, bumping knees. Six boys, six girls. Celeste, of course, formed the bridge to the boys, sitting next to William but without touching. Jennifer, the last to sit, tried to schmoosh herself between the Lynn-Lynnes, a futile move. She moved to perch an arm's length away from Glasses-'n'-Braces, only I'd seen in the match-light that he'd taken off his specs for the occasion.

It seemed to make more sense to me to begin with Truth or Dare instead of the other way around, in that Spin the Bottle required action of some kind or another immediately, whereas Truth or Dare allowed the "out" of a truth until we worked up some nerve. Celeste's sisters, of course, had filled us in on all the games, and Celeste and I had, in turn, told the other girls.

Nobody spoke. The sound of the water bounced off the walls. William smoked, the cherry of his cigarette getting brighter and then dimming with each drag. Another boy coughed. You could hear the fabric of our pants and windbreakers rub on the rough planks of the floor as we fidgeted in the dark, all staring at William's cigarette cherry. Celeste took my hand and squeezed it. I squeezed back. Slowly the outlines of two small suspended boats came into view against the open cutouts of a moonlit night sky. Then silhouettes of heads, shoulders. A girl hiccupped.

"Gimme a puff," Josh whispered to William.

The glowing cherry moved sideways a foot and grew brighter, casting an orange glow on Josh's features, on his perfect face and the scab on his temple. I hoped that it wouldn't scar.

"Pass it," William whispered to Josh about the cigarette, and the Salem began to move around the circle. None of the boys or girls in the oval before me tried it, but I had experience. I'd had clandestine puffs of my dad's before, and I knew how not to really inhale and make myself cough. I put the cigarette up to my lips, thinking about how it had touched Josh's lips before mine, and pulled some smoke into my mouth.

"You smoke?" another boy whispered.

I quickly blew out. Loudly. "Mmm-hmm," I answered, trying to sound cool.

"No, you don't," William teased, but in a way that you couldn't tell if he really knew either.

"I have," I said quietly.

"She has," Celeste said, taking the cigarette and trying to pass it back to William. He seemed to take a long time getting it out of Celeste's fingers.

"I drank a gin and tonic at a party," Lynne P. said.

"*What* party?" a boy teased. "Your birthday party?"

"No!" She huffed in the shadows. "At a Hanukkah party where my mom and dad were. I had a 7UP and I switched it with a gin and tonic." The confidence in her voice trailed off, as she must have realized she'd put more words out into the space of the boathouse than anybody else. "On the buffet table . . ." she tacked on.

"I ate a raw oyster," Glasses-'n'-Braces said.

"Ew!"

"That is so gross!"

"It tasted like a huge snot," Glasses-'n'-Braces said proudly.

Jennifer made a really girly, disgusted, fake throwing-up noise.

"Vomitorium-orium," a boy said.

"A huge gray loogie," another one said.

"That's *so* gross."

"Not as gross as calamari," Celeste said.

Josh asked, "What's that?"

"It's gross," I interjected.

"It's really chewy," Celeste said.

"And grosser than a raw oyster," I said. I knew what it was, but I'd never tried it. I also knew that Celeste loved it; she'd sworn me to secrecy.

"What is it?" William asked.

Celeste looked around the group, everyone faintly visible now. Nobody knew. Well, I knew. "It's *octopus*!" I told them.

I saw Josh shudder exaggeratedly.

"You ate a . . . an octopus?" William sounded flabbergasted. He stared at Celeste.

"No way," she said, and an elbow jerked into my arm. "I ate, um, I just tasted a piece of one."

"Was it a tentacle?" a boy asked.

"Or a gigantic eye!" Lynn L. screeched.

"A suction cup!" a boy sort of shouted, getting into it.

Celeste didn't respond except to dig her short nails into my leg. I wouldn't tell. She didn't have to worry.

"The head! The head is a piece of one!"

"Shh!" William spit. "You wanna get caught?"

We shut up. I took it upon myself, being the scout that I was, to stand and go to the door, crack it, and look outside. The boathouse was well away from any of the other structures. No lights, no lantern jogs from Mr. Rahdart. I drew my head back in and whispered, "All clear."

William pulled a green ginger ale bottle from behind his back, placed it on its side, and spun it. It spun faster than I thought it would. I closed the door and sat down. We were silent, as silent as children mesmerized in the face of something important to learn.

The bottle slowed down until William grabbed it off the floor and said, "First time, I go, since it's my bottle. First round . . ." He looked at Celeste. "What should first round be?"

"What do you mean?" Celeste sounded nervous.

"Well," he said, and if I'd known a leer from a hole in the wall at the time, I'd have recognized William's look. "Well, we could call a kiss on the cheek or a kiss on the lips or making out, for ten seconds or something." Obviously William knew his way around a game of Spin the Bottle.

"It should be something else to start," Celeste said quickly.

"Like what?" a boy asked, his voice cracking.

"Like what?" William repeated.

"I don't know," Celeste whispered, "like hugging or something."

William scoffed. "*Hugging?!*"

Somebody else whispered, "Holding hands."

"No," Lynne P. whispered. "Holding hands until somebody gets somebody else. Like you could hold hands for over a minute."

"Yeah."

"Yeah."

"Okay."

Everyone nodded. William sighed. "You're such babies. You're supposed to kiss."

"We might," Celeste said, low, clearly, "but give us a chance to get used to it."

"It'll be light by then," some random boy said.

"Shut up, dork," I said.

"You are," another boy whispered, and then William shut us all up again by spinning the bottle. Thinking, now, it sounded not unlike a pestle in a mortar, grinding.

And the bottle spun and spun and finally slowed to point at one of the nameless boys. "A do-over," William said, grabbing for the bottle.

"Uh-unh," I told him. "You didn't say anything about do-overs."

"Look," William said, sounding very much like my father when he'd tired of my purposefully tedious questions or some other form of bad behavior, "there's no hand-holding or kissing boys with boys or girls with girls. Well, if you want to hold hands or whatever, fine, but not for the game. That's how it works." He spun the bottle. It slowed.

And it stopped, pointing at my knee.

William sort of pitched past Celeste and grabbed my hand. "Now what?" he asked. "This is dumb. Look at what'll happen."

I was only thankful that it was dark and nobody could see the blush that I felt creep up my neck. Both William and I were leaning in toward Celeste, our hands joined over her cross-legged lap.

"Now it's supposed to be your turn?" William asked me. "You're supposed to spin the bottle and then you have to hold hands with somebody else? This isn't Twister. This won't work."

Everybody acknowledged William's point, nodding, picking at mosquito bites, mouthing tendrils of hair. William's hand, not sweaty or anything, let go of mine, and he sat straight again. I followed his lead and fixed my posture. "What about just Truth or Dare?" I asked.

"Yeah."

"Yeah."

Whispered agreement all around.

"All right," William said, snatching the bottle and putting it behind him. "You better hope none of you get me on a dare."

Celeste tapped my leg. I tapped hers back.

"You go first, then," William said, meaning me.

"Fine." I looked around our oval, this misshapen clump of kids. "Wanda," I said.

Wanda looked up from the good fray she had going at the hem of her blue jeans. "What?" Wanda stared right at me.

"You," I said.

"Me what?"

"Truth or dare?"

Wanda's fingers froze. "Um, truth," she said.

I had nothing prepared, even though I'd brought this on myself. I thought back to how Wanda said she'd been making out with the boy from her confirmation class. I looked at her two-toned fingers, the darker skin on top, the paler skin of her palm, the difference visible even there in the shadowy boathouse. I recognized her blackness then, her being different from the rest of us. But we all knew Wanda, and she wasn't the only black student at our school. There were maybe twenty blacks. Her race shouldn't have anything to do with the game. I would just ask. Out with it. "How many times have you made out with the boy from your confirmation class?"

Wanda looked up into the rafters. The water sloshed. We all studied her carefully then, the light inner side of her fingers unfurling from her dark, closed fists like petals from a flower in a time-reduced science film. She counted silently with her mouth. "Seven," she eventually said.

Some boy sighed, I assumed wistfully.

I did the math in my head and knew Wanda had lied somewhere, either before in our cabin or there in the boathouse. Confirmation class didn't meet more than once a week. I didn't think so, anyway. Maybe hers did. Never mind.

"My turn?" Wanda asked.

"Yes," I said.

"You." Wanda pointed at Glasses-'n'-Braces.

"Me?" Glasses-'n'-Braces pointed at his own chest.

"You," Wanda said again.

Nobody said anything.

"You have to ask," Josh said.

"What?" Wanda looked confused.

"Ask 'truth or dare,'" Jennifer peeped.

"Truth or dare," Wanda said.

"Me?" Glasses-'n'-Braces continued to point at his own chest.

"Jesus! You!" William flicked his dead cigarette butt at the boy.

"Truth," the boy spurted.

"This isn't gonna get us anywhere," Josh said, and my ears prickled from listening so hard.

"Let him go," Lynn L. whispered.

"Fine," Josh mumbled.

"Do you have wet dreams?" Wanda asked out of the blue, and suddenly the game got better.

"Oooh . . ." Both William and Josh exhaled in admiration of Wanda's question. Other boys laughed nervously.

"What?" Glasses-'n'-Braces stammered.

"Do you have wet dreams?" Wanda asked again, carefully enunciating, as if she had repeated, "How much is the floral fabric per yard?"

"I . . . What?"

I felt sort of sorry for the boy then. Who would want to answer that? But I was curious, too. Supposedly all of them did at some point, but was Glasses-'n'-Braces old enough? Maybe he had pubic hair!

"Do. You. Have. Wet. Dreams." Wanda was getting into it, and we all laughed.

"Shh!" William scolded. "Answer," he commanded the boy.

"I . . . I . . ." The boy looked around for help from his cabin mates, all of whom suddenly had to bite nails and clear throats and look away.

"Of course," Celeste said.

"What?" the boy asked yet again.

"Of course you do," Celeste said calmly. "All of the boys in this boathouse do."

Like a cuckoo-clock figurine, miniature wooden mallet hidden behind my back, my head jerked ninety degrees toward Celeste. *What?* I stared. This was my friend? Sometimes she said the weirdest things you could imagine. What if people started thinking she was too weird? Then what? I looked at Celeste, my eyebrows raised for effect. I looked at her cheeks and at her thick eyelashes and, from my angle, the glittering surface of the orbs of her eyes. And I could tell. Already. They wouldn't abandon her. At least not in sixth grade, I decided. And I couldn't. If I'd been able to verbalize what I felt, studying her face, I would say that I'd quickly deduced that Celeste already had too much power, with her beauty, to turn off a few insecure boys, not to mention the secure ones.

I know now that sitting there in that lumpy oval those boys must have been sweating and begging and praying to get Celeste. "Let me get her let me get her let me get her let me get her, pleeeeeease." Their identical mantras must have been ricocheting around that boathouse like the echolocations of bats.

And *I* had thought we were all interested in—what, the game of it?—the play, the fun, everybody. . . . Even as I hoped and prayed, as I sent up my own mantra—"Josh Josh Josh Josh Josh . . ."—another game played itself out in everyone else's heads. Twelve different imaginary games.

The first real show of guts came from Jennifer, of all people. We'd gone probably eight turns of truths, everyone resorting to making the pickees say who they would most like to kiss in the room. Nobody asked me, and nobody asked Josh, but we found out—big surprise—that Celeste wanted to kiss William and William wanted to kiss Celeste. Another boy diplomatically answered, "Any of the girls," and one other thought that Wanda would be his ideal. He caught no flak.

Jennifer, answering a nameless boy's question, said, "Dare."

My heart beat faster.

The no-name boy saw his chance, and, all credit due him, said, "I dare you to kiss me."

Communal "Ooooooh . . ."

"Where?" Jennifer asked.

"Over there," the boy said, flinging his attempt-at-casual, limp-wristed arm toward the dark corner.

"She means where on your face," Celeste interpreted.

"It's a dare?" The boy glanced at William for reassurance.

William answered, "You can pick. It's your dare."

"I pick my lips," the boy told Jennifer.

Communal "Ooooooh . . ."

"Come on," Jennifer said, and stood up, walking toward the corner.

My legs vicariously quivered for her. The boy stood and followed Jennifer like a zombie into the dark. The rest of us couldn't see anything, really. We didn't hear anything either except for some windbreaker arm-swishing noises.

And then they were back.

"You *kissed*?!" Lynne P. spurted.

No joke. They were walking clichés: deer in headlights. Duh. Jennifer nodded, just barely. The boy sat fast. Another boy punched him in the shoulder. The kissing boy didn't flinch and only brushed at the spot where he'd been socked.

"Who's next?" Josh asked, and then answered his own question: "You. Lynn Whoever. You're up."

And the game started rolling. "A-rockin'-an'-a-rollin'!" William said enthusiastically, forgetting his volume for an instant.

Even though we were perfectly capable of it, we weren't very creative in our subsequent dares. They involved only kissing, although they didn't necessarily involve the darer. Lynn L. chickened out, losing her mind completely, after having been kissed on the neck by a no-name guy, and only dared Lynne P. to kiss Celeste on the arm. Big deal, although I'm sure with hindsight that the boys undoubtedly enjoyed the display.

And then. And then, after two more turns without my getting picked once, it came to be Josh's turn after he'd been bullied into kissing loudmouth Lynne P. on the forehead by a no-name boy.

"Your go," William told Josh.

"I dare . . ." Josh deliberated; I assumed fake-deliberated. "I dare . . ." he repeated. I was already blushing. "I dare Celeste to kiss me on the lips."

I didn't quite react right when he said Celeste's name. I actually sort of grunted.

"For ten seconds," Josh added. "You count, William."

Celeste looked at me, and I'm sure—I remember this; I think I remember this—I just sort of numbly shrugged. We were in the jaws of an unstoppable game. My crush had called the name of my best friend. It hurt at the time no less than when now your mate calls out the wrong name, the name that isn't you, the mistake name, at the most wrong moment of all.

You're so young. You've never really had that queasy, limb-tingling, scalp-floating feeling before. Your head just floats, more or less, over the stump called your neck, and you sort of shrug, pretend that your best friend can go and kiss your crush because he asked her to.

"Outside," Josh added, late.

I must have raised my eyebrows and tilted my head in a casual, why-not sort of gesture to Celeste. The two stood and departed.

They did. They got up and went outside.

And then, eventually, after some horrible looks from the girls, Celeste and Josh returned. Celeste took her seat again next to me and studied her lap. She was breathing faster and louder than when she left. I wanted to take her face in my hands then and kiss her. Kiss the mouth that kissed Josh. Maybe I just wanted to kiss, and maybe I just wanted to kiss Celeste on the mouth; I don't know. But at that moment I wanted to suck on Celeste's lips and inhale her breath and feel her nose on the side of mine and slap her so hard she would cry out.

Instead, I said to her, "Your go." It was, after all, her turn.

"William," Celeste said. She cleared her throat.

William's white teeth shone, his smile a shiny crescent in the boathouse. "Dare," he said without being asked.

Celeste didn't flinch. "I dare you to make out with Colt for thirty seconds outside."

"What?" William asked, looking dumbfounded.

"Make out with Lisa for thirty seconds outside."

William seemed to resign himself to the task, lowered his chin, and double-checked with a look to Celeste. "You sure?"

"Yes," Celeste said.

"Make out," William triple-checked.

"Yes," Celeste said.

I knew what she'd meant to do, what she was trying to do.

I can't tell you how I got from sitting inside the boathouse to outside behind a rough-barked tree. I could make something up, but I'd be lying. I don't remember. What I do know, though, is that William's understanding of some words was different from mine, or Celeste's, or Rachel's and Diana's. I remember William putting his hands on my chest where no tits grew, in the places where tits should be—even some sort of little buds, but there weren't any; there was nothing there—and, upon discovering my lack of pubescent mammary glands and fat, pushed me up against the rough-barked tree.

"Thirty seconds," he said.

I didn't answer. I looked at his handsome face and closed my eyes in preparation. I remember feeling relieved that I was up against the tree; otherwise I might have fainted under the pressure.

But then a hand jabbed down into my pants and into my underwear. I didn't say a thing. I didn't peep. What was he doing? Kissing? I opened my eyes to the top of William's head. He was ducked at my waist; he could have been fishing for correct change.

And then the finger. William's finger started squirming deep into my underwear, in between my legs. And he pushed and wiggled. I could feel his fingernail scratching. And then the finger started pushing harder, and I tried to climb away from it, off of it, against the rough-barked tree, but I had nowhere to go, and then some part of me gave. William's finger burned, burned like the exhaust pipe of a motorcycle singeing a permanent divot into your calf as the motorcycle lies on top of you so heavily you cannot escape it, weighing you down on top of your own road rash and mistakes, your own stupidity.

Just a bit of skin, right? So much like a church song, a hymen, a nothing-much-important part of the whole Mass. Just a hymn.

He kept his head down the whole time, as if he might be able to fit his face into my pants and see what he did. I could have told him he wouldn't be able to see.

"Thirty seconds," he said, and pulled his hand out of my pants, out of me. He wiped the backside of his fingers on the leg of my jeans, then the palm side. *My* jeans. "Colt," he said, and smiled. You would hope that he wouldn't—you'd want him not to do it, not to, really—but he raised his finger, his index finger, to his nose and sniffed.

I felt scorched between my legs. I felt scraped from the bark at a spot on my back where I could feel my jacket had inched away from my jeans.

We went back into the boathouse, I don't know how.

"So?" Celeste whispered when I'd sat again.

No idea at all. I don't have a clue what I did. Certainly nothing.

"So?" she asked again, eager to know, no doubt, that she'd done right.

I think I nodded.

The game stopped abruptly when something huge-sounding splashed in the water just outside one of the boat entrances. A fish? A raccoon out for a swim? A dead body? A mass murderer diving into our midst? Everyone bumped out the door and ran back to the cabins at full speed. Safe once again inside our spider haven, we girls squealed the night away. I tried to squeal as enthusiastically as before. I wondered what William might report of our exploits against the tree, but I somehow doubted he would hamper his chances with Celeste in the future by revealing too much. Even he probably sensed she would have called him the name of the ugly creature that he was.

As for me, I wouldn't tell. I didn't tell. There wasn't much blood.

Celeste sheepishly presented me with a Hostess cupcake for my birthday the next morning, apologizing over and over again. I just wanted to forget, but instead I told her I loved cupcakes. She looked like she was going to cry.

NOMEANSNO

The band has traveled along the edge of the world to stand where it is now. It has followed the curved northern line that runs through Purgatory. Examine for a second—the exact amount of time for which you are able—the path that you have chosen. Your brain hitches inside your skull. Say the word *path*, and then the word *way*, and then the words *kung fu*. Say *grasshopper*. Remember how, at the start of every show, David Carradine brands his own forearms carrying the cast-iron pot from the fire. Imagine such repetitive pain. Roll up your sleeve. Take your cigarette and begin a circle in your pale flesh. Your skin stinks sweetly. Think bacon. Think pork cracklin's.

The next day do your other arm.

Notice that she doesn't stop you.

$\mathcal{C}$ELESTE AND I didn't have such an easy time in junior high school. At the start of seventh grade we were teeny, without the smallest signs of breasts still, young, and for the first two weeks literally lost. My combination lock stuck and looked as though it'd been hit with a hammer. I had anxiety dreams about leaving books for weeks at a time in a locker I didn't know I even had, losing my locker altogether, remembering and forgetting yet another new combination. The worst dream recurred regularly: The school itself expanded magically, like some creepy organism under our biology microscopes. It birthed long umbilical cords of endless hallways; ugly gray-green linoleum-tiled classrooms multiplied, splitting and dividing so that I had to walk farther and farther to get to a number and floor that hadn't existed the day before.

Celeste's nightmares involved her losing significant parts of herself. Clumps of hair clogged her brush. She told me she dreamed of parting her hair just above her ear and bobby-pinning long, coming-loose strands over a big bald patch on the top of her head. Teeth crumbled in her mouth when she ate in the cafeteria. She had to run to the bathroom and spit molars into the sink. Toenails and fingernails peeled away like orange rind from her flesh. She woke one morning, still dreaming, and looked down to see she'd lost both baby toes. She thought she wouldn't miss them too much, but wondered how she'd get through the mandatory swimming and lifesaving section of gym class coming up that winter without being laughed at by the already developed girls. Their boobs grew and grew, even as Celeste dropped away, bit by bit.

Our dreams weren't too tough to figure out.

We did, however, as they say, have each other. Junior high school was a much bigger place than our sixth grade, and while neither of us suddenly became ugly, we simply stayed the same. We hadn't lost our baby chick down, and we sort of peeped around the perimeter of the big, big school yard. Rather than on us, all the boys' eyes invariably fell upon the newly abundant mounds of breast flesh bouncing through the halls, all the new boobs hanging like Tantalosian treasures over water fountains and desktops and library file drawers. Somehow a pretty face, a cute nose, didn't seem to carry much weight at all. Celeste may still have had plenty of personality, and we both aced tests, completed all of our home-work perfectly, and participated in every class, but we were simply beaten down by boobs. We were forgotten for a time.

The two of us sat in the Diamond kitchen after school eating another Celeste favorite, garbanzo beans soaking in a puddle of red wine vinegar. I swear, that's the kind of girl she was. With those kinds of tastes. Celeste and I fenced with our forks momen-tarily, but junior high had killed the spirit of our play. We'd been in school just over three weeks. I looked out at the Diamonds' pool in the backyard, closed now for the season. A few yellow leaves somersaulted onto the blue cover.

"Do you want to join the Glee Club?" Celeste asked.

The tongs of my fork scraped the ceramic bowl. "Why would you want to join the Glee Club?"

"I don't know," she answered. "It'd be something different to do, at least." She stood and went to a drawer for a spoon and came back to her chair. She started slurping vinegar. "Diana was in the Glee Club."

Diana, Celeste's oldest sister, had left for college the month before. Celeste seemed to be on a bit of a Diana kick since her departure, talking about Diana at Brown University now, about what Diana was so good at, about how Diana used to do something or other better than anybody else. Archery, for example. Diana was better at archery than anybody else, boy or girl.

I had no desire to sing up on a wobbly set of risers. "But why *Glee Club*?" I implored with my eyes for her to drop the idea. Because I knew I'd have no choice. I fished out the last garbanzo bean, giving her my best hangdog.

Celeste slurped and talked. "Diana says that a girl who can sing, even if she has to learn in Glee Club, will get a lot of attention when she grows up."

To my ear, it didn't sound much like Diana, but Celeste had made the pronouncement. A Dianaism. A new one to adopt with appropriate fervor. And, then again, I should be so lucky as to grow up the way Diana had been able to. Glee Club? I could try. Wasn't it for dorks and squares though? "We would sing?" I had to ask.

"*You* already sing like Diana Ross," Celeste said, the repetition of her saintly older sister's name surely not accidental.

"Nuh-uh," I said. "*You* sing like . . . like a *rock star!*"

"Come on, Lisa. Let's do it."

It wasn't as if we'd joined on for any other extracurricular activities. Fine. Maybe we could make friends with some eighth-graders who could help us assimilate better than we currently were. "Okay."

"It meets Tuesdays and Thursdays before first period. At six forty-five. I'm going to write Diana a letter tonight and tell her about it." Celeste carried the bowl to the dishwasher. Case closed. "Do you want to do geometry or social studies first?"

We had five classes' worth of homework total that night. I dug through my backpack and suddenly realized I'd left my English book at school in my gym locker. Six forty-five? Or had I left it under my desk in class? Oh, no. Where was it? Singing in the morning . . . We'd have to get up when it was still dark out. If I had to buy another English book, my dad would give me one of his money-responsibility lectures. Hopefully it was in my gym locker. "Geometry," I said.

We rode our bikes to school. Tuesday and Thursday mornings Celeste pedaled to my house even earlier than usual, and we headed to Glee Club, held in the music room of the junior high's Cecil and Beverly Anastakis Fine Arts Building. Celeste ended up being an alto, which she hated, although not enough to quit. For some reason girls *had* to be sopranos. And while I was one, I was a lousy version, breathy and thin-voiced. My turdy brother, David, made fun of my practicing in the bathroom. He sang scales in his mocking falsetto at the dining room table, peas falling out of his mouth. My father laughed. My mother wasn't around.

Celeste had it better. I tried to get myself invited over for supper as often as I could. The entire Diamond family—minus Diana now—knew the lyrics to what seemed to me to be hundreds of Broadway musical songs. I learned number after number from *Fiddler on the Roof*; *Oklahoma*; *A Funny Thing Happened on the Way to the Forum*; *South Pacific*; *Hello, Dolly*.

Mr. Diamond encouraged everyone to sing loudly. Loudness alone, in fact, seemed to be half the point of it. We belted. We shook the Diamond house to its foundation. We even made the neighbors call once, at which point Mrs. Diamond, by far the quietest of us, told us to pipe down, though she couldn't suppress a smile. She returned from the kitchen a few minutes later, producing a clove-studded dessert of baklava and a china teapot of strong, red-colored tea.

Mr. Diamond always slapped the table edge and sang off-key in his croaking baritone until he coughed and laughed and then sang some more. He directed us, his big arms swinging, and invariably toppled his coffee cup or wine goblet or overturned a plate. Ravioli flew. Grapes rained down like pennies from heaven. Mrs. Diamond shook her head knowingly and let her husband finish the song before starting to clean up after him.

Celeste's and my favorite, for obvious seventh-grade reasons, was the extended refrain from *South Pacific*'s "A Wonderful Guy." We begged to sing it whenever I was there. Beautiful teenage

Rachel helped, and even Mrs. Diamond sang with real gusto then, Mr. Diamond going quiet to beam at his ladies. The long string of *"I'm in love"*s—sixteen, seventeen of them?—bounced off the walls. I counted on my fingers under the tablecloth. Mr. Diamond took to trying to throw us off after weeks of the incredibly repetitive chorus, but you could tell he really did watch us with true adoration. He touched the cheeks of his family and made a habit of rubbing the top of my head with his warm, fat palm. I couldn't remember the last time anyone in my family had touched me in an affectionate way. I thought I loved him.

Lately I sing Elvis Costello songs with my daughter—a little P.I.L. or old ska, innocuous stuff—and think about the nights at the Diamonds'. I wish I knew if they sang as much when I wasn't there, or if I actually made it better or more fun and they sang because I *was* there. It's possible they did it all for me, the special food, the special attention. A gift from them, to me. I never thought to ask Celeste. I just inhaled them. I suppose I needed their family to survive and didn't even know it. They must have, though. Celeste, too. She knew. She had to have known. Catching myself absentmindedly humming Blondie, or sometimes a Pretenders hit, I tell myself that now: She must have known what she gave me.

In November, as the days grew colder and gloomier, and our backpacks grew ever heavier, Mrs. Diamond decided that Celeste and I should go to dance class. She would be treating both of us, she said one afternoon as we studied at the kitchen island. "I don't want to hear another word about it, Lisa."

We all knew my dad wouldn't pay. He'd tell me to participate in a team sport at school for free. "It's why we moved into the neighborhood in the first place, isn't it?" he'd drone, sitting in the garage at his toolless workbench smoking a Salem. "For the district. For you kids." Our father, Mr. Smith. Plain as plain as plain could be. His no-frills approach to our upbringing, aside from a few biased indulgences for my brother, David, got us by, but it wasn't exactly what I'd wanted.

You can guess what I wanted. Within a week of moving to Kansas City I'd decided to become a Diamond. Fuck the dull, saltine-cracker Smiths. Screw our father with his boring grass lawn trimmed right up to the house foundation with no flowers or bushes or trees, his bland baked pork chops, his awful spaghetti. We had no original art, no unique furniture. We had no pets. Our father said that our mother, the ghost in the bedroom, wouldn't allow them. Not even fish, not even a stinkin' furball guinea pig.

I know he did what he needed to do, and maybe even all that he could do.

Our father understood some things, though, just fine, and one of them was that his children were reflections of him. David and I learned to be the ones to bear the burden of his projections, of his expectations for our success. We needed to balance the black hole of his failed marriage, his absentee wife, our invisible birth-giver. We needed to be smart, courteous, proper Smiths. We didn't need to be artistic Smiths. Or singing Smiths. Or dancing, prancing, showy Smiths.

I never even asked my father if I could go. He was a chemical engineer.

"I want you to try all four dance styles," Mrs. Diamond said in her usual bossy monotone. Just recently I had figured out how to hear the underlying kindness in that voice, on Halloween, when Celeste and I helped Mrs. Diamond hand out full-size candy bars to the neighborhood kids. Mrs. Diamond was a green-faced witch, and Celeste and I were nondescript ghouls in shredded Mr. Diamond shirts dirtied with shoe polish. (I have no recollection of what my family did for Halloween, that year or many others. Did they—we—turn off the lights and go to bed?) "Four weeks at a time," Mrs. Diamond told us. "Modern, jazz, tap, and ballet."

Were we klutzes? I don't know. I don't think so. Anyway, the thought of being treated to such a gift erased any apprehensions I might have had concerning leotards and strangers. "Thank you," I said as sincerely as I could.

"You girls need a diversion," Mrs. Diamond said flatly. "Some fun."

"What if I don't want to take ballet?" Celeste asked.

"Do you know anything about ballet?" Mrs. Diamond countered.

"*The Nutcracker*," Celeste said. "Twyla Tharp." Celeste twisted the squeaky sole of her tennis shoe back and forth on the rung of her counter chair.

Mrs. Diamond said, "Twyla Tharp uses modern-dance technique in her choreography."

"The nutcracker?" I asked. I had no idea what they were talking about, food or dancing.

"The ballet," Celeste said.

"It's a holiday production," Mrs. Diamond said. She absently fondled her loose gold watchband. "Christmas-leaning," she added, "but delightful." The Diamonds were Jewish.

"Oh." I didn't really understand.

"We'll go next month," Celeste told me, picking up her pencil and flipping over her French-verb worksheet. "Okay, Mom," she said to her paper, to *a manger, a dormir, a écouter.*

"Good," Mrs. Diamond said. "You'll take tap and jazz for the first four weeks. Monday, Wednesday, and Friday afternoons, starting this coming Monday."

"*Three* days a week?" Celeste almost whined, looking up. "We have homework, you know."

"Oh, I know," Mrs. Diamond said. "You have too much homework for your age. *Two* dance classes, *three* times a week. Tap and jazz at the Plaza Dance Academy. We'll have to take the two of you to get your gear. Shoes and tights and whatnot. Can you go, say, on Saturday, Lisa?"

I could get away after Saturday-morning cleaning chores. "Probably in the afternoon," I said.

"Ask your dad," Mrs. Diamond instructed. "You don't need to bring any money." Mrs. Diamond left the kitchen, no good-byes.

"God," Celeste muttered. "Three days a week."

Celeste and I already studied all five weekdays after school at her house. I wouldn't need to say a thing to anybody in my family. "Just think," I said. "Soon we'll be *dancing* singing stars."

She smirked, then smiled. "*Je danse, tu danses—*"

"*Nous dansons,*" I completed.

Celeste rolled her eyes. "Watch out," she said. "Here come the gazelles."

You had to giggle.

Better we started with jazz and tap than modern and ballet. Jazz class followed tap class, an insipid, counting-oriented form, as far as I was concerned, taught by a Mr. Chris. First or last name, I wasn't sure. Even though I didn't yet have a label for his self-presentation style, anyone could see Mr. Chris was a true pansy, a prissy fag, a bottom without question. He openly made fun of us nine girls while praising the uncoordinated efforts of the two boys, one pale, buck-toothed, and thin to a fault, the other a mixed-race boy named Westley who showed us the very first day that he could run up the wall, do a flip, and land on his feet. I'd never seen such a trick. Celeste applauded, eliciting a "Shush!" from Mr. Chris. Mr. Chris seemed to be processing both the mixed-race boy's natural ath-letic ability and the probability that Westley would never be gay.

Tap class sucked: shuffle-ball-change, shuffle-ball-change, shuffle-ball-change. Big arms. "Beeeiiiiiiig arms! Beeeeeeeeeiiig arms!" Splayed fingers. Fake grins. After two weeks of Monday, Wednesday, and Friday tap classes, we figured out that we could skip and not be found out. Mrs. Diamond dropped us off in the alley entryway of the Plaza Dance Academy. We went in, hid behind the women's dressing room partition until we saw the Volvo station wagon pull away, and then ran back outside to sit on the kitchen stoop of a nearby German lunch restaurant until it was safe to start dressing for jazz class inside. No loiterers allowed.

Mr. Chris caught us more than once at the changeover, but he didn't seem to mind our skipping at all. Instead he exhaled, "Why, *hello*, girls!"

Celeste and I liked jazz dance class, however. I should say we *loved* jazz dance class. It transformed us, and, thank god, we were both equally good. We could wiggle our itty square hips with equal aplomb. Westley and three other boys, the skinny one fortunately absent, took the class too.

A short-haired young woman named Ms. Elswit taught us. She played great music and complimented everyone in the class. "Nicely executed, Tabitha!" she'd effuse. "Oh! Big! Yes, Westley! Yes! Run, Lisa! Oh, leap, leap, Celeste!"

"We're going back years, now," Ms. Elswit would say, prepping us for a rehearsed number we'd learned the previous class. "Follow me." We bent, we crunched, we swooped, we went left, we ran right, we clapped, we—yes—we shuffle-ball-changed. But, of course, it was a different beast altogether.

Ms. Elswit made us think our bodies had a sense of humor, had grace no matter what, had strength, had connection to New Zealand, Africa, Ireland. She purposely made us laugh and flub steps and go through three more sets with no break and pant and sweat.

She asked Celeste and me if we'd be taking the class again the following session.

"We have to do ballet and modern next term," Celeste said.

"Stick with the class anyway," Ms. Elswit said. "Trade one of the others out for it. You girls are fantastic."

"I don't think we can," Celeste told her. "Not right away."

"Well, find out." Ms. Elswit pulled at the sweaty crotch of her leotard, adjusting. "You're welcome additions."

I wished we could stay in the class, even if ballet or modern turned out to be good.

As it turned out, ballet and modern both sucked. Still, even years down the line, those classes would prove useful for a good laugh at least: Celeste and I developed an alcohol-induced modern dance routine. Truly fuckin' funny. But at the time, we quickly came to realize the sheer inanity of both disciplines. Ballet: Pinch a quarter between your ass cheeks. Squeeze. Produce two dimes and a nickel. Present change to butthole-mouthed old lady teach-

ing class. Modern: Squat. Pretend you are shitting to the drum-
beat. Slap your hands on invisible tits. Pretend to shit some more.

So we skipped and just went to jazz instead. Ms. Elswit must
have fixed it in the office. And if Mrs. Diamond ever found out,
she played dumb. Besides, the shoes had heels.

Celeste and I took jazz until we left for college. Eventually we
ruled the class. We even outdanced Ms. Elswit; she graciously
curtsied to us in tenth grade, and we knew we'd accomplished
something special. By then we could kick over our heads as easily
as we braided our hair or applied fruit-flavored lip gloss. Second
nature. And the splits! All three directions, like pie. Westley hung
in there too. He even may have been as good as we were. Okay.
He was. Years later, Westley and I eventually had a July Fourth
weekend of heated groping while Celeste was on vacation in
Greece with her whole reunited family.

My family, of course, eventually found out about the dance
classes but believed for all those years that I'd received a scholarship. Celeste and I took dance breaks from our homework. We
made up our own routines to radio songs. We hummed in Quanti-
tative Chemistry and stepped in time under the lab tables. And
Mrs. Diamond just kept paying. I stopped thanking her after a few
years because she never reminded me. Never.

Oui, nous avons dansé, nous avons dansé. Mrs. Diamond had
been right.

The August before eighth grade, Celeste's second sister, Rachel,
left for college. Celeste seemed normal enough. For about a
week. Mr. and Mrs. Diamond, too, tried to maintain their emotional status quo for a while. But Rachel's absence was soon felt all
over their house, at poolside in the dog days of her late-summer
disappearance, at the dinner table, in front of the TV at night.

And so two weird things happened. One, Celeste almost acted
as though she needed me, a confusing, monopolizing display of
attention and demand from her, most noticeably around other
friends. Two, I became a surrogate Diamond. Not that I wasn't

one already, but as we entered eighth grade, I was now allotted certain Diamond duties—mostly cooking.

My family, in turn, seemed to accept my complete defection without protest. My brother, David, continued to trail me through school, born just those ten months later than me, and our father sort of hovered peripherally, never daring to venture too close.

Neither of them actually asked me to do anything *with* them, ever. David and I had never gotten along for whatever reason— maybe, I realize now, because he stole nearly all of the attention of the one good parent left. And my father? My father had no clue about anything having to do with me. But sometimes they'd ask me to do things *for* them. David finally admitted—nearly squint-ing with the pain it caused him to consult me—that he didn't know where the cool kids shopped. "It's not like you ever go either," he'd said, "but, well, you *know* where they go. Tell me."

"You think I'd tell *you*?" I countered.

He threatened to spread lies about me at school if I didn't. That I had crushes on teachers and queer-baits. I told him that I'd tell Celeste he masturbated, and that when he did, he called out her name.

We reached an immediate if uneasy peace.

My father made small requests: I needed to make an appear-ance at the block party; I needed to remind him of the parent-teacher conferences by writing memos to him. I swear he used the word *memo*.

Meanwhile, my mother deteriorated. She had occasionally left her bedroom door open after we'd first moved to Kansas City as a sign, I figured, an enticement for me to come and get the woman-to-girl knowledge I was surely lacking. But once I met Celeste and her sisters, I rarely took the invitation, and my mother's door began to remain closed more and more.

Behind the closed door lay Janice Joy. The slow-rolling, moss-collecting stone, the nearly inanimate object of our little affection, Janice Joy. Unfortunately, should alliteration concern you, my mother's maiden name was Jones.

In our case, the conventions of a wealthy Midwestern city

upbringing mandated some kind of an explanation for a mother like Janice Joy, and we all—our father, David, Celeste, and I— happened upon an acceptable one. "She's ill, and the doctors can't quite get to the bottom of the illness." It wasn't a lie. We just skipped the part about Janice Joy Jones living in her nightgown, in her own bedroom, for no discernible reason. My father dutifully took her to a physician every six months, probably hoping against hope. Hoping for Janice Joy to be diagnosed with terminal cancer? Or simply to hear the words spoken once and for all: "She will never get better"? He must have hoped he'd be given something, anything, find out something new, but despite minor muscle atrophy from lack of activity, my mother had nothing physically wrong with her.

A series of ineffective psychiatrists kept Janice Joy barely afloat with a series of ineffective medications. Early sedatives, I suppose. Or early uppers. I never knew what the different colors and sizes were for exactly. Whether the medications fed into her blank stares, her zombiehood, hardly mattered. She seemed no different when she ran out of pills, and sometimes days would pass before anyone noticed and refilled her prescriptions.

Her voice, when I heard it, sounded as though she'd been dramatically, exaggeratedly hypnotized. A voice for effect, for an audience. Only she wasn't faking. I don't believe she ever faked it, whatever "it" actually was.

Our family's vague dismissal of Janice Joy's problem worked well enough in the school district, anyway. My mother never went out. As the rest of us found few reasons to be in our house beyond supper- and sleep-time, few people came to visit after Janice Joy's initial failure to answer the doorbell. Hardly ever, in fact.

As my new Diamond duties increased, my ownership of my mother waned. It had to. I could not be related to "that." All possibility of a sane future for me hinged on not being my mother in any way. My dad's DNA alone comprised my makeup. At an age when most girls worry about inheriting their mothers' hips or coarse body hair, I worried about inheriting a piece of my mother that couldn't even be identified. And so I dismissed her whole.

I assume now that my mother's illness came down to chemicals, or I'd be screwed. Janice Joy Jones' body regulators, her seratonin levels, her brain-helping glands, clearly played a crappy game of chemical poker, losing over and over on a daily basis, and they produced a creature incapable of dealing. Something either ran out or quit working in my mother, but somehow all my own some-things worked fine. They still all work fine.

So I imagine I put up precious little resistance when the terri-ble, terrible arm-twisting began, to spend significantly *more* time with the Diamonds. Both Tuesdays and Thursdays, our long days beginning with Glee Club—as opposed to our long Mondays, Wednesdays, and Fridays ending with jazz—Celeste and I were responsible for supper at the Diamond house. For the first several months, those meals pained each and every one of us four at the table, but both Mr. and Mrs. Diamond insisted we find our way around the kitchen on our own. It was a family tradition, and a way to "develop a cooking style." Food counted. Food mattered. Eventually Mrs. Diamond broke down and left out some of her favorite, trusted cookbooks on the counter. Gastronomical peace offerings. With bookmarks. And so our bloody, undercooked, plain roast chicken—gizzard and other internal organs still stuffed in their wet paper package inside the cavity—picked up root veg-etables, rosemary, fifty degrees more of oven temperature, and another forty-five minutes of suntanning time. Lost the organs and got stuffed with real stuffing. We asked Mrs. Diamond to buy chestnuts.

Later we requested Roquefort, fresh herbs, dark mustard, water chestnuts, bean sprouts, a pepper mill, ramekins, capers, sherry, lamb chops, an entire duck, anchovy paste, a citrus zester, dates, slivered almonds, rare olives, sesame seeds, honey, a spring-form cake pan, phyllo dough, bitter Swiss chocolate, new pota-toes, filet mignons, crabmeat, lobsters. A fifteen-pound turkey. Pâté.

Under the protection of friendship and camaraderie, Celeste and I competed in the kitchen eventually, trying to outdo each other for the highest praise from her parents. We had never competed so openly before; I'm not sure Celeste had ever competed with me at all, but once our cooking nights were established, she competed with gusto. We loved the challenge. Alternating Tuesdays and Thursdays, one of us took on a main course and the other prepared two side dishes.

Mr. Diamond grew bigger still. I'd swear he gained as much in height as he did in girth. Unfortunately for our egos, however, he never failed to praise Celeste and me equally. Mrs. Diamond, on the other hand, never failed to offer a piece of advice or suggestion concerning every menu item. A pinch less salt. More butter. As with jazz class, there seemed to be no discernible winner between us. We didn't care, not yet.

One Thursday, over an admittedly brilliant pan of lasagna, a real egg-yolk Caesar, and a sautéed-zucchini side dish, Mr. Diamond effused, for the umpteenth time, "You girls are becoming some wonderful cooks!" He whistled "The Surrey with the Fringe on Top" between bites.

"They are," Mrs. Diamond said, and we waited for her usual amendment. She looked up at the ceiling for a moment, chewing, before it came to her. "I actually think the Caesar could use a touch more garli—"

"Give it a rest, Mona," Mr. Diamond suddenly said.

"What?" Mrs. Diamond seemed not to have heard her husband.

"I said, 'Give it a rest, Mona.'" Up until recently, Mr. Diamond had referred to Mrs. Diamond, in my presence, as Mama. He delivered the nickname in a way that didn't make it sound silly, but rather used it in a kind of pet way, as if he'd called her that ever since baby Diana uttered the word. Lately, though, since Rachel left, Mr. Diamond had used his wife's first name much more often.

"Give what a rest?" Mrs. Diamond said a bit quickly.

"Mona, you know exactly what I mean," Mr. Diamond said. "Everything on this table is delicious." He indicated the entire table with the wide span of his arms. "It's perfect," he added.

"It is *not* perfect," Mrs. Diamond snapped. A look tried to alight itself on her face; she reddened, fighting something. "I mean to say, I agree with you, but . . . but everybody can always improve."

"They're in eighth grade!"

I had never heard Celeste's parents quarrel.

"Yes," Mrs. Diamond said. "They *are* in eighth grade. And it's plenty time they learned some basic skills."

"What about algebra? How about essay writing?" A fleck of salad dressing clung to his upper lip. "They're reading Shakespeare, for god's sake!" Mr. Diamond's voice rose. "What sort of skills are you implying they're lacking? Embroidery? *Dreidel carving?*" He actually pounded his fist, holding a fork, on the table. He seemed as big as Goliath suddenly.

I'd spent most of my life, in my house, being quiet so as not to disturb my mother. While I'd grown used to Mr. Diamond's booming singing voice, I didn't know his arguing one at all. I wanted to slide out of my chair and out of the room like an oiled noodle off a fork.

"*She's* going to go, too," Mrs. Diamond said loudly. She pointed with her knife at Celeste. "Celeste is going to grow up and leave this house, and there is nothing you can do about it."

"Of course she will. She'll go." Mr. Diamond blinked twice. "But for god's sake, Mona, don't push her so far that she never comes back."

Mrs. Diamond's mouth fell open. I understood her suggestions for cooking improvement. I did. I for one didn't think she was as bad as Mr. Diamond was suggesting. She just came across rough, but she wasn't really. Besides, she was even usually right. "Celeste's maturing," Mrs. Diamond retorted.

What? I wondered.

"What?" Celeste asked, making a horrified face.

"Your body is maturing," Mrs. Diamond said to Celeste with obvious impact. "I can smell your underarms," she added.

Uh-oh. Mrs. Diamond had gone too far. At the dinner table. Over our lasagna. That's what it felt like, anyway. Even better than that noodle, I decided at the moment, would be the chance to impersonate the meatball in the song about the mountain of spaghetti and the meatball getting to roll onto the floor and out the door. I might have started singing the song under my breath. I don't know exactly what I did, but when I looked up from my napkin in my lap, the three remaining Diamonds stared at me.

"Mom!" Celeste stood up when I looked at her. She tried to walk away, but her loose sweater sleeve snagged on the wrought-iron arm of her chair. She pulled. Her sweater ripped. "I can't believe you just said that!" Celeste gracelessly stumbled out.

I could hear myself swallow. If Celeste actually got embarrassed, then it must be true. She wouldn't have cared at all a few months ago. Did *I* smell?

"Really, Mona! Really . . ."

"What?! What's so terrible about noting the fact that your own daughter's growing up? There's nothing terrible about the human body, and you have to come to terms wi—"

"Lisa," Mr. Diamond said.

Me? "Yes?"

"You're free to go up to Celeste's room if you like," he said.

"Thank you," I said, sensing that my saying that, too, was inappropriate. Climbing the stairs, I heard Mrs. Diamond pick up where her husband had cut her off.

"—come to terms with your children living as adults, participating in adult activities."

"Some behavior belongs to children," I thought I heard Mr. Diamond say.

Celeste sat barefoot on her bed shaking a bottle of nail polish. She said, "As soon as I leave for college, I'm doing exactly what I want. I just won't tell them. How stupid can Diana be?"

"What do you mean?" I asked.

"Diana moved in with a boy. With a guy. He answered the phone. She could have just . . . I don't know. My dad is really mad."

Wow. I knew then, even if Celeste didn't, that Diana didn't have it in her to lie any more than Celeste did. "Is your mom mad?" I couldn't think fast enough to ask a better question.

"Not as much as Dad," Celeste said, scratching her knee. "God. I can't believe that my mom said that."

"Said what?" I pretended. I knew she meant about the armpit smell.

"You know," Celeste said, opening the bottle of polish, painting her toenails.

Of course. It took all the self-control I had not to lean over and take a big whiff. Did she stink? "Oh," I said. "No, you don't."

"But I do," she muttered. "I smell different lately."

She did? Why didn't I? I should, too, then. "You do?"

Celeste raised her arm casually. I sniffed. She was right. She smelled different, like her sisters used to, sweating by the pool. I didn't smell like that. I looked quickly for a budding chest. I couldn't see any new breasts under her sweater. "Are you growing boobs too?" I asked.

"They hurt," she said. "Really badly."

They did? "They do?" I looked again but didn't see any signs.

"Uh-huh." She moved the stiff brush down the row of her delicate toes.

Why the hell didn't my boobs hurt? We were both maturing late, but at the same time. It was supposed to be at the same time. We were alike that way. We'd figured that out: We were the same.

"A lot. They hurt a lot." She finished her nail painting. "Let me do yours," she said.

I shook my head.

"Come on. It's Pouting Pretty." She held up the bottle. The stupid name did not escape me.

Eighth grade grew ever more painful as I enviously watched Celeste's body change. In leotards, at jazz, the physical proof became undeniable. She messed up dancing more, while I continued to excel, but the small discrepancy between our performances did little to quell my desire to trade bodies with my best friend.

My brother, David, harassed me about my obvious lack of physical development behind my father's back, while more and more my father's back seemed to be the only part of him I saw. I suppose he faced what he could and denied the rest in much the same way as everybody then.

I have a vivid memory still of seeing my father's hunched form from behind at about that time. He was bowed over absolutely nothing at his desk. He didn't seem to hear me when I called out to him from the hallway; only after I'd entered his study did I realize that he'd fallen asleep. His breath sputtered quietly, in, out, in. He was a sort of lip snorer.

I looked around at the bare study walls. He rarely used the room, preferring the garage for smoking, the den or his bedroom for TV watching, the bathroom for reading. Just another empty room. A desk, a file cabinet, and a few technical books on almost empty shelves. Suddenly Celeste's most recent story of bra shopping and my father's sad, empty study mated and produced in my mind a new baby thought. For the first time, I swear, I wondered whether or not my father had a girlfriend. It wasn't a moral issue for me. I suppose I thought he *should* have one. Where did the color, where did the fun in his life come from?

I left him there to sleep, having forgotten what it was I'd wanted to ask him anyway.

The vibe at the Diamonds' changed for a short while after "the Fight" before easing back into something a little less than normal. Mr. and Mrs. Diamond seemed especially nice to me. We all suffered my lack of growth. I'd like to say that I accomplished my goal of riding out my extended hiatus, my prepuberty marathon as maturely as I had envisioned, but I didn't. I bemoaned my situation more than a touch and inflicted plenty of juvenile wrath around me. I tried to throw myself into my homework, into jazz, into Glee Club, and ignore my never-changing front.

Boys no longer seemed to know I even existed. A fast-passing shadow from something you never saw the solid of, I became a distant echo from grade school at the side of Celeste the Babe,

Celeste the Brick House. She may not have had much to display yet, but she had something. And her undeniable beauty made up for the rest that had yet to grow.

I, on the other hand, had nothing; no matter what I wished, no matter what I prayed at night, I was an empty physical entity inching ever closer to becoming my mother. I knew there was no god.

Once, in a group of mixed company in the cafeteria, when Celeste used my name as I stood, clearly, by her side, William Hirsch, the very one-and-only finger fucker, responded with an irritated-sounding, "Who?"

Eighth grade was a very bad year.

BUTTHOLE SURFERS

The band sings something about the pope. You hate the pope. Yell at your boy thrashing next to you that you wish you could kill the pope and that you want more. You want enough to fill you up. You want more cocaine and more vodka. You want more of all of them, of men, of the things that stick out of them, egos and Marlboro reds and dirty words about banging your perfect ass. With your body, force your boy to stand still during his favorite song about the pope. Watch his face go black with anger. See a storm. See a bad spanking. See your boy is ugly. Decide your boy is the pope. Blow the pope away with an imaginary gun. Fellate your own fingers afterward.

Dig in the pope's pocket for the bullet, the brown glass vial with the magic top. Snort. Taste chemicals running down the back of your throat. Snort again. Ignore the band. Ignore the pope. Move to the bar to look for your other part, your monster twin. You don't see her. Feel the burn of your boy's eyes between your shoulder blades.

Order vodka—say that, say just *vodka*—and decide you would rather bring home the bartender. You would rather bring home any other boy in the place. You even consider the idea of leaving with a thing possessed. You could do it. You have to do something. You have to do someone.

Decide then as you set your jaw and clench your teeth that you will get rid of your boy. Promise yourself this. You will get rid of your boy as soon as the cocaine and money run out. Promise yourself. Try to remember the word. Promise. Swear.

_I_ DOUBT MY coming of age was very different from most any other woman's, and mine likely doesn't make for much of a story. Fortunately the bigger story is Celeste's, so I'll wrap up all the minor physical details.

Three inches. I grew an inch a month the summer before high school. One morning in July I woke up to a hard lima-bean lump under my left nipple. A week later another one showed up under my right. The lumps hurt when I pressed on them. I decided I might have some weird nipple cancer until I remembered what Celeste had said so many months earlier.

Lima beans became plum pits became tangerine halves.

In August I sat peeing on the toilet, looked down, and saw pencil marks, like fuzz, shading the pale vee where my legs met. I licked my thumb and tried to rub the marks away. Hair! Hair! I looked and looked. The thin, sparse patch was the ugliest thing I had ever seen. How did it suddenly appear there without my knowing?

By Christmas I had procured a monthly fund from my father for what I "needed." He handed over far more than necessary for tampons. I used the extra—he forked out twenty bucks a month beyond my decent allowance—to found my cosmetic collection.

I'm proud to say I took my hyperspeed maturation completely in stride. The faster the better. I'd been ready for years. Despite the fact that I had problems recognizing myself when I stood naked in front of a mirror, I intellectually welcomed all physical changes. No, that's a lie. A pencil-mark hair sprouted from the edge of my areola in those first months, and I almost threw up. I bought tweezers and pulled it out, my eyes watering from the sting. No more grew. There. Luckily.

I didn't really like bleeding every month, but it didn't hurt. I figured out how to use a tampon from the instruction pamphlet the company put in the box. If you did it right, you couldn't even feel you were wearing one. And if bleeding every month meant that Celeste and I were once again more alike than different, all the better.

New Year's Eve, I wore the best gift I'd ever gotten to my first real party: a slinky purple dress. The Diamonds had given it to me for Christmas.

For Hanukkah I gave the Diamond family a cool African carving of an ibex from the UNICEF import store along with a tin of my own homemade cookies. I gave Celeste a trendy, long knit stocking cap. She gave me the perfume Lauren because she knew I adored it; I sprayed on too much of it at the department stores we wandered through in the Country Club Plaza.

Of course, Christmas with my own family was undeniably painful, as usual. Our mother, decorated, dolled up for the day in a new quilted bathrobe, sat as silently as a prop in the corner, on the only wooden chair in the entire living room. As if David or I actually needed evidence of our mother's decline, evidence with some special holiday oomph, our presents had been signed only by our father that year, although we could tell he'd tried unsuccessfully to imitate her handwriting just below or above. No question the gift-wrapping department had taken care of the khakis and Polos we had registered for at Dillard's to make it easier for Dad. Perfect bows, fancy paper.

Our father even helped the prop to unwrap her own gifts, as if she were a true cardboard cutout or enfeebled quadriplegic. Explaining what he was doing as he bent over her lap. Our father, I'd decided, had *better* have a girlfriend.

I suppose I was so enraptured with my new body and my recently revived status as living, breathing girl at school that December 25 in my house was one more day to be simply endured. Dinner, which I agreed to warm in the oven, had been delivered the previous afternoon by a decent caterer. I could hardly wait to be excused to go to the Diamonds' after we'd eaten, after I cleaned up the dishes and the prop went back to her room.

Later, in front of the Diamonds' menorah, in my purple dress, I looked older, sexier, nearing some high school approximation of youthful sophistication. Celeste told me that her mother had brought home three different dresses and that Celeste and her dad had decided which one I would get. When I put it on and paraded out of Celeste's room and down the stairs, they applauded. Mrs. Diamond, small-footed as she was, loaned me a pair of black, strappy shoes as well as a black-beaded necklace and purse.

I thought I loved her, too.

Lynne P.'s parents were letting Lynne P. host the New Year's Eve party, mainly for freshmen and sophomores, in her family's gigantic brick house with white pillars out front. The official mailed invitations said that a home-based employee (the live-in maid) would be supervising, along with Lynne P.'s older brother, who was home from college. Her parents were celebrating in the Bahamas.

I had arranged to stay at Celeste's, of course; we, in turn, had agreed unconditionally to call at quarter after twelve to check in, and then again later no matter what the time to have Mr. Diamond pick us up. He promised not to be mad, while we promised to eat something significant for every drink he knew we'd be having, even though neither of us had ever had more than a glass of wine apiece under parental supervision. "Cheese, meat, or sandwiches, or more than two real hors d'oeuvres count," he said. "A celery stalk does not. A stick of Bubble Yum does not. You promise, I promise. Deal?"

"Bubble Yum comes in cubes," Celeste said.

"Seal the deal, young ladies," Mr. Diamond said. He held out his hand to shake.

We shook.

Mrs. Diamond dropped us off at the corner of Lynne P.'s block so that Celeste and I could walk up unencumbered by the stigma of adult supervision. "Have fun, girls," she said in her usual flat voice.

We got out and waved good-bye nonchalantly. Before pulling away, Mrs. Diamond lowered the automatic window on the passenger side. "Kiss somebody cute at midnight," she said, then gunned the Volvo's engine, just a bit, and drove off smiling.

A granular dusting of snow blew across the sidewalk in wispy patterns. Not wanting to topple over and wreck our outfits, we clacked along carefully. Celeste wore shiny red satin pants, a white ruffled blouse, and expensive dyed-to-match red satin high heels. Mrs. Diamond had let us wear two of her jacket-length furs. My purple dress slipped across my thighs, over my nylons, in a noticeably new, tactile way. Celeste had convinced me that the dress looked better without underwear under the panty hose, so I didn't wear any. My long hair whipped around my face and stuck in my thick green-apple lip gloss. Celeste wore cola. We were, without question, sugar-mouthed jailbait.

Celeste started, "Diana and Rachel said that you're supposed to—"

"I know, I know," I said. You were supposed to kiss as many cute boys as you could after the midnight countdown. Evidently everybody kissed everybody, almost. We clicketied up the long front walk of the house. I checked Celeste out. "You look like . . ." I said. "You look really, *really* good."

"You look the best you've ever looked," Celeste said.

The old sixth-grade bursting-at-the-seams sense of excitement had changed little in two and a half years, but we'd learned how to manage the surges better.

"Thanks," I said, barely concealing a squeal.

Celeste pushed the glowing doorbell, and the world as we knew it opened wide.

"Shut the door!" at least a dozen people yelled as a sophomore boy ushered Celeste and me into dazzling chaos.

Lynne P.'s huge marble-floored foyer teemed with kids from school, everyone dressed up, wearing cologne and perfume, drinking punch in champagne flutes or eating food from toothpicks and laughing too loudly and moving like ants, efficiently, using invisible antennae, checking each other out in clusters and then moving on to sniff at another group, everyone moving around the foyer and into the living room and dining room and art gallery and kitchen and library and den and sitting room and long hallway and back again, all following the same winding route, following the marked, scented path to earthly delights.

"My! Ladies . . ." said an older guy in a tuxedo whom I didn't recognize. He swayed in patent-leather shoes in front of us. It was nine thirty. Was he dancing?

"Hi," I said amenably enough, or so I tried.

"Hello," Celeste said nicely.

"Allow me to take your coats," he said. Black curly hair, gorgeously out of control, sprang from his head. "I'm Charlie. Lynne's brother."

Charlie was so *cute*. Charlie was in *college*.

"Mmm-mmm, ladies, ladies." He raised a crystal glass to his lips and took a sip of something dark, something that smelled dark too. "Please. Your coats. It's my duty."

Celeste dripped out of her fur. I drooled out of mine. Whoops! Oh, silly us! Woo-hoo! There go the coats! Tee-hee-hee . . . I wonder what we'll get rid of next? What did you say your name was again, you handsome hunk of manliness?

"Perfectly *lovely* jackets," Charlie said in a fake something-or-other accent.

"Thank you," Celeste said.

"I'm Lynne's brother," Charlie repeated. "Her older brother."

Yes. Of course he was. In a tuxedo. Answering the door. Charlie's wolf ears twitched under Granny's sleeping bonnet.

He raised our coats, draped over his arm, to his nose. "Ladies, you smell good," he said. "And look good. Good enough to eat."

Flattered to the brims, we reluctantly stepped away from Charlie's charming smile and went looking for his sister.

We spent half an hour following the ant trail around the first floor of the incredible house. Classmates stood much closer to one another than they normally did at school. Most of them drank soda or punch, but a few sophomore boys brazenly swigged at cans of Budweiser. In the library, a girl named Georgia frantically pushed past, her baby-blue angora sweater wounded with the telltale orange-red grease splotch of a loosed cocktail weenie. Everyone we encountered told Celeste and me how nice we looked, how pretty, how grown-up. Two sophomore girls, purported to be cigarette-smoking brains who gave blow jobs readily, girls who'd never spoken to us at school, left their dates' sides and approached us. "I like your dress," one told me, her breath smelling stronger than Charlie's.

"Thanks."

"Where'd you get your pants?" the other asked Celeste.

"Can you wash that?" the first one asked me. She reached toward my hip and fondled the material. I thought she would squeeze my butt if she could, for a firmness check. Instead she poked me in the stomach in some undisguised sophomore-to-freshman comparison move. I'd become a mattress.

"Why'd you do that?" Celeste asked the girl.

"What?" the girl asked, obviously having heard.

"Why did you poke Lisa in the stomach?"

"Oh, my god," the other girl said to her friend. "They are *so* young!" She turned to Celeste and poked Celeste in the stomach. "Just like little snookems." Poke, poke. "Little muffins." The girl giggled, continuing to poke at Celeste.

Celeste slapped the girl's hand away, hard enough that you could hear the slap above the conversational din and The Rolling Stones on the stereo. Some nearby people looked our way.

"Oh, my god!" The girl clutched her wrist.

"Don't do that," Celeste ordered, still managing to sound nice, a mother scolding someone else's child. "Don't poke." She smiled sweetly at the sophomore slut-brains, the brain-sluts. "You shouldn't touch people who don't invite being touched."

The poker blushed obviously, unprepared for an immediate comeback. "And still," the other one eventually said, squaring her shoulders as if she had a good something to say, "you *do* invite it." She flicked her hands at our outfits. "You're inviting every guy here to feel you up in those."

"You shouldn't be jealous," Celeste said simply. "You're pretty. There are enough boys to go around." Celeste's delivery, her word choice, couldn't be dismissed. She was as socially adept as anyone twice her age. She would have the sophomores frazzled in thirty seconds.

As if commanded, the girls looked around the room at all the boys, then directly at their dates. The girls' reddened moon pie faces returned to Celeste and me. Both girls' heads rose and lowered, scanning our slippery, slinky, shiny, slick, seductive fronts.

"Ladies," I said primly. I curtsied then, my best low, low, jazz-class curtsy. I stood, arched my back, and blew two kisses at the sophomores.

The real beginning, ours, stood almost panting in the wings, seconds away.

The original poker reached for my long hair and grabbed a hunk. "You snotty little bitch!" she said. She pulled, and I tried to hold my ground. My curtsy was good. But now I decided it was time to practice my high kick: *thwack!* In Mrs. Diamond's fancy shoes, I kicked the girl in the ear. In the ear!

"Fight!" some guy yelled somewhere very far away.

The first girl let go of my hair under the impact of the kick, and so my head was free, but she grabbed my dress going down as she fell backward. Celeste hung on to my shoulders from behind to keep me up, but it didn't work. Evidently the other sophomore had a strong hold on Celeste's hair, and the four of us toppled onto the library floor in a polyester-sheathed heap.

"Honky Tonk Woman" was playing. We scrapped and scrabbled. I felt yanking mainly. Apparently the grabby sophomore wanted my dress. Off of me. A guy nearby clapped. Another refereed, shouting, "Below the belt, below the belt!" repeatedly, as though that was what he really wanted to see.

I was sort of afraid of getting scratched, but I didn't think about the fact that I wasn't wearing any underwear or I might have been afraid of my dress riding up. Mainly I tried to hold the wrist of the hand that was twisting and yanking and threatening to ruin my beautiful purple gift. As soon as I could I jabbed into the girl's chest with my free elbow.

The sophomore with a hold on me spit in my face.

I jabbed with my elbow again and hit soft boob flesh.

She screeched; I saw her wince close up. Finally she let go. Then somebody else, some part of one of the other two, clocked me hard in the head. My leg burned. I pushed off of the spitter and looked back to see the other sophomore raking her shoe along my shinbone just as Celeste ratcheted down on the girl's head. The crook of Celeste's arm was pinched on the girl's neck in a prowrestling move. Celeste cranked down, pulling her fist toward her body with her free hand. The sophomore pedaled her feet, trying to get out of the hold, catching me another time in the shin.

Then the spitter bit me. She *bit* me on the inside of my arm, on the thin, nervy skin right up by my pit. I howled. I screamed to beat The Stones.

And suddenly I was on my feet. Tuxedoed Charlie held me from behind by my forearms, while I watched a large older woman in a black velvet suit pull Celeste and the other girl up from the floor, still attached to each other, Celeste's arm still clamped around the girl's neck. "Stop that!" the older woman said, placing a manicured hand on each of their faces and pushing.

Celeste let go. One of her silver barrettes had shifted in the fight, and a mound of hair rose from the side of her head. The other girl's nose bled. The spitter held her tit and the ear I'd kicked. I rubbed at my shin with my other calf and ran my tongue over my lower lip, tasting blood.

"You should be ashamed of yourselves!" the older woman scolded, shaking Celeste and the other sophomore. "New Year's Eve!"

"No shit, Sherlock," the spitter dared to say to the woman.

"That's it," the woman said calmly. "You are going home. What is your name?"

The spitter clamped her mouth shut and stared defiantly.

Lynne P. suddenly appeared. "They started it, Irina!" she declared, swinging a pointing finger between the two sophomores, then gestured at Celeste and me. "*They're* my friends." The hostess always carried the clout.

Charlie spoke up then too, releasing my arms. "These two were just defending themselves," he said. Still behind me, Charlie patted and smoothed the back of my dress. My body tremoloed, it vibratoed, from the excitement. I looked around the rest of the room for the first time. The entire party seemed to have crammed itself into the library.

"It's true, Irina!" Lynne P. said emphatically. "Please don't make my friends go." Irina, evidently, was the live-in-maid-person-in-charge along with Charlie. Above Charlie.

"All right. We *will* talk about this tomorrow," Irina said under her breath to Lynne P. "You two girls have to go," she said to the sophomores.

The spitter scoffed audibly.

On cue, Charlie produced the sophomores' dates. "Time to take your dates home. Gentlemen." He gripped the guys mock-good-naturedly around the shoulders, one on either side of him. I decided Charlie was a minor god.

I have learned much about fighting since that New Year's night of 1979, and about girl-fighting in particular. I know that girls who are enraged will forget to protect their faces or breasts, but sheer instinct will usually make them protect their baby-makers; when you're fighting, it's easy to draw an opponent's fists down to guard a gut, whether that gut belongs to a guy or a girl. And I've learned that once struck, an amateur will try to protect far more than fight, will fail to punch well, will fail to react quickly enough. I've also learned that the sharper the edge and the closer to the eye, the more afraid a human will become. Unfortunately, I've also learned that all the hard-earned fight knowledge in the world makes no difference when a handgun shows up.

Oh! God bless the flesh! I gave thanks for my new appendages, painful as they were just then. Our induction was complete. Celeste and I accomplished all that freshmen girls might possibly aspire to and more. Having put our best flesh forward, in our best packaging, and having had that packaging yanked and torn asunder by unknown sophomores who helped to call attention to our new developments, we had risen exponentially in the grand scheme of high school.

Lynne P. and her brother, Charlie P., and their long-term maid and overseer, Irina, put on a grand party that night, and Celeste and I now found ourselves the stars. Every guy recognized us. Every girl recognized us. The kick-assers. The ass-kickers. The fighters. The chicks who made the freshman class proud.

A could-be-cute, blue-eyed boy I'd only known peripherally and never spoken with before told me in the kitchen, "Hair looks good." He burped into his shoulder. "The punch has . . . the punch has rum eenit now."

"Yeah?" I said. I flipped my hair from one side to the other. "Does it taste okay?" I'd never had hard liquor before. I'd never wanted to try it.

"Nah," he said, seeming kinda weird. I didn't yet know how to recognize the signs of drunkenness. "Buttit works."

His name was Jim. Two years later I'd get to know Jim very, very well, but that particular New Year's Eve, I had other, bigger game in mind. "Maybe I'll try some," I hedged, trying to be friendly.

"I'll go an' get you some."

"Um, I think I want some food first."

"Oh. Yeah. Get me to get you . . . later . . . you want some punch later."

"Okay."

"Okay."

"Well," I said, looking over Jim's shoulder, "I'm gonna . . . I'm going to go find Celeste."

"Okay." Jim waved at me with his plastic punch cup. "See you 'gator."

My fellow inexperienced Country Club Plaza High School students and I were soon to be on our merry way to "inebriation annihilation," a favorite expression of Jim's come junior year, when I often heard his retelling of "The Spiking of the Punch of 1979." Had he used rubbing alcohol that night, he wouldn't have managed to get us all drunker than he did.

I found Celeste easily enough, following the rerouted ant trail to her giant cluster. She happened to hold court as effortlessly as any preternaturally ordained being might. She saw me and called me in as she retold the story of our battle, allowing me to interject whenever I wanted. Playing court jester to Celeste's impending class ruler, I went for the humorous asides. I was the silent, slapsticky, deaf-signer-in-the-oval girl to Celeste's narrator, and I—we—had freshmen and sophomores doubled over as I pretended to bite and pull hair and kick.

"We need a toast!" someone hollered.

Lynne P., in the immediate group, yelled, "Time for punch!"

We initiated a mass drive to the watering hole, an exaggeratedly large, shell-shaped behemoth of a punch bowl protruding from the center of the dining room table. ("Well, shit," Jim would say years later, "that bowl had to've had ten gallons of 7UP and Kool-Aid in there already. We *needed* to add the three bottles of 151. You can't catch a buzz if there's not enough booze," and his blue eyes would twinkle with pride.)

Right then, before the running of the herd began, I probably should have said something about the punch being spiked, but I honestly didn't know that rum had such potential for wreaking havoc. What was a little rum? I honestly didn't know. Evidently everybody else did, though.

"To Lisa and Celeste," Lynne P. said, lifting her plastic champagne flute. Dozens went up around the room.

"To raising the standard," Charlie said, holding his dark drink aloft.

"To fights!" some guy yelled.

A lot of cheering.

We glugged the punch. All I tasted was fizzy cherry Kool-Aid—finishing with a weird back-of-the-throat sensation after I swallowed. I considered whether or not Jim might have lied to me; the punch *tasted* perfectly, normally bad. Nobody else seemed to taste anything out of the ordinary.

"Another toast! Fill 'em up!"

I turned around. It was Josh, long-gone Josh, Josh from summer camp, Josh who had ripped out my heart and chewed on it while trying to give Celeste a hickey. While I'd thought about Josh plenty in the three years since camp, nothing kind really came to mind during those pointless ruminations.

At Josh's loud suggestion of a toast, Celeste shot me a look. After the shadow of the events of Camp Evergreenshade had finally thinned to a mere sliver, we both had decided that neither of us would pursue William or Josh. They weren't worth the wedge they would have shoved between us. I shrugged my shoulders at Celeste.

People had already bellied up again. Lynne P. sloppily passed the glass ladle over the tops of outstretched flutes. More people came in. The ivory linen tablecloth began its inevitable decline toward a Grateful Dead mottled fuchsia.

"To the ladies!" Josh shouted. "To Colt and Celeste!"

"To the kickers of ass!"

Eventually kids started dipping their flutes into the bowl and changing to bigger cups. Somebody switched out the music. Jim Morrison purred and rumbled, and Lynne P. told us to go dance in the foyer instead of the sitting room. Irina continued to bring out pans of finger food and plunk them into warmer trays over Sterno canisters.

The Times Square ball drop led us on the P.s' TV. We screamed from ten on down, buzzing the windowpanes.

Somebody took hold of my arm from behind and spun me around. "Happy New Year." Hard knock of teeth on my own. Wet lips. Grab of my thigh. Yuck. I pushed the body away from me. It belonged to a creep from algebra.

The foyer and living room were awash, a swelling crush of limbs and bodies. Another one, some body, grabbed my shoulders and pulled me left. I saw Celeste get pulled right not more than five feet away by William. Good ol' William. She saw me, too. Celeste caught my glance in the swift tide and then she was gone.

"Hi." Josh's face rose in front of me.

"Hi."

On my shoulders, Josh's hands, hot, unholy, burned to my fluttering core. I wish I could say he was unwelcome. Instead I wanted to swallow his entire head. I wanted to grow a snake's or frog's tongue to unfurl down his throat.

"Happy New Year, Colt," Josh said. "You look *so* good."

"Thanks."

He kissed me: a sweet, essentially perfect, perfectly essential kiss. In that first moment I fully imagined Josh kissing Celeste at camp, but then I succeeded in forgetting. Josh kissed me, and my body before my brain noted his perfect balance, his delicate measure of pull and press.

"Kiss me back," Josh said.

What? Wasn't I? I thought I had been.

I leaned into Josh with all of my small weight, smashing a breast against his shirt buttons, and tried to copy his mouth motions with my own. A new warmth bounded, puppylike, up my spine from my pelvis.

So this was what drove the masses.

Josh had grown early and grown well since sixth grade, one of the few boys in our freshman class to do so. I felt his chest muscles flex beneath his oxford.

He pulled away. "That's more like it," he said, smiling. My body agreed. He wrapped his arms around mine, picked me up, and pivoted 180 degrees. He set me down and spun me. When he stopped, I faced William.

"Happy New Year, gorgeous," William said and proceeded to stuff an ashtray-tasting tongue past my guffaw. I kept my eyes open but didn't shove William off like I should have, brute shit that he was. He kissed me while I watched Josh take Celeste's face in his hands, turn it, pull her ear to his lips, and say something that made her smile.

What had he said? She returned Josh's gesture, saying something close in his ear.

"What is that?" William asked me, abruptly pulling away from his relentless pursuit of tonsils. He caught me with one eye half-open. "What are you doing?"

"Huh?" I responded dumbly.

"What are you, in a coma?"

Obviously William wanted me to kiss him back, too. You know what I thought then? I thought, "Fuck you, William. Get your mean, mean fingers and your stinky tongue away from me." What I said was, "Happy New Year," and pushed straight past him, banging my shoulder purposely into his arm.

I stepped to Celeste. Celeste and Josh. They were, like weirdo Frenchmen, loudly kissing each other's cheeks on both sides, back and forth. Then they laughed. They made me smile, I was so relieved. And then a guy, a pimpled, cowlicked tenor from Glee Club, lunged my way.

"Whoa, there, sport." Charlie! Charlie! It was Charlie to my rescue, one hand on the tenor's chest, the other hand on the back of his neck.

"Happy New Year!" I yelled to Charlie. Oh, I really wanted Charlie. "My hero," I said, blowing punch breath at him. "My man divine. My anti-Hamlet! You one-who-acts, you!" I flinged. I flung. I surely catapulted myself at Charlie's manly-man college-boy being, his dark hair and dark drink and expensive tuxedo that fit far too well not to have been his own, and I kissed him madly. Like Jim Morrison sang about, or so I thought.

But Charlie barely kissed back before he stopped, and, oh, no, Josh and Celeste stood watching. They'd found me. Found me out.

"Hey!" the tenor said grumpily.

Celeste remembered that we had to call her dad. "He's too old for you, of course, you know," she announced as we climbed the winding staircase to use Lynne P.'s bedroom phone.

"Who, Charlie?" Of course I knew who she meant.

"You know who I mean."

"Charlie," I stated.

"Josh has always liked you," she said.

"Bull." She knew better. And I knew better.

"I has," she said. "He told me so."

"You just said, 'I has.'" We bumped through the hallway leading to Lynne P.'s room. Did I need to be embarrassed about kissing Charlie?

"I did not," Celeste said.

"What?"

"I didn't say 'I has.'" We opened Lynne P.'s bedroom door. Pink carpeting undulated within; a lace-covered canopy bed laden with white and pink stuffed animals bobbed in the center of the room.

"Yes, you did."

"Josh has always liked you," Celeste said.

"You—we should call your dad."

Lynne P. staggered in. "He loved it," she said.

"Huh?"

"He told me, 'I curse you for your friends,' and then he said, 'I can't kiss a ninth-grader, damn it.'"

He swore about me? "He swore about me?"

"I just *said* he said, 'I curse you for your friends. I can't kiss a ninth-grader, even if I wanted to.'"

"You skipped him saying he wanted to," I said, grinning despite myself. He wanted to kiss me back! Charlie in his tuxedo with that hair wanted to kiss me back!

"Charlie farts," Lynne P. said. She backed up toward her bedroom door. "I grew up with him. In the bathtub." She butted into the knob. "With bubble bath. To make bubbles. Are we going downstairs or what?"

On the phone, Mr. Diamond told us we weren't eating enough.

Someone had thrown up in the kitchen sink, and nobody was saying who. Irina frowned as she dealt with it, cleaning pukey dishes with the vegetable sprayer. She turned on the garbage disposal. Kids scattered like flies off kicked shit.

In the foyer, the midnight kissing had stopped and the serious dancing had begun. The marble floor tiles were wet and dirty, but nobody seemed to care. Disco screamed from the stereo, several years out-of-date but conducive for optimal contact with the opposite sex. All the dancers did the bump until some of the guys decided to bump too hard, sending girls flailing into the walls. Suddenly Celeste got it in her head for us to do one of our routines from jazz class.

I had slipped one of Lynne P.'s bikini bottoms on over the outside of my nylons. I don't know what I was thinking. I wanted to keep my dress on. My dress had gotten me kisses. But I wanted to do high kicks without worrying, and the bottoms were all I could find. Celeste and I scootched the others off the floor and wiped it down with some embroidered hand towels. At the same time, we pointed our fingers and said, "Hit it!" to our Glee Club lackey manning the stereo.

The Emotions sang "Best of My Love," and Celeste and I spun and stepped and kicked as high as we'd ever kicked. We wiggled our little hips in some attempt of groovin', and we really did get there. We could dance for sure. Again we drew a crowd, and lots of people clapped. A few girls clapped lightly, I noticed, maybe a bit sourly. They were just drunk, I decided.

I can still see Celeste dancing, and it's how I remember myself, how I imagine myself too, dancing the same steps. Her big smile, her hair swinging, her hands moving fast, her bottom cute as a peach. Innocence and sex wrapped up in a tight package, the best I'd ever be.

After the dancing but before the making out came the fire. Some beer-drinking sophomore guy had started lighting paper napkins from the Sterno cans, and Lynne P.'s dining room table went up. He swore he'd put the napkins out completely, but with everybody oddly, momentarily turned away from the detritus, the nearly empty punch bowl and the crumbs and oily cheese slices and limp parsley sprigs, the table suddenly burst into flames. That's what the closest witnesses told the firemen, even though Irina had already put the fire out with the extinguisher by the time they arrived.

That's how the whole party got kicked out into the snow, and how I came to be making out with Josh against the neighbor's lumpy stone house. All over the place horny, wriggling teenagers waited for their rides.

Josh pushed down the top of my dress and had me turn Mona's fur coat inside out and put it back on. Then he unbuttoned his shirt! He took it off, pressing his bare chest into the coat with me, palming my new breasts. I could barely breathe. It was the sexiest thing I could have imagined. Something chemical and horribly powerful raced around my body and made me heady.

An arm's reach to my left, her body flattened against the same house, stood Celeste with some guy's face at her chest. As Josh moved his warm mouth down my neck toward my nipples, I watched Celeste roll her eyes toward the night sky and heard the crisp scrape of her fingernails on the stone. I looked up, too. Bright stars, sharp pinpoints of light, filled the entire rectangular, framed view between the houses. The past few painful years disappeared into the magical suck.

Lynne P. was grounded for two months. The dining room table had been an antique. Celeste hadn't been lying about Josh liking me, at least not in 1979. Josh and I fondled and fumbled around on our way to sophomore year, never really committing to couple-dom. We wanted so many people, so much. Charlie P. went back to college, and Celeste and I went on to high school celebrity status.

We never looked back.

You don't even make it inside the club. You stand with her next to the others in a ragged loop in the parking lot and pass around a jug of grape-flavored rotgut and a jar of pig poppers and spit-soaked clove cigarettes and a box cutter. In that order you slug and huff and smoke and slice your own initials into the skin on the underside of your arm. Watch how your flesh opens in red maws with the pulling of the rusty blade. Count the number of people who have done this before you.

You have some of her, of all of them, in your skin now, in you.

Huff more and listen to the world echo itself.

Stare at palm trees with their limbs ruffling like huge bird feathers in the night wind. Decide that the trees do not go with the parking lot. Decide that the trees do not go with purple hair. Decide that the trees do not go with scars or the plaid sofa that tilts on the edge of the asphalt as though it were dying. Decide that the trees belong someplace else.

As ICING coated as a gingerbread house, sophomore year came and went, a sickly-sweet and nearly perfect dream for the two of us Renaissance women. We spoke French in the halls to each other. Girls and guys both joined the Glee Club in droves. (Mr. Dolan couldn't believe that first crowded Tuesday morning. He almost dropped his coffee along with the sheet music when he walked in.) Mrs. Diamond kept up the payments to the Plaza Dance Academy, and we kept up our ends, our chins, our kicks and attitudes. We refined our beurre blanc, our ratatouille, our chocolate mousse, our piecrust, our gravy, our presentation.

Unquestionably, too, we flaunted our weaknesses, lest we be viewed as less than human. Celeste could not, for the life of her, create one single thing with clay that didn't list, tilt, buckle, or collapse. I, for that matter, could not render a bowl of fruity orbs or an arrangement of dusty wine bottles for all the charcoal in the world. Still, we fell in lust with the art world of Kansas City, such as it was, over the summer before junior year.

The Nelson-Atkins Museum of Art presented its pillared facade not far from our high school. Across the street from the museum sat a collection of converted old mansions and full-frontal contemporary buildings that comprised the Kansas City Art Institute. Walt Disney was said to have attended the Institute long ago but hadn't graduated. The reason as to why he'd dropped out was not entirely clear, but the two overriding rumors seemed to center around his purported homosexuality and/or his taking a bunch of acid and drawing cartoon characters for all of his assigned projects—talking mice and the like.

Celeste and I had grown bored of hanging out at her pool all day, lying around in the sun. Reading or discussing guys only went so far. And the usual parties had become exactly that—the usual parties.

As good kids might want to do, we went looking for some clean diversion. Actually, we went looking for new guys, guys we didn't know. I'm not sure whose idea it was to check out the neighborhood around the museum and the art school, but that's where we set out to forage, to find some older, better, arty guys, guys who cared about more than sports, possibly an older European visitor-type exchange kind of guy. We set out in short shorts and bikini tops, all the better for shopping the numerous balconies of the adjacent apartment buildings, student housing, and campus dormitories.

Slogging through the July heat on our first excursion out, flip-flops slapping, we encountered no new guys. The sun beat down mercilessly, and we frowned and squinted. (Sunglasses would have left terrible raccoon-eye tans.) We understood quickly that we were idiots, roaming the melting blacktop streets and ant-frying sidewalks in the middle of the day. Where were the guys? We surmised that the interesting European ones with whom we would try out our French had to be in some air-conditioned location. Some life-drawing class—god, to get a naked *guy* for a model!—or some restaurant, or some wood-paneled room at the Nelson-Atkins Museum proper. But you couldn't get into the museum showing so much skin, so we hoofed it back to the Diamond house, cursing the fact that neither Celeste's parents nor my dad would loan or buy us a car.

We changed into jeans and faded summer Izods, and returned to the museum to pay our student dollar. Inside, the central atrium rose for stories. The cool of the stone and concrete and the air all around us made Celeste's arms pebble with gooseflesh. I shivered and let my eyes adjust. Suits of armor flanked the halls leading to the galleries. Egyptian pottery rested inside tomblike glass cases. From the right came the distinct sounds of dining, of cutlery noise and genteel conversation and ice in glasses. We followed the smells of real ingredients wafting our way.

Past an archway an enormous room appeared, and this second tree-decorated atrium swarmed with people eating lunch. The patrons all had "the look," paint-splattered and rumpled or mon-eyed and tweeded. The patrons wore their superior aesthetics on their sleeves. At least that's what their plated chicken breast and new asparagus seemed to say: The painters didn't paint houses and the tweeds didn't hunt foxes. They didn't need to bother with *real* work. Well, they didn't have to work a regular schedule, at any rate, as many a painter had to buy gesso and canvas and many an original trophy wife had to get on the horse at some point.

Busers, the bus people—drones, we would soon learn to call them—picked up dishes and refilled tea and looked down their young noses at the diners. One female bus person sprouted blue tufts of hair from her temples like horns. Another guy had hair the color of blood, fresh-sprung, thick and scary. A tall, thin, graceful, adept, smiling, Chinese-looking person of completely indecipherable sex bused the tables, too, his or her chin-length hair a shiny, flirty curtain.

Celeste and I had found our venue. "Do you have any money?" she asked.

I dug in my jeans pocket as I surveyed the room. I didn't feel uneasy. I saw no one I knew, but lots of people I'd like to. I loved the sensation of the place immediately and wondered why it'd taken us so long to get there. "Yeah. Twenty . . . two, three, twenty-eight dollars."

"Let's eat something," Celeste said, heading toward the incomparably chic cafeteria line. Waiting and watching a really hand-some scooping-serving guy with five (five!) little silver ring earrings and short hair so severely short that without the earrings you would have thought he was in the military, I was suddenly reminded of Christmas trees. The workers fought their bland uniforms with color and shine and glitter. These people, I realized, feeling clever, were their own pieces of art.

In short order, Celeste and I got to know the servers. We infiltrated the staff deftly by tipping atypically well for a couple of high school–looking girls and—well, fuck it, fine, I admit it—eating at the art museum nearly every weekday for the rest of the summer.

Celeste had the sense to have us stop wearing upper-body insignia. No more Polos or Izods. Plain or bizarre T-shirts replaced our preppy shirts, and we opted for the oldest jeans in our dressers. Thread by thread we unwove perfectly good blue-jean knees—you couldn't have the holes looking like you'd just made them. I can only imagine how neon-bright our want had been those first few weeks, how baldly we had been courting attention. I'm embarrassed just to think about the deliberateness of our plan, the extra mascara, the switch of shoes, the attempts at "unusual" hair without actual cutting or dyeing.

There was a core of seven Kansas City Art Institute students who worked regularly at the Nelson-Atkins dining room. Surely by the time the troops broke down and decided to include Celeste and me, it had become a matter of pity, or more likely a matter of fuckability, a five-syllable system by which every visible human was rated. Celeste and I did rate high on the fuckability scale.

It was Brooklyn who bridged the gap. Formerly Brooke, Brooklyn was a server with a black-dyed, spiked weed patch of hair. (All of the crew could be immediately identified by hair alone.) Brooklyn was in the process of becoming a man, although she still happened to be in the money-saving stages for counseling and surgery and airfare.

Taking her time to water us and compliment some something of our beings—always startlingly observant and frighteningly honest compliments along the lines of "Your thighs look very strong" or "Your eyebrows are perfectly raw" or "You wouldn't need to wear a bra if you didn't want to"—Brooklyn trotted out the other busers one by one, instructing them to wipe or snatch or refill at our table.

"Drone Mack Truck," Brooklyn said as the guy with the blood-red hair lazily ran a drippy rag over our glass tabletop.

"Drone Pia Stream," Brooklyn barked when an itty-bitty

blonde minced by. "Come here." Pia did as she was told. "These tasty young women would like to meet us. Pia, Lisa, Lisa, Pia."

"Hello," I said as casually as I could.

Pia just looked at Brooklyn.

"Say 'hello' back, you bitch," Brooklyn said lowly.

"Hello," Pia tinkled, her voice light and sugared. We would come to learn she sprinkled and sprayed when told and that she was a slave of sorts, belonging exclusively to Brooklyn.

"Pia, Celeste, Celeste, Pia."

Again, Pia looked only to Brooklyn. We hadn't put anything together yet, and Pia's behavior confused Celeste, I could tell, as much as it did me. "Say 'hello'!" Brooklyn pushed.

"Hello," Pia said nicely again.

"Go away," Brooklyn instructed.

We met all seven within two lunches. Brooklyn had held the position at the art museum restaurant the longest, making her the head drone, or boss of the busers. We met Drone Blue Rose, the girl with blue hair thorns at her temples, and Drone Ing, the truly genderless Chinese person whose drone name, when directed toward another drone, indicated wishy-washiness, as in, "Stop Inging and make up your fucking mind." We met the drone who made us drool, the very handsome and pierced Drone Ess—"Like the letter, but spelled E-S-S."

The spelling information, evidently, proved you to be an insider. Ess was often asked what the S stood for, being the singer in his own band. He would tell each and every inquirer something different. An ongoing, underground argument revolved around whether S stood for Satan, See More, or Saliva. Ess apparently was not necessarily always creative and had repeated his top suggestions for the capital letter more than a few times. Celeste and I decided, dopily, that the nonexistent S stood for Sexy.

We also met the seventh, Drone Gigantus Khan, said to have a huge cock hanging between his scrawny, pale legs. Gigantus Khan spoke in a put-on British accent, having visited London with his family for a summer when he was eight. He claimed to have been greatly influenced by the dialect because he had been in the pivotal formative year of his youth, and thus simply couldn't help it. Nobody particularly liked Gigantus Khan. He was retained as a sort of sideshow ringer, one that was put up against the freaky keepers of other tribes at hardcore shows when needed. A secret weapon, albeit with a shitty British accent. The runt with the gigantic wanker. "Shall I free my willy?" he used to ask. Years later when the movie came out, I laughed out loud at the ridiculous title.

All too soon, however, Celeste and I had to return to Country Club Plaza High School, just two weeks after the drones them-selves had returned to KCAI and largely disappeared from the restaurant at the art museum.

Still, the museum itself intrigued us more than a bit, and even after the busing staff changed its weekday face, we continued to visit for both the food and the art. I loved the primitive pieces for what I could imagine, for the hands through which the pottery and fertility figures must have passed, for the strange worlds I would have loved to experience for more than just an hour or two. Celeste, on the other hand, seemed drawn to the classical paint-ings, like a butterfly to hollyhock. But then I could sculpt; she could draw. Perhaps our predilections made a little sense.

Junior year, year of the PSATs, ultimately took Celeste and me deep into the realms of test anxiety, precalculus cramming, and vocabulary quizzes, and so our summer fling with the unusual faded into the past, a crated donation in storage. We would revisit before the year was over, but by the outset of our second junior quarter, we just didn't have time for artistic drones.

In February that fated year, when every brown, ice-coated lawn crunched underfoot, when the bitter prairie wind came stalking to kill everything it could with its cold breath, when granular snow hard as grit scratched at every exposed surface, my mother, Janice Joy, froze.

We remaining three stalwart Smiths were used to her turns for the worse, turn after turn, but this was The One. What happened was that word got out. I always figured the leak came from my younger brother, David, being what younger brothers always are with a family secret: just plain bad. Unfortunately my usual mean dismissal of my mother may have had something to do with it as well. I complained about my mother to Celeste without paying much attention to the classmates around us who might have been listening in. I jabbed at Janice Joy in the cafeteria, whining about how my mother uselessly took up space. In the halls I bitched about how her room stank. Whatever cruel fastball I could smack Janice Joy's way as Celeste and I played indoor tennis in gym class, I did. I know now that I used my mother to redirect the pressure of too much homework and the slow-cooker temperatures of a college-prep high school, of adolescence, of having a goddess of a best friend, but it's hard not to feel guilty. I might have been responsible, too.

After The One, Janice Joy went away. The rest of us put her away. I try, try, try not to feel guilty. Engaging in guilt, like worry, doesn't do a damn bit of good, you know?

I had a boyfriend a few months after my daughter was born who told me about his dog that he had to put down because it licked and chewed itself into being put down. The dog had these hot spots, my boyfriend said. It licked first at some invisible something in its coat, then chewed away the hair, and then chewed at its own skin, and then licked and chewed away at these noncancerous, non-flea-ridden, nonallergic spots till its flesh bled, bled and wept and oozed and bled, and the dog made more spots, and made the spots bigger, and if a spot was over a bone, it gnawed down to its own bone. The boyfriend was a decent man who didn't abuse the dog, I don't think. The dog licked and chewed because it hurt, and it hurt because it licked and chewed. But the crux lies with the initial nibble, doesn't it? Starting a new hot spot, giving in to the desire to begin another time.

The same goes for guilt and worry. So, I try not to worry. And I try not to feel guilty about my mother. What can ever be undone? I can't take back what I said about her. But it's hard knowing how contemptible I was, how horrible I was behind her back. And right to her face. I swear I understand that poor, sick dog better than I do a lot of people.

So, somehow word got out that our mother was one of the undead. The murmuring bothered me at school, sure, tugged at my teenage guts to deny what I heard, to fight for her, but I knew the time was as right as any to get rid of my nearly literal closet ghost. Her outing had come. And so I decided to unite with the persecutors in attitude if not action. A small part of me relished the name-calling of the person whom I most despised, the person whose love I never felt. I had wanted a real mother so badly. . . . I joined the mad masses, at least in spirit, to bring forth the creature, to call the monster by her name and be rid of her for good.

After days of my feeling the burbling undercurrent, two boys from my brother David's class got loud about Janice Joy, late during fifth-period lunch. Wanda, Celeste, and I were flicking a triangular paper football over finger goalposts and drilling one another on the week's worth of irregular French verbs. One of the boys, a cocky little jerk who wore his Docksiders with the heels purposely broken and flattened, said from the neighboring table, laughing, "Well, the *Smith mother* is retarded."

A second boy, one with bangs and slitty eyes, laughed and looked our way. "Naw. She can't talk at all. That makes her a mute, you *retard*." Both of them laughed and slapped their table till the first boy knocked over his half-empty soda can.

Celeste stopped conjugating, caught our paper football, and held it in her hands, staring pointedly at the boys.

"You are *way* wrong," Docksiders said. "Mutes don't shit their pants!" They both laughed again, fake and loud as hell, purposely knocking around their lunch garbage. Cheese puffs sprinkled across our table.

Celeste flicked the football at Docksiders. It caught him square in the forehead. "You are *so* wrong," Celeste said. Unhesitatingly. Of course.

He looked at Celeste and blinked. "That's not what I heard," he said.

"She's not sick is what I heard," the slitty-eyed boy said. "She's a *lunatic.*" He retrieved our football from the puddle of spilled Coke and flicked it back to us. Wanda grabbed it out of the air.

"Bull," Celeste told him.

Celeste was sticking up for me again, and I had the odd urge to tell her not to, so instead I said to the boy, "Yeah, she is *craaazy*. So what?" I jerked my chin up an inch.

"She—" And then the boy stopped. "Cool," he said.

"No, it's not," I said, paused, then added, "She uses the toilet." I wanted to tack on, *But she doesn't flush*, but didn't. As if she'd read my mind, she let me have it: Celeste's kick under the table left a bruise.

That night, sometime after eleven o'clock, the show began on the front lawn of our house. I was asleep, but evidently for their extremely short production, the cast wore pajamas and paper bags over their heads à la *The Gong Show's* Unknown Comic. That's what our father said to the police. The screeching of car tires woke David and me up. "It was just a dark car down the street," he told the uniformed team sitting properly in our living room after midnight. "A shiny car. Like it'd had a washing recently."

The boys evidently drove off right after my father opened the front door and turned on the outdoor lights. I can picture him, rushing out into the frozen dark, trying to make sense of what was happening. The last boy had to light two matches. The first that he tossed toward the lawn went out in the air. But with the second match, the lighter fluid took. And the words the boys had spelled out flamed to life. The words that clearly only my mother could read from the second floor.

I'd love to know why my father didn't resod. I think sometimes about asking him still. How expensive could it have been? It was ridiculous, terrible. Instead, he just reseeded over the burned black letters in spring. The words grew brighter green than the rest of the lawn until August of the next year. The verdant letters. KILL THE FREAK! they read. The exclamation mark dribbled away in splotches toward the direction of the getaway car, across the corner of the Nielsons' yard. Dad reseeded the Nielsons' dribble marks too.

Poof. Janice Joy saw it all, and afterward failed to rise for anything. Not for anything. My brother, David, spent the night at a friend's house, and I made sure to sleep over at the Diamonds' the day the expensive people my father had hired took my mother to the home, so early in the morning that none of the neighbors were witness to the occasion. The expensive people had practice in such transfers, and they evidently moved Janice Joy without incident.

The look that surely crossed my father's face must have been one of . . . one of what? I couldn't have guessed what his features must have given up as his wife plodded down the front walk, never looking back. It's the one bit of information he ever gave us: "She never looked back."

She, on the other hand, I imagined clearly, stood at the window staring at the fiery letters with amazement that night, the slight heat of her palms leaving no mark on the panes. She watched and breathed a heavy sigh of relief. Her excuse had finally come. Her excuse to pee the bed and refuse to eat the regular crumbs and not to make the insane effort to rise again had finally come. She'd been delivered. As her husband made his futile dashing way down the street after the getaway car, her heavy and grateful sigh left a mist on the pane. She drew a heart in her own breath and pierced it with an arrow. I swear I thought I could picture her doing it.

The casting out of my mother took some work to get over, if I must be honest. Her undoing couldn't have come at a worse time in terms of my psychological maturation. When alone, I slept fitfully. I bit my toenails while I studied at night. My brother caught me once and threatened to tell everyone that I pretended to be a monkey in my room when nobody saw. I picked at anything: my nose, a scab, my scalp, the tiny hairs on the back of my arms with my teeth. I brimmed with restlessness. I felt like I could stick my finger in a socket and make my ears light up for all the pent-up energy I had.

The Diamonds added another couple of suppers to the preexisting schedule, allowing my father to get in some much-needed one-on-one bonding with his unruly teenage son. Celeste and I cooked most every night at her house, and I spent the night at least twice a week. They made me think it was my idea. A couple years later, during one of our long-distance telephone conversations, Celeste let me know that my father and her parents had hammered out a sort of intervention for me. I'd had no idea I'd needed any such thing or that plans were put into effect behind my back.

I realize now what a fool I had to have been, becoming the ass that I did, but I felt free! Crazy free! I'm sure I hurt horribly, but all I remember is being daring, being adventurous, being willing to try anything once. Or twice. Free, free, free!

Jim—remember him from the New Year's Eve party? the punch spiker?—played basketball, and played it well. I liked basketball least of all the regular guy sports, but our varsity team, by some accounts, was heading toward the play-offs. Jim was the second-best player and still only a junior. He'd grown spectacularly in all ways since our first encounter, and without even the specter of a mother anymore, I'd grown suddenly reckless. In a few mere weeks, while picking at pieces of myself in private, I'd become a brash thing in public. Celeste and I had our ever-present following. Of course, I'd remained the clown of the two of us, wisecracking Bones to handsome Captain Kirk. But suddenly I couldn't contain myself in any way. I needed to fill myself up with attention, all the attention I hadn't gotten from Janice Joy all those years, I suppose. And the more attention I received from guys, the better.

Jim, I decided, would be the one to give me what I needed.

"I can't *believe*," Celeste said.

"I *know*," I said. We'd come to our first basketball game of the year at the urging of classmates. Walking in, we were amazed at the number of students and overzealous parents who filled the bleachers already, the game still fifteen minutes away. Why weren't they doing homework? I pretended to fall walking up the bleachers. A freshman girl gasped. Celeste saw my move in the making and caught me easily in my standard position, one of my dancing legs high, tennis shoe toe pointed. We smiled and waved at classmates. A guy whistled. But really—why weren't they doing homework? The past two nights we'd done extra in Honors English and European History to make room for the game. (Our report cards only ever varied by a plus or minus here and there. PSATs: I took her in math; she beat me in verbal.) "Guess KU is calling their names," I added, sitting down.

"KU is fine—"

"I know KU is . . ." Two of our team members jogged to their bench and pulled off their warm-up pants. The sight of their bare legs, in shorts, in the middle of winter, stirred something under my breastbone. ". . . it's okay, but you know what I mean."

"If it's the only place that gave somebody money—yeah," Celeste said, "I know what you mean." Occasionally we found it difficult to belie the advantaged girls that we were. KU pretty much stank.

Jim jogged over to our team's bench then and started talking to Coach Wolfsheim. Jim nodded and shook his legs one by one, then his arms, then started again with his legs, his head bowed to the short coach. Random voices in the bleachers called out, "Jim!" or whistled more and shouted dumb, wordless crowd ululations, howls and barks. And then. Then Jim took off his warm-ups. It couldn't have been simpler or less intellectualized. I looked at his legs and made my decision, however unconscious at the time. The instinct to perpetuate the species attacked my brain like an ax.

"Come in, Lisa," Celeste said.

I grinned stupidly and turned to Celeste. "When did he get so cute?"

"I don't know," Celeste answered sincerely. The senior center came off the court toward Jim then, a ball tucked under his arm. He looked like a man. He could have been an astronaut or a senator already. The notion scared me a little, and when the center took off his warm-ups, the dense hair on his legs made me feel small, young. A man like that could hurt me. He could lie on me in a bed, and I wouldn't be able to escape. Or be able to breathe. The swarthy center lifted his five-o'clock-shadowed face to the crowd and looked around. His eyes found me. Or Celeste. Us. Jim looked at the center, and then Jim found us, too. I smiled my flirtiest half smile and wiggled a few fingers at him in a wave. Jim smiled and lowered his head. The center stared. Lechery, I believed, darkened his brow.

"Stay away from the center, what's-his-name," I warned Celeste.

"Why?" Her lavender angora sweater made her eyes glow, reminding me of a fifties pinup calendar. At the moment she approximated April, or maybe May.

"He's scary," I said.

"You think so? Naaaw."

"He is. Look how hairy his legs are."

"Hair doesn't make him scary. He's . . . he's just hairy, not scary." We giggled.

Some girls we hung out with during lunch period sat down next to us, and we all talked about what we'd had for supper and the family trees of European monarchies. We suspected a pop quiz the next day. Just then the loud buzzer sounded, and the chaotic-looking bouncing and running on the court stopped as the two teams gathered at their benches. Our school's stiff cheerleaders cheered a peppy cheer. The smell of popcorn and hot dogs wafted in through the sets of double doors. Somebody dropped a soda can. A fart. An answering belch. A few mean-faced teachers scanned the seats for the culprits. More whistling. But I only had eyes for Jim.

Jim moved better than the other guys out there, I decided early in the game. He seemed more graceful somehow without looking faggy—Grecian, or Roman, in the way that you might imagine the original Olympians looking, only Jim was obviously taller than they would have been. I wanted to sculpt Jim out of clay in art class and give his own likeness to him as a gift: Here, here you go.

See your jersey number? There, on the back. I could've written Jim an ode.

The hairy center, Jim, and one other guy, another senior, seemed to have a plan going that worked well. I couldn't really figure it out, but the three of them kept making all the baskets. By half-time, our team was ahead by eighteen points. Jim and the others retreated to the locker room. The pom-pom girls galloped onto the floor and began a terrible dance routine. Celeste and I looked at each other, bug-eyed. We were so much better, but, oh, well.

"Who's their choreographer?" Celeste asked.

"They do their own," said one of our lunch-period acquaintances, Jordan. "I don't understand why they put themselves through this week after week." Jordan's skiing tan had started to fade, although her nose still presented the pink, tight-skinned results of a terrible burn. She was the sort of girl who never touched zinc oxide, sensitive as she was about the size of her nose already. White expands, we all knew. Black recedes. Perhaps if black zinc oxide had existed, Jordan would have used it. Still, Jordan was generous, acerbic, droll. "Oh, look. The poor dears."

The pom-pom squad consisted of six somewhat unpopular girls who, despite jeers and general disapproval, shook about for every sport in every season they were able, field hockey, wrestling, and water polo included. They were very bad.

"It *is* hard to figure out why they would continue," Celeste agreed.

"They're so . . ." I searched. ". . . so—oh, god!" The biggest of the pom-pom girls had just gone to jump-kick when her supporting ankle twisted gruesomely beneath all her weight. I watched the heavy girl wince and flop into an ungraceful kneel. Laughs erupted in the bleachers. The girl's squad continued, but now in a confused and halfhearted way, as if their actions were suddenly sacrilegious. The heavy girl stood and hobbled off, twirling her hand in a gesture that indicated the others should finish. "That had to kill," I said. Nobody applauded the exiting casualty.

Some guy shouted, "That's right, lard-ass!"

The pom-pom squad didn't really have a coach or anyone else

in charge, Jordan told us. They ordered and paid for their own costumes.

"That must have *killed*," I repeated.

Celeste looked in her lap, then bit at the writing callus on her middle finger.

"We must remember, 'survival of the fittest,'" Jordan remarked, adding, "Anyone want popcorn?"

"I do," another lunch-period girl answered.

"Is the butter real?" Celeste asked.

Jordan looked into her own eyebrows.

"No, then," Celeste said. "I'm going to go to the bathroom."

"Same here," the other lunch-period girl chimed, following Celeste down the bleacher stairs.

"Do you know Jim?" I asked Jordan. "The player—"

"I know who you mean. He lives two blocks away from me." Jordan *tsk*ed and shook her head. Jordan didn't date inside our school district for some reason.

I smiled. "He made a pass at me freshman New Year's."

"Ah, yes," she said. "Your coming-out party. As it were."

"You're *not* being nice."

"Never, darling, never. He's a . . . I don't know . . . bird of a different feather? I've never seen him with a girl. And he's not shy, either. Just, he seems so involved. Or maybe preoccupied . . . You know."

Jim wasn't the sort of guy you suspected of being gay. Maybe he had a girlfriend outside the district. "What's with him?"

"Go ask him after the game. I dare you, Lisa. Crack that shy boy out of his shell. Want some popcorn? Oh! Do you want a raffle ticket? They're giving away a limo ride for Sadie Hawkins."

The dance! I could ask Jim to the dance. I could ask him and get him to pick me up and play pony with me on his big knees in the back of a limo. Or something like that. I wanted that. "Love one," I said.

"A raffle ticket it is," Jordan said.

"Would you get Celeste to come back? I need to ask—"

Jordan wagged her finger at me. "You two should never, ever vie."

"Who's vying?"

"You know better than that," she said somberly.

"What?" Did Celeste like Jim? I didn't think so.

"There's an expression, darling: Never shit where you eat."

I laughed as if I understood. Jordan left for popcorn and raffle tickets. More often than not expressions like that, the kind a kid might call "grown-up" expressions, left me truly perplexed. I blamed it on my unsophisticated father and absent mother. The sort of savvy so many of my classmates possessed skipped me over entirely, though I always tried to play along. I'd been denied a slice of adulthood, somehow, and it'd take me ages to catch up. Ketchup. So what. I'd make up whatever I lacked in other ways. Quickly. Fast, fast. Gimme my cake. It was time to fuck.

Celeste lagged behind, like I said. I should have let her stay there. I really should have.

She came back and sat down next to me. "I think she broke it," she said, a piece of black tissue paper stuck to her lavender sweater.

"What?"

"Kira."

"Who?"

"Kira. You know, who fell."

"Oh, yeah." It looked like it had killed. We won the game by twenty-six.

I always found the expression "losing your virginity" stupid and sort of technically incorrect. Celeste and I knew that virginity didn't actually mean an intact hymen. Which was good, since William the finger fucker had done away with mine long ago. Still, I couldn't help wishing it had been more tangible, as though I'd really given up something. A piece of me, you know, something along the lines of an appendix or tonsils. Still have your tonsils? No, lost 'em years ago, heh, heh. Wink, wink. I don't know. Nothing was gone. If anything really changed it was just that now even more of the outside world managed to stuff its way into us.

You know, when a portion of you is filled with a piece of someone else, you can't help becoming some smaller percentage of the total. If you are a woman, technically you constitute less of the aggregate when being fucked than before the fucking. Assuming the outer borders of your own body are the actual limits of the measured entity, of the circle, of self, you are, by definition, less yourself when having sex.

I somehow wanted it to be different. Here. Have an earlobe. Oh, no, I have more. Keep it. Go on, as a memento, a part of me. Have it. My virginity. I insist. I'm *giving* it to you.

Yes, my decision to offer up my virginity was voluntary. (And in his family's attic, Jim was kind and sweet.)

I suppose Celeste's offering was voluntary, too, insofar as she'd had control enough at the time to say, "Keith, we should have sex now." In the grass, by the War Memorial, at night.

Imagine his reaction. Imagine looking at a young woman such as Celeste was then, the purest, most unadulterated beauty around for thousands of miles, her beauty incontestable all the way to the towering mountains of Colorado, to the Great Lakes of the North, to the vast cotton seas of the South, to the far reaches of the Eastern shore. Her beauty was wide-ranging and complete, enough to challenge any goddess'. And, lo and behold, enter the beauty's mortal of the moment, Keith. Keith the water-polo player. Lucky, lucky Keith.

It hurt, she said, a lot. Later she would know that, by comparison to most guys, Keith was hung like a minotaur, notwithstanding the Speedo that had made it all look so manageable. For a minute she hadn't even thought that they'd be able to do it, and then they did, and it stung so much her eyes watered, although she wanted to make sure I knew that she hadn't cried.

She healed quickly and told Keith somewhat unkindly that she wasn't happy with their going out together anymore. He in turn announced to every guy he could that he'd gotten Celeste and that he had the blood on the blanket to prove it. Keith failed to achieve the desired effect, however, as Celeste's reputation merely changed to one of "woman," as in *"You make me feel like a natural woman."* Experienced, but hardly slutty. They wanted her all the more.

So I held on to her tight after that. What else could I do?

Our girls' track team went to state our junior year. Celeste and I ran the first and fourth legs of the 440 relay. We placed third all-around, a feat for our small prep school, one that has astonishingly yet to be repeated. I also placed sixth in hurdles, Celeste seventh. Jazz-class leaping had its benefits.

I kept Jim a while longer until a few weeks into June, when his family went on an extended vacation to Majorca. I hated the idea of him surrounded by bikinied girls, his great body a magnet. But by then we'd really had enough of each other anyway. A mutual decision. No hard feelings. Best of luck and all that. He told me not to write about who I started going out with next. He said he couldn't stand it. No worries. Friends. What we both wanted. Honestly. Duh, I swear, cross my heart.

And, so, the summer leading into senior year spread itself in front of Celeste and me like a banquet. We did not resist. We had no reason to whatsoever.

THE SKULLS

Decide you like the voice of Jack-in-the-Box. Crawl across the driver, a boy you plan to know better in an hour, and say, in your best Marilyn, your absolute best slurring-drunk Marilyn, "Jack, baby. Hey, Jack." Wait for Jack to speak.

The clown says nothing.

Solicit a response. Tug on the low V-neck of your black shirt and lean farther out the window. You don't wear a bra. Expose and push. Make cleavage for Jack. Grind your knees into the driver boy's lap.

Silence.

Tell everybody in the car, the five others and the driver boy, that Jack is blind. Collect agreement. Collect Fuck, yeahs! When you sit back in the seat you share with her, look down at your chest. One tit remains free, slung in the stretched-out neck of your sweater. Leave it there and laugh. Point to yourself. You are hilarious. Collect loud laughs. Laugh until you make her cry. Laugh until your tit pops back in. Tug at your sweater. Put yourself back out there. Move to perch on driver boy's lap. Collect encouragement to drive through just as you are.

Say, "Oh, Jacky-wacky," as you grab bags of tacos.

Feel stirrings in the lap where you kneel.

Try to force your lone tit onto Jack's hand as he passes sweating waxed cups of soda toward you and driver boy. Watch Jack's face go crimson when he and your soft flesh finally collide. Feel the power that a single tit can wield. Wonder if you can scoop up the other one too. Cram your hand in. Fish for the mate. Watch Jack turn and leave the window.

See him with others talking in the back. They are not uniformed. They are agents. They are secret service. They are Jack's protection.

Try to reach the rest of what belongs to you before driver boy peels out.

The car trails shredded iceberg, cheese, lyrics. Between bites, belt out "I Walk the Line." Feel your might.

HER OLDEST sister, Diana, sent Celeste a letter in June. We greeted the cheery mailman in our swimsuits. Instructions on the back of the envelope directed Celeste to read the letter in private. We poured apple juices, avoided Mrs. Diamond, and headed upstairs to Celeste's bedroom. In the letter Diana wrote that she had met the man with whom she wanted to spend her life. She wrote that, wrote "with whom." Diana had recently dropped out of graduate school, knowing that this man was the one for her. He also happened to be Diana's professor. And Diana happened to be pregnant. And the two had happened to elope at the end of the previous term.

From Diana's details, we did the math. The professor impregnator husband had to be all of about three years younger than Mr. Diamond.

"Lisa!" Celeste squeaked, then whispered, "How could she drop out of school?"

"Oh, my god, you'll be an aunt."

"She was on her way to New York. Now where's she on her way to, barefoot?"

"What?"

"Barefoot. Barefoot and pregnant, Lisa." Celeste widened her eyes at me and opened her mouth in a silent scream.

"You're gonna be an aunt."

Celeste looked confused, her pale blue bikini light against her tan skin.

"If you're the sister of the mother—"

"Shut up. I can't believe Diana did this."

"With her professor." I tried to imagine having sex with one of our teachers. I could not thoroughly think the act through with any of them. The fat, the skin, the age. How horrible.

Certainly thinking the same, Celeste flexed her stomach muscles and looked at her belly button, then plucked at the skin on the underside of her upper arm. "I just don't see why"—*pluck*—"why she would say she's not going back to graduate school." *Pluck, pluck.*

I thought about the fact that the letter was a secret, why Celeste was to have read it in private. What would Mr. Diamond say about his oldest daughter running off with her professor? Obviously nothing kind, if Diana's pleas for a few more days or even a week without telling their mother and father were a true indication. "What about your parents?" I asked.

"Are you joking? The sky's going to fall!" She looked at me agog.

I dropped my jaw, trying to mirror Celeste's expression.

"Oh, no!" she lamented.

"Oh, no!" I commiserated.

That night for supper Celeste and I went the extra mile. We baked bread from scratch, decorated the table with petunia petals, and composed gorgeous lump-crabmeat salads, exactly the way that Julia Child suggested. We sautéed fresh mushrooms with onions to top porterhouse steaks. Earlier we'd dragged out the ice-cream maker and bag of rock salt and had improvised rocky road, feeding chunks of Hershey bars and pecans and expensive toffee into the top of the hand-cranked relic of Mrs. Diamond's, dotting the swirling, thickening surface of the chocolate contents with more treats, more distractions.

At the dinner table, I noticed that the upholstery of my chair chafed the back portion of my legs not covered by my tennis skirt. I looked at Celeste. Despite the lovely presentation her halter top offered, her shoulders looked angry too. So early in the season, we'd been a bit careless with the baby oil and iodine, our magical basting solution, our anointment extraordinaire.

"You must have been inspired today," Mrs. Diamond intoned, looking at the table, at our pinked cheeks. After her first bite of salad, she smiled. "Delicious." She'd had her hair cut that afternoon, and she seemed pleased with the results. The flirty-looking bob made her look impish. Much younger. It occurred to me that Mrs. Diamond might be trying in some way to replace the missing daughters. More interesting to consider, though, I decided, chewing bread, would be Mrs. Diamond's desire to attract the attention of her own husband, to be dressing up, fixing herself up for him. The two were such a bizarre but perfectly right couple.

"To what do I owe this fine meal, my dears?" Mr. Diamond bellowed. He took a swig of wine and raised his glass to us. Looking at the barrel-round girth of his chest, I decided that Mr. Diamond would surely have to elevate himself above Mrs. Diamond some, if he were on top in the sack, as she would entirely disappear beneath him. He would eclipse her.

"Really, girls. Why such a special dinner?" Mrs. Diamond stopped her fork just before stabbing a premium chunk of crab. Even with her new haircut, I couldn't picture Mrs. Diamond, Mona, sitting astride Mr. Diamond's hips. I just couldn't.

Celeste looked at me. She had a lot of trouble lying outright. "Well," she started. "Well, I was sort of missing Diana. And Rachel." She swallowed. "And I thought that they would almost come home for a meal like this." The fact that neither of Celeste's sisters had yet returned home for the summer was a matter of some vexation for Mr. and Mrs. Diamond, although they both pretended that they believed young women needed to form their own personalities through experience. Rachel had taken off for Ibiza until August, at which point she would come home for a week before the start of her new semester. Of course, Mr. Diamond paid. Diana's absence, on the other hand, had been glossed over, though not entirely successfully. Both parents were grumpy about their eldest daughter missing the opportunity to spend time in Kansas City with family. Still a privileged outsider to the twelve-month workforce, Diana did not yet toil for her own upkeep. And now Celeste and I had insiders' knowledge. Unless the professor was a dud, Diana probably never would. Married and all. Baby and all.

"That's a nice thought," Mrs. Diamond said to Celeste. "I think you've certainly cooked enough for your sisters to have been here too."

"There's ice cream for dessert," I interjected as my attempt at diversion.

"Ice cream!" Mr. Diamond boomed. "Please don't tell me, darling Lisa, that it's homemade."

"It's homemade." I smiled.

He leaned over to rub my head like he had for years, and I pulled away then as I had for nearly as many. It'd become a game: He tried to mess my hair up horribly. Then he'd laugh riotously if he managed to get me in a headlock and produce big fluffy rats' nests. I minded just enough to try to avoid this but not enough that I always succeeded, so he still got me every once in a while. I certainly must have valued his touch. Since going through puberty, my father seemed frightened of my body and avoided touching me at all. If we accidentally bumped into each other getting in or out of the car, or if we so much as reached for the salt at the same time eating eggs for breakfast and his hand touched mine, he'd apologize. But fortunately, Mr. Diamond was nowhere near as timid. His lunge over his salad to grab my head and mess up my hair missed, so he sucker punched me in the arm instead. "Uhh!" he grunted.

"Didn't hurt," I said.

"Did too," he shot back.

"Did not."

"Why I oughta'," he teased, making a fist.

"How long will you two persist?" Mrs. Diamond sighed.

Far away, Celeste fished for shreds of crabmeat hidden in lettuce. I knew she was thinking about Diana, the sister who was about to become a mother at the hands—at the dick!—of her own professor. I stared at my soft pat of real butter on its proper plate and wondered how our dinners, how our family—the Diamond family, I mean—would change shortly. In hindsight, I think that Celeste already knew what would happen, that the brunt would fall on us, that her father would weep to see us go, that he would cling to us so tightly we would wriggle away straight into the jaws of savage beasts, to be torn limb from limb. Celeste knew her father would send us there, wherever, away. She knew we would seek escape.

I picked up the entire pat of butter with my knife and slathered my second slice of freshly baked bread. "This bread is *goob*," I said with my mouth full, grinning at Mr. Diamond.

"Oh, yeah?" he challenged. "Pass me some of that '*goob* breb.'"

"Honestly," murmured Mrs. Diamond. I finally knew her well enough to know that she wasn't actually upset; in fact, I believe she secretly enjoyed her husband's repartee with me.

We finished our salads, and then Celeste and I cleared the plates to make room for entrées. The steaks under the broiler were nearing perfection. Taking the lead from local barbecue restaurants, we'd sliced sweet potatoes into fries. They baked, individually rubbed with corn oil. I turned on the oven light and peered in at the orange sticks, our little gastronomic children. "Should we flip them?" I asked Celeste.

"I don't know," she said. "Do you think it will be a boy or a girl?"

I frowned at the sweet potato fries. "Maybe we should. I don't know. What do you think?"

"I think a girl, a strong one like Diana."

"We should flip them, I think," I said, opening the oven door. The earthy, sugary scent of sweet potatoes hit me in the face. "What if it's a boy?" I pinched two pot holders and lifted the baking pan out of the oven. "A baby Cupid."

"It'll be a girl," Celeste said with authority.

"You never know. Come here." Celeste stepped to my side. We both stared at our sweet potato babies.

"Flip," she decided.

"I think so too."

Sticking her head through the swinging kitchen door, Mrs. Diamond asked, "Do you girls need help in there?"

She never asked us that anymore. It was the steaks she was worried about.

"We know, Mom," Celeste said. "Medium."

"Your father doesn't really care for too much blood," she said.

"I know," Celeste answered. "'A little blood is good. Too much a disaster.'" He said it all the time. Celeste's imitation of his expression, all nose and chest and baritone, came strikingly close.

Mrs. Diamond grinned at her youngest daughter and swung her head back through the door. "I like your haircut," I told her too late.

"Something good from a book," Celeste said.

I knew what she meant. I almost always knew what she meant by then. For years. "How about Emily?"

"The Brontës? Hmm. Get me tongs." We flipped the fries and stuck them back in the oven.

"She could be a Catherine," Celeste countered.

"Ooh. Or an Elizabeth."

"So many syllables. Everybody would say, 'How cute, Little Lizzy!'"

"Maybe not, but, yeah, Diana would have to repeat herself a lot. 'No, not Liz, *Elizabeth*.'"

"It's just so weird," Celeste said, turning on the flame under the onions and mushrooms.

"I know." I knew what she meant. I'm sure I did. "I guess we could be her, sort of," I ventured. "It could be us pregnant."

"Exactly."

I thought about what I would name my own daughter if I had one. Duh-hay. That was an easy one. "Celeste," I said.

"What?"

"No. I mean Celeste for a name."

"You think so?" She smiled at me then in a way I hadn't seen yet, in a way that made me want to cry, she was so open, so much more than I would or could ever be, in a way that exuded love for me and for an unborn baby who could get named for her sake and for an idea, for the notion of continuation, for sincerity, for innocence. Aw, it really was a look to beat the band.

"Hey!" we heard Mr. Diamond's voice roar from the dining room. "Where's my dinner?!" He was backed by rhythmic percussion; I was sure he pounded his utensils on the table. And within the beating of that fork and knife I realized with a small start that Mrs. Diamond was the tolerant one. She put up with his theatrical, childish behavior. She'd lived with it for years. Little, hard Mona. Mona, the Jewish saint. Okay, so maybe I'm misremembering a bit. Not a saint. But Mona kept it together.

"Bring!" Thunk. "On!" Thunk. "The!" Thunk. "Grub!"

"Your dad's in a good mood tonight," I said.

"Just wait," Celeste said glumly, stirring the onions and mushrooms.

"Well, don't tell him then," I offered.

"How can I not?"

"What do you mean? Just don't tell him."

"But he'll know that I knew ahead of them. He'll look at me and know. And maybe if I tell him instead of Diana, he won't get as mad, because he won't shoot the messenger."

Another expression I wasn't sure about. But I did understand the basic tenets of lying. You just did it. "Celeste," I directed impatiently, "just don't tell them. When they find out, whenever they find out, just say, 'What?!' and make a face." I made the face she should don.

She looked at me and laughed.

I frowned. "What?"

"You should see yourself."

"Ha-ha. You don't have to tell them. You've not told me things before. *Don't* tell them."

Celeste sighed and opened the oven door. "These are just going to have to be done, even if they're not."

"They're done. *Don't* tell them."

We carried in our prizewinning dinner. Mr. Diamond stuffed himself, Mrs. Diamond seemed pleased, I gobbled everything—being out in the sun always made me feel like I was starving—and Celeste, the dope, ate like a bird. She had all of two bites of porterhouse and maybe one sweet potato stick.

"You're not eating," Mrs. Diamond urged.

"I'm just not very hungry." Celeste looked at me out of the corner of her eye.

I tried to kick her under the table.

"Ouch!" Mr. Diamond said.

"I'm sorry." I'm sure my burned cheeks flushed more. "Sorry, Mr. Diamond. I di—"

"Diana is married and pregnant."

"That's all right, Lisa."

"To her professor."

Mrs. Diamond was the first to actually hear Celeste. "What did you just say? Celeste?"

"What is she saying?" Mr. Diamond asked Mrs. Diamond.

"Diana married her professor, and she's pregnant," Celeste repeated.

Mr. and Mrs. Diamond—it was really weird—both sort of cocked their heads at Celeste like confused pets not comprehending a human's words.

"What did she say?" Mr. Diamond asked me then.

It couldn't have been a matter of hearing. Celeste had spoken plainly. "About Diana," I said, ashamed.

"Say it again, Celeste, and tell me how you think you know this," Mr. Diamond said, his voice low and flat and scarier than I'd ever heard.

Celeste's eyes started to fill. Mrs. Diamond wiped her mouth with her napkin, her haircut suddenly looking flip, disrespectful somehow. "Which professor?" she asked.

"He's three years younger than you," Celeste told her father, and with a single sweep of his powerful arm, Mr. Diamond cleared all the dishes near him onto the floor. He opened his mouth to speak, but nothing came out.

Mr. Diamond was alternately overbearing and despondent that summer. He had never needed us to be in a hurry to grow up, but now there seemed to be something almost manic in his desire to keep us young with his childish teasing, his persistent questions about the happenings at pool parties and backyard gatherings, his oppressive congeniality, even his down-in-the-mouth moping. If we said we were only going to the laundromat by UMKC to play Ms. Pac-Man, we had to return with scores. If we went to a movie, a thorough plot summary became a given. He hovered in the kitchen, his enormous presence getting in the way of any real cooking, and by the time July bloomed, heavy and scented, we began to make mistakes. I burned when trying to sauté. Celeste's soufflés failed to rise. We both spilled milk.

Celeste slowly grew increasingly frustrated with her father's inability to accept what she had taken to calling, complete with an academic tone, "the circumstances of his daughters' realities." I wanted to laugh, but she was serious. She seemed to want to punish him. It was Celeste who decided on the peanut-butter-and-jelly dinner. No shit. I was sent home rather than be allowed to spend one of the usual nights over.

You really wonder, years later—don't you?—what feeds into the final making of a person. Do specific events alter the course of somebody forever after? I mean, of course they do, but wouldn't it be interesting to go back in time and have the hand of a god point her finger at the exact moment in the reel of your life where you veered? The spot where you changed your own destiny? Certainly Celeste's following my virginity-loss lead began her alternate tack, but had the mess—bad word, maybe *the new route*—had our new route actually started with the first lie about my nonexistent virginity? Had it started at the basketball game when I first laid eyes of lust all over Jim? Had it begun two nights before, when Celeste and I doubled up our homework to make room for the basketball game? Don't you ever wonder? I do.

I'm sure I'm obsessing on the wrong issue, that the virginity loss isn't the right moment, but it is a marker in a life. Celeste's life. And the way she went about everything afterward had to make you think.

Anyway, an unfortunate confluence of attitudes and events occurred in July to redirect Celeste and me. Me and Celeste. Celeste and me. Her dad had gone berserk in his behavior toward us, and Celeste, having given it up to a water-polo player at the end of the school year, decided that there had to be better fucks walking the streets of Kansas City, Missouri, than the one she had chosen for her deflowering. There just had to be, I'm sure she was thinking.

A nice equation: Newly promiscuous daughter + newly protective father = Ah! you say. Yes, I see. Of course you do. And so after a bit of a slow start out of the gates, Summer of '81 went surging down the straightaway. Summer of '81 would take it by three lengths. No, looks like four, folks. Yes, four.

The trip to visit my mother for the first time since she'd been locked up—put away, shelved indefinitely, committed to the booby hatch loony bin nuthouse cuckoo's nest pasture—brought all the perspective I needed. Shed more than a little light.

Celeste believed that we new women, we two women of new worldly ways, could reach Janice Joy; we could tap into a common pool of female psyche and understanding and bring on a revived consciousness in my mother. I considered begging to differ, but I didn't. In fact, I'd been curious initially. I hadn't seen Janice Joy in months. Celeste convinced her mother, the one sane parent left, to let us borrow her car for the afternoon.

The facility rested, unprotected by trees or significant hedges, in a flat and dry lake bed, the water of which must have evaporated many millennia before. Despite the crunch of the groomed gravel drive and the creak of ornate, wrought-iron gates, the squat brick buildings of Easy Prairie Estate seemed to me as scattered and forlorn as teeth kicked from a crumbling skull. Throwaways, I thought of the inhabitants as Celeste spoke to the guard outside the gates. Gone-for-goods. Shells. How much did it cost to keep my mother here? And who paid? The insurance? Or just my dad?

I knew the answer to the one question that mattered, though: never.

We were expected and provided with a yellow paper parking pass to hang over the rearview mirror. Short balsa-wood crates of simple-care summer flowers, marigolds and snapdragons, sat piled near the buildings where neatly trimmed lawns tidily met the brick facades. I understood immediately why my father had chosen Easy Prairie Estate. It was his kinda place. I bet you could see into every corner. Clean. No hiding places behind bushes or looming trees, no sloping, ill-defined borders between building and earth, nurse and patient, depressed person and crazy woman.

"How sad," Celeste said without pretense as we walked toward the tastefully painted beige-and-black front door of Meadow Hall #6.

"No shit, Sherlock," I said as lightly as I could. The door was locked. I pushed the glowing orange doorbell, its color nearly disappearing in the summer sunlight. We heard approaching footsteps, hard-soled, from behind the beige-and-black door.

"Welcome," a young male attendant no older than we were started to say upon opening the door. He looked surprised to find Celeste and me on the other side.

We stepped inside and an icky sense of déjà vu nearly overtook me in the plain, large entryway. "We're here to see Mrs. Smith," Celeste said. She smiled a proper smile at the attendant and added, "Janice Joy Smith."

"Come in," the attendant said. "Sign here." He tapped a fingernail on an open record book. We'd signed two already, one at the front gate, and one in the main building. I should have had the nerve to write *Farrah Fawcett* or something, but I didn't. I dutifully signed my name beneath Celeste's, considering momentarily whether or not I should look for my father's distinctive scribble in the preceding pages. "Janice Joy is in the viewing room," the attendant told us.

"Viewing what?" Celeste asked.

I glanced around. The attendant didn't appear to be offering any directions. "Where's that?" I asked.

"Down the hall." The hand came out again. "To the left." Point. "To the end, then right." Point.

"Viewing what?" Celeste asked again.

"Oh, the scenery and such."

"They look at the celery?" Celeste asked.

"*See-ner-ee*," the guy repeated.

With no further elaboration from the attendant, Celeste and I flip-flopped our way down the tiled hall. Celeste's multilayered, multicolored, and stacked flip-flops were orange in the center, mine blue.

My father had warned us not to expect too much. What he'd actually said was that the doctors were "making continual adjustments with her medication," and that "her appearance is dissimilar to what you're familiar with." Who talks to his child that way? I understood him to mean that Janice Joy looked like dirt.

"Should we be whispering?" Celeste whispered.

I shrugged.

"Naw." She shook her head, then hummed the opening bars from "Age of Aquarius." I joined in. We flip-flopped right. We stopped. The hall opened up onto a sort of terrarium, a room lined with windows, although what greenery grew did so on the other side. A glass box surrounded by grass. And insignificant clumps of cheerless marigolds. Dusty snapdragons. No television provided viewing in the viewing room. No art. No card tables. No big Indian, no Jack Nicholson, no nothing.

An air-conditioning vent thrummed quietly in the ceiling. A faint tan stain spread from the vent across the plaster in the shape of the perfect amoeba, the one from all the books: blob and frozen tentacles, delineated edges.

And there she was. *Was* it her? I frowned. Three women sat in three wingback chairs facing three of the four corners of the earth. Janice Joy was Baby Bear, staring out onto the shaded east lawn. I took Celeste's hand as we approached. "Mom?"

"Hello, Mrs. Smith."

Getting a decent look at her, I could see what Dad meant. Something had sunk in her, around the eyes, in the face, the posture. She seemed tiny, smaller than I'd remembered. "Mom?"

Janice Joy blinked at the green grass, moved her head ever so slightly toward the sound of my voice, and visibly sank in the wingback. I thought I heard a hissing. Oh, no. My mother pissed herself like a child in fear. She began to shiver. "Mom?" As if palsied, her left hand curled into her left wrist. I thought of steamed lobster tail. She was a tiny girl in her nightgown, only she wasn't, wasn't a girl, wasn't young at all. "Oh, my god," I said when Janice Joy clenched her jaw. I knew what she was about to do. "Let's go, Celeste," I said, trying to hurry away.

"No," she said. "Wait."

"No," I said. "I want to go."

"Wait. We can talk. She's just sca—"

Janice Joy grunted. Oh, god. "Please, let's go."

"It's okay," Celeste said as my mother emptied her bowels into her nightgown.

I was not, despite my recent impressions of a class clown, very vocally expressive. If I'd had the sense to scream at her, to tell her how difficult she'd made my life and how painfully she humbled me and how I wished I could have been born a Diamond instead, who knows? Things may have turned out differently. But I didn't yell or scream or stomp my feet. Instead I pivoted and ran, kicking off my flip-flops, and something about the bare expanse of room funneling into the long, polished hallway made me want to fly, out and away, but I could only leap, so I leaped as high and as far as I could and I ran and leaped and flung my arms as if I myself were housed there and needed to escape, as if I had been forced to live with Janice Joy in Meadow Hall #6 like a fellow fucking lunatic, like a fucking viewing room decoration, only I possessed the knowledge of my existence, such as it was, and understood—understood what? I just leaped. And leaped and leaped.

I draped myself across the hood of Mrs. Diamond's navy car, scorching against my face. My tears should sizzle, I thought, but they didn't, slinking hotly, silently instead along the length of my neck where it met metal. Not knowing exactly why, I cried a river. I'd never had much of a mother, really. But for her to do that, what she did—I don't know. It made me . . . *own* her for a moment. She was mine. My mom. My mom did that. She looked at my face and peed herself. You couldn't help but think of beaten dogs, caged and ruined animals. I'd made her pee. *I* had. And then worse.

Celeste came out a long time later, maybe half an hour later, holding my flip-flops together like a kind of fat taco. "Here," she said. "You left these."

"Thanks," I said, my cheeks dry.

Celeste went to the passenger side, unlocked and held open my door. I felt queasy from the sun and the smell in the place and everything else. I wanted to ask her what she'd been doing, but I vowed to myself that I'd wait for her to tell me, no matter how long I had to wait. I would wait years if I needed. I would not ask about the time that my mother and Celeste had spent together without me. Jackals couldn't drag the question from me.

"What took you so long?" I asked even before we backed out of the parking space.

The car vroomed forward, and Celeste slammed on the brakes. "God!" she said, flustered. "I hate that you can't tell when this car is in drive or reverse."

We both knew Celeste would someday cause a disaster; she always did that, forgetting to reverse. I asked a different way. "What did you do in there?"

"Nothing much," she said evasively, placing her arm behind my seat and backing out by the book.

I tried to reangle the right-side air-conditioning vent. "You were gone for forever." I wouldn't ask again. I wouldn't.

Celeste drove past the gates and pulled onto the main road. I turned the radio on, then turned it off. I sat, sick, watching out the side window, wondering how much any friend would take. How far would a rich teenager from a stable environment go for a freak like Janice Joy?

Some ten miles down the road, she said quietly, "I couldn't do anything."

I stared at the ceiling, afraid I'd cry. "What did you try to do?"

"I just told her about you," Celeste said.

"What?" In the smell, with Janice Joy grunting?

"I thought she'd want to know."

"Know what?" That her daughter was being raised by Jewish wolves? That despite all her efforts to crush her offspring's spirit, Janice Joy's daughter had bloomed like a desert flower—no, wait, like a flower on the arctic tundra? What the fuck was Janice Joy entitled to know?! "Know what!?" I wasn't going to cry. I wanted to slap Celeste. Or I wanted her to turn the car around so I could march back into Meadow Hall #6 and slap my mother hard across her shriveling apple head.

"About you," Celeste said. She wasn't a cool driver yet. She sat upright with her hands at ten and two. Stiff. "What you're like, that you dance."

"As if . . ." I started, and immediately lost my thought.

"How you're a good student and you'll go to a good college on scholarship."

My father said he'd told Janice Joy the same things when he visited. So it wasn't like Celeste had been doing anything special. Why would she think it'd make any difference?

Like poison, the thought of Celeste's turning on me seeped into my brain, of her using what she'd seen of my mother against me someday in the future. Distrust of my best friend crept in on spider legs, into my ear to lay eggs.

"What good do you think that would do? None, Celeste. God. You stood by her in that sm— You kept talking to her? Why didn't you come with me?"

"I just thought . . . I just thought."

"No, you didn't." I was mad. Ahead, a couple of crows on the road pulled at something furry and ribboned. Bloody.

"Move!" Celeste warned the windshield as we approached. Engaged in a macabre tug-of-war, the birds flopped away at the last possible second.

"She should hear that stuff from somebody other than your dad, Lisa."

I twisted in my seat. The birds were back at the carrion. "She doesn't hear anything," I said.

"She can hear," Celeste said.

"Is that your professional opinion?" As if she knew anything about *my* mother.

"You know she can hear," she said, and I hated the knowing tone of her voice. I knew Janice Joy's ears worked fine, but I also knew that she didn't listen, couldn't listen and let the world into her head ever again. I knew her better. I knew her best.

"You should have come with me. I *asked* you to." I raised my voice. "I don't understand why you couldn't do me the favor of coming with me! You had to stay there with *my* mother?!" Celeste came to me in a sort of daytime nightmare then, a waking apparition: She sat at a lunch table surrounded by classmates, making an *sss* sound through her teeth, the sound of pee. "She's *my* mother!" I sort of hollered.

What Celeste should have said was, "Praise be to God, and thank you, almighty Jesus, for delivering me from such a fate," but she just said, "I know."

"She is!"

"I know she is," she said.

A tan-and-black mass appeared on the side of the road ahead. I wished it to be an abandoned sweatshirt or piece of tire.

"I just thought I should try," Celeste said.

"Well, it was a dumb idea." It felt good to be mean to her. She wasn't perfect, you know? She had flaws.

As we drove closer I could see the mound of something had been alive once. A dark, bloody tire track led to the lump. The poor thing had been dragged. What was it? A dog? No. What was that?

"What was that?" Celeste said, wincing.

"I don't know."

"It's so sad. I hate seeing things run over. Knock wood, I haven't hit anything yet."

"What does that mean?" I asked. I was sick of it.

"What? I haven't hit any animals yet. Since I started driving."

"No," I said. "I mean, what does 'knock wood' mean?"

"You know," Celeste said, taking a rare glance away from the road in my direction.

"No, I don't. Like on a door? Knock on a door? I don't get it."
I'm sure my voice sounded peevish, ticked off as I was at Celeste
Nightingale.

"Really? You've never heard that before? You know, 'Knock
wood,' like, um, 'Guard me against it actually happening.'"

"Like what happening?"

"Like, 'Keep me from hitting an animal when I'm driving.'"

Feeling slow and stupid, I figured it out suddenly. "You mean,"
I said, "like, 'Knock wood my mom never takes a Janice Joy turn
for the worse.'"

"No, Lisa, like, 'Knock wood, I haven't hit any animals yet.'"

"Maybe we should take her for a wheel-around in her chair off
the Easy Prairie Estate grounds," I entertained. "We could push her
out onto the road in front of cars. In front of a big Trailways bus."

"I think it was a coyote," Celeste said, ignoring me.

"Or one of those trucks that carries cars on two levels. Those
have to weigh tons. Splat! Just like a, a squirrel. A mute . . . pissing . . . a mute pissing and shitting squirrel."

"Stop it."

"What?" The impulse to continue grew by the second. All the
horrible thoughts about my mother that had stewed and fer-
mented in my gut for years wanted to come up my throat like ran-
cid beer foam. "We could wheel her to a bridge and—"

"Stop it!" Celeste blinked, her eyes watery with tears.

I turned away from her and looked out the side window. *And
push her over the edge,* I mouthed at the glass.

We drove most of the way into the city in silence. What a horrible idea. I'd never, ever go back. I wouldn't, I swore. Not until she
was dead. I disowned Janice Joy there in Mrs. Diamond's car.
Completely.

Finally, as we passed through Westport, Celeste said quietly, "It
looked like a coyote."

"I don't think there are any coyotes in this part of the country,"
I said nicely. I didn't actually want her to defect.

"I know." Celeste swallowed loudly. "But . . . it looked . . . like
it had that kind of fur." She swallowed again. "And I saw the eye."

"That'd be sad," I said.

"Everything's sad," she almost whispered.

I sighed loudly. "What should we cook for dinner?" I asked.

"Lisa."

"What?" I tried to cover the annoyance in my voice. I didn't want to talk about it anymore.

"You decide," she said. "I don't feel very good."

Well, you shouldn't have stood talking to the piss-and-shit monster for half an hour. "What about fettuccini?" I asked. "With some of that tasso stuff from New Orleans that your mom bought from that catalog."

"Huh?"

What did she mean, "huh"? She always listened. We always got each other, twins with our own secret language. "That tasso stuff."

"I think I'm going to throw up," Celeste spurted.

"Pull over pull over pull over—"

She gagged and scraped the hubcaps on the curb trying to park in front of the liquor store on Main, cars whooshing by. She opened her door and vomited onto the street.

She had the flu, supposedly. Unlucky me, I got to spend the next three entire days with my father and brother. She wouldn't tell, I told myself. Maybe Mrs. Diamond, but nobody else. She wouldn't.

Jello Biafra makes you wet.

Duck low. Both of you, through hips and legs, press to the front where the violent boys are, where Jello can see your bravery and might. Show him your worth. Show him your nipples clear as day, hard as Jujubes through your thin, sweated-through tanks. Show him that you can survive the entire encore, that you can survive California, *über alles.* Spread your boots wide and stand still in the middle of the noise and the fury and stare straight at him, waiting to be pummeled, waiting to take what you know will be elbows to your ears, fists to your temples, high knees to your tailbones.

And it comes. Not what you expected, but good nonetheless. A 40 oz. can of beer, heavy and unopened, crashes into your exposed collarbone. Just yours. Think that it was meant for your head, or maybe hers, and as you think this, look at what it got instead. The hard top edge of the can hasn't just damaged you, just welted you; it has gouged you as if you were made of wax. Imagine holding a paring knife and leaning in toward one of Madame Tussaud's favorites. Take a chunk, put it in your pocket, and walk away.

But you bleed. Wonder if the scallop of flesh and chip of bone the size of a front tooth is still clinging to the warm can rolling on the dirty floor. See clearly that a piece of you is missing. Remember a bus ride into the wilderness.

Wonder why it is that you feel no pain.

Look around behind you with a whip of your head. Left. There are cops here. You saw them when you came in. Right. More. Others. But you have impressed those closest to you. Look to the stage. Look to her.

Brace yourself.

You know the worst is yet to come.

EIGHT

ALL THINGS Janice Joy seemed forgotten and laid to rest when I saw Celeste next. In the sun on a chaise by their pool, she looked a little funny-colored but otherwise fine. A recuperating color. "My father was in seventh heaven," she said, flipping onto her stomach. "He waited on me hand and foot, even after I missed the pot . . . and the throw-up hit his *slipper.*"

"Really?" Mr. Diamond's slippers were older than the hills, larger than most shoe boxes, deep maroon and embroidered with gold figures so long obscured that the decorations resembled swirls of evaporating mist. If you looked at the slippers from the right angle, you could see that the embroidery had been worn away to gold fuzz. He adored his slippers and donned them the very instant he walked in the front door. They were what he said the king of the castle wore to relax. "On his *slipper*-slipper?"

"Yup!" Celeste said. "The sad part was that he didn't even get mad. He just held my hair out of the way while I threw up." I could picture Mr. Diamond perfectly. "My eyeballs felt like they were going to pop out of my skull—I was hanging over the side of the bed—and all I kept staring at was this gigantic drop on the holy slipper."

"Ew."

"I know! I had crackers. Saltine crackers and 7UP."

"Can we talk about something else?" I sat up, reached for the magic solution, and began basting my legs. My summer goal was a warm mahogany.

"Okay," she said. "Have you changed your schools?"

"Nope." My list of prospective colleges had stayed the same: UW Madison, Brown, Yale, Duke, University of Chicago, and, at the insistence of my father, Mount Holyoke. (As if I'd go to a "women's college.") "Yours?"

"Mom had me add Berkeley, but we haven't told Dad yet. With Diana and all."

"California? You'd cross the Rockies?" Mr. Diamond would keen. Celeste would be as good as dead, she'd be so far away from him.

"Well, it's up there, school-wise."

"Yeah." I lifted the right hip strap of my bikini bottoms to check my line. We only had Brown and Yale in common. I didn't like to think about the year after next. "We should do something."

"Like what?"

I felt like kissing new boys. "I don't know."

"I don't know either." She passed me a lemon half.

I squeezed juice over her hair and thought of having a salad for lunch. Still on her stomach, she ran her fingers through her locks. I watched her shoulder muscles flex. "Your highlights are coming out," I told her.

"Thanks."

"We need new boyfriends."

"But not the same old school people." She fanned her hair out on her towel to bake.

"*Je voudrais un peu de, de . . .*"

"*Garçons!*"

"*Oui, oui, mademoiselle!*" I effused. "*Garçons français.*" We were constantly engaged with the idea of finding those elusive foreign-exchange guys, if not with the actual pursuit.

"They all have foreskins," she said matter-of-factly.

"Have you seen one?"

"Seen a foreskin?"

"No, Celeste. A French guy." I made a retarded sound. "Have you?"

"Just a foreskin? It's attached, you know, not, like, sitting on the table next to your change."

"Duh, but what does it look like? How can a penis be the same with or without one?"

"Well, I don't know. Sort of how an earlobe is part of an ear but you could cut it off if you had to. You'd still have an ear."

"An ear without an earlobe would look weird."

"Lots of people don't have ear*lobes*. You know, from biology—attached or detached."

"But they come out of the womb that way. They don't . . . A rabbi doesn't cut off earlobes in an earlobe bris."

Celeste flutter-kicked her legs against her chaise. I ran through a section of one of our jazz routines using just my arms. We sang several rounds, faster and faster, of "The Ear Song": *"Do your ears hang low?/ Do they wobble to and fro?/ Can you tie 'em in a knot?/ Can you tie 'em in a bow?/ Can you throw 'em over your shoulder like a continental soldier?/ Do your ears hang low?"*

We tried, but we really just imitated professional tanners. We lacked the stay-still, corpselike stamina.

I thought about biology. "I don't remember seeing a picture of a penis with a foreskin."

"Me either," she said.

"Well, then, how do you know about them?"

"I don't."

"Celeste . . ."

She started laughing. "I'm serious! I don't."

"Yes, you do."

"That's how it seems like it would be—I don't know!"

"Like an earlobe?!"

"No!" she laughed. "Like a *penis* without an earlobe."

I laughed. I was glad she was better. It sucked when Celeste was sick. The last day of her quarantine, my brother, David, and I had watched afternoon TV on the couch in our den, only he was shirtless, alternately flexing his minuscule pec muscles over and over. "Look, Lis! They dance! They dance!" He was making fun of me. Of course I couldn't ignore him after a while, and we'd started fighting. He couldn't pin me because I was too flexible and used my legs to get out of his moves, but we rolled around on the floor until we crashed into the TV cart. The canned laughter of *Gilligan's Island* disappeared with loud *ka-thunk*. Somehow the television still worked when we set it upright and replugged it, but the picture arched on the bottom afterward like a tent pulling away from its stakes. David and I completely denied knowing what had happened when our father pounded on top of the set later that night. Our father had sighed and lit a cigarette, saying we needed a new TV anyway.

I flipped over and lay on my stomach. "I want to see one," I said to Celeste.

"What? A French guy?"

I barked a seal laugh. "Actually, yeah. A French guy *and* his French foreskin."

"Really?" She patted her fanned hair. You knew it was done when it was crunchy. "Okay. Me too."

"The same one? You have to find your own—although obviously you won't have any trouble."

She smiled. We stayed out another hour in the noon sun, concocting different plans of foreskin attack. Eventually we talked our way back to the Nelson-Atkins. The museum seemed to provide one of the few all-ages options for us, as we weren't ready to go the fake-ID route yet. "You're right, Lisa. You're definitely right." She stood up. "We could still make lunch there."

I'd begun to get excited again, thinking about the good-looking Ess. Drone Ess. Maybe he wasn't a drone anymore. If Brooklyn had left the hive—she sort of gave me the creeps anyways—maybe Ess had risen in status. "Let's go." We grabbed our towels and headed inside the Diamond house.

"Just wear some of my clothes," she said, as if I didn't already. The air-conditioning in the big kitchen hit us full blast.

"Maybe we could get Ess to get us into one of his shows!" I said as my nipples hardened. We had more than seven weeks left of summer vacation.

"First things first," Celeste said. "I doubt he's French, though."

"We should ask."

We had lapsed in our maintenance of scruffy clothing, and getting ready took longer than we anticipated, as we couldn't quite figure out if we should dress for potential foreign-exchange foreskin bearers or the drone set. I wouldn't let Celeste rip a new pair of Liz Claibornes just for the afternoon, though. We settled on cut-offs and plain Ts.

By the time we flip-flopped our way in, we'd missed lunch. The enclosed atrium looked the same as it had the summer previous, but for some reason I felt less sure of myself. We stood at the entrance archway.

"We could have tea," Celeste suggested, looking around.

"And crumpets," I said. A few hoities and a few toities (socialites and dirty, painted artist types, respectively) languished at a half dozen bistro tables. "I'm hungry. I wish we'd gotten here in time."

"Maybe they still have those croissant sandwiches."

"Look." I pointed discreetly with my shoulder. "Isn't that, oh, what's-her-face, she had blue horns last year."

"Blue Rose," Celeste said. "My middle name."

"Right." Blue Rose's nearly shorn head was now decidedly magenta. "Magenta Rose?"

"Drone Magenta Rose to you. Look—they still have the sand-wiches. Let's go get some and say hi."

I didn't see Ess. I wanted guys. "After we eat we should wander around," I said.

"I want to see the Russian show," Celeste said, nodding, entirely missing the point. We migrated as casually as we could to the sandwiches, the slapping of our flip-flops bouncing off the stone walls. A small, paint-dappled man raised his head from his sketchbook and stared at us lewdly.

Drone Blue Magenta Rose stepped behind the counter. "Yeah?" she asked, as dull as dirt.

"Hi," Celeste said. "It's Celeste. And Lisa." She pointed to her own chest and mine and then to the row of cellophane-wrapped sandwiches. "Two, please."

Drone Rose chewed on a toothpick, looking tired or bored or both. "Who?" She checked me out and frowned.

"Lisa," I said, "and Celeste. From last summer." No look of recognition came to Drone Rose's face. The sandwiches had been sat on. They looked completely squashed. "What happened to the sandwiches?"

"Ess," Drone Rose said.

"He's still here?" Celeste asked brightly.

"Sure the fuck is," Drone Rose answered, and began rubbing her belly. Beneath her loose apron, an obvious mound of pregnancy appeared as she ran her hand in circles. "What kind?"

"What?"

"What kind of sandwich? Not the ham. Ess put the ice bucket on the hams."

I didn't want a sandwich anymore. "Where is Ess?" He must have gotten Drone Rose pregnant. "Is he the dad?"

Celeste stepped on my foot.

Drone Rose squinted at me. "Who are you?" I could have sworn she was drunk.

"I'm Celeste, and she's Lisa. We met you last summer. Brooklyn introduced us."

"That bitch is gone," Drone Rose said.

"Did she graduate?" I asked.

Drone Rose shook her head. "Stupid bitch got hit by a train." She licked her chapped lips and singsonged flatly, *"The worms play pinochle on her snout."*

Brooklyn was dead?

"How did it happen?" Celeste asked right away.

"I just said she got hit by a train—you deaf?"

I knew what Celeste was asking: whether it was on purpose or not. Brooklyn had seemed like one of those people you might not see again. I hadn't known anyone who'd died, really, up until that point—although I hadn't known Brooklyn well. It was bizarre to think about.

I wanted to know where Ess was and whether or not he was procreating. And why wasn't Drone Rose on the pill, being a college student who had sex and all? "Drone Ro—" I tried.

"Don't fucking call me that."

"It's how we were introduced to you," Celeste said.

Just Plain Rose stared morosely at the sandwiches.

"Is Ess here?" I asked. She wasn't very nice, so I wasn't going to be nice either. Besides, she was pregnant, almost bald, and what? Renamed Thorn now?

"Ess won't fuck you," the magenta-headed girl said.

Could she see me flinch? My water-off-a-duck's-back attempt at a nonreaction to her hardcore comments wasn't working well. I was certain she could tell that she shocked me with her words, which was what she obviously wanted to do. "So?" I said dumbly. What did she mean? Why wouldn't Ess fuck me? What was wrong with me that he wouldn't?

"What about Ing?" Celeste asked. "And, um . . ."

I knew she was thinking about the long-schlong guy . . . um . . . oh! "Gigantus Khan!" I remembered.

"Khan?" Rose asked with a touch of interest. "You know Khan?"

"And . . . and Mack," Celeste said. "Mack Truck."

"And Pia Stream," I added.

"Wait a minute." Rose squinched up her face and looked from me to Celeste and back. She pointed. "I remember you two. You're the rich girls." She nodded and poked her pointing finger into her ear and itched at something. From the looks of her, the something could have been the kind of mites that cats get. Pregnant Rose looked pretty awful. "You're the ones Brooklyn wanted to steal and sell as sex slaves and then get ransom for out of your paren—You're the *rich girls*! Hey!" She reached across the counter and pushed Celeste on her breastbone. "It's the fuckin' rich girls!" Suddenly she grew flamboyantly animated, nodding her head and slapping the counter. "The rich girls! Man, we missed those tips."

I considered telling her that they were the ones to go back to school first but got hung up on her "rich girl" comment. I had

never considered myself a "rich girl." My definition of self in relation to others had been primarily formulated by my weird family
and by my subsequently trying to fit into some kind of an acceptable, albeit superior, norm. Education, intelligence, and talent
represented and defined me, sure, but money? I'd never actually
realized that my family had superfluous amounts of anything but
freako behavior. I mean, yeah, I understood we weren't poor,
but . . . I looked at Celeste, whose cheeks had colored. "You
remember us?" Celeste asked, lightly fingering the spot on her
chest where she'd been pushed.

"I do!" Rose said. "Damn! The rich girls are back!" This she said
loudly enough to raise the heads of several patrons, the lechy-
looking man included. "The rich girls are back," she repeated
again, and smiled as big as if she'd be eating steak that night after
a month of choking down potatoes.

"Hi," I said, and gave her a fake smile. I pointed at her belly.
"You're pregnant."

"Yeah," she said casually, scratching, all nice now that she
thought she'd get money from us. "I'm gonna have a midget."

"A midget?" Celeste looked horrified.

"A little person," I explained. "A baby." I was pretty sure I
understood Rose just fine.

"Yeah," Rose said. "A little person."

"You and Ess?" I fished, lest I'd forget the point of our visit.

"Here," Rose said. She handed us two croissant sandwiches.
"Get a tray. These are the best."

"What are they?"

"Not ham," she said.

"Heeeeyy! It's the . . . the girls!" Ess appeared from behind a
divider near the kitchen.

"It's the rich girls!" Rose repeated yet again. "Hey, fucker, it's
the *rich* girls!" Now I was sure I could smell alcohol on her breath.
Ess looked really good, the same as the summer before.

I wanted to be cool and bold, and I wanted to know if Ess and
Rose were going out or married or whatever. I really wanted to

kiss him. I wondered how old he was. I had to be casual, and I had to—

"Are you two the parents of the midget?" Celeste asked.

I scoffed but watched Ess laugh a real laugh at Celeste's question. "Me? Me and Rose Bitch? Hell, no." He took a few steps toward Rose and slung his long arm around her shoulders. He pulled her toward him with a jerk. "Rose Bitch and me are just friends. Isn't that what we're tellin' the rich girls, honey?" He spoke into her magenta scalp and squeezed his arm again. I watched his bicep pop up like a bun.

Rose looked into Ess' face. "That's right, honey." She patted him on the chest. "That's what we're telling the rich girls. Add two more sandwiches to the list, huh?" She looked at Celeste and me. "We're treating you to your sandwiches!" She rubbed her belly again and shoved Ess' arm off of her. She grinned a schizophrenic grin.

I looked for some kind of boss. How was it that these two workers could get away with what they did, swearing and touching each other? Was their behavior part of some adult artists' game I didn't get yet, kind of like how I didn't understand weird sayings? It sort of felt the same, or made me feel the same way, a little out of it. Four-and-twenty blackbirds baked in a pie. Why not twenty-four? What did "What a tangled web we weave" mean? "Keep your powder dry"? Or "A bird in the hand"? Which hand? The left or the right? Ess and Rose being allowed by some boss to act the way that they did on the job made me feel like those expressions did, irritated and confused and somehow out of the loop, maybe the way somebody faking his way through an English class would feel when he really didn't know how to read.

"Are you two together?" Celeste asked.

"Aw, that's cute," Rose said. "Honey, the rich girl wants to know if we're 'together.'"

I could tell by the way that Ess checked us out that he wanted to kiss us and then some, which was more than fine by me, but we obviously had to find out what the situation was with Rose. She was pregnant, after all.

"Rose Bitch, knock it off," Ess said, suddenly serious.

"What?!"

"That midget's not mine," he told us, and looked at Rose in a hard-to-figure kind of way.

"His witto fishies don't swim wight," Rose whispered to us.

Huh?

"Fuck you, you skank!" Ess was gone behind the screen in a flash. I looked around the room, at the patrons, for the boss. Not a soul had reacted. Maybe the drama of the atrium dining room was part of the package. Could they be actors? Were their colors designed to be art by the ones who hired them rather than by the intentions of the drones themselves?

"Ha, ha!" Rose barked at the screen. "Ha, ha!" She turned back to us. "Take your sandwiches," she said. "And don't forget to *ti-ip.*"

"May I have a water?" Celeste asked.

"Lemon?" Rose almost sneered.

"Yes, please," I piped up.

Rose slopped ice water out of a silver pitcher into two wine-glasses for us and jammed lemon wedges onto the rims, three on each. "Here," she said, holding out the glasses. "Here you go. Now fuck off." She turned on her heel and disappeared behind the screen. A big-sounding pot clunked on the stone floor and bounced around, the noise magnified in the huge atrium.

Celeste and I walked to a table. "Oh, my god," I said under my breath as we sat down. They were honestly bizarre. Grown-up. Foreign. Rose was so, so *mean.* Still, a big and compulsive part of me wanted to win her over, to make her actually like me. Why would I feel that way? "Why the hell would I want her to like me?" I asked Celeste, trying to sound facetious.

"I know. I do too," she said with complete sincerity. Celeste unwrapped a sandwich and sniffed. "Brie." She took a bite. "And strawberries."

I unwrapped mine and took a bite. "And jam. Blackberry."

"Mine's boysenberry," Celeste said quietly. We both bent over our sandwiches and chewed, nearly huddling in the aftermath of Rose. I tried to rationalize why it was that I would want a person like Drone Magenta Skank Rose Bitch to like me. It made no sense.

"What happened to Brooklyn, I wonder?" Celeste said suddenly.

"Here." I pointed at my own front teeth. She had a seed stuck in between hers. "Go like this. I don't know, but doesn't it seem like that's not so surprising?"

Celeste picked at her teeth discreetly, chin lowered. She smiled.

"Got it," I said.

"As if Brooklyn was destined to die young? I agree. Do you think she did it on purpose?"

I thought and chewed. "Probably," I decided. "Maybe they said she was going through the sex change for the wrong reason or something."

"Or maybe it'd take too long to save the money, or her heart hurt her too much."

I made a face. "I can't imagine Brooklyn's heart ever hurting."

"Sure you could," Celeste said.

"I wonder what happened *exactly*," I said.

She crumpled her cellophane wrap. "I don't want to know."

I did. I wanted to know, intensely, exactly what happened. Who was there? Was there an audience? Did she leave a note? Did she straddle a rail? Lie down across the two? Die right away? Try to roll off at the last second and not make it? Who picked her up? Who picked up the pieces of her? What was left after a whole train passed over Brooklyn's body? "I want to know," I said finally.

"You would," she said.

I didn't say anything. We looked around and caught the eye of the short, lechy guy. He was actually kind of cute, but too old for us, and sort of creepy. He looked like he could be a soccer player. Small, strong. He smiled. I smiled back even though I hadn't intended to.

"Let's go look around," Celeste said, pulling on my elbow.

I tipped a last ice cube into my mouth and chewed. I wanted to talk to Ess.

"*Garçons, oui?*" she reminded me.

"*Oui, oui, oui.*" I oinked like a pig. We stood, intending to wave good-bye, but no other drones had made any sort of appearance, and Ess and Rose had not come back out from behind the screen.

I didn't particularly care for the Russian collection, decorative eggs and cloisonnéed iconography and miniature, detailed triptychs. I knew the collection was supposed to be rare and very valuable, but it felt like I was walking through some rich grandmother's dining room, staring obligatorily into her hutches and glassed corner stands. Celeste, on the other hand, seemed absorbed, although she could have been faking it. After a while she sighed loudly. "Out of context, they just don't have the same appeal."

"You've seen Fabergés *in* context?" I didn't necessarily think that she hadn't, but if she had I didn't know about it.

"No, but, you know, they look a little dumb sitting there all glassed in. Can't you imagine having a bowl of them in your palace by . . . by the sofa, and you could pick them out one by one and turn them over in your hands?"

What was she talking about? "A bowl of eggs in my palace?" I asked.

"Sure," somebody said behind us. We stopped bending over and turned. It was the short soccer lech. Just behind the lech stood Ess.

I was struck dumb. Celeste didn't react either.

"Well, now," the lech said. "We have two pillars of salt, Ess. What, pray tell, does that make us?" The lech's eyes were bright blue, rimmed with black lashes. He couldn't have been more than two inches taller than I was.

"This is Hank," Ess said, gesturing flat-handedly to the lech, "and . . ." He moved his upturned hand between Celeste and me. "And these are the ladies."

We remained rooted.

Hank extended his dirty-fingernailed hand. When we still didn't react, he took Celeste's hand and brought it to his mouth. He kissed the backs of her fingers and then continued to hold her hand near his face. He inhaled and stared. I smelled cigarette smoke coming off of him, emanating from him like the smell of cooking meat from a roast in the oven, from his pores. I looked at Ess. He didn't know our names.

"Lisa," I said to Ess.

"Celeste," she said, looking directly at me.

I shrugged. Why not?

"Riiiiiight . . ." Ess said, nodding, handsome and cool, his sinewy arms crossed in front of his chest. Celeste pulled her hand out of Hank's.

"Nice to meet you, ladies. Lisa and Celeste." He smiled with his lips closed, his eyes shifting between the two of us. He seemed to have a second thought, sort of, an additional idea all of a sudden, and snatched my hand before I even realized he had moved in my direction. "Lisa," he said, and lifted my limp hand to his mouth. Did he have a lisp? He sounded like he might, but it was well covered if he did. A thick tongue. His eyes were white-blue, they were so light colored. He exhaled onto my knuckles and then he flipped my hand over completely, cupping it in his other hand, and kissed the translucently pale skin there at my wrist. Too long. A hot press of his mouth. A finger flutter in my gut. I pulled my hand away and looked at Ess, then Celeste. I clasped my hands behind my back.

"Hi, again," Celeste said to Ess.

"It's very nice to make your acquaintance," Hank said to the two of us.

"That's so true," Ess said. "I wondered where you two went this last year." He gave a quick glance to Hank and winked as if conspiratorially.

"You did?" Celeste asked.

"Sure!" Ess smiled, all nice white teeth, and unfolded his arms. "You like the eggs, Celeste?"

Celeste turned and stared at the glass case as if for the first time, as if it had been beamed there in a *Star Trek* transporter. Hank dropped his gaze to my boobs and kept it there. I crossed my arms in front of my chest. "Ah," Celeste said, "I do, um, like the eggs, but they, they lose some, some magic or . . . or tactile value when they're behind glass." She bothered the waistband of her cutoff jeans with her thumb.

"She needs a palace," I helped.

"I understand completely," Hank said. "Cloisonné should be touched, don't you think? Why else develop the form? So small, so jewelrylike—well, it *is* jewelry—and jewelry is tactile, certainly." He looked at me then. "Meant to be touched."

An image of the basketball player with all the body hair flashed in my mind. I could see the swarthy center standing in a huddle around Coach Wolfsheim. What did the basketball player have to do with this Hank? I didn't like him. I didn't. "What do you do?" I asked Hank.

"He's an artist," Celeste said.

Where the hell did that come from?

"I'm an artist," Hank said, "and a teacher."

"He's our guy!" Ess said enthusiastically. "Our sculpture deity!" Ess slapped Hank on the back. I wondered why Hank was covered in paint if his specialty was sculpture.

"At KCAI?" Celeste asked. Politely.

"Yes, yes," Hank said.

I sneaked a good look at Ess. He was tall, six-two or six-three probably, and tan and lean. He wore a lot of silver rings on his fingers besides the ones in his ears. Hank's fingers, by contrast, seemed overstuffed, Popeye-like. I looked at his digits hanging off the ends of his stained hands. He diddled his fingers by his thighs at that moment as if to say, *I see you.*

"You paint your sculptures?" I asked.

"Aha," Hank said. "An observant one."

"She is *so* observant," Celeste said. "She notices *everything.*" She checked herself, knowing, I understood, how young-sounding her multiple emphases must have seemed. "I think Lisa has a little recorder in her head sometimes."

"Oh, yeah?" Ess asked. "Tell me what I said last summer."

Before I could even become embarrassed, I said, "Not a lot,

because you never came to our table except for the time when Brooklyn introduced you. We heard more *about* you than we did from you." My voice didn't even quaver.

Ess' grin faded some. "Oh."

"You said, 'I've seen you in here,'" I told him.

"That's all you said?" Hank asked. "You met these fine specimens and all you could think to say was, 'I've seen you in here'?"

Ess tilted his head just slightly in acknowledgment. Despite Ess' punk predilections, you could detect the relationship between the teacher and the student. It was weird, as creepy as the teacher was. I checked out Hank's shoes. He wore old work boots that must have been fawn-colored when they were new. Now they were paint covered and clownish, almost. "That's all he said," I pronounced as assuredly as I could, looking at Ess, daring him to respond.

"I must have had something in my eye," Ess said.

"What?" Celeste asked.

"To not see the two of you and say more," he answered, smiling at Celeste.

I could feel Hank's eyes boring into me. I was but a mere wooden shed; he was a mature nest of termites. I was a slim young cheese round; he was fast-growing mold. I recrossed my arms and angled myself away from Hank's view and toward Ess'. I knew I fought an uphill battle to win the tall man of my newly formed dreams, as Celeste—damn it, she was my friend, and I'd tried to accept the fact that I was friends with the best-looking girl for miles and miles and miles and miles—well, as Celeste seemed to be considering Ess too.

We hadn't really talked about a plan, so it was nobody's fault.

The four of us carefully made our way through the Russian exhibit with its extra guards posted in each room. Hank actually really knew his art and didn't talk to us as though we were still in high school. He gave us a minilecture on the history of triptychs and the trinity in Orthodox religions. I must admit that he made me feel as though I were Celeste's equal (a skill that shouldn't go unnoted).

Hank's eyes were bright, and they reflected a clear intelligence as well as something else I'd never seen. And, hell yes, hindsight is 20/20, but even then on that day walking through the Russians, I felt Hank to be unique among men. He *studied* Celeste and me, and I know all women say this of a man at some point in time, but he saw *through* me. At least that's what I thought Hank capable of, there in the museum. He saw me naked, and he saw my thoughts as clearly as though they were printed on my forehead. He saw parts of me that I'd never revealed.

We'd just about finished with the exhibit when Hank leaned my direction and said into my ear, "You're a sculptor, aren't you?"

Cheesy as hell, but, still, how did he know that of the two of us I was the one who was better at clay than charcoal? We'd revealed nothing of ourselves art-wise, although between Ess and Hank, they were getting a lot more information out of Celeste and me than we normally would have let slip. I tried to give Hank a frowning, serious look. "Why would you say that?" I asked him. So my pots didn't explode in the kiln like Celeste's, but how would he know?

"I can tell," Hank said cryptically.

I hated him already, and yet I wanted him to give me more attention, along with Ess. Hank felt dangerous, nearly as much so as any French exchange student could. He had to have been in his early thirties. What could he do to me? What could I entice either one of them to do to me? "But how?" I asked.

"Because of how you move your hands," he said after a while, leaning into me, exhaling hot air from his nostrils onto my neck.

We'd already told them both where we'd applied to schools, trying to show off, but as it happened I actually had wondered a little bit about pursuing art. "How?" was all I could manage.

"Your hands," he said again, and watched me to make sure that I lifted my own appendages to my face to study.

They weren't frail, I knew and noticed again, but they weren't chubby paws either. "So?" Before he even said anything I understood that he'd studied hundreds of girls' hands. How could he determine what mine were best at? Didn't they write essays and complete complicated equations better than nearly every other girl's besides Celeste's? I stepped over to Ess. "Let me see your hands," I demanded of him.

Ess smiled and glanced over my head. I turned in time to see Hank lift his eyebrows at Ess. "What?" I asked them both.

"What?" Ess repeated, holding his hands out to me as if having his nails inspected.

I moved my own hands, palms up, beneath his, feeling weight, texture, warmth, and gave a little bounce, indicating that we'd be playing the game, the Bet I Can Slap Your Hand(s) Before You Pull It/Them Away game. I had a trick, a sneak attack, and I rarely lost.

You weren't supposed to look at the hands. I stared into Ess' eyes; they were browny-green, sort of hazel. I looked at his smooth-lipped mouth and white, even-toothed smile and felt my ears warm.

"Your go," Ess said.

I glanced down at his forearms, their fine covering of golden hairs, his silver rings, his lean wrists, and jerked my hands in a fake impending slap. Ess pulled his hands away—not a bad reaction, time-wise. The very nanosecond his hands landed back on mine like tentative dragonflies, I attacked cross-handed, crushing his stately right. The slap rang out in the museum room.

"Fuck!" Ess yelled, then started nodding his head, replacing his hands. "I see how this is going to be."

I got Ess eight times before I just barely missed. Hank stood by surveying, a thick-bodied presence. "Ho-ho!" he said loudly when I missed. "I get the winner." With that, I purposely left my hands hanging there for Ess to slap over and over till we quit, my skin stinging. I let Ess be the winner. He and Hank didn't play each other, of course.

Celeste remained engaged by some icon or other until we all

left the exhibit, returning to the arched entryway of the restaurant. "What're we doing?" Ess asked, scanning the group. "I'm off. Done for the day."

"You have a critique on Friday," Hank said to Ess.

Ess turned his head away, looking into the restaurant atrium, and wiped at the corners of his mouth with his ringed thumb and sexy forefinger. I knew where I wanted his long digits: tangled in my hair, pulling my head back, running up from my hips to my collarbones, stopping and pausing at all the right places.

"You're in summer school?" Celeste asked Ess.

Hank said, "Summer classes. Summer session."

"Not as punishment," Ess added. "Independent study."

"You're good then," Celeste said.

"Depends on who you ask." Ess still looked around the restaurant, empty except for a single table of tea-drinking ancients.

"He's good," Hank said, "but whether or not he's ready for his critique on Friday is 'another bloody issue entirely.'"

"You're pretending to be what's-his-face," I pointed out.

Hank grabbed his own crotch. "Giganto Schlongo."

"Khan, right?" Celeste asked.

Ess turned his attention back our way. "Talk about a disproportionate human figure. I sketched the wanker for homework and got a fuckin' C from Biljana."

Hank had obviously heard Ess' Sketching Gigantus Khan lament before. If I remembered correctly what Brooklyn had said about Ess, his memory didn't always serve him well. We walked slowly toward the exit. God! Brooklyn was dead. She was dead and gone and it seemed weird. Unreal. I would try again. "What exactly happened to Brooklyn?" I asked the guys.

"Now there's a story," Hank said, shaking his head theatrically. "Why don't we head over to my house—I have a pool—and we'll tell you all about the poor child."

Even Celeste, I could tell, saw straight through Hank's thin disguise. Oh, yeah, right. "We'll talk about how Brooklyn died and then I'll ask you to model for me, mmm, yes, you adorable bunnies, you bouncing bundles. . . ." I gave Celeste a look. But. Then. There was the prospect of Ess. I checked him out sidelong. And the prospect of Ess' fingers. "Where do you live?" I asked.

"Over on Oak," he answered. "Close. Walking distance." We stopped just inside the front doors of the museum.

"He lives in the stone house," Ess told us. "With the sculptures."

"That house?"

"The sculpture house?" The sculpture house was famous, having been owned by a series of Art Institute instructors who added to an ever-growing outdoor sculpture collection and voluntarily left the works behind to the property in perpetuity. It'd been in the newspaper and on the news. It'd even been featured in *Architectural Digest,* as the house itself had been built by some Frank Lloyd Wright contemporary or other and was, in its own right, spectacular.

"How did you get it?" Celeste asked.

Hank smiled a snake smile at my friend, his lips spread wide and pale, and then he shoved just the little tip of his tongue through at the corner. I had the almost undeniable urge to push it back in with my index finger, push it the way you'd push a typewriter key. "I got it," he said, and slurped his tongue back in, "by unscrupulous means."

"He fucked the old bag," Ess said plainly, looking as though he'd heard the story a thousand times.

I was momentarily suspicious as to how close Ess and Hank were that they seemed tired of each other's tales, but then I forgot my brain completely as the museum entry's automatic double doors opened and a musky, hot wind blew through. It lapped obscenely at my bare thighs. My glands and sturdy, pumping heart took over, a one-two knockout to my higher reasoning abilities. Ess' shirt clung to his chest. I couldn't even remember what we were talking about or why we were standing there.

"What old bag?" Celeste asked.

"The fuckin' crone," Ess said, and repeated what seemed to be a habit of his, touching his own chest. Could I swoon there on the marble? I thought about mouth-to-mouth, about Ess giving me mouth-to-mouth, and then about how we'd had to learn CPR the previous spring and had to perform it on a dummy named Annie with rubber flesh the color of the crayon called Flesh, and how her lips needed to be wiped with rubbing alcohol after each one of us, and that the rubbing alcohol or maybe all our mouths, all those clumsy student mouths, had sort of worn away her fake lipstick and flesh-colored skin around her mouth so that she looked like she'd been eating a powdered-sugar doughnut or maybe had just had one thrown right on her mouth, one of those minidoughnuts, and how when we knelt over her and locked our elbows and inter-laced our fingers and practically bounced on her with all our weight we still made the light light up only every other time and how her chest actually clicked like a . . . like a broken thing, a bro-ken toy, one of those cans with a label of cows on it that when it's tipped over it moos, only it's broken so all it does is click, and then I was breathing fine and remembered that we were talking about how Hank had gotten his house, the sculpture house.

". . . the heiress gave it to the Art Institute, and every ten years the school in turn allots it to the 'most promising artist-instructor.'"

"Rent-fucking-free," Ess added.

"Wow," Celeste said. "So you slept with a very old woman in order to be granted a rent-free house for a decade."

Hank paused, his look hard to read. "No," he finally said after Celeste and I had moved our stares to our own feet, "I orally manipulated the last dean."

Ess cleared his throat to hide a laugh. "I don't know if you two are ready for that story."

"I dare you," I said to Ess.

"Well, let's go then," Hank said.

I smiled and shrugged my shoulders in Celeste's direction, but she was already beelining it out the door.

"Where are you?" Mr. Diamond hollered. The phone was covered with melted candle wax and resembled an aging gnome with a dial in its chest, the receiver when hung up a huge bow tie. Who homemade a phone? I immediately passed the receiver to hovering Celeste.

"Hi, Dad," she said.

Standing at least two feet away from Celeste, I could still hear him bellow, "Where are you!?"

"Can you have Mom make dinner?" Celeste asked. She leaned toward me and tipped the receiver. I leaned in.

"Damn it, young lady, tell me where you are right this minute. Your mother said you two left for the museum at two ten! It is now nearly five hours later!"

"We're at an Art Institute faculty member's house, Dad. We're at the sculpture house. We met people at the museum—"

"What people?!" God, he'd really lost it since Diana.

"Artists. *Faculty* members." Mr. Diamond respected academicians. Celeste's tack, I thought, might work.

"What are their names?" he asked, his tone minutely better. "Where do they live?"

Celeste pressed the receiver into her stomach and mouthed, *What's your last name?* at Hank.

Cigarette dangling from the corner of his mouth, Hank walked over with a pen and wrote on Celeste's wrist: "MAnSoN, bRothEr oF."

Celeste giggled.

Even though the phone was buried in Celeste's suntanned midriff and I couldn't actually hear Mr. Diamond's voice at the moment, I nonetheless knew as well as Celeste that if her father said anything, if he wasn't waiting silently and very impatiently on the other end, he was in the process of saying, "Celeste Rose Diamond, you will shortly be in a serious amount of trouble!"

Hank wrote, "Dixon."

"Dixon, Hank Dixon, Dad. What's the matter? We're *fine!*"

"You're at Hank Dixon's house?" Mr. Diamond's voice changed entirely. He paused. Hank's reputation had evidently preceded him. "Well. Ah. Then. Are you eating? When can I come to pick you up?"

"There's so much to see, Dad. This place is incredible! Maybe you could come over sometime too."

"All right, then. When shall I pick you girls up? Late is fine. Just say a time and I'll be there."

"Hold on," Celeste said, and smashed the receiver into her butt. "Will you give us a ride home?" she whispered at Hank.

Nodding, Hank tossed his head at Ess, who lounged on one of the four sofas. "He will," Hank whispered back.

"Hank said he'd give us a ride, Dad. Do you need us to call again?"

I hoped and willed Mr. Diamond to say the right thing. It was a summer vacation night, even if it wasn't a weekend night.

"Ah," he hedged on the other end. "Ah, no, that's all right. Please be safe, though. And," he dashed off, lest he be hung up on, "and take some mental notes. I want to hear all about the art tomorrow, and that magnificent house."

"Tell Mom there's pâté and stuff if she doesn't feel like cooking, okay? Thanks. Bye!" Celeste tried to hang up the phone, balancing the receiver on the pointed gnome hat.

Hank casually put the gnome's bow tie back in its proper place, took Celeste's elbow, all gentlemanly-like, and led her back to the sofas. Neglected though as I was at the moment, I couldn't have been happier by Celeste's sudden and impetuous infatuation with the old guy, as it left the gorgeous young one open to my inexperienced attempts at seduction.

Hank had shown us around the sculpture gardens, the pool a mosaic-tiled extravaganza in the middle, but since then we'd sat in the living room drinking exotic blender concoctions that our host had prepared noisily in his talisman- and trinket- and found-object-filled kitchen. We listened to loud, unfamiliar reggae music, Hank and Ess affable and smooth and questioning, knowing just exactly how to make a couple of young and thirsty girls comfortable. It had been my idea to call Mr. Diamond. I thought that buying more time might well produce the desired results that Celeste and I had settled upon so many hours earlier, when the sun at its midday zenith had baked our oiled skin.

"Dinner then?" Hank asked.

Hank, not the soccer player I'd imagined but rather a rugby player—one of the starters and stars of his team, if you could believe anything he said—had dumped briquettes into the hibachi on the back terrace before we called home, but he hadn't lit them. Now he stood in the living room and shook a box of wooden matches as a percussion accent to the band on the stereo. Celeste had drunk more than I had, at least a whole handblown chalice's worth, but I didn't think the alcohol was what had swayed her in Hank's direction. She seemed to find him utterly irresistible, and so I decided that I should, too—not as much as I did Ess, but . . . What about this intense small man could Celeste possibly like? His age? His artwork? His ego? None had me pitter-pattering.

Ess, on the other hand, turned me into a bowl of quivering, nubile jelly. "Time to eat!" he said enthusiastically from his Dionysus-like pose on the couch.

"Yes, indeed," Hank said, finally drawing a match from its box and lighting it, I guessed for the hell of it, there in the house. "Yes, indeedy-deed."

The tale of Brooklyn, we'd learned while strolling through the sculptures upon our arrival, was one of love, betrayal, and loss. A classic. Brooklyn hadn't recognized the good thing she'd had with Pia until it was too late. Pia fell for another woman, a sad, beaten woman in the oldest of professions, and Brooklyn couldn't win her slave back. "Suicide on the train tracks!" Ess had bayed at the sky. Clearly thinking himself clever, he'd added, "Now Pia's a whore's whore."

We all worked at dinner, and through the kitchen window, I watched Celeste glug down big swallows of another one of Hank's blender drinks, standing close to the short man as he smoked a cigarette and turned bratwurst. Inside, I thrilled to the fact that Ess had elected to help me with the salad and a bag of frozen French fries. I stood barefoot on Hank's kitchen floor and did my best to sexily peel carrots. Ess clearly had dibs on me now, it seemed, and I chose not to question what hidden reasoning or arrangements he and Hank had. I simply reveled in my success. Ess poured too much oil on the tray and babbled about his drummer at their last show. "You shoulda seen the guy," he said. "He was a wasted motherfucker."

I looked out the window to check on Celeste and stopped peeling, awestruck. She and the old guy were making out, the long two-pronged grill fork erect in his hand.

"That man moves faster than the speed of light," Ess said at my shoulder.

I didn't think it'd been Hank to make the move. I pivoted then, my bare feet squeaking a little, and faced the handsome college guy with his earrings and ripped, sleeveless T. Carrot in one hand, peeler in the other, I had to have been obvious. "What?" Ess asked. "You want that, too?"

I rose up on my toes. Yes, I wanted that, too.

Ess flung the oily pan into the sink with a loud clank. He looked out the window again, now behind my back, and then put both hands on my waist and hoisted me to the counter. "You don't weigh a damn thing," he said, and opened my knees to stand between them. He leaned in, smelling like something wild in his ragged army pants. I closed my eyes and felt his warmth move my way, but no kiss came. I opened my eyes again to Ess inches from my face. "Aw," he said, "you're too sweet." He pulled back maybe a foot and looked me up and down.

"What?" I asked.

He moved in then and kissed me hard, hard. He sucked my tongue into his mouth, scraping the edges with his teeth, then pushed his tongue past my incisors, beyond the mid-molars, deeply, thickly as if to see how far it would go, how it would fit. He yanked his tongue back and said, "You'd let me, wouldn't you?" he asked.

I stared, sort of out of breath. Let him what?

"I can be nicer," he said. "I should be nicer. Want me to be nicer?"

I thought I did. My mouth hurt. "Okay."

He took my head in his hands then and twisted it to the left. He started talking, talking and alternately sticking his wet tongue into my ear so that his voice came and went, gloopy-sounding and hot, then cool, blowing, more words, tongue, spit noises, blowing. He . . . was older. He was so cute. He was in a band. "Wanna hold you over" tongue in my ear. Noisy blowing—"and then turn you around"—huge sticky spit sounds—"like that, wouldn't you?" He pressed on my skull, turned my head, and stared intently into my eyes. His pupils seemed uneven, one bigger than the other. "That's it for now, cutie-pie. You're gonna learn." He rubbed his lips together as if smearing on lipstick. "Learn to beg."

What? I looked out the window at Celeste and Hank. They too had stopped kissing, and I caught Hank making an OK sign, a chubby O with his thumb and forefinger, at Ess. I turned back. "I'm going to what? What'd you say?"

"You heard me."

"I'm going to *beg* you?"

"You heard me," he repeated, smiling humongously.

I couldn't help it. I grinned as wide as my mouth would manage. Ess was gorgeous, leaning into his shoulders there on the kitchen counter. I wanted more than his dirty, wet notions in my ear. I glanced again out the window.

"He won't touch her till she's ready," Ess said.

"Huh?" I swiveled back around.

"You're both safe with us."

What did that mean? "What . . . what?"

He said, "We know what we're doing."

What, exactly, was that? I saw Ess' forearms flex again, his eyes twinkle, his white teeth flash. I leaned in for another kiss, prepared to show Ess exactly how well I could kiss back when I wasn't stunned by his unfamiliar tactics, but he dodged. He moved his head off to the side, and I met air. Nothing.

"Hey, *chica,* you two need some food."

What the hell? You kiss somebody and then you back off? I

looked out the kitchen window for a third time and saw Hank talking to Celeste as though he were explaining something, instructing her through some complex portion of a sociology postulate. The barbecue fork twirled in curlicues and stabbed obelisks in the air, and Celeste nodded and finger-combed her hair behind her ears. I hopped off the kitchen counter and went for my blender drink, a soupy, warm thing by now, but I didn't care.

"What's the oven supposed to be on?" Ess asked, picking the oily tray up out of the sink.

How the hell was I supposed to know? I chewed soft chunks of unblended banana. "Where's the bag?" I asked brightly.

"I don't know."

"The temperature would be on the bag."

Ess opened the refrigerator door and stuck his head inside. Hmm. "Ess, they're frozen fries."

"You don't thaw them first?"

Despite Ess' question, I believed Hank when he'd said that Ess was a talented artist. I did.

The bratwursts were great, the fries burned, the salad bland. We sat with our feet in the pool, waiting to digest, and then Hank said it: "I'm sorry I don't have swimsuits for you ladies."

Now, I know you know as well as I did that something of the sort was coming. That the transparent plan to get Celeste and me naked and fucked had been built into the evening from the very first moment Hank laid eyes on us in the atrium of the art museum that afternoon. You could tell just by looking at him, without knowing him at all, without knowing he was a semifamous artist-lech, a lech-artist, that he would set up the situation the way that he did. Even I had known. Some men just didn't hide it very well, it being their intentions to screw. Or maybe they chose not to hide it at all.

"We don't need them," Celeste said.

I looked to her with my face that said, *I'm hiding the real face I'd normally be making because I don't want the guys to see that one, but what the hell do you mean by saying it's okay that we don't need swimsuits?*

She ignored my look completely. "Do we?" Celeste asked Hank.

Hank started to say something and then stopped, looking at Celeste as though she'd caught him in a corner. I guess she sort of had. "Of course not. I have—you can—whatever you like is fine by me."

"We could, say, swim in your rugby uniforms then?" she asked.

"Fuck," Ess said. "I don't know about you all, but I'm swimmin' in my birthday suit." He stood and wrestled off his T-shirt. In the late light of the setting sun, he was golden colored and lean, his stomach muscles moving beneath his glistening skin. He should have had wings, I thought, should have sprouted them there, poolside, and taken me for a fly around the garden. The rest of us sat and watched as Ess unbuttoned his pants and stepped out of them. He wore no underwear at all. His tan appeared complete, all his skin the same beautiful amber.

"Our man," Hank said, "obviously has no qualms about nudity." Hank looked at his student as if assessing a hillside, a desktop, a usual subject.

"He shouldn't," Celeste said, standing.

I sat still, staring, rigidly self-conscious, my toes puckering in the water. Ess' pubic hair was a light brown, almost red. His penis, I noted, smooth and tan too, was longer than Jim's. Or what I remembered of Jim's. I sensed I would soon be unable to recall a single distinct detail of my first lover's body—although I wouldn't have called him that yet, used that word, called him a "lover."

Hank stood, too. Celeste walked to the large modern sculpture on the other side of the pool, the one that looked like a teepee collapsing, and began a nonchalant disrobing. Both Hank and Ess, it was quite clear to me, purposely ignored Celeste then, as if they saw this sort of thing all the time, as if she were merely another model in a drawing class. I was the only one who knew better, though. When they looked at her, when they really looked at her naked, they would certainly see her. They wouldn't, couldn't, pretend not to. I knew that much. With her body half-hidden in angular shadows, Celeste seemed comfortable enough taking off her clothes in front of these strangers, in front of Hank, who, for all I knew, could be nearly thirty-five, nearly twice our age.

Celeste and I had skinny-dipped tons in her pool at night in the last few years. It wasn't the act itself that concerned me. Honestly. It was the company.

And the comparisons.

She hung her shirt on the end of one of the teepee poles and reached around to unhook her bra. I'd seen the freeing of her breasts plenty but still sat glued to the show. I looked quickly to see if the guys were coarse enough to watch, but they were pros. Some three sculptures away from Celeste, Hank, obviously having done all of this before, nothing new about it for him, hung his paint-splattered pants on the horn of a life-size copper ox, its young patina an iridescent orange-and-green muscular swirl. He hooked his red boxers on the other horn, and his shirt over the arched tail. I looked at Hank's body as he approached the pool. He looked nothing at all like what I'd expected, I realized, even as I understood that I hadn't known *what* to expect. His nakedness, his nakedness did what? It seemed to siphon everything toward him. His nakedness was a vacuum. His nakedness was masculinity of a kind, of a sort, of a something I'd never known or seen. I felt my bones and skin and lungs and psyche want to move without me toward Hank. He was not thin; nor was he hairless. Thick scars dissected both of his knees. But. And oh. I looked. And looked again. He was solidly muscled, and paler nearer his center than on the extremities of his limbs. And he pushed in front of him what I can only think to call the perfect penis.

Unlike Ess' form, Ess' gorgeous, idyllic spread of youthful self, Hank's frame was marked with the world. You know: with Experience. I couldn't stop looking, running my eyes over the sinew of his back, the shine of another scar splicing hamstring and glute. And then, as soon as I could bring myself, I studied it. The—his— penis wasn't particularly long or thick or red or stiff or anything at all else that you might imagine made up a perfect penis. Only years later, now, I've figured out that it was quite elegantly and simply the most balanced of all of those elements, of all the proportions and hues and values. Hank's penis fit the da Vinci man-in-the-circle equation. Hank's was, exactly, the ideal one. And right away, too, I knew that Celeste had figured out in her usual, quicker way, too damn long before I had, that Hank was a skilled artist with his god-given gift. There, at the side of Hank Dixon's cunnilingus-obtained, statue-surrounded swimming pool, dead smack in the middle of the city, I changed my mind. I wanted to give Celeste Ess and take Hank back, if I'd even had him in the first place.

Ess cannonballed. I got soaked. "Get naked!" he shouted at me, shoving big waves of water into my lap with his beautifully muscled arms. Ah, he was so pretty that summer. "I can tell you want to," he told me.

Hank dove into the pool, and Celeste, her timing perfect, followed. I believe I was the only one who saw her go in.

"Chicken," Ess teased me, and sixth grade came flooding back.

"Am not," I said. And then, of course, I had to. I dropped off over the edge, knelt on the bottom of the pool, and rose like a dolphin, spitting water. (The shallow end. Easy.) I bent and removed my shorts, twirled them over my head, and let them sail toward the ox, where they slapped his copper flank with a sodden thunk. The shirt next. In loud encouragement, which I appreciated to no end, Ess whistled as I unhooked my bra and sent it aloft. I tried to dance, move with the articulated kind of abandon that Ms. Elswit encouraged in jazz.

We can only hope.

The three of them applauded. I crouched, removed my underwear—Celeste's underwear actually, as I'd started my day at her house and changed into her clothes after swimming at her pool—and demurely trotted them to the intricate tiled edge, where they clung the rest of the night like a pale pink question mark.

Who makes up the protocol for such nude gatherings? Celeste and I, when alone and naked in her pool, always swam around for a while, talked on the pool steps with the lights out, or played in the dark, usually scoreless pool volleyball or catch or some other mindless game.

I know. You imagine young women, grown girls, playing games, naked, in a backyard pool, the big house's eyes glowing yellow-white in the dark, and you feel a flutter in your groin, or pity for what's to come, or you feel your breath catch in your chest for what you remember, what you lost, what's still exactly there in you right the fuck now, and you can almost know how we would do what we were about to do. I should shut up, I know. But, really, we all still have it in us. Us, you, me, whatever. We can all still feel. Can all still grab at life.

Protocol, though. What's right? Celeste and I had no idea. We only had what we already knew going in. Try to be normal, smile. Make a joke. Say something smart. But Hank's pool was bigger than the Diamonds', more elaborate, more disguised.

Like good dance partners, we let the men lead the way.

"Marco Polo," Ess said.

"No." Hank sidestroked toward a floating kickboard in the deep end. Celeste flipped a somersault in the water, and I followed suit. We could both manage nine without a breath, but we stuck to singles while the guys figured out how to play with us. Naked and all.

The earth continued spinning and we four rode it like everyone else always did, too, and in our unconscious doing, the sun dropped out of sight. We swam in the warm water and talked a little, dusk closing in. For entire moments as I stroked along beneath the surface, I forgot that two grown men with grown bodies were swimming just a few feet away. But Celeste and I were approaching our eighteenth birthdays, and we couldn't forget for long.

The water, silken, slipped over us. Standing in the shallow end, I arched and dipped my long, long summer-streaked hair into the water behind me. I lifted my feet and floated and spread my arms and felt the strange, seaweed slinking of my own locks against my skin. The sensation was heavenly and lush, and I watched as Celeste saw me and then did the same. Our hands brushed once or twice in her long hair, in mine, and then there were no more splashing sounds, no more casual talk from Ess and Hank. I stood first.

"Please," Hank said. "Go back. Keep floating."

Celeste stood too.

"Please," he repeated.

"Why?" Celeste asked.

"It's beautiful," he said.

So we did. We went back to floating the way we had, although after what Hank said it felt like hurdles at a meet or a dance number at a recital. You knew you were being watched and it wasn't quite the same. I forgot the feel of my hair, of the water, feeling only the stares of Hank and Ess running over me, how my breasts swelled up through the smell of chlorine, how the air cooled the flesh beneath my small tuft of pubic hair rising into the night between my sharp hip bones.

I knew, too, that the differences between Celeste's body and mine were becoming more apparent with each passing sweep of the men's eyes. We were both equally fit, yes, but the subtle disparity of our dimensions, our proportions, the smoothness of her curve between waist and thigh, my sharper protrusions, her longer limbs, my bigger rib cage, all floated there between us.

Would the men kiss us? Would they approach us as we stared up into the tree branches and dusty aubergine sky and kiss us upside down? I wanted them to. I wanted both of them to kiss me, Ess softer this time, my hand drifting down to touch his beautiful stomach, then Hank, feeling his weathered mouth move over mine, touch his penis in the water, feel it stiffen in my grip. I wanted their wet hands running my full length, imagined four hands skimming my edges. My nipples tightened. I heard Celeste breathing, breathing, breathing, and then I heard splashing, wet footfalls moving away. We stood up.

"He's getting the sketchbooks," Ess said.

Hank strode toward his house. "I didn't hear him say that," I said, feeling very naked.

"I know him. We have to draw you. Damn, you should see this!" Ess squeegeed his short hair with a pale palm and added, "It's fantastic!"

"Huh." Celeste slapped the surface of the water as if it were a baby's bottom, as if she were calming it down.

"I mean, you're fantastic! Trust me on this."

I looked at Celeste and shrugged, did a few somersaults and resurfaced. We waited around for Hank to come back out, the pool water clapping hollowly in the drain nearby, the blender grinding away at ice cubes back inside the house. I wondered what Celeste was thinking, how she felt about being drawn naked, what she wanted to do with Hank, how she'd known that he was so desirable so early, what she thought would happen before we went home. I didn't say a word. Electric light throughout the sculpture yard broke into the dark in a wave from left to right. The pool glowed.

"Ess. Grab these." Hank dropped towels on the ground. He had huge pads of paper and the blender and goblets and his actually really, really good body, too, even good-beside-Ess good, and charcoal sticks behind his ears and a cigarette in his teeth and that big damn smile dimpling his cheeks. And the penis. I knew I shouldn't stare, but too bad. I did. I couldn't take my eyes off it, and Hank saw me. He winked. I immediately looked to Celeste. She hadn't noticed, busily scrutinizing her own crescent of toe point, left-right-left, treading water like a synchronized swimmer. Ess pushed himself up out of the pool and picked up the towels. I wondered how he could keep such a good body without playing a sport, just going to art school, drinking lots, sculpting, and singing in a band. "There," Hank said, nodding with his head. Ess dropped a towel in a lump, and Hank sat down cross-legged on top of it near the edge of the pool. Ess took the other towel, dried off his butterscotch skin, and followed suit. "Ladies," Hank said. He tipped out a thick drink for himself. "If you would indulge us, we would be forever grateful, and your likeness may join the ranks of the garden."

A naked sculpture of us? Hadn't Hank meant to say "your like-nesses" rather than "likeness"?

"Please," Hank said.

We floated for over an hour.

By the time the two of them reluctantly let us get out of the pool—"No no no, just pee in it, I don't care," Hank had told Celeste halfway through—we were pruney and crabby and frustrated. They had sketched and sketched, flipping pages and making faces and mumbling and drinking more blender drinks, not offering us any, away in their own little worlds. I was mad. So was Celeste.

"You're going to give us a ride home," Celeste, already dressed, told Ess as I fumbled with my damp shorts, my fingertips dead-fish white. I was happy for Celeste's straightforwardness. Ditch the asking thing. Tell them what to do. No more, "Hang in there, hold, hold. Nice. Can you spread your hair again? No, with your other hand. You, um, no, I mean Celeste, Lisa."

Screw them! Why did we even do it?

I couldn't find my bra, Celeste's bra. I went searching through the sculptures, remembering soberly how I'd stupidly flung it away over my head. Strip-dancing and "artistic modeling," I con-cluded, didn't contain a single common denominator. And I bet that neither of them, done for a living, was much fun at all. I slapped at a mosquito biting my ankle; my wet hair dripped a cold trail into the crack of my ass.

We gathered around the sketchbooks, the empty blender, the damp towels. Celeste and I stood behind the two seated men, their laps hidden by the giant rectangles of paper, and looked over their shoulders as they compared and discussed and pointed. They turned page after page of dusky water, dark charcoal hair, arms and hands, and there was my profile! I saw Celeste's mouth, her breasts, my foot, and then the both of us from a greater dis-tance. The drawings were astonishing—fluid, skilled, delicate, auda-cious. And they were of us. Us!

I felt the change in Celeste even as I felt it in myself. These were art. We were art. With each new page, I wanted to fuck the teacher and his student more. Celeste did, too. I knew it.

"Time to go home now," he said when coming upon, finally, the first virginal white sheet.

"Yeah." Ess sighed. "You ready?"

SONIC YOUTH

IRVINE, MARCH '83

Another bitch, a blond slash wearing a bass. You watch her pluck, the curtain of her bangs obscuring her eyes. You don't need to see her. Not really. From the bar where you stand you watch her head bobbing, her hair swinging, and you are reminded of long-hair days from your formative years. Wonder how those years play out now. Wonder how they got you here. That's the real question anyway, isn't it?

NINE

THE GUYS packed us up and shipped us off. In the car, Ess stared straight ahead, his focus elsewhere. On his drawings, the sculpture to come, the night as it had played out, I wasn't sure, but I knew his concentration was no longer on me. Or Celeste. Not in the flesh anyway, not there in the car. He banged some unrecognizable song out on the steering wheel and hummed. I couldn't get his attention. I couldn't wait to have him. I couldn't wait to see him again.

Pulling up to the curb, Ess ducked his head past me and looked up to the Diamond house through the passenger window. Sitting in his rusty convertible I saw with his eyes all of a sudden, saw what Celeste's house really looked like. Huh. It was a mansion. After the hours we'd just spent at Hank's trim and eccentric sculpture house, the Diamonds' just didn't seem the same. Too big. Uselessly big. And sort of beige, even though it wasn't. I was sure Celeste felt the same way.

And then I was struck: With no sure way of contacting the men again, we had few options left. "Don't you want our numbers?" I asked.

"Hey," Ess said, continuing to look past me. "You know where to find us." Casual as casual could be.

"You have your critique on Friday, right?" It always took me longer to figure out how to play along.

"Hey. Whenever, *chica*. It's fine. You know."

"Bye, then," Celeste chirped from the backseat, and gave my shoulder a shove. "Go. I can't get out till you do."

I opened the door.

Mr. Diamond was kind.

I hadn't even thought about him again until I walked the flagstone path to the front door. He was going to have all kinds of questions. I'd lost a flip-flop; I thought I'd sprained both my wrists from all the water-treading and hair-caressing; and I was certain my eyes were still neon pink from chlorine. We opened the door and punched in the alarm code (a combination of all three Diamond daughters' birthdays, a number I remember to this day).

"You made it back, did you?" Mr. Diamond called out from the dining room. He sat at the table reading.

"Yes, Dad," Celeste called back, and continued moving toward the stairs. I bolted down the hall alongside her.

"I don't want to see tired faces tomorrow," he said. "You girls get some sleep."

And he nicely, for once lately, let it be.

That night, my dreams were churned things, watery, dark, scary things. Beside Celeste in her big queen-size bed, I rolled and swam and struck out at creatures.

It's interesting to think about how some part of your brain gets hold of the meaning of an event, of the significance of happenings, faster than the other parts of your brain. But it sucks that it's usually the part of your brain that doesn't connect with the rest, generally. You think about vestigial parts of the human body, the mind, things that belonged to us for a purpose hundreds of thousands of years ago. Did we used to have gullets like chickens? Eat a few stones to help digest our fern lunches? Did that part of our brain that knows things first tell us what to do? Was it our built-in warning system? Bulls, when entering the ring, can smell the fear and blood and death of the bulls that came before. Their sense of smell is part of an intricate alarm series. Where'd ours go? Our sense of smell blows chunks. Do we still have an alarm system and just not know how to use it anymore? I wonder sometimes. I wonder if a bull has ever escaped and barreled away down the streets to some sweet pasture, to any real heaven on earth. I hope so. I really, really do.

In the morning, the world still seemed changed. "I want to go back," I told Celeste.

Her yawn beside me was only faintly sour. Yogurt-breathed. "You do?"

I had visions of Hank and Ess dancing in my head. "It . . . they . . ." I searched. "Don't you want to go back?" We hadn't made clear plans before falling asleep.

"I don't care," she said.

I didn't believe her. "Really?" I had never seen myself in drawings before. I wanted to see more. I wanted to see more of me through their eyes. "It feels, I mean it felt like—" I tried again. "Like, like worship."

She stretched and scratched under her back. "Like love."

"Fame," I said, smiling.

Celeste put both her feet on my closest thigh and pushed me out of bed.

"Oh," I groaned from the floor. "Oh, Ess. I need resuscitation."

"Is that what you're calling it today?"

"Hank, Haaaaank," I falsettoed, I Celeste-ed, "give me what I want. Give me that manly manhood of yours, that masculine, manly manhood."

"Shut up."

I sat up. "You really don't care?" I looked down at my feet and wiggled my toes. They were tan. "Really?"

"I don't know," Celeste said.

She had to want these guys. "But they're so different," I told her. "They're our *garçons*. Better than *garçons*. They're artists."

"So?" She swung her legs out from under the covers and over the bed's edge. "So they're artists."

"But they're different," I tried again. "They're not the same as everyone else. They have guts."

"And dicks."

"Yes." I grinned the evil grin. "Let's go back. Please let's go back. Let's go back let's go—"

"Why? So they can sit there drawing us again?"

"I didn't mind," I said. "I mean, I thought it might be humiliating—I mean, it could have been humiliating—if they weren't any good or weren't actually drawing us. . . . But they were great. Come on, you thought so too."

"It wasn't humiliating because we chose not to let it be," she said, walking to her dresser.

"You think that people are in control of their own humiliations?" Where was she going?

Celeste pulled tangled bikini tops and bottoms from her drawer. "Sure. For the most part. Don't be embarrassed by other people's actions. It's in your control."

I wasn't sure I believed her; she'd started to wander. "I think they're both good artists," I said.

She tossed me a suit, a bright striped bikini. "You think they're both *sexy*."

"Don't you?" I stood.

"Of course. But their being artists has nothing to do with their being sexy."

I stepped into the bottoms and pulled Celeste's nightgown over my head. "I think it does," I said into cotton flowers. "You don't think they're good artists?" I tried to pull the nightgown free but my hair was caught on a button.

Celeste turned to me, her breasts pale against the brown of the skin over her ribs. She had pink nipples. I did, too. "I think good artists have talent, but I . . . I don't believe that talent equals sexiness."

"Well, then, why do you think they're sexy?"

"Confidence."

One word. I could have come up with twenty and the one she chose wouldn't have been on the list. What seventeen-year-old in 1981 knows to list confidence as her ultimate turn-on? Not me. My best friend was clearly a freak. I hooked the back of the top and tied the strings behind my neck.

"But they *are* artists," Celeste said, "and so it'll be hard to know, you know? Know if they're interested in us as us or us as specimens."

"Does it matter?"

"It does if you ever want to ride those ponies."

"You are so gross!"

"It was your idea," she said.

"You were naked before I even stood up!"

"Your idea to go hunting for new guys."

"So."

"Well, if you hadn't noticed, they sent us home. Untarnished."

"It's a game for them," I said. "I want to play."

"Why should it be a game?"

"Pleeeeeease." Sometimes I found her exasperating. I looked at my reflection in her mirror. "You don't think they're *good* artists?" I couldn't just let everything slide away.

"I'd like to reserve judgment."

"But you think they're sexy. So why wouldn't you want to go back to the sculpture house, or the Nelson-Atkins or wherever and try to . . . try to get them again?"

"It's not that." Celeste bit her bottom lip. "It's. They're." She frowned and scanned her bedroom ceiling, looking, I guessed, for some kind of clarity of expression. She seemed to be after something that completely eluded me. "They could be dangerous," she said finally.

"But how, when they didn't—really—touch us?"

"Exactly."

I had no idea what she meant. "Art makes a difference," I tried. "Art . . . counts. It makes them different."

"It's not art," she said. "Not that makes them different, anyway."

"I want to go back," I said again. I couldn't be more plain. She'd get done by a master, I would bet.

"Lisa."

"Please."

She paused. "Fine."

"Yea!"

"I don't know about 'yea.'" She swung her arms the same way that Hank had the night before, as if she were warming up for a sporting event. "Think Dad's gone by now?"

We walked downstairs. I was chipper as could be, and to top it off, Mr. Diamond had already left for work. We sat there at the kitchen table, both of us in Celeste's swimsuits, eating big wedges of watermelon.

I think, now, she could smell what I couldn't. It was there, right there, raked just under the bullring dirt.

Putting our plates in the dishwasher, Celeste suggested we not go back that day, the very next day. "We should try to find them on campus Friday," she said, "after Ess' critique."

"But we could miss them," I said. "We don't know where they'll be on campus."

"It'll be fine. We know where the sculpture department is, and we know where Hank lives."

I didn't want to wait two days. Why couldn't we go to the museum right away? "Why not today?"

"Because," Celeste said. "Because." She seemed to deliberate. "They shouldn't see how eager you—we—are."

"What's wrong with that?" I asked. "They don't like eagerness?"

"I don't mean enthusiasm," she said.

"Well, what do you?"

"We're at a disadvantage, Lisa. Why don't you see it?"

Huh? "How do you mean?"

"Every way possible."

"I don't think Ess is smarter than I am," I said.

"No, but he's older."

"So?"

"He's more experienced."

"So?" I thought I knew what she was driving at, but I wasn't going to concede so easily. "If they'd wanted to hurt us, they could have already."

"Not that measurable of a hurt," she said.

"Oh," I breathed, "the unmeasurable kind of hurt."

"Exactly."

"*Im*measurable," I said, pointedly correcting the intentional mistake that Celeste had chosen to ignore. I paused. "Well, what's wrong with having sex with an older guy anyway?"

"Nothing."

"Then what? *What?*"

"We should wait until Friday, Lis."

I didn't want to, but I didn't want to fight about it, and Celeste was making me feel funny. Sort of icky. "Well, what are we going to do until then?"

"Whatever we want. We could go to—well, there's Wanda's party Saturday. You know there'll be different guys there!"

Why was she talking about Saturday and different guys, obviously black guys? Her false enthusiasm irked me. "Until *Friday*," I repeated, irritated. "What will we do until we see Ess and Hank again?"

"The same things we did before we met them."

I looked at her. I couldn't decipher how she meant that, whether she was being mean or simply straightforward. "Ha, ha," I said. She could take *that* however she wanted. I opened the kitchen door out to the backyard. "Swimming?" I asked.

"Sure."

The dew had nearly evaporated from the grass. The Diamond backyard, nothing like Hank's, was green upon green with preppy-colored accents. Clear yellow honeysuckle wove along a far portion of the fence. Periwinkle spread under the shade of two mimosas donning their pink pompon flowers. A brick pathway dissected the yard into neat squares and rectangles, separating to create the edging around the concrete pool slab and the border planters, merging again to provide a solid footing for the stone birdbath. The yard was pleasant and pretty. But now it felt plain. I contemplated the yard, the Diamonds' yard, so different from my own family's.

I'd not been home much and felt missed even less. My brother, David, and my father had begun a regular eating-out schedule most nights. My absorption into the Diamond family seemed nearly seamless, actually, and I rarely stopped to think about how my slow migration into a house that wasn't technically mine wasn't exactly normal. Of course I made a show of returning to my "real" house a couple times a week, spending a night here or there, talking to David and my father at breakfast. Sadly, I never cooked for them. In the Smith kitchen, I never really shared what I'd learned in the Diamond house over the years. David and I argued over the most trifling school issues, over when the blue test booklet prices were going to go up, when the construction of the new administrative and counseling building was beginning, and our father sat and read the paper, tapping his hard toast on his saucer in some semblance of time to my brother's and my bickering.

But my father and David appeared just as content to have me gone as I was to be rid of the sanitary confines of that plain, utilitarian house. The arrangement of losing first the mother, and then, largely, the daughter, seemed to suit the Smith men just fine. Oh, well. Screw 'em.

Now, though, as I measured the Diamond yard against "mine" in my mind and against Hank's sculpture yard, I came to the conclusion that the Diamonds' was far closer to the neighborhood norm than it was to anything artistic. Until then, I had found the place a sanctuary. Indeed it was still familiar, still safe and comfortable, but now it lacked the proverbial *je ne sais quoi*. Certainly Mona Diamond hadn't replanted overnight or redesigned the yard into what it hadn't been the day before. But. But, unlike the Diamond yard, Hank's yard presented itself with lust, I now saw, with vigor, spirit, and freedom freedom freedom. (Too young, I couldn't see through all the Bohemian obviousness. Just a serial home for seductions. A home for serial seductions.)

Celeste skimmed the Diamond pool surface with the long-poled net, snagging bee carcasses and floating roly-polys. I dove in after she finished and swam nearly to the other end underwater, thinking about Ess, about how I needed to practice kissing different guys so that I could respond more quickly. I needed to be more adept at reading a guy's kiss and then kiss back in that style. Like singing. Don't break into Pink Floyd in your R & B voice. I had to figure out what Ess liked. If you kissed a guy hard on your end, maybe his kissing so hard to begin with wouldn't hurt as much.

I gulped air and burst into song, into *"We don't need no thought control. . . ."*

Celeste tiptoed on the edge, preparing to back-dive. "Don't sing about teachers," she said, and sprang like a sprite.

We swam laps for a while, then took our usual chaises. After half an hour I was bored. "I'm bored," I said.

"Then read something," Celeste said, turning over.

We'd agreed that we'd conquer some of the classics over the summer. Celeste struggled through a few mid-Brits, but I hated them, pompous, whiny things that they were. All the social suffering, blah, blah, blah. I'd defected to *Vogue* and *Mademoiselle* in June, because as much as I'd begun to dread the serious junk, I didn't enjoy the fluff any better. I found romance novels insipid. Soap operas too. The Lynnes had formed a club over the summer around *General Hospital*, a "daytime drama" I tried to like but couldn't. Celeste and I were equally dismayed, equally bored. I knew it, even if she wouldn't admit it.

"It's nine thirty in the morning," I said. "And it's Wednesday." I scratched my butt. "I've read every magazine in the entire city." I looked at her and cut her off. "That I *want* to read. My tan is fine. My nails are fine. My hair is fine."

Celeste groaned into the chaise pillow.

"You *know* I don't have my period. . . ." Celeste and I had been bleeding together for nearly two and a half years.

"Ssshhhhhh."

"Celeste, please?"

"Lis, I'm going to kill you."

"Not if I kill you first. Please, let's go to the Nelson-Atkins for lunch."

Another groan.

"Please."

"What if Pregnant Rose is there?"

I knew I had her. "Pregnant Rose? I won't let her bother you, Celeste."

She flipped onto her back again and pointed into the sky. "Look. A clown with an anteater nose. But she makes me feel bad."

"Me, too," I admitted. "But . . . but it seems like Ess and her aren't really going out."

"I wasn't accusing you of intervening. I just feel bad for her, drinking and pregnant. That can't be very good for the baby."

"Maybe a beer or two is okay," I ventured.

"Maybe," she said. "But I don't think she's drinking one or two beers a day."

I sat up and stared at the Diamonds' pool, the pretty, pretty rectangle of limpid blue. "Please, Celeste? We *have* to do something. Art is good."

"*Art* is good. The museum is good. That doesn't mean everything in the museum is good. It's an easy logic problem."

"If A is red," I countered, "and B is boring, then what would C be?"

"A horny monkey," Celeste said. We laughed.

Three hours later we were back at the Nelson-Atkins, the second day in a row. I had won, and Mrs. Diamond had agreed in advance to let us stay out. She understood the smothering her husband was capable of. "You watch out for each other," Mona had said, and given us each a ten-dollar bill.

We'd decided to eat a late lunch in the hopes of Hank lingering around the same time—the thought of which made my heart pitter-patter—and to view the Russians again in the meantime, with the new knowledge Hank had given us. To see if knowledge made a difference with art. But before we even set foot into the exhibit, I'd decided that the only way knowledge might matter was if it included information along the lines of people being murdered for art, good, scandalous, real-life stories, where you could look at a painting and think how cool it was that it had been stolen and sold and stolen again, and then rescued, all for what it was to somebody willing to pay for art, for what that painting was, or showed, or represented, or made that thief or millionaire feel. That was cool. That would make me want to touch a cloisonnéed egg. Roll it around in my hands, balance it between my breasts as I floated in Hank's pool.

Egg held at throat. Egg resting in the crevice of thighs near perfectly rendered knees. A charcoaled orb between pointed toes. I could see the eggs, see Celeste and me, see Hank and Ess seeing me, and Celeste, seeing the eggs.

I was on a roll.

Walking through the exhibit, I suppose I appreciated the triptychs a little more than I had the first time, but the eggs . . . well, I just kept seeing the eggs on our bodies at Hank's. Celeste hadn't even let me peek into the atrium restaurant to see if Hank or Ess was there. We had to pretend we'd come for the art.

We moved into Egypt, into the small rooms with carved stone and hieroglyphs. These I wanted to touch. I could barely keep my hands off of the minor prince's tomb on its pedestal. To touch something that had been around thousands of years ago, had been touched by other hands—the slave's carving hands and the artist's sensitive hands and maybe even the hands of the people who laid the mummy to rest—to touch that now was almost to connect with the dead, to take away time. I couldn't exactly figure out my compulsion, because it was more than just that too, but finally I allowed myself to gently stroke a stone corner.

"Lisa . . ." Celeste warned as a guard walked in.

"Please do not touch the exhibit pieces," the woman said.

"Sorry."

The woman stood with her hands clasped behind her back, her feet spread. You could tell she'd been in the military. I resented her immediately. "What a bitch," I whispered in Celeste's ear.

"She's just doing her job," she whispered back.

"Fuck her," I whispered.

"Angry today, are we?" Whispered.

"No," I said in a regular tone of voice. "I'm going downstairs." I turned and headed toward the door. A strong hand grabbed my arm. Celeste.

"Wait," she said. "I need you to promise."

"What?"

"Promise me that you won't leave me. No matter what. No matter what happens."

Jesus. She sounded like we were going off to war. "What's going to happen, Celeste?"

"No matter what you do. No matter what I do. We stay together, okay?"

"Okay, okay."

"Promise."

"I promise."

"Swear."

"I *swear*, Celeste."

Hank sat downstairs in the restaurant atrium at a table by himself save for a journal-size sketchbook. We stood at the entrance, easily thirty yards from where he sat, and he looked up from his drawing immediately. I wondered, suddenly, about his sense of smell. He smiled at us, and then he turned his gaze to the workstation where Ess stood in his full white apron, a bus tub in his hands. Ess gave Hank an impatient, questioning look, and Hank nodded our way. Ess made an obvious "Oh!" face then and turned to us with a grin straight from *Alice in Wonderland*. A shit-eatin', canary-chompin' grin.

Okay, so Celeste had been right. Screw it. We were there now, and we couldn't very well turn tail and walk back out the door. Hank seemed to sense our discomfort and waved us toward him. Friendly enough. Being friendly. Polite, actually.

We walked over to him. I tried to keep my shoulders leveled. Squared. Stay proud. Be elegant. Walk gracefully around the other tables, toward the penis, chin up, light brush of fingers on a chair back. Think, think of something clever to say.

"Hi, Hank," Celeste said.

"Ladies," he said, and I wanted to fuck him. He took Celeste's hand, and then he took my hand in his other, and he brought both to his mouth. He kissed mine, then Celeste's, then mine again. "The very affectionate French kiss in threes," he said, still holding our hands.

"*Trois*," I said dumbly. I wanted to look at it. I wanted to, I wanted to, an Egyptian wonder, a rugby penis—I stared straight into Hank's eyes.

"*Oui*," he said.

Celeste smiled—I knew in spite of herself—and pulled her hand away. I reluctantly withdrew mine too.

"Have a seat," he said.

"We're going to eat," Celeste told him.

I nodded and smiled.

"Ah, good. I already ate," he informed us, "but I'm sure our friend Ess will be happy to see you."

I followed Celeste to the food, to Ess, like a calf to slaughter. Doe-de-doe-de-doe, I tripped along behind her.

"Hi," Ess said. "Um, Celeste. And Lisa." I still believed, having seen his sketches, that he was a talented artist. At least he remembered our names. Obviously. His smile could have taken an eye out it was so bright.

"What's good today?" Celeste asked.

"Now there's a setup if I ever heard one." Ess rubbed distractedly on the front of his apron, the part that covered his light, golden-red treasure trail. The abdominal muscles.

"What?" I asked.

"'What's good today,'" Ess repeated.

"She asked *you*," I said.

"For a joke," Celeste said to me.

"What?"

"Forget it," Ess said. "The pasta. The pasta's good."

Celeste told him, "I'm not in the mood."

"For pasta," I said, and elbowed her.

"I seeeee," Ess rumbled. "A salad perhaps? The spring vegetable soup is most divinely excellently superb as well."

An ancient tweed cleared her throat behind us and pushed her tray ever so accidentally into my lower back.

"We'll be with you in a moment, ma'am," Ess said flatly.

I shot the tweed a frown. "It's July," I flirted. "Wouldn't that make the spring vegetable soup a little *old*?"

"Huh?"

"Never mind," I told him. "I'll have the pasta, please."

"Look look look!" a high voice said. Ing appeared from behind the screen. "They're back! Don't you both look delicious! Why, hello!" Ing flung two floppy hands at us.

You couldn't help but smile. Celeste and I said hi. Ess told Ing to help the tweed behind me.

"The lasagna," the woman directed, a long fingernail clacking on the glass guard. "That one."

"So what brings you two ladies in here?" Ess asked, all smiles. As if he had to ask.

"You," I said. What else would have worked?

"Me?"

"Mmm, mmm," Ing said, lifting out a slab of spinach-and-blue-cheese lasagna with a spatula that was clearly too small for the task. "The girls are here for you, you lucky bo—" and the square of noodles and speckled filling flipped back into the pan.

The tweed gasped, truly gasped, then said, "I certainly hope you're not intending to give me that now, young woman."

"Young woman?" Ing asked her, raising eyebrows.

We watched the tweed struggle with Ing's gender identity.

"Or young man?" Ess teased the woman.

The tweed shook her head and looked disgusted but held her ground.

"Pasta," I instructed Ess, drumming my fingers on my tray, smiling.

Ess smiled back and drummed his own fingers on his chest. "Yes, ma'am. The lasagna, was it, or the linguini and asparagus?"

My-oh-my. Eenie meenie minie mo. Either man would be more than fine for me. Ess was so nice to look at. "Linguini," I said, "and make it snappy."

Ess didn't smile. "You're getting a spanking for that."

"You be nice," Ing said, managing to get a second piece onto the tweed's plate. Ing handed the food to the woman, set down the spatula, and clapped.

"That's a frosting spatula, you know," Celeste said.

"Is it?" Ing looked at the spatula as though it belonged in a glass box in one of the exhibits. A relic, a strange stone carved for an archaic task.

At the table with Hank and our food, plans were made. "Come swim," he said. "It's hot as a witch's tit out there today."

"What'd you say?" I asked.

"Lisa isn't all that familiar with sayings," Celeste said.

"Like the Mojave," he said.

"Like the underside of a magnifying glass," Celeste said.

"I get it, I get it. But why would a witch's tit be hot? Why not icy cold?" I really didn't understand.

"It's just a saying," Celeste said.

"That's a good question," Hank said. "It almost makes more sense for a witch's tit to be icy cold." I couldn't tell if he was repeating for the pleasure of saying the word *tit* or not.

"Witches are close to demons," Celeste said, "and hence live in hellish places. Where kettles boil."

"And trouble brews," Hank added.

"Why would anybody come up with that in the first place?" I asked. "I mean, who would think about a witch nursing?"

"Ho! Now I hadn't even thought about measuring temperature with a mouth." Hank smiled at me, and I felt my face warm. "No, no. Don't get embarrassed. That's wonderful. That makes me want to sketch such a sight. Pointy hat, warty nose, and a cherubic baby at her tit! That's great!"

"Or touching a witch," I mumbled. "Anywhere on her body. I mean, they're fake anyway."

"Not if you lived in Salem," Celeste said.

"You two could very well be considered evildoers," Hank said, leaning back in his chair. His blue eyes pierced through me. Eye skewers. Pupil daggers. Straight through. "In the seventeenth century."

I wanted to call him a, a—damn, what were they called? "A warlock!" I shouted.

"Where?" he asked, all big blue eyes, pretending to be scared. All dark lashes. Sexy dark lashes.

I decided that the rest would be easy. The rest of the day, the night. I barely touched my linguini even though it was good. Celeste didn't finish her soup-and-half-sandwich combo either. I wished she'd be more herself, stop flashing me looks. I, for one, loved the idea of the unfamiliar. God, men! They were real men! Who cared if we had no idea what we were doing with them. They would have to know what they were doing with us, and I couldn't wait to find out what that would be. What could Ess do to me? How would he touch me? Taste me? I wanted to know about Hank, too, but . . . well.

The short walk back to Hank's had us sweating. Past the locked gate, Ess, Celeste, and I raced each other to the pool and jumped in, completely clothed. Hank walked toward his kitchen. "Now what are you going to wear?" he asked.

I looked at Ess, his shirt clinging to his deliciousness. I looked down at my own hard nipples announcing themselves as plainly as if I'd been naked. I looked at Celeste, but she was underwater, a thin manta ray, moving along the sinuous drop of shallow to deep.

"Like I give a fuck," Ess told Hank.

"No," Hank said, stopping at the door. "I don't suppose you would."

I couldn't make out Hank's tone, but I didn't care, as thirty seconds later muffled reggae began to ring out from the house. Hank opened the windows and moved the speakers into them, then started to make something or other on the closest counter. He didn't look up, just chopped away with an enormous knife.

"What's he making?" Celeste asked, rising beside me.

"Don't know."

"He has a thing about fruits," Ess said, struggling to take off his black jeans in the pool. I stared. "Joining me, ladies?" he asked.

I dropped underwater, took everything off, and slopped it into a pile on the tiled surround. I'd learned my lesson last night—no flinging away key pieces of body coverage. The afternoon sun felt wonderful. Ess trotted through the water and piled his clothes directly on top of mine. I thought of him sitting on me, pinning me in a wrestling match. I wondered how much he weighed.

"Already?" Celeste asked, and then got naked as if she did this in front of other people every day of her life. She made her own clothing pile next to mine, just barely touching, our bra straps holding hands. We had hoped we'd end up in Hank's pool, even considered bringing suits, but in the end decided against it. Naked felt better. And naked was closer to sex, wasn't it?

"Marco Polo," Ess said, clapping his hands to rally us, a private-girls'-school dream of a naked gym teacher. Beneath the noise of his clap, his rings clanked metallically. "Who's first?"

"You go first," I told him.

"Fine by me." He shut his eyes, turned his back, and counted to ten. "Marco!"

"Polo."

"Polo."

Celeste and I had swum to the deep end, opposite corners. Ess swam our general way, eyes closed. "Marco!" he yelled louder.

"Polo."

"Polo."

He'd drifted nearer Celeste, who pushed off the wall and quietly glided toward the center. I loudly treaded water and said again, "Polo." I couldn't swallow the giggle that escaped afterward. Ess moved his head my way, then rotated his body and extended his muscled arms in front of him. I wanted to shout, "Polo Polo Polo!" at the top of my lungs, but instead backed into the corner and propped my elbows, arms outstretched, on the lip of the pool. The sun bounced off my white breasts.

"Marco!" he yelled louder still.

"Polo." Mouselike in my peep. And then his hands found me, found my waist first. I giggled. He kept his eyes closed. His rings were colder than the rest of his palms. He hummed along with the reggae song and pretended to be blind, moving his hands up my front, over my breasts, circling my neck, feeling the shape of my face. He tried to fit a finger in my nostril. I slapped his hand away. "*Stop* it!"

He opened his eyes. "It's you. I couldn't tell if it was you or her."

I couldn't decide if I was flattered or hurt.

"You're no sculptor yet then," Hank said, appearing with a platter of sliced fruit.

"I knew it was Lisa."

"Why did you say that then?" Celeste asked.

"I don't know." Ess caged me, his feet perched on the pool walls on either side of me, his hands gripping the edges. He bent forward and down and tilted his head and kissed me as sweetly and gently as anyone ever had on the side of my neck. Celeste and Hank looked on. I melted. I dropped into the water and slid through Ess' legs. Oh, oh, oh. The mosaic swirls of waves and seaweed and serpents glittered in the daylight. From beneath the surface I saw the warbled figure of Hank bend toward the edge of the pool and set down the platter. I burst into the air.

"What are these?" Celeste asked, swimming toward the food.

I was reminded of a Gauguin spread, of halved, exotic, womb-looking spheres. Hank had created a beautiful plate for us. And Ess had thought I was Celeste with his eyes closed, or wished that I were. I pushed it away, the thought, and swam to see what Hank had put together.

"Where do you get these?" Celeste held up a half of a yellow-skinned orange fruit brimming with black roe, wet seeds like premium caviar. "Is this a mango?"

"Papaya," Hank said, and knelt.

Ess splashed around in the water behind us, yawning loudly, trying to float on his back.

"Kiwi, right?" Celeste pointed to fuzzy, round slices of green.

"What are those?" I flicked at a small pile of things that looked like warty eyeballs with no irises.

"Lychees," Hank said. "Try one."

"You first," I said to him.

He took one and popped it in his mouth. "They're pitted," he said after he swallowed. "Fresh are better, but I haven't found them yet."

Ess yawned an MGM lion's roar of a yawn. "See the starfruit?" Ess asked without looking. "California. He has 'em shipped every month."

"They're beautiful," Celeste said.

"Taste," Hank directed. He sat down on the ground and drew a joint out from behind his ear. I'd seen joints at parties before, and a hookah too, but pot wasn't a big drug at school. The kids who did stuff usually went for the pharmaceuticals. Word was that Valium and gin was a great combination for a car crash. A few smoking-lounge kids made bongs in art class, and a guy nicknamed Billy Browneyes sold his mom's prescription uppers, but Celeste and I had never touched anything except alcohol. We'd never even had so much to drink that we'd puked.

Hank leaned back to pull a lighter out of his pocket. "Puff?" He lit the little twisted end and the pungent scent wafted our way. Celeste looked at me. I didn't know. Drugs seemed like a waste of time, but maybe trying them would be fun. "Have you smoked before?" he asked, and then Ess was right there in between us, bumping shoulders. He held his thumb and index finger out to Hank.

"I take it that fraternizing with the students isn't perceived to be a big deal at KCAI," Celeste said.

"You can say 'Art Institute,'" Ess said, taking the joint and turning his back on me to face her. Over his shoulder I saw Celeste press her naked front into the pool wall.

Hank drew a slow finger over the platter. "For you, Miss Lisa . . ." he said. "I believe an Asian pear is in order." Hank leaned my way and fed me a piece. Sweet, crunchy, perfumed, juicy. I smiled.

Ess coughed through his nose, snorting thin smoke like a

waterlogged dragon. "Hell, no," he said in a voice tucked up into the top of his lungs, a tight voice with no air in it. "It's a school to study *art*. They couldn't keep us apart. Hey! I'm a rhymin' machine!" He exhaled loudly, then took another puff.

"The school's a bit different from your usual college," Hank said, and put an eyeball—what were they called again?—into Celeste's mouth. He brushed something imaginary off her lower lip after feeding her. Pool water, maybe.

"More like how you'd want it to be," Ess said in the squeezed voice again, then seemed to get an idea. "Shotgun," he eked, and grabbed the back of my head suddenly. He pulled my face to his, mashing his lips on mine. He stuck his finger into the corner of my mouth to pry open my teeth, and then blew all the smoke in his lungs into my throat. "Breathe, breathe, suck it in!" he said excitedly.

I did as I was told and felt everything start to burn at once.

"Hold it! Hold your nose!"

I couldn't help it though. The smoke was nothing like cigarette smoke. The cough came out as if it didn't belong to me. A long, jerking, face-tingling coughing session. Finally I stopped.

"Just breathe," Hank said. "Slow. Slow."

"Will you do me?" Celeste asked Hank.

"Really? You want that?"

Celeste nodded. "I'll try to hold it better."

"Good luck," I croaked, and coughed again. I watched Hank suck in smoke, then lean to lift Celeste's chin with his fingertips. He pivoted and repositioned himself, smoothly, in one move, to lie stomach down, bringing his face within inches of hers. I coughed again. He slowly took away the gap, and in the sunlight I could see the sheen of sweat on his upper lip. We were all that close.

Celeste—good god, we knew her to be what she was then, at that sun-bright moment backdropped by a Plains-baking sky—closed her silky eyelids and parted her ripe lips that put the fruit to shame and waited for Hank's mouth to find hers. Hank used his tongue to open her more, to make room for the smoke, for the breath of him, and then sealed his lips to hers. I watched his chest contract. I saw her intake of him. And then they were done. He kissed her in parting and lay staring, the only dry, clothed one of us. Celeste closed her mouth and opened her eyes. She pinched her nose like a girl, and somehow looked perfectly natural.

But we were so much the same. She would cough like I had. I waited and watched her hold her breath until finally she asked Hank with her eyes. "By all means," he said, and she plunged into the water and blew a stream of bubbles. They burbled on the surface, releasing a faint haze, a celestial mist of sweet breath.

I wanted to hate her.

"It is hot today," Hank said, standing. He put the joint out on the leg of his paint-covered jeans, walked to a table and set it in the ashtray, then pulled his shirt over his head. "Are you all fine in your birthday suits?"

We had been the night before. Why wouldn't we be now? Why did Celeste's body look longer underwater, mine shorter? My breasts appeared severe, hers perfectly rounded handfuls. Birthday suits? Ess backstroked away into the middle of the pool; Celeste nodded, treading water and smiling at Hank; and I prayed for dusk to come quickly, come slinking in quickly on silent cat feet.

Hank stripped to his boxers only, then dove in.

"What's wrong with your birthday suit?" I asked him when he came up.

"Absolutely nothing." He grinned at me, his eyes the color of the blue tile behind him.

"Well?"

"I'd like to keep it that way," he said.

Lifting himself onto the edge, back muscles flexing, Ess said, "Can't sunburn the shrine."

"What?" I was slow enough to ask.

"Where they worship," Ess clarified. "The ladies. Can't sunburn the shrine."

And I felt naked, naked, naked.

By suppertime, Celeste and I wore two of Hank's oversize cotton button-downs and boxers. Our long hair had dried. I left my shirt unbuttoned far too far, trying to feel sexy. I did, sort of, but couldn't help but think Hank had given Celeste a better shirt and a better pair of boxers. Hank had opened a bottle of white wine for us ladies. They drank Buds and both wore Hank's shorts and worn-out T-shirts with rugby stuff on them. We sat in the room with all the couches while a chicken, nestled among chunks of onion and carrot, baked in the oven.

For a while, earlier after smoking, I had felt truly funny, wondering how long I'd been in the pool, wanting to ask how much time had passed, and then wondering whether or not I'd actually asked or just thought about asking. I managed to get across to Celeste what I felt, and she agreed, nodded and smiled. I wasn't sure if I enjoyed the pot, but Celeste seemed perfectly at ease, the same way she nearly always did. Whatever worry she'd had earlier had disappeared.

I felt better now, on my second glass of wine, the sun behind the tops of the trees and sculptures. The colors of some changed with the new light, metallic silvers and chromes going blue or orange, others bouncing with the yellow-greens of sunlight through leaves. The four of us lounged on the sprawling, fabric-draped sofas, and I wondered, minute after hour, when the seduction would come. When would it happen? Would I have to ask Ess for it, like he'd said the night before? I wondered if they would only draw us again. How could we indicate that we were "ready"? Was the power in Celeste's and my hands? Is that how it worked with real men? I briefly considered the difference between Hank and Ess, their degrees of man-ness, but decided that even though Ess was significantly closer to being a barely man, a man just barely, he was still a good distance away from any guy in high school. That's what I thought, what I decided with my feet up on Persian silk and Indian saris, looking out into the sensory overload of the sculpture sunset.

Hank took out a small metal pipe, an ornate, pretty thing, from a drawer in the hand-carved African coffee table, and then a small wad of tinfoil. More pot, I guessed. He broke off a small chunk of the lump inside the tinfoil with his thumbnail and dropped the pitch-colored bit into the end of the pipe. He pulled an extra-long wooden matchstick from a ceramic vase, struck the match on a red brick that was acting as a paperweight atop loose sketches and handwritten notes, and sucked in through the pipe. "Mmm," he said. "Good for the appetite."

"This is great shit," Ess enthused, reaching.

"Is that the same?" Celeste asked.

"Hell, no," Ess said, taking the long, still-lit match from Hank.

"What is it?" she asked.

"It's hash," Hank said.

Honestly? I had no idea what hash could be, beyond the corned-beef kind that I didn't like. I knew, though, that anything that I said now would be dumb.

Celeste stared at Ess, who held the match on the pipe and sucked. "What does it do?"

"It's mellow," Hank said. "Nice. You don't have to try it, though, if you don't want to. It's like pot." He watched Ess continue to suck on the pipe. "Sort of."

"What's it going to do to me?" she revised.

"It's *great*," Ess said in the weird voice. "It relaxes you. Way nice."

"Try just a little," Hank suggested to Celeste, and she held her hand out to Ess. She didn't even look at me. Not a glance.

"Bowl's hot," he warned.

"Don't hold it by the far end." Hank stood and took the pipe from Ess, showing Celeste how to hold it by the thin stem.

If she tried it, then I would.

Celeste put the skinny pipe end in her mouth, and Hank held the match over the teakettle part. "Draw some in," he coached. She sucked, and then sucked again. "Try to hold it in your lungs. Down deep."

She passed the pipe back to Hank then, who pulled on it repeatedly. "Done." He smiled at Celeste, who smiled back, her dancer's legs tucked up beneath her, her eyes glowing with the perfectly matched color of Hank's shirt. I watched him watch Celeste hold her breath.

"You can let it out," Ess finally said.

I sat up. "We can hold our breaths forever."

"Forever?" Ess laughed.

"A long time," I said defensively.

Celeste pursed her lips finally and blew. Very little smoke came out. "Where'd it go?" I asked.

"She might not have taken in much," Hank said. "Miss Lisa, would you care to try?"

I hovered at the ready. Of course I did. "I guess."

"Here." Hank sat and cut off a tiny little chunk with his thumbnail and dropped it into the teakettle. He blew out the long match, nearly all charcoal now, and lit a new one.

Ess reached over and punched me lightly in the ribs. "Coughing only gets you higher," he said, smiling.

Ah. So maybe I'd been higher than Celeste in the pool, and that's why I'd felt weird. I wouldn't cough this time. Hank stood and came over to me, put the pipe in my mouth and moved my fingers to the stem—it was heavier than I thought it'd be—then lowered the flame over the teakettle. The three of them had sucked loudly on the pipe, so I knew I'd have to as well. I sucked the way you would giving yourself a hickey on your forearm as a kid. Yes, that hard. And the small burning rock of hashish oil and whatever else sped like a pinball at full speed past the mouthpiece of the pipe, past my lips, over my tongue, under my uvula, and into my throat, where it clung for a moment until my wet windpipe recognized its threat and expelled it at great force to the back of my tongue. I couldn't help but swallow it. Hank pulled the pipe out of my mouth. I would not be the baby of the bunch. I would not cough. I would not make a scene. I tried to cover, clearing my throat, wiping my watering eyes. I coughed just a little, primly, into my fist.

"Where the hell did that go?" Ess shouted, knocking his rings on the table edge. "Lady Leather Lungs! Yes!"

"Did you just swallow that?" Celeste asked.

I nodded. "Accidentally," I said, quick to brush it off.

"Damn!" Ess whooped. "She ate herself some good times!"

Hank rubbed my shoulder. "Are you okay?"

I nodded.

"Really?" Celeste's eyes were dreamy behind her question.

"Really," I said, and even though my throat burned, even though I'd somehow made a fool of myself again, I'd managed to contain the damage, control my idiocy to some degree. I thought. Which was good enough for the time being.

I'd love to say that I didn't remember a thing after that, that the chicken and carrots and wine and salad disappeared. That I couldn't even remember what I ate. That I just didn't remember a single minute of the rest of the night. But I can't. I can't say that. I remembered everything, took in every minute physical detail, saw every thread on every fabric surface, every glistening pore of onion layer I peeled away with my fingers from oily wedges, every meaty chunk of white meat torn from breastbone.

While the other three talked, I watched. I observed hand gestures and facial movements, body positions and foot tappings. Now and again somebody would ask me something or talk to me or the conversation would grow interesting enough for me to listen to, and then it seemed incredibly smart, interesting and creative and rare, precious eggs of conversation—I said that even, "These are eggs of talk," and none of them seemed taken aback by what I said. They didn't make fun of me, didn't laugh at me except when I was actually trying to be funny.

After supper, we wandered outside. The sky was a midnight blue, dark and rich, and in my head I invented a new chocolate: navy chocolate. With blueberry undertones. And then Ess was on me. He and I had managed to get into the sculpture garden pretty deep, and we were talking about the different properties of various clays—red, common, white, porcelain—and then I said, "I want you to have sex with me."

He smiled and asked, "Do you know what you're asking?"

I nodded.

"No, you have to say it. Out loud."

"I know what I'm asking you," and he pressed his full body against me and the marble monolith of a sculpture behind me, an ancient-civilization-remnant-looking thing covered in nonsensical writing, in nobody's language.

"Tell me," he said.

"What?"

"Tell me what you want me to do to you."

Was it that simple? Ask and thou shalt receive? I could try it. Where was Celeste? I wasn't supposed to leave her. "Where's Celeste?" I called out loudly.

A clonk of ox sounded under the chocolate sky and a sugared giggle told me she was fine. "Over here," she said. I heard her clear as a bell, clear as clear water, clear as good glass. Clear, clear. I knew what I was doing. So did she.

"I want you to kiss me," I said, and added, "nicely. Not too hard."

I swore I could see Ess smiling in the dark. "Standing or lying?"

"Standing first," I said, and he bent his neck to make his mouth meet mine, and his kiss was nice. Almost soft and nice, and his lips were wet, and mine were too, and I tasted salt as his tongue found its way into my mouth. I didn't know what I was supposed to do, and I didn't care, and it seemed that what mattered more was that I told Ess what to do and he would do it, that he was waiting for me, and this much equaled a teenager's best stab at wonder, at delight, at nubie heaven. With his better kisses, Ess' careful and supple sucks and nibbles, his presses and bigger body presses, I could feel his erection rising and rising and rising, feel each blood pump rising, what I wanted to know in the full flesh of skin and blood in my hand, my grip, each vein and hair, feel it all.

He ground against me after a while, a rhythmic pushing, and Hank's button-down now bunched up around my middle. Ess pulled his mouth off mine and leaned back, his pelvis a hard force keeping me against the monolith. My throat, my stomach, my groin beat as if my heart had split itself and migrated. "Now what?" Ess asked.

"What do you want?"

"No," he said. "You have to tell me."

"I want you to take off your shirt," I managed shakily. I could see blades of grass. I could see fireflies, their lights sharp as lasers at the planetarium. I could see the individual hairs of Ess' eyebrows. He took a step back. Ess pulled the old rugby T over his head, and I could see each of his stomach muscles flex, a ripple that swam like schools of fish up his entire front. I could see the gooseflesh rise from his belly button. I could see his Adam's apple. I could see him swallow. He dropped the T to the ground and stood. My sculpture. My private showing. A piece of my heart traveled to the top of my spine, there to block reason from interfering with the rest of my body's workings.

He just stood there. I could see the strain of him inside the shorts of Hank's. "Yes?" he asked.

How much harder it was to ask for it, I thought, just barely thought, my piece of heart forcing loud blood through my eardrums. I knew where I wanted to get but hadn't thought about the trip getting there. I could see each of his earrings. I could see his fingernails pale against his tan hands. "Unbutton my shirt," I half whispered, "and take it off."

He did.

"Touch me," I said hoarsely. "And kiss me."

Ess stepped forward. He knelt and placed his hands on either side of me, put them on the carved words of no language, and covered my stomach with kisses like feather strokes, moved his mouth to my right side, narrow there, between hip and rib, and opened his mouth full, took the slim muscle between his lips. He bit down carefully, snaked his wet tongue over my skin, and my side muscle danced, contracted, shuddered and sang. I put my hand beneath his chin. "Here," I said, and bent my knees to move my breasts to his mouth. He kissed lightly, ever so, until I pushed his mouth on me harder, pushed on the back of his short hair, on the hot back of his perfectly shaped head. He liked it. I could tell. He gripped my thighs and squeezed, and I could feel his arms shaking, and my legs grew weak, and I lowered to my knees, and then we kissed harder, just as hard as the first night now, but this time I wanted it. I pressed back. And it didn't hurt, not that I could have been able to tell then.

Ess moaned—in need, I supposed—and his voice vibrated from his throat to my lips and into my face, my head. I put my hands on his throat and he moaned again, and the vibration jumped into my fingers. His hands found my ass and he cupped each cheek, each muscle. "Now what?" he said into my hair.

Now what? Oh, god, all the rest. "Take our bottoms off."

Ess sat on his heels and pushed the boxers I wore down to where my knees sank into the grass, and then he stood. He unzipped his shorts, Hank's shorts, and let them drop around his ankles. He stepped out of them. I stayed put. His penis was hard, straight, the tip glistening. He took the shaft into his hand and squeezed, and a drop of clear liquid slid from the tip into his fingers. I leaned forward and licked, looked up and saw his head drop backward. He rumbled, "Now what?"

I opened my mouth and wrapped my lips around his tip but he pushed my head away. "Now what? You have to say."

"I suck you," I said.

"Where?"

I would say anything, anything, and so I said, "Now I suck your dick," and I put both of my hands over his one, gripping, and he let go. I moved his tip into my mouth and tasted him, a drop of seawater, and I let him plunge. He pounded against the back of my throat and I tried to guard my teeth, the sensitive insides of my lips cushioning my sharp edges. I thought of Jim, my first experience, momentarily, thought of the feel of him in my mouth, and concentrated on what I knew to do, moving my circled fingers along with my mouth, my entire head. I looked up. Ess reached down and pulled my hair away from my face, tangled his fingers into my summer-bleached locks and kneaded and circled and clutched and pulled.

"Uuuhhhh," he moaned into the sky, and then, behind, beneath his utterance, I heard another one. I heard hers. Celeste's voice, the voice that came from her when she sang, broke into Ess', hers a single noted pant, quiet, distinct, growing faster. "Jesus." Ess gasped and grabbed his penis, pulling it from my slick mouth. "Jesus." Celeste's quiet note echoed as if bounced through a metal room. It reverberated off sculpture after sculpture till it found me, us, found its way. And I was, for a moment, her. I pushed my own light breaths over my vocal cords and matched her, sang with her, just quiet enough for me. I don't know if Ess heard me or not, but I imagined what Hank was doing to her then, moving in and out, and I lost myself. I could see the individual beads of sweat on Ess' calves. In the garden I could see, in its web straddling the legs of a small stone nymph, a spider inching toward center. I could see the feathered remains of moth wings in the sticky trap. I could see myself with Hank.

Ess collapsed onto the ground, onto his back. "Tell me what," he said, his body glossy in night shadow. "Now. What now." And Celeste's repeated note, like a ventriloquist's, bounced and came in from behind us.

"Have sex with me," I said, collapsing to the ground too, kicking free of the boxers finally.

"You need to tell me exactly," Ess said, exasperation close enough to hear.

For the first time I wondered why. Why did I have to tell him exactly?

"Tell me," he repeated, and he gripped himself again.

I didn't like any of the other words I knew for sex, and I hated the expression *do it*.

He groaned, sounding pained now.

"I, I want to put your dick inside me. And then I want you to come on my tits." Just my mouth said the words. My brain had become a pinpoint of thought, of nearly nothing.

"You're good," he said. "Damn, you're good for a little high school girl." He flipped to his stomach and straddled me, and I could feel I was wet without touching.

"Slow?" I asked, and he knelt over me on knees and hands, and then with one arm shoved under the small of my back, picked the whole of me up off the grass. He put me back as gently as he would a baby.

"You're teeny," he said, and I'd swear to this day I heard a sort of reverence in his voice, as much as a man like Ess would ever show.

"Please," I said.

He pushed my left leg out and moved his right knee inside it, then my right and his left. He arched, dropped himself toward me. I lifted my hips to meet Ess. I used my hand to direct the tip of him, and he waited, and I said, "Please," again. He pushed then, hard, hard, and he yelled out into the sculptures, into the burble of the pool, into the flickers of fireflies and spiderwebs and buffed modernism. Into the world from inside me, and I gasped at the shove of it. I gasped at the raw. At the new.

He lowered to his elbows, and I reached around to hold the wings of his shoulder blades. The shock of him, the pain of his size, of his thrusts, pushed me away somewhere, deeper, but the hash, I suppose, brought me back. The swallowed nugget of hash languorously paddled its way through my bloodstream; it bobbed my head above the waves.

Ess thrust and pulled and thrust, and I heard Celeste's quiet voice rise till it became someone else's, till Hank owned it, till he finessed it into a long and quavering cry. She stopped, and I heard a shudder, I swear, her reflex, and then quiet. Ess grunted and pulled himself out. He stroked himself twice with his hand and a warm string of ejaculate rained onto the front of me from my neck to my stomach. He rolled away onto his back and then rolled onto his stomach, onto his erection, onto his face, onto his chest, onto his knees.

I could see blades of grass stuck to his sweaty skin. I could see a diminutive flake of golden leaf attached to his Achilles' tendon. I could see me, my hands, as I held them up in front of my face, the lines on the palms intersecting, wondering what they said, what Hank saw, what Celeste knew.

In her bed that night, late, Celeste told me what she and Hank had done to each other in the garden. I could see it with my hashish vision. She had climbed atop the ox, laughing. Hank had taken her hands into his and turned them palm-up to the moonlight, or maybe into the reflected light of the pool. He kissed her wrists and up her arms as far as he could reach as she sat on the sculpture, then moved to her nearest thigh. Had she bent and leaned over, she'd have seen that he'd risen up on his toes, his leg muscles clenched into rugby knots, in order to kiss her there. He reached her knees, descended her shinbones, knelt, took her foot in his hands and massaged the arch, pressed hard on spots that he had memorized, had studied in books. Celeste's breath caught. She instinctively reached for a mane but didn't find one on the copper ox. He moved her foot to his mouth and slowly, like hard candy, sucked each of her toes.

A zing of pleasure traveled up her leg. "Come down out of the sky," he said.

"I'm not," Celeste said, and her freed mind let her say with no forethought, no regret, "I'm on a beast of burden."

Hank chuckled, stunned with the opportunity at foot, in hand. He'd had plenty, plenty more than he could likely count, but this mortal's close invitation to her perfumes was such a one as he could never remember. She was beyond beautiful, his skilled eyes knew, beyond ordinary access, too. He knew his luck, and so he would treat her to what he could, what she would let him. He took off his shirt and laid it down on the grass beside the ox. "Come down in any case," he said, then thought to add, "unless you'd like me up there with you."

"I'll come down." She swung her leg over the beast's head and planted both feet on his T, lest he think she were ignoring his chivalry.

"I would like to kiss you," he said. "May I?"

"Yes," she said, and so he took her waist, spun her, braced his back against a flank, or maybe the broad metal rib cage, and pulled her into him. Smoothly, gently. He kissed her the way he had when passing her smoke in front of the others, carefully. And he found her mouth magnificent. He could spend hours there, the taste of youth. He could smell her breath as a cat might, put his nose to her opened O of magenta, of berry, of a color he couldn't name in the world.

But the beauty took more of him, drew his tongue in to move on top, beneath, hers, took his wrists and placed his hands, over his very own shirt, on her breasts. He would need to wait for all that he wanted, all that he might manage to contain, but he could fondle. And fondle he did. He had spent more years than not with clay, and he knew how to cup his hands just so. To caress in the thick centers of his palms any pliable person, any alive surface, and so the beauty leaned into him, pushed her tongue deeper, forced her sweetness into his recesses. He made her murmur with his hands on her breasts alone. He knew what he could do to the rest of her. He knew he could make her sing. "May I do more to you?" he asked the beauty.

"Yes."

With concentrated purpose, he unbuttoned and removed all that she wore, certain to keep a warm hand in contact with her skin, always, because he didn't want her to care about her own nakedness. He wanted her to feel her own flesh in air, her flesh beneath, astride, atop his own flesh. Not to care. He knew he could bring her there.

And I saw her—his—clothes come off her perfect body, saw her muscles flex, the tautness of skin from ankle to forehead. I could see her lungs expand. I could see her veins' valves open and close. I could see her pecan-shaped ovaries. I could see her through and through.

He pushed her back, held her at arm's length, and took in her shapes, her lines, with his eyes first. And then he reached, reached for hair with one hand, hamstring with the other, begged her forward with his touch, and she came into him readily. You could say happily. Stepped in and kissed him with all her tongue. Her hands found his erection in his shorts. She inhaled. He exhaled into her.

He needed to taste her. Could she be so succulent? Could she taste a new way, a way he didn't know? Could she be possible? "Would you let me lay you down?" he asked.

"Yes."

He picked her up in his arms then, her flank smooth against his belly, and knelt with her. He placed her on the fragrant grass, where she stretched like a child waking from a nap, and the sight made his heart thunk in his chest. Where had she come from? Who made such beauty? She didn't seem to notice or care. He thought of orchids.

She smiled up at him and draped the backside of her hand over her cheek, took a knuckle between her beautiful lips, and bit. Her teeth flashed white.

How could he waylay the inevitable? How could he stop himself? "May I take off my shorts?"

"Yes."

He did and then lay on his side next to the beauty, head propped in his hand. He hoped he could make her roll into him. And so he kissed her again, bowed his head and gave her all of him through his mouth, placed his hand on the perfect mound of breast nearest him and caressed again, released her and drew the lightest of fingers across her stomach until he raised a quiver, a tremble from her core. She rolled toward him then, her long hair a gorgeous tangle, a laurel leaf caught in dark gold strands. She kissed and kissed, her breasts a firm insistence. Her fingers sought his nipples, and she pulled on them, traced the end of her fingertips around and around.

He could feel her rising. He could feel the blood in her rushing into the zones he knew better than clay, better than fruit.

And with her slight weight then she pushed him to his back. Had he lost himself so soon? Before he could stop her, she'd attached her beautiful lips to his nipple. While she sucked, barely bit, pulled his being to a single small gathering of nerve endings, she moved her hand slowly over his stomach, down, down, brushing the hair beneath his full erection, down, down farther, to his scrotum. Ever so lightly she teased small designs, cloisonné patterns, over the contracting surface. He pulsed. He reeled. He could release himself in thirty seconds. And, he knew, he would disappoint her if she continued. If she straddled him then, he would find her too much to bear. How had she managed this? She had drawn off his control, tapped his practiced resolve.

He pushed on her chest. "Please," he said. "I'd like to taste you. Will you let me?"

"Where?" she asked, and he knew she asked honestly.

"Here," he said, and reached between her legs. "Here," he said again.

She had never known a skilled mouth there, but the thought filled Celeste with shivering delight, with desire she couldn't contain. "Yes."

She softened in his hands, allowed herself to be put on her back. He spread her legs. He thought of lilies.

He lay between her legs and sent moist breath into the light hair of her pubic mound first, kissed her there, stroked the hair with his fingers, and then moved lower, his lips parted, breathing out slow and heavy dampness until she startled him by moving herself onto his mouth. And so he began. He licked her completely from the top of her graceful petals to the bottom, her lubricant floral waters, cucumber, the Caribbean, the softest of slippery near the seeds in his treasured starfruit. She was like no one he had ever known. He closed in, found her clitoris, used all he knew.

She began to sing, maybe, a sustained sort of quiet single note. Was this her moan? Her guttural cry? Her fingers dug in the grass.

She let him lift her knees slowly, open her open her open her. He used his fingers now, just two, as she felt small, and the very discovery of this forced his hips into the earth, had him moving now, the cushion of thick grass soft enough.

She felt his rhythm and found it with her own hips. She danced on his fingers, under his tongue. Her voice grew strong as a small bell. She tightened around his digits. Her hands went into his hair, and he felt himself edging toward the reckless peak. They quickened and quickened, and as her contractions came hard and fast around him, over him, they moved through him, and he spent himself—despite all that he had hoped to contain—there in the grass at her feet. He had come with her, he realized with fascination and regret. He had never done such a thing in his life.

I saw her smile. I saw him smile back. His mouth, much of his face, gleamed with her wetness. And she laughed. She looked at him and laughed, more bells, more of her, escaping out into the garden. Into the night her voice went. I could see her delight. I could see his wonder. And I could see my future.

MINOR THREAT

POMONA, JULY '84

Waiting for the band to appear for sound check, play mumblety-peg outside with the roadie. He is your temporary guardian, for you have proven yourself, finally. You have earned the privilege to be abused by those behind the doors. By those with microphones and fists.

You have built a reputation for yourself as one of two dicksucking trajectory sensations, as one of two who improve the show backstage and front. You have taken to the leap and dive and crash like a Jim Jones devotee. Birdbrained and wingless, you hurl yourself into the frothing dancers. They all, the all of them, admire your flights.

Remember, this is important: Never trust that you will be caught by the outstretched hands.

Asking if you have eaten cunt lately, the roadie distracts himself from the game and misses. His knife drills into the cracked leather of your boot, tongue side of the steel toe. Figure you will bleed, but no more than usual. He feels bad, however, and even tells you as much. With his accent and pained look, wonder how he has made it so long. Wonder if he has lied about his time on the road.

Wiggle your toes in your boot. Ask him if you can shave his head. Consider carving a swastika between his eyebrows. Consider taking him home.

Remember, this is important: Never trust that you will be saved by anyone.

See the band coming. The van in which the members ride does not slow enough, though, takes the curb, and plows into the small pile of black garbage bags mounded in front of the no-parking sign. The bags contain the band's own clothes. The bags are luggage. You and the roadie have forgotten to move the luggage into the dressing room.

Expect punishment. Look to the roadie who could mete out the lashes, but he is already at the garbage bags, talking, tugging as if they were humans. Recognize the error of your ways. Realize that you have made a brief miscalculation in judgment. A small failing. Nothing. A few garbage bags. A few grains of sand. You have made too many errors to count.

Remember, this is important: Never trust that you will be redeemed.

TEN

Mr. DIAMOND had a fit. We didn't get in till two in the morning, and, in an uncharacteristic move, he held us hostage in the kitchen while he called my father. Mr. Diamond sat, teakettle-like and steaming over the remains of a cereal bowl, as the other line rang, shaking his head, glaring. He'd never made me feel ashamed before. In the quiet, bland, peace of the Diamond kitchen, I didn't like his silent accusations at all. I was my own person, and I could do as I pleased. Ess pleased me, sort of.

I could almost hear my groggy father answer. "Hello?" he would have asked—did ask—disoriented.

"Hello, Lawrence." I'd nearly forgotten my father's first name. It sounded odd coming out of Mr. Diamond's mouth—that and the fact that most people called my father Larry. The two fathers spoke infrequently, not necessarily because they didn't like each other, but because their paths rarely crossed.

My father responded in some way. I looked at Celeste. At the kitchen island, she stood defiant, the way I'd hoped she would. We'd had a great day, a great night, the kind I thought that all young women had a right to, and Mr. Diamond shouldn't be allowed to diminish such an experience. I would hold on to the night like a lucky stone, a four-leaf clover folded into my wallet, dried and pressed into my cheesy teenage heart forever. No matter what my father said, I decided, I would tell Mr. Diamond only what Celeste and I had agreed to say. If I were grounded for forever, then I would simply leave. I would ask Hank if I could stay at his house. I would model for him whenever he asked. Ess could come and visit and together they would sculpt me into the miraculous. A viewer would look at the piece and be unable to decipher where Celeste ended and I began.

"Yes, yes," Mr. Diamond said. "Sorry for the late call." He waited a few beats, then added, "No, not an emergency. I apologize for the inconvenience." He listened again.

I grabbed Celeste's hand and squeezed. I mouthed, *Stick to the plan.*

She nodded. Of course she would.

"I thought you should be made aware of the fact that your daughter, Lisa, arrived home tonight with Celeste just minutes ago." He frowned at the remains of cereal floating in his bowl. "Yes, at two o'clock."

I could smell the chlorine coming off of Celeste and me. I wondered if Mr. Diamond could smell the pot, the hash, the sex. Then I wondered if a parent would actually ever want to smell that emanating from a child. Could a parent will himself into processing what he was actually smelling? Hmm. And then I realized that I could still be stoned. The thought brought a rush of blood to my groin, to where I half bled, to where I'd been so wanted and needed and pounded. Stoned wasn't so bad, although of the two options of stoned presented during the evening, I'd preferred the hash, even if it'd been accidentally eaten.

"It is," Mr. Diamond said into the receiver, actually pointing his finger at Celeste as he said it. "Yes, they just arrived."

What would happen? I couldn't remember a single instance when my father had been a disciplinarian. I though momentarily that my brother, David, would think higher of me.

"I understand," Mr. Diamond said. "Just a moment." And I was given my father at the end of a telephone line.

"Hello," I said noncommittally.

"Mr. Diamond tells me—" he started.

"The car—well, you know the famous artist? You wouldn't know him, but he's famous, and he actually lives here, well, we were at his house earlier, and then we were getting a ride home from one of his students—"

"What does this man teach?"

"Sculpture. In the sculpture department. At KCAI." Should I dare call him Dad? I never did. I watched Mr. Diamond stare at me intently, hanging on what I had to relay.

My father cleared his phlegmy throat. "You don't need to lie, Lisa."

But I wasn't. Not yet, really. "I'm not."

"Were you safe?" he asked.

"Yes." The conversation darted in a direction I hadn't expected.

"Are you hurt?" He sounded so tired.

"No."

"In the future, you call ahead of time to let the Diamonds know if you're going to be late."

Was my father being cool? Was it possible? "Of course." I'd do it. I'd say it. "Dad."

He yawned loudly, and then his breath caught, the beginning of his nightly smoker's cough. He hacked into the phone line.

"Sorry," I told him, and I was. Sorry to wake him up, sorry to make him start coughing.

"That's all right. But you know, without your mother around," he said, something rumbling in his lungs, "we're really a household of adults now. So you need to act like one, Lisa."

"I know." Celeste stepped on my foot, wanting to know what he said.

"Apologize to Mr. Diamond and tell him it won't happen again. Put him back on the line, please." If my father told me he loved me after that, I wouldn't have known. I'd already handed off the receiver.

Mr. Diamond nodded and frowned, listening. I turned my head toward Celeste and mouthed the word *cool*, giving her an OK sign. She looked astonished. I shrugged. Who'da guessed?

"But certainly, Lawrence, they weren't up to any good at this time of the night." Mr. Diamond pinched his temples with his gargantuan thumb and middle finger, covering his eyes with his vast hand. "Yes . . . I see. You have different rules in your house, however. . . . Well, in September, yes. Legal, yes, I understand." Mr.

Diamond moved his thumb and finger in circles. "As a favor to you. Fine. But for the record I do not believe that such behavior is acceptable." He pulled his hand from in front of his eyes and looked icily between Celeste and me. My back itched something fierce from the grass at Hank's. I fought the urge to scratch. "Yes. Fair enough. Okay, Lawrence. Sure. Good night then." Mr. Diamond hung up the phone, not taking his eyes off of us.

"Dad?"

"No," he said quickly to Celeste. "Now you listen to me. This sort of discourteous, worrying behavior is not acceptable in this household, do you understand? What you did to your mother and me—the both of you—is inappropriate and worthy of punishment." I looked down. Mr. Diamond's slippers seemed even more tattered than when I'd seen them last. "Do I even want to know where it is you've been?"

Hell, no. I imagined Mr. Diamond, clad in sequined purple tights, slamming Hank and Ess into the rubbery ropes of a wrestling ring and then crashing the men into each other. Hank and Ess would collapse onto the mat, at which point Mr. Diamond would climb up to the top corner ropes and soar, landing on the two with his full weight, his elbows to the backs of their heads. Ka-boom! I smiled at the thought. I couldn't help it.

"Is something funny, Lisa?"

"No." I bit my lip, but the image of Mr. Diamond in tights held tight. I started giggling silently, my whole body shaking.

Celeste drilled me with her elbow.

"Lisa?" Mr. Diamond was getting mad at me, getting really mad at me—I could tell by the tone of his voice—but I couldn't stop. The laugh finally escaped, bursting out into the quiet kitchen.

"I'm sorry," I said, and laughed again, holding my stomach.

"Celeste, maybe you would like to tell me what's so funny."

"I don't know." She looked at me, pained. "What? I *don't*."

New peals blew out of me, over my windpipe. It was just so funny. So completely funny. I squatted and held my stomach. Tears welled, and still I kept laughing.

"That's it," Mr. Diamond said, and lifted me from the floor in a single swift move. "Explain yourself." His face was turning red, a squall rising.

I recognized the seriousness of the situation and tried to calm myself. I wiped at my eyes. "I'm sorry. I just, sorry. I had this, I saw this image in my head. Sorry. Mr. Diamond." I apologized to the kitchen island. I knew I couldn't look at him.

"Celeste, is Lisa hallucinating?"

"*Dad!* No."

"What the hell happened tonight?!"

"You don't have to yell." Celeste's voice cracked. "God!"

"*Where were you?!* Tell me right this goddamn minute!"

The kitchen door swung open, and little Mona Diamond marched into the kitchen in an eyeleted white nightgown. "That's enough!" she yelled at Mr. Diamond as loudly as he'd just shouted at us. "You leave those girls alone this instant, and I do mean leave. Leave them here. I will meet you upstairs." She glowered at her husband. "Do not cross me, Sol." I'd never heard her use his given name before. I sobered completely, cold and quick.

Mr. Diamond left then, without another word. His slippers made no sound.

Mrs. Diamond, barefoot, calm, slowly went to the stove and lit a burner. "Tea?" she asked.

"Please, Mom."

"Yes, please."

"Sit down, girls." She looked at us and corrected herself. "Young women." She rummaged in the refrigerator and pulled out cold cuts, a jar of horseradish sauce. Dark bread from the counter bread box. "Dinner around here has been less than exciting without you," she said.

She made cups of tea with honey. Slivers of lemon rounds floated like lace on top. "It'll clean your systems," she explained, then pushed plated roast beef sandwiches our way. "If you eat, you won't be as sick in the morning." Listen to Mona.

With my foot, I found Celeste's leg. She tapped my foot with hers and bit into her sandwich. "Mmm," she said.

I bit and chewed. Oh, it tasted *so* good! Mona watched us eat and started making two more. "You women are just that," she said, piling rare slices of beef onto bread. "Women now. I hope that you can conduct yourselves as such."

I watched Celeste nod. I nodded too, mouth full.

"Women should be courteous," Mona suggested flatly, slathering. "Which entails calling. So that other women don't worry."

"I'm sorry," Celeste said.

"I'm sorry," I said.

"I know." Mona cut our new sandwiches on the diagonal and put the triangles on our plates. She sat down to her own cup of tea and blew around the lemon slices. "Was it worth the wrath of your father? I hope?"

Celeste looked at her mother and smiled, nodding.

"You had fun, then."

I nodded too.

"Do you girls need to go on birth control? Would you like more honey?"

"Yes," Celeste said without pause.

Mrs. Diamond didn't even look at the honey jar as she spooned from it. "Lisa?"

"Yes."

She sighed, but not in a terribly sad way. Just in the way you might sigh on a Friday afternoon after work, on your way home, when you get stuck in traffic. You're done for the week, but you can't quite relax yet. "We'll make appointments at Planned Parenthood then," she said. "I suppose the sooner the better."

"Probably," Celeste mumbled into her sandwich.

"I don't believe we'll need anything from your parents, Lisa, but if so, I'll talk to your father." She sipped her tea. "I don't imagine he'll want to endure that conversation with me for long."

Nothing was required of my parents. Not in 1981. Celeste and I both chose the lightest of the Ortho-Novums. We stayed on the same cycle for years to come.

I don't think Mona ever filled Mr. Diamond in entirely on what had transpired, but for the rest of the summer he was distant and polite. He never yelled at us again, but then he never sang or laughed again either. Not that summer. Not around us. He knew, I think, that we were gone, even as we still remained under his very roof. Solomon was a wise man.

We agreed to call if we were going to break our new curfew time of twelve thirty A.M.

We called often. Summer was barely half-over.

Less than twenty-four hours after our first carnal encounters with Ess and Hank, Celeste and I came to the realization that, as much fun as we'd each had, neither of us had undergone a fully satisfying experience. Intercourse but no orgasm in my case; and in hers, orgasm but no intercourse. We set out to remedy the situation, to see if, as they said, things got better with time.

The first two weeks of our new liaisons, the men seemed content with the status quo. We modeled for them, we ate, we smoked, we swam, all at the sculpture house. Sometimes we worked our way around to sex, always at the same time, it seemed, as if the guys had some sort of preordained schedule. But never in the house. Never in a bedroom, or even on a couch. And neither Celeste nor I had gotten it right yet, been given it right exactly yet, still. Even stranger, more often than not the men denied us. They kissed us, got us high, teased us into a frenzy, only to back off. I didn't understand it, as I could see that Ess was obviously ready for more. Celeste said the same was true for Hank.

Day after day we returned. We learned which artist had created which sculpture. We were told which works were insured for hundreds of thousands of dollars by the school, and which could have toppled to the ground without being missed. I took to touching the most valuable pieces every time I visited, trying to mark them with a scratch from my fingernail, a burnish from a ring. I removed a barrette from my hair once and scraped my initials into one of the rear hoofs of the ox as I lay, stoned, in the grass beneath him. I didn't think anyone saw.

Celeste and I experimented with makeup, thinking that maybe we were too young-looking, that maybe we should behave more like grown-ups—although Celeste pointed out that we behaved exactly the way that Hank and Ess did.

And with each nightly return to the Diamond house, the family home of Celeste lost more of its luster, more of its charm. It felt less secure without the warmth of Mr. Diamond spread through it. But more than that, it grew pedestrian. The art on the walls was serviceable, but lacked true flair; the furniture sat, prosaic, on standard Orientals. Where were the kilims? Where were the risks?

At the start of August, a chunk of rock as big as a king-size box spring and mattress set appeared in the sculpture garden. Two deep ruts cutting into the grass led to and away. "Forklift," Ess said.

"That'll be you," Hank said. "You two in stone."

Oops. That's right. You said *stone*, not *rock*. "Really?" I stared at the marbled golden yellow. I couldn't see it yet. I couldn't see us in there at all.

"You'll be floating." Hank smiled.

"On the ground?" Celeste asked.

"No. Eventually it will be set into the top of a poured-glass platform."

"That'll be *so* great!" I gushed, losing my attempted artsy indifference.

"Above or below eye level?" Celeste wanted to know.

"About a foot below standard," Hank explained, "so the eye skims over the surface of your figures and the glass water."

"*Niiiiiice*, huh?" Ess patted the stone. "The Hankman has some work to do."

Hank raised his eyebrows in a don't-I-know-it look.

"Whaddaya say, Hankman? A year? Thirteen, fourteen months?"

"Hard to say, Ess."

"How 'bout some smoke to celebrate? I got paid this morning!" Ess took a little chunk of foil out of his shorts pocket and bounced it in his palm like a ping-pong ball.

"I'm in," I said.

"In," Hank said.

"Celeste?" Ess walked up to her as she studied the stone. "You game?"

"What?"

"Smokin'," Ess said.

"Oh."

"No? But this is dee-licious."

"She said 'oh,'" I clarified.

"Well, Miss Chickadee?" Ess missed the foil ball. It fell into the grass. I could fall after it, let go, just flop down. I felt like washing off all the new cream blush I had on. I constantly saw my mascara-coated eyelashes out of the corners of my eyes now, mistaking them for birds, for peripheral things I could never quite focus on. Yeah, just flop down, just follow the bouncing Ess ball into the grass.

"Ah." She looked at me. "Okay." I knew what she thought. Noon was still an hour away.

Hey. It'd whet our appetites.

"Hankman, you sure you fixed all your pipe screens?" Since I'd swallowed the chunk of hash, the question had become one of Ess' favorites. I appreciated Ess' support of my honest mistake that night, as apparently the pipe's screen had tipped or tilted or come loose somehow, but I was growing tired of Ess' repeated joking. Hank, however, seemed to have infinite patience for the guy.

"Yes, Ess, I checked them all. But why don't you do us the favor and go pick one out. Make us some lunchtime drinks, too. And some lunch. While you're at it."

Both Celeste and I laughed, and Ess said good-naturedly, "Fuck y'all," then went inside to do as he was told.

"Do you need us to model today?" I asked Hank nonchalantly, hoping.

"I believe I have all the sketches I need right now. Later on if—" he said, and stopped.

What came next? If what?

"When I get into the stone some, I may need to check proportions."

I laughed. "Is that what you're calling it now?"

Neither Celeste nor Hank laughed. "Get it?" I couldn't understand their lack of reaction. Celeste, at least, always teased me about the same thing.

"He means our *limbs*, Lisa."

Well, now, I knew that. Why did she say that? "Gee, really?"

Just looks. Plain ol' looks from the both of 'em.

Ess walked right back out with beers. "Lunch is served," he said. We clinked brown bottles and drank. Celeste and I sipped. Ess pulled a small, red-glazed pipe from his pocket and presented it to the three of us. "Now for the appetizer."

Hadn't he misordered? Appetizer hash should come before beer lunch. Oh, well. So he wasn't a genius. He was talented. He was gorgeous. He wanted to be with me. I guessed.

We smoked and smoked, and the day got better. I thought at one point we should eat some lunch, but then Hank brought out fruit and we ate that and I wasn't as hungry anymore. Hank carried out the sketchbooks to the stone and wandered around and around the chunk, flipping pages of us till he made me dizzy and tired. Celeste fell asleep in the garden. I sat at the edge of the pool and hung my feet in for what could have been five minutes or an hour, hard to say. I never tired of gazing at the mosaic tile, the feel of water, the movement of me through another medium. Ess played drums on two overturned clay pots and sang whatever songs, ones that went nowhere, ones I didn't know. Then Hank was sitting by me. "Tell me, Lisa, what it is you want to be when you grow up."

At the moment I thought a nothing would be pretty great. I could be a nothing who hung out around pools all day and smoked hash and modeled sometimes. Not a nothing, then. I could be an inspiration. Yeah, an artist's inspiration. One particular tile on the bottom of the pool looked like an eye. An eye hiding behind seaweed. "An eye," I said, and pointed.

"I wondered who might notice that," he said. "You're the first to mention it."

"An inspiration," I said.

"Mmm." He paused. "Now there's an ambition. In what field?"

"Just like Celeste. That way." The eye winked as a piece of something, a butterfly wing, a fairy shoe, floated between it and my own eyes. I knew my ambition was impossible.

"What way is that?"

"You know." I fluttered my feet.

"You have a freshness about you, Lisa."

I wanted beauty about me more. "So?"

"I'm being sincere. You're your own person."

Duh. Sometimes I thought that smoking hash made the guys dumber. I didn't tell Hank that though. Where'd Ess gone? The clay-pot drumming had stopped; I wasn't sure when.

"Life is richness in many forms. We should all find our own." Hank picked up my hand from where I'd braced it on the lip of the pool and again studied its lines. You'd have thought I held the secret of the world somewhere between my pinkie and wrist, the way he stared. Maybe more like a crystal ball. Yeah, my palm was a crystal ball.

"What's there?"

"Just you," he said.

"That's not what I mean!" I nudged him with my shoulder.

"But it is what I mean," he said.

I sat and wished he'd kiss me, and then a wasp buzzed my face. I swung my arm at it, clocking Hank in the forehead. He started laughing. I thought immediately about how he must be used to getting hit in the head in rugby. Why hadn't we ever seen him play? I thought I'd like to see him play a game, watch him run around in his shorts and cleats or whatever their shoes were called.

"Hey, there, Slugger," he said. "You all right?"

"Where'd the wasp go?"

"What wasp?"

"The wasp. I wouldn't just hit you."

"Hmm." Hank rubbed his forehead and shot me a sly half smile out from behind his forearm. He had good forearms. Maybe if we smoked more hash he would kiss me.

And then Ess was there, right there. "Beer?" He held one out toward the two of us. For me? Hank. The beer was for Hank. For me? "Beer?"

"Lisa?" Hank asked.

Oh. "Sure, I could drink a beer." Was I hungry? I couldn't tell.

Hank stood up. He'd had one leg in the pool, one out, the whole time. Just the one dripped now. Maybe he had one wrinkle-skinned foot and one normal one. "Time to get back to work."

"You okay?" Ess asked me.

I watched Hank's wet leg stride away next to his other one and wondered how long it took a leg to dry. He shuffled sketchbooks he had laid all over the top of the slab.

"Did you want this?" Ess asked, still holding out the beer.

I took it. "How come we never go anyplace but here?"

Ess looked around. "No better fuckin' place that I happen to know of."

I thought about that. Maybe it was true. I nodded. I took a few swallows of beer. "We should still go someplace else," I said. My toes would be little, flesh-colored prunes.

"Yeah," Ess answered. He sat next to me and dropped his feet in as I took mine out. I stared at his belly button. You could see how pale he'd normally be by the little patch of untanned skin just inside and high.

"We should go out," I said. "Outside."

"We're sittin' outside, knucklehead."

"You know what I mean."

"Yeah, well."

Well what? "Well?"

"Well," he said again. "You know."

What did I know? "Know what?"

"You know. You guys."

Who was he talking about? Us guys. What guys? "Celeste and me?"

"Yeah."

"What about us?"

"You know."

I didn't. "I don't know."

"Come on, Lisa."

"I have no idea what you're talking about."

"You and Celeste. Your age."

Our age? Oh. Oh, my god. We were kids to them. Oh, my god. They kept us holed up because they thought we were kids.

"You know." Ess glugged beer.

Oh, my god. "You're embarrassed of us." How could we not have figured out what the deal was before? Of course they were embarrassed of us. How dumb could we have been? Two dumb girls acting dumb in front of guys who knew it was dumb to be seen with us in public. How dumb were we? I wanted to go wake up Celeste from her nap and tell her we had to go. Had to leave. Because we were dumb.

"No," Ess said unconvincingly. He rubbed his big tan hand over his short hair and looked around, away.

"You *are* embarrassed."

"That's really not true. You, she . . . I mean, you're really some-thing."

What the fuck did that mean? "What does that mean?"

"Where's Hank? He can explain."

Some dangerous tincture of what I'd had or hadn't had that day suddenly infused me. "Fuck Hank," I said, trying to throw back Ess' own language. "What do you mean?"

"Hank would say it better." For a fraction of a second I thought I could see the boy in Ess, the smile going out of his eyes com-pletely. Poof. Out with a breath.

"Try saying it yourself." That wasn't enough. "Fucker," I added.

"Hey, come on. It's not a big deal."

"You're an idiot." The words plopped out of my mouth like a bone too big for a little dog's mouth. Dogs were loyal. Dogs were dumb. Dogs would trot around after two men who didn't even want them.

"Why are you calling me names?" His soothing tone was one reserved for toddlers.

"Screw you!" I tried to slosh beer out of the narrow-necked bottle into Ess' face but with little success.

He started to laugh. "You're great! You really are. Hank was right." He wiped his chest. His silver rings caught the afternoon sunlight.

"About what?" I threw my half-full beer bottle into the pool and watched it bob. "Stupid bottle. Fucker." I was winding up. "Why don't you ever take us away from here? Why don't you invite us to hear you sing?"

"For starters, Miss Smartypants, we're booking starting in September. For two, name someplace we could go. You want us to take you out to dinner? How 'bout a movie?"

I realized I didn't know exactly where, but, sure, a movie would be fine. "What's wrong with going to the movies?"

"Nothing, Lisa. But think about it. The wrong person sees us out, Hank loses it all."

I didn't know what he meant. "What?"

"Y'all are death sentences. You aren't even *seniors* in high school."

"We're *death sentences*?" My limbs felt tingly.

"You're just kids. And we're—"

"Assholes." I stood up.

"Hey, hey." Ess rose beside me, forgetting his beer. "You're so damn feisty!"

I tried to slug him. I wanted to but only managed to sort of bump him in the chest with my fist, on his perfectly formed pectoral muscle. The left one. "You're such a jerk," I said, and then my voice jammed in my throat. I didn't understand why.

"Lisa." He grabbed my wrists, and I started crying out loud. "Lisa, Lisa." I was a black-and-white manic movie star, the madwoman throwing a fit who had to be controlled by the handsome, sane, masculine lead. The tall one. Ess drew me into his chest and hugged me. "Hey, there."

I sobbed. What the hell was wrong with me? I hated myself for crying, and the instant I thought about crying, the worse I cried.

"It's not your fault," he said. "You were just born *later* than we were."

"Hi," Celeste said, suddenly there. "What's the matter?"

I pulled out of Ess' arms. What could I tell her? We weren't grown-ups. "We're stuck here," I said, and sniffled.

"What do you mean, Lisa? What's the matter? What did you say to her, Ess?"

"Nothing."

"Nothing." I rubbed tears off my cheeks and looked at their mascara blackness on my fingertips. "I'm an idiot."

Celeste moved her eyes over me the way she might a car that had just been recovered, looking for scrapes, dents. "What happened?"

Ess shrugged.

"I'm fine." She and I had discussed the two of them for weeks, their less-than-usual behavior. Now I knew the deal: They just couldn't be seen with us. Here Celeste and I were, all of a few short weeks away from being through the first round of the pill. Pregnant-proof, wrapped up in invisible armor, good to go. Nearly ready for anything, and the guys didn't want to take us outside of the yard. Could our age be affecting their libidos? Why wouldn't they sleep with us normally, or like normal guys would want to? Then I considered the fact that neither Celeste nor I had found the right opportunity to work our way around to telling the guys about our visit to Planned Parenthood. Were they worried they'd get us pregnant?

"You're still stoned," she told me matter-of-factly. I saw a flicker of Mona in her daughter.

Hank and Ess would never take us to a movie. Never to a nice restaurant. Never to the prom—not that we needed to go. Well. "No. I'm fine."

"We should eat something more."

"I know." It might be nice to go to the prom, though.

"Let's go make something. Hank'll let us cook."

I wanted macaroni and cheese. I wanted turkey potpie. I wanted Celeste to cook for me while I watched TV on the couch. In the air-conditioning, under a blanket. Chocolate milk. Or a rootbeer float! Tater tots. Nothing that took hours, nothing from another country.

"Think we can make some real food?" Celeste asked Ess.

"Fuck, yes!" Ess grinned a happy grin and pinched my cheek. "You okay, you little nut?"

I nodded.

"Y'all gonna cook? I'm starving." Ess brushed the hair away from my face, relaxed his eyes, and then sort of petted me. I wanted to melt. I slapped his wrist and punched him in the gut. His pretty, pretty gut.

He screwed up his mouth. Elvis. "Why, thank ya. Thank ya vury much."

I—we—could still go to see Ess sing, I thought, watching him gyrate and hump the air, and if Hank happened to be at the same show, who could blame him for talking to us, right? Maybe we could even work it out so that our seats were next to Hank's. Listening to Ess talk about the places he played, though, I guessed everybody would be dancing instead of sitting. Those shows were his favorite. Hardcore, he said, and I imagined lots of people who looked like the drones showing up and screaming at Ess, girls holding their spiky heads. Celeste and I had never been to anyone's concert. Ess didn't like the word, though. He'd told us that the clubs in Westport and Lawrence where he played weren't at all typical halls. They were clubs. I tried not to ask too many questions and hoped he would continue to describe one of his shows in some kind of way that made sense to me. I wanted to seem like I already fit in when I got there. I wished Ess or Hank would let us know if our new makeup worked or not.

"Come on," Celeste said to me, taking my hand. "I was thinking about tabbouleh." How could tabbouleh be her version of "real food"? "Hank," she said. He still walked around the stone, around and around. "We're going to cook a meal."

He stopped. "Sure. You'll have to make do with what's in there, though."

"Thanks," she said. I thought that the stone, once it became us, would be looped with a dirt circle.

We went inside and started looking for food. How could Celeste want Middle Eastern and I want Middle American? Since being at Hank's, I sometimes felt as if I knew her even better than ever, and then sometimes hardly at all. "I want grilled cheese," I said, walking to the connected big couch room, trying to find the TV. "And tomato soup."

"He doesn't have a TV," Celeste said, reading my mind. "It broke and he never had it fixed. Finally he threw it out."

I looked at the stack of expensive stereo equipment. I'd blow the stuff up before I succeeded in playing anything. "We need some music," I said, and then Celeste stood right beside me. (How did I not notice people moving toward or away from me? My vision seemed to work in spliced film clips when I smoked.)

"Here," she said, and pushed about twenty buttons, after which Bob Marley, the now familiar Bob, sang away.

"What's there to cook?"

"Not a lot. Come help."

We made a substantial if odd salad and baked garlicky bread sticks from scratch. Ess went and bought another case of beer. We ate outside on a big blanket on top of the stone. To give the stone our auras, Hank said. To give it our energy. The evening shimmered as beautifully as any evening could. We sat for hours in firelight. We debated the merits of Kandinsky, Miró, Dalí, migrated to Warhol, Pollock, returned to ancient Greece, leaped forward to the Renaissance.

No, we didn't have sex again, but then Celeste and I had not yet found the right inroad to that discussion. To look at the night, a person would have to wonder: What more could two seventeen-year-olds ask for?

BAD BRAINS

SANTA CRUZ, NOVEMBER '84

A Bad Brains show downtown. You march into the slam-ming, all balled fists and big combat boots. By now you're terrier-mean when you have to be, too smart for your own good, head crowned with a military flattop dyed cherry red. You are the only girl out on the floor, and you are small. Your boots rub against your bare shins. The top edge of your corset chafes a raw line just above your nipples.

You want to hurt somebody. You want to hurt a boy, really. One too soft behind the eyes. One who is just pretending. You pump your elbows. Head goes down. Knees and boots up, the music just one long throb of speed, beer, noise, and sex and—the word you don't truly know yet—angst. Loud, in-your-face, fucking-suck-my-dick-you-cum-sponge angst. Faster faster faster. You spin and hunch up and pitch and bounce. You try to aim for arms and shoulders if you want to go more than a minute. Slam your whole side, jumping, into the backs of giants, into the thighs of Herculean, early-school skinheads there to start a riot, there to draw blood, there because they have their own bands named White Pride and F.T.N. Let the two cross-tops and junk gin and four no-filter Camels make your heart pound. Spin in faster circles and punch and kick at the blurred mess of smells and flesh.

Make a giant swear at you. Make another one, one from your past you have let stick his tongue into your everywhere he can, pick you up and throw you against the rest. Some go down, but you fall on the concrete slab instead of on top of anyone. Your knee doesn't feel right when you stand again. Dig your nails into the meat of your palms. Make bigger fists. Head down. March. Punch. Watch for the eyes. Find the weak one.

Fuck him. If you had a dick you would rape him there on the floor. Kick him in the balls instead with all of your might. Forget to watch for his friends. Forget to remember that everyone comes with backup. Yours, your other, your backup, stands on the edges. She will be too late to save the pretty, slight arc of your small nose.

You don't even see the swing.

$\mathcal{H}$ANK'S DIDN'T change much. The status quo had been established, and neither Celeste nor I had enough experience yet to make what should have happened happen. Of course, plainly obvious (as anyone with distance could see), we were being strung along, two temporary parts of a long-ranging, practiced, and ongoing plan of seduction. I really want to tell you that we got out quickly, that we were wise and careful girls. But, alas. Not a hope, a prayer, a fuckin' song.

Did we care? Sure. Did we know we were being manipulated? Probably. But the more they gave, whatever bit Hank and Ess had planned for that particular day, the more we waited, seals, orking and clapping our fins to be fed slippery appetizers. Enough to keep us alive.

The school year approached for us in its black-winged chariot, and we had to hop on. To give up our summer days at the sculpture house . . . oh, we pulled out our hair and gnashed our teeth. What girls in our positions wouldn't?

Ess and Hank had sex with us the last Sunday night before the Labor Day holiday, the Sunday preceding the first day of school. The details, clearly, had been prearranged. Hank's bedroom and a guest bedroom. We'd finally made it into the house. I couldn't come though, no matter what, and Celeste couldn't keep Hank from coming too soon. Still, leaving the sculpture house that night in Ess' junky old car, I fought back tears. Celeste sniffled in the backseat. The men had succeeded at what they'd set out to do.

Think about it. If you're so inclined, you can keep young women the way you might raise ermine. They both result in a kind of luxury. And the girls don't smell nearly so bad, they cook for themselves, and, if trained properly, won't bite your dick off when presented with it as a treat.

So what did we do? I told you. Gnashed teeth. Went back to dance, finally. Studied, as always. And made some decisions.

You can imagine what high school felt like after six weeks at Hank's. Placated and talked down to by teachers and administrators. They presumed all of us in our class were ready to leave and made little attempt to teach us much; you could tell the difference senior year. While capable of learning, I decided I would simply maintain, and, I believe, as much as she fought the instinct, Celeste did the same. We were, once again, bored to tears.

We didn't skip school, and we didn't necessarily disappoint our teachers. But we simply found no place for ourselves at Country Club Plaza High School anymore. We were too old there now, and yet too young for Hank's, too young for the Art Institute crowd to take us in completely. We were displaced by our own desires, our own doing, and we suffered for it.

Our schedules didn't allow us much time to hang out at the art museum, but the pressure to participate in senior class activities eventually spurred us to find time for other afternoon and evening activities. As leaves ruddied brown and maroon, and stiff-armed jackets came out of our storage closets, Celeste and I found ourselves at the head of the homecoming float committee. After all, we were the freshman girls who had kicked sophomore ass on Lynne P.'s floor.

As had been the case for two years running, our class built its float in Lynne P.'s five-car brick carriage house, with the college student renter who lived above kicking in to do the grunt work of buying and transporting the kegs.

Celeste and I hadn't seen the Artists, as we now affectionately called them—as in "Hey, wouldn't the Artists tell us to get the hell out of here right now?"—in over a week. Our last two visits had found Hank pacing back and forth in front of the stone with his chisel. We decided the stone needed a name. The Flintstone

UFO, maybe. Hank had sort of rounded all the edges of the rectangle and made dimples, as if a flying space oval had been dented by space debris.

The stone wasn't actually all that far off from our senior class proto-float-in-progress. 1981's float category was extraterrestrial films. Our football team, bad as it was, comprised of prissy tight ends and jaded socialites-to-be, would be battling a redneck farm community team for their honor, a team from cowtown middle Missouri. Thus: Close Encounters of the Herd Kind. Our senior class float design, a mildly funny deal with helmeted cows, had been approved before we'd made the more serious bovine modifications. Celeste and I loved the artistic challenge, so to speak, of bringing in a new attitude. Ours was a top-secret affair. We hoped we would be punished. Mildly, of course.

But as for Hank's. Neither of the last two visits had commenced as planned. Ess didn't own a phone and couldn't be contacted. Yes, Hank had seen Ess in class, but Hank was busy with committees and panels and his work. His *work*. Hank just paced, absorbed with yellow stone. He behaved as though we weren't breathing right in front of him, but rather buried alive, suffocating in lodes of earth tones. In there strangling in veins of gold.

So we left. Given the fervent attentions of guys at school and the imposition of an actual schedule, we somehow found the wherewithal to give Ess and Hank a bit of their own medicine. Of course, ours lacked the hardcore narcotics, the illegal substances, and the years of detailed research. But, hey, at least we tried. We left the men entirely alone. A wormhole behind us closed completely, and our summer liaison, perfectly encapsulated, shot light-years away.

Still, Celeste and I had changed. Clearly. We couldn't deny the experience of the summer. Nor did we want to. We'd left our village, walked less than a mile, and seen the world. Corny but true. How the fuck could you go back to high school guys?

We tried. Yeah, we flirted as we stuffed maroon and white tissue paper into chicken-wire Hereford frames. The guys were fish in a barrel. But two weeks before homecoming, Celeste and I had yet to be asked to the homecoming dance, a bigger deal than the end-of-the-year prom. Sure, rumors abounded: This guy was gonna ask, that guy was gonna ask, blah, blah. We thought we should consider attending the dance for the fond memories we were told we would make—the ones we'd latch onto in the old-age home, rocking away, gripping wooden armrests. "Remember senior dance, Lis? What a hoot!"

We had some sense that we should consider the future, but it's difficult, so terribly difficult, to think of much of anything beyond a month away when you're in that zone, the superhuman-senior-in-high-school zone. We had lived our summer for the day. Who cared if we went to homecoming dance? I thought right away about how great it would be to have Ess take me. We could make an appearance and then leave, the dust settling around everyone's expensive shoes. But I knew the impossibility of such a scenario. And I couldn't imagine Hank there with Celeste at all. So who cared if we went.

What a bunch of bullshit, though. I, for one, had started to get nervous. Of course you want to go to your senior dance. You want to be beautiful and dance and dance and have the entire class envy your every graceful, carefree move. So, maybe, then, we needed to consider asking the guys.

The Saturday night two weeks away from homecoming, wearing gloves with the thumbs and forefingers cut off to better handle the slippery crepe paper, Celeste and I leaned into each other with our beer breath and said nearly at the same time, "Let's just ask the fuckers" (me), and "We should ask the guys if they're too chickenshit to ask us" (Celeste). Both our tolerance for drinking and our proclivity for swearing had risen markedly since our days at the sculpture house.

"Who then?" I asked.

"Does it matter? It's the experience, right?"

Well, now, that was crap. It was all about being seen. Sort of. "I have an idea." I had it in my head to choose the most dangerous, handsome, out-of-the-loop guys we could. Guys we probably didn't know well. Guys who would secretly be flattered, but tell us when we asked, "If you want. Okay," and take another drag of their cigarettes. "Let's get refills," I told Celeste.

We walked toward the crowd at the keg, the first of two collectively purchased for the night. The float-building scarcely disguised the parties. Most of the senior class milled around in jackets and newly purchased fall clothes, lavender Dickies, wide-wale cords, duck boots you knew just made the wearer's feet sweat without a hint of frost on the ground. A good autumn weekend party. Our float of the football helmet–wearing cows—clearly members of the rival team—bursting from the top of a flying saucer, had a long ways to go. The auto mechanics class guys promised to build a kick-ass fiberglass saucer around the base of the three cows, but so far no saucer had materialized. We still had two weeks. The auto guys, like nearly all students at our school, were "gifted." They had beer to drink and aesthetic discussions to hold before they finalized their rockin' design.

Waiting in line for the keg, I glanced over my shoulder at our framing. Could we get away with it? We'd purposely propped the chicken-wire hooves of one Hereford, with horns, onto the back of another Hereford, with horns. Supposedly, one could argue, the three animals were simply struggling to get out of the narrow saucer opening. Really, though, we hoped to incense the opposing team. Celeste and I, along with our good ol' friend in crime Wanda, hadn't yet decided on the actual final-minute amendment we'd be making to the official sign for our float. (The Lynn-Lynne contingency, half of the governing body of our class, would likely have to stay on, possibly into morning light, to finish last-minute crepe-paper stuffing, but even they wouldn't see the final sign until we presented it.)

Celeste and I had tossed around plenty of options but felt we were not living up to our creative potential. We were falling into the same trap as the auto guys.

"Here's my idea," I told her, ready to present her with my brilliant script.

"Hi," Jordan, the sophisticate, interrupted, gushing.

"Hi," I said back.

"Wow." Celeste couldn't contain her surprise. Jordan clung to an East Indian guy we'd never seen, a guy who had to have come from another school, as per her rule. Quite beautiful, he grinned at us both, empty beer cup in hand.

"Celeste, Lisa, this is Raj."

"Hello, Raj."

"Hi, Raj."

"Raj is an exchange student at Central Prep."

He looked good, but did he speak? I knew what a drone would ask. "Got any brothers, Raj?"

"Why, Lisa," Jordan exclaimed, clearly delighted by my compliment to her.

"Only a sister in Bombay," he answered.

"Nice accent," I told him.

Celeste inched toward the keg. "That's where you're from then?"

"Yes. And thank you." Raj smiled at me and stood up straighter, checking out—you could tell just by how his eyes moved—Celeste's legs and my hair. Jordan tried to snuggle her way back under the crook of his arm without being too obvious.

We shuffled toward the beer.

"I've convinced Raj to accompany me to that horror called 'the dance,'" Jordan said, pronouncing the A of dance like "ah."

Celeste pumped with one hand and expertly filled Jordan's cup with the other. We'd all learned proper keg etiquette early, the tilt, the ideal placement of the nozzle, pump-to-flow ratio. Raj's cup came next. "Thank you," he said, and removed his arm from around Jordan to take the beer from Celeste.

"You're welcome." Her everyday, every-purpose smile often bewitched strangers. You could clearly see its effect on Raj. She directed her attention to Jordan. "Well, we haven't been asked yet. Maybe we should follow your lead and do the asking ourselves."

"Oh, I highly recommend it! Highly." She gazed at Raj, who looked down at his shiny penny loafers.

"I have a plan," I told them. "Actually, I was just about to spring it on Celeste."

"Ooh. Do tell." Jordan gripped Raj's upper arm and leaned into him. She seemed to want to wear the guy.

Taking my full cup from Celeste, I smiled what felt like a sly smile. "If it works, you'll know it."

"Aren't you being coy, Lisa." Depending on the circumstances, I thought Jordan could be either hilarious or grating. With Raj at her side, I decided she wasn't so funny.

"No," I told her, "I'm not being coy. Celeste, a conference?"

"Yes, go make your plans," Jordan said, and flicked her hand at us.

Celeste very kindly laughed at Jordan's snooty routine. "Nice to meet you, Raj."

"Likewise."

Celeste and I walked into the expanse of Lynne P.'s backyard forest and conferred. "Here's the plan," I said. "Actually it's not much of a plan, but it'll be good."

She waited patiently.

"Let's ask somebody totally different. Guys from the smoking lounge. From auto class. Let's ask freshmen. Or UMKC guys."

"We don't know any UMKC guys."

"So? That's the point. Let's ask somebody that'll make everybody else say, 'Holy shit!'"

Celeste swallowed beer. "Why?"

"What do you mean, 'Why'?"

"Well, what would be the point?"

What was she talking about? I'd just explained. For something different. For a, a change of pace. "For a change of pace."

"For a change of pace, maybe we just shouldn't go."

"Really?" That sorta hurt. I wanted to go. "You don't want to go?"

"I do." A sigh.

"You miss Hank."

"Yeah."

"Well, he can't really take you, Celeste. I don't think it'd be a good idea for him to go to a high school dance."

"I know." She drank more beer.

"It could be fun," I tried.

"Possibly." She gave me a weak smile.

"Come on. Somebody *different*."

"Well, who?"

I looked around in the dark as if our potential dates would pop out from behind two trees. "Well, what about Tommy Jackson and . . . and Riley What's-His-Face?"

"Those guys? We've never talked to them."

"So. I bet they haven't asked anybody, and they're *cute*."

"They smoke."

"So does Hank, Celeste."

"They're juniors. And they're antisocial."

"I had Quan Bio with Tommy. He's in all AP now, and he's a class behind us. You know he's gotta be smart."

"What about Riley?"

I knew next to nothing about Riley other than that he hung out with Tommy in the smoking lounge and looked good in his faded jeans. "I don't know."

"Lis." She scrunched up her nose.

I thought my idea was a good one. I did. "What?"

"Maybe Raj has some friends."

"He's preppy."

"That's a little hard to avoid around here."

"*We* avoid it," I said, growing cranky. Why couldn't we at least go to the dance with Marlon Brando–style bad boys, if we were going to ask unknowns?

"Let's think about it. We'll figure it out. I like that we don't just sit and wait to be asked." Celeste nodded as if convincing herself that I was right. "I do. So we'll ask the guys ourselves. Let's just, you know. Ask the right ones. Okay?"

"Tonight, though."

"If we can."

"Tonight, Celeste. Then we can plan."

"What, our dresses?"

"The whole night," I told her. "Where we eat, how we get there, maybe a dance. All of it."

"Are we going to pay for it all too?"

"*Lawdy* no! We'll just make them think they came up with it all on their own."

"Aw, Lis. You're, you're . . ."

"I'm what?"

"Precious."

"Okay, *Mom.*"

"I meant that in a good way."

I tapped a dried leaf into pieces with the toe of my shoe. "We should buy some hash for the dance."

Celeste scooted a different leaf toward her with her foot and started tapping too. "I don't know. Do you think it would be the same? The sculpture—Hank's house was always so . . . humm. Comfortable."

"Safe."

"Yeah. Safe."

"I think it'd be fun."

"Maybe."

Well, a maybe was closer than a no. "Back to the cows?" I rallied well. Time to act! Time to make decisions!

"Sure." We walked toward the carriage house. Celeste veered kegward. "More?"

My cup was half-full. Half-empty. "Why not?" I couldn't think of a single damn reason. Not one.

You could say we split the difference. Tommy Jackson and some of his derelict genius friends were at the keg party that night. Either my excellent persuasive skills or enough beers eventually swayed Celeste into flirting with this alluring circle of questionables. Jackals, the boys fought over the bait. Well, almost. Celeste and I tossed in our bits of meat and waited.

G. J. Muldoon and Benny Waize, the two victors, asked us, and we agreed.

At the homecoming game, Celeste and I had a sixty-second window of opportunity behind the field house to change our float's posterboard nameplate on the front of the riding lawn mower that towed our spectacle. Our dates for the evening stood guard.

Due to time constraints, we'd had to eliminate the third cow. The two Herefords that remained had been separated, bent apart for the judging in the morning. Now, however, we reunited them in perverse love, exactly the kind that prodded teenage males to madness. I had sculpted a long papier-mâché tongue for the occasion and quickly inserted it into the humping steer's mouth. We staple-gunned the replacement signs over the originals on either side and then walked back into the stands, our dates flicking their cigarettes into the parking lot, real casual, fucking proud as could be. What discipline we all exhibited, I thought, sauntering. Our squealing had been so, so long ago contained.

Of course, the floats were lined up in order of class, so when the crowd finally saw the senior's, the effect proved significant. Our home-team crowd, used to refined suppression, went berserk. And then a chant went up, exactly as Celeste's and my newly redesigned placards had laid it out:

> "CLOSE ENCOUNTERS OF THE HERD KIND:
> Oops! Excuse Me! Hope You Don't Mind.
> Just Too Bad You Had to Drop That Pass
> 'Cause Now You'll Have to Take It UP THE ASS!"

Repeat.
Repeat louder. Again.
I don't know why Celeste and I did it. Honestly. Some wire, some connection, had kinked in my head. Or between my spine and cortex. And, wonderfully, Celeste had suffered the same malfunction. Whatever had happened, we'd run with it.

Looking back, you have to wonder why the driver sitting in the lawnmower seat didn't call somebody's attention to the alterations. Hadn't he noticed? To this day I have no idea who the man was—some football player's uncle, some maintenance guy's brother, who knows. But for whatever reason, he just drove along, following the juniors' jiggling, tissue-shedding E.T.

The cowtown crowd, tremendously challenged in their current environment, both academically and socioeconomically, fully understood our float. Their football team led the way, some beefy defenseman the first to throw down his helmet. And, behind the defenseman, a wave of visiting team players and classmen surged across the field toward our players, our bleachers, our people. Us. Us wimpy preps, the succored elite.

Not only did I bare my teeth and growl, I made fists and shook them over my head. I don't know that my own noise was unique or could even be heard in the middle of the home-team din. The virus, the feeling, the rush, had found me, taken root around my hip bones, fed on my blood and marrow. It had fed on sun and fruit, had smoked great hash, drunk chlorinated water, and sucked up summer. The thing in me had grown lanky and fucked-up. I loved the thing and decided there, as our pink-cheeked and healthy rivals stampeded closer and closer, the bursts of their nostril steam clearly visible against the green grass of the field, that I would cultivate it.

My date was the third to stand up against the horde moving toward our bleachers, behind two of our football team fathers. I followed. I stood fourth. We readied to take them on.

Despite the fact that parents broke up the fight before it had barely started, the tale of the riot of '81 is always only delivered in reverent tones. To this day. I swear.

Celeste and I escaped unscathed. I hadn't even wanted to, necessarily, but so many fathers had decided to attend the game that one managed to grab me before I reached the fence around the track loop.

An ambulance came. A second ambulance came.

Everybody made it to the dance, though. After the ambulances left with a few cases of abrasions and contusions, Principal Legros announced over the speaker system that those responsible for the instigation of the "scuffle" would be thoroughly investigated and prosecuted. "To the fullest extent that school policy allows."

Celeste and I were gonna get laid that night.

The night of our senior dance, Celeste and I dressed in up-to-the-minute, one-piece pantsuits, mine silver, hers black. They were polyester, shirred up the front and back center seams, and entirely clingy. Mona brought three tiny glasses of champagne into Celeste's room as we applied our makeup in shades of purple and pearl.

"Ladies," she said, "to truth in love."

"To beauty and truth," I answered, taking a flute.

Mona glanced at her daughter and then at me. "Celeste. Don't you want to make a toast? It's your senior homecoming dance."

"As if I don't know that." Celeste stood in front of the mirror with a curling iron stuck in her long hair. "Ow!" She reached for the third flute. We looked at her. "Cheers."

"Cheers."

"Cheers." I plucked at the front of my bodysuit. The ensemble, belted with silver buckles at the back of my neck and bra line and waist, felt too short between crotch and collar. The center seam rode high. I looked at Celeste's to see if hers fit the same, but to my dismay I noted yet again, for the ten thousandth time, that Celeste wasn't as long-waisted as I was. Hers draped perfectly. Shirred perfectly. Whatever. It fit. Mine almost did.

"Lisa." Mona admonished my continual wiggling and plucking.

I stopped and sipped. We'd instructed the guys to bring white rose wrist corsages. Neutral. No pink or yellow, nothing to pin onto and wreck our fine-knit bodysuits from Saks. I wondered what Ess and Hank would have brought us. What they would have made us wear. The thought made me sad, watching Mona sip champagne. I bet Hank would have flown in some rare, exotic blooms. Yeah, he would have, probably flowers that resembled animal penises and human vaginas. Then we would have been forced to wear them, sex on our sleeves. That'd be just like them.

Maybe going to the dance with G.J. and Benny would be just fine. They were young, sure, but acted as though they'd been around every block possible. Smart and jaded. They'd do.

Half an hour later, the doorbell rang. Mr. Diamond was conspicuously absent for G.J. and Benny's entrance. He'd left "on an errand," Mona said. A part of me wanted him there, seeing me off to my senior dance, raking the guys over the coals, making sure that Celeste and I were in good hands. It felt like he didn't care about us anymore.

I know now, of course, that he cared too much. That he had watched the last of his girls leave with such finality, make such a determined and obvious exodus into adulthood, that even if we'd tried, we wouldn't have been able to skulk back into childhood. Even as Mr. Diamond saw us every day, ate dinner with us every night, we were, like the Femmes song says, *gone, Daddy, gone.*

"Hi, Benny," I said, walking over to him. He looked uncomfortable in his tuxedo, holding a box with a bow. He needed a cigarette, I thought, needed to take off his tie and unbutton the pleated shirt. He looked good, though.

G.J. stared at Celeste. Almost too handsome, I thought, and decided I was happy with the way we'd paired up. "You look great," he told Celeste.

"Aren't my ladies beautiful?" Mrs. Diamond asked.

"Yeah," Benny agreed, handing me my box.

Celeste stepped over to G.J., a tall guy, and looked up at him. "Is that for me?" she finally asked.

"Oh, yeah."

We unwrapped our corsages, the expensive Plaza Florist embroidered ribbons proof of the guys' perfectly acceptable upbringings. Mona posed us for pictures in the foyer and on the staircase, then sent us off with kisses and a tightly folded hundred-dollar bill pressed into each of our palms. "Just in case," she said. "Don't forget *breakfast.*" Mr. Diamond did not approve of our school's all-night-long tradition for seniors, but Mona had defended it, mentioning that nearly legal adults should be allowed to do whatever they saw fit, and certainly partaking in a decades-long custom would not suddenly turn us back into little girls and place us in harm's way. After all, the young gentlemen had hired a limousine with a driver for the entire twelve hours. (Another Country Club Plaza High tradition.) What could be so wrong with that? Mona had tried to warm Mr. Diamond up to the idea with a hug then, a rare show of physical affection, but he hadn't hugged back. Sometimes, as much as I still loved him, I wanted to hate him.

Once inside the back of the limo, Benny and G.J. lit cigarettes and tugged at their collars. The evening was extremely hot for October. "We bought champagne," G.J. said, lifting the self-evident bottle from the built-in ice bucket.

"And Southern Comfort." Benny reached into his jacket and flashed a smile and a flask.

I began fiddling with buttons, the glass divider between the white-haired driver and us rising and lowering with a mechanical whir, the windows, the sunroof. That was the one I wanted. Not quite dark, the sky appeared in the expanding rectangle.

"We're cruisin' the Plaza for an hour," G.J. said, tossing his head casually in the driver's direction. He'd removed the wire cage from the champagne. He aimed toward the open sunroof, pressing with both thumbs. With a loud pop the cork shot from the bottle, hit the roof, and ricocheted off my head. "Shit," G.J. said, the champagne foaming over his hand and onto the floor of the limo.

"Are you okay?" Celeste asked. She seemed to be the only one to have noticed the trajectory of the cork.

"Fine," I said, not rubbing, not wanting to call attention to the mishap. Sometimes I wondered if my head wasn't the size of a truck for the sheer number of times it got in the way of flying, falling, and otherwise misdirected objects.

"What?" Benny asked, exhaling cigarette smoke.

"Nothing," I said. "Nothing, nothing."

"You sure?" Celeste asked.

I shot her a shut-up look. "Champagne!" I reached for a glass and held it out to G.J., who had just stuck the bottle in his mouth. Guess he didn't want to waste. His cheeks swelled. We all laughed, and G.J. spit foam onto the floor. We laughed louder.

Maybe the night would be okay. It could be. We didn't know each other even slightly, but it might make the events more interesting. Despite too much cologne and perfume and pretense, we four had a good deal more freedom, I suspected, than other couples. Our expectations of one another were both high and entirely non-existent. Celeste and I hoped that the guys would live up to their seedy reputations, and the guys probably hoped the same from us. Other than that, pretty much anything was fair game. Our float alterations had already established that we were no longer your typical, rule-complying young women. Maybe some laws would get broken. I, for one, would try.

We rode around the Plaza for an hour, drinking two bottles of champagne. We stood through the limo sunroof, taking turns wearing Benny's dark sunglasses, pantomiming singers on the radio and feeling *Saturday Night Live* cool. Finally we stopped for our dinner reservations at The Steakhouse on the Plaza. Benny and G.J. ordered mixed drinks with their fake IDs and let us share. Six cocktails, four chateaubriands, and a round of flambéed desserts later, we left. Celeste and I tried not to feel funny when the driver stood at the curb, ushering us into the car. We needed to grow better accustomed to service, I thought. I imagined what Jordan might do and patted the driver's hand resting on top of the door. "Thanks, hon," I said.

"What did you call him?" Celeste said, reaching for the third bottle of champagne, chilled over dinner.

I kicked one of the empties on the floor. "I said, 'Thanks, hon.'"

"You did *not*!"

"What?" Benny asked, crawling across me to the other side of the seat.

"Did you hear Lisa call the driver 'hon'?" Celeste loosened the wire cage and suddenly the cork blew on its own. Champagne sprayed the upholstered ceiling, the front of Celeste's pantsuit, and all over Benny's ass. G.J., still standing outside talking to the driver about the upcoming route through town, ducked his head in, looked around, and ducked back out. I heard him say something about a cleaning fee.

"Aw, man!" Benny complained, smiling, brushing at his pants.

"Don't sit down!" I stopped Benny with a hand on his back.

"What the hell am I supposed to do?" He stood up through the sunroof.

"Take 'em off," I said.

Celeste wiped the front of her with one hand and swigged from the champagne bottle with the other. She swallowed and hooted. "Yeah!"

"You can dry them out the window," I suggested.

"Yeah!" Celeste said again.

G.J. got in. "I leave you alone for *two* minutes," he scolded us in some Mr. Cleaver kind of accent, "and now look. I'm very disappointed. Very."

"Hi," Benny, still standing through the roof, said to the driver as the man walked to the front of the limo.

I patted Benny's ass. "They'll never dry otherwise, and you wouldn't want to ruin your tux."

"Oh no," Celeste said, and passed me the bottle after swigging again. "You definitely wouldn't want to do that."

"No, no." I patted again, then let my hand slow down a little. The guys were smoking-lounge bad, smart, and rich. Even though they smoked all types of tobacco, both swam for our school and usually placed at state. I wondered how it was Celeste and I had never considered dating them before. Huh. Before the summer a lot was different, I supposed. I ran my hand over Benny's well-developed hamstring and decided I wouldn't mind getting high if they offered. "You should really get out of these wet pants."

"Fine," Benny huffed, as if he actually minded.

An hour later we arrived at the school's Special Events Building—the one built primarily for dances and fancy functions—with the four of us crammed together out the sunroof opening. We held Benny's black pants flapping behind us like a pirate's flag. We'd consumed four bottles of champagne total and had broken into the Southern Comfort. G.J. had a key to the natatorium, where we planned to sneak in later and smoke a joint.

Students stopped their milling out front and stared at us, the four happily drunk and drunkenly happy seniors. They must be jealous, I thought. Look how much fun we're having. Look how daring we are. Look how *different*.

We almost didn't get inside the actual event, as none of us had bothered to RSVP. "But we're seniors," Celeste pleaded with the new sophomore geometry teacher at the greeting table. "You should have known we'd be here." Well, at least she said something. The rest of us sucked our peppermint Life Savers and stood behind her, studying the floor tile.

"Have you been drinking, Ms. Diamond?" The new geometry teacher was young herself, and her use of "Ms." sort of impressed me.

"Yes," Celeste said. "I'm eighteen years of age."

"The Missouri drinking age is twenty-one," the teacher countered.

"We dined and drank in Kansas," Celeste lied. She lied! I wasn't sure when I'd heard her lie before. She rarely even fibbed. Damn. She'd made some progress pretty quickly.

"Well," the teacher hemmed.

I should have moved forward and joined Celeste. Instead I reached behind Benny and patted his ass. His pants had dried. He reached behind me and patted my ass. I was *really* hoping to get laid. Celeste and I were safe as safe could be on the pill now.

"Look," Celeste told her. "We made an honest mistake. We each thought the other had already done it."

"I'm not sure I believe you," the teacher said, training analytical eyes on Celeste, "but it is your senior dance. Okay. Go ahead and sign in."

I watched as Benny scribbled a totally illegible signature. Walking into the dance, he told me he'd written Benjamin Franklin, same as he usually did. I didn't even care about the immaturity of his move. Who fuckin' cared anyway? This was for fun. This was for the hell of it, for the old-folks' home.

Inside, the class leaders had again chosen the safe-and-staid look, but the room bounced with students, the lights low, and a decent band played loud music up on the stage. We four parted the waters. The guys had taken off their bow ties earlier, along with Benny's pants. The pants were back on but the ties had stayed off; the shirts got unbuttoned. I unbuttoned Benny's myself. We danced till we sweated, and G.J. and Benny were actually good! Really good. We may all have been out of it, but we didn't care. We had fun, and we drew a crowd, and you could tell that even when the superstiff kids didn't want to look at us, they felt compelled to. For posterity, Celeste and I broke into a little disco-jazz routine we'd learned back in seventh grade. We were gonna get laid. You could tell by the way Benny and G.J. looked at us.

Some indecipherable time later, we transgressed our way into the natatorium. G.J.'s key worked fine. Inside, the pool glowed pale turquoise, and I wondered momentarily why my life seemed cordoned by swimming pools and water, tile and stone. I didn't contemplate for long, however. We sat on a heavily lacquered bench and passed a joint. "Nice," I said after inhaling, the skunky-sweet smoke passing over my tongue.

"Swim?" G.J. asked.

I'd spent too much time on my getup to lose it all, I thought, but looked to Celeste just in case she happened to be game. "No," she said, drinking the last of the SoCo from Benny's flask.

"You mind if we do?" Benny took a long hit on the joint and passed to Celeste, stood and took off his jacket and shirt.

"Do we mind if you swim?" I figured he'd have to skinny-dip or put his pants on over wet underwear. I felt like hollerin' a big ol' "Hell, no, we don't mind!" Instead I said, "Not if you don't mind strippin' for us, we don't."

"I just might do that then. You comin', G.J.?"

"Right there," G.J. eked out, holding in smoke.

Celeste and I watched the two swimmers leisurely undress. We'd already seen Benny's fine form in the limo, the bottom half, anyway, in his little black undies—I didn't even know what to call them—but G.J.'s physique was still a complete mystery. We were not disappointed. Both of them were fit and lean. When down to their skivvies, the young gentlemen turned their backs to us, stepped out of their underwear almost seamlessly, and dove in.

Celeste turned to me as the guys butterflied and crawled. "So we're gonna have sex, right?"

"I hope so. Don't you think?"

She nodded enthusiastically, the pot kicking in. "You bet!"

"You bet!" I said back, and giggled, and then we were on our way to a full-fledged giggle fit.

"Hey!" Benny splashed our way. "Shh!"

"Sorry. We forgot." More giggling.

"Seriously!"

A bigger fit.

"They'll hear us!" Heavy-handed whisper.

Full-out laugh.

"Shh!" And then, treading water, G.J. and Benny both began to crack up themselves. "Shut up, damn it!" Benny laughed.

In the middle of my laughing I started wondering where we would have sex. Hotel rooms were for sluts, and they had to know we weren't sluts. Was either set of parents out of town maybe? "Now what?"

"Man, gimme a cigarette, Lisa," Benny said, and coughed.

"Where are they?" I asked. He pointed over to his pile of clothes. He should have said, "In the jacket pocket with the condoms," as I found them soon enough. I could've called him on the latex, but I didn't. I guess I was stoned and happy we were all on the same page.

G.J. and Benny cupped themselves appropriately enough for high school guys as they emerged from the pool, and then turned their backs, flicking and squeegeeing their limbs as if they were at a swim meet. I realized, watching, that a human being with short hair could get pretty dry without a towel. I wondered what it felt like to have really short hair. How long had we been in the natatorium? "Should we go?" I asked as the guys turned to us, zipping flies, hopping and stepping into shoes without socks.

"We've been here ten minutes," G.J. said.

"It's two thirty," Celeste said, looking at her mother's slim watch by the light of the pool.

"We've been in here an hour?"

"No, we got here twenty minutes ago."

"No! More like two hours!"

"We should check on Malcolm." Malcolm was the name of our driver. We'd made friends once he realized that Benny's father's credit card receipt would include Mr. Waize's customary 25 percent tip.

"I can't believe we've been here that long."

"When did we get here?"

Hell. I didn't care. Would you? But where were we going to get laid? We didn't have a sculpture garden.

"The brick wall is a cinch," I said, the limo gently rocking along toward Westport and our favorite backyard. Celeste and I had talked up the place without letting G.J. and Benny know our exact relationship with the resident or what our actual intention was once we sneaked in. We said we'd taken art classes there over the summer and that the place was something you just hadda see.

"Nobody'll be there?" Benny asked again.

"No," I stated. "Nobody the fuck at all will be there."

Celeste slapped my leg. "Onward! Henceforth, Malcolm. We will soon be amongseth the sculpturests."

Malcolm, of course, couldn't hear us, or had at least chosen not to hear us earlier in the night. But since he'd found out about the tip, he'd begun talking to us periodically through an intercom system. "Ladies," he said just then. "You have us making our way toward a very controversial homestead."

Interesting, this white-haired Malcolm. I wondered what he'd seen in his lifetime of chauffeuring. But Malcolm was obliged to wait for us, I decided, even if we were in the act of something illegal.

"Malcolm," Celeste said, pressing the intercom button.

"Yes."

"Have you been to the sculpture house before?"

"Oh, yes."

"You've been here before?"

"Never inside, miss."

"It's nice, Malcolm," I said. "You should see it."

"So I have heard, miss." I decided that Malcolm put on the accent for us. Maybe he was even making fun of us.

The Southern Comfort had vanished. The champagne was gone. "We can drink that, right?" Celeste pointed at the square crystal bottles of bar booze in the limo.

"You wanna drink whiskey?" G.J. asked.

"Is it good?" Celeste wanted to know.

"Not unless it's with sour mix, it's not," he answered.

"What's the clear stuff?"

"Probably vodka."

"Well, we have Coke here," Celeste said, opening a small cupboard. "And Tab." Cans fell on the floor. "And 7UP. Do any of those go with vodka?"

"The 7UP could," Benny told her.

"But I like Coke better," she said, hugging a can between her breasts.

"Well, have a vodka and Coke then," G.J. suggested.

The combination didn't sound too good. I didn't want to drink anything else till I could pee someplace. "Can we stop at a gas station?"

"What for?" Celeste pulled the tab from her Coke can.

"Ladies' room," I said.

"Good idea," she said, and held out a crystal rocks glass to G.J. "Vodka, sir."

G.J. took the stopper out of the bottle and smelled. "Whew. That's *gin.*"

"Malcolm," I said into the intercom. "Stop at a gas station, please."

"Yes, miss."

"I don't care," Celeste said. "Gin'll go with Coke."

"It's your funeral," G.J. said, clearly happy. He lifted the bottle from its place and poured. "Two fingers." He showed us the measure of gin. "Wait, Celeste. Ice."

"No," she said. "Ice is *cold.*"

"Isn't that the point?" Benny asked her.

"I'm tired of cold drinks." Celeste poured Coke into her two fingers of warm gin. "I'm tired of cold."

We hadn't wanted to spoil our pantsuits' lines by wearing coats, but now we missed them. Unfortunately the classic Indian-summer day, or night, or now really the morning, had grown chilly and damp.

Celeste continued pouring Coke in her glass till it overflowed. "Nothing shows on black," she said.

"Good thing," G.J. said. "Gin, anyone?"

"No, thanks." I crossed my legs. We were still a couple blocks from the nearest gas station that I could think of.

"What about Scotch?" Benny asked.

"You like Scotch? Man." G.J. shook his head. "That stuff'll kill ya. My brother drank Scotch all night and had to go to the fucking hospital. They pumped his stomach."

"Huh?" Celeste drank warm Coke from the can.

"That's what they do. Stick a tube down your throat and pump out everything in there."

"Imagine if it was spaghetti!" Celeste said.

"What?"

"If they pumped out spaghetti!"

"Gross," I told her.

"Or oysters!" she continued. "That would be really gross!"

"Len just had Scotch in his stomach," G.J. said.

Celeste squawked. "Is that short for *Leonard*?"

"So?"

"Nothing," she said. "I like that name. I do!" She looked around. The limo went over a big bump. "Hey! Somebody else should have some. Benny, have some Scotch. What if it was eggs? It'd be all chunky and yellowy pasty."

Benny said, "I will if you stop talking about pumping up food."

"Or pea soup! Like *The Exorcist*! Bllleeeeeeeeeeccccccckk!"

"I think I better have a Scotch if she keeps this up." Benny smiled at me and handed G.J. a glass.

I saw the gas station up on the right. Malcolm pulled in. "Anybody else?" I asked.

"Me!" Celeste shouted.

"Yeah."

"Yeah."

All four of us filed out as Malcolm held the door. Inside, after she peed, while I went, Celeste said, "I hope Hank sees us. I hope he watches with his new *belle du jour* and hates himself. I hope he pulls G.J. off of me and fights him and then takes his place!"

Had she smoked more pot? "Seriously?"

"No, Lisa! Not seriously. *Yes*, seriously."

What? "The fight part too?"

"I'm not serious! I hope G.J. can go longer than Hank. That would get Hank good."

I thought for the first time that Ess could be there too, there with a groupie, some dumb, ugly girl, and I thought how Celeste wasn't being all that kind about Hank. She sounded more like me than me. "We need blankets or something. It's kinda chilly."

Celeste chortled. "We'll make our own heat." She burped. "Ooh."

"Really."

"You fuckin' bet," she said.

We filed into the limo again, the interior of which you could now smell standing outside the open door. The mix of odors zapped me back to a party my parents had thrown at our house in Chicago when I was really young, maybe three or four. The limo smelled like grown-ups. It smelled like grown-up stuff, anyway.

"Malcolm," Celeste said, the last in line, "can you just drop us off down the block? We're surprising our artists—our . . . teachers."

"Are you certain?" Malcolm sounded mildly concerned. "You are aware of the time?"

"Yes, yes. Yes! That'll be perfect."

We knew where to sneak in: around the back, where the neighbor's bushes grew brambly and thick and the brick wall stood no taller than me. Ceramic heads arose from the wall at regular intervals, crazy busts of Medusa and Cerberus and Hades. I loved them, but understood why the neighbors would encourage the wild undergrowth. "I'll go first," I said, and stepped into the bushes. The three of them followed close behind. We crunched along, getting scratched.

"Hey!" Celeste whispered loudly. I stopped and Benny bumped into me. "Hey, Colt!" she said. I could hear the smile in her voice. "Colt the scout."

You had to smile, too. It was sweet she remembered. "I've got it covered," I said. We crept along again until I found a spot that I knew corresponded to a decent clearing on the inside of the garden. Somewhere between Pan and another satyr, I stopped and said to Benny, "Give me a boost. Put your fingers together like this." I took his hands in the dark and showed him. "Okay. I'm going to step in them. Can you two guys pull yourselves over?"

Benny just made a noise that obviously meant yes; they had it under control. He boosted me up onto the wall. I sat on the top, took off my shoes, and hopped down on the other side. Except for the faint glow of the pool, the garden was dark. Celeste appeared on the wall next and handed me her heels. She jumped and fell forward onto her hands, laughing.

"Shh."

"Oh, let 'em."

Let 'em what? I wanted to ask, but then G.J. clambered up, stood, and jumped completely over Celeste. Benny climbed up and sat, then hopped down next to me. "Let your eyes adjust," I said. "It's really great."

We stayed by the wall for a few minutes, the familiar forms of the sculptures taking their shapes slowly, as if sucking matter from the dark. "Damn," G.J. said eventually. "This place is crazy."

"No shit," Benny agreed. I heard him unscrew the cap of his flask, now full of Scotch.

"Gimme some of that," Celeste said, swinging her shoes from their straps around her wrist.

"Shh," I told her again.

"Oh, shh you."

The guys laughed lowly. We stood there till I could distinguish everyone's breathing. Well, what now? Was I going to have to do this whole thing myself? "You wanna see some of the sculptures?" I asked Benny, touching his jacket sleeve.

"Yeah. Let's go," Celeste said loudly. "There's a giant sculpture of Pick Up sticks over here. And a spaceship."

"Celeste!" I hissed.

"What? He's in bed." She took off.

"Who?" Benny asked.

"The artist who lives here," I whispered, chasing after Celeste and grabbing her arm. "What are you doing? I thought you wanted to"—I looked over my shoulder—"have sex with G.J."

"I do."

"You're not acting like it. I don't think he would know that."

"Sure he does."

I made out the ox's silhouette. "Go back there with him."

"Why?"

"*Celeste.* What are you going to do? Have sex from a distance?" I could see the guys standing with their hands in their pockets, moving in a slow circle, nodding to each other at some sight or other. The sculpture garden was a crazy place in the dark, that was for sure.

"Fine. Maybe I could just go inside." She dropped her shoes.

"Celeste!"

"Fine." She walked back to the guys. I picked up her shoes and followed. She stepped to G.J., put her hand behind his neck, and pulled his head to hers. He seemed to accept her advance happily enough. Quickly, I set her shoes on top of her bare feet, took Benny's hand, and guided him away toward the monolith. The ground was solid there, level, the grass as soft and manicured as anywhere in the garden. I leaned with my back into the sculpture and grabbed Benny by his lapels. He straddled his legs, put his hands above my head, and pressed into me. Ah, it was always the press that got me. The want.

I tried to concentrate on the kissing. Benny wasn't bad, but he kept moving his tongue in the same way, as if he were spelling the same word over and over in cursive. I wanted to tell him to write a whole story. Not too sloppy or hard, though. He tasted like ashes and smoke, cigarettes and Scotch. My back was icy against the sculpture but my front was fine.

Benny seemed afraid of my tits almost. He'd rub a hand over one and then breathe hard through his nose, a sort of sigh, put his hand back on the monolith and grind his groin into my waist, going back to spelling the word again. I moved my hand between us and into his shirt, over his smooth chest. I traced the ripples of his stomach muscles lower, lower till he shivered. I gripped his erection through his pants and he moaned. His enthusiasm spurred me onward to his belt buckle. "Lisa," he practically panted when I tugged down his underwear. A new body. A good body.

I backed him up and went to my knees. Benny's hands went into my hair, and I didn't think about anything, anybody else. I didn't. I wouldn't.

I tried not to.

I teased, sucked a little, all the while unbuckling my pantsuit and pushing it down my thighs. I lay back on the grass and took off my outfit completely. Benny stood over me, his face dark, the sky looking as though it were lightening behind him, a dusky purple to match my makeup. He whistled a quiet whistle. He was nice. Benny was a nice guy, a good bad guy, a smoker who paid nice whistle compliments before he got laid. He knelt and carefully lay on top of me, his erection off to the side on my thigh. "I have rubbers," he said.

"I'm on the pill."

"Kick ass." He kissed me again, spelling. I was ready enough, I supposed, even though I wouldn't have minded a little more specific attention, when the retching began. It wasn't delicate. Or quiet. Or G.J.'s. Celeste whimpered between gags, and then the real vomiting started. She had to have been just on the other side of the monolith. You could discern splashing on stone.

"Oh, my god," I said, banging my head in the grass.

"Jesus," Benny said. He rolled off of me as Celeste puked what sounded like buckets.

"Benny," G.J. called from farther away. "Lisa."

I found my pantsuit as Benny groaned, "Uuuuh. Bad timing."
He wasn't kidding.

"Benny. Lisa. Where are you?" I could tell G.J. was moving in
the wrong direction, toward the pool and the house.

"Pssst! Here. Don't go that way!" I stood up, trying to get my
feet into the right leg holes. "Over here." I should have told G.J. to
follow the puke noise.

"Son of a bitch!" Poor Benny. He'd gotten so close. Now he half
hobbled, stooped in his dress shirt like a blind man searching for
his dropped cane. "Do you see my pants?" he whispered.

Celeste started crying then. "I'm sorry," she said. She could certainly hear us as well as we heard her. "I don't feel very well."
More puking ensued as I tried to buckle the backside of my
pantsuit. I realized I had it on inside out when a clunk sounded
from the other side of the monolith. No more Celeste noises.

"Celeste?" I called out softly. Nothing. "Celeste?"

We disheveled three converged on my best friend on the other
side of the sculpture. She lay, passed out, in the grass, her face
resting in her own puke. Something didn't look right, and then I
realized Celeste was bleeding from her nose. I saw a dark bump
on her forehead. Shit. Shit, shit, shit. "Shit!"

"Holy shit!" G.J. said.

I rolled her onto her back.

"No!" Benny said. "Remember first aid? She'll asphyxiate." He
rolled her onto her side, halfway into her own puke again.

"She's not throwing up, though. I think she's unconscious. Look at
her head. At her nose!" Jesus, I didn't know what we should do. Mr.
Diamond at the side of a hospital bed. My old room at my old house.
My brother, David, every damn day. "I have to go wake up Hank."

"Who?"

"Who?"

"The guy who lives here. The artist."

"Fuck that," G.J. said. "My dad's gonna kill me."

"Why?" Benny asked stupidly. "We can just take her back over
the wall."

Was he an idiot? "No, we can't. Stay here. Stay here, and I'll be right back." I looked at Celeste, still as every other sculpture in the garden. "Make sure she's breathing," I said, and ran toward Hank's kitchen door.

I pounded. "Hank! Hank! It's Lisa!" And pounded. "Hank! Celeste is hurt! Hank!" I pounded till my arms and fists ached. "Hank!" I looked behind me. The sky was definitely lightening. I couldn't see any of them. I had no idea what time it was. "Hank!" Hank didn't answer his door. I didn't hear a single sign of life inside the house.

I ran back to the monolith. Celeste lay there alone. In her puke. They'd fucking deserted us? Malcolm wouldn't, though. I bent down and stuck my finger under her nose. She was breathing. I pushed back her hair and then decided I should go see if Malcolm and the limo still waited down the block. Where would we go? To a hospital to have her stomach pumped? I shredded my nylons climbing over the wall, scraped my knees through my pantsuit, scratched my face and arms and neck crashing through the bushes, and burned my feet running barefoot on the sidewalk.

No limo. No Malcolm.

What could they have told him to make him leave?

Celeste.

I ran back the way I came, almost crying this time, thinking about living at home again, about what could happen to me. And Celeste. As I dashed into the neighbor's bushes, a car turned into Hank's driveway. I crouched and watched Hank get out of the passenger seat. Music, laughing, spilled my way. By the light of the overhead, I could see the car was full of people, six, seven, eight of them in a little yellow Toyota. "And Goethe, too!" I thought Hank said, to which the people inside laughed. He jingled keys and walked to his gate as the Toyota backed up and drove away.

I ran at him. "Hank! Hank!" He swung his arms and jumped. "It's me! Me, Lisa! Hank!"

"Lisa?" He squinted.

"Hank, Celeste is really sick. She's in the garden."

"Lisa? Lisa, what's wrong?"

"She's in the garden. Celeste is sick."

"What's wrong with you? What the hell happened?" Suddenly I heard the Hank I knew come back, appear in the moment. "Are you hurt?" I didn't even need to look down at myself to know what he saw. My pantsuit was still on inside out. For starters. He reached toward me and pulled a stick out of my hair. "Lisa, where's Celeste? Is she hurt?" He gripped my face in his hands, his warm hands.

"Inside," I said as clearly as I could.

"Inside my house?"

"In the garden," I repeated again.

Hank unlocked the gate. I ran and he followed. I rounded the corner of the monolith and looked. She was gone. She was gone? Where was Celeste? I walked around the monolith twice, thinking that I'd mistaken the sides, but I knew I hadn't. "There! See?" I pointed at the vomit, the evidence.

"Lisa," Hank said, and held my shoulders. "Tell me what happened. Why are you here? What happened to you?"

"She's bleeding," I said. "She could suffocate. *Where is she?*" I jerked away from Hank and started looking behind other sculptures. "The guys fucking left us! Malcolm left us. I can't believe it! Where is she? Celeste? Ce-leeeste! Where are you? It's okay. Hank's here. Ce-leeeste!"

Hank stayed with me. "What guys? How did you get in here?"

"It's our dance," I told him, and then actually started to cry. "Celeste! Ce-leeeste! Our senior dance."

"Lord. We'll find her." And then we did. We found her. Celeste crouched at the pool, scooping water, trying to clean her face, trying to drink.

I wanted to push her in or punch her. "Why didn't you answer?"

"I have a bloody nose," she said, sticking her thumb and index finger in her nostrils.

Hank turned Celeste's face to him. "Who the fuck did this? Lisa, who are these guys? Celeste, who did this to you?"

And then, slower than slowly, I figured out why Hank was so

concerned. What we looked like. Think about it: We looked worse than bad. "I'm okay," I told him. "Celeste, Celeste drank too much and got sick. She was passed out. I was afraid. We're okay."

"Why are your clothes . . . Look at . . . Lisa, don't be afraid."

"I'm not. I'm not now." I crouched next to Celeste beside the pool. She had a chunk of steak in her hair. She smelled terrible, and the bump would be a huge bruise.

"I'm going to call the police," Hank said.

"No, no, no! No! Hank," I tried, "we're fine. I mean, it was our fault."

Hank didn't call the police. He brought us into the kitchen and put ice on Celeste's head, made coffee, and opened a box of crackers. We explained, more or less. At one point Celeste, still drunk, spoke to him in French—which he didn't understand—telling him that she hoped he felt her pain. She pounded her chest as she said it, her accent perfect. He guided her to his shower, then came back to me. "You're next. When were you expected home exactly?" He walked to the coffee table and opened his drug drawer. "I don't drive, you know."

We didn't know. "Why not?"

"A long story. Eat your crackers."

"We can walk."

He raised his chin and lowered his eyes toward my heels. "Right."

"We have cab fare. We'll tell Mona we said good-bye at breakfast."

"Would that be before or after you lost your night's clothes and came home in T-shirts and shorts?"

I drank Hank's sucky coffee and said—said for Celeste, said for me, said for the both of us, said for stupid, chicken, immature girls everywhere trying just to grow another day or week or month older and learn how to deal with men when we didn't have a clue—said, "Mona got us on the pill. She'll be cool."

"What?" Hank asked, but I could tell he'd heard me. And then his face did something funny. His mouth drooped and he started blinking big watery blinks. I thought he might cry the same way I just had.

It would take me years to understand what I saw happen to Hank right in front of me: I had watched the eyes of the beholder change. And he wasn't even lookin' at Beauty at the time.

She wasn't a girl anymore.

VIOLENT FEMMES

SAN DIEGO, MARCH '84

You heard the band was not the usual, but you go anyway. You go because somebody said that they were raw. Raw as in sometimes no amps at all. Watching next to her, you now understand that raw meant raw meant raw. Like raw cashews. Raw, no salt. Raw, not burned or toasted or even blanched. Raw in that they make you feel lucid for the first time in years at a show, raw in a way that makes you want to mock them and whip your plastic cup of shit keg beer at the ridiculously tall one and the ridiculously big acoustic guitar and charge the stage and kick them all in the kidneys till they piss blood and beg you to squat over them and lay a hard, small turd in each of their rank, pale belly buttons.

You can't remember when you took a dump last.

You hate this.

You need more something.

*T*HANKSGIVING APPROACHED like a frozen turkey down a luge track. The semester had all but disappeared, and Celeste and I had removed ourselves almost completely from any events pertaining to school other than classes. We'd mailed out our college applications.

We just waited.

Having cleared our social calendars of anything resembling what we'd come to disdain—and no, after Benny and G.J.'s desertion, the word *disdain* wasn't too strong—we spent many of our afternoons again at Hank's. He let us come and get high and watch him work. He was affable with me, and much to Celeste's delight, now able to maintain an erection for extended periods of time before coming. As the weather grew colder and we donned newly acquired old black leather motorcycle jackets, I wondered why he allowed us to come back. Hank had never kicked us out, but his lenience since the vomiting and our break-in seemed almost too nice.

Lately I wonder if he didn't feel responsible. Or perhaps he simply understood our need for a haven, a halfway house into an artistic adulthood. More likely, he saw unmistakably where Celeste and I were headed in the hands of high school boys.

Ess appeared occasionally, and he'd greedily screw me whenever I let him, which was whenever he was there. Hank's entire house became fair game. No more teasing, no more dry humping and backing away. I remember thinking once that we'd made it.

That Celeste and I had been fully inducted, whatever the hell that meant.

With our shorter senior schedules, we were often home in time to make dinner and sober up, get to jazz class, and complete our homework halfheartedly. Mr. Diamond warmed some as the days chilled, but he never really did recover from our first late return from Hank's so many months before. We could have been friendly ghosts he smiled at and talked to.

"Kids grow up," Celeste said one night as we threw together box-mix tacos. "He should realize that, and if he can't, it's his own damn fault."

"Yeah," I agreed. What else was a displaced girl to say?

Eventually I realized that Ess visited Hank's just for the nooky and to spy. Sure, Hank acted as Ess' mentor and teacher, but mainly what Ess wanted to watch was Hank's progress with the sculpture. Other students came around to watch the progress now and again, too, some of them drones, some new people. I can recall, clearer than clear, as if the day had been shot on digital video, when I made the decision to try to sleep with one of the other ones.

Ess hadn't appeared for over a week, but on this particular Thursday, three other guys had. The fact that the sculpture department attracted far more male than female students had not escaped my attention.

Drone Mack Truck had been coming around, despite—or maybe because of—his photography major. He no longer scowled at me. When he didn't scowl, he was positively flawed in the best of ways. I liked his crooked smile and how wiry and brooding he looked. Beyond that, if only because he almost never talked, Mack seemed smarter than Ess. Perceptions, of course, counted for most everything. No question Ess was knock-down, drag-out sexy, but almost in too obvious a way, if that makes sense. A little too close to perfect. And, I'd finally come to realize, a little too dim-bulbed.

Mack, you could say, wadn't purty, but he was hot. Raw sexy.

Menacing sexy. An epitome of sorts, too, but not any kind of golden boy. Not Bring on the Babes 'Cause I Am a Man. More of a You Might Not See Me, But When You Do, You'll Decide I'm Sexy.

I saw Mack. His hair, which used to be bloodred, was now green and growing out mild brown. You wouldn't think green hair could ever flatter anybody, but green hair on Mack looked good. With his almost black eyes and his warm complexion, the green didn't wash him out. He wore it in short spikes and nodded at Hank as he chiseled away at the flying saucer. I saw a leg emerging. Mine or Celeste's, I had no idea.

Mack strolled the garden with his camera. As far as I could tell, he usually took photos of angles and curves, pieces of sculptures rather than the wholes. You'd see him crouching in some nearly impossible contortion between the bronze legs of a cubist Apollo, shooting crotchward, or lying flat on his stomach, his long lens trained on Hermes's Dada-esque ankle wing. Then too Mack would point his big Nikon at people. He'd get in your face, forcing you to finally stick out your tongue or give him the finger. When you did, the shutter clicked, a big mechanical eye winking.

The Thursday Mack moved his camera toward my ear and said only, "Gorgeous whorls, Lisa," the wind carried wood smoke and pine, and the sky was a pale November blue, and my mind was sharpened like a stick. Mack had chosen my ear, rather than Celeste's. I would remember the moment forever. I made my decision immediately, quick as the shutter click, quick as his eye for a good-looking ear.

Celeste and Hank didn't have sex when other people were around. (Except for me, but of course I wasn't right there in the room with them. I'd be sitting in the cold sun scribbling inanities on my worn-out Jack Purcells or studying my hair for split ends.) In the presence of others, they behaved like good acquaintances, although I tend to think the usual gang knew.

Hank didn't let just anybody come by, however. He had an elite group of students, probably the ones he perceived to be the most talented or beautiful or interesting. Or trustworthy. Certainly trustworthy had to be key. With the smoking and drinking and all. So while not a whole lot of people in general would have suspected Celeste and Hank of having sex, the invited few pretty much understood what was going on between the handsome teacher and the beautiful high school girl. A few might have mumbled about them now and again, but never so loudly or rudely that Hank would have kicked them out.

The people at Hank's liked to be thought of as special. You know, how everybody wants into the exclusive group. So Hank got away with fucking his high school girl on the pill, and I got away with pursuing Mack under Hank and Celeste's protection. Actually, I think, Hank somehow thought better of me for picking Mack. I didn't know at the time that I was but one of many regular screws for Ess, but I'd suspected. I decided not to care. I decided to screw Mack instead. Move on.

So I did.

Pretty quickly, Mack came into the know about Hank and Celeste. The Wednesday before Thanksgiving, the weather turned ugly, sleet sending the few extra hangers-on home. Everyone but Celeste, Mack, and me. Ess probably hadn't been around for five or six days again. The four of us went inside and smoked a big bowl from Hank's new hookah. Celeste and Hank went down the hall. Mack and I got the munchies and started dinner. Mack was a good cook, but not very happy to take the compliment when I paid it.

"Fuck, no," he said. "Just wasn't anybody else at home when I was hungry."

I wondered what sort of family Mack came from. I'd never wondered about Ess'. I never cared about anything when it came to Ess except for the immediate. "Where'd you grow up?"

"Here and then Jeff City. Dad's a judge."

Not what I'd expected. With the green hair and earring. "Really?"

He nodded. Definitely not much of a talker. He added dried basil leaf to our sauce for pasta. Mmm, nothing like a big bowl of spaghetti on a cold night. And nothing like a new guy. The time felt right. I went in for the kill, stepping up behind Mack while he stirred, and kissed the back of his neck. I watched the stirring stop, the wooden spoon tip. "Turn around," I told him, and he did.

We were panting and half-naked, Mack's back splattered with marinara, when Celeste whispered in my ear, "Guest room."

I nearly jumped. I hadn't heard her approach at all. I grabbed Mack's hand and showed him the way.

Smaller, shorter than Ess, lanky, Mack was almost hairless on his body, the way I imagined Japanese or Indian men to be. Visibly excited by my birth control information, he sat on his heels on the bed and pulled me by the back of my knees toward him, draping my legs over his angled thighs. He licked his thumb and with it found my clit. He rubbed small circles and inserted just the head of his cock inside me. I swear I came in under a minute. When he felt me come—he could tell!—he fucked me full-on till I actually made noise.

He smiled at that and kept going. He took my ankles and lifted up my legs till they were closed, my view of Mack's face blocked. He leaned forward and slid me backward on the bed. My knees inched toward my chest till I was folded in half, my shinbones on either side of my nose. Thank god for jazz. He stopped, hot breath hit my calves, and I felt him pulse into me. Mack! He let go of my ankles and carefully straddled my legs so I could lower them. Mack Truck! He kissed me. He pulled a pillow out from the covers and shared it with me. I got it. I loved him. Sort of.

We lay quiet. Mack took an imaginary picture of my face. His left eye squinted closed; his index finger nodded.

A knock on the door. "We finished making the pasta," Celeste said.

"I'm starving," I said, and smiled.

Mack smiled back and nodded. "Me too."

Celeste and I were responsible for getting up at six thirty in the morning to stuff and tie and insert the monstrous buttered bird into the oven. After that we went back to bed and got up again at nine.

"Happy Thanksgiving," Mona said, blowing on a mug of tea in the kitchen.

"Happy Thanksgiving," I told her. I believed it would be a happy day, because I got it. I understood now. I understood how it could actually work with a guy, the sex thing.

"I figure we should start basting in an hour or so." Mona spread jam on a bagel.

"Yeah." Celeste yawned.

"Go brush your teeth, Celeste."

"Why? They're fine." She pulled her lips back in a grimace.

"Stop that."

"It's my cur," she said. "I'm doing my cur imitation."

Mona shook her head and raised her mug of tea. "That's a lovely one," she said sarcastically.

We began cooking what in my mind is still the best meal I've helped to create. I know that on my own I've never duplicated it. My father and brother were coming over, along with two international Ph.D. candidates from Calcutta via KU; they'd been assigned to the Diamond family through Mona's Crossing Borders volunteer work. Mr. Diamond tried not to show his disappointment in the last-minute news from Celeste's sister, Rachel, that she wouldn't be back for the feast.

I should describe it. You should at least hear what we did, the three of us there in the Diamond kitchen.

Into the bird in the morning had gone the most traditional of stuffings, the herbed bread stuffing with celery and onion. We added two baking dishes later, one of cornbread dressing, one with that Midwestern rarity, oysters. We cut autumn leaves from pastry to decorate our rolled piecrusts, filled them with pumpkin, apple, and mincemeat. We warmed a honey-pineapple glaze and painted a perfect ham. We boiled and chilled appetizer shrimp. We stewed cranberries with fresh raspberries and sugar. We turned a mountain of sweet potatoes into a casserole for royalty: a pound of butter, a pint of heavy whipping cream, a cup of brown sugar, pinches of spice, a cup of pecan halves. We baked a fresh green-bean casserole and fried our very own onion crisps for the top. Polished silver. Boiled pearl onions and Brussels sprouts, bathed them in herbed cream, more cream. Candied carrots. Whipped ten pounds of russets. Baked crescent rolls from scratch. Warmed a wheel of brie, added fresh horseradish to our own cocktail sauce, made sure the chairs were comfy, tossed romaine with Granny Smiths and raisins and water chestnuts and walnuts and blue cheese, filled bowls with pistachios, decanted wine into crystal, filled boats with savory gravy, took ice cream out of the freezer to soften, positioned chargers, lit candles, decorated water goblets with grenadine-tinted ice cubes, turned down the dining room chandelier rheostat, and gave our thanks.

You'd think there would have been leftovers to fill refrigerators for miles, but I'd never seen a group of five men consume more food. The Indian guests from Calcutta were well acclimated to America. Two homely bachelors, paunchy and thrilled with their luck at drawing the Diamond card of the KU Thanksgiving lottery, they ate until I do not believe their stomachs could have expanded further. Mr. Diamond topped himself. My brother, who had recently overtaken me in height and then racked up another six inches, ate to fill his hollow leg. My father did better than expected, too, eating two pieces of pie with our amaretto-flavored whipped cream.

All through dinner, I found myself daydreaming about making marinara. Mack had stolen my appetite, of course, and it's hard after smelling what you cook all day long to really be hungry, but I tried not to let anyone know. Everybody watched everybody. Mona, with each additional request to pass another dish around for the second or third time, expanded in her seat, grew bigger with pride, until her presence verily towered over Mr. Diamond's. One of the Calcutta guys said, "I would favor some more of that delicious yam—the seasonings remind me of home." She must have been keeping count. It must have been his fourth serving. Mona grew big as the entire room then, reached toward Celeste and me, who flanked her on either side at the end of the big mahogany oval—we were her prodigies, her offspring, her tutees, her pride-and-joys—and patted our forearms. I figure it came as close to a kiss as Mona would ever give. She beamed. She glowed.

My brother and father left a few ungracious minutes after finishing their desserts, but the Indian guys stayed to help clean up. They were appreciative and friendly. I barely saw them, fixated as I was on the previous night's events, but I tried a little as I scraped and covered and rinsed and loaded.

And that was that.

And, as was our habit, Celeste and I barreled into the future.

Throughout the Christmas holiday break, we fucked like bunnies. Mack and I humped all around Hank's house and KCAI's deserted dormitory. Mack melted me. Turned me to goo. Made me, officially, a horn dog. I couldn't get enough of him. His dick was my desire, his mouth my daily reward. My loins, my flesh, ached from the use. He taught me gorgeously perverted techniques. He produced vegetables from beneath his trench coat. He personally introduced me to the pleasures of battery-operated paraphernalia. And I did not resist, had no aversion to anything experimental. Must have had something to do with mother issues. Or having been friends with Celeste for so long. Otherwise being fucked with a zucchini might have rung a few alarm bells.

I didn't sense that Mack had me strung along with other girls, but I also didn't sense he felt like taking me out in public. Same ol', same ol' with these Art Institute guys. I sort of understood, though. I lapped up all that he gave me, but I knew all the while that I wouldn't see Mack after I left Kansas City. We weren't sweethearts doing everything we could to be together forever after. We were, simply, in love with sex with each other. It's a sort of love. It is. Maybe he wasn't bowled over by me, but he never let on. Each day after Christmas, Mack and I and Celeste and Hank smoked, played board games in the afternoon, and then screwed. Celeste and I generally won at Scrabble and no longer coughed when inhaling.

Did I still desire Hank? Well, sure, but I'd decided that Mack was able to fulfill my every desire for now. Besides, desire was one thing; need was another. And clearly I didn't need Hank. Celeste might have, though. On the couch or arguing over team chess, they seemed *close-close*. Mack and I beat them every time, but I saw Celeste defer to Hank when she knew better. Why would she do that? Where had she gone? As talky as Celeste and I were when we went home, she hadn't really let me in on what transpired behind the scenes with Hank emotion-wise. I fished; she wouldn't give. I decided she would be pragmatic about Hank. She knew she'd be leaving, too. She knew better than to get attached to a teacher who couldn't really be seen with her. I was certain of it.

Vacation sped by in a blur. New Year's Eve we spent in the KCAI sculpture department at a small party, as close as Celeste would get to a public outing with Hank. Mack was one of the few students who stayed over the break in the dorms. He'd visited his family in Jeff City for exactly two days, Christmas Eve and Christmas Day, and said, "That's it. No more."

He and I rang in the New Year in style.

New Year's Day, a freezing-cold day the color of young guilt, I tried to reconcile my growing obsession, this base sexual fascination with guys, with what I knew would too soon be the act of committing myself to years and years of study. If I were going to be using my brain in the future, I reasoned with myself pretty pathetically, it'd be fine to focus on using my body for the time being.

My conscience buzzed like a bee dying in a jar. Eventually I'd learn how to leave it on a windowsill.

Back to school in January, the days dragged, icy or gritty with sandblasting Plains storms. Celeste and I stayed frozen in the stone outside in Hank's yard. In the dead of winter, our forms looked covered in snow even when they weren't. We were under there, in there; you could see us at that point—at least where our heads and limbs and torsos were. Just stuck, stuck in Kansas City in the shit season.

Familiarity set in during March, soggy and punctuated by two blizzards. Rachel, Celeste's sister, called with news of her elopement with a fellow environmental studies graduate student. Diana had given her professor husband a son, Jacob. Mack and I saw less of each other; he was engrossed in his photography and art history and whatever else he was taking. As I waited for envelopes from colleges, I began to understand that Celeste and I would likely not spend the next four years with each other. The weeks inched by. College acceptance letters, and a few rejections, started coming in. I felt mildly obligated to spend a bit of time with my father, as he'd be paying my expensive way wherever I went. Sometimes Celeste went to Hank's without me. But, for the most part, our holding pattern remained the same.

By April, amidst daffodils and hyacinths, we'd determined where we were going to school. I'd be attending the University of Wisconsin at Madison, which had awarded me a partial scholarship. Celeste, to Mr. Diamond's complete horror, would attend the University of California at Berkeley, having won a grant that covered her entire freshman-year tuition, including room and board. Mona was ecstatic, her husband nearly inconsolable.

Did you know that it only takes seven days to establish a bad habit but thirty to actively rid yourself of it?

Clearly we'd spent more than seven days at Hank's.

May whispered of freedom. We'd defined ourselves at Country Club Plaza High School as the outsiders, the girls who wore strange clothes and talked about art as if the world revolved around it, the girls who had gone from popular to untouchable. We didn't care. We understood that normalcy meant death. We understood that our classmates were losers.

Hank had started serious work on our sculpture again. While we had our schoolwork distractions, Celeste and I still spent at least a day or two a week at Hank's, often with Mack. The honeymoon was over for all of us by now, so when Ess showed up, as he did from time to time, I grew tempted. He'd heard about Mack and me and hadn't seemed to mind. Ess was his usual self, gorgeous and dumb. But Mack and I knew each other's bodies inside out now, so visiting with him still had its advantages. Celeste and Hank's relationship appeared, for all intents and purposes, the same. Treading water. Holding ground. Whatever.

The sculpture, though, had begun to take form in realistic seriousness. I could tell the difference between the figures and looked forward to each visit. Hank—if nobody else at the Art Institute—had true talent.

One of the last times I slept with Mack, he presented me with the photo of my ear. His hair had grown out and he'd bleached it platinum. He wore it in longer spikes, à la Johnny Rotten. I wasn't sure the new color suited him as well as the green had, but it mattered little. I'd been preparing myself for separation. In a week Mack would leave for a summer-long road trip into Mexico and Central America. I told him I thought that for safety's sake he should shave his head and let his brown stubble grow in before he left the country. He didn't even acknowledge the comment.

I have the ear photo still, framed and hung on the inside of my bedroom closet door. I didn't feel right hanging it elsewhere, as intimate a photo as it is. It's a good photo, I think, every time I open my door in the morning. A good photo.

And then June. Caps and gowns. Graduation. Gifts. Hugs and drinks with tearful classmates whom Celeste and I had blown off most of the year.

Dinner out with my father and brother, an almost pleasant affair at one of the overcrowded and overpriced barbecue restaurants on the Plaza. My father gave me a check. My brother gave me a card signed only with a crude drawing of stick-figure kids looking like they were humping and a TV with a tongue sticking out of the screen and Xs for eyes. A dead TV. I got David's joke. He'd included a fifty-dollar bill. I didn't hug him or kiss him, but I smiled so that he knew I understood.

Then dinner another time, a better time, with Celeste and Mona and Mr. Diamond and Diana and her husband and their baby and Rachel and her husband. We requested the private room at the Japanese restaurant where the chefs cooked at the table and chopped out a teriyaki steak beat on the huge metal surface, flung shrimp and made bad jokes. We loved it. Celeste and I were allowed hot sake like all the adults. And I was part of a big family. I actually thought how lucky I was to have my mother locked away. I felt safe in her inability to ruin my graduation.

While we never said as much, I'm sure the weaning process Celeste and I undertook was purposeful. Possibly because we had graduated from high school and now felt different, significantly more grown-up, we agreed to stop going to Hank's. How difficult the process must have been for her! How different a relationship she'd had with Hank than I'd had with either Ess or Mack. How different an experience altogether. And how selfish I had to have been not to see her pain. How much of an idiot I'd always, always been. How.

We never resumed our summer visits to the art museum. Instead, we started going out to clubs. Practiced being adults. Mack had made some very good fake IDs for us before he left on his road trip, and we put them to use.

The dance clubs in Westport were fun enough at first but contained too much of something I couldn't pinpoint. Too much clean, maybe. Too many busy lights. Too much fakeness or desperation. Too much money. Just no art, really. Well, no, not exactly that either. I suppose we just found live music more interesting. Dancing to live music beat prerecorded hands-down. Even when the band wasn't very good, the people there felt sincere. Real. (As opposed to unreal people? Hmm.) We ran into Westley from dance class at a reggae show on Main at the end of June. He and I traded phone numbers, as soon I was going to be desperate for company. The Diamonds were going to Greece for two weeks for a family reunion, and my father had forbidden me to go, saying only over and over again, "Not that far away. That's just too far."

I had yelled and told him I would be happy to be rid of him "just like Mom." He didn't change his mind.

Westley and I fooled around while the Diamonds were gone, but we both recognized a certain lack of passion. I don't know if our dancing together for so many years played into our feelings, seeing each other in leotards and tights, watching each other mature. But whatever it felt like for Westley, I felt like I was kissing my brother. We did hook up a few more times to see some music, though. He was different, artistic, smart, and talkative. And, of course, we could dance.

I began to read the flyers stapled to the telephone poles around Westport—a weird kind of poetry when you read them from top to bottom on a covered phone pole. I bought *Rolling Stone* at the newsstand.

I also had my hair cut while Celeste was gone, at a cool salon where all the cutters had hair that looked like the drones'. Long hair had drifted out of style, and I couldn't very well start college with people judging me as less than up-to-date. The woman who cut nearly a foot off my hair told me she was a "stylist" and sold me gel to make spikes when I wanted, then showed me how to hang my head upside down and use hairspray to make them stiffer. Before I left I studied her makeup, her severe eyes, the slash-blushed cheeks, the purple lipstick. My brother, David, called me a "freaky punker" when I arrived home. I told him he was so out of it, he didn't even know the right word. "Punk," I told him. "Only dorks say 'punker,' dork." He never failed to reduce me to a six-year-old. In the shower, I couldn't believe how much less hair I had to wash. But I felt lighter. Ready to go.

Celeste returned with her hair in a hundred braids, some with colored thread and thin pieces of leather woven into them. She let me touch them as we sat on our bed. Her bed. I hadn't been in the Diamond house in what felt like years. "I met a girl from Berkeley when we were in Mykonos. She braided these for me on the beach. Can you believe it? What are the chances of meeting somebody from Berkeley? She goes to Tulane—her name's Fatima—

but she told me all the cool places to go in the Bay Area, where to buy organic produce—she's a vegetarian. She doesn't even eat fish."

"How do you wash it?"

"What? Oh, just up by the scalp and then you let the soapy water sort of rinse through the rest." She looked really different.

"Did you meet any guys?"

"Yeah! Rachel and Diana were jealous. But their husbands are nice, and Jacob is so cute. Actually Diana's old man *is* an old man. Rachel's husband is gnarly, though. Totally." She sounded really different.

"Gnarly?"

"You know. Awesome."

"Oh."

"Let's go swim. I'll tell you all about the handsome Greek men." She made a purring sound and pulled off her tank. She didn't have a tan line on top anymore!

"You sunbathed nude?"

"No. Just with bottoms. Topless. Everybody does. Rachel and Diana, too. Mom wouldn't—until the last two days! Can you believe it?"

Mona sunbathing topless. "What did your dad do?"

"What do you think he did? He made sure to get the best cabana there! He was totally up at, like, six in the morning with his books, ready to head down to the beach. He loved it. He wants to go back every year! I don't think he ever read more than a chapter, though, as busy as he was admiring the view, ha, ha."

How could two weeks change Celeste so much? "Did he sing?"

She tossed me a bikini. "No. He whistled. Every damn day in the shower. Your hair's way different! I like it! You're not tanning so much. I guess it goes with the look." So chatty. I hoped she was happy to see me.

"Westley and I fooled around."

"What?!"

"Not what you'd imagine."

"Huh. I guess we've known him too long." She stepped out of her blue jeans and underwear. She had shaved! She hardly had any crotch hair left!

"You shaved."

"Well, the bottoms are teeny. Look." She held up a new bikini bottom. It looked like string. Pink crochet.

"Wow."

"Yeah, exactly what I said when we saw what everybody was wearing on the beach, but, when in Mykonos . . ."

What? I was lost. When in Mykonos what? "Yeah."

"Oh, here. Don't put that one on." Celeste walked to me naked and took the bikini back. "Here. I got you one, too." She extracted a baby-blue crocheted bikini from her half-unpacked suitcase. "Do you like it?" Her braids made noise on her back when she swung them around over her shoulders. They sounded heavy.

"Thank you," I said, trying to sound sincere. Baby blue hadn't really been part of my preferred palate lately, but I didn't want to seem ungrateful. She had thought of me while she was away. I had looked forward to her return.

"Have you heard from Mack? Fatima says that Central America is a dangerous place to be right now. And what about Hank? Have you been over there lately?" She looked at herself in the mirror and cupped her own breasts in her crocheted bikini top, the triangles no bigger than half Kraft cheese slices cut on the diagonal.

"No," I said. That seemed to about cover it.

"I guessed. Do you think we'll be disappointed by the sculpture?" She let go of her breasts. "I wonder if he'll sell it for big bucks or leave it there for history? Have you ever contemplated the breakdown of the word *history*? *His story*?"

I hadn't. No doubt I should have. I was going to Wisconsin, and Celeste was going to California. I wondered how I could break that down. Unlike all the algebra and calculus I'd taken, though, I couldn't find the key, the way in.

We swam. We became reacquainted. My new suit didn't do much for me, but I didn't complain. It fit.

August, and the end was imminent. Celeste and I became physically inseparable, spending most every minute of every last day together. But we had similar tendencies. We'd been nurtured together for years by the same people. (Oh, if only we could have been twins separated at birth.) And with those common tendencies, we chose similar courses of action. If I hadn't shut down some, hadn't diverted my energies into the practical aspects of packing and moving, my heart would have sprung an unstoppable leak. For what it's worth, I sensed Celeste's behavior indicated she felt the same way and that she closed some of the same doors I did in order to stay sane.

We'd been best friends since sixth grade.

I lived at her house.

We slept in the same big bed.

We agreed not to go to Hank's before we left. We would see the sculpture at Christmas break, we promised ourselves, once it was finished. We'd go to Hank's gallery show newly returned and mature in sexy cocktail dresses. It would take Hank and Ess and Mack and all the other guys nearly ten minutes to recognize us. They would want dates we wouldn't give them. They would beg to take us out on the town. We would say that we were busy. We'd have other plans. We would give in only if they pleaded.

We agreed to call each other long distance three times a week.

We agreed to write long, honest letters.

We agreed to search for art, for unusual people, for free speech, for original thought, and for cool clothes.

We two little Kansas City girls agreed, and then we went out into the world.

You knew Exene would be good. They said she was the undisputed champ with a cunt on the West Coast. What you didn't realize is that she would be this good, that she could go it alone up there onstage if she needed to. But she doesn't even. She has a band to back her up as tight as any group of killers you've heard yet, as fucking fast as the best of the best.

The bitch is your new musical *krishna krishna,* your new *rama rama.*

Decide to try not to be jealous. Decide not to try to be a singer because you know you cannot write this music, and you cannot sing your better half's tunes. Believe, at the moment, that you are not original enough. Let your bum brain draw its slow lines around the notion of *original* versus *original enough.*

The hash you smoked half an hour ago purses its lips on your sphincter and kisses. It decides to deep-throat you. Know that you and the dark Turkish pitch are a combustible duo, and that tonight's show will either be very good in outcome or, diametrically opposite, that you will remain unsullied.

Decide, then, that it's time to meet the band. Decide you must stage-dive the bitch herself in order to overthrow the monarchy.

Somewhere between the time she mentions the New World and the time you find yourself facedown in the terribly proverbial dark alleyway, fetid with all fluids human, all castoffs and discards, tuna cans and burger bags and pizza boxes and sanitary napkins and deflated blow-up dolls and all those dirty needles, all those nasty, nasty pricks, discover that you have been penetrated.

Wonder by what. Sniff your fingers.

THIRTEEN

My NEW life was a hill. The campus of UW Madison sat at the edge of a lake on an immense sloping hill. As the fall semester progressed and the oh-so-fucking-cold weather set in, the hill would often become slick with ice. A big, frozen hill: a sledder's paradise and a book-toting student's nightmare. I fell, he fell, she fell, we all fell. I saw a fellow classmate from Life Drawing slip and fall late in October when he was about two-thirds of the way up the half-mile-long hill and watched him follow his sketch pad down for over a block before somebody stopped him. I'm not kidding. You know the hill if you've ever been to a pot rally or gone to Madison just to hang out.

I developed a stopping technique for when I was feeling brave and had the right clothes on. If I saw somebody coming down the hill, clutching at nothing, spinning, I'd stop, spread my feet, and bend my knees. Then I'd put a gloved finger on the hill, on the ice, and carefully step left or right to line up with the careening student. I'd always wanted to play football. You had to lean forward. Keep your center of gravity low. Sometimes when I was lucky I'd slow the person down without falling myself. Usually, though, we'd both go down. All in the name of camaraderie. A great way to meet people.

I stopped Carl with my special hill tackle. I had been admiring the great ass in his worn-out blue jeans, the clank of his motorcycle jacket's buckle. I could have told him combat boots were no good in sleet. Most of the rest of us carried umbrellas, but Carl was pretending to be cool. He looked cold as shit, his shoulders hunched, holding a notebook over his head, when his footing went.

I'd been missing Celeste for months already and coveting her warm California existence. We'd kept up on our promise to call each other at least three times a week—we called five or six, easy—but the rest of our promises proved harder to live up to. Challenged for the first time in years, I actually worked on homework. I was a perfectionist when it came to grades.

I saw interesting people and cool clothes and heard plenty of free speech, much of it about the benefits of hemp, and I encountered some original thought in my classes, but most of that happened to be coming from the TAs, which meant that their original thought had been practiced, if not rehearsed in a mirror the night before. So I'd not been very active in much of anything but my own junk, when I saw Carl—whose name I didn't yet know—nose-dive into the hill and start sliding.

Carl, a gangling, towheaded product of a Scandinavian union, had grown up a local of Madison, Wisconsin, and thus suffered from something of an inferiority complex. In his view he humbly attended the local college. But I was no dummy. (Nor, actually, was he.) Carl's lack of confidence was to my advantage. I moved in swiftly.

Out on the West Coast, Celeste had gone hog wild. By the time I met Carl, she had bedded three boys on three separate occasions. In a new dialect that continued to evolve, she told me how each boy had been uniquely disappointing compared to Hank. She'd started to believe that boys had no interest in anything she desired. "I swear, Lis, they just go ahead, doing whatever. It's as if you're not even there as a whole body with a brain. Just boobs and a warm spot between your legs."

Hmm. Not such good luck yet, but what exactly did she expect with hippie guys, with unshaven, stinky boys? "Well," I said, "maybe you're not choosing them with care." I laughed a little, since she couldn't see my face.

"That's true. You're right. I'm not at all."

"Why *are* you picking them?"

"They look like they would know what they're doing."

"But they don't."

"One guy tried. And I tried to help him, but it was awful."

"How?"

"He wasn't in tune, you know? Like, he totally didn't read me. If he'd paid better attention, he might have understood, you know, my rhythms."

Aha. "Yeah."

"Well, what about you and Carl?"

Carl and I had been rolling around in his off-campus apartment for nearly a week, getting the hang of things, of each other. "It takes practice," I said, wanting to add, "with the same person."

"Yeah," she said, exhaling heavily into the phone.

"Are you smoking?"

"Just a little toke to get me in the homework mode."

Carl smoked every day. I could hardly fault Celeste. One girl's can of beer was another girl's joint. "My liberal arts core class has oral presentations this week," I told her, a bit bored. "I'm giving a talk on sculpture. Rodin."

"Yeah? I miss you, Lisa."

"Me, too." We had pretty much relayed as much about our lives to each other as we could without switching skins, without changing places completely. Sometimes I wished I had a roommate. My partial scholarship pleased my father so much that he had sprung for a single dorm room, my own space. But sleeping at the Diamonds over the years I'd gotten so used to another body in the bed at night that I now felt utterly isolated. Carl was wonderful to fall asleep with, but shortly afterward he'd break into an almost snore, a throaty breathing that woke me up. For those first few seconds, I never knew exactly where I was.

Carl was a good guy, though. Sweet, clean, considerate. Trying to be a bad guy, but just too nice. He had truly blond pubic hair. I decided he must have been one of those white-haired kids with red-rimmed eyes, an All Light kid. I knew I probably wouldn't keep him, but he was warm under the covers and made some great lamb curry. I liked that Carl wasn't a vegetarian or a No-dairy-I-eat-weird-food-because-of-allergies-I-swear-I'm-allergic-to-*everything*! person like all of Celeste's new West Coast friends. Carl would do, though I felt little passion for him.

Actually I hadn't felt much passion at all since I'd arrived in Madison. I felt challenged as a student, and challenged as a new adult, trying to get through the registration lines in one piece, to get where I needed to be on time, prepared, making acquaintances on the dorm floor. Part of me, however, didn't want to fit in. I wanted to be a Hank, an Ess, a Mack. I hadn't declared my major, but I found myself leaning—worse than Pisa, worse than a frosh at a fraternity keg party—toward fine arts.

I heard Celeste's intake of breath again. "I'm thinking," she said, "I'm thinking of staying here over Christmas. There's this soup kitchen. . . ."

I'd never heard the term before, but I knew immediately where I'd be, come December. My father would have to understand. I vowed to reward him with straight As, or as close as I could get. I owed him that much. It was David's last year at home. They'd be fine. My father had been hinting at a Hawaiian vacation too, anyways. "A what?"

"A soup kitchen. Where you feed poor people."

"On Christmas?"

"Well, Hanukkah, too, actually."

"They eat soup?"

She laughed. I could hear her buzz. "Lis, Lis. Even in Wisconsin you're still the same."

"Why wouldn't I be?"

"There'd be turkey or something on Christmas. I'll spoon out gravy."

I couldn't think of a more depressing way to spend the holidays. I wanted Mrs. Diamond to make a fuss, buy me a dress, hear Mr. Diamond sing nondenominational carols. "Could I come and do the carrots?"

"Oh! Lis! Would you? God, that'd be totally awesome! Would you? I'd love it! We could wear Santa hats when we served and go out to dance in San Francisco at night!"

"Okay." The dancing idea wasn't so terrible. "I'll try. Should I really try?"

"Do. Do! I'd love it. It'd be totally great!"

"Are the dorms open through the break?"

"Our suites are. Special cases and all."

And then I saw him as if I were actually spying. I cleaned my multifaceted eyeballs, a fly on the kitchen wall. I saw Mr. Diamond's slippers. His slumped girth. The empty cup in front of him. How could she do that? "But what about your parents?"

"Oh, no big deal. Diana and the baby will be there and maybe her husband."

Yeah, but Diana wasn't Celeste. *"Celeste."*

"He doesn't run my life!"

"But—"

"And he's not paying my way, anyway. He has nothing to do with my being here or what I'm doing at all."

If Celeste had been a toddler, I would have shushed her or taken her out of the room. "Hey," I said, turning up the radio. "Listen to this song." The college radio station played some pretty decent music.

"Old," she said.

Was it? "Oh."

"You should really ask, Lis. Try. Please? Pleeeeease? I have some money if you need it. My fund."

I had one of those too. "I don't think I'll need money—let me see."

"Do!"

"There's no hope of snow, is there?"

She belly-laughed into her end of the phone. "Damn, we're gonna have a blast!"

A blast? Who used that word? I didn't like the idea of Christmas in California. But I had no choice. I had to get her back.

By finals week, I'd become friends with the speed dealer on my dorm floor. Andy was kinda freaky-cool, a big-time Doors fan and a proud, newly practicing Buddhist. He told me he could reconcile his drug dealing with his religion because he'd not yet risen beyond searching for the ox. I had no idea what he meant, but what he sold me helped me stay up late and find the time I needed to study for fifteen credits' worth of what I really hoped would be As. Carl didn't approve of my taking speed, but when I stopped telling him about it and just started brewing pots of coffee at night, pouring cold cups down the toilet, he seemed to believe little ol' me from Kansas City had stopped taking anything naughty. He held firm to the belief that only what sprouted from the earth was worthy of ingestion. Manmade=bad. Manmade=bad for body, bad for mind. I found his opinion rather Neanderthalish, but, hell, he let me stay over. And he was warm. (Did I say that already?) What harm did a little coffee brewing do?

You could check by phone. I'd made two straight As, two A-s, and one B+. I think it was the first B I'd gotten since grade school in Chicago. I wasn't devastated, but I was definitely peeved.

David said on the phone that our father really did want me to go to Hawaii with them, but that they both understood how I would want to spend my time with Celeste. David also said that our father had a girlfriend.

"What?"

"Yeah."

"What do you mean?"

"'Tard. He has a girlfriend."

"You've met her?"

"Not yet."

"Well, are you going to?"

"I think Dad's going to introduce her in Hawaii."

I actually paused, thinking about David and his life for a second. We were nothing alike, though, so I didn't pause long. "Have you seen pictures?"

"No, but I've heard him on the phone with her."

"You shouldn't do that."

"I wasn't *on* the phone. He was in his office and I was acciden-tally in the hall. She's somebody from work."

My mother's odor, her fingerling mist, snaked its way into my dorm room where I'd been collecting dirty laundry to do down on the second floor. Telling David, telling my mother, I said, "He *should* have a girlfriend."

Silence. Finally, "Yeah?" David was ten again, his horrible skinned knee between us as I took the sting-y orange stuff from the medicine cabinet. "I promise," I had said to him. "Fast. Then it's over."

"Yeah," I said.

Another long pause. "You should come to Hawaii," he said.

"I'm going to California."

"I know." I could actually hear him rub what sounded like a soft beard on the receiver. I could have, should have, ribbed him, but I was so shocked by his sudden maturity that I forgot to. I realized we'd never wrestle again. Never break another TV.

"She's dead," I said. "Pretty much." I craved more speed all of a sudden.

"I know."

"Right?"

Silence.

"Right?"

"Okay," he said. As if I made it true. Maybe I did.

"Why don't you ask to come visit in California?"

"I'm seventeen."

"Oh, yeah."

"His girlfriend's way younger, I think."

"I hope she's a good lay."

"No shit," David said, and I knew he was my brother.

Celeste met me at the gate with her friend Joaquim. They were coed suitemates along with four other grant people. As the winter sun flagged, about half an hour away from giving itself up to the Pacific, we rode back to Berkeley in Joaquim's fifties convertible Cadillac. It was smooth as a boat, huge, and pink. "You pronounce it Wah-keem!" Celeste half yelled from the front seat as we drove on the highway, her hair rising up behind her like a tempest. "Joaquim is gay." I knew all about him already from our phone conversations, but evidently she wanted him to believe I hadn't heard much about him. Her covering surprised me. She pointed near my shoulder. "The top doesn't always work." She'd taken out the tiny braids and dyed her hair lavender, only it sort of looked gray in spots. She wore a string around her neck, just a plain red string, and another dirty macraméd one that looked like it must have been white at some point. She had silver lipstick on, and, for some reason, she looked great.

"Okay," I shouted. What was I supposed to say to Joaquim being gay or to his broken car top?

"Just so you didn't go making goo-goo eyes at him," Celeste called out to me, showing me teeth, pretty and white next to her silver lips.

I lifted my hands and shoulders. I saw Joaquim grinning in the rearview. He looked beautiful, like a model. In fact, he and Celeste made a gorgeous couple, even though they would never be one. Joaquim reached into a center compartment and dug around, not really watching the heavy traffic. "Hey, Celie, find the one-hitter."

"Celie?" I asked.

Celeste shrugged. "It's fine by me."

Why hadn't I thought of that? "I like it."

"Yeah. It fits out here." She pulled out a mini brass pipe.

"Guests first, dear," Joaquim said, and twinkled his fingers at me in the rearview. I wondered what the rest of the suitemates were like.

"Here," Celeste said, pushing the round end of the pipe into a film canister. "It's so gooooood."

"Yeah?" Jesus, I thought, I'd gone all but mute. San Francisco surrounded us on I-80 along with the tangy, fresh smell of the sea. The bay twinkled. Celeste handed me the pipe and a lighter. "Here?" I asked.

"Duck down," she said. "It's windy."

"Right." I should have added, "Duh." What was wrong with me? I popped back up after the hit and passed to Celeste. "Some left," I eked.

She laughed. "No! Where'd your lungs go?" She stuck the pipe in her mouth and finished my hit for me. Repacking, she turned to Joaquim. "When Lisa—when we were less practiced, Lisa swallowed a whole chunk of hash. She was stoned for fuckin' days."

"I was not!"

"We *both* were." She ducked down beneath the dash, popped back up after smoking. She exhaled into the wind and raised her arms up as we crossed the bridge. "Lisa's here!"

The pot was good. I mellowed, patting my suitcase on the seat beside me, and watched other drivers as we started to slow down in traffic. A group of manual laborers sat in the back of a pickup. They whistled. "I love you too, sweeties!" Joaquim called out.

"No! Da ladies!"

I blew them kisses.

"Lis likes to encourage people," Celeste told Joaquim.

"So do I!" Joaquim blew kisses till the guys started swearing and screeched over to a lane farther away.

"Joaquim grew up in San Francisco. So there wasn't ever any real coming *out* of the closet. His mother says she knew from the time she can remember. Oh! Lis! I brought this for you. I have to show you it. I swear, I don't know what's wrong with him."

"Joaquim?"

Celeste opened the cinched top of her patchwork bag. "No, idiot, my dad. Wait. You have to read this." She handed me a letter she'd clearly read more than once. "Read it."

I recognized Mr. Diamond's handwriting from kitchen notes, from to-do lists on Saturdays. I remember much of the letter still. Whole sections, actually. It was an elegy, a dirge, a requiem. It was horrible. While Mr. Diamond didn't say Celeste was actually dead to him, the letter relayed in no uncertain terms that he was saying good-bye, that her disappearance was exactly that, a disappearance. That she'd clearly not cared to contact him the last several months except to inform him (and his dear wife) of her intentions to remain as far away as possible. That she'd not inquired after his well-being. That she had abandoned her own flesh and blood. She'd become lost to him as a daughter, lost, dropped over a cliff, swept to a foreign land.

"Some pretty good purple prose in there, huh?" Joaquim asked me.

I didn't answer. Obviously Celeste had shown the letter to Joaquim. I wondered for a second about the sanctity of such things, letters, special, private things. Celeste must be devastated, I thought. She wouldn't do that otherwise, share her father's letters with college suitemates.

"Can you believe it?" Celeste laid a tan arm over the white seat back. "I mean, what happened to him?"

What had happened to *her*? Granted, Mr. Diamond hadn't been exactly warm the last months of summer, but what had inspired him to write such a letter? Celeste and I had talked nearly every day. She never mentioned anything like this. What the hell had Celeste done to her parents to have them more or less disown her like that? He sounded devastated. And I felt crushed. Like he did. Where was the mention of *me* in the letter? Had he dismissed me too? Was I just Celeste's keeper? I didn't understand. I'd become like a daughter to him, to both parents, hadn't I? "Wow," I finally got out.

"I know. Totally. It's pretty deep."

Deep like a pond? Or like, "Man, heavy." When would she start saying *groovy*? The pot was good, but I felt ill at ease. "Yeah." I handed the letter back to Celeste, who laughed and waved it in circles over her head as if she'd let it loose any second and have it fly away. Maybe into the back of the truck with the guys that Joaquim liked.

"So we got a tree!" Celeste said.

"What?" How could she really do that to them? Didn't she remember the infamous visit to my mother? Surely Celeste couldn't have forgotten how good she had it.

"We all bought a Christmas tree. Well, it's in burlap with a root-ball. After we use it for Christmas we're donating it."

Where would you donate a rooted Christmas tree? "Where?" Back to the tree farm?

"Oh, I don't know. Maybe the projects in Oakland, or wherever. We haven't really thought it through yet."

We stopped completely now, in line for tolls.

Why hadn't I thought to write Mona and Sol? I might have been able to do something, to stop this from happening. "You'd plant a Christmas tree somewhere without permission?"

"Not without permission. I don't know. You know. Give it to a good cause."

Even as Celeste said it, I had visions of inner-city kids pulling the tree out of the ground and tromping on it, shouting that Santa never gives nobody nothing. "Maybe in a park or something," I suggested. Mr. Diamond would be a perfect Santa Claus.

What had Celeste done?

"Yeah. We could have a planting ceremony! So anyway, we're having people over tonight for a tree-decorating party. The suites— I told you, right?—are some of the only places left open. With all the out-of-town students and stuff. God, not stuff. They're people. How rude of me!"

I couldn't put my finger on it. Something had gotten away from me, sort of, but was still right there. Like bobbing for apples. Like going after the bamboo shoot in chow mein with chopsticks. I nodded to myself and watched a station wagon full of girls in red and yellow sports uniforms inch past on the right. One of the girls, maybe twelve, looked at me, squinted her eyes, stuck out her tongue, and then brought her thumb and index finger pinched together to her lips, taking a big imaginary hit. They grew up early out here. Well, screw her. I looked forward. I needed to try to get more out of Celeste. "Is your mom okay?" I asked Celeste.

"I guess. She's called since the letter from Dad. She thinks it'll blow over with time."

It hadn't sounded like that to me. "You think?"

Celeste shrugged as if she didn't really care. She had to be aching. "We've been cooking all day for the party. And we have plain popcorn and cranberries. For the tree. And an area set up in Tram's room to make ornaments."

"Really? What kind?"

"They'll be horrendous," Joaquim said. "Construction paper atrocities."

"They'll be *fun*, asshole. That's the point of a party. To have fun."

I realized that Celeste was actually throwing her first real party. She socked Joaquim in the arm and turned back around to me. Something twitched in my belly. A snake tail, a frog leg, something green.

"You'll help when we get there, right? We said nine o'clock on the invitations. I hope people know that means to eat beforehand. We just made, like, finger foods."

"Of course," I told her, meaning I'd help her. I didn't know if people in California expected to be fed dinner at nine o'clock or not. "Is it dress-up?"

"Oh, some of us special people will be—have to be. Joaquim is dressing up, aren't you?"

We rolled up to the tollbooth. Joaquim tossed coins into the toll and whipped an imaginary scarf around his neck. "Would *you* like a costume?" He pointed at me over his shoulder. His fingernail was painted with clear polish.

"Sure," I said, entirely unsure. "Are you?" I asked Celeste.

"Of course. All hosts and hostesses have to dress for the occasion."

"Everybody in the suite stayed?"

"We've found solidarity in our orphanhood," Joaquim said, seeming pleased with the notion.

"We borrowed a bed for you from the suite across the hall before they left. Just for you." Celeste smiled one of the smiles I knew, the beneficent one. The caregiver smile.

"Thanks." I looked back across the bay at the glittery silhouette of San Francisco, the one needle-looking building distinct against the rest. "What's that one? The sharp one?"

"The Pyramid," Celeste and Joaquim said at the same time. "Jinx!" They poked each other and set off on a fit of giggles. The green thing inside me kicked like a fetus.

We exited at University Avenue. The street was bleak, heavily trafficked, and lined with cheap-looking hotels. I wasn't much impressed. At least the Madison campus was pretty. Celeste read my mind. "It gets better," she said. "Shit! We have to buy ice. Joaquim, stop at the gas station. We need ice for the party. We need ice!"

"I heard you the first time. Ice. Yes, yes, ice." He sped up and swerved from the left lane all the way into a Standard station on the right side of the road. The tires actually made that screeching movie noise.

Celeste raised herself up before we'd even stopped and vaulted over the car door. "Be right back," she said, walking toward the grimy station's dim glow.

"So you live near here?" I asked Joaquim.

"I know what you're thinking." He laughed. "You'll see. It gets better in no time."

"No. I didn't mean that—"

"I know what you meant. Your Celie is safe in Berkeley. Wait two more minutes and you'll see."

I watched Celeste hand money over to the cashier, then step out and pull six bags of ice from the outdoor freezer, clopping them on the concrete. I vaulted the car door myself, really just because I wanted to see if I could do it and it looked fun, then went to help carry. I picked up four bags.

"Hey, Colt," she said, and smiled. "Still got some muscle, huh?"

"Are you kidding? It's all the cheese." My dairy reference to the state of Wisconsin definitely wasn't original, but Celeste was nice. I watched her eyes skim over my hair, a messy, time-consuming hairdo. I'd dyed it black the night before.

"You look so new," she said. "Madison must be a great place to go to school." We tromped back to the car. "Pop the trunk, baby," Celeste called to Joaquim.

"Top no worky, trunk no worky," he said.

"I forgot."

Joaquim pulled out into traffic the same way he had left it for the gas station. I fishtailed across the backseat. "Yee-ha!" he called.

Celeste swiveled around, grinning ear to ear. I recognized this smile too, the Fun! smile. The one she couldn't help.

The neighborhood did get better, all within about a block. We crossed a heavily populated street with venders and pedestrians and kites and balloons and interesting food smells and then continued up onto a winding road, eventually pulling off onto the drive of what was clearly a mansion. Set back from the road and nestled into the hillside, the four?- five?-story house sat there with the assuredness of a happy, wealthy grandmother. Joaquim pulled around to the side and into a decent-size square parking lot carefully disguised with large stone planters and a veritable copse of trees at its center. The grounds were meticulously groomed, some fragrant garden scent distinct as we got out of the car. White and porched and balconied and shuttered and gorgeous, the house stunned me. "You live here?"

"We live here," Celeste said with the tiniest drop of pride in her voice. I guess, after all, she had earned it. She lived here for free, all expenses paid.

"May I get your bag?" Joaquim asked, reaching into the backseat.

"I can get it."

"You two grab the ice."

An almost warm breeze. It couldn't have been less than fifty degrees out. It wasn't Christmas weather, but it wasn't Madison weather either. Birds swooped in the evening light. Lush, unusual vegetation grew in well-kept clusters in the part of the large side yard I could see. I could live here, I thought. I'd have no problem living here. "Can you stay here after freshman year?" I asked.

"Alas, no," Joaquim said. "But we can continue our grants if we succeed this year. Then we tippy-toe down the road."

"The sophomore house is half a block down."

I hadn't seen distinct blocks, but I recognized the privilege they'd earned.

"Come in, come in!" Joaquim unlocked the side door and held it open for us ice girls. "Welcome to our humble abode."

Nothing about the interior bespoke "dorm." Not a thing. Celeste and Joaquim and their suitemates and the other gifted freshmen at U Cal Berkeley lived in fucking splendor. I understood why the suitemates had purchased a live tree. And I understood why Joaquim would call construction-paper ornaments horrendous. "I'll show you the common space downstairs later," Celeste said. "Let's go up and drop off all this." We wound our way up a broad hardwood staircase to the third floor. There, a wide hallway spanned the entire length of the mansion. Only two doors opened off the hallway, one left, the other right. Staircases at either end continued upward.

Joaquim unlocked the left-side door and smiled. He had a great smile. You wouldn't have known he was gay at all till he started talking.

"Do you have any straight brothers?" I asked.

His smile grew. "If I had a nickel," he said, and carried my suitcase down another stupendous, long hallway toward a well-lit room. What? I didn't pursue it. Original prints on the walls. Hardwood floors. Pretty sure an authentic Oriental runner. Chrome sconces. Glossy taupe paint. Art-gallery lighting. With each step my decision solidified. Jesus, a Warhol? The hallway poured itself into an incredible space. The suite was hard to describe in its attitude, its sense of history, its space, its vibe. Trust me when I say you wouldn't want more as a freshman at college ever. The furniture, Celeste said, had come with the place. I wondered how freshmen at college could find the respect required to care for such things, but then Celeste explained that there was a biweekly "cleaning service"—she made the quoting sign with two fingers on each hand—to come and take care of what they could not. I guessed the suitemates only suffered internally if they didn't respect the gift of adult responsibility the suite afforded. *That* was it. . . . Evidently Berkeley chose its grant recipients well. For the past two decades, the donating millionaire's desires had been honored by teenagers. Clearly, they were light-years beyond their peers in terms of respecting adult stuff. You'd guess it anyway, looking at the place. I wondered what a party would do to the grand room. Four, five, six couches. More chairs and lamps and small tables than I could count.

"Gimme those," Joaquim said, taking all six ice bags. He had great shoulders. I traded for my suitcase. Celeste led the way to her bedroom.

"We rearranged for you a little," she said before opening the door. I'd known that Celeste had her own room, too. Like me. But she'd never described it on the phone. So I had done the same thing anybody would, I guess, imagining her single-person room to be much like my own dorm room, only California-ized a little. A palm tree outside her window, maybe, some sunnier paint on the walls. I knew though, before we even went in, how wrong I'd been. She flicked on the overhead. Yup. French doors to a balcony. Beautiful antique furniture. A walk-in closet. Serious framed art hanging from, wow, real picture molding. Two double beds. We could have fit in one double. Why had they brought in another? "In case we get lucky," Celeste said, smiling again.

At least I could tell she was happy to see me. She even hopped around a little, being goofy, then stopped and blushed, as if embarrassed by her own actions. Holy shit, where was the Celeste I knew? Since when did she let herself be embarrassed by anybody else, much less herself? I wanted to give her a hug. I wanted to shake her back into her body.

Instead I said, "You're totally blushing." I'd never used the word *totally* before and decided to try it out. It felt dumb coming out of my mouth. I'd have to work on it.

"Shut up. Put down your suitcase." She turned away and glanced at herself in a gilded mirror over the room's double dresser. "I *am*," she said. "Blushing, I mean. How weird."

What did we do now? Should we squeal? "Remember dancing at Lynne P.'s New Year's Eve party?" I asked.

"And the fire?! That's when you and Josh started going together, right? God, doesn't that feel like a lifetime ago?"

It felt like yesterday to me. I checked out the room. A neat stack of books sat on a fancy desk that better resembled a dining room table. I walked over to read the spines. *Finnegan's Wake*, *The Great Gatsby*, somebody I didn't know, an art crit book, a Carver collection, not a textbook in sight. "Like a fucking lifetime ago," I said.

She looked at me looking at her books. "They're my—I don't know what you'd call them—standbys maybe? The ones I know, and the ones I'm still trying."

"Where're your schoolbooks?"

"I sold them back. Take a load off, Lis. God! You're here on vacation! Or maybe actually you could come help me? There's so much to do! We're trying to create safe areas, you know? Like where it's safe to eat and not so safe, like on the couches? I hope people have fun. Oh—we put the tree in the dining room. I'll show you." I was regretting the fact that I'd brought only my tiny reserve of speed.

Like trying to catch a feral cat.

Like swinging at a piñata at a birthday party.

Like the fucking bamboo shoot, stuck to the bottom of the plate.

THE RED HOT CHILI PEPPERS

LOS ANGELES, SEPTEMBER '84

You want to fuck the singer, but you would suck on any of them. A rim job, a piss shower, wouldn't matter. The band plays in nothing but tube socks hung over their cocks and sacks. They can make the socks swing like giant tittie tassels. You've never seen anything so sexy.

You don't have a way backstage, though. Not yet, and your night's mix, half a bottle of crap rum, three bad burner lines, a black beauty, and four beers, is kicking in. Your skin tingles. Your scalp crawls. The hair on your arms stands up. You want a finger in you, in your mouth, your cunt, your ass. Anyone, any finger, soon, will do.

Light a Bidi cigarette, your little green bomb of nicotine, and pull the smoke low into your lungs. Go for the head rush. Now smash your mouth on the boy with the mohawk and pretty lips standing by the speaker, nodding his head with the fast bass. Bite the pretty lips because you can't help yourself. Taste iron. Taste salty blood.

Take the punch Mohawk gives you hard in the back of your skull. Hang on to his lip like a pit bull. Thrash and growl. Scratch at his neck. Take three more punches, knuckles hard as fucking rocks making the music roar, before you let go.

See him look at you.

The room swirls, halts, changes direction. You feel hot blood, yours, his, roll down the gentle curve of your chin.

Draw a big circle with your tongue around your lips and fling your middle fingers in his face. Waggle your head. Show him how crazy you are.

Make him grab you and slam your body against his. Make him yell crude nothings into your ear. Cram his hand down the waist of your camouflage pants. Make him pick your little body up off the floor with the shove of his fingers. Growl again in the dark. Bite his ear. Wrap your legs around Mohawk's slim hips and ride.

Proudly lift your smeared face to the singer. Smile.

Show your teeth.

FOURTEEN

*T*HE TREE stood at least twelve feet tall. "We had to use a wheelbarrow to get it in," Celeste said. "Who knew dirt was so heavy."

I looked at it. "*You* didn't do the lights, huh?" The cords and connections showed all over the place in the branches, big loops of droopy lights carelessly arranged.

"Of course not." She rolled her eyes. "Honey did."

There were signs of other people in the suite, voices audible from other rooms, but I hadn't met anybody else yet, and then, in one of those bad pot moments, all the suitemates tumbled into the dining room at the same time.

"Hey, everybody!" Celeste called out. "This is Lisa, Lisa, everybody." Celeste swept her hand around. Evidently Berkeley admissions could not only detect responsibility and intellect from afar, they could detect beauty, too. I wanted to shrink. I would not. Lots of heys and hand raises came my way. Celeste moved around the semicircle. "Lisa, Tram. Tram, Lisa. Tram is from Vietnam. Her mother is Vietnamese and her father's Anglo." Tram smiled. "And Honey. What can I say about Honey?" Everyone except me smiled and nodded. "Honey is from all over. She grew up in free-living communities—um, communes." Honey made a peace sign and clasped her hands behind her back, rocking on her heels. "Joaquim, you met." He blew me a kiss.

Damn. The suitemates, a perfectly diverse ensemble, all looked like they had just wrapped filming for the day. "Hey," I said back to them all.

"And Noah. He's our Black Power man." Of course, gotta have one of those to round out the cast. He made a fist while his face stayed serious. "He's from—"

"The neighbor*hood*," he said. Was he for real? But then he smiled, and everybody else laughed. Oh. Okay. He leaned toward me and used his fist to tap my shoulder. "Hey."

"And Nanci with an I. She's from the Bay Area, too."

"Just tell her," Nanci said, sounding as though she were from New York.

Some of them laughed again. "Nanci's Jew—"

"She's our resident JAP," Joaquim said. "She grew up in *Sausalito*." I had no idea where that was.

You could almost see the guy scheming with the photos of the prospective grant recipients, all lined up: "Yellow goes with brown, professed homosexual goes with Kansas City girl. . . ."

Celeste walked to me and put her arm around my shoulder, squeezing. "It's good, huh? Two kikes, a fag, a nigger, a Charlie, and a fuckin' hippie."

What had she just said?

"It's okay," Tram said without a trace of an accent. "It's our little saying."

And then they all said it again together: "Two kikes, a fag, a nigger, a Charlie, and a fuckin' hippie."

I widened my eyes. I tried to smile. "Do you like our tree?" Honey asked. Her long hair—longer even than Celeste's or mine had ever been—grew as blond as nice Carl's did back in Madison. Blonde-blond. Yellow-white. She was honey incarnate. What was *I* incarnate? We all knew what Celeste was. I'd seen the slide in my art history class of the sculpture in the Louvre. But what about me?

Whatever I was, I'd say it right back. As I labeled I pointed at the same time: "Two kikes, a fag, a nigger, a Charlie, and a fuckin' hippie." They laughed.

"So what're you?" black Noah asked.

"What am I?"

"Yeah, you!" he said with what I guessed was mock seriousness, with a brooding Gary Coleman from *Diff'rent Strokes* sort of fake anger. Who were these people? Where was the flirty Hank? The dumb Ess?

I knew through and through what I was. But I would tell him something else. "I guess I'm the WASP," I said, trying to wear my label proudly, hoping beyond hope I might magically transform into some other acronym, another minority, another somebody.

"Jesus, another one?" Nanci groaned. "I'm kidding, I'm kidding!" She looked like a young Joan Collins but prettier. (I know what you're thinking. A younger Joan Collins in *1982*.) "Oh, what in the name of your savior is burning? Can't you *smell* that?!"

"The quiche!" Honey chirped, and sprang away.

"Somebody," Celeste said in her new accent, "help me with the eating stations, please?"

"I will," I said.

"But somebody else," she said. "I mean somebody else *too*! God, Lis. Sorry! I didn't mean that to sound like I didn't want your help."

I knew that.

"Okay." Joaquim clapped his hands. "Let me supervise. I'm in charge." He pointed and delegated and ordered around. No one left without telling me they were happy to meet me.

I stuck by Celeste in the dining room as she arranged stacks of small white china plates, pulling them from a flip-top wooden crate. "Rental," she said by way of explanation.

How much did that cost? How much money did the suitemates have? "How many people are coming?" I asked, moving to the tree to fix the lights.

"Cheese board here. Spinach puffs . . . Well, if everybody we invited comes—I don't even know how many people we invited."

"You don't?"

"A lot."

"Like how many?"

"Maybe a hundred? A hundred and fifty? I'm not sure. It's an invitation-by-mouth party."

Didn't she mean *word of mouth*, or *invitation*? Visions of Madison snowshoed through my head with my crowd. A place like this, a party at a place like this one? They'd be doomed. The Warhol wrecked. The furniture covered with cigarette burns. "But this *place*."

"We invited good people. A lot are sticking around just for the party and then leaving town tomorrow!"

Ah. The good people. The California type. Maybe it'd be fine. I didn't know what to say. "What kind of ornaments are we making?"

"Do you really want to know?" Celeste grinned.

"Tell me."

"It's an invitation-by-mouth party, Lis."

I had no idea what she was talking about. "Isn't it *word* of—"

"We're making *windowpane* ornaments."

"What?"

"You know about windowpane at Madison?"

"What?"

She frowned, scratching at a plate with her thumbnail. "You know." She looked at me. "You really don't know what I mean?"

"No."

"Acid, Lis. Windowpane is a kind of acid."

As in LSD? "You mean tripping acid, acid?"

"Bingo."

A hundred and fifty people were going to take acid in their suite? "All those people?"

"Oh, no! But it always brings good people. People know it's a treat, a good party, somebody went to some effort. You know, like buying kegs in high school or whatever. It makes a good party."

"Oh."

"It's see-through and sometimes square. Hence the name."

Hence? "How many people are going to, um, make ornaments?"

Celeste laughed and laughed, holding her stomach. "I *love* you, Lis!"

"People are really going to make them?"

"Yes! I just said that. Aw." She walked toward me. "I'm sorry." She gave me a big squeeze of a hug. "They're making ornaments if they want to, and they're dropping acid if they want to. Only if they want to."

"Do you want to?"

"Oh, Lis, it's so much fun! This stuff is good, not too strong. I mean, I've only dropped a few times, but you'll *love* it."

I wanted to ask her if she promised, but I knew better. Instead I asked, "Where is it?"

"Where's the acid?"

"Yeah." Where did somebody keep a big stash of drugs?

"It's in Tram's safe."

"In her safe?"

"Her mother has this thing about money and protection and all that. It's not like you couldn't get the safe out of her room with a dolly, so I guess if somebody really wanted to take the whole thing, he or she could."

He or she? What had Berkeley done to her? "I'm kinda . . . I, ah, just didn't understand."

"Aw, Lis! I think you have jetlag. We should have some drinks."

I rewrapped a branch with lights. How could we do the upper half without a ladder? "Is there something to reach the top?" A drink would be good.

"Beer or a martini? We have real glasses!"

I didn't understand her perpetual enthusiasm. I recognized her as Celeste, but somehow she'd become this "Celie" too. What time was it? How long would the night be? The blue spruce smelled wonderful, but its needles were sharp, and the instant I thought about how sharp the needles were with my stoned brain, I stuck myself. I put my finger in my mouth, tasting sap, remaining mute.

"Let's have martinis, okay? It'll make the decorating go all the better."

"I have speed," I ventured.

"Cool, daddy-o. Me, too."

Plainly, hers would be better than mine. "Martinis and speed," I said. "Sounds good to me."

I'd remember to talk to her about the letter later.

None of the suitemates had really gotten it together by the invite time, so at a certain point they just cleaned up the kitchen and started dressing. There were two dishwashers, something I'd never seen before. Who had enough dishes to fill two dishwashers?

I hadn't brought anything dressy. I figured Celeste would cover my ass with some new California skirt or pair of leather pants. We'd taken a pink-and-black-speckled capsule each, along with two martinis, Tanquerays, with splashes of tonic. We called them T-and-Tinis. We were proud of ourselves.

"This?" Celeste held up a supershort black skirt with zippers running down both sides.

"Where'd you get that?"

"A shop in San Fran. We have to go."

"Black's my color." I could hardly keep from chewing off the inside of my cheek.

"It's yours." She tossed it my way.

I'd brought a little pink T-shirt, a laundry accident of Carl's. He'd been mad for weeks, but Eraserhead fit me perfectly now. A skirt, a T, a pair of black fishnets, and some four-inch pumps. I'd stand a whopping 5'6". I smiled. I liked my outfit laid out there on my very only own double bed. I chomped on the inside of my lip and downed the rest of my martini. "Is there more?" I asked just as I saw Celeste slug hers back. We weren't really all that different yet.

"Of course!"

"What are you wearing?"

"Oh, look!" She walked into her closet and said, "Malibu." She came back out with a salmon-colored gown straight out of the sixties. "Look."

It did not shout Christmas. It did not say Santa Claus. And it didn't even come close to spelling Hanukkah. It simply purred California sex-kitten goddess. And it wasn't even on her yet. Well, I could rip the T-shirt. "That totally looks like Malibu," I agreed.

"Marabou," she said. "The feathers." The dress sprouted a wreath of feathers around its off-the-shoulder neckline.

"Oh."

I watched her eyes run over my black hair. "Hey, Lis. Why don't you try it on? I bet it'll fit you better." She walked the dress to me as if she were a saleslady.

What would we do, trade? "No," I protested because I thought I should.

"You know you want to. I can hardly breathe in it. Look, it's velvet."

We had different definitions of dressing up. I gnawed on the side of my tongue. "Okay, let me try it." I would need sixties plat-form heels to go with the dress, or I'd drag the thing on the ground. I held my arms out as if accepting a baby or a crystal vase. "You want to try—here," I told her. I wanted to offer her some-thing in return. "Try on my shoes."

As I stepped out of my clothes, I looked at her little stack of books on her desk. I could almost swear I saw dust on the small pile, but then I decided I was imagining things. "Zip?" I turned my back to her.

She pulled. "It fits! Turn around, turn around."

I looked at Celeste. Celie. "Yeah?"

"Yeah."

Did I want to wear the thing? It went with martinis and tuxes. I wasn't sure it went with huaraches and embroidered shirts. "What kind of people are coming?"

"All kinds."

Ah. All kinds. Like my dad and her mom and Hank and dead Brooklyn and my anise-burping lab TA for French. I thought about college. I thought about the world. I thought about all sorts of things. You know, everything I might have thought about at that point. The speed rapped its knuckles on the inside of my skull: "Hell-oooooo. Anybody home?" Echo, echo, echo.

I looked at Celeste as she sauntered around her room in my heels, her hands on her slender hips, her long lavender-gray hair swinging. I touched my own. Celeste turned and caught me in the gesture.

"It's really great," she said, sounding as if she meant it. "It's really, um, what do I want to say? Gutsy! And progressive."

I had progressive hair.

"*Au courant*," she said. "I've gotta get mine cut. Long hair is so passé." Somehow she didn't look passé. "So, you'll wear it, right?"

I turned in front of her mirror. I knew that no matter which I wore, her dress or my own outfit, I'd want to wear what she wore. Win-win, lose-lose. Guess who was which. "I don't know."

"You don't have to wear it, Lis. I just thought you might like to."

"You picked it out for you." I decided I'd rather show off my legs. Be able to move around a little in case people danced. "Unzip me?"

"Yeah," she said. "It is a little much, isn't it?"

"You're a hostess. You're all supposed to be getting dressed up, right?"

"God!" I saw her jaw working. "You've *got* to see Joaquim's out-fit. He looks just like Frank Sinatra. He has this pale, um, moss-colored sharkskin suit? He's gorgeous in it! The suit's gorgeous. He's gorgeous! Too bad he's gay."

"Totally," I agreed, taking off Celeste's dress and sitting on my bed. Could he get excited with a girl, I wondered, or would nothing at all happen? I pulled on the black fishnets.

"Sexy!" Celeste whistled. "We are going to have so much fun! Oh, here." She stepped out of my shoes. And into her dress. "Zip?" I zipped her in and looked. I knew I'd choose the wrong one.

Celeste's speed kicked my speed's butt. By the time guests started arriving, I'd had four T-and-Tinis and had barely stopped chewing on my own mouth. I felt sober and out of place. I tried hard not to cling, though, acting as much like an adult, as much like a friendly, socially comfortable visitor, as I could. The party itself, as more and more people came, felt like a child born of an unlikely mar-riage: East Coast socialite and Moroccan world traveler; blues musician and marathon runner; drug addict and Unitarian minis-ter. A few guests came dressed like me; a few like Celeste and Joaquim; and quite a few more like Honey, in her beaded Grate-ful Hemp creation. Much like the suitemates themselves, the guests were diverse to a fault. In 1982, though, of course, diversity wasn't yet something to celebrate much (but then Berkeley's always been ahead of the game, hasn't it?). I hadn't been in California long enough, and couldn't help but feeling I was at some junior UN meeting, some mock global convention, something edging in toward too smart and a tad too dorky. I talked to Black Power Noah, the deejay for the party. He'd made nearly three dozen mix tapes over the last week, he explained, organized by music theme and cross-referenced by tempo. He could fake cool, I decided, but under the surface he was still a bright nerd like all the rest of us. I looked around the room for a speed-clear second, with crystalline insight, and saw a space teeming with insecure seventh-graders, all the ones who wore braces or glasses or both, the ones who stooped to hide nonexistent breasts, the ones who laughed too loudly to overcompensate for a lack of friends.

I asked Noah if he had anything by The Pretenders. I liked Chrissie Hynde's look. He consulted his clipboard. He had four decks feeding into the system and the cue number of each song on each tape written in a grid slot on his clipboard. "Scheduled for the eleven-o'clock set," he said gruffly, but I understood already. I'd seen him in junior high, the kid whose pants were too short and who knew all the tricks of his expensive new Texas Instruments calculator before the rest of his class. "This is the request sheet," he said, tapping the top sheet with a mocha-colored finger, "but I'm not playing requests until midnight. So, oddly, if you don't place a request, you'll hear your selection sooner."

I smiled. "Thanks. Guess I'll abstain from requesting a song then."

Celeste carried a foot-long cigarette holder, its end jammed with an enormous unlit joint. She'd quickly become the epicenter of the party in her Malibu Marabou Fabulous Frock. She'd had me wrap her long lavender tresses into a towering bun with a few enticing tendrils loose at temple and nape. Her other hand held a perpetual martini. Two occupied hands meant that she had to call people darling and kiss cheeks. She had a great act. I would have done the same thing.

For the most part, guests seemed to be behaving themselves. Every now and again people in groups of two or three would emerge from Tram's bedroom carrying construction paper snowflakes in teal and aqua and white to hang on the white-lighted blue spruce. Not so tacky at all, I thought. Were only acid takers making ornaments? I hadn't decided yet if I was going to or not. I thought I might try, but Celeste would have to be accessible. I wasn't sure I'd like to wander around tripping by myself.

I plucked a cherry tomato off a branch of a wrought-iron table-top sculpture filled only with things red: strawberries, cranberries, cherry tomatoes, radishes. The effect was pretty if not particularly gastronomically coherent. "Nice gams," somebody said behind my back as I went after a radish.

I turned around. Ooh. Hello. "Yeah?" I bit, crunching my radish to early James Brown. I hadn't quite deciphered the logic behind Noah's arrangement.

"Best in the place," the stranger said, moving his gaze over the front of my legs on up to my face. He wore a fifties pinstripe suit, two-tone shoes, and a hat.

"Nice lid yourself," I said, nodding at his fedora.

"Good kicks, too." He moved his martini toward my spike heels.

"They double as weapons when needed."

"I can see that."

"You could use a tommy gun."

"Hey, I'm no gangster."

I smiled, addressing him with my remaining radish half. "That's right. You just sing for them, right?" I felt proud of my quick thinking, of my knowledge of period slang—thanks to Mr. Diamond's fascination with the era.

"Not a note."

"Aw. That's too bad."

"You wouldn't say that if you heard me sing."

"I wouldn't?"

"Trust me."

What color were his eyes? He had a nicely shaped face, a strong jawline. I wanted to get in under the hat and get a better look. "Give me one good reason, tommy gun."

"I talk to my mother every Sunday."

"Ah, love of family. Or should I say *famiglia*?"

He laughed then. "What's your name?"

"Lisa."

"I haven't seen you around before, Lisa."

I was aware of his immediate use of my name, of how doing that was supposed to help you remember. He'd probably used three dozen girls' names in the last two hours. "I'm visiting Celeste for the holidays."

"You're not going home?"

That couldn't be explained over a half radish and nearly empty martini glasses. "What's your name?"

"Lawrence."

Weird. My father's name on a different person. Huh. On this guy, it had some soul to it. Interesting. "So, Lawrence," I tried out. "Looks like we could both use refills."

"I'll second that. Please." He held out his hand for me to walk first. "The view is ever so lovely."

Now, as I'm sure you've figured out, I've always been a bit of a sucker for a smooth talker, for a guy who pays me compliments. But I know some women who immediately distrust a man who throws out lines like he's feeding chickens in a yard. An alarm goes off in their heads. Not that they're not attracted to him, but it's as if they can see the future, see his forgetting to call, his fibs, his coming in later and later. They hear in his smooth talk the fact that he can't help himself. They hear he'll fuck up.

I could rationalize. Or I could desist. But I don't even try. I know exactly who the Lawrences are, and I take them into me, into my life, knowing full well exactly where we'll end up. I relish the potential for destruction. The plot arcs of my time with these men are familiar and thrilling. Huge soaring faces, rocky cliffs, jutting ecstasy, utter destruction on the other side. Give me Lawrences any day. Bring them to me in truckloads. Make me feel.

We walked into the large kitchen, people crowded around both ends of the center island mixing cocktails. Nanci with an I, the suitemate whom I could most easily imagine in junior high school with Celeste and me, had just mixed a full martini shaker. "Hey, Lawrence!" she exclaimed. "Don't you look dapper! You and Celeste, you know, Sinatra and Mia Farrow. Before the haircut, of course."

Exactly like Lynne P., I thought, as we held out our classic glasses. I liked my Eraserhead T. I did. It fit well, and only the brave came up to talk to me. Nothing wrong with that. Anybody could dress like Nanci with an I any old day in an expensive red shantung chemise. She had beautiful collarbones, golden skin, and an ugly voice. I wondered if Lawrence happened to be one of the three guys Celeste had already slept with that semester, or if Nanci with an I had simply meant that both Lawrence and Celeste were similarly turned out. I should have been paying better attention to Celeste when she named them over the phone.

I was amazed at how far away Madison felt, thinking momentarily about Carl at his apartment off campus, going home to his lanky Scandinavian family for latkes and hard spice cake. I pictured my clothes hanging in the dorm room closet, my piles of papers and textbooks stacked hastily on top of my desk. How far away.

"Cheers," Lawrence said. He clinked his glass on mine. "Lisa." He said it as though he'd just remembered.

"Cheers," I said.

"Cheers!" Nanci with an I said.

I looked around the kitchen and noted how the party had remained contained. Behaved. I thought about Hank's and the basic respect everyone had always shown his place. Interesting, I thought, still feeling far too sober. Utterly different from high school. And different from what you would expect. Disentangling ourselves from the line, Lawrence and I left Nanci with an I and walked toward the living room.

"Mmm-mmm," Lawrence said behind me as I did my best model catwalk-sashay. I smiled, walking, and played with one of the zippers on the side of the skirt. The speed was mellowing a little, finally. Maybe California at Christmastime could be all right. Snow, schmo.

Back in the big gorgeous living room, people sat and stood and conversed. Like adults. I supposed I'd have to try to do the same thing. I moved to a just-freed ottoman pushed up against a wall. "Share?" I offered, sitting down delicately, aware of how far Celeste's skirt was riding up my thighs.

Lawrence sat and knocked the bridge of my nose with the brim of his hat. "Apologies," he said, taking it off with his free hand. I could see his scalp through his almost completely shaved light brown hair. His eyebrows were nice, dark but not too thick, and his eyes were . . . well, what? Hazel. Pretty. Thick lashes. His eyes looked smart and then something else more. Familiar. "You're from Kansas City, too?" he asked, the gears shifting.

"More or less."

"What does that mean?"

"My family moved there right before I hit junior high."

"Ah. Where were you actually born?"

"In Indiana, but then I lived in Chicago before Kansas City."

"You don't look like a Midwest girl."

"Thank you?" I said, attempting irony. I sipped my martini, not nearly as good as our T-and-Tinis had been. Where was Celeste? I hadn't seen her in an hour. Not that Lawrence wasn't interesting. I wondered what time it was and what was keeping my Pretenders. "Where are you from?"

"A little bit of everywhere. I was born in Memphis."

"That's kinda cool." I thought of Elvis right away. "You go to Berkeley?"

"No."

No?

"I'm between schools."

"What do you do?"

"I play music."

"I thought you didn't sing."

"I don't."

"So what do you play?"

"Lead." He reached over to my thigh and began playing with the zipper on the skirt. "I like these."

He wasn't exactly subtle. "Yeah?"

"I like what's under them."

Had he slept with Celeste already? Where was she? She wouldn't have taken acid without me, would she? "Do you know Celeste?"

"Who?"

"*Celeste.*"

"Oh, yeah. Pretty girl."

I couldn't get a read. "What kind of music?"

"You should come see us sometime."

"Who told you about the party?" He was starting to bug me. I wanted to fuck him.

"I've known Tram for years."

"I thought she was Vietnamese."

"On her mom's side."

"So . . ."

"She came here when she was a kid."

Did he belong to Tram, then? I didn't want to step on toes. I should try to be a decent guest. Where was Celeste? I sipped on my martini and looked around the room. Noah had Prince singing through the speakers now, fine by me. "You two go out?"

"Tram? I've known her for years."

He had a knack for evasion. Evasion and smooth talking. "I should find Celeste," I said, watching Lawrence stare at my thigh. Guys who were leg men were always good. Legs were my best feature.

"Have you two made ornaments yet?" he asked, fingering my fishnets, weaving a finger in and out of the large mesh. His touch felt casual, random, as if he were doodling on his own pant leg while a professor lectured away. I looked at him closely. Celeste had told me sometimes you could tell from people's pupils; Lawrence's pupils were significantly dilated.

"No. No ornaments. I can't decide. Have you?"

"Yes. Two of them."

He had double-dropped? I could hardly tell except for his eyes. I didn't know what else I expected, although those lingering images from drug education seminars came to mind, I had to admit. 8 mm reels of re-creations, of girls gone mad, jumping to their deaths from thirty-story balconies, bad actors screaming laughable nonsense at the top of their lungs, pretending to be crazy, man, crraaaazzzzy. "You must have had practice. At making ornaments."

"Since I was fourteen." He appeared proud of the fact.

"Wow." Maybe he wasn't as normal as he looked.

"Celeste," he said, staring straight into my eyes.

"No. I'm Lisa."

"She's there," he said, still staring directly at me. "Peripheral." He pointed toward the center of the room, his eyes remaining fixed.

I looked. "Oh. Thanks."

"You do have the best legs in the room, Lisa."

I took the compliment with a smile and stood. I wanted to do a high kick for Lawrence right then, give him a really good look, but I had to consider the fact that I was miles and miles away from high school. I couldn't just show off anytime I wanted to anymore. "See you later?"

"You bet, Lisa." He sat there on the ottoman, appraising me as if I were a painting. Something two-dimensional. Maybe that's how the acid worked on him.

"Celeste." I broke into her circle.

"Where have *you* been?" she asked. Most of the joint in her long holder had been smoked.

"Sitting over there." I pointed at Lawrence.

"Danger, Will Robinson, danger!"

"Lawrence?"

"He'll have you for dinner," Celeste said.

I grinned. "I'd let him eat me."

"Lis, Lis. I'm serious." Celeste pushed on me with her empty martini glass and directed me back over to Lawrence. "Lawrence."

"Hey, Celeste."

"Lawrence, you leave Lisa alone. Do you hear me?"

He'd put his fedora back on his head. He jutted his chin out at her. "Why's that? She looks plenty tasty to me."

"I mean it, Lawrence. No, no." Why was she scolding him like a naughty pet who'd crapped the carpet? "Lisa's my friend. *Friend.* Do not touch my *friends.*"

He laughed. "You may be underestimating your friend. She keeps up just fine."

Celeste turned to me. "You dropped without me?"

"What?"

"You took the acid already?"

"No."

"What are you talking about, Lawrence?" She jabbed the base of her empty glass on his lapel.

"She keeps up *talking*, Celeste. Just talking." The way he said her name made me realize they'd had some sort of interaction already, a one-night stand, a flirtation that had gotten screwed up, something.

"I mean it," Celeste said again to him. She was fighting back a smile, I thought. Were they just friends? "I do."

"I know you always mean what you say, don't you?" he told her, touching the brim of his hat in a sort of salute.

Celeste shook her head. "Lis, Lawrence is no good."

"Oh, now," he said.

"We must be going," she said, doing her best snoot. "Come along, Lisa." She pushed me toward the kitchen.

"What's wrong with Lawrence?"

"What isn't?"

"Wha-at?"

"He gets around."

"Well . . . it's not as though I'll be here forever. He's . . . he looks good in a suit."

"He looks good out of one, too." The suite was filling up. We bumped our way through people in the hallway.

"Is he one of the one-night stands?"

"No. No, no. But he sleeps with Tram. Sometimes. They don't go out, but they have sex. I guess when they're both without somebody else. He's just . . . he's without values, Lis."

"Why do you say that?"

"He hits on anything with two legs."

He liked my legs, damn it. "Well . . ."

"He walked out of Tram's bedroom one morning after she'd already left for class."

Mincing through the hallway in the opposite direction, a guy wearing socks with those ugly brown sandals said hello to Celeste. She leaned to him and kissed his fuzzy cheek. "Hey," she told him. We kept inching forward. "He walks out of her bedroom naked. I'm no prude, but I don't know him all that well, and everybody else is gone."

"I bet he looks good naked," I said.

"But that's not my point. He pours himself a bowl of cereal and starts eating while I'm at the table reading the newspaper."

"And?"

"I try to ignore him. What else should I do? I figure it's easier to not make a big deal out of it, that he'll finish his Frosted Flakes and go back to Tram's room."

"But he doesn't."

"But he doesn't. He leans back in his chair when he's finished eating and says with a full-blown hard-on, 'Wanna ride?'"

"And he looks good?"

"He looks incredible, Lis, but you're missing the point."

Maybe, maybe not. "But you already know that Tram and Lawrence don't actually go together—aren't an item, right?"

"Yes, she told us the second week here, but—"

"Did you climb on?"

"Lisa! You're as bad as he is!"

I liked the thought. "So?" She seemed to be skipping something about their encounter.

"So nothing. No, I did not '*climb on*'!"

"I would have."

"Lisa!"

"Well?"

"He's bad to the bone. Take my advice. Or leave it with your clothes on the bedroom floor."

"Ha, ha."

We'd made it to the kitchen. "Olives?" somebody asked Celeste. We stepped into the pantry.

"Maybe I like bad bones," I said.

She rolled her eyes and gave me an old familiar face. "You are such a dork."

"I know you are, but what am I?"

"Do not say I didn't warn you."

"Fine. Are we going to take acid?"

"I wanted to see how you felt about it, Lis. It's totally up to you. I didn't wanna, you know, *push drugs on you* or anything."

"Celeste the pusher."

"Shut up."

We brought out the olives and made a shaker of T-and-Tinis. "They're good," I told a curious girl who stared and stared at the shaker.

"Wow," she said. A lot of her hair was woven with the colored threads that Celeste's had been the previous summer.

"Anyway," Celeste said as we walked away, "what about Carl?"

"What about Carl?"

"I thought you had a—"

"Good thing going?"

"Yeah. I should find a light. Feel like a hit?" She wiggled her long holder the way we used to pencils, making it look as though it were made of rubber.

"Sure." I waited for her to bring up Carl again, but she'd apparently forgotten.

"What's the verdict on the ornament making?" she asked instead.

The euphemism had begun to grate on me. Enough already. "It'll be fun?"

"I think it's a lot of fun."

I still trusted her. So I would. "Okay."

"Okay?"

"Yeah. Why not?"

"Woo-hoo! Let's light this up, then head on in there!"

I couldn't stay away from Lawrence. We were, you know, like, in the same place, floating around the room together, and Celeste wouldn't let me out of her sight. Every now and again something would sort of swim. The upholstery on the sofa would undulate or the carpet would vibrate as if made of visible cells, as if it were alive like everything else. I understood how we were all connected to one another, how we were of the same universe, how we were the *same.* I thought about what my speed dealer back in Madison had told me about Buddhism and tried to tell them about my immediate and profound revelations concerning life.

"I can love you," Celeste said to Lawrence as the three of us sat squeezed next to each other on a love seat, me in the happy middle. "I understand. We need to love. Everybody. I can love you, too, Lawrence."

Lawrence had drifted to a slower place. He was less quick, less chatty. Warmer. "Thank you," he said to Celeste, then continued to stare at my fishnets. Apparently, they moved. "See?" He wiggled his hands in front of his face, imitating the motion of something organic in a gentle current. "Liquid," he said.

As he said it he made it true. I was amazed. The motion of his hands slid to my fishnet stockings, and the stockings began to ripple, invisible slow-motion raindrops falling there at my ankle, plip-plopping on my knees. "Cool," I said.

"Cool," Celeste said.

"Liquid," he said again.

"Yeah."

"Love, spreading."

"Fuck love," Lawrence said.

"Fuck," I said, listening to the word that meant nothing, listening to the sound of the hard consonant ending. My desire for sex had disappeared, even as I sat half on top of Lawrence, smelling his unique smell, even after Tram had left her bedroom, the distributing done, and had smiled at me sitting between Celeste and Lawrence and had told me to enjoy myself, had told me that "Pleasure is good."

"I still have love for you," Celeste told Lawrence. "I have love for everyone in the room."

I looked around at all the people. So many colors. So colorful, they vibrated and shimmered like tropical fish. I liked how they looked, but I didn't think I felt anything for them. I wasn't sure I even cared about anybody. Except Celeste. And maybe her parents. I cared about them. I would talk to her about the letter. And then I forgot and came back around right away to there being love in the room.

Celeste was the only one I loved for sure, though. Without reservation. I thought I would tell her that, but instead the word *fuck* came out of my mouth another time, my bottom lip fascinated with the feel of my upper teeth scraping to make the hard F. "Fuck. Fuck." I felt my whole mouth form the word, thought about how we made sounds that created meaning. "Fuck," I said, again and over and again.

THE GERMS

ESCONDIDO, AUGUST '83

Onstage, he says, "This is sex, boy." Maybe he says, "This is 'Sex Boy.'" You don't know, and you don't care. You're having a bad night, bad in that you can't find your way, and you can't find her. Your feet hurt and your cunt hurts and your asshole hurts and your scalp hurts where you carved the anarchy symbol above your ear. Hoof and slit and pucker and noggin. You ache everywhere.

Consider quitting. Consider going back. Consider the muscled piece of revulsion in the crowd with that symbol on his jacket. His bald head.

Recognize your descent as you consider entertaining such a white, white cock.

$\mathcal{T}$HE NEXT week we spent in a continual California state of surrealism. Having survived the party more or less intact, the suite now served as an upscale boutique. People came in; substances went out.

Tram clearly had more than the stash of party acid. I was still afraid to take much of it, but Celeste seemed to want to be free. And loving. She dropped a hit every couple of days. I knew her, so I didn't berate her about her decisions, assuming she would eventually figure out what she was doing.

In our room on Christmas Eve, a non-acid-dropping day, she gave me a ribbon-wrapped handwritten book of gift certificates. I could tell she'd spent hours putting it together, and it held coupons for all sorts of services, either performed by her or to be purchased from others to be performed on me. Scalp massages, foot massages, favorite breakfast, trip across the Golden Gate, Chinatown soup, the best sand castle ever.

"I know Hanukkah is over already, sorry." We had always exchanged gifts on Christmas Eve. "Here." I handed her the wrapped gift I'd brought with me from Madison.

"You shouldn't have," she said, and I knew she actually meant it. She tore through the wrapping paper with abandon. "Yea! A present!" Inside the box sat twenty-one other boxes. None were expensive, really, but they were all pretty, clean, and square.

The first I had seen in a junk store. I'd asked to buy the pale blue velvet box rather than the old watch that perched in it. The man had thought me dim-witted but eventually indulged me.

Now Celeste had it, along with twenty others: wooden, leather-covered, tiny, small, medium, embroidered, carved, painted. Inside each I'd placed something entirely inconsequential, stuff I'd collected over the years: barrettes she would recognize and stones from sixth-grade camp and an ancient jawbreaker and pennies from the year we were born.

"They're so pretty. Lookit. Look how great these are." She began opening them, covering her mouth with her hand in recognition, holding stuff up. "And what you put in them!" She started crying.

"Don't." My gift looked so lame suddenly. Boxes. Rocks, a lock of hair, an unopened Gobstopper, they shouldn't make a person cry.

"You thought about me while we were apart," she said, sniffling.

I smiled and nodded. "Duh." Not like we hadn't talked on the phone almost every day.

"Wow."

"They're just dumb." God, they looked so dumb, spreading out across her bedspread. "Don't."

She laughed. "I thought about you, too." She wiped tears off her high, perfect cheeks. "Our presents are so similar."

I hadn't even noticed. "I . . . yeah."

"Will you cut my hair?"

"Celeste."

"Please?"

"On Christmas Eve?" I thought we'd just hang out with some of the others in the suite. They were watching old black-and-white movies on TV, drinking eggnog with rum or acid or both.

"It's so tangly and ugly. I want something new."

"Wouldn't, I—wouldn't Joaquim do a better job?"

"Maybe. He can direct you, but *you* should do it, Lis."

We were scheduled to help serve the next day at noon at the soup kitchen, La Cocina del San Francisco. Celeste had warned me that it wouldn't be fun, but that it'd be worthwhile. "How 'bout after tomorrow?"

"No, Lis, tonight. It's the right time."

"How do you want it?"

"I want it how you would do it."

"Celeste."

"Please."

"How short?"

"I'm sick of being a hippie."

"You're hardly a hi—"

"I want to look like you."

When we were finished, Celeste's haircut resembled mine, sort of, though neither Joaquim nor I—despite what we thought were aesthetically honed sensibilities—had much in the way of practical experience. We seriously botched the job. And still she looked amazing. Gorgeous-girl-with-crazy-haircut amazing. She said she wanted to dye it a darker purple as soon as she could.

Watching Celeste delight in her short hair, running her fingers through it, tossing her head, I saw how much she and I had departed from each other physically. Less than two years ago we'd posed for Hank's sculpture, probably the exact couple of months that we most resembled each other. Now, though, beyond our general shapes and skin color, she looked nothing like me. At nineteen, I was what everyone would have to call petite. My hips, in their circumference, had never progressed much past my waist, had never smoothed themselves even a little, had never provided any real difference between the measurements of the two essential parts. Celeste's hips hadn't spread, per se, but she'd somehow made herself—shrunk herself—a waist. She flowed from toe to throat, comprised of smooth lines and length of limb.

Her neck was longer, her fingers thinner, her knuckles less knobby. Her eyes were more tilted, her lips redder, her lashes darker, her arms wickeder, her wrists finer, her tits just visibly, painfully, better. Somehow the shitty haircut only brought all of those features to the forefront. She'd lost a layer of herself. About a foot and a half of hair. In my lopping I had managed to uncover the prize completely.

But, well, what was really new, huh? She was her same incredibly beautiful self. You just saw her differently for a few days, noticed different aspects you hadn't paid attention to in a while. As always, she pretended to love what I'd done to her.

I made a phone call to Hawaii, but my father and brother weren't in their room. I left a message at the desk for them to enjoy themselves and have a Merry Christmas. My father had sent me a check in a holiday card with the Budweiser Clydesdales on it weeks ago already. I couldn't tell if he thought the card was funny or not. My brother and I had stopped exchanging gifts sometime in high school.

Celeste and I made glüg, a hot red-wine drink she had a recipe for, and sat around with the other suitemate orphans watching *It's a Wonderful Life*. Celeste cried.

I began to wonder about her.

We woke up early Christmas day and talked to each other in the calm low light. I'd not managed to work my way around to the letter yet. Maybe I didn't want to anymore. Eventually she padded over to my bed and climbed in. "It's stupid to talk across the room to each other," she said. Her hair, having been slept on, poked from her head every which way. I laughed. "What?" she asked.

"Your hair."

"Oh! I forgot!" She patted her head, smiling, feeling how big and mad her hair was. "I *love* it!" She enthused about everything now, I'd noticed.

"It's crazy."

"Just like yours!" She smiled at me, reached over and patted my head. I watched her eyes scan my hair, my face. "I miss you, Lis."

"I'm right here. We're together."

"You know what I mean."

I did. What could we do about it? "Let's make a big breakfast for everybody."

Her face lit up. "Good idea!" Her breath smelled like booze and cloves. She hugged me, and for a second her body felt so foreign, so unfamiliar, that I didn't know who she was at all.

In the middle of our making everything that we could find in the kitchen, biscuits and soy-sausage gravy and scrambled eggs with brie left over from the party and broiled grapefruit with brown sugar and a pitcher of Bloody Marys and fresh-squeezed orange juice for mimosas, Lawrence walked into the kitchen. Naked. With a red bow tied around his penis. "Merry Christmas!" he bellowed as loudly as Mr. Diamond would have. "Ho, ho, ho!" I hadn't seen Lawrence since he'd disappeared from the party around three in the morning several days ago. But I was liking the view. What could I say? I was really liking the view.

Celeste glanced up from frying sausage and looked back down. "How did you get in here?"

"Well, I climbed down the chimney, of course!" He rubbed and slapped the muscles of his flat belly. "Ho, ho!" I watched the bow bob slightly. "Jesus," he said, suddenly seeming to get a good look. "What the hell did you do to your hair?"

"What does it look like?" I asked. Maybe he was an asshole. He was gorgeous, though. He had two tattoos on his shoulders, the cartoon Tasmanian Devil on one, a thorny black heart on the other.

"Who the fuck did that?" he asked.

I felt my face redden. I dotted grapefruit halves with butter.

He looked at me. "What'd you use, Lisa, a lawnmower?" I kept my eyes down on my job, not sure what to say. "And why are you buttering grapefruit?" he pushed on.

"They get broiled, you classless fucker," Celeste said. "Now I know my haircut's great. If Lawrence doesn't like it, then it's gotta be good."

"Hey, hey. Merry Christmas, remember? Oh." He scratched his back. "Right. You're one of the two kikes in that little saying of yours . . . that's right." He sat down at the kitchen table and propped his elbows on the chair back.

Celeste banged at the sausage in the frying pan with a metal spatula.

"Where'd all that *love* go, Celie? I got some for *you* right now. Didn't you even see your present?"

She continued to massacre the sausage, not looking at him.

"Come on," he said. "Don't you wanna unwrap it?"

I did. Like a great big candy cane.

"Lawrence," she asked in falsetto, "dear Lawrence, why aren't you at *home*?"

I knew at this point, from having talked to Celeste and Tram in the days after the party, that Lawrence lived out of his car. What money he had he made from playing with his band and petty dealing, delivering for Tram sometimes. Tram was perfectly willing to have him sleep in somebody else's bed, she said, because they'd had plenty of each other for years. She claimed not to be possessive. Something about her made me afraid of her, though, as if she were capable of murdering me in my sleep. Creep up with a knife between her teeth and slit my throat before I made a noise. And, because Tram felt dangerous, Lawrence did even more. I'd fluttered around him like a moth since his very first compliment. I wanted him to turn me to ash.

"Ah!" He picked up a spiraled wooden honey dipper off the table and jabbed it at his chest. "I should go home, eh? You got me good there, Celie. You got me good." He smiled and stuck the honey dipper between his nice lips, pretending to brush his teeth with it.

"Stop it! Don't ruin that!" She stomped to Lawrence and batted his hand away from his mouth. The honey dipper fell to the floor.

"Ooh, angry girl. I'm getting a stiffy."

"Fuck you."

"Look, baby, I'm ready."

Celeste looked down in his lap. "What is wrong with you? Get out of here."

He looked at me out of the corner of his eye. "Lisa doesn't want me to go, do you, Lisa?"

I didn't. I shook my head no before I realized what I'd done. He grinned ear to ear.

"Lisa!"

Why was she so angry? The situation sort of reminded me of swimming with Hank and Ess. Maybe Lawrence was a little meaner, but he was still just teasing. And naked. "He's just teasing, Celeste."

"No, he's not." She bent to pick up the honey dipper and

Lawrence spanked her butt. In a single swift motion she swung around and punched him in the side of the head.

His hand went to his ear and he winced. "Damn!"

"That's not yours." She meant her butt, I guessed. Or maybe the honey dipper. I couldn't figure her out so easily lately. Celeste walked to the sink and opened the cupboard beneath it, tossing the honey dipper in the garbage.

"A goddamn slugger," he muttered.

She tilted her head at him and smirked. "You were just leaving, weren't you?"

"Thought I'd have some breakfast first. What're you making besides baked grapefruit?" He rubbed his red ear. "Come on, Celie. It's Christmas, for fuck's sake. Don't turn me out on the street today."

"What's your problem? What *is* your problem?"

"I wouldn't know where to start," he said. I wondered if he meant it, but when Celeste turned her back to open the refrigerator, he winked at me, pointed to his lap, and tossed his head in a come-here gesture.

I really wanted to. I shrugged my shoulders and looked toward Celeste. "Are you going to help, Lis," she snipped, talking into the top shelf, "or are you going to stand there and stare at the asshole?"

"I was thinking I'd stare at the asshole," I said in an attempt to lighten up her mood. It didn't work.

"Your loss," she said meanly, trying to open a jar of pickled peppers, I assumed for the Bloody Marys. Maybe she just needed a drink. She'd been fine to Lawrence when we were tripping. I just—I just felt like I couldn't read her all the time now. I looked down and wiggled my toes. Cooking in underwear and a little T-shirt wasn't the same as being naked with a bow, was it? I should do splits. High kicks. "Goddamn it," she muttered, struggling with the jar lid. Finally she went to a cupboard, pulled out a shot glass, poured herself some warm vodka, and tossed it back. "Ah!" she sort of spit. "Merry Christmas, everyone."

"Merry Christmas," I said to Celeste honestly, and then Tram came traipsing in wearing a jade-colored silk robe, her eyes gummy with sleep.

"What time is it?" She frowned. Lawrence reached his hand back and untied her sash. I caught a glimpse of her brown skin and a dark triangle of pubic hair before she rewrapped the robe. "Lawrence." It didn't even sound like she was scolding him. A teacher calling a student's name maybe.

"Your asshole is not behaving himself," Celeste said, turning back to the soy sausage, pouring herself another shot of vodka.

"What's new." Tram yawned. "You should just fuck him and then he'd leave you alone."

These suitemates might have been the nerds as kids, but they'd grown into something else completely since then. "Hi, Tram," I tried.

"Merry holiday," she said. I returned to my grapefruit halves, sprinkling on brown sugar. Tram sat at the table with Lawrence, laying her head down and snoring exaggeratedly. "Hey, Celeste," she said, perking up all of a sudden. "You still have some of that sensimilia?"

"Yeah. Lis, would you mind getting it?" Celeste directed. "It's in my dresser, top left."

"Sure." I was happy to get out of the room.

I rummaged around in her sock drawer till I found the baggie. Both Joaquim and Noah were standing in the kitchen when I came back. Bare-chested, they waited as Celeste made them Christmas morning cocktails. Nobody paid Lawrence's nudity any mind. Were Celeste and I so, so . . . I didn't think we were prim. Were we? "Here," I said to nobody in particular, holding out the baggie.

"Gimme," Tram said, snatching the three bagged buds right out of my hand. A little lightning-quick Vietnamese ninja, she was. "Hookah morning!" she said, running out of the kitchen.

"Oh, no," Noah groaned. He took his screwdriver from Celeste and tasted it. "I still say they're better with Tang."

"Just because you grew up drinking your urban vodka with

urban mixer doesn't mean the rest of us have to," Joaquim said. Damn, he was purty.

"Oh, justh shut up, you!" Noah flung his hand at Joaquim.

"Nnnnnnn," Nanci with an I said, walking in, looking hungover in her too-small nightgown. "Don't ever give me that glüg shit again." She arched her back, walking with her toes turned out. "Smells good."

I couldn't get over how unreal the suitemates felt. These people were simply beyond bizarre, their particular combination a basement-science-project mishap. Bleach and baking soda. A Bunsen burner and closed can of mixed vegetables burbling away. "Bring plates to the table, would you, Lis?" Celeste asked, more like herself again, kind of.

A few minutes later Honey appeared, bushy-tailed as a Madison squirrel, carrying a basket full of small cloth-wrapped gifts. "Merry Christmas!" she piped. "Merry Christmas! Take one, take one, you too, Lisa. Take another one! Merry Christmas." They smiled politely as if they all knew what the fabric hid. Later I found out that they did indeed. Honey had been tie-dyeing bandannas and beading belts and painting tiny clay animal figurines for months. Since she'd arrived. She sold them at street art fairs. Now she was giving away her leftovers. Still, I suppose the gesture was a kind one, more or less in the spirit of things.

Tram returned with her hookah and Celeste's baggie, an entire bud short. She had a small tray and a few tiny bowls of powders, brown and white. I grew anxious immediately. "Brown or white?" she asked.

"White, please," Noah said.

"Definitely white," Lawrence said.

"White."

"White."

"White!"

"White."

"Lisa?" Tram looked at me and cocked her head. How could she just be my age? Change the setting, the year, and she'd make me piss my pants.

I had no idea what they were choosing but thought it better to go with the flow, with the majority, than to buck a system I didn't understand. I suddenly missed my Buddhist speed dealer back in Madison with his old-fogey compartmentalized pillbox, his low-key pitch and lack of pressure. He'd always told me exactly what I was buying and where it'd get me. "White," I added.

"Aw. It's Christmas. Nobody wants to make it special?"

Evidently nobody did.

"Fine. Come on." She set the tray and the big gangly hookah on the kitchen table.

"Save it till after breakfast," Lawrence said. Naked in his chair. "They're going to the trouble to make it."

I thought that pot made a person hungrier. Why would we want to wait? I looked down again at my underwear and T-shirt. I looked at the cookie pan of grapefruit halves I'd been working on. I thought about the homeless shelter Celeste and I would be at in less than two hours, and I just didn't really know where I was.

I glanced at Lawrence. He stared directly at me. *Nice ass*, he mouthed, and I saw that he was slowly stroking himself under the table, his arm muscles flexing, his shoulder moving in a slow rhythm. He was jacking off in a room full of people? On Christmas morning at breakfast?

"That had better be soy sausage," Nanci with an I said to Celeste.

"Of course," Celeste said sweetly.

"Are those going under the broiler?" Joaquim asked me. He came and stood close. "We need to fix her hair," he whispered, pressing his index finger into the spilled sugar on the pan.

I nodded. "Maybe you should, though."

"He should what?" Lawrence asked.

Joaquim looked up. "He should—Jesus, cut that the fuck out, Lawrence."

"Make me."

"Tram," Joaquim said, "I thought you'd housebroken him. Please leash that thing."

Tram looked over at Lawrence. "Stop that!"

"At least use the bathroom," Honey suggested.

Celeste opened the oven door. "How about everybody wears both a top and a bottom for Christmas brunch?"

Noah scratched his chest. "Cool."

We ate and talked about what our families might be doing at the moment. I said I thought that my father would be snorkeling with his *lover*—going for the impact of the word, although none of them reacted the way I'd hoped, only nodded or kept chewing—and that my brother would be on the beach, watching girls. Surely I could have come up with something more interesting for David, couldn't I? But I didn't really know him very well anymore. Even as kids we'd never interacted that much. The fact that he'd been nearly as big as me or bigger for our whole lives technically meant that I wasn't really a big sister anyway.

I pressed my fork into a gravy-smothered biscuit and thought about the time David had gotten his arm caught in the bottom flap of a vending machine when he was six. He'd not had any money and had wanted a pack of gum. I'd pulled and pulled, finally getting his arm out, scraping his wrist till he bled, but he hadn't cried. My father had already trained him in proper Smith protocol.

Celeste wrung out her grapefruit half above her mouth when it was her turn. We went quiet watching. That's just the way it always was. I was used to it, year after year. The rapt stares. "Another normal day," she finally said in reference to her family. "Kikes and all," she added, licking her lips.

The hookah appeared again. Tram packed the bowl and used her pinkie fingernail to sprinkle on what I found out was coke. When I asked what the brown was, Celeste said, "Dangerous."

"Oh, come on," Tram said, scooping up another nailful. "I don't know why you won't try."

"Nobody's as stupid as you," Lawrence said.

"I'm not stupid."

"*Horse* stupid," he said.

I didn't get it.

"You're an idiot," Tram said. "Take a hose, everybody. Well, okay, double up."

Celeste and I shared. With the cocaine in the bowl too, the pot wasn't so dopey-dreamy. We all sat around the table and talked about the idiot president and his minions, a topic on which nobody disagreed. I didn't want to go to the soup kitchen. I didn't feel like going anywhere. Maybe Celeste would forget. Forget about the soup kitchen the way she'd forgotten about her parents. I watched her inhale a second bowl with Lawrence and Tram.

And she did. Celeste completely forgot about serving homeless people on Christmas Day. I debated whether or not I should say anything; she'd been so enthusiastic about it before I'd arrived, talking about how important giving was. I didn't say anything until an hour after we were supposed to have been there, when I thought we'd be safe.

"What time is it? Oh, my god!" She stood up. "Lis, we have to go!"

"They ate their ham and peas by now," Lawrence said.

"Well, maybe we can still help clean up. Shit! Why didn't you say anything?"

"I forgot," I lied.

"Damn it. What's wrong with me?"

I looked at her madwoman hair and her frenetic hands and cracked up. She was a mess. "Stop it," she said. "What?" She sort of giggled, and then everybody busted a gut, the sensimilia laughter contagious.

Lawrence stood up, looking around in false panic, imitating Celeste perfectly. The laughter grew. Honey held her stomach. Noah brushed away tears.

When we caught our breath Celeste said, "I really wanted to go feed the homeless."

Why we found this so funny I have no idea, but now we burst into new peals. She was hilarious. Absolutely hilarious.

We all spent the day doing nothing but talking and smoking, drinking mimosas, listening to music. Lawrence said he knew of a good band playing over in Oakland later. By dinnertime I'd cajoled Celeste into going. She let Joaquim touch up her hair. Tram brought out more coke and cut lines for everybody on a mirror she'd taken off the wall. She rolled up a hundred-dollar bill to use as a straw. I wasn't sure I was getting much of the coke up my nose until I sniffed hard after passing off the rolled bill to Celeste. You could feel it up in there like a live wire. Somebody showed me how to rub it on my gums.

After the lines, unable to sit still, Celeste and I began to clean compulsively. We vacuumed and dusted and sang while we did it. I sat still for a second and felt my heart race. I stood up and kept going. Being still felt terrible. We skipped dinner, showered, and dressed.

"No other takers, huh?" Lawrence stood in the living room, looking mean in some camouflage pants and a white tank, a leather jacket slung over his shoulder.

"Don't freeze out there, tough guy," Nanci with an I said from the couch, a bag of potato chips in her hand.

"Slamming will keep me warm."

Celeste rolled her eyes. As much as she seemed to hate Lawrence, she *had* agreed to go. I wondered if maybe she didn't really kind of want him. We'd both dressed carefully, putting to use what we'd learned from the Art Institute people at Hank's. Black clothes, dark makeup, our hair headfuls of chaos. We still had our fake IDs that Mack had made us. We didn't look like the girls in the photos anymore, but they did match up with our other IDs, credit cards and student IDs. Lawrence said we wouldn't have a problem anyway; he knew the doorman.

He drove us in his car, a little piece of shit. Despite what we pretended in front of Lawrence, Celeste and I had never been to a real hardcore show, which is what he said he could guarantee us. Outside the crappy little club, waiting in line for the doors to open, I wondered where I'd be in ten years. You have moments like that sometimes, you know? You catch yourself going, "I wonder where I'll be? Who I'll be with?"

Celeste had been civil with Lawrence in the car, almost flirty once, which was great for the night, but standing there checking out all the people in line, I already knew I wouldn't end up in Oakland. Not with Lawrence. Still, he could be good in the way I'd found Mack to be good, useful, if only for a short time. Not long enough to get tired of him. Just long enough to have him learn me.

Celeste and I had gone in together on coke for the three of us before we left. Tram had given us the coke in a vial with a mini spoon attached to a chain attached to the screw-on lid. It made me think of dollhouses. Lawrence had two flasks in his pockets, both full of vodka. He also told us he had a knife in his boot, and that if anything happened to come get him. Visions of *West Side Story* shadow-danced in my head. I couldn't quite remember the great line about a cigarette and your dying day, but I wanted to. I smelled somebody smoking one of those sweet cigarettes, the ones that smelled like incense. I just tried to be cool. You know. My usual self. Ho, ho. It was Christmas, I kept reminding myself.

Somebody cranked the house music inside.

A couple guys approached Lawrence and called him Lawless, slapped at his face and jacket and acted like they hated him when you knew they were just showing affection. The third-grade aspect of the gathering was evident. As a matter of fact, the entire street scene seemed to be about doing dumb shit, the sort of dumb shit you'd do in grade school.

A huge guy with a shaved head unlocked the three dead bolts, and the house music surged out with the opening of the door, and people started shoving with their dog-collar bracelets, and the huge guy swore at the whole lot of us and said the cover was four dollars and then more shoving started, big shoving, and Celeste smiled at me, her forearms up to protect her front and she yelled, her mouth all cocaine tight, "This is great!"

"Yeah!"

"We should go to more of these!"

"Yeah!" I got pushed from behind and nearly knocked down. "This is going to be great!"

I could see her grind her teeth. "Yeah!"

We got in, no problem, and then lost Lawless Lawrence almost immediately. Inside, the place was dark enough to not see your feet. It smelled like spilled beer and rotting citrus fruit. When Celeste and I went into the same stall to snort from the dollhouse spoon, the odor of puke reigned supreme. We were having a blast. I said, "Do you think this is what we missed out on with the guys in Kansas City?" The instant I said it I wanted to suck it back in. I didn't want to break the mood.

She pushed the mini spoon into her right nostril, holding her left closed with a slim finger and said, "Hardly." What did she mean? She handed me the spoon, the lid dangling. "I've never really liked coke before," she said.

I liked it a ton so far. I scooped and handed her the vial. "It's fun," I said stupidly, rapidly, as fast as my mouth could move.

"It *is* fun. I dropped out of school." She gave a dazzling smile.

"Yeah?" She dropped out of school. "Wait—what?" I stood straight, the spoon halfway to my nose.

"In November."

"Why?" My gut already knew she had, but hearing her actually say it freaked me out more than a little.

"I don't think it's what I'm about."

What the hell did that mean? "What do you mean?"

"Have I told you I just *love* you?! I don't want to be in school. Not right now. I want to experience. I want to create. Fuck studying bullshit and taking classes from cabbage-munching Chinese graduate students you can't understand."

I couldn't remember hearing her say a single crappy thing about another culture before. "Do the suitemates know?"

"No. Well, probably not. They might suspect. Lawrence does, I guess."

I snorted and handed the spoon back to her. "Now I get it." And right then, finally, Mr. Diamond's letter made sense. He suspected. Damn, he could read the writing on the wall. He knew. That's what it was all about, and Celeste had shut down, shut him out, because she couldn't break the news to the man who believed his youngest and most beautiful daughter would be academically knighted. Win a Pulitzer. Discover the cure for war.

"Yeah. The Lawless man is blackmailing me." She stuck the spoon in her left nostril. The white powder disappeared.

"What does he want?"

She made a face.

"Get the fuck out, you coke whores!" somebody yelled. A kick on the stall door came next.

"All fucking right!" Celeste yelled back, recapping the vial. "Okay!" God, she knew how to stick up for herself plenty well in a place like this one. With these kinds of people. She'd somehow learned so much more in one semester than I had. We left the stall.

The kicker already had her pants undone and drooping around her thighs. "Cunts."

"Cunt," Celeste snapped back.

Ketchup. "Cunt," I tacked on. Ketchup, Lis, ketchup. The girl pushed past.

"Yeah," Celeste said. "I just thought, 'Let it go.' I dropped in November."

"You said that already."

"In November." She went to the sink to wash her hands. "Boring. It was all so boring."

"But in November we were talking on the phone and you were telling me about your classes."

"I was?"

"Yes." I snorted a deep snort, only I swallowed. My phlegm tasted like chemicals.

"I was worried you wouldn't come out to stay with me. To Berkeley."

"I came out."

"But I was worried."

"Fucking Berkeley cunts," the girl in the stall said.

"Oakland skank," Celeste answered. The coke made her quick, even if she didn't mean what she said. You could tell she didn't mean what she said. That she just said it.

Two beers and three visits to the bathroom stall later, Lawrence reappeared. "They're good, I fucking swear," he said of the head-liners. "Trust me." The opening band had played to a dead house. Nobody'd moved; nobody'd applauded. They were booed and pelted with somebody's dinner remains, fries and half a ham-burger, the crescent moon of the bun silhouetted for one flying second in the stage lights. Everybody milled around now, waiting. Lawrence took a few steps away to talk to a plump ugly girl. She had a black eye.

I leaned over to Celeste. "So Lawrence says he'll tell if you don't do him?"

"Not exactly. He implies it, though."

"What if I took your place? You know. Like, went in your stead. I'll calm him down." I winked. "I mean, what would happen if the suitemates did find out about your dropping?"

"If they told on me I'd get kicked out of the suite." Her lower jaw twitched. "My staying there is contingent upon performance. No. Not performance. But I have to remain enrolled."

"Are you?"

"I didn't take any finals, Lis."

"You flunked?"

"Believe it or not, no. Cs and Ds. My grades were good before I dropped. Before I stopped going to class. I never technically dropped."

I couldn't imagine doing such a thing, just stopping like that. It was the sort of move that school anxiety dreams were made of. You hadn't gone to class for weeks and woke up one morning real-izing you had a final exam that very day you hadn't studied for. It made me sick to think about. How could Celeste have done that? I knew her dreams through and through. She must have flipped out. I couldn't figure it.

"The real problem is that I haven't registered for next semester. It's only a matter of time. I figure by the second week of classes they will have found me out. The administration. Never mind the suitemates."

"What will you do?" The pudgy girl with the black eye held her forearms out to Lawrence. What was she doing?

"I'm working on it," Celeste said. "Maybe I'll work on it here."

"What?"

"Working on it. A plan, Stan. Don't need to discuss, Gus. Get myself free." Her jaw jerked back and forth, back and forth. "I need some booze," she said, tapping her fingernail on her front teeth. "Not a thing. You could drill a huge hole. Right. Fucking. Here." Clack, clack went her fingernail. "Tell you what. Why don't you go get Lawrence. Or I will. Maybe we should both fuck him later. There's an idea. Go be nice to him now, though, so I can have some vodka."

Now she was talking. I'd get him away from Pudgy. "Yeah. Vodka would be good right now." I stepped over, running my tongue over my gums.

"Looks like Lisa needs to slow the fuck down, doncha, little Lisa?" He slapped Pudgy on the arm and threw his head at me. "Straight outta the chute."

Pudgy nodded knowingly. He really could be an asshole. No wonder Celeste had a problem with him. I didn't ask him. I just went for his jacket pocket and asked, "Didn't your mother ever teach you any manners?"

"My mama's dead."

I stopped my pocket fishing. "I thought you called her every Sunday."

"Oh, I do. Every Sunday morning, after every Saturday night, I look up into the sky and cry, 'Mama, fix my achin' head!'"

Pudgy laughed too hard. Fuck that. "She really kicked the bucket?" I asked. I bent my leg and rubbed him with my knee.

"Yup." He looked down at me. I couldn't tell if he was telling the truth or not. I liked his profile, though.

I dug around for a flask. Cigarettes, a Zippo, money, flask. I pulled it out. "You share, we'll share," I told him.

"Hey," he told Pudgy, shrugging, "sometimes you gotta follow your nose." Lawrence and I stepped back over to Celeste, who was talking to some guy.

"Lisa, this is Papa."

"Aaaay, Papa Cherry! Dude." Lawrence pounded the fleshy side of his fist on Papa's shoulder. Papa Cherry looked a little like Hank—older, great eyes.

"Hey," I said, unscrewing the flask and taking a swig. My throat had to be numb too. I didn't even feel the vodka go down.

Celeste took the flask and filled her mouth, swallowed twice. "Papa?"

He took it and drank.

"You'd best share what you've got too," Lawrence told Celeste.

"Depends on what you want to share," she said, and then actually smiled at him.

"I thought you college types had free will."

"She's mine 'n' I'm hers," she said.

"Can I watch?" Papa Cherry asked. "Better yet, stick me right in the middle."

"Fuck Papa. Forget him, little ladies. I'll stick you," Lawrence said. "I'll stick you right."

The coke had numbed my body, but my head liked the sound of it. "I bet you would," I dared.

"I'd split you wiiiide open, little Lisa," he said.

I imagined myself halved like a freestone peach. I thought about the skin lamp shades the Germans were said to have had during World War II. Where was my brain going?

"That'd be hard to do," Celeste said. "She can do all three splits."

"Mmmmm." Lawrence grabbed his crotch. "Down, boy, down."

"Bullshit," Papa said.

"Celeste, too," I told him.

"You're full of shit."

I looked around. There was no way I was going to do the splits in the club. No way at all. "Trust me," I said.

"Show me," Papa said.

"What are you," Celeste asked, "from Missouri?"

"Home, home on the range," Lawrence sang, as poorly as he had said he did. "I think you're full of shit too."

I had an idea. I looked around. The place was dark enough, nobody else really paying attention to our little foursome. I turned to face Lawrence. "Here. You're this tall. I'm this tall. I'll put my foot here." I scooted into him, aligned my feet on either side of his right, pressed my crotch into his leg, and found my balance. I raised my booted foot to my knee, undergripped the arch, straightened my leg, and set my foot on his shoulder, saying, "And put my other foot here."

He grabbed my calf. My black jeans had ridden up and exposed a few inches of my shin. He licked.

Papa looked at me, then Celeste, and said, "Come to Daddy!"

She followed my move on Papa. How many thousands of times had we done exactly the same thing in dance class? Then your partner walks backward, working your stretch. Big deal. I felt Lawrence's other hand stroke my supporting leg's thigh. He grunted, leaned to me, and said with liquored breath, "You're *mine* later, you hear me?"

I knew not to commit right away. Papa snarled and bit the toe of Celeste's combat boot. I saw Pudgy approach. I wiggled my leg to get Lawrence to let me take it down. He tightened his grip on my calf at the same time Pudgy shoved on his back. "Fuck you!" she shouted as we lost our balance and fell on the floor, Lawrence's full weight onto my splits.

"Hey, cunt!" I heard Celeste yell.

"Fuck you, too!" Pudgy yelled. I struggled to get out from under Lawrence to see. Over his shoulder I watched Celeste take her leg down and Papa cock his fist at Pudgy, punching her hard in the face. She staggered back a second before driving her little fist ineffectually into Papa's stomach. Now he pounded her again, this time, I could see, smack in the nose. Damn. That had to hurt. Her hand went to her face. She looked at her bloody fingers.

"Yeah," Lawrence said in my ear, rolling to look at her. "Stupid fat bitch."

I hoped Lawrence would prove as creative as Mack had been. I'd developed a taste for that kind of stuff, and I liked his dirty weight on me. "Mind if I take my leg back now?" I said coolly.

He looked at me and my calf by the side of my head. Sort of surprised. "Guess I believe you," he said.

I bit at the tongue of my boot.

"Fuck, that's good," he said.

Finally the band came out and played. Celeste and I made our only wise move of the evening, staying clear of the dancing. Out of the slamming. We met more of Papa's friends, all of them in a band from LA, up visiting the scene for the holidays. I guess everybody had to go somewhere for Christmas.

Would Mr. and Mrs. Diamond write me back if I wrote first?

Later, we caught a ride with Papa's band, along with Lawrence. We'd run out of coke but not out of time. Somebody knew about an after-hours place. Every last one of the guys in the car looked good to me. I'd found my candy store. The zits, the greasy hair, none of it mattered. They stank. And they were works of art. Maybe, I decided, Lawrence would be even better the next day. Maybe he'd want me even more if I chose somebody else in the car for the night.

Which one, which one?

You pick a fight with a girl. You have never done this before, but something about the look of her mouth reminds you of the only other mouth you love now, and it can't belong on the face of this girl too. No one else is allowed to wear it. Not here. Decide to fix her mouth so that it will never look like the other again.

Begin with her fast tumble. Do not move so that she trips. When she catches herself on her hands and knees, kick. Feel soft fat, fat stomach, and know that your decision is correct. Fat does not belong anywhere on a body with that mouth.

The girl is not afraid, though, and in her rising from the floor, from the rank range of horked spit and meaty feet, you realize you will likely lose. You see she is big. She is big as a house. Big as death. Her enormous tits have escaped her ripped, marker-lettered T-shirt. Notice that she has gotten the second word of the band's acronym wrong.

Do something. Now. You won't have another chance. Think about pulling your illegal Tijuana stiletto from your boot. Think about going to stick her, about carving her thick middle. Think twice, and then think again. Push your fist into her gut. It is not what you'd meant, exactly. Your hit contains indecision from someplace lost and long wrong, and it fails to do what it should as the girl with the mouth plunges her bulk into you. Your entire hand is lost in flesh.

She screams. Her grotesque tits smother your face, and

you cannot breathe as her weight in all its slow-motion horror tips you backward. The mountain of what you have come to hate surrounds you.

In the crush you only feel the break. You do not hear the crack of your own wrist bone.

It is nowhere near over.

_I_ LEARNED A new expression. Actually, I learned a lot of new expressions, Californiaisms, you could say. Celeste and I—here's one—_snagged_ ourselves a few _decent_ fucks in the back rooms of a stranger's house in the wee hours of the morning and decided to spend the rest of my vacation time traveling to see music with the LA band and Lawrence. We'd be going on the road, catching one band after the next. That morning, early, after not sleeping, Celeste and I went back to the suite and showered, threw clothes in a duffel, woke up Tram and bought an eightball (another new vocab term), and told her to say good-bye to the other suitemates for a while. Papa, Lawrence, and the rest picked us up. Good odds for us, 5:2, in our favor. I would learn, actually, that they, the odds, were almost always that good in the world we were choosing, sometimes better.

We drove south. Neither of us had slept with Lawrence the first night out, but as I'd guessed might be the case, it only made him try harder, pretending not to care about either of us. He copped a feel whenever he could. I suspected in the eyes of all people punk, we were very fresh meat. None of them cared that we'd been with two of them less than twelve hours previous. Been through two of them.

I forgot about Mr. and Mrs. Diamond.

In Fresno, Papa rented a single hotel room for the lot of us. We had hours to go before the show, four cases of the cheapest beer I'd ever had, and an eightball. I watched as band guy after band guy took his turn cutting lines. The process fascinated me. We removed the olive-colored top of the toilet tank and set it on the coffee table to use as our slick surface. The two mirrors in the place were permanently affixed to the walls, and X-Ray, evidently the band member with the best handyman skills, couldn't figure out how to detach the old medicine cabinet door without ripping it off. He'd wanted to, but Papa bitched at X-Ray, said he had a fucking credit card down at the front desk and that he'd take it up the ass if they completely trashed the place. I looked at Papa as he chopped at the coke. He had the longest eyelashes I'd ever seen on a guy, black, blinking now and then over icy white-blue eyes. Despite his stage name, the only name of his we knew, he felt trustworthy. The older statesman.

Celeste had screwed the drummer, because, she said, he had the best arms. She'd admitted when we were packing the duffel that she'd not remembered his name at the time they'd had sex.

"So?" I said.

You could tell by looking at the guy sitting there across from her in the hotel room that he'd flipped for Celeste—I mean, how many humans in his usual circles did he know who challenged Aphrodite?—but he was trying not to show it. Casual and all, no big deal. They said "casz," like Zsa Zsa, as in *casual.* It took me two days to figure out what they were saying. Longer still to figure out all the other stuff.

Myself, I'd given the bass player free reign with my body for a few wet, thrusting minutes. He didn't hide the fact that he wanted more turns but seemed to accept the fact that I might not give them. He was interesting to look at, fair, skinny, his hair dyed black as soot. He wore eyeliner. I'd liked his stomach when he'd taken off his shirt at the after-hours house. I'd suggested he follow me into the empty bedroom. He did. He didn't talk much.

I decided I liked coke a lot better than speed. The only thing I didn't like about it was running out. Or doing too much. I didn't like feeling like I needed to go jog around the block a few times. Celeste and I weren't as big as the rest of them, obviously. Pacing seemed to be key, but then coke also seemed to be a treat the band guys didn't always have, and they snorted the stuff up pretty greedily. I thought about the straws filled with flavored sugar you bought as a kid, that you poured into your mouth, orange- and grape- and lime-flavored sugar, yum, yum. That's how the band liked coke. Celeste and I were making friends, though, so we kept sharing. After the guys had all done four lines, and we two girls half that each, we let the pile of white powder sit. It didn't glitter on the toilet lid, but it whispered. It promised. It, it. Hmm. Yes, it was it.

"Beer?" Papa asked.

Every one of us had just swigged ours. A round of yeahs. Papa fetched beers from the bathtub they'd filled with ice and water, scooping ice from the ice machine with wastepaper baskets, making bowls out of the stretched-out bottoms of their T-shirts. I made a mental note that none of them planned to bathe in the next, oh, day.

The problem with coke if you're a guy—as with Ecstasy or some of the other ones—is that your libido is affected. I'm not a guy, so I don't know for sure, but that's what I know anyway. Problem when you're a girl is that your libido is still there, sort of, but you're hinged at the hip with the guys who are also doing coke. You decide they're the only ones on the same level as you, so you're just stuck on them. And—see, now you're understanding what I'm getting at—they're only interested in doing more coke. Or maybe being pricks. Coke does strange stuff to testosterone, too. But whatever.

You could tell Papa ruled the room. He kept the peace. In retrospect, I suppose that if he hadn't been there, Celeste and I would have had a very different trip to Tijuana for New Year's Eve. Via the hardcore route from Oakland on down. Papa imposed order. Celeste and I may have been out of control, but he kept everybody else in some sort of preordained line. I'm sure what he said was, "Give the kids a break."

You gotta start somewhere, right?

So Celeste and I did, with a vengeance. 1983 trumpeted itself. You could see the newborn year on its way. It sounded like the deejay Hellin Killer. That's what the band said, anyway.

We drank beer and later did a few more lines. We talked about shit, but I don't know what, none of it intelligible. For some reason the guys showed us a modicum of respect, and they didn't gang-bang us. Thank god for coke sometimes, you know?

Or maybe thank god for Papa. Hard to say. I don't really remember. Days blurred into other ones. But that first day traveling wasn't the same as all the rest because I'd had so few other ones yet at that point. I remembered more of Fresno. Fresno, then the car breaking down and the repair work that Celeste and I each kicked in a hundred bucks for, Bakersfield, down to Chula Vista, across and into Mexico on the thirtieth for two nights in Tijuana.

In Fresno I went after Lawrence. He faked indifference at first at the club, but after he'd sweated out his coke, he ended up fucking me so hard in the station wagon later that I had bruises on my sit bones the next day. He moved my legs every which way. I pointed my toes for him.

The scenery, I thought, would be better, better than scrubby half desert and ugly nonarchitecture. But as we drove south, the Bay Area heated and dried into dung-colored suburbs, strip malls and billboards and gas stations with help-wanted signs in the windows held with yellowed tape. Celeste tried Lawrence out in Bakersfield while Papa waited patiently.

I knew I'd have no attachment to these people in less than a week, other than Celeste, if you're wondering how I managed to be so unemotional about the events. And now that I'd grown up and learned how things worked, I could share with Celeste. I thrilled at being desired, sharing the spotlight with Celeste. I didn't see any other girls in any of the places we went who held a candle to either of us. I'm not sure what that said about Celeste's and my choice of company, but I didn't care. We were stars, and I tried to play along.

Something in Celeste seemed to have jangled loose, though. After we finished the coke, she doled out speed and acid. The fact that she'd dropped out of school had not entirely left my conscious state. I was on Christmas break. She was on a permanent vacation. I couldn't get a straight answer out of her as to what she'd do after Berkeley discovered her nonenrollment. I suggested Madison and tried not to think about the next semester.

Tijuana felt dangerous and bleak. Even for breakfast, I shied away from drinking anything but beer, as did Celeste. We'd heard the water was bad, the food bad, the local law enforcement bad. Dirty, barefoot kids begged at midnight. During the day, hunks of strange meat hung on hooks on outdoor carts in the raw sunlight, the vendors busy fanning their chopped vegetable toppings and stacks of tortillas to keep off the flies. Shops sold bright plastic objects and cheap toys. Bad souvenirs. In one really depressing section of the city, people lived in boxes. Refrigerator boxes, bigger boxes pieced together with that rippled carport roofing, den siding boxes. I showered less and drank more and began to understand why the band, why these punks, were attracted to the bedlam. Life was so close to the surface. It was there in your face. Nobody on the earth, practically—well, a really small percentage—lived like Celeste and I did. Had. Back in Kansas City. What was stuff anyway but that? *Stuff*. Life was about experience, not stuff. The truth lay just underneath, but it took bravery to go down there.

Celeste and I were brave.

We rang in the New Year by completing our rounds, going through all five guys each. We didn't agree on our favorites, but then we knew that'd be the case. On the big night Celeste dose-and-a-halfed and gave Papa the ride of his life. I'm sure that's what it had to have been, anyway.

The bus trip all the way back up to Berkeley sucked Tijuana donkey dick. Lawrence, Celeste, and I rode the Greyhound from LA, where the band stopped and we disembarked. We were hungover, cash-poor, and out of all our good substances. My flight back to Wisconsin left the next morning, back to Milwaukee, where I had to catch another bus over to Madison. On the bus to Berkeley, I resigned myself to the task of returning to school and finally fell asleep, only the third time in a week, as the diesel-and-chemical-toilet-stinking dog rumbled its way up Interstate 5.

The three of us staggered into Joaquim's car at the station, napped some more, stumbled past the Warhol and the magnificent root-balled Christmas tree still standing in the dining room, muttered our hellos, and went straight to bed. Lawrence went easily, familiarly back into Tram's bedroom, and for a moment I hated him. But then I realized it wasn't in keeping with the spirit of the trip, so I tried not to. I asked Celeste for her alarm clock, went back out to remind Joaquim that he was giving me a ride to the airport in the morning, noted the slightly irritated nod he gave me, and went to sleep.

Celeste didn't get up to ride with me in the morning, just mumbled, "Bye" into her pillow. I wasn't sure she was even awake. Her newly darkened purple locks looked coarse. A strange texture. I patted her head, kissed her stinky hair, and said "Good-bye."

I tried to be nice to Joaquim on the car ride to the airport. I gave him a pared-down PG version of our escapades. As I spoke I realized that we hadn't encountered a single gay person during our adventures away from Berkeley. Maybe two black guys. I wondered what that meant.

My flight was long and mindless and routed through St. Louis with a three-hour layover. I bought a fashion magazine, which bored me. How overdone and insipid the models looked. They were wearing *costumes.* I threw it in a garbage can with a flourish and lit myself a cigarette. My lungs didn't exactly like them, but they filled the time. I realized that people were staring at me, at my hair and my boots and my dirty Eraserhead T-shirt and my leather jacket and the zipper skirt of Celeste's that I'd made my own. I loved that how I looked kept most of the people at a distance. I didn't want to deal with anybody. I didn't want to talk to anyone. Fuck 'em all.

Carl met me at the bus station in Madison, the wind brutally cold, the blowing snow melting as it hit my torn fishnet-covered legs. "Look at *you*!" he said with a huge smile.

"Hey," I said.

"Hay is for horses," he said.

And that was it.

He tried, though, much to my dismay. He had dinner nearly ready at his apartment, a good ol' Wisconsin casserole, glutted with cheese, in the oven and a salad chopped to bits in a bowl on the counter with a bottle of Thousand Island standing guard at its side. He banged a pop-open cardboard roll on the countertop and dispersed biscuit dough in slabs across a cookie sheet. Who owned a cookie sheet? If it came with a suite and suitemates, maybe, but a guy who bought a cookie sheet? Where did this person come from?

I opened the refrigerator door, looking for beer. I wanted my cheap beer. And a couple shots of tequila. I saw only a slender green bottle of white wine. I reached for it, looking at its label— Gewürztraminer, ick—and stood. Carl approached me from behind, encircling my waist with his slim, unscarred arms, and kissed the side of my neck. He had tried to kiss me when we got in his car. As an excuse not to kiss him for real, I'd told him I tasted like cigarettes. That I wanted to brush my teeth. "Hay is for horses." Jesus.

He pressed into me, the back of my skirt, and said in my ear, "I missed you so much. You look so sexy."

I held up the bottle. "You got a corkscrew?"

"Sure, I got a corkscrew," he said, attempting, it seemed, some sort of libidinous double entendre, pressing again.

How gross. "Where is it?" I moved toward the counter, half dragging him. I shrugged, trying to get him off. I should have asked him to drop me off at the dorms. My mistake. "Don't," I told him.

"You need to relax," he said good-naturedly.

"Fuck, yes," I said, and watched as he squinched his eyes for a flash of a second, as if my voice had hurt his ears.

I should have had an appetite. I hadn't eaten much for a long time. I'd bought some truckers' No-Doz at the Milwaukee bus stop, though, and now all I wanted was alcohol. At another time I'm sure I would have loved the smell of a bubbling casserole and baking biscuits that a perfectly good-looking Norwegian guy—wait, he was Scandinavian, right?—who was interested in sex with me had prepared all for my benefit. But I didn't give a shit. My hands were ice-cold, my feet frozen. I shivered.

"Aw," he said. "You've been away for too long. Look at you." He rubbed my arms vigorously.

I wanted to strangle him. Armies of ants made their way across my scalp. "Don't," I said again.

"You need a sweater," he said, and left for his bedroom.

Why would he persist? I opened drawer after drawer looking for a corkscrew when it dawned on me. He wanted to fuck. He wasn't outright asking for it, and he wasn't simply taking it the way the guys had in California, the way I'd allowed them to. At least the Californians were straightforward. Carl was *worming* his way to a fuck. Ew. "I'll cook for her and be nice and warm and then she'll give me what I want." I'd rather he just get it over with. I took off my clothes.

Over my shoulder I watched as he walked back into the kitchen with one of his thick-knitted fisherman sweaters. I turned away. Naked, I bent over his counter. I stared at the corner where the fake linoleum tile backsplash met the side of the refrigerator and the avocado countertop and said, "Wanna fuck?" I just waited. I didn't hear anything. I'd expected him to drop to his knees or to unzip or to say something appreciative. Nothing.

Finally, as I thought about how clean his kitchen was, wondering how often he scrubbed his counter and what sort of cleaning products he used (did he buy bottles of Mr. Clean?), he said, "Maybe you should go."

He was rejecting me? Nobody in California had rejected me.

Carl had no idea. None. Fuck him and his shitty Gewürztraminer. I turned around. "You know what, you Midwestern pathetic piece of shit? You have no idea. Fucking none."

He looked at me oddly. He said, "I think maybe I do, Lisa."

I picked up my clothes off the floor. I didn't like the idea of walking back to the dorms with my suitcase in the snow. I needed sustenance. "I'm taking the wine. Fucker."

"Maybe you should take some food too."

"Fuck your food. You don't want to fuck me. You just lost out, Carl. You blew it big time, baby."

"I 'blew it big time, baby'? What're you on?"

"Dick. Fucking dick."

"What happened, Lisa?"

I stepped into my skirt, forgoing the stockings that provided zero warmth anyway. "Nothing fucking happened. I'm tired. All you want is to get yours anyway. Or am I wrong? I dare you to tell me you didn't want to fuck. I fucking dare you."

"What the hell happened?"

"Fuck off. Leave me the fuck alone."

"Obviously that wasn't the case while you were away."

"What?" I pulled my T-shirt on and stuffed my bra in my jacket pocket, stepping into my boots without relacing or tying them.

"Take a look at yourself."

"What?"

"Forget it."

"Fuck you too," I said, clomping into the living room and hefting my suitcase. "Have a nice supper. Asshole." I slammed the door. On his stoop I opened my suitcase and nestled the wine bottle inside.

The walk back to the dorms was a brutal one. I fell once on an icy patch of sidewalk, slipping forward and landing hard on the ball of one hand, my other wrist twisting, stuck in the handle of my suitcase. I was miserable and missed the California weather. I wondered what Celeste was doing. She'd probably crawled out of bed a few hours before dinner. She'd be all steamy and clean from the shower, nice to her suitemates. She'd probably have cooked dinner. Something good. Something without pounds of cheese. Not a casserole. Not some pale-assed salad with Thousand Island.

I followed the curve of the lake. Sucking up my pride, I eventually bent over to tie my boots. A pickup truck clanking along with loud snow chains honked and kept on going. I looked for the high-rise dorm lights, but couldn't see them. The trees were bare, my feet numb. I should've been able to see them. You could usually see the dorms half a mile away at night. A few blocks away finally, my hands alternately screaming in the cold as I switched the suitcase from side to side, I began to fear what I thought I remembered: The dorm didn't reopen for another two days.

By the time I got to the front of my building, I knew it. I tried the door anyway, pounded on the heavy glass. I sat down leadenly on my suitcase and started crying. Like a baby. Like a stupid fucking baby. I hated myself for it. I didn't know anybody else besides Carl and his parents who lived outside the dorms. Few cars and no cabs drove by in the dark, the snow heavy, everybody else holed up, cozy squirrels inside their tree forts. My cheeks burned from my crying. I'd never been so cold.

Pub. I had no choice. I needed shelter. I sniffled, shots of ice to the brain, wiped my face on my cold leather jacket, and set out. Six blocks. I could do it. With each painful step into the wind, I hated Madison, Wisconsin, more. I hated the hemp and candle stores, the bicycle shops, the vegetarian restaurants. I said it as I tromped, as I stepped in snow higher than the tops of my boots. "I hate the bookstore. I hate the mailbox. I hate the co-op. I hate the fancy-ass diner. I hate the crystals store. I hate the fucking library." Up ahead, the Hound's Tooth glowed in the night. I knew they'd take my ID there. I just wanted heat.

I stomped my boots inside the door. The warmth hit me in a wave and my knees actually buckled. I regained my composure, but not before a guy at the bar had noticed. He stood. "You all right?"

I looked. He was a regular customer of my speed dealer. I recognized his face. "Hey," I said, my cold ears burning. I dropped my snowy suitcase on the floor.

"I know you," he said. "You're the crazy girl. Hi, crazy girl."

"That's what you call me?"

"That's what Andy calls you. You know." He seemed almost apologetic. "Your hair and all." He checked out my all. "Aren't you frozen?"

I gave him a look.

"Of course you are. Sorry."

I glanced around. All I could feel was my exposed skin thawing, not a particularly pleasant sensation. The bar had maybe a dozen people in it. I should have reached up to the tip of one of my ears and cracked it off like a potato chip. Instead I said, "Buy me a drink."

"You look like you need one," the guy said.

"I do." We walked up to the bar.

"What's with the suitcase?"

"I forgot the dorms aren't open yet."

"Ooh. That's too bad."

"Yes."

"What's your poison?"

He'd never guess. "Tequila," I told him instead.

"Really?"

"Yeah."

"I've never met a, a woman who drinks tequila."

"Now you have," I said, smiling, lest he change his mind about buying. I took off my jacket before realizing I was carrying my bra rather than wearing it.

"Nice shirt."

"Mmm. Excuse me." I brought my jacket with me to the bathroom, leaving my suitcase to sweat, to be stolen if the guy so desired. In the mirror I looked pink and thin. I went into the stall to pee, sat, and suddenly understood what Carl had meant. Fuck. The bruises. I still had yellowing bruises on my sit bones from Lawrence. Worse still, I had full-blown finger bruises from What's-His-Face. Eight fingertips and two thumbs on my thighs. Fuck, fuck.

Oh, well.

I peed and went back out into the bar. Evidently the bartender didn't need to see my ID. A shot of tequila with a wedge of lime waited for me at the bar, along with my suitcase and the guy. I didn't think I knew his name. He obviously knew me only as the crazy girl. "Thanks." I gulped the tequila and felt the heat spread from my stomach as if I'd swallowed gasoline. Might as well have. I tried to remember what I'd eaten last. McDonald's? No. Oh, right. The Chik-a-Stiks I'd found and eaten at the bus stop in Milwaukee before the truckers' No-Doz. The Happy Meal was the day before.

"You want a beer?"

I nodded, then remembered my manners. "What's your name?"

"Bob."

"Hi, Bob. I'm the crazy girl." I laughed and felt the tequila sledgehammer into my head. "Lisa," I introduced myself. "Nice to meet you."

He shook my hand. "So it's a beer to chase that?"

"Yeah." I checked Bob out. He was baby-faced with thinning, curly orange hair. From what I remembered of him, chatting with my dealer, he was funny. But what else could you be when you had that Bozo thing going on?

He ordered two High Lifes. Right. Back in Miller country. "Cheers," he said, handing me a bottle and clinking his against it.

"Cheers." I had options. I did. I ran through them in my head. I could go to a hotel, call my father, and tell him what happened, sort of. Prepare him for the extra charges on the emergency credit card. I could call Carl and apologize. I could drink till closing time and then go to the twenty-four-hour coffee shop, then to the library all day and hold out till Hound's Tooth opened for happy hour and do the whole thing again for one more day. I had options. I did.

"What's your major?" I asked.

Bob was fine. He was fine. Eager and quick. His apartment was dirty, but warm as hell, the radiators broiling hot, ticking and clanking. My appetite came back at dawn. I minced naked around the dirty clothes on the floor and out toward what Bob had called his *cocina Americana.* I didn't get it and I didn't ask. It was a closet kitchen. I looked in the dorm-sized fridge and found a block of cheese, a fucking hunk of moldy cheddar. The irony did not escape me.

When Bob was having sex with me, his curly orange pubic hair bumping me softly, his thin penis gently sliding in and out, in and out, I wondered how Celeste was doing. I would call her as soon as I could.

I hung in there till the dorms reopened. As long as I needed. I never even said hello to Bob on the street again.

You don't even know how you got here. Imagine a spaceship. Imagine a space creature with a purple club of a dick, hard and long as a femur. Shudder. Pick up a beer bottle that isn't yours and swig warm cigarette sludge. Squint in the dark against the noise. Look for her and the other somebodies you must have come with. Had to come with.

On stage a bleeding man bounces and sing-talks. Look at the veins bulging in his neck. Think baby snakes. Think tapeworms.

Smell this place you are in. Think dirty women. Think underpants. Think feet. Think cunnilingus breath and metal and unwashed hair and puke and smegma and a rained-on dog. Think dirt. Think wiped shit on a bathroom wall spelling WHAT. Think think think how you got here. Think go. Think find.

Wonder what is happening. Remember art.

$\mathcal{M}$Y FATHER offered to fly me home for a late New Year's visit the week before classes began. I considered the option but decided that I'd rather return with Celeste for double impact. I would have loved to see Hank, Mack. Ess and everybody else. I recognized my homesickness and hated myself for it. I missed Celeste the most. On a good day I trudged down to the dorm cafeteria at least once. I figured that with my limited activity I didn't need too much to sustain me. I'd carry miniature boxes of cereal back up for my dinner. Every morning when I woke in my single room and looked out at the gray sky, I came closer to what I'm sure you can already guess.

But I tried.

I had a few good internal struggles while reading Joyce for an upcoming class.

I began to imagine two different futures, my head splitting. In one I shriveled like something freeze-dried or salted, a filet of haddock, or maybe cod, with spiky black hair. People like Bob would pick me up and thaw me out occasionally, soak me in tequila. I would start to stink. In the other, I flourished like a tough plant, maybe a flowering agave. People like Papa Cherry and Lawrence would give me daily attention and I would smell all the sweeter as I grew bigger prickles.

Two weeks into the new semester the plan began to take a clear shape. As clear in my mind's eye as Hank's finished sculpture must have been in his when he started. I asked a few questions in the right places and found out that I could still get a 90 percent refund on my semester's tuition. I'd have a check for thousands of dollars! I called Celeste to tell her about my plan, about the agave future I would make come true.

Noah answered the phone. "Hey. You missed her by twenty-four hours," he said.

"What do you mean?"

"She got caught."

Shit! "Where is she?"

"We don't know, exactly."

"What do you mean?"

"Come on, Miss Madison. You know what the words 'We don't know, exactly' mean, don't you?"

Fuck him, the fucking snob. "What do you mean by '*exactly*'?"

"She told Lawrence she was going to LA. She didn't leave an address or phone number. Maybe Lawrence knows."

"Is he there?"

"No, he left, too."

"They left together?"

"No. He's just doing his usual coming and going, although I'm sure Tram gets more of his coming."

What an ass. "Is Tram there? Does she know?" I tried to keep my panic contained.

"Yeah, she's here. I don't think she knows, though. Do you want me to ask her?" He yelled out her name. Somebody else yelled something back. Honey, I thought. "She's in the bathroom," he said. "I can go ask her through the door. Hang on." I heard him set down the receiver and walk away.

What the hell had Celeste done, and why hadn't she called me? Certainly she must be planning on calling me. She wouldn't just disappear, would she? No, I told myself. No, she wouldn't do that. She was just getting settled, wherever she was in LA.

"No," Noah said. "She doesn't know either."

"What exactly did Celeste say? What happened exactly?"

"She left us a note. We were in class."

"When?"

"Yesterday. She said she loved us and hoped that we'd get a better suitemate than her. That's all. And that she was moving south."

"That's exactly what the note said?"

"Lisa, I think if we knew we'd tell you." Silence.

"Who was she with the last week?"

"Nobody, really."

"What?"

"Nobody but us. Honestly, Lisa. I'm sure she'll contact you. She's a bright girl. Very bright, actually. Did you know she didn't even fail any of her classes? She missed over a month, and she still passed them all."

"How do you know that?"

"One of Joaquim's friend's works in records. I don't know if he was the one to blow the whistle or not."

"Can I talk to Joaquim?"

"Look. Nobody knows anything else." He paused. "Joaquim is busy right now."

I stumbled. I felt like I might fall. "Will you call me if you hear from her? Please?"

"Sure, Lisa. We'll call you. Take care—"

"Don't you need my phone number? Noah, wait!"

"Hey. Calm down. I've got a pen."

I gave him my number and made him repeat it back to me. "Please tell all the suitemates to tell her to call me if she calls, okay?"

"I don't think she will, but yeah. I mean, of course, we'll tell her."

"Oh, god. Please, okay?"

"Okay, okay."

"Why don't you think she'll call?"

"Lisa."

"Will you tell Lawrence to call me as soon as he comes back? Please, Noah?" I heard the desperation in my voice. I couldn't help it. I couldn't control it at all. "Please?"

"Yes. I'll tell Lawrence."

"Please."

"Yes, Lisa. I'm going to go now, okay? Bye." He hung up.

"No." Oh. Oh, god. Oh, no. I needed to book a flight. I needed to pack. I needed to get a tuition refund. When had I talked to her last? It'd been, what? A week? Too long. We'd never gone so long. She had said things "were a-brewin'." But when I'd asked her what she meant, she wouldn't tell me exactly.

"I don't want to jinx it, Lis."

"Jinx what?" I tried.

"Please. I'll tell you if and when it happens."

Now I sat in my dorm room thinking I should have forced the subject. What did I need to do?

One. I had to get the money first. And I had to drop out officially; that way if I ever decided to go back . . . I knew what I could do: I could call the circumstances a family emergency. I pulled on my big workman boots and down jacket, wrapped my head up burka-style with a double-wide black scarf, and hit the campus. Four hours later I'd been promised an emergency check by the next afternoon.

Two. I hiked to the UW Madison travel agency and for an arm and a leg found a one-way flight for the next evening via Minneapolis–St. Paul. My father's credit card went through, so I'd get there, at least. I hoofed it back to my room.

Three. I called Andy, the speed dealer. He made a delivery.

Four. I decided I needed to tell my brother at least. I would make him swear not to tell our father until I told him myself. Just not right away. I needed to try to find her first.

"Bullshit!" David blurted on the other end of the phone line.

"David . . ." I heard our father rumble in the background, then hack his cigarette cough.

"Really, Larry," I heard some woman say, "you should stop smoking so much. For David's sake at least."

"Who's that?" I asked.

"Let me switch phones," David said. A series of clunks and clicks, David yelling, "I got it! Hang up!" Another click.

"Who was that?"

"That's Marla. Dad's girlfriend."

"No way!"

"Yes way."

"What's she like?"

"Didn't he tell you about her?"

Had he? "I don't think so."

"He told me he invited you home."

"He did. But I don't think he told me about—what's her name again?"

"Marla."

"What's Marla like?"

"You know your typical blonde bimbo?"

"Yeah?"

"Well, she's not like that."

"David, tell me!"

"I can't believe you're dropping out. That's so lame, Lisa."

"Not forever. Celeste has *disappeared*. I have to go find her. She's the one who's really dropped out. I'm just on emergency leave for a semester."

"But it's not really an emergency."

"Maybe it is."

"It's *Celeste*."

"What does that mean?"

"You know what I mean," he said. "It's, it's *Celeste*. The *goddess*."

"Well, then her ugly friend Chopped Liver is going to go get her."

"That's not what I meant. I'm not calling you chopped liver."

"Whatever. Look. I just wanted to tell somebody where I'd be. Please don't tell him. I'll get around to it when I'm there. I don't want him to worry more than he needs to."

"Does he need to?"

"No."

"Li—"

"What's Marna like?"

"Marla. She's all right. A little bossy. Up-to-date."

"Is she pretty?"

"Not exactly. She has kids, too. Two. Remember Joel Schumacher?"

"No."

"Never mind, then. That's her son. And Dana. She's divorced."

"He's not."

"Does it matter?"

Of course it didn't. David knew I knew that. "Duh. Don't tell, okay?"

"How can somebody get in touch with you?" he asked, his voice serious for the first time.

"I don't know." I hadn't thought about it. "Okay. Um. Here. I'll give you Celeste's old suitemates' number. I'll stay in touch with them."

"Who?"

"Where I was this Christmas."

"Oh. We have that number."

"Well, that's how you can find me."

He paused. "Lisa?"

"Yeah, David?"

"Be careful. Don't do the really bad drugs, okay?"

He could be sweet. He really could. "Keep studying."

"Yeah, right. Look where it'll get me."

"Take care of him." I hadn't called him "Dad" since the phone-call mess with Mr. Diamond years previous, when Celeste and I were in trouble. When we'd gotten hot-'n'-heavy at Hank's. I had a pang of nostalgia, regret, something all of a sudden.

"Like I don't already do everything," David answered.

"Okay. Bye, then."

"Okay."

"*Bye.*"

"Bye." He hung up. I wouldn't talk to him for ages.

I told my RA that I had an emergency. He agreed to send my two boxes of cold-weather clothes and books and papers home for me the day after I left in exchange for my room stuff, the fridge and bedding and stuff. I bought some beer from the beer guy two floors down and swallowed a speckled pink, wondering how I'd go about finding Celeste when I got to LA, where I'd stay. I could look up Papa Cherry. Somehow. He might know something or put me up or both. For all I knew, that's where Celeste was staying anyway. I needed a decent plan. I paced and paced and drank a few beers, smoked a cigarette, waited for the phone to ring, and then the sun came up.

Twenty-four hours, I thought. Only twenty-four hours late. But who knew? Maybe I was already months late. It's hard to say, you know?

The plane to Minneapolis–St. Paul was a toy plane. It sat twelve. I'd had no idea it was so small when I booked the flight. It bounced through the air. You couldn't hear yourself think. I smoked three cigarettes in the backseat. Nearly everybody did. And drank. Millers all around. I was happy to get off. On the next flight I daydreamed about the beach. Last visit I'd only seen the beach and the crashing Pacific from the back of the band's station wagon. None of the guys had wanted to stop and get wet. I guess it's the same everywhere, if you grow up there. Maybe the Grand Canyon becomes old hat too if you live there.

LAX was crowded. I didn't even want to breathe. I was afraid I'd book the next flight back to Kansas City and beg Hank to stay at his house. The loose "plan" I'd finally worked out involved getting a decent hotel room by the week in Venice. I liked the look of the place in movies I'd seen. Not rich. Sorta cool. I'd have to ask a cabbie to take me to a decent, halfway-cheap hotel. Or a motel. I didn't exactly understand the difference.

I wondered how much a cab ride to Venice would cost. I'd cleared out my checking account before leaving Madison and had $356 cash exactly. If I spent a dollar a day I could stay almost a year. I also had the family credit card that might get me through the first week at a hotel before my father canceled it. And, last but not least,

I had a check from the University of Wisconsin Madison for $4,671.13. I decided not to pay attention to the cents. I'd find her.

Why I scanned the crowd looking for a familiar face as I followed the signs to baggage claim, I'm not sure. I needed to quit doing that. You don't know anybody in a new city, but suddenly everybody you set eyes on looks exactly like somebody you know or used to know, or something about his walk or her hair makes you think that person *could* be somebody you know. Or used to know. I felt muffled in wool, pale, out-of-it among the hordes of pretty people. I needed an X-Ray at my side. Even a Gigantus Khan would do. A little companionship. A big dick on a little guy. Solidarity. I told myself that I should call Hank and fill him in. Maybe he'd even heard from her.

You have to try hard not to be intimidated by LA. I put up my best front. Between the celebrity treatment and the climate, the cars and the temperament, the apprehension factor loomed large. At the luggage carousel, I stood next to a couple passengers I recognized from my flight. Soon a few more joined us. We watched as an ill-taped cardboard box circled and circled. On its tenth round I considered claiming it. What would everyone do? Would they accuse me of stealing? What could I get? What was in the box? My compulsion knocked loudly.

Have you ever sat on the rooftop edge of a big building, your feet dangling over? What did you feel? I've always wanted to throw myself off. Not because I've ever actually wanted to die, but simply because pushing myself over seemed to be what should be done under the circumstances. What begged to be done. It's hard to explain. I've had it since I was a kid. The urge to touch priceless art. The urge to staple my own finger. It was an abandoned box. A forgotten, unwanted box. I could offer the box a home. I could take it off the endless carousel. I stepped forward and picked it up; I turned it over in my hands, looking for a clue to its insides. There were no words. I set it back down on the carousel.

"I was about to do the exact same thing," a man in a business suit unafraid to talk to me said, kind of smiling.

Eventually our luggage came pooping out of the black hole in the ceiling. The box continued its circling. I hauled my suitcase off, squared my shoulders, and turned toward the automatic doors opening and closing onto the sunny smog beyond. I'd find her. I looked back at the carousel, trying to see the box. I could still go back and get it. I don't know why I wanted it so badly. It was just a stupid box. And it wasn't mine. I stepped outside.

Rows of cabs idled at multiple curbs. I wanted a nice-looking driver. Instead I had to go stand in line by a glass booth with a bossy black woman inside. People would tell her where they were going and she'd point out a cab for them. The big yellow inch-worms of taxis crept forward.

When it was my turn I told the woman, "Venice."

She looked me up and down, plain disgust on her dark face. "That one," she said, jabbing her index finger. I dragged my suit-case over to the cab she'd pointed at. I moved to the back, waiting for the driver to get out and put my luggage in the trunk. Instead the trunk latch popped. Through the rear windshield I watched the driver take a drag off his cigarette.

I could do this. I could find her. Celeste would be worth all of it.

The driver took me miles out of the way, I thought, the meter ticking past thirty dollars. I had no choice. Finally he dropped me at an ugly two-story motel the color of Pepto-Bismol. I paid for a week—$115—and asked for a second-floor room. A narrow bal-cony ran the length of the building, and if I stood on my toes, I could see the ocean. Even when I couldn't see it, I could smell it. I didn't miss Madison. My room, tidy, decorated in textured gold wallpaper and a nubby gold bedspread, fit the bill. I hadn't expected much. The bathroom sported teal tile, the kitchenette a hand-lettered sign saying, NO HOT PLATES.

Now what? I decided to see if Lawrence had resurfaced at the suite in Berkeley. The room's phone had no dial tone. I went back to the front desk, where the nice fat lady behind it told me that the pay phone on the corner worked. "You're a little peaked," she told me in a strange accent. "Go take a nice walk by the beach. Get some fresh air." She puffed on a brown cigarette that smelled like pipe tobacco.

"Do you have change for a five-dollar bill?"

She shook her head. "The laundromat has a machine," she said. "Out the door, left two blocks. Nice and close. Just down Mildred."

"Who?"

"That's the name of our street, little thing."

"Oh."

"You dress like you're tryin' to be tough, but watch out for yourself, all right?"

Why had I thought beach towns were safe? Weren't they? "Thanks."

I went walking. My years of French would do me no good here. On the way to the laundromat I saw two groups of not-nice Mexican-looking guys and a lot of beat-up cars. A teenage mother with three kids. She couldn't have been any older than I was, hollering at two and carrying a little one. An old black woman with bright yellow hair. "Hair is good, hair is good," I thought she mumbled as I passed. I got five dollars' worth of quarters and headed back toward the pay phone. I decided if I passed another punk on the street that I would ask him—most likely a him— where a good show was. I had to start somewhere.

I didn't see any. I called the suite. The phone rang and rang. Finally somebody answered breathlessly. "Hello?"

"It's Lisa. Celeste's friend. Who's this?"

"Hey, Lisa. It's Nanci." Nanci with an I. "What's up?"

"Is Lawrence back? Has anybody heard from Celeste?" A horn honked. A loud motorcycle rumbled by.

"—o."

"What?"

"Lawrence was here a while ago."

"Is he still there?"

"I don't know."

"Would you check? Please?"

She huffed a little. "Hang on." She set her receiver down heavily. Another motorcycle. Nanci with an I yelled something in the background.

"Hello?" It was Lawrence.

"Lawrence! Where is she? I'm here. I can go get her."

He laughed a big laugh at my expense.

"Shut the fuck up. Do you know where she is? Lawrence!"

"Where who is?"

"Fuck you."

"You should be nice, you little slut, or I might not tell you."

I would grovel if it got me any closer to Celeste. "Please?"

"'Exactly' I really don't know. Papa's got himself a rich friend, though. They were up here visiting again last week. We had a good ol' time."

"Who? What's his name?"

"He drives a DeLorean. Everybody calls him DeLo. A real pretty boy but crazy as shit. You should meet him. How's your little pussy?"

"Fine. DeLo lives here?"

"Where are you and your little pussy, Lisa?"

"Venice Beach."

"Now what did you go and do, you dumb little pussy? You didn't drop out, too, did you?"

"I'm here, aren't I?" The phone asked for eighty more cents.

"Aw, damn it." He actually sounded genuine. "Why'd you go and do something dumb like that? You dumb little pussy-slut."

"I was just following my role model. *You*, Lawrence."

He woofed a fake laugh. "You so funny, funny like Charie Chan! Look—my money's on the rich dude. He fell for little Miss Celie pretty hard."

"What's his real name?"

"No idea."

"What's Papa's real name?"

"Couldn't tell ya. Sure you don't want to come back up here? You suck some mighty fine dick, you dumb little pussy-slut."

Lawrence lucked out, being hundreds of miles away: I had good sharp teeth. "She hasn't called there then is what you're telling me?"

"Not that I know of. Maybe she called you, since you're *in love*."

"Fuck you."

"I warned you, didn't I? You use profanity one more time and I'll just have to hang up this phone."

"Please, Lawrence. What's Papa's band's name again?"

"What're you gonna give me if I tell you?"

"What do you want?" I felt a thousand years old just then. And I couldn't believe I couldn't remember. How could I not know? They had to have said it a dozen times back in Tijuana.

"I want some dumb little slut pussy."

"Fine."

"Fine what?"

What did he want me to say, "sir"? "What?"

"Fine what?"

"I don't know what you want me to say, Lawrence." Two Vespas zoomed by, loud as lawnmowers.

He waited.

"What?" I asked.

He sighed. "You're just a little too serious for me, pussy-slut. They're called Jenny's Dead. Got it?"

"Who's Jenny?"

"I don't have a clue," he said. "But whoever she is, she's dead, huh?"

I asked the nice fat front-desk lady if she knew where people like me hung out.

"You all are just lost. If you get to know you, you can be real sweet."

I waited for her to say more.

"Down on the boardwalk. And Ren. Ren cleans for me. I guessed nobody else would hire him with the mohawk haircut and all."

"My name's Lisa," I told her.

"I know that, silly. You filled out the rental form."

"Right." What was her name?

"Everybody calls me Madam, like a name, what with some of your neighbors and all."

I was so lost. "I should call you Madam?"

She smiled. I could see a molar had been pulled, way back in her mouth. "You can call me Teeny, Miss Lisa Smith."

"Lisa."

"All right then."

"I'm going to the boardwalk."

"Be careful."

"I will." I couldn't call her Teeny.

"That's a good girl."

I went upstairs and made my hair bigger, overkilled on black eyeliner. I made fists. I looked at myself in the mirror and told my reflection it wouldn't be long. I considered calling my brother and giving him the name of the motel. I considered calling Hank. Frowning, I decided I did look a touch peaked. All the better to get what I needed.

Maybe I needed to call everybody who might have heard from her. Well, I could hardly call her parents for the risk of it, but she wouldn't have called them anyway. My dorm phone had been disconnected by then, and I'd packed the phone itself to be shipped home. Would she call my house? Would she call Hank? I didn't think in my heart of hearts that she'd do either, but I could try. Likely she'd get settled somewhere and call my dorm room to tell me where she was, only to find out that my number had been disconnected. I thought about the millions of people in Los Angeles.

I set out to locate Papa. I figured he was my best lead. Celeste wouldn't have called anybody else. She had enough sense not to scare my father or appear needy to Hank. That's what I deduced. That's where my big-time detective work led me.

How would I carry my jacket walking down a beach boardwalk? Maybe I shouldn't bring it. Maybe just hanging off my hand, swinging a little, or over my shoulder? Fuck it. I threw it on the bed, took off my shoes, and switched to old, ripped blue jeans.

One of the same pairs I wore my sophomore year of high school. They were finally faded enough, the knee blown out on one leg.

I was trying too hard. I was nervous.

I was more than a little lost.

Madam Teeny said good-bye to me when I left. She said I looked better already. "Some of that good ocean air. Be careful."

I headed to the coast, to the edge of America. I'd never put a foot in the Pacific. I decided I couldn't wait any longer. Why do we do that? Not experience what we can when we can? We're there, within thirty yards or thirty feet or thirty football fields of incredible, beautiful, natural treasures, and we just sit dumbly in a car. Look out at stuff like we're watching a movie. Somewhere between meeting the now-dead Brooklyn and walking down this boardwalk in Venice Beach, California, I'd decided that there was something to be said for living life. Truly. You know, by the horns and all that. Only Celeste and I actually had. Grabbed.

These days, watching my daughter throw a frisbee with her friends at the park, I try to explain the scars and whatever else the other moms notice about me. To the moms who have brand-new, fresh, just-picked kidlets with their neutrally colored buggies and shit, the ones who are still sort of surprised to see somebody like me with a kid—the ones who are curious and young and desperate for conversation with an adult who isn't their absent other—I say that I had been a younger somebody interested in being able to speak from experience before I said anything. I wanted to know what I would be judging. Bring on the drugs, I had said, though not to the nursing mother at my side. Bring on the poverty. Jesus, I'd grown up so privileged, it was pathetic. Bring on the dark side. Try to *kill* the meat that you eat. Try as I might, though, with some infant gurgling and snorking at a tit next to me, I could never exactly explain it. Our decision to go where we did, that is. You can't, really. Explain it. You try.

Despite all my efforts to thwart the kid in my bones, to control the Midwesterner escaped on the sands for the first time, the beach captured me. It got me. I can't tell you how happy I was to have left my leather jacket in my motel room. Oh! Sand between your toes feels so good, even if you have pitch-black manic hair.

The waves spoke my name. The beach had lost its tanners, the midday sun long gone. I zombie-walked to the water, a mindless lead fleck to a magnet. I could have been approached from behind by an entire gang of unsavories and I wouldn't have noticed. The scent! The sound! The warm nothingness and everythingness about it. The ocean. I felt home, dumb as it sounds.

Now I just needed her.

I strode out to halfway up my thighs, grinning hugely at the speckling of late surfboarders and boats. Above the horizon, the sun was a hand width away from setting. A few hours before dark. Down the beach I saw the Santa Monica Pier and the Ferris wheel. She could be riding it. She could be walking near here. She could be on one of the fancy boats out in the water. The magnitude of my search threatened to undo me. I walked out of the water and along on the harder wet sand for a while, moving slowly in the direction of the Ferris wheel. Clumps of seaweed with onionlike pods were strewn for miles, a few crawling with tiny crabs or stinking with dead fish. Seagulls cawed to each other, at me. I knew I was a long way from home.

I walked for probably fifteen minutes before a tall fuchsia mohawk caught my eye. It stood on a guy in a group of people I thought I might ask about Papa and his band. "Hey," I said when I got close. They turned their heads, but nobody answered. They hadn't been watching the shore. I may have surprised a few. Every one of the five of them blatantly checked me out, their chins and eyes rising and lowering and rising again. Four guys, one girl. She glared.

"Hey," I tried again in greeting.

Still no response, but one darkly tanned, short, short-haired guy jerked his chin at me as some sort of indication that I should continue speaking. What—they were some kind of sign-language punks?

"I just moved to town."

Nothing.

"I have some friends here, but I don't have their phone number. They're in a band."

The mohawk raised and lowered his eyebrows quickly with half-lidded eyes in a gesture of so-fucking-what?

"Jenny's Dead," I said.

"I know them," a third guy in a plain white T said. "North Hollywood."

"Do you know where I could find them? Do you have a number?"

"Who d'you know?"

"Papa—Papa Cherry—X-Ray. All of them."

"Where you from?" Short Hair asked.

What should I say? I needed to be smart. "Bay Area," I said.

A few subtle nods. They didn't question me. "Naw," White T said. "I don't know them good like that. Just know the ass-wipes a little."

I nodded like I understood they were ass-wipes, like I hadn't slept with all of them. I guess the one fact didn't preclude the other. I'd try another way. "Any of you know DeLo?"

"Hoooo . . ." Mohawk yowled. "He's a rich motherfucker."

"And I'd fuck his mother," White T said.

"Fuck, yeah," the girl agreed, which made the guys all laugh.

They obviously knew DeLo. "A friend of mine—she's hangin' out with him right now."

"Up in the Hills? Idn't she the high-priced cunt."

Did they think they could shock me? I'd show them it wasn't possible. "No more than me," I said.

The girl sniffed. She had low, loose tits in her tank. A no-threat girl. "Huh," she said, scanning my front again.

"Anybody have DeLo's number?"

"Who's looking?" Mohawk asked.

"I'm Lisa," I said, and took a few steps forward, closer. "Li'l Lisa, Papa calls me."

"Yeah," White T said. "Sounds like him."

"You know how to get in touch with DeLo?"

"No," Mohawk said. "But I might know somebody who does. At a show tonight."

"Where?" I asked, trying hard not to sound too eager.

"Here," Short Hair said. "Venice."

The one guy who hadn't talked yet, a small, tight-bodied guy, said, "Stick around. We'll take you." Right away, the way the others reacted to him, I knew he was the boss.

"Much appreciated," I told him, then looked down at my bare feet, my wet jeans. The boss followed my look.

"Where're you campin'?" he asked.

"Up on Ma . . ." God, what was the name of the street again? "Ma—Mildred."

"Mamildred," Mohawk said, and they chuckled.

People were really the same everywhere, you know?

We were on foot. The five of them followed me back to my motel room before the show. I tried to avoid Madam at the front desk, but she was gone anyway, a thin, balding man in her place. I thought about the sayings you learn as a kid, the one about the eighty-inch-wide bride, the skinny-as-a-broom groom. I smiled. We'd bought beer at the 7-11 with my fake ID. You could always buy beer friends, I'd remembered. Two twelve-packs of Budweiser seemed to put me in their favor once and for all.

I shivered. After the sun went down, the beach had cooled fast, the warm air turning chill and damp. The constant breeze made my ocean-facing ear ache. Inside my motel room I lugged my suitcase off of the bed so they could sit. I hadn't even unpacked. I opened it on the floor as the others immediately made themselves at home, opening the mini fridge, turning on the TV, picking up the phone receiver and noticing the lack of a dial tone.

I'd learned their names. The Swing Low Sweet Chariot girl was Candy, because she was supposed to have a sweet pussy—I supposed despite her less-than-sweet-looking tits. White T was Whitey, easy enough to remember, a Jim or John or Joe White. Mohawk was Boo Boo. Short Hair was Mike. And Boss Man was

Jesus. He had a huge cross tattooed on his back. Boo Boo said that Jesus had found the Way to survive prison. A matter of necessity, evidently. I would have guessed he was too young for prison, but small people can be deceiving. He could have bought the beer, I thought. I needed to watch my money.

I pulled out a blue skirt and my combats, and wondered whether it'd be stupid for me to enter the bathroom to change while they all took up residence in my room. I decided to change my pants in front of them, in the corner, sort of pretending that none of them would care.

And they didn't. They acted like it, anyway. But you could tell how they held themselves a little still as I unzipped and took off my jeans, the way they remained so engaged in exactly what they were doing, that they did actually notice. Ha! I figured I could fit into their tiny little world as well as anybody.

You always had to prove you had balls. I had gigantic ones, despite what my nickname might lead them to believe. That's what I told myself. And that's how you get them, anyway. Tell yourself you have balls, big balls, over and over. Big balls. Big balls. It works. Trust me.

The person who Boo Boo thought might have DeLo's number didn't show up. Other people there knew DeLo, too, but nobody had his number. They thought he might actually come. He didn't. I waited till the bitter end, and then I set my sights on Jesus.

THE RAMONES

LOS ANGELES, APRIL '83

Fuck the fact that they're the granddaddies. Their long hair looks stupid.

O<small>N THE</small> third day I found her. As I suspected he could have done within minutes of my meeting him, Jesus made some calls, got DeLo's number, rolled over, and handed me his phone. "Dial," he said in his usual direct way. "Whoever answers, ask for Celeste."

I sat up and hung my legs over the edge of the bed. A woman who wasn't Celeste answered. My heart beat madly, pounding in my neck. "May I speak to Celeste?"

"Who's calling?"

"Lisa. Lisa Smith."

"Oh! My, yes. One moment, please." I heard footsteps, definitely high heels, moving away across a hard floor.

And then there she was again. She *was* again. "Hello?"

"Celeste?"

"Lisa?"

"Where are you?"

"Lisa? Lisa?! Where are *you*?!"

"I'm here," I said. "LA."

"What?!"

Jesus walked out of the room. "In LA. Venice. Venice Beach."

"I called and called Madison, your number. You weren't there, it just rang, and then finally I got the no-longer-in-service message. I wanted to call your dad but I was worri— You know. I wasn't sure if you hadn't just taken a little trip or moved in with—what's his name—with Eric? Is he with you?"

"Carl? No. Where are you?"

"You called me."

"I don't even know where I called, Celeste." I looked around at Jesus' spare bedroom, the small dresser, nothing on the floor but my clothes.

"I met a guy, Lis."

"DeLo."

"How'd you know?"

"Celeste, I'm here to find you. Well, I mean to move out here. Both. You know what I mean."

"Really?" I thought the sound I heard was her smiling. "Really?"

Now if I tell you this part and you don't believe me, I can sort of understand. Not only did everything take place years ago, but these events took place out in California, under the regular influence of many illegal substances and the perfect portion of sky, the right sun and the right moon and the right span of earth. You know. California. That right span of earth that people said would someday break off in an earthquake and fall into the water. That one.

Jesus borrowed the neighbor's car and we drove away from the water. DeLo did indeed, as Jesus and his friends had said, live up in the sky. Well, the Hollywood Hills, closer to heaven than where the rest of us resided. The house that Jesus and I arrived at was a castle. Celeste sat on the broad stone steps waiting, wringing her hands. She jumped up when she saw me in the passenger seat through the windshield and nearly got herself run over, Jesus stomping on the brakes.

I whipped open the door and we collided. We hugged, hard enough to hurt. I suppose we stopped just short of kissing each other. Rib bumped rib. I wanted to take her face in my hands and slap her. I wanted to tell her that she'd been very, very bad. Instead I cried like some lucky sap at the lost and found. Celeste laughed and wiped my face. "Stop," she said, smiling. "I'm fine."

I smiled and remembered myself enough to introduce Jesus,

who still sat in the car behind the steering wheel, the Datsun idling poorly. "Celeste, Jesus; Jesus, Celeste."

"Hey."

"Hey."

"You can park over there," she directed him, pointing to a cul-de-sac for cars. He could pull up between a Rolls-Royce and a Jag, or take the space next to one of three identical DeLoreans. He chose the first. Both Celeste and I stood and watched. When Jesus killed the ignition, she said, "I can't believe you're here. For good?"

I looked around. "Well—"

"You could stay here with me," she said. "There's so much room. I'd love the company."

Who was she, Rapunzel locked up in a tower? I looked at the gleaming stone house, at the pillars and palms. I'd be "company"? The Datsun door opened with a creak. I saw with one look at Jesus' face that he knew before I did what I was going to do.

We went inside, up through that stunning house, across all of the marble floors, past room after room of white and gold, white and silver, white and cream and ecru. The same soft music played everywhere, a duet for cello and violin. I looked for speakers, for speaker wire. I recognized a soft-colored Hals, a delicate Delaroche, an Ingres. On the staircase wall hung a large portrait of DeLo's mother, a beautiful movie star from the fifties. She'd obviously made a ridiculous amount of money. Or married into it. Or been born into it. Or been given it by admirers. In the portrait, she was nearly as beautiful as Celeste. We went up the stairs, down another corridor, and through a pair of giant pocket doors. Celeste had her own suite, two sitting rooms and a bedroom, a dressing room, a bathing room, a room containing nothing but a toilet and a bidet.

In the first sitting room, an enormous peach space that made Celeste glow, we sipped champagne—I'm not joking—and ate caviar and watercress on crackers thin as communion wafers. Jesus sat quietly, knocking back the Dom Pérignon, forgoing the snacks. Celeste broke open a jeweled box after we nibbled like mice and used a small silver spoon to scoop out at least three grams of cocaine. "Dinner is served," she said. She cut out a portion and drew perfect lines with a blade directly on the mirrored top of the glass coffee table. "Dig in." She handed me a short gold straw. I didn't need to be offered twice. Jesus followed.

I looked at Celeste and the room. We would catch up shortly, the cocaine and champagne loosening our tongues, but for a few moments longer I tried to piece together the puzzle. Her hair was pale pink now, the color of bubble gum. She dressed the same, her perfectly lithe legs disappearing into a pair of men's old blue jeans, her lean torso, leaner now, barely covered with what had to be a kid's faded T-shirt with the letters KROQ printed across the front, stretched prettily across her chest. I recognized her as the Celeste I'd known for years, and then looked again, blinked, and she was gone, replaced by a stranger. I blinked and blinked till I made a movie, till the persistence of vision kicked in and they became the same, singular beauty, the one Celeste.

We stayed up all night, snorting lines and drinking champagne. I asked where DeLo was. Celeste said that he might stay away because we were there. I asked what she meant. She shrugged and said she thought he might be in a different room of the house. Around six in the morning Jesus left. Near ten, Celeste drove me back to my motel in one of the DeLoreans, no different from either of the others except for the license plate. I packed up while Celeste looked around the room. I twisted my toothpaste cap and bagged dirty socks. She opened the mini fridge and took a beer. She went outside and stood on the narrow balcony. I moved small stacks of clothes from the dresser to the bed and watched as she figured out how to rise on her tiptoes to see the water. "We should go to the beach," she said.

"Let's go up by the pier," I told her. "You shouldn't leave that car around here for long."

"Why?" I could tell she really didn't know; she never looked into any future except the kind one.

I was given my own suite, a smaller one down the hall. Only after living in his family's house for over four days did I meet DeLo. He entered Celeste's suite late one night as we lay around on the sofas wondering what to do.

By the light of the television, I could see he was intensely handsome in an early black-and-white-movie-star way. Chiseled jaw. Perfect posture. Liquid eyes. I thought he could be one of the most beautiful men I had ever seen. "Hello, Lisa," he said.

"Hello," I said, sitting up.

"Are you enjoying California?"

"Fuck, yeah," I said. "Thanks for the room—rooms."

"It's all Ma." He hummed the *Beverly Hillbillies* theme song. "She's from another place, you know. Celeste. I'm outta here. Might be back later. You around?"

"We were thinking of going out," she said. I expected her to ask if it was okay that we left, but she didn't. "Wanna meet us?"

She'd been so evasive, so closed about him, that I sat pretty stiffly, waiting for him to reveal something, anything about himself, but he didn't.

So Celeste and I lived in the mansion. It seemed to me that Celeste's beauty was enough to keep us there. I could find no other reason why anybody would house us for free in such a place. Obviously I was being allowed to stay because she was allowed to stay. Occasionally I felt the tiniest bit the servant girl, doing all our laundry, making social arrangements, but whatever tasks I'd been given or taken upon myself were far less than could be expected of the free-living friend of a beautiful concubine. And she was allowed to stay because DeLo believed her to be his.

I sent a postcard home to say that I was alive, well, and living in the Hills. After a while, I simply, actively, discontinued contact. When you lived the life that Celeste did, that we did, you could do things like that. I deposited my tuition refund check but rarely took out any money. DeLo left Celeste cash on her dresser several times a week for her to do with whatever she wanted. She always shared with me.

Nobody mistook us for each other anymore from behind or in passing. You would think that Celeste lived a chaste life, one filled with meditation, high colonics, and wheatgrass, the way she began to burn so brightly. Every abuse that she inflicted upon herself seemed only to serve as some special tonic, some magical powder. Her eyes glittered, and her body—her body radiated.

I kept her as close as I could. If Celeste were staying with those of us domesticated enough to understand captivity, you could say that she had too much wolf in her.

Close, close as I could.

Maybe two months after I arrived, she began to cheat on DeLo. We would go out to see music, and somewhere along the line she decided that DeLo wasn't her one desire. Desire wore a studded collar. Sometimes Desire wore self-inflicted scratches across his chest or blue jeans so dirty they were gray or his dead father's Vietnam dog tags. Once Desire wore a vibrating butt plug, she said, because she had asked him to. She'd never tried one before.

She always picked her men. She decided who Desire might be.

Through Lawrence and the Berkeley suite, Celeste's sisters eventually got hold of her whereabouts. As Mr. Diamond had sort of officially abandoned her, her sisters could come visit without repercussions on their end. They could keep secrets. All sisters can keep secrets.

Celeste's sisters arrived on the same flight and fell all over her at the airport, hugging and crying. Diana had not brought Jacob, as I'd hoped she would. I thought it might be wonderful to lay eyes on a child who might resemble his aunt Celeste. Rachel and Diana both gave me hugs as they said hello, but then virtually ignored me, hanging on Celeste and touching her face and little waist. Both of them had grown bigger, older. Life showed on them.

We'd driven one of the DeLoreans to pick them up, and when we lifted the doors, the sisters' mouths opened. "This is yours?" Rachel asked Celeste.

Celeste just shrugged. How could you explain? I suppose she could have said, "As long as he keeps me it's mine to drive," but that wouldn't have sounded too good, and she had a hard time lying. So she shrugged. We squashed in and headed back. If that had been their reaction to the car, then I knew how they would react upon seeing the house.

And they did. Celeste tried to downplay the place, but there was no getting around the fact that she—we—lived in a castle. She modestly pointed out a few of the great paintings while I noisily directed their attention every which way, making them look at the molding, the chandeliers, the inlays of this and that. You'd think I was the one fucking Pretty Boy for all the bragging I did on his house.

They both had only a weekend to visit. Diana bitched about her professor husband being too old and too incompetent to deal with Jacob for longer than two days. She grew red-faced as she related his constant need for naps and his addiction to hard candies she'd never heard of before they married, horehound drops and root-beer barrels. She swore the codger would choke Jacob with one and fail to administer the Heimlich properly. Rachel whined about her own husband constantly being sick, about how he got hives, was allergic to everything, how he'd lied to her about why he'd gone into environmental studies in the first place. She said he had some idiotic theory that the chemicals everywhere could make you allergic, sick, that you shouldn't dry-clean clothes, that you shouldn't use insecticides. And, she added, he claimed that the sun was dangerous. "The sun!" she practically spit. "Who's *allergic* to the sun?!"

Of course, Celeste and I couldn't really take Diana and Rachel to the shows and after-hours places we usually went. Celeste had gone to great pains to hide the drugs and stay relatively sober. She believed her sisters needed to carry home the news that she was prospering. That she was living the good life. Our hair alone had initially caused exclamations of disbelief, however, and we quickly understood the impossibility of introducing the sisters to any friends, much less DeLo. He gladly stayed away. I made up the lie that he had traveled to New York for a shoot. In fact, he looked good enough to be a model, I'd decided. So he could certainly be one for the purposes of hiding his utter insanity from Celeste's sisters.

I'd gotten to know DeLo slightly, primarily from watching him when he and Celeste and I went to hear a band together. He was every bit as crazy as his reputation, the frightening one that preceded him. Maybe it was his use of heroin that scared me most. Celeste swore to me that he didn't force it on her, and that he was able to function perfectly well. At night, anyway. She'd never even really seen him in daylight.

DeLo's mother was in Europe or somewhere.

Celeste's sisters seemed to buy the whole show, and they left laden with gifts that had been bought with all the money DeLo showered down on Celeste. I hoped they'd tell Mr. and Mrs. Diamond that both Celeste and I were living high on the hog, in the land of gold, surrounded by flowers and palms under a benevolent sky. Who knows what they said, but we never got another letter from Mrs. Diamond. Instead Rachel and Diana both began to call Celeste's private line and tell her that they hadn't seen any mention of the model "DeLo" in the East Coast gossip columns. They called early in the morning, catching us before we'd gone to sleep yet, tricking Celeste into saying things that she shouldn't have. They planted the seed of doubt.

The sisters didn't really suspect DeLo's habits as Celeste and I knew them to be, but they wormed their words, their doubt, into their sister's head, making her wonder how he really did spend his time, where he went away to, how he spent all those hours and hours away from her. Finally, Celeste's wondering got the best of her.

She and I had dropped a blotter each, no big deal but for the extra lick of bravery it gave us, when we decided to set out through the house to find him. We could see that all the cars were home.

He'd be somewhere in the cavernous place, doing something. Celeste had the idea to light an actual antique oil lantern, one you might see in old engravings accompanying Poe stories; she wanted us to make our own ghost story. I didn't like the idea of tripping on acid in the dark and being scared, but I just followed at that point.

We crept from room to room, room to room until, clutching each other and squealing as if we were back at sixth-grade camp, we entered a third-story wing that used to be old servant sleeping quarters. In the days after I first arrived in the Hills, we'd walked through the entire house. But after the first three or four servant bedrooms proved to be nearly identical—each one containing a slim single bed, a small dresser, a few storage boxes, and dust—we hadn't bothered opening the rest of the doors in the wing.

Now Celeste drew in the dark with the lantern. She swung it side to side. Its orange-gold glow, its acid-born tail, *thhrrrrattt*ed as she waved the spirits away, the lamplight echoing into itself. The blotter had hit, and as we moved through the hall, we knew we'd find nothing more than the results of our drugs. Good visuals anyway.

We moved from room to room, watching spectacular shadows fly over the walls.

And then we opened another door.

The room smelled different. Warmer. Closer. Alive. And there in the lamplight, on a small single bed, lay DeLo, the syringe still in his right hand, a candle dripping onto the metal lid of a water-color set. He did not see us, nor we him after that first glance. Celeste lifted the lantern, and the walls—the walls crawled with unexpected icons, drawn and painted and hacked into scratch-board. The room, now redolent, now stinking, now foul, now toxic, swelled with images of Celeste. An easel stood in a corner. Acrylics and oils, inks, amateurs all. They were horrible. Terrible. And they were all her. Every last visible inch of wall had been cov-ered with Celeste. A coarse caricature of Celeste nude on horse-back; Celeste chaste upon a chaise; Celeste topless, a cross floating above her head. She had not posed for them. I knew this. I had no doubt.

To see her through his eyes: She was worshiped. In the swift course of but a few seconds I understood myself as I never had. I was not her equal. I never could be.

Celeste stared. She recognized, I believe, for the first time in her life, the impact she had on the world.

She dropped the lantern.

The flames lit the floor like a magic pond. Celeste stood frozen.

The fire felt cool, actually, as I walked through it over to DeLo. I had the strength of a thousand women as I pulled him away from his obsession, as I rescued him from her.

We were, as you might guess, cast out. We weren't meant to see.

DeLo went into rehab. None of us ever saw him again.

Our reentrance into the ordinary hardcore world wasn't necessarily a difficult one. In our social circles, our reputations preceded us, mine for my rescue, Celeste's for just being Celeste, being the impetus for all of it.

She had socked away thousands, and I still had my bank account. We went in on a little rental house back over in Venice. We both admitted to loving the water enough to succumb to the newcomer syndrome, moving close to the beach. We didn't mind.

BAD RELIGION

VENTURA, OCTOBER '83

In the john the lighting is good, you realize. You have been let into the club early, hours before others, by the boy who jizzed straight into your sinuses, by the boy who lets you go behind the bar before the manager arrives. Finish the dregs of your rum grotesquerie and lift your skirt. Look as closely as you can because your crotch has crawled for days. Sit on the toilet seat lid and hunker over yourself, digging through your pubes like a monkey. See them. Step out of your ripped underwear. Decide to do away with your hair altogether.

Use your switchblade dry. Hear the scrape. Put a booted foot on the stall door and try to shave your labia.

The outcome resembles mange. Bleed from self-inflicted cuts. From accidental slips over lip.

And they are there. There they are. Trying to hide, they are still there, unshavable, beige specks with legs flattened onto your skin. Think how they cling to life. Pick one off with the sharp tip of your blade. Squat. Place the speck on the toilet seat. Scrutinize. Understand why they are called crabs. Crush it with the backside of your fingernail. It pops. Think of sushi, of roe between your teeth. Imagine eating sushi again someday, then set yourself to the task at hand. You must kill families.

Hurt your neck straining to see if you have cleared them all away.

Stand straight, done. Pull down your skirt. See the blood-speck-covered seat. Leave the stall. Wet a paper towel and return. Wipe down your deed. Flush.

You will have to tell her about them. She will have to check too.

You go. You go out, eventually Into the Unknown, and you are desperately disappointed. You had heard as much. Nothing that comes through synthesizers can fix you, or give you your fix. Nothing here.

$\mathcal{O}$NCE UPON a time, on a rare September day less than two weeks into the school year when my mother was lucid or happy or medicated enough to want to interact with me, a day when she'd left her bedroom door wide open and had actually stood in the jamb waiting for me to come home from school, we had a talk. Sort of.

"The circus is coming to town, Lisa! Take your friends," she said. "My treat."

The circus? I'd never been, nor did I have any actual desire to go. And I'd only made one real friend so far. "Why?" I refused to be gentle with my mother. I wanted to jab her all over with my finger and give her a polka-dotted bruise suit.

"The circus is wonderful," she said, sitting on her neatly made bed. It was a good day for her. I could tell she had a memory movie showing, the way she tilted her head and looked up into the corner of the room.

I rolled my eyes, giving her my best junior-high-schooler-to-be. "Pppssshhh," I said, or something close to it.

She was undeterred. "Really, Lisa, you'd be surprised. The performers are very skilled. I used to walk on stilts as a child."

"What?"

"Yes," she said, smiling as though she were tasting something delicious. She nodded, and her eyes closed. "It's delightful to be very tall."

My mother was worse than a dork. She was a freak. She wanted me to go to the circus to watch her family. She sat there with her eyes closed, daydreaming of lions and tigers and bears. "Radio Tokyo. Come in, Mother. Hell-*o*."

"Oh, stop it." She opened her eyes. "The aerialists are superb. I don't think you could do that, even as athletic as you are." She suddenly colored the shade of a pale pink rose. She corrected herself: "As athletic as your father says you are." She'd never really watched me do anything physical.

Was she daring me to go to the circus? I wouldn't go. Especially if she wanted me to. "The clowns? Mom? They're idiots. Why should we suffer idiots gladly?" I'd give her a little Mr. Diamond. See what she'd do with that.

"They're silly, yes, but they're supposed to be. Some are highly trained. Have you ever heard of Marcel Marceau?"

Duh. Celeste and I had seen *Silent Movie* over the weekend with her sister Diana. "Yes," I said, nearly belligerent. I wanted to put my knapsack in my room, grab a snack, and go over to the Diamonds'. "So?"

"Well, he could be considered a clown of sorts."

I tilted my head and waited. What did she want? Life was *outside* of this room, not in it.

"I'll treat," she said again.

I sighed. What was the big deal with the circus? "You weren't actually *in* the circus as a kid, were you?"

"I thought about it often." She copied my sigh. Or, oh no, I must have copied hers. Whatever. My mother's sigh had come out of me. I decided I needed to change that. "Running away from my life often seemed desirable."

"Huh?"

"There's a reason why you don't know your Grandmother and Grandfather Jones."

"Why?"

She gave me a look, a false-stern look, one meant to shut me up. "They were very controlling. We'll leave it at that."

Wait. Hold on. She wouldn't get away that easily, teasing me with something interesting for the first time ever. "Well, what did they do?" I tried.

She frowned.

"What?"

"Lisa."

I wanted to know. I had never really thought of my mother as having been young. She had begun when I was born, hadn't she? I knew better, actually, but I'd still always thought of her, my mother, as a sick fruit tree, withering but refusing to die. And like a still-healthy graft, I'd stretched away from her as hard as I could, straining toward the sun.

Some people were orphans, I reminded myself. Starving in India and China with cargo planes' worth of leftovers simply never reaching them.

Grandmother and Grandfather Jones. "Why don't I know them?" I asked. She almost seemed receptive, and my father was nowhere in sight.

She fussed with the itchy-looking lace at the collar of her day robe. I looked at her hands. They were mine, still unlined, the knuckles pronounced. "Do what you want to," she finally said to me. "No matter what other people do, do what you want to do."

What did she mean? She needed a few classes with our home-room teacher, Ms. Watsky, to straighten out that nonspecific language of hers. Or a few days around Mr. Diamond. That'd teach my mother to be clear. I wanted her to keep talking. "What if I *don't* want to do something? What if I don't want to play dodgeball in gym?" I loved dodgeball.

She frowned. "Oh! By all means, play that game! Girls weren't allowed to play dodgeball when I was in school. Play, play! Women—young women—should do whatever they want to do."

I looked at my all-but-entirely-bedridden mother with incredulity. Where were these words coming from? I just stared. She couldn't have been much bigger than I was. Just a little stinky half breath of a woman. And she had wanted to play dodgeball?

"Staring is rude, Lisa."

"Sorry." I looked down at my own hands. My nails were dirty, and the bump on the side of my middle finger by the nail rose sore and red from all the writing we'd done for homework lately. I waited for her to say something else. Nothing came. I studied the bedspread. How could my father . . . Hmm. She'd filled me with questions I knew wouldn't get answered.

"Why don't you ask your friends," she said finally, standing, indicating that I should be going now. That she would be getting tired. "About the circus. You might be surprised." She paced in a slow circle. "I know," she said, and then made an odd noise, one that I thought she wanted to be a chuckle, a nice little mother-daughter-camaraderie laugh. "I know you think you're too old for it, but you could go unchaperoned. By yourselves. I'd get your father to just pick you up and drop you off. An outing with the girls."

"I'll ask," I told her, knowing I'd do no such thing. "Bye."

"Bye."

The suggestion stuck, weird as it was.

After math, before art class, as we walked through the halls, I asked Celeste. "You wouldn't want to go to the circus, would you?"

"The circus?"

"It's coming. My *mother* thinks we should go." Celeste had some understanding of Janice Joy at that point, as much as I'd confessed so far.

"Sure!"

"Really?"

"Why not? It would be fun."

"I guess." We passed by the lunchroom and its noise. The lunchroom's disorder—slight to severe, depending upon the teacher on duty—undid me a bit. My previous school in Chicago had required us to eat our lunches at our desks. "What?" I asked Celeste, not having heard her.

"I didn't say anything."

"Have you ever been to the circus before?" We'd been studying all the verb tenses and irregular conjugations in English. I recognized my innate use of the past perfect tense in my question and felt strange, the way I had when, after eating braunschweiger my whole life, I found out that it was ground-up liver and spices. To name things, from food to verbs and everything in between, to break them down to their components or to isolate them out of context, made my sixth-grade head sort of float. I knew it made no sense. I just felt weird sometimes. I felt weird knowing that I had used the past perfect tense for years without knowing what it was, and then I felt weird using it and recognizing my using it right in the middle of saying something in the past perfect tense.

We walked into the art room. "I went to the circus once when I was really little," she said. "All I remember is eating cotton candy. I'd never had it before. And this woman who hung from her hair and spun in circles."

"My mother says she'll treat. And that we can go unchaperoned."

Celeste smiled that dazzling smile I hadn't gotten used to yet. "Let's go, Lisa!"

"Okay." I smiled back, happy suddenly. "We can invite other girls, too." Her enthusiasm was contagious. We took our yarnbutton-small-object-construction-paper-and-glue projects-inprogress from the sixth-grade flat file and found two seats next to each other at one of the long tables. We didn't have assigned seating in art. I loved that about art.

"Can we invite boys?" she asked.

Boys? "Why?"

"I was just wondering." She looked down at her yarn octopus and jewel-filled button treasure chest.

"I guess." I didn't want boys along. I looked at my aquatic scene. I'd copied the idea from her. My fish, though, with their sequin scales that weren't sticking to the paper very well, seemed to have aquarium rot.

"We don't have to," she said.

"If you want to." To shoot spitballs at them from across the room was one thing, to flirt from a distance. To go after a certain boy's flag in flag football. But to sit next to them, close to them, for hours?

"What do you think?" she asked.

I tried to read her mind. It looked like Celeste wanted to go to the circus with boys. I would concede, of course, and began to rationalize. Somebody had to begin the inevitable. We'd all have boyfriends someday, wouldn't we? "You pick them, okay?"

She gave me her big smile again, the one that felt like a present. "You help."

I looked around the room at the sixth-grade prospects. My heart pounded. I wasn't ready. But I was a quick learner. I could do it.

To this day I don't know what it was about the circus that my mother so desperately wanted me to see with my friends. The best I can figure is that she wanted me to see possibility. Maybe in her life one of the few forms freedom had ever taken was that of a woman in fishnets standing on top of a jogging elephant. I don't know. I never did bother to ask.

God, sometimes it's hard not to beat yourself up about stuff, you know?

So we went to the circus: Celeste, myself, the twins Jennifer and Jessica, who just seemed to be the right people to bring to the circus because they were twins, after all, and two boys brave enough to take Celeste up on the invitation—although I always suspected that their parents forced them to accept because they lived on the same block as the Diamonds did. Celeste had simply walked over to their houses and rung their doorbells, asking a parent both times if first Dominic and then Stuart could go to the circus on Saturday.

My father had suggested that it would be nice if we brought my brother, David. I'd told him, "No way!"

All of us kids were too nervous to say much in the car, riding silently except to answer my father's random questions. "How are your classes going?"

"Fine."

"What are you studying in math?"

"Fractions."

"Do you like school? Dominic, is it?"

"It's okay, I guess."

"And you. Stuart, is it?"

"It's all right."

"Girls, do you enjoy gym as much as Lisa does?"

"I do, Mr. Smith," Celeste said. I adored her.

The drive, much to my humiliation, was not a short one.

As my mother had promised, my father finally dropped us off near the arena parking entrance and said he would meet us back in the same spot in two and a half hours.

As my father tooted his horn and pulled away slowly, waving as he looked into his rearview, I just wanted to disappear.

"Imagine if *my* dad drove us," Celeste said to the group. "Well, only Lisa knows him, but we are *so* lucky her dad brought us. My dad is crazy. He would have made us do word games or something." Her chattiness made the rest of us relax a little.

"I have fifty dollars for food and stuff," I said. My father had gone overboard so that I could treat everybody.

"I have twenty."

"My mom gave me a ten."

Everybody else had brought money too. We had over a hundred dollars to spend between us. We walked with the crowds toward the arena, feeling very grown-up as kids several years older glanced at us enviously, trying to pull away from their families, their own parents calling out to them to slow down or hurry up.

My father had driven out during the workweek to pick up tickets, expensive good ones near the front, but we didn't know they were right at the bottom, second row in from the sawdust, until one of hundreds of teenage girls wearing red rubber noses and striped shirts showed us to our seats. We bought programs and popcorn and hot dogs and warm peanuts and Cracker Jack. We bought Cokes and 7UPs and pop-up clowns on sticks that sprang from their own inside-out smocks. We bought corn dogs and caramel apples and cotton candy. We bought key chains and pressed-wax camels and marionette monkeys. One of the twins bought a baseball jersey–style shirt with a dancing pink horse on the front of it. We never sat still, somebody rising every few minutes to buy something else. Everybody but Celeste, of course. While she shared my popcorn, had two bites of my caramel apple, and peered into my kaleidoscope with its cardboard outer tube decorated with a scene of horn-playing seals, she stayed in her seat the entire time.

The pink horse, one of five white ones that had obviously been dyed or painted, pranced around one of the three rings with a purple one and a yellow one and an orange one and a green one. The five of them circled in a tight line while a woman whose costume was riding up her crack hopped from one to the next. "She must have rubber on her shoes," I said to Celeste.

"I don't think so," she said. "They look like ballet slippers. See?"

"Looks like a lotta butt to me," Dominic said, nudging Stuart.

"Butt?" Stuart asked. "Where's a butt? I don't see any butt." They laughed till I thought they'd be sick.

"Who wants ice cream?" Jessica, or maybe Jennifer, asked.

It was hard to pay attention to all the acts at the same time. Our seats were nearest the center ring, but I attempted to practice my peripheral vision. I tried to see from end to end all at once, looking straight forward, till I gave myself a headache right behind my eyeballs, like a brain freeze from a Mr. Misty.

A guy shot from a cannon and landed in a net. Clowns drove tiny bicycles and toy cars. Tigers jumped through plain hoops and paper hoops and flaming hoops. A woman walked a high wire and did the splits on it. A man juggled five balls at the same time and never dropped a one. And all the while, as I sat there thinking that we were sitting next to boys, *boys*, Celeste only had eyes for the circus. She gasped when Stuart grew brave and tried to flirt with her outright, placing a large wad of cotton candy on top of her hair like a puffy pillbox hat, but she gasped for the trapeze artists flipping in the air. She never even knew about the cotton candy at all. The boys giggled and I waited for her to feel it, but she didn't. Finally I took it off her hair myself. "What?" she asked.

I looked at the boys. They looked away, feigning interest in the act that used a seesaw to fling acrobats onto other acrobats' shoulders.

"Never mind," I told her.

She gasped again, her hand going to her mouth.

I took the opportunity to study the profile of this girl, my new friend. She struck me as perfect. I didn't believe it possible to ever view her differently. I held the cotton candy from her head in my lap. I raised it to my mouth and took a bite.

"Gross," Dominic said as I did it. "That was on her hair."

"So?" I stuck out my tongue at them, opened wide, and crammed the whole wad past my lips.

You know how different cultures believe that eating a piece of something or other will imbue you with the properties of what you eat? Asians are famous for such beliefs, consuming testicle-soup this and ground-bull-horn that. They say it's how mad cow disease got started, cows eating cows in their own feed. The Native Americans have legends to keep their people away from cannibalism even when entire tribes are starving to death in winter.

But I swear, if I could have leaned over and taken a bite of Celeste's arm or shoulder or thigh rather than that cotton candy, I would have. I would have taken her into me gladly, consumed her there in front of all the other freaks, in front of anybody who would watch.

I did not know she would consume me.

The mass of cotton candy melted across my tongue and disappeared. I opened my mouth to Dominic and Stuart. Look, boys, look. None of her left.

The club kills the lights, and in the dark while the band members take their places the voice of a calm professional British woman says in a prerecorded announcement: "Serious assaults on individuals include the offense of grievous bodily harm."

You all roar.

"The offense is set out in the Offenses Against the Person Act of 1861. If you cause or inflict grievous bodily harm on somebody or wound him or her, cutting the skin, the maximum penalty is life imprisonment. If the person dies, the charge may be murder or manslaughter. If the injury is less serious, such as bruising or grazes, the charge may be assault occasioning actual bodily harm, with a maximum penalty of five years' imprisonment."

The lights fly up. The singer grabs the microphone and screams, "Aren't you fucking glad you live in America?!"

You go mad with the first chord.

$\mathcal{S}$HE BEGAN, not slowly as you might think she would, but nearly immediately to try to make herself ugly. As if she were punishing herself for DeLo's obsession, for his bad, bad art. But none of what she did really worked. The instant you looked at her, saw her move so fluidly across the room, you saw nothing but beauty.

Eventually Celeste and I became creative in how we supported ourselves, occasionally receiving shipments from Tram by way of Lawrence to dirty up a bit and sell. Because our little house had two bedrooms, we often took in temporary boarders, one or the other of us moving into the other's bedroom for the week or two weeks or month that the boarder stayed. If the boarder was a guy, he'd usually sleep with one of us eventually, and then we'd switch up bedrooms again. But as soon as he began to feel as though he no longer owed us a boarder's rent, that his services warranted a reduced rate—"Fuck, at least just a third, you bitch. Make it fair! Split it three ways."—we just kicked him out, made a few more phone calls, sold a little more of something.

We had what we needed and then some. We were fine.

Celeste often sat at the Formica kitchen table with the scale, measuring and weighing and packaging. She had a knack for folding what became her signature glossy-magazine envelopes that she cut carefully from high-end publications, making sure that some artistic scene appeared properly centered on the smooth side. Pretending occasionally to move single grain after single grain from one pile to another, she would call out to Rumplestiltskin to come put an end to her toiling.

The months passed. The Fourth of July, our birthdays, Halloween, Thanksgiving, Hanukkah, Christmas, New Year's again. Spring. Summer. Autumn another time. Celeste and I became notorious fixtures at hardcore shows. The original trip to Tijuana, the one with Lawrence and Papa and his band through Southern California, had been our initiation. Now after more than a year on the local scene, everybody recognized us. The weather fluctuated only a little, and I thought about Kansas City less and less. I sent my father and brother a few short postcards, our address scribbled after my name at the bottom, and found out through equally brief postcards back that mine, luckily, had been forwarded to them; David was in college at SMU, and my father had moved in with his girlfriend.

I suppose I may have secretly fantasized about my father trying another intervention of the kind he had so many years earlier when he sent me over to the Diamonds' more nights a week, that he might try again to send me someplace better—parents rescuing their kids from cults were so publicized and weirdly popular in those days—or at least him visiting me, but no such luck. David seemed to consider me a goner. Neither of them ever called, but then again, I didn't want anything to do with the robots, the "System"-loving automatons that I believed them to have become. I said it, anyway. Said the words like everybody else did.

You had to do away with them somehow. Those other people from your other life. You were supposed to not care. Not about anything but the scene. And maybe anarchy—but you could fake that one. I was allowed to keep Celeste because I belonged to her, or she to me, but beyond that, no attachments. No soft spots. The people we saw every week were the same as us, we thought, made of bile and salt and shards of glass.

You couldn't care, or you wouldn't make it. You wouldn't survive.

I never did write Mona and Sol.

Celeste and I had fun. We did. We believed we did, then. Our twenty-one-year-old bodies were strong. We smoked and drank and slept little. We huffed and popped and snorted. We stayed on the pill and ate when we remembered to. We fucked strange men often. We visited the free clinic. We made scars.

We never made future plans. We lived near some imagined precipice, some edge of a cliff. We needed to. We didn't know where else to live anymore.

I still don't know if she wrote her parents. I only know they never called. And I never asked.

We didn't have meaningful discussions about art. We didn't read much, although sometimes we tried. We didn't cook except to warm up canned ravioli or drop a slice of bread in the toaster. We didn't shave our armpits for a while until we decided they itched. We didn't miss snow. We didn't swim in the ocean enough. We didn't exercise except to brave the slamming. We didn't use condoms. We didn't wear heels. We didn't consider that we'd made bad choices. You just couldn't.

Like any other night before going out, we strapped and snapped and clipped on gear. We zipped and buckled. We dropped our stilettos into our boots. It was, really, a perfectly necessary habit.

We were going to see Gun Club play over in Simi. Our boarder-of-the-moment, a tall, muscled bass player from Seattle trying to make it in LA, had heard about the show and had offered to give us a ride. I suspected that he and Celeste would begin sleeping together soon. He had nice legs. Long.

In the car, the boarder, who called himself Heinrich, cracked open a beer with one hand and drank the whole thing. He seemed wired with something we didn't sell, something all speed, all thrashing fast beat. He reached toward Celeste's feet in the passenger seat well and pulled another can off the six-pack ring. He pounded the second as fast as the first. "You heard Gun Club before?"

I'd heard of them, although I actually never paid much attention to most of the music, far more interested in the people who played it and listened to it than the noise itself. I'd stop short of saying it wasn't music, but really, it was the visual scene I went for.

I didn't know, honestly, if Celeste felt the same way. I can't speak for her on that count. People made us tapes and left albums at the house. We listened to some and let others get dusty. I've managed to resurrect a few in the past couple of years, some of the ones with a hint of melody.

I sat behind Celeste and stared at Heinrich. He reminded me of somebody I couldn't place, somebody from somewhere whom I hadn't entirely liked before.

Neither Celeste nor I answered. He repeated himself. "You heard 'em?"

"Probably," Celeste said.

"What does that mean?"

"That she has," I said. "Or maybe not. She means, 'Probably.'"

He swung his arm over the seat back and dropped his beer can at my feet, then reached for another. "You'll like them," he said, more a command than an opinion.

"I heard about 'em," I said, and pulled out my bullet. I took a bump, the super-stepped-on coke knowing the way now, my nose knowing where the cheap rush was going. I tapped Celeste on the shoulder. She turned and took it.

"Cheers." She'd picked up the expression from a recent British fuck. I didn't like it, but didn't tell her.

"*De rien*," I said. We almost never used our old favorite anymore. Our French was fading. Still, I liked the feel of it in my mouth.

"*Sprechen sie Deutsch?*" Heinrich asked.

"*Nein*," she said immediately.

"Too bad. I like the sound of it between a *fräulein*'s lips."

"Fuck off," I told him, and he started to laugh.

"Aren't you a pint-sized toughie," he said. He looked at Celeste and shook his head. "*Both* of you are little idiots."

"So fuck off twice then," I said, and he laughed louder, sitting still as the light turned green. The car behind us honked.

"Go," Celeste said. He still didn't drive. "Go." He sat. The car behind us honked again, longer. Celeste packed the bullet, snorted loudly, pulled a beer can off for me, and passed it back along with the bullet. "Here." She pulled another off for herself, daring Heinrich to challenge her about taking two of his remaining three beers. He didn't say anything. He crept forward finally.

The ugliness of LA whizzed past the windows, the 7-Elevens and the rest, the short, squat buildings containing nothing necessary, everything that could be dumped in a ravine and not be missed: cheap furniture, ugly clothes, bad sports gear, California rednecks.

"Look," Heinrich said eventually, pulling something from his jacket and waving it in the small space between the three of us. It was a gun. "Get it?" he asked. "A gun for the Gun Club."

I got it.

She got it, too. "Put it away," Celeste said. He did.

We pulled up to the place, a grimy little club with painted-over front windows protected with grid wire. At some point people from the inside had started scraping at the paint, writing in bad backward lettering, using keys or jewelry to scratch out erect penises and anarchy symbols. A bare bulb hung over the entrance. In the circle of light and extending down the block for a hundred feet stood the crowd we knew, milling, loosely lined up, ready. Heinrich found a parking space around the corner.

We got out, Celeste swinging the single can left in the six-pack ring, and cruised the line. Both Papa and Lawrence were there, hangin' out with different people. I thought I should try to count the guys I'd slept with. Or, better yet, count the guys *we* had slept with.

Celeste and I introduced Heinrich to a few people, doing our jobs as social ambassadors. We threw odds or evens for a gulp at a Jim Beam fifth from Jesus, my first Venice lay. Heinrich lost, but both Celeste and I called it right. The brown liquor went down easy. I coulda been in Westerns, I was so good with bourbon.

Actually, we were both incredibly good at anything you put in front of our mouths. But she was better. Celeste had conquered abandon. She owned abandon. And those hyper-red lips of hers, you just stood spellbound. Mesmerized. Like a sixth-grader staring at a spinning bottle.

Minute after minute ticked by.

I remember looking around at the crowd that night, at Celeste, and thinking how I could view my whole, current life in one sweep of my eyes. Like a group portrait. I thought that. Frozen in a moment, our past screws, the easy and not-so-easy conquests, dotted the sidewalk, strung together like a strand of pearls laid on a table. Pearl after pearl. Look at them all. And Celeste, I decided, was the gem, the central diamond or ruby or whatever. She was the real Jesus at *The Last Supper*. I laughed and tried to tell her what I was thinking: "Look! It's Da Vinci. But you're the Jesus."

"Jesus gave us the bourbon," Celeste corrected.

"I know," I told her. "I'm not that fucked up."

It was hard to always think clearly.

We waited and waited some more. We smoked part of a guy's cigar, the end juicy-slobbery. Celeste had slept with him once before. I remembered her telling me afterward that he'd been insecure. I had yapped a callous laugh at the time and said, "You mean he's got a little weenie? A wittle wankie weenie?"

"No," she'd said. "He's insecure." She had scratched her crotch as she'd sat on our crappy couch that we'd found in a parking lot, the missing leg replaced with a stack of Yellow Pages stolen off our neighbors' porches. Scratch, scratch. "Yeah, fuck 'im," she had said, scratching again. She'd rarely betrayed them so blatantly, at least not to me.

Waiting for Gun Club to show, I enjoyed hooking my index finger over the thick cigar, playing the old-time mobster. I took another goobery drag and Hank's fingers suddenly, clearly, rose in my memory's vision. I wondered how my weird group portrait there on the sidewalk might change with the insertion of Hank. And Ess, too. Maybe Mack and Ing. Older disciples. It's possible we could have composed a similar portrait in Kansas City if we'd stayed. Would Celeste and I still be the same people? Would we have become different people if we'd not moved away? What if we'd gone to the Art Institute? Living in California, I thought about the guys more than I'd still like to admit—I mean, how could I not?—but a person has to give up on some people for real sometimes. You can't always hang on forever.

After another half hour of waiting, the usual bordering-on-bad restlessness began, the usual frustration with adhering to normal conventions. The waiting. The civility. The waiting. To look at the crowd you'd wonder why we hadn't torched the place already. Beer bottles arced into the street, then toward the lone bulb at the entrance.

The door opened.

We piled into Club Hell and quieted. Once inside, Heinrich stood even taller. I looked and looked at him, trying to remember who he reminded me of. Somebody. And then, as he raised his hands over his head while talking to Celeste to bat at an old beer banner, I saw it. The connection, the similarity. The gesture made me remember. Heinrich looked like that tall center, that basketball player way back from Country Club Plaza High. The big, scary fuck. Heinrich had far less hair, but all of the attitude, the posturing, the immediate sense of security in a crowd. I remembered his gun in his jacket pocket.

The band appeared, far past schedule, and as always, the chaos reorganized itself toward the stage. I took another bump of coke, preparing myself for a night of injury, when Celeste looked at me slyly and asked if I wanted to go for a drive. "I have his keys," she said in my ear beneath the band's noise.

I nodded.

We slipped away from Heinrich slowly and merged backward into the crowd as he pushed forward. He didn't notice our departure.

"I have to pee first," she said, heading toward the bathrooms near the exit.

Inside there was one stall with no door. The broken toilet seat rested on the gluey floor. "Be my guard?" Celeste asked.

"Always," I said, her soldier. As always.

Outside, we found Papa. I thought of him as a lesser Hank, a sort of kind, sexy father figure who fortunately was not actually your father. "Oh, yesyesyes," he said. "My favorite Midwestern ladies." He gave us each a sexy kiss.

We said our nothings and I shared my bullet. Afterward Celeste and I turned to leave, stepping out into the street to go for a little joyride. A little nothing. A *nothing*. But Heinrich was right there behind us all of a sudden. "Where the fuck are you going?!" he spewed. The skin on the back of my neck crawled. Celeste lifted her chin and turned around. I followed.

"Hey," Papa said.

"Fuck you," Heinrich said. "Stay away from my bitches."

"I don't think you should call them yours," Papa said.

"I pay them; they're mine."

Heinrich had just lost his place in our house. I would happily toss out his crappy clothes on our brown lawn and keep his guitars to sell. Guitars always brought in money.

"Heinrich," Celeste said. "Stop it."

"I pay you," he said, his body tense and tall and spelling danger every which way you looked at it.

Papa stepped between Celeste and Heinrich. Fuck. Most every show something happened. Scuffles, fistfights, all the time. A bunch of bullshit.

I wondered again what Heinrich had taken, what he'd put into his system, when Celeste stepped around Papa and approached Heinrich, her hand on his huge chest. "Stop. He's our friend."

I don't know why it didn't work or why Celeste's gesture provoked him. Something. Heinrich pulled the gun out of his jacket pocket and flailed it around like the enormous, drugged, displaced, fucked-up musician that he was. God.

I think it was just for show. I think that had to be the case.

But Papa didn't wait. He's told me since that he had enough experience to know that when a gun came out you needed to make it dead, get the gun down as absolutely fucking fast as you could. It's what he did. He shoved Celeste away and lunged his entire weight into Heinrich the way a linebacker would. The gun fired into the sky, and I actually thought, It was loaded. I reached for my boot at the same time I saw Celeste go for hers.

Heinrich was so big. He was a giant. He wouldn't go easily, we all saw in a slow-motion second, and as he collapsed clumsily onto his ass, onto the pavement, something told me we'd overstepped. We had moved into territory we never should have.

The gun fired again. You wouldn't believe what a gun sounds like until you're close. A gun sounds louder in the movies. Louder in your imagination than in real life. Heinrich's just sounded like a pop beneath the muffled music seeping from the club. A firecracker.

Papa moved funny, backward and sideways, and his arm swung weirdly. It was hard to make sense of it.

She didn't hesitate.

I did.

We wouldn't get a do-over.

She clicked open her stiletto and lunged at Heinrich on the sidewalk, the knife in front of her. And she shoved it into his chest. I watched. I saw her. I saw her do it. Square-on. Dead-on.

But she was so little, you know?

And so.

And so he screamed brutally like an ox, like a bull, like a moose, like something that didn't belong there on that street, and Celeste, sweet Celeste, wasn't anything more than a terrier.

He fell backward with her on top of him. I watched as his hand raised the gun off the asphalt. I moved in, in slow motion, and kicked with all my might, the hardest I've ever kicked. The gun came loose. It spun away and slid heavily for a yard. A yard and a half.

Heinrich's other hand held her by the throat. I gripped my stiletto and, tripping, plunged the blade into his ribs. It met curved bone and halted. My ears roared in my head. I twisted my knife and it slid through, past, a weird puncture sensation traveling back up through my arm.

Even as it happens, you know what you're doing. I knew right from wrong. I had always known. To protect Celeste would always be right. I didn't question it.

Heinrich screamed an unholy noise. My hand slipped off the handle. I staggered to stand and fell over my feet, and as I did, I saw his huge paw grip my stiletto.

I don't think I could have done anything. I don't. But.

He took my knife, my very own knife, and pulled it from between his ribs. He raised it so high that for a single, split-second chance I saw room enough for me to dive between it and her. And then, in the most fantastical, horrendous moment of my life, Heinrich stabbed Celeste in the back.

She reacted almost as though she'd expected it. As though it had been choreographed. "Oh, no," she said plainly, and Papa fell upon Heinrich's throat with his knee. Heinrich's neck made a funny noise, and he stopped moving. It was over as quickly as it had begun.

I scrambled to Celeste and reclaimed my knife, pulled it from near her spine. With its extraction came a sigh of breath. I should have known to leave it.

I couldn't let it be, just that, so simple and so stupid.

So damn ordinary. Not for her.

Papa would go to jail, but before he did, we both took Celeste off that huge monster and rolled her onto her back.

"Oh," she said.

"Celeste," I said.

She looked straight at me, her eyes clear. "I think I'm going to die," she said.

"No."

"I do, Colt. I'm sorry."

And then she left.

Cruisers and ambulances came. The entire human contents of the show bulged around us outside and stood staring, not wanting to put fingerprints anywhere. Papa, shot through his shoulder, the hole in the back of him worse than the one in the front, bled a big puddle.

We sat on the pavement next to Celeste. Next to her body.

They put her on a gurney eventually. They could have put her on Mars.

Celeste was dead.

FEAR

LOS ANGELES, JULY '83

Feel around with your hands when the power goes out.
Grope strangers and call her name.

Where is she? How could you have lost her?

TWENTY-ONE

THE SUN poured in through the opened metal blinds. I sat at the side of the desk and shook and shook as I repeated the Diamonds' Kansas City address for the detective as he wrote it in a notebook. He picked up the phone and told somebody to get him the Country Club Plaza police station in Kansas.

"Missouri," I said.

"What?"

"It's in Missouri."

He nodded. He was loose-skinned as though he used to weigh much more, and his nose was pocked with old acne scars. His desk was marked with rings from coffee cups. I wanted to be anywhere else. Anywhere else at all. "Missouri," he told the somebody on the phone. The somebody would send an officer to the Diamond front door.

I could not fathom what was to come. I could not fathom the now. I could not imagine tomorrow or the next day or week or year.

I was not allowed to go far from home. I would be questioned again. "Can I go back to Kansas City for the funeral?" I asked him as he waited. The dirty phone receiver pressed to his ear looked diseased from use.

"Did you forget the rules already?" I saw disgust in his eyes. Clearly, he thought I should be wherever Celeste was too. Earlier I'd heard him say to another detective, "Fucking punks. Let 'em rot."

I wondered who would come to identify her. Her body. I imagined Mr. Diamond looking down at his youngest daughter in a drawer in a morgue, Mona standing next to him. I didn't even know I was wailing until the detective plugged his ear.

That night at home, I tried to pack her things into my suitcase. I couldn't find hers; I didn't know where it'd gone. I expected that her family would want some of her stuff, but I couldn't figure out what. Not her clothes scattered around on the floor, her beat-up boots and shoes. Wasn't her high school diploma and all that in Kansas City already?

I went through her top dresser drawer and found bikini tops tangled with fishnets, pennies from our birth year, my old barrette. I sagged to the floor. I picked up the nearest dirty T-shirt and buried my face in her smell. I cried myself to sleep. When I woke in the middle of the night, for a split second I thought I'd dreamed all of it, but when I lifted the damp T-shirt to my nose, it only smelled like me. I knew.

Days crept by. I didn't eat or drink or do coke or bathe or speak to a soul. Nobody from her family called me, and I realized they probably never would.

Papa was the one to raise me from the dead. "You should come visit your old Papa," he said on the phone. "Don't know when you'll get to see me next."

My hoarse voice barely worked. "Where are you?"

Club Hell closed. Papa did time for manslaughter, more than he should have, but the local community demanded he be made an example. They were sick of punks. The same people realized, however, that prosecuting me could have the opposite effect. A tiny girl going to jail because she had tried to help her dying friend battle a giant might not aid relations between the factions of Simi Valley. And so I was unceremoniously let off the hook.

I stayed in California. I began walking the shore in the mornings. I didn't know who, or how, to be.

A surfer one day, pulling on his wet suit, asked if I'd like to try. A few months later I finally did.

I made a handful of new friends. I never really touched drugs after that night, never went to the same clubs. I slowly learned to live with myself. I took a waitressing job at a chain restaurant. I applied to UCSD and got financial aid. I moved to an even smaller place closer to school. I sent my father and brother more postcards.

Nearly two years after Celeste, my mother died. My father called me and told me that it was finally over. And so I flew back to Kansas City for the first time since I'd left for college. I carried two suitcases.

My father was living with Marla in Westport, not far from our old neighborhood. I thought that I would get a hotel room on the Plaza, but they insisted I stay with them. Marla especially seemed adamant. They had two nice guest rooms set up for both David and me. My brother looked much older, a man, handsome if I had to admit it. And Marla was kind. I was happy for my father. He and David and I nearly picked up where we had left off, only we were a little more courteous to one another. I didn't know them anymore, nor they me, but that felt natural. We hadn't ever been close. I vowed to begin trying.

The funeral was incredibly small, with a closed casket. I didn't cry. Atop the cherry wood, a photo of my mother from the early sixties showed her happy in a yellow dress. I'd never seen the photo. I asked my father if I could have it, and he smiled.

The day after, I looked up Hank in the phone book. He sounded genuinely happy to hear from me. We talked for hours. I explained. He agreed to go with me the next afternoon after classes, and he said he'd even have Ess drive. Ess had been accepted as a new instructor at the Art Institute, teaching incoming freshmen in the Foundations program. They saw each other often.

Ess got out of the car first and hollered, "You ain't never gonna get any bigger, are you?" He looked like an older, nicer version of his same self. His hair was still short, his face handsome as ever. He actually ran at me and picked me up, spinning. When he set me down, finally, Hank was right there. I looked at him and smiled. He hugged me hard. I burst into tears.

We drove in Ess' new Volkswagen Jetta. He'd gone legit. I couldn't believe it. I'd be lying if I said I wasn't disappointed with the news that he'd married six months before that. No, he hadn't married Rose from the old crew, although she was doing all right, living with her son. Ing had moved to San Francisco. Mack, great-lay Mack, had become incredibly successful in Chicago. He worked in advertising. Gigantus Khan had gone off to New York. Hank said he'd bet money the wanker had gone into porn. "No," Ess said, bringing the conversation back around to his own marriage. "I married a nice, normal girl. Kinda like you."

I suppose I did look sort of normal again. I realized that nobody from Kansas City except Celeste had seen me during the in-between time. I smiled and cried a little more.

I stared. It was just a piece of rock, facing the same way as all the rest in the Jewish cemetery, toward the rising sun. Just the name, just the dates. I took the pocketful of sand I'd brought with me and poured it in a little pile on top of the stone. It'd blow away or wash away fast, I knew, but there wasn't much more for me to give her, not there anyway.

Hank and Ess stayed with me for a long time. Ess, in his usual old way, sat on the grass after a while and started picking at the blades. Hank sat, too, and finally I joined them. We told good stories.

"You ready?" Hank asked when we'd settled into quiet, when we'd found the right time to go.

"Yeah."

Ess drove us back to the sculpture house. I knew from talking to Hank the night before that he'd finished the sculpture and that it would be traveling abroad in a major exhibition. Eventually, though, it would come back to the yard. "It belongs here," he'd said.

We actually went in the front door. Not much had changed inside. We walked into the kitchen, where I asked Hank if he would make me a blender drink for old times' sake. He happily obliged me. As he gathered ingredients and Ess used the phone to call his new wife, I went out the back door and into the garden.

And there she was.

Floating in a glass pool of pale turquoise near my knees, Celeste smiled serenely at the sky, her hand stroking hair, her ankle bracing toes. You'd swear her ribs were expanding and contracting, as alive as she seemed. My eyes followed her lines, her limbs, to the other one. To me. I could barely breathe with what I saw. I stood transfixed with my own form. I could not comprehend. I did not believe that I had been that beautiful when we'd posed.

I looked and looked.

And then the sculpture explained. There. Right there. It was so simple. Celeste's beauty moved in a direct current from her to me. She gave herself to me. You could see it plain as day.

Hank stepped to my side with two bright red tropical concoctions, clearly proud at having captured what he had. He looked at the sculpture and blinked. "She always loved you best," he said.

The next morning, hungover and puffy-eyed, I decided to go. I showered and pulled on plain jeans, a plain T-shirt. I walked. I carried the suitcase for blocks and realized how often I had repeated the same action in such a short life.

They'd had the shutters repainted. I wondered if anybody used the pool anymore.

I knew they were inside. I walked the last few steps and rang the bell.

Mona opened the door.

I will tell my daughter the entire story of her namesake soon, when we go back to Kansas City again.

And when we visit, Mr. Diamond will sing.

THE SEX PISTOLS

LONDON, JUNE '77

You're not there. You couldn't have been there. But you can imagine it.

Sid, Johnny. And the both of you.

The crowd jumps in a single motion. Everybody. Every last human being including those in the band. Even the drummer picks his ass up off his seat with every jump.

And for a few seconds, the room, in its unity, fills up with unadulterated joy.

Only joy.

ACKNOWLEDGMENTS

*F*OR THEIR belief that I could be anything I wanted to be in life, and for reading to me nearly every night as a child, I'd like to thank my parents, Sandy and Bill Buege. They fostered an affection for words no number of rejections could ever undo.

I fear I have not been much of a model eldest sister to Meg and Emily, yet they both remain unwavering in their love and encouragement. They tempered early drafts, and they share their families with me—Lance, Amelia, Alex, Steve. Somehow they've always made me believe that what I attempted in writing was as important as what they did and continue to do every day. Amazing.

Mary Anne offered tea and biscotti, a shoulder, on a day when I needed it most. I will not forget her understanding. Gladys, Franz, Cheri, Jim, Travis, Josh, Spanky, Karen, Rudy, and Barbie have always supplied enormous familial support. They are never far from my thoughts; nor are the memories of Deloris Weckauff and William Albert Frank Buege.

Optimistic people urged me to pursue writing when I was younger. Special appreciation goes to Rod Shene and Alison Creed, and to Dr. Russell Hogan, one of many compassionate former teachers at Clayton High School in St. Louis. Thanks as well to those whose long-ago friendships helped to color this novel: Joy, Elizabeth, and Laura; Sarah and Brenda; Lisa B., Lisa N., Theresa, and Lynne G. The not-always-painless memories of others helped me to render a unique world: Matt, Gregg, Rich, Angie, Rommie, Darren, Bobbie, Adam. I hope life is good for each of you.

Most current friends are easier to keep track of, and many have helped me with my fiction and with New Orleans life in general. Some have volunteered as spotters when I hung by my ankles overhead. Several have read drafts. For great kindnesses I wish to acknowledge Jennifer and Shelley, Matthew, Jarret, Joey and Sarah K., A.C. and Bill, Simon, Neil and Eric, Linda T., Lisa Dunn, Zandrah, Heather and Mike, Laurel and Kevin, Arin, Rakia, Marcus, Chrys, and Marc. As well, my Canadian in-laws help to warm up this thin-blooded American when I visit. Thanks especially to Jacob and all the Boyden ladies.

I owe much to Rick Barton and Joanna Leake, professors and writers extraordinaire. I wish Jim Knudsen were around for just one more rainy night at the Parkview. What you three created, the University of New Orleans MFA program, is stunning, all the more so when considering the adversity of Louisiana state higher education. Many people affiliated with the MFA, and the English Department of UNO, past and present, have my gratitude. Nancy Dixon and Bill Lavender, *muchas gracias*. The early constructive criticism of Bill Rhode, Steve Hughes, and Charlie Rehor has always stuck with me. The companionship and easy temperaments of Kris Lackey and Jane Haspel make the weekly grind more than worthwhile, and the hallway roamings and administrative kindnesses of Les White, Kim McDonald, Dan Doll, John Cooke, and Peter Schock have not gone unnoticed. So many UNO graduate writing students, too many to name, have taught me more than I might ever impart to them. They overflow with talent and will go far.

One former student in particular must be recognized for both her friendship and for the ball she set in motion. Sarah Debacher listened when I desperately needed an ear, and she also introduced me to Claire Smith. Claire, in turn, recommended an agent who's since worked miracles.

Rob McQuilkin made the impossible happen. Not only is he a fantastic agent with contemporary skills, he is of the rarest and most old school; he actually edits. His passion for rhythm, for balance and measure, has my utmost praise, as does his resolute belief in my work.

Rob put my manuscript into the hands of Jennifer Jackson at Random House, a talented woman who has changed my life. As an editor, Jenny is unflinching, patient, thorough, and unbelievably enthusiastic. As a reader and new friend, she is infinitely generous. I am, profoundly, in her debt. A thousand thanks to Sloane Crosley, a publicist par excellence.

And, dear Joseph, last but never least: You taught me the importance of heart and gave me yours, both gifts impossible to measure. To that porch, only in imagination or in real life, cheers.